Lecture Notes in Computer Science   8877

Commenced Publication in 1973
Founding and Former Series Editors:
Gerhard Goos, Juris Hartmanis, and Jan van Leeuw

Advanced Research in Computing and Software Science

Subline of Lectures Notes in Computer Science

Tie-Yan Liu Qi Qi Yinyu Ye (Eds.)

Web and Internet Economics

10th International Conference, WINE 2014
Beijing, China, December 14-17, 2014
Proceedings

 Springer

Volume Editors

Tie-Yan Liu
Microsoft Research
Haidian District, Beijing, China
E-mail: tyliu@microsoft.com

Qi Qi
The Hong Kong University
of Science and Technology
Kowloon, Hong Kong
E-mail: kaylaqi@ust.hk

Yinyu Ye
Stanford University
Stanford, CA, USA
E-mail: yinyu-ye@stanford.edu

ISSN 0302-9743   e-ISSN 1611-3349
ISBN 978-3-319-13128-3   e-ISBN 978-3-319-13129-0
DOI 10.1007/978-3-319-13129-0
Springer Cham Heidelberg New York Dordrecht London

Library of Congress Control Number: 2014955020

LNCS Sublibrary: SL 3– Information Systems and Applications,
incl. Internet/Web and HCI

Typesetting: Camera-ready by author, data conversion by Scientific Publishing Services, Chennai, India

Printed on acid-free paper

Springer is part of Springer Science+Business Media (www.springer.com)

Preface

This volume contains the papers presented at WINE 2014, the 10th Conference on Web and Internet Economics, held during December 14–17, 2014, at the Academy of Mathematics and Systems Science (AMSS), Chinese Academy of Sciences, Beijing, China.

Over the past decade, researchers in theoretical computer science, artificial intelligence, and microeconomics have joined forces to tackle problems involving incentives and computation. These problems are of particular importance in application areas like the Web and the Internet that involve large and diverse populations. The Conference on Web and Internet Economics (WINE) is an interdisciplinary forum for the exchange of ideas and results on incentives and computation arising from these various fields. This year, WINE was held in cooperation with the ACM and was co-located with the 11th Workshop on Algorithms and Models of the Web Graph (WAW 2014).

WINE 2014 received 107 submissions. All submissions were rigorously peer reviewed and evaluated on the basis of originality, soundness, significance, and exposition. The Program Committee decided to accept 32 regular and 13 short papers. We allowed the accepted papers to be designated as working papers. For these papers, only 1-2 pages of an extended abstract are published in the proceedings. This allows subsequent publication in journals that do not accept papers where full versions have previously appeared in conference proceedings. Of all the accepted papers, four are working papers. The conference program also included six invited talks by Robert Aumann (Hebrew University), Xiaotie Deng (Shanghai Jiao Tong University), Noam Nisan (Microsoft Research), Christos Papadimitriou (University of California at Berkeley), Andrew Chi-Chih Yao (Tsinghua University), and Peng Ye (Alibaba Group). In addition, WINE 2014 featured three tutorials on December 14: Computation of Equilibrium in Asymmetric First Price Auctions, by Nir Gavish (Technion),Theoretical Analysis of Business Models, by Kamal Jain (eBay Research), and Price of Anarchy and Stability, by Martin Gairing (University of Liverpool).

The successful organization of WINE 2014 is a joint effort of many people and organizations. In particular, we would like to thank Baidu, Microsoft Research, Google, and Facebook, for their generous financial support to WINE 2014, the Academy of Mathematics and Systems Science and Tsinghua University for hosting the event, as well as the Operation Research Community of China and National Center for Mathematics and Interdisciplinary Sciences of China for their great support. In addition, we would like to acknowledge the Program Committee for their hard work in paper reviewing, Springer for helping with the proceedings, and the EasyChair paper management system for providing quality and flexible support during the paper review process.

October 2014   Tie-Yan Liu
                                                                                Qi Qi
                                                                               Yinyu Ye

Organization

Program Committee Chairs

Tie-Yan Liu	Microsoft Research
Qi Qi	Hong Kong University of Science and Technology, Hong Kong
Yinyu Ye	Stanford University, USA

Program Committee

Allan Borodin	University of Toronto, Canada
Peter Bro Miltersen	Aarhus University, Denmark
Yang Cai	University of California, Berkeley, USA
Bruno Codenotti	Istituto di Informatica e Telematica, Italy
Jose R. Correa	Universidad de Chile, Chile
Nikhil R. Devanur	Microsoft Research
Edith Elkind	University of Oxford, UK
Qizhi Fang	Ocean University, China
Amos Fiat	Tel Aviv University, Israel
Nir Gavish	Technion-Israel Institute of Technology, Israel
Dongdong Ge	Shanghai University of Finance and Economic, China
Vasilis Gkatzelis	Stanford University, USA
Gagan Goel	Google Research
Mordecai J. Golin	Hong Kong University of Science and Technology, Hong Kong
Martin Hoefer	Max-Planck-Institut für Informatik, Germany
Krishnamurthy Iyer	Cornell University, USA
Kamal Jain	eBay Research
Ming-Yang Kao	Northwestern University, USA
David Kempe	University of Southern California, USA
Peter Key	Microsoft Research
Piotr Krysta	University of Liverpool, UK
Ron Lavi	Technion-Israel Institute of Technology, Israel
Mohammad Mahdian	Google Research
Azarakhsh Malekian	University of Toronto, Canada
Evangelos Markakis	Athens University of Economics and Business, Greece
Nimrod Megiddo	IBM Research

Vahab Mirrokni	Google Research
Hamid Nazerzadeh	University of Southern California, USA
Cheng-Zhong Qin	University of California, Santa Barbara, USA
Aaron Roth	University of Pennsylvania, USA
Rahul Savani	University of Liverpool, UK
Guido Schäfer	Centrum Wiskunde and Informatica, The Netherlands
Maria Serna	Universitat Politecnica de Catalunya, Barcelona Tech, Spain
Yaron Singer	Harvard University, USA
Xiaoming Sun	Institute of Computing Technology, CAS, China
Shang-Hua Teng	University of Southern California, USA
Aviv Zohar	Hebrew University, Israel

Additional Reviewers

Adam, Elie	Garg, Jugal
Alaei, Saeed	Gentile, Claudio
Anshelevich, Elliot	Haghpanah, Nima
Aziz, Haris	Harks, Tobias
Barman, Siddharth	Hsu, William
Bei, Xiaohui	Huang, Chien-Chung
Bhaskar, Umang	Huang, Eric
Bilo', Vittorio	Huang, Zhiyi
Brânzei, Simina	Iwasaki, Atsushi
Chen, Po-An	Jaimungal, Sebastian
Chen, Zhou	Jeż, Łukasz
Chiang, Chao-Kai	Jiang, Bo
Christodoulou, George	Kanellopoulos, Panagiotis
Colini Baldeschi, Riccardo	Kern, Walter
De Keijzer, Bart	Klimm, Max
Dehghani, Sina	Kodric, Bojana
Deligkas, Argyrios	Kollias, Konstantinos
Ding, Yichuan	Kong, Guangwen
Drummond, Joanna	Kulkarni, Janardhan
Dworkin, Lili	Kyropoulou, Maria
Ehsani, Shayan	Lahaie, Sebastien
Elbassioni, Khaled	Lai, John
Fanelli, Angelo	Lev, Omer
Feldman, Michal	Lewenberg, Yoad
Frongillo, Rafael	Li, Yuqian
Gao, Alice	Liu, Xingwu
Gao, Xi Alice	Lucier, Brendan

Ma, Weidong
Mahini, Hamid
Malec, David
Mansour, Yishay
Mehta, Ruta
Meir, Reshef
Morgenstern, Jamie
Moscardelli, Luca
Mu'Alem, Ahuva
Nehama, Ilan
Niazadeh, Rad
Nikolova, Evdokia
Nikzad, Afshin
Okamoto, Yoshio
Oren, Joel
Oren, Sigal
Piliouras, Georgios
Qin, Tao
Rahn, Mona
Rubinstein, Aviad
Ryan, Christopher
Röglin, Heiko
Seeman, Lior
Sheffet, Or
Singla, Adish
Sompolinsky, Yonatan
Steele, Patrick
Sudhölter, Peter

Talgam-Cohen, Inbal
Telelis, Orestis
Tong, Chaoxu
Tzamos, Christos
Uetz, Marc
Vassilvitskii, Sergei
Von Stengel, Bernhard
Vondrak, Jan
Wagner, Lisa
Wajc, David
Wang, Changjun
Wang, Chuan-Ju
Wang, Zizhuo
Weinberg, S. Matthew
Wu, Zhiwei Steven
Xiao, Tao
Zadimoghaddam, Morteza
Zhang, Chihao
Zhang, Hongyang
Zhang, Jia
Zhang, Jialin
Zhang, Jie
Zhang, Jinshan
Zhang, Peng
Zhang, Xiaodong
Zheng, Bo
Zhu, Ruihao

Table of Contents

Short Papers

Cake Cutting Algorithms for
Piecewise Constant and Piecewise Uniform Valuations

Haris Aziz[1] and Chun Ye[2]

[1] NICTA and UNSW, Sydney, Australia NSW 2033
haris.aziz@nicta.com.au
[2] Columbia University, New York, NY 10027-6902, USA
cy2214@columbia.edu

Abstract. Cake cutting is one of the most fundamental settings in fair division and mechanism design without money. In this paper, we consider different levels of three fundamental goals in cake cutting: fairness, Pareto optimality, and strategyproofness. In particular, we present robust versions of envy-freeness and proportionality that are not only stronger than their standard counter-parts but also have less information requirements. We then focus on cake cutting with piecewise constant valuations and present three desirable algorithms: *CCEA (Controlled Cake Eating Algorithm)*, *MEA (Market Equilibrium Algorithm)* and *MCSD (Mixed Constrained Serial Dictatorship)*. CCEA is polynomial-time, robust envy-free, and non-wasteful. Then, we show that there exists an algorithm *(MEA)* that is polynomial-time, envy-free, proportional, and Pareto optimal. Moreover, we show that for piecewise uniform valuations, MEA and CCEA are group-strategyproof and are equivalent to Mechanism 1 of Chen et. al.(2013). We then present an algorithm *MCSD* and a way to implement it via randomization that satisfies strategyproofness in expectation, robust proportionality, and unanimity for piecewise constant valuations. We also present impossibility results that show that the properties satisfied by CCEA and MEA are maximal subsets of properties that can be satisfied by any algorithm.

1 Introduction

Cake cutting is one of the most fundamental topics in fair division (see e.g., [7, 17]). It concerns the setting in which a cake is represented by an interval [0, 1] and each of the n agents has a value function over the cake that specifies how much that agent values a particular subinterval. The main aim is to divide the cake fairly. The framework is general enough to encapsulate the important problem of allocating a heterogeneous divisible good among multiple agents with different preferences. The cake cutting problem applies to many settings including the division of rent among housemates, disputed land between land-owners, and work among co-workers. It is especially useful in scheduling the use of a valuable divisible resource such as server time.

In this paper, we approach the cake cutting problem from a mechanism design perspective. We assume that each cake recipient, which we will refer to as *an agent*, has a private value density function over the cake. Throughout the paper we focus on the fundamental classes of value functions called *piecewise constant value density functions*.We also consider *piecewise uniform valuations* which are a restricted class of

T.-Y. Liu et al. (Eds.): WINE 2014, LNCS 8877, pp. 1–14, 2014.

piecewise constant valuations. We consider three of the most enduring goals in mechanism design and fair division: fairness, Pareto optimality and strategyproofness. Since many fair division algorithms need to be deployed on a large scale, we will also aim for algorithms that are *computationally* efficient. Strategyproofness has largely been ignored in cake-cutting barring a few recent exceptions [9, 10, 14, 15, 20]. The main research question in this paper is as follows: *among the different levels of fairness, Pareto optimality, strategyproofness, and efficient computability, what are the maximal set of properties that can be satisfied simultaneously for piecewise constant and piecewise uniform valuations?* Our main contribution is a detailed study of this question including the formulation of a number of desirable cake cutting algorithms satisfying many of the properties. A few works that are directly relevant to this paper are [8, 9, 10, 11]. Chen et al. [9, 10] presented a deterministic, strategyproof, polynomial-time, envy-free and Pareto optimal algorithm for piecewise uniform valuations. They left open the problem of generalizing their algorithm for piecewise constant valuations. Cohler et al. [11] and Brams et al. [8] formulated linear programs to compute envy-free allocations for piecewise constant valuations. However, the algorithms are not Pareto optimal in general. Two of the algorithms in our paper rely on transforming the problem of allocating a cake to agents with piecewise constant value density functions to an equivalent problem of allocating objects to agents where each agent has a homogeneous preference for each object. The transformation is done by pre-cutting the cake into subintervals using the union of discontinuity points of the agents' valuation function. This transformation allows us to adopt certain well-known results of random assignment and market equilibrium to the problem at hand.

Drawing the connection between cake cutting and random assignment, we present *CCEA (Controlled Cake Eating Algorithm)* for piecewise constant valuations. CCEA is polynomial-time and satisfies robust envy-freeness and robust proportionality, which are stronger than the notions of fairness that have been considered in the cake cutting literature. The main idea of an allocation being *robust* envy-free/proportional is that even if an agent re-adjusts or perturbs his value density function, as long as the ordinal information of the function is unchanged, then the allocation remains envy-free/proportional.[1] CCEA depends on a reduction to the generalizations [1, 13] of the *PS (probabilistic serial)* algorithm introduced by Bogomolnaia and Moulin [4] in the context of random assignments.[2]

If we insist on Pareto optimality, then we show that there exists an algorithm which we refer to as the *MEA (Market Equilibrium Algorithm)* that is deterministic, polynomial-time Pareto optimal, envy-free, and proportional for piecewise constant valuations. The main computation of MEA lies in solving the Eisenberg-Gale convex program for market equilibrium. Although similar ideas using linear programs and market equilibria have been used explicitly to compute envy-free allocations in

---

[1] Although full information is a standard assumption in cake cutting, it can be argued that it is unrealistic that agents have exact vNM utilities for each segment of the cake. Even if they do report exact vNM utilities, they may be uncertain about these reports.

[2] The CC algorithm of Athanassoglou and Sethuraman [1] is a generalization of the EPS algorithm [13] which in turn is a generalization of PS algorithm of Bogomolnaia and Moulin [4].

cake-cutting[11, 8], they do not necessarily return a Pareto optimal allocation. In a recent paper, Tian [20] characterized a class of strategyproof and Pareto optimal mechanisms for cake cutting when agents have piecewise uniform valuation functions. The algorithm of Tian involves maximizing the sum of concave functions over the set of feasible allocations. It is worth noting that MEA when restricted to the piecewise uniform valuation setting is a special case of his algorithm. We show that for piecewise uniform valuations, CCEA and MEA not only coincide but are also group-strategyproof. Previously, Chen et al. [9, 10] presented a deterministic, strategyproof, polynomial-time, envy-free and Pareto optimal algorithm for piecewise uniform valuations. We prove that for piecewise uniform valuations, CCEA and MEA are in fact equivalent to their algorithm and are group-strategyproof instead of just strategyproof.

Although CCEA and MEA are desirable algorithms, they are not strategyproof for piecewise constant valuations. This is because the incentive of the agents for the piecewise uniform valuation setting is rather limited: each agent only cares about obtaining as much of their desired pieces of the cake as possible. On the other hand, for piecewise constant valuations, agents also care about the tradeoff in quantities of having pieces at different levels of desirability. Another difficulty of obtaining a strategyproof algorithm via the aforementioned transformation is that the discontinuity points of each agent's valuation function is private information for the agent. In particular, unlike the setting of allocating multiple homogenous objects, where it suffices for an algorithm to output the fractional amount of each object that an agent will receive, the method of *conversion* from fractions of intervals into an actual allocation in terms of the union of subintervals is also a necessary step of the algorithm, which may be subject to strategic manipulation by the agents. To drive this point further, in the paper we give an example of an algorithm that is strategyproof in the random assignment setting, but is no longer strategyproof if we implement the conversion process from fractions of intervals to the union of subintervals in a deterministic fashion.

To tackle this difficulty, we present another algorithm called *MCSD (Mixed Constrained Serial Dictatorship)* which is strategyproof in expectation, robust proportional, and satisfies unanimity. For the important case of two agents[3], it is polynomial-time, and robust envy-free. To the best of our knowledge, it is the first cake cutting algorithm for piecewise constant valuations that satisfies strategyproofness, (ex post) proportionality, and (ex post) unanimity at the same time. MCSD requires some randomization to achieve strategyproofness in expectation. However, MCSD is deterministic in the sense that it gives the same utility guarantee (with respect to the reported valuation functions) over all realizations of the random allocation. Although MCSD uses some essential ideas of the well-known *serial dictatorship* rule for discrete allocation, it is significantly more involved. In contrast to serial dictatorship, MCSD achieves *ex post* fairness. Our main technical results are as follows.

Theorem 1. *For piecewise constant valuations, there exists an algorithm (CCEA) that is deterministic, polynomial-time, robust envy-free, and non-wasteful.*

Theorem 2. *For piecewise constant valuations, there exists an algorithm (MEA) that is deterministic, polynomial-time, Pareto optimal, and envy-free.*

---

[3] Many fair division problems involve disputes between two parties.

Table 1. Properties satisfied by the cake cutting algorithms for pw (piecewise) constant valuations: DET (deterministic), R-EF (robust envy-freeness), EF (envy-freeness), R-PROP (robust proportionality), PROP (proportionality), GSP (group strategyproof), W-GSP (weak group strategyproof), SP (strategyproof), PO (Pareto optimal), NW (non-wasteful), UNAN (unanimity) and POLYT (polynomial-time)

Algorithms	Restriction	DET	R-EF	EF	R-PROP	PROP	GSP	W-GSP	SP	PO	NW	UNAN	POLYT
CCEA	-	+	+	+	+	+	-	-	-	-	+	+	+
CCEA	pw uniform	+	+	+	+	+	+	+	+	+	+	+	+
MEA		+	-	+	-	+	-	-	-	+	+	+	+
MEA	pw uniform	+	+	+	+	+	+	+	+	+	+	+	+
MCSD	-	-	-	-	+	+	-	-	+	-	-	+	-
MCSD	pw uniform	-	-	-	+	+	-	-	+	+	-	+	-
MCSD	2 agents	-	+	+	+	+	-	-	+	-	-	+	+

Theorem 3. *For piecewise uniform valuations, there exist algorithms (CCEA and MEA) that are deterministic, group strategyproof, polynomial-time, robust envy-free and Pareto optimal.*

Theorem 4. *For piecewise constant valuations, there exists a randomized implementation of an algorithm (MCSD) that is (ex post) robust proportional, (ex post) symmetric, and (ex post) unanimous and strategyproof in expectation. For two agents, it is polynomial-time, robust proportional and robust envy-free.*

Our positive results are complemented by the following impossibility results. These impossibility results show that the properties satisfied by CCEA and MEA are maximal subsets of properties that can be satisfied by any algorithm.

Theorem 5. *For piecewise constant valuation profiles with at least two agents, there exists no algorithm that is both Pareto optimal and robust proportional.*

Theorem 6. *For piecewise constant valuation profiles with at least two agents, there exists no algorithm that is strategyproof, Pareto optimal, and proportional.*

Theorem 7. *For piecewise constant valuation profiles with at least two agents, there exists no algorithm that is strategyproof, robust proportional, and non-wasteful.*

Some of our main results are also summarized in Table 1. Some of our results even extend to more general domains with variable claims and private endowments. As a consequence of CCEA and MEA, we generalize the positive results regarding piecewise uniform valuations in [9, 10] and piecewise constant valuations in [11] in a number of ways such as handling richer cake cutting settings, handling more general valuations functions, achieving a stronger fairness concept, or a stronger strategyproofness notion.

2   Preliminaries

Cake cutting setting. We consider a cake which is represented by the interval [0, 1]. A *piece of cake* is a finite union of disjoint subintervals of [0, 1]. The length of an interval

$I = [x, y]$ is $len(I) = y - x$. As usual, the set of agents is $N = \{1, \ldots, n\}$. Each agent has a piecewise continuous *value density function* $v_i : [0, 1] \rightarrow [0, \infty)$. The value of a piece of cake X to agent i is $V_i(X) = \int_X v_i(x)dx = \sum_{I \in X} \int_I v_i(x)dx$. As generally assumed, valuations are non-atomic ($V_i([x, x]) = 0$) and additive: $V_i(X \cup Y) = V_i(X) + V_i(Y)$ where X and Y are disjoint. The basic cake cutting setting can be represented by the set of agents and their valuations functions, which we will denote as *a profile of valuations*. In this paper we will assume that each agent's valuation function is private information for the agent that is not known to the algorithm designer. Each agent reports his valuation function to the designer.

Preference functions. In this paper we will only consider *piecewise uniform* and *piecewise constant* valuation functions. A function is *piecewise uniform* if the cake can be partitioned into a finite number of intervals such that for some constant k_i, either $v_i(x) = k_i$ or $v_i(x) = 0$ over each interval. A function is *piecewise constant* if the cake can be partitioned into a finite number of intervals such that v_i is constant over each interval. In order to report his valuation function to the algorithm designer, each agent will specify a set of points $\{d_1, \ldots, d_m\}$ that represents the consecutive discontinuity points of the agent's valuation function as well as the constant value of the valuation function between every pair of consecutive d_j's. For a function v_i, we will refer by $\hat{V}_i = \{v'_i : v_i(x) \geq v_i(y) > 0 \iff v'_i(x) \geq v'_i(y) > 0 \ \forall x, y \in [0, 1]\}$ as the set of density functions *ordinally equivalent* to v_i.

Properties of allocations. An *allocation* is a partition of the interval $[0, 1]$ into a set $\{X_1, \ldots, X_n, W\}$, where X_i is a piece of cake that is allocated to agent i and W is the piece of the cake that is not allocated. All of the fairness and efficiency notations that we will discuss next are with respect to the reported valuation functions. Within the cake cutting literature, the most important criteria of a fair allocation are *envy-freeness* and *proportionality*. In an *envy-free allocation*, we have $V_i(X_i) \geq V_i(X_j)$ for each pair of agent $i, j \in N$, that is every agent considers his allocation at least as good as any other agent's allocation. In a *proportional* allocation, we have $V_i(X_i) \geq \frac{1}{n} V_i([0, 1])$, that is, each agent gets at least $1/n$ of the value he has for the entire cake. Envy-freeness implies proportionality provided that every desirable part of the cake is allocated. An even stronger condition that envy-freeness is *equitability* which requires that each agent is indifferent between his allocation and the allocations of other agents.

An allocation is *Pareto optimal* if no agent can get a higher value without some other agent getting less value. Formally, X is Pareto optimal if there does not exists another allocation Y such that $V_i(Y_i) \geq V_i(X_i)$ for all $i \in N$ and $V_i(Y_i) > V_i(X_i)$ for some $i \in N$. In the case where Pareto efficiency cannot be satisfied, we also consider a weaker notion of efficiency called non-wastefulness. For any $S \subseteq [0, 1]$, define $D(S) = \{i \in N | V_i(S) > 0\}$. An allocation X is *non-wasteful* if for all $S \subseteq [0, 1]$, $S \subseteq \cup_{i \in D(S)} X_i$. In other words, an allocation is non-wasteful if every portion of the cake desired by at least one agent is allocated to some agent who desires it.

For fairness, we do not only consider the standard notions envy-freeness and proportionality but we also propose the concept of *robust fairness* — in particular *robust envy-freeness* and *robust proportionality*. An allocation satisfies robust proportionality if for all $i, j \in N$ and for all $v'_i \in \hat{V}_i$, $\int_{X_i} v'_i(x)dx \geq 1/n \int_0^1 v'_i(x)dx$. An allocation satisfies robust envy-freeness if for all $i, j \in N$ and for all $v'_i \in \hat{V}_i$, $\int_{X_i} v'_i(x)dx \geq \int_{X_j} v'_i(x)dx$. The main idea of an allocation being robust envy-free is that even if an agent re-adjusts or perturbs his value density function, as long as the ordinal information of the function is unchanged, then the allocation remains envy-free. The main advantages of robust envy-freeness are less information requirements and envy-freeness under uncertainty. It also addresses a criticism in cake cutting models that an agent has the ability to ascribe an exact number to each tiny segment of the cake.[4] Note that even equitability does not imply robust envy-freeness because by perturbing the valuation function, equitability can easily be lost.

Let us fix a piecewise constant value density function v. Let $(I_1, I_2, \ldots, I_k)$ be the *positively* valued intervals induced by the discontinuity points of the value function sorted in the order of decreasing preference, that is, $v(x)$ is higher on I_i than it is on I_j if $i < j$. Let x and x' be two allocation vectors whose i-th component specifies the length of I_i that is allocated to the agent, then we say that x stochastically dominates x' with respect to the preference ordering if $\sum_{i=1}^{j} x_i \geq \sum_{i=1}^{j} x'_i$ for every $j = 1, \ldots, k$. It can be shown that an allocation x for the agent with valuation function v is robust envy-free if and only if it stochastically dominates any other allocation x' with respect to the preference ordering. Moreover, it can be shown that an allocation x is robust proportional if and only if $\sum_{i=1}^{j} x_i \geq 1/n \sum_{i=1}^{j} |I_i|$ for every $j = 1, \ldots, k$. Both robust envy-freeness and robust proportionality require each agent to get a piece of cake of the same length if every agent desires the entire cake.

Properties of cake cutting algorithms. A *deterministic cake cutting algorithm* is a mapping from the set of valuation profiles to the set of allocations. A *randomized cake cutting algorithm* is a mapping from the set of valuation profiles to a space of distributions over the set of allocations. The output of the algorithm in this case for a specific valuation profile is a random sample of the distributional function over the set of allocation for that profile. An algorithm (either deterministic or randomized) satisfies property P if it always returns an allocation that satisfies property P. A deterministic algorithm is *strategyproof* if no agent ever has an incentive to misreport in order to get a better allocation. The notion of strategyproofness is well-established in social choice and much stronger than the notion of 'strategyproofness' used in some of the cake-cutting literature (see e.g., [6]), where truth-telling is a maximin strategy and it need not be dominant strategy incentive compatible. Similarly, a deterministic algorithm is *group-strategyproof* if there exists no coalition $S \subseteq N$ such that members of S can misreport their preferences so that each agent in S gets at least as preferred an allocation and at least one agent gets a strictly better payoff. A deterministic algorithm is *weak group-strategyproof* if there exists no coalition $S \subseteq N$ such that members of S can misreport their preferences so that each agent in S gets a strictly more preferred allocation. A randomized algorithm is *strategyproof in expectation* if the expected utility from the random allocation that every agent receives in expectation under a profile where he reported truthfully is at least as large as the expected utility that he receives under a profile

---

[4] Let us say that a cake is part chocolate and part vanilla. An agent may easily state that chocolate is more preferable than vanilla but would require much more effort to say that if the vanilla piece is α times bigger than the chocolate piece then he would prefer both pieces equally.

where he misreports while fixing the other agents' reports. We say that a cake cutting algorithm satisfies *unanimity*, if when each agent has positive valuation for at most $1/n$ of the cake and the interval of the cake for which he has positive valuation does not intersect with intervals of the cake for which other agents have positive valuation, then each agent is allocated the whole interval for which he has positive valuation.

Relation between the properties of cake cutting algorithms. We highlight some important relations between the main properties of cake cutting algorithms.

Remark 1. For cake cutting, *a*) Envy-freeness and non-wastefulness $\implies$ proportionality; *b*) Robust proportionality $\implies$ proportionality; *c*) Robust envy-freeness $\implies$ envy-freeness; *d*) Robust envy-freeness and non-wastefulness $\implies$ robust proportionality; *e*) Group strategyproofness $\implies$ weak group strategyproofness $\implies$ strategyproofness; *f*) Pareto optimality $\implies$ non-wastefulness $\implies$ unanimity; *g*) two agents, proportionality $\implies$ envy-freeness; *h*) two agents, robust proportionality $\implies$ robust envy-freeness.

The free disposal assumption. We may assume without lost of generality that every part of the cake is desired by at least one agent. If that is not the case, then we can discard the parts that are desired by no one and rescale what is left so that we get a $[0, 1]$ interval representation of the cake. Notice that this procedure preserves the aforementioned properties of fairness and efficiency. The free disposal assumption is necessary to ensure the algorithm of Chen et al. [10], which is a special case of two of our algorithms, to be strategyproof for piecewise uniform valuations. The existence of a non-free disposal algorithm that satisfies all of the desirable properties in the piecewise uniform setting remains an open question. Now we are ready to present our algorithms.

3 CCEA — Controlled Cake Eating Algorithm

CCEA (Controlled Cake Eating Algorithm) is based on CC (Controlled Consuming) algorithm of Athanassoglou and Sethuraman [1]. Since the original PS algorithm is also known as the simultaneous eating algorithm, we give our algorithm the name *Controlled Cake Eating Algorithm*. CCEA first divides the cake up into disjoint intervals each of whose endpoints are consecutive points of discontinuity of the agents' valuation functions. We will refer to these intervals as *intervals induced by the discontinuity points*. The idea is to form a one-to-one correspondence of the set of cake intervals with a set of houses of an assignment problem. In an assignment problem, we have a set of agents and a set of houses. Each agent has a preference ordering over the set of houses. Given two houses h and h', we will use the notation $h \succsim_i h'$ to indicate that agent i prefers h over h'. In our case, the preferences of agents over the houses are naturally induced by the relative height of the piecewise constant function lines in the respective intervals. The technical heart of the algorithm is in CC (Controlled Consuming) algorithm of Athanassoglou and Sethuraman [1]. Note that even though in the standard assignment problem, each house has a size of one and each agent has a demand of one house, the CC algorithm still applies in the case where the intervals corresponding to the houses

have different lengths and there is no constraint on the total length of an agent's allocation. Once CC has been used to compute a fractional assignment p, it is straightforward
to compute a corresponding cake allocation. If an agent i gets a fraction of house h_j,
then in the cake allocation agent i gets the same fraction of subinterval J_j.

Input: Piecewise constant value functions.
Output: A robust envy-free allocation.
1 Divide the regions according to agent value functions. Let $\mathcal{J} = \{J_1, \ldots, J_m\}$ be the set of
   subintervals of $[0, 1]$ formed by consecutive discontinuity points.
2 Consider $(N, H, \succsim, size(\cdot))$ where

   - $H = \{h_1, \ldots, h_m\}$ where $h_i = J_i$ for all $i \in \{1, \ldots, m\}$
   - $\succsim$ is defined as follows: $h \succsim_i h'$ if and only if $v_i(x) \geq v_i(y)$ for $x \in h$ and $y \in h'$;
   - $size(h_j) = 1$ for $h_j \in \arg\max_{j \in \{1, \ldots, m\}}(len(J_j))$;
     $size(h_j) = \dfrac{len(J_j)}{(\max_{j \in \{1, \ldots, m\}}(len(J_j)))}$ for all $h_j \notin \arg\max_{j \in \{1, \ldots, m\}}(len(J_j))$;

3 Discard the houses that give every agent a utility of zero from H to obtain H'.
4 $p \longleftarrow CC(N, H', \succsim, size(\cdot))$
5 For interval J_j, agent i is an allocated subinterval of J_j, denoted by J_j^i, which is of length
   $p_{ih_j}/size(h_j) \times len(J_j)$. For example, if $J_j = [a_j, b_j]$, then one possibility of J_j^i can be $[a_j + \sum_{n=1}^{i-1} p_{ih_j}/size(h_j) \times len(J_j), a_j + \sum_{n=1}^{i} p_{ih_j}/size(h_j) \times len(J_j)]$.
   $X_i \longleftarrow \bigcup_{j=1}^{m} J_j^i$ for all $i \in N$
6 **return** $X = (X_1, \ldots, X_n)$

Algorithm 1. CCEA (Controlled Cake Eating Algorithm)

CCEA satisfies the strong fairness property of robust envy-freeness.

Proposition 1. *For piecewise constant valuations, CCEA satisfies robust envy-freeness
and non-wastefulness.*

Proposition 2. *CCEA runs in time $O(n^5 m^2 \log(n^2/m))$, where n is the number of agents
and m is the number of subintervals defined by the union of discontinuity points of the
agents' valuation functions.*

Although CCEA satisfies the demanding property of robust envy-freeness, we show
that CCEA is not strategyproof even for two agents. Later (in Section 5), we will present
a different algorithm that is both robust envy-free and strategyproof for two agents.

Proposition 3. *For piecewise constant valuations, CCEA is not strategyproof even for
two agents.*

If we restrict the preferences to piecewise uniform valuations, then CCEA is not
only strategyproof but group-strategyproof. We first show that in this restricted setting,
CCEA is in fact equivalent to the algorithm of [9].

Lemma 1. *For piecewise uniform value functions, CCEA is equivalent to Mechanism
1 of Chen et al. [9].*

Since the set of valuations that can be reported is bigger in cake cutting than in the assignment problem, establishing group strategyproofness does not follow automatically from group-strategyproofness of CC for dichotomous preferences (Theorem 2, [5]). We show that that CCEA and hence Mechanism 1 of Chen et al. [9] is group strategyproof for piecewise uniform valuations.[5]

Proposition 4. *For piecewise uniform value functions, CCEA is group strategyproof.*

For piecewise uniform valuations, CCEA is also Pareto optimal. The result follows from Lemma 1 and the fact that Mechanism 1 of Chen et al. [9] is Pareto optimal.

Proposition 5. *For piecewise uniform value functions, CCEA is Pareto optimal.*

4 MEA — Market Equilibrium Algorithm

In the previous section we presented CCEA which is not Pareto optimal for piecewise constant valuations. If we relax the robust notion of fairness to envy-freeness, then we can use fundamental results in general equilibrium theory to formulate a convex program that always returns an envy-free and Pareto optimal allocation as its optimal solution. For each valuation profile, let $J = \{J_1, \ldots, J_m\}$ be the intervals whose endpoints are consecutive points in the union of break points of the agents' valuation functions. Let x_{ij} be the length of any subinterval of J_i that is allocated to agent j. Then we run a convex program to compute a Pareto optimal and envy-free allocation. Once we determine the length of J_j to be allocated to an agent, we allocate any subinterval of that length to the agent. We will call the convex program outlined in Algorithm 2 as the *Market Equilibrium Algorithm (MEA)*. MEA is based on computing the market equilibrium via a primal-dual algorithm for a convex program that was shown to be polynomial-time solvable by Devanur et al. [12].

Proposition 6. *MEA is polynomial-time, Pareto optimal and envy free.*

We mention here that the connection between cake cutting and computing market equilibria is not completely new: Reijnierse and Potters [16] presented an algorithm to compute an approximately envy-free and Pareto optimal allocation for cake cutting with general valuations. However their algorithm is not polynomial-time even for piecewise constant valuations [21]. MEA requires the machinery of convex programming. It remains open whether MEA can be implemented via linear programming. Cohler et al. [11] presented an algorithm that uses a linear program to compute an optimal envy-free allocation. The allocation is Pareto optimal among all envy-free allocations. However it need not be Pareto optimal in general. Similarly, Brams et al. [8] used a similar connection to a linear Fisher market as MEA to compute a maxsum envy-free allocations. However the allocation they compute may not be Pareto optimal even for piecewise uniform valuations (Theorem 7, [8]). Although MEA is not robust envy-free like CCEA, it is Pareto optimal because it maximizes the Nash product. What is interesting is that

---

[5] Chen et al. [9] had shown that their mechanism for piecewise uniform valuations is strategyproof.

Input: Cake-cutting problem with piecewise constant valuations.
Output: A proportional, envy-free, and Pareto optimal allocation.

1 Let $J = \{J_1, \ldots, J_m\}$ be the intervals whose endpoints are consecutive points in the union of break points of the agents' valuation functions. Discard any interval that gives an utility of zero to every agent. Let x_{ij} be the length of any subinterval of J_i that is allocated to agent j.

2 $l_i \longleftarrow len(J_i)$
3 Solve the following convex program.

$$\min \quad -\sum_{j=1}^{n} log(u_j)$$

$$\text{s.t.} \quad u_j = \sum_{i=1}^{m} v_{ij} x_{ij} \quad \forall j = 1, \ldots, n; \quad \sum_{j=1}^{n} x_{ij} \le l_i \quad \forall i = 1, \ldots, m; \quad x_{ij} \ge 0 \quad \forall i, j.$$

4 Let $u_j^\star, x_{ij}^\star$ be an optimal solution to the convex program. Partition every interval J_i into n subintervals where the j-th subinterval J_i^j has length $x_{ij}^\star$.
5 $Y_j \longleftarrow \cup_{i=1}^{m} J_i^j$ be the allocation of each $j = 1, \ldots, n$.
6 **return** $Y = (Y_1, \ldots, Y_n)$.

Algorithm 2. MEA (Market Equilibrium Algorithm)

under uniform valuations, both MEA and CCEA are equivalent. In the next result we demonstrate this equivalence (Proposition 7). The proof requires a careful comparison of both CCEA and MEA under uniform valuations.

Proposition 7. *For piecewise uniform valuations, the allocation given by CCEA is identical to that given by MEA.*

Corollary 1. *For piecewise uniform valuations, MEA is group-strategyproof.*

Thus if we want to generalize Mechanism 1 of Chen et al. [9] to piecewise constant valuations and maintain robust envy-freeness then we should opt for CCEA. On the other hand, if want to still achieve Pareto optimality, then MEA is the appropriate generalization. In both generalizations, we lose strategyproofness.

5 MCSD — Mixed Constrained Serial Dictatorship Algorithm

Thus far, we presented two polynomial-time algorithms, each of which satisfies a different set of properties. CCEA is robust envy-free and non-wasteful, whereas MEA is Pareto optimal and envy-free. This naturally leads to the following question: does there exist an algorithm that satisfies all of the properties that CCEA and MEA satisfy? The answer is no, as there is no algorithm that is both Pareto optimal and robust proportional (Theorem 5). Similarly, there is no algorithm that satisfies the properties MEA satisfies along with strategyproofness (Theorem 6). Lastly, there is no algorithm that satisfies the properties CCEA satisfies plus strategyproofness (Theorem 7). Consequently, we may conclude that the properties satisfied by CCEA and MEA are respectively maximal subsets of properties that an algorithm can satisfy for piecewise constant valuations.

We saw that CCEA and MEA are only strategyproof for piecewise uniform valuations. In light of the impossibility results established, it is reasonable to ask what other property along with strategyproofness can be satisfied by some algorithm. It follows from (Theorem 3, [19]) that the only type of strategyproof and Pareto optimal mechanisms are dictatorships. Chen et al. [10] raised the question whether there exists a strategyproof and proportional algorithm for piecewise constant valuations. The algorithm MCSD answers this question partially.

Before diving into the MCSD algorithm, it is worth noting that there is a fundamental difference between the setting of assignment objects to agents where the agents have homogeneous preferences over the objects and the cake cutting setting. In the former setting, the objects that we are allocating are well defined and known to the public. On the other hand, in the cake cutting setting, the discontinuity points of each agent's valuation function is private information for the agent. In order to illustrate this difficulty, consider the uniform allocation rule. The uniform allocation rule (that assigns $1/n$ of each house) is both strategyproof and proportional in the random assignment setting. However it cannot be adapted for cake cutting with piecewise constant valuations since strategyproofness is no longer satisfied if converting $1/n$ of each interval (induced by the agent valuations) to actual subintervals is done deterministically. Chen et al. [10] resorted to randomizing the conversion process from fractions of intervals to subintervals in order to make the uniform allocation rule strategyproof in expectation.

Proposition 8. *No deterministic algorithm that implements the uniform allocation rule can be strategyproof if it also satisfies the free disposal property.*

In order to motivate MCSD, we first give a randomized algorithm that is strategyproof and robust proportional in expectation. The algorithm is a variant of random dictatorship. Under random dictatorship, if the whole cake is acceptable to each agent, then each time a dictator is chosen, he will take the whole cake which is unfair ex post. We add an additional requirement which is helpful. We require that each time a dictator is chosen, the piece he takes has to be of maximum value $1/n$ length of the total size of the cake. This algorithm *Constrained Random Serial Dictatorship (CRSD)* draws a random permutation of the agents. It then makes the allocation to agents in the order that the lottery is drawn. Every time that it is agent i's turn to receive his allocation, CRSD looks at the remaining portion of the cake and allocates a maximum value $1/n$ length piece of the cake to agent i (breaking ties arbitrarily). Notice that CRSD is strategyproof, as in every draw of lottery, it is in the best interest of the agents to report their valuation function truthfully in order to obtain a piece that maximizes his valuation function out of the remaining pieces of cake. We will see, through the proof of Proposition 10, that CRSD is robust proportional in expectation.

MCSD is an algorithm that derandomizes CRSD by looking at its allocation for all $n!$ different permutations and aggregating them in a suitable manner. The algorithm is formally presented as Algorithm 3. Although MCSD does not necessarily require $n!$ cuts of the cake, it is #P-complete to implement [3, 18] and may take exponential time if the number of agents is not a constant.

Proposition 9. *For piecewise constant valuations, MCSD is well-defined and returns a feasible cake allocation in which each agent gets a piece of size $1/n$.*

Input: Cake-cutting problem with piecewise constant valuations.
Output: A robust proportional allocation.

1 **for** each $\pi \in \Pi^N$ **do**
2      $C \longleftarrow [0, 1]$ (intervals left)
3   **for** $i = 1$ to n **do**
4          $X_{\pi(i)}^{\pi} \longleftarrow$ maximum preference cake piece of size $1/n$ from C
5          $C \longleftarrow C - X_{\pi(i)}^{\pi};\ i \longleftarrow i + 1$.
6   **end for**
7 **end for**
8 Construct a disjoint and exhaustive interval set $\mathscr{J}'$ induced by the discontinuity points in agent valuations and the cake cuts in the $n!$ cake allocations.
9 $Y_i \longleftarrow$ empty allocation for each $i \in N$.
10 **for** each $J_j = [a_j, b_j] \in \mathscr{J}'$ **do**
11   **for** each $i \in N$ **do**
12   Let $p_{ij} = \frac{count(i, J_j)}{n!}$ where $count(i, J_j)$ is the number of permutations in which i gets J_j.

13   Generate $A_{ij} \subseteq J_j$, which is of length $p_{ij}|J_j|$ according to some subroutine.
14          $Y_i \longleftarrow Y_i \cup A_{ij}$
15   **end for**
16 **end for**
17 **return** $Y = (Y_1, \ldots, Y_n)$

Algorithm 3. MCSD (Mixed Constrained Serial Dictatorship)

Proposition 10. *For piecewise constant valuations, MCSD satisfies robust proportionality and symmetry.*

Unlike CRSD, MCSD interprets the probability of allocating each interval to an agent as allocating a fractional portion of the interval to that agent. Unless the actual way of allocating the fractions is specified, one cannot discuss the notion of strategyproofness for MCSD because a deviating agent is unable to properly evaluate his allocation against his true valuation function in the reported profile. Contrary to intuition, MCSD may or may not be strategyproof depending on how the fractional parts of each interval are allocated.

Remark 2. MCSD is not strategyproof if the fraction of each interval of $\mathscr{J}'$ is allocated deterministically.

In light of this difficulty, we will implement a method (Algorithm 5) that randomly allocates the fractions of intervals to agents. For every interval, the method chooses a starting point in the interval uniformly at random to make the cut. Agent 1 receives the left-most subinterval from the starting point with length dictated by MCSD, followed by agent 2, so on and so forth. To generate this starting point for all subintervals, it suffices to use a single bit of randomness together with the proper dilation and translation for every interval. With this implementation, MCSD is strategyproof in expectation.

Proposition 11. *MCSD implemented with the aforementioned random allocation rule is strategyproof in expectation.*

Although MCSD is strategyproof in expectation, it fails to satisfy truthfulness based on group-based deviations no matter how the fractions of each interval are allocated.

1: Generate $U_j \sim unif[a_j, b_j]$.

2: For $a_j \leq x \leq 2b_j - a_j$, let $\mod(x) = x$ if $a_j \leq x \leq b_j$ and $x - (b_j - a_j)$ if $x > b_j$. Let

$$A_{ij} = [\ \mod(U_j + \sum_{k=1}^{i-1} p_{kj}(b_j - a_j)),\ \ \mod(U_j + \sum_{k=1}^{i} p_{kj}(b_j - a_j))]$$

if $\mod(U_j + \sum_{k=1}^{i-1} p_{kj}(b_j - a_j)) \leq \mod(U + \sum_{k=1}^{i} p_{kj}(b_j - a_j))$ and

$$A_{ij} = [a_j,\ \ \mod(U_j + \sum_{k=1}^{i} p_{kj}(b_j - a_j))] \cup [\ \mod(U_j + \sum_{k=1}^{i-1} p_{nj}(b_j - a_j)), b_j]\ \text{otherwise.}$$

Algorithm 4. A subroutine that converts fractional allocation into subintervals via randomization

Proposition 12. *For cake cutting with piecewise constant valuations, MCSD is not weakly group-strategyproof even for two agents.*

Moreover, for cake cutting with piecewise uniform valuations, MCSD is not weakly group-strategyproof since RSD is not for random assignment for dichotomous preferences [5]. On the fairness front, even though MCSD satisfies both proportionality and symmetry, it does not satisfy the stronger notion of envy-freeness.

Proposition 13. *MCSD is not necessarily envy-free for three agents even for piecewise uniform valuations.*

Another drawback of MCSD is that it is not Pareto optimal for piecewise constant valuations. However for two agents, it is robust envy-free and polynomial-time.

Proposition 14. *For two agents and piecewise constant valuations, MCSD is (ex post) robust envy-free, and polynomial-time but not Pareto optimal.*

6 Conclusion

We presented three deterministic cake-cutting algorithms — CCEA, MEA, and MCSD. We then proposed a specific randomized version of MCSD that is truthful in expectation. All the algorithms have their relative merits. Some of our results also extend to the more general cake-cutting setting in which agents do not have uniform claims to the cake or when agents are endowed with the cake pieces [2]. Cake cutting is a fundamental problem with numerous applications to computer science. In order for theory to be more relevant to practice, we envision exciting work in richer models of cake cutting.

Acknowledgments. The authors acknowledge the helpful comments of Simina Brânzei and Jay Sethuraman. NICTA is funded by the Australian Government through the Department of Communications and the Australian Research Council through the ICT Centre of Excellence Program. Chun Ye acknowledges NSF grants CMMI-0916453 and CMMI-1201045.

References

1. Athanassoglou, S., Sethuraman, J.: House allocation with fractional endowments. International Journal of Game Theory 40(3), 481–513 (2011)
2. Aziz, H., Ye, C.: Cake cutting algorithms for piecewise constant and piecewise uniform valuations. Technical Report 1307.2908, arXiv.org (2013)
3. Aziz, H., Brandt, F., Brill, M.: The computational complexity of random serial dictatorship. Economics Letters 121(3), 341–345 (2013)
4. Bogomolnaia, A., Moulin, H.: A new solution to the random assignment problem. Journal of Economic Theory 100(2), 295–328 (2001)
5. Bogomolnaia, A., Moulin, H.: Random matching under dichotomous preferences. Econometrica 72(1), 257–279 (2004)
6. Brams, S.J.: Mathematics and Democracy: Designing Better Voting and Fair-Division Procedures. Princeton University Press (2008)
7. Brams, S.J., Taylor, A.D.: Fair Division: From Cake-Cutting to Dispute Resolution. Cambridge University Press (1996)
8. Brams, S.J., Feldman, M., Morgenstern, J., Lai, J.K., Procaccia, A.D.: On maxsum fair cake divisions. In: Proc. of 26th AAAI Conference, pp. 1285–1291. AAAI Press (2012)
9. Chen, Y., Lai, J.K., Parkes, D.C., Procaccia, A.D.: Truth, justice, and cake cutting. In: Proc. of 24th AAAI Conference, pp. 756–761 (2010)
10. Chen, Y., Lai, J.K., Parkes, D.C., Procaccia, A.D.: Truth, justice, and cake cutting. Games and Economic Behavior 77(1), 284–297 (2013)
11. Cohler, Y.J., Lai, J.K., Parkes, D.C., Procaccia, A.D.: Optimal envy-free cake cutting. In: Proc. of 25th AAAI Conference, pp. 626–631 (2011)
12. Devanur, N., Papadimitriou, C.H., Saberi, A., Vazirani, V.: Market equilibrium via a primal–dual algorithm for a convex program. Journal of the ACM 55(5) (2008)
13. Katta, A.-K., Sethuraman, J.: A solution to the random assignment problem on the full preference domain. Journal of Economic Theory 131(1), 231–250 (2006)
14. Maya, A., Nisan, N.: Incentive compatible two player cake cutting. In: Goldberg, P.W. (ed.) WINE 2012. LNCS, vol. 7695, pp. 170–183. Springer, Heidelberg (2012)
15. Mossel, E., Tamuz, O.: Truthful fair division. In: Kontogiannis, S., Koutsoupias, E., Spirakis, P.G. (eds.) SAGT 2010. LNCS, vol. 6386, pp. 288–299. Springer, Heidelberg (2010)
16. Reijnierse, J.H., Potters, J.A.M.: On finding an envy-free Pareto-optimal division. Mathematical Programming 83, 291–311 (1998)
17. Robertson, J.M., Webb, W.A.: Cake Cutting Algorithms: Be Fair If You Can. A. K. Peters (1998)
18. Saban, D., Sethuraman, J.: The complexity of computing the random priority allocation matrix. In: Chen, Y., Immorlica, N. (eds.) WINE 2013. LNCS, vol. 8289, p. 421. Springer, Heidelberg (2013)
19. Schummer, J.: Strategy-proofness versus efficiency on restricted domains of exchange economies. Social Choice and Welfare 14, 47–56 (1997)
20. Tian, Y.: Strategy-proof and efficient offline interval scheduling and cake cutting. In: Chen, Y., Immorlica, N. (eds.) WINE 2013. LNCS, vol. 8289, pp. 436–437. Springer, Heidelberg (2013)
21. Zivan, R., Dudík, M., Okamoto, S., Sycara, K.: Reducing untruthful manipulation in envy-free pareto optimal resource allocation. In: IEEE/WIC/ACM International Conference on Web Intelligence and Intelligent Agent Technology, pp. 391–398 (2010)

Network Cournot Competition[*][**]

Melika Abolhassani[1], MohammadHossein Bateni[2], MohammadTaghi Hajiaghayi[1], Hamid Mahini[1], and Anshul Sawant[1][***]

[1] University of Maryland, College Park, USA,
[2] Google Research, New York, USA

Abstract. Cournot competition, introduced in 1838 by Antoine Augustin Cournot, is a fundamental economic model that represents firms competing in a single market of a homogeneous good. Each firm tries to maximize its utility—naturally a function of the production cost as well as market price of the product—by deciding on the amount of production. This problem has been studied comprehensively in Economics and Game Theory; however, in today's dynamic and diverse economy, many firms often compete in more than one market simultaneously, i.e., each market might be shared among a subset of these firms. In this situation, a bipartite graph models the access restriction where firms are on one side, markets are on the other side, and edges demonstrate whether a firm has access to a market or not. We call this game *Network Cournot Competition* (NCC). Computation of equilibrium, taking into account a network of markets and firms and the different forms of cost and price functions, makes challenging and interesting new problems.

In this paper, we propose algorithms for finding pure Nash equilibria of NCC games in different situations. First, we carefully design a potential function for NCC, when the price function for each market is a linear function of it total production. This result lets us leverage optimization techniques for a single function rather than multiple utility functions of many firms. However, for nonlinear price functions, this approach is not feasible—there is indeed no single potential function that captures the utilities of all firms for the case of nonlinear price functions. We model the problem as a nonlinear complementarity problem in this case, and design a polynomial-time algorithm that finds an equilibrium of the game for strongly convex cost functions and strongly monotone revenue functions. We also explore the class of price functions that ensures strong monotonicity of the revenue function, and show it consists of a broad class of functions. Moreover, we discuss the uniqueness of equilibria in both these cases: our algorithms find the unique equilibria of the games. Last but not least, when the cost of production in one market is independent from the cost of production in other markets for all firms, the problem can be separated into several independent classical *Cournot Oligopoly* problems in which the firms compete over a single market. We give the first combinatorial algorithm for this widely studied problem. Interestingly, our algorithm is much simpler and faster than previous optimization-based approaches.

[*] Supported in part by NSF CAREER award 1053605, NSF grant CCF-1161626, Google Faculty Research award, ONR YIP award N000141110662, DARPA/AFOSR grant FA9550-12-1-0423.
[**] Full version publically available on arXiv since May 8, 2014. See http://arxiv.org/abs/1405.1794.
[***] Supported in part by ARO grants W911NF0910206, W911NF1160215, W911NF1110344, ARO/Penn State MURI award, Israel Ministry of Defense Grant 4440366064.

T.-Y. Liu et al. (Eds.): WINE 2014, LNCS 8877, pp. 15–29, 2014.

1 Introduction

In the crude oil market the equilibrium price is set by the interplay of supply and demand. Since there are several ways for transporting crude oil from an oil-producing country to an oil-importing country, the market for crude oil seems to be an oligopoly with almost a single worldwide price[1]. In particular, the major portion of the market share belongs to the members of the Organization of Petroleum Exporting Countries (OPEC). The worldwide price for crude oil is mainly influenced by OPEC, and the few fluctuations in regional prices are negligible.

The power of an oil-producing country, in market for crude oil, mainly depends on its resources and its cost of production rather than its position in the network. [2]

The market for natural gas behaves differently from that for crude oil and matches our study well. Unlike the crude oil market with a world-wide price, the natural gas market is segmented and regional [40, 35]. Nowadays, pipelines are the most efficient way for transporting natural gas from one region to another. This fragments the market into different regional markets with their own prices. Therefore, the market for natural gas can be modeled by a network where the power of each country highly depends on its position in the network. For example, an importing country with access to only one exporting country suffers a monopolistic price, while an importing country having access to multiple suppliers enjoys a lower price as a result of the price competition. As an evidence, EU Commission Staff Working Document (2006) reports different prices for natural gas in different markets, varying from almost 0 to €300 per thousand cubic meters [15].

In this paper we study selling a utility with a distribution network—e.g., natural gas, water and electricity—in several markets when the clearing price of each market is determined by its supply and demand. The distribution network fragments the market into different regional markets with their own prices. Therefore, the relations between suppliers and submarkets form a complex network [11, 39, 10, 18, 15]. For example, a market with access to only one supplier suffers a monopolistic price, while a market having access to multiple suppliers enjoys a lower price as a result of the price competition.

Antoine Augustin Cournot introduced the first model for studying the duopoly competition in 1838. He proposed a model where two individuals own different springs of water, and sell it independently. Each individual decides on the amount of water to supply, and then the aggregate water supply determines the market price through an inverse demand function. Cournot characterizes the unique equilibrium outcome of the market when both suppliers have the same marginal costs of production, and the inverse demand function is linear. He argued that in the unique equilibrium outcome, the market price is above the marginal cost.

Joseph Bertrand 1883 criticized the Cournot model, where the strategy of each player is the quantity to supply, and in turn suggested to consider prices, rather than quantities, as strategies. In the Bertrand model each firm chooses a price for a homogeneous good, and the firm announcing the lowest price gets all the market share. Since the firm with the lowest price receives all the demand, each firm has incentive to price below the

---

[1] An oligopoly is a market that is shared between several sellers.

[2] However, political relations may also affect the power of a country.

current market price unless the market price matches its cost. Therefore, the market price will be equal to the marginal cost in an equilibrium outcome of the Bertrand model, assuming all marginal costs are the same and there are at least two competitors in the market.

The Cournot and Bertrand models are two basic tools for investigating the competitive market price, and have attracted much interest for modeling real markets; see, e.g., [11, 39, 10, 18]. In particular, the predictive power of each strongly depends on the nature of the market, and varies from application to application. For example, the Bertrand model explains the situation where firms literally set prices, e.g., the cellphone market, the laptop market, and the TV market. On the other hand, Cournot's approach would be suitable for modeling markets like those of crude oil, natural gas, and electricity, where firms decide about quantities rather than prices.

There are several attempts to find equilibrium outcomes of the Cournot or Bertrand competitions in the oligopolistic setting, where a small number of firms compete in only one market; see, e.g., [27, 36, 34, 21, 20, 41]. Nevertheless, it is not entirely clear what equilibrium outcomes of these games are when firms compete over more than one market. In this paper, we investigate the problem of finding equilibrium outcomes of the Cournot competition in a network setting where there are several markets for a homogeneous good and each market is accessible to a subset of firms.

The reader is referred to the full version of the paper to see a warm-up basic example for the Cournot competition in the network setting. In general due to interest of space, all missing proofs and examples are in the longer version of this paper on arXiv (http://arxiv.org/abs/1405.1794).

1.1 Related Work

Despite several papers that investigate the Cournot competition in an oligopolistic setting (see, e.g., [36, 21, 20, 41]), little is known about the Cournot competition in a network. Independently and in parallel to our work, Bimpikis et al. [6] (EC'14) study the Cournot competition in a network setting, and considers a network of firms and markets where each firm chooses a quantity to supply in each accessible market. The core of their work lies in building connections between the equilibrium outcome of the game and paths in the underlying network, and changes in profits and welfares upon coalition of two firms. While Bimpikis et al. [6] (EC'14) only consider the competition for linear inverse demand functions and quadratic cost functions (of total production), in this study, we consider the same model when the cost functions and the demand functions may have quite general forms. We show the game with linear inverse demand functions is a potential game and therefore has a unique equilibrium outcome. Furthermore, we present two polynomial-time algorithms for finding an equilibrium outcome for a wide range of cost functions and demand functions.

While we investigate the Cournot competition in networks, there is a paper which considers the Bertrand competition in network setting [3], albeit in a much more restricted case of only two firms competing in each market. While we investigate the Cournot competition in networks, there is a recent line of research exploring bargaining processes in networks; see, e.g., Bateni et al. [4], Kanoria et al. [24], Farczadi et al. [16], Chakraborty et al. [9]. Agents may cooperate to generate surplus to be divided based on an agreement. A bargaining process determines how this surplus is divided between the participants.

The final price of each market in the Cournot competition is one that clears the market. Finding a market clearance equilibrium is a well-established problem, and several papers propose polynomial-time algorithms for computing such equilibria. Examples include Arrow-Debreu market and its special case Fisher market (see related work on these markets [14, 13, 23, 12, 19]). The first polynomial-time algorithm for finding an Arrow-Debreu market equilibrium is proposed by Jain [23] for a special case with linear utilities. The Fisher market, a special case of the Arrow-Debreu market, attracted a lot of attention as well. Eisenberg and Gale [14] present the first polynomial-time algorithm by transferring the problem to a concave cost maximization problem. Devanur et al. [13] design the first combinatorial algorithm which runs in polynomial time and finds the market clearance equilibrium when the utility functions are linear. This result is later improved by Orlin [33].

For the sake of completeness, we refer to recent works in the computer science literature [22, 17], which investigate the Cournot competition in an oligopolistic setting. Immorlica et al. [22] study a coalition formation game in a Cournot oligopoly. In this setting, firms form coalitions, and the utility of each coalition, which is equally divided between its members, is determined by the equilibrium of a Cournot competition between coalitions. They prove the price of anarchy, which is the ratio between the social welfare of the worse stable partition and the social optimum, is $\Theta(n^{2/5})$ where n is the number of firms. Fiat et al. [17] consider a Cournot competition where agents may decide to be non-myopic. In particular, they define two principal strategies to maximize revenue and profit (revenue minus cost) respectively. Note that in the classic Cournot competition all agents want to maximize their profit. However, in their study each agent first chooses its principal strategy and then acts accordingly. The authors prove this game has a pure Nash equilibrium and the best response dynamics will converge to an equilibrium. They also show the equilibrium price in this game is lower than the equilibrium price in the standard Cournot competition.

1.2 Results and Techniques

We consider the problem of Cournot competition on a network of markets and firms (NCC) for different classes of cost and inverse demand functions. Adding these two dimensions to the classical Cournot competition which only involves a single market and basic cost and inverse demand functions yields an engaging but complicated problem that requires advanced techniques to analyze. For simplicity of notation we model the competition by a bipartite graph rather than a hypergraph: vertices on one side denote the firms, and vertices on the other side denote the markets. An edge between a firm and a market shows that the firm has access to the market. The complexity of finding the equilibrium, in addition to the number of markets and firms, depends on the classes that inverse demand and production cost functions belong to.

Cost functions	Inverse demand functions	Running time	Technique
Convex	Linear	$O(E^3)$	Convex optimization, Potential game formulation
Convex	Strongly monotone marginal revenue function[3]	$\text{poly}(E)$	Reduction to a nonlinear complementarity problem
Convex, separable	Concave	$O(n \log^2 Q_{\max})$	Supermodular optimization, nested binary search

We summarize our results in the above table, where E denotes the number of edges of the bipartite graph, n denotes the number of firms, and $Q_{\max}$ denotes the maximum possible total quantity in the oligopoly network at any equilibrium. In our results we assume the inverse demand functions are nonincreasing functions of total production in the market. This is the basic assumption in the classical Cournot Competition model: As the price in the market increases, it is reasonable to believe that the buyers drop out of the market and demand for the product decreases. The classical Cournot Competition model as well as many previous works on Cournot Competition model assumes linearity of the inverse demand function [6, 22]. In fact there is little work on generalizing the inverse demand function in this model. The second and third rows of the table show we have developed efficient algorithms for more general inverse demand functions satisfying concavity rather than linearity. The assumption of monotonicity of the inverse demand function is a standard assumption in Economics [2, 1, 30]. We assume cost functions to be convex which is the case in many works related to both Cournot Competition and Bertrand Network [28, 42]. In a previous work [6], the author considers NCC, however, assumes that inverse demand functions are linear and all the cost functions are quadratic function of the total production by the firm in all markets which is quite restrictive. Most of the results in other related works in Cournot Competition and Bertrand Network require linearity of the cost functions [3, 22]. Next comes a brief overview of our results.

Linear Inverse Demand Functions. In case inverse demand functions are linear and production costs are convex, we present a fast algorithm to obtain the equilibrium. This approach works by showing that NCC belongs to a class of games called *potential games*. In such games, the collective strategy of the independent players is to maximize a single potential function. The potential function is carefully designed so that changes made by one player reflects in the same way in the potential function as in their own utility function. Based on network structure, we design a potential function for the game, and establish the desired property. Moreover, in the case of convex cost functions, we prove concavity of the designed potential function (Theorem 6) concluding convex optimization methods can be employed to find the optimum and hence, the equilibrium of the original Cournot competition. We also discuss uniqueness of equilibria if the cost functions are strictly concave. We prove the following theorems in Section 3.

Theorem 1. *NCC with linear inverse demand functions forms a potential game.*

---

[3] Marginal revenue function is the vector function mapping production quantities on edges to marginal revenue along them.

Theorem 2. *Our designed potential function for NCC with linear inverse demand functions is concave provided that the cost functions are convex. Furthermore, the potential function is strictly concave if the cost functions are strictly convex, and hence the equilibrium for the game is unique. In addition, a polynomial-time algorithm finds the optimum of the potential function which describes the market clearance prices.*

The General Case. Since the above approach does not work for nonlinear inverse demand functions, we design another interesting but more involved algorithm to capture more general forms of inverse demand functions. We show that an equilibrium of the game can be computed in polynomial time if the production cost functions are convex and the revenue function is monotone. Moreover, we show under strict monotonicity of the revenue function, the solution is unique, and therefore our results in this section is structural; i.e., we find the one and only equilibrium[4]. For convergence guarantee we also need Lipschitz condition on derivatives of inverse demand and cost functions. We start the section by modeling our problem as a complementarity problem. Then we prove how holding the aforementioned conditions for cost and revenue functions yields satisfying *Scaled Lipschitz Condition* (SLC) and semidefiniteness for matrices of derivatives of the profit function. SLC is a standard condition widely used in convergence analysis for scalar and vector optimization [43]. Finally, we present our algorithm, and show how meeting these new conditions by inverse demand and cost functions helps us to guarantee polynomial running time of our algorithm. We also give examples of classes of inverse demand functions satisfying the above conditions. These include many families of inverse demand functions including quadratic functions, cubic functions and entropy functions. The following theorem is the main result of Section 4 which summarizes the performance of our algorithm.

Theorem 3. *A solution to NCC can be found in polynomial number of iterations under the following conditions:*

  1. The cost functions are (strongly) convex.
  2. The marginal revenue function is (strongly[5]) monotone.
  3. The first derivative of cost functions and inverse demand functions and the second derivative of inverse demand functions are Lipschitz continuous.

Furthermore, the solution is unique assuming only the first condition. Therefore, our algorithm finds the unique equilibrium of NCC.

Cournot Oligopoly. Another reasonable model for considering cost functions of the firms is the case where the production cost in a market depends only on the quantity produced by the firm in that specific market (and not on quantities produced by this firm in other markets). In other words, the firms have completely independent sections

---

[4] It is worth mentioning that Bimpikis et al. [6] prove the uniqueness of the equilibrium in a concurrent work.

[5] For at least one of the first two conditions, strong version of condition should be satisfied, i.e., either cost functions should be strongly convex or the marginal revenue function should be strongly monotone.

for producing different goods in various markets, and there is no correlation between production cost in separate markets. In this case the competitions are separable; i.e., equilibrium for NCC can be found by finding the quantities at equilibrium for each market individually. This motivates considering Cournot game where the firms compete over a single market. We present a new algorithm for computing equilibrium quantities produced by firms in a Cournot oligopoly, i.e., when the firms compete over a single market. Cournot Oligopoly is a well-known model in Economics, and computation of its Cournot Equilibrium has been subject to a lot of attention. It has been considered in many works including [37, 25, 32, 29, 8] to name a few. The earlier attempts for calculating equilibrium for a general class of inverse demand and cost functions are mainly based on solving a Linear Complementarity Problem or a Variational Inequality. These settings can be then turned into convex optimization problems of size $O(n)$ where n is the number of firms. This means the runtime of the earlier works cannot be better than $O(n^3)$ which is the runtime of the most efficient algorithm known for convex optimization. We give a novel combinatorial algorithm for this important problem when the quantities produced are integral. Our algorithm runs in time $O(n \log^2(Q_{\max}))$ where $Q_{\max}$ is an upper bound on total quantity produced at equilibrium. The following is the main result of Section 5.

Theorem 4. *A polynomial-time algorithm successfully computes the quantities produced by each firm at an equilibrium of the Cournot oligopoly if the inverse demand function is nonincreasing, and the cost functions are convex. In addition, the algorithm runs in time $O(n \log^2(Q_{\max}))$ where $Q_{\max}$ is the maximum possible total quantity in the oligopoly network at any equilibrium.*

2   Notations

Suppose we have a set of n firms denoted by $\mathcal{F}$ and a set of m markets denoted by $\mathcal{M}$. A single good is produced in each market. Each firm may or may not be able to supply a particular market. A bipartite graph is used to demonstrate these relations. In this graph, the markets are denoted by the numbers $1, 2, \ldots, m$ on one side, and the firms are denoted by the numbers $1, 2, \ldots, n$ on the other side. For simplicity, throughout the paper we use the notation $i \in \mathcal{M}$ meaning the market i, and $j \in \mathcal{F}$ meaning firm j. For firm $j \in \mathcal{F}$ and market $i \in \mathcal{M}$ there exists an edge between the corresponding vertices in the bipartite graph if and only if firm j is able to produce the good in market i. This edge will be denoted (i, j). The set of edges of the graph is denoted by $\mathcal{E}$, and the number of edges in the graph is shown by E. For each market $i \in \mathcal{M}$, the set of vertices $N_{\mathcal{M}}(i)$ is the set of firms that this market is connected to in the graph. Similarly, $N_{\mathcal{F}}(j)$ denotes the set of neighbors of firms j among markets. The edges in $\mathcal{E}$ are sorted and numbered $1, \ldots, E$, first based on the number of their corresponding market and then based on the number of their corresponding firm. More formally, edge $(i, j) \in \mathcal{E}$ is ranked above edge $(l, k) \in \mathcal{E}$ if $i < l$ or $i = l$ and $j < k$. The quantity of the good that firm j produces in market i is denoted by q_{ij}. The vector $\mathbf{q}$ is an $E \times 1$ vector that contains all the quantities produced over the edges of the graph in the same order that the edges are numbered.

The demand for good i denoted by D_i is $\sum_{j \in N_{\mathcal{M}}(i)} q_{ij}$. The price of good i, denoted by the function $P_i(D_i)$, is only a decreasing function of total demand for this good and not the individual quantities produced by each firm in this market. For a firm j, the vector s_j denotes the strategy of firm j, which is the vector of all quantities produced by this firm in the markets $N_{\mathcal{F}}(j)$. Firm $j \in \mathcal{F}$ has a cost function related to its strategy denoted by $c_j(s_j)$. The profit that firm j makes is equal to the total money that it obtains by selling its production minus its cost of production. More formally, the profit of firm j is $\pi_j = \sum_{i \in N_{\mathcal{F}}(j)} P_i(D_i)q_{ij} - c_j(s_j)$.

3   Cournot Competition and Potential Games

In this section, we design an efficient algorithm for the case where the price functions are linear. More specifically, we design an innovative *potential function* that captures the changes of all the utility functions simultaneously, and therefore, show how finding the quantities at the equilibrium would be equivalent to finding the set of quantities that maximizes this function. We use the notion of *potential games* as introduced in Monderer and Shapley [31]. In that paper, the authors introduce *potential games* as the set of games for which there exists a *potential function* P^* such that the pure strategy equilibrium set of the game coincides with the pure strategy equilibrium set of a game where every party's utility function is P^*.

Next we design a potential function for NCC if the price functions are linear. Interestingly, this holds for any cost function meaning NCC with arbitrary cost functions is a potential game as long as the price functions are linear. Furthermore, we show when the cost functions are convex, the potential function is concave, and hence any convex optimization method can find the equilibrium of such a Network Cournot Competition. In case cost functions are strictly convex, the potential function is strictly concave. We show the equilibrium that we find is the one and only equilibrium of the game. The pure strategy equilibrium set of any potential game coincides with the pure strategy equilibrium set of a game with the potential function P^* as all parties' utility function.

Theorem 5. *NCC with linear price functions (of quantities) is a potential game.*

We can efficiently compute the equilibrium of the game if the potential function P^* is easy to optimize. Below we show that this function is concave.

Theorem 6. *The potential function P^* from the previous theorem is concave provided that the cost functions of the firms are convex. Moreover, if the cost functions are strictly convex then the potential function is strictly concave.*

The following well-known theorem discusses the uniqueness of the solution to a convex optimization problem.

Theorem 7. *Let $f : \mathcal{K} \to \mathbb{R}^n$ be a strictly concave and continuous function for some finite closed convex space $\mathcal{K} \in \mathbb{R}^n$. Then the convex optimization problem $\max f(x) : x \in \mathcal{K}$ has a unique solution.*

By Theorem 6, if the cost functions are strictly convex then the potential function is strictly concave and hence, by Theorem 7 the equilibrium of the game is unique.

Let $ConvexP(\mathcal{E}, (\alpha_1, \ldots, \alpha_m), (\beta_1, \ldots, \beta_m), (c_1, \ldots, c_n))$ be the following convex optimization program:

$$
\min \quad -\sum_{i \in \mathcal{M}} \left[\alpha_i \sum_{j \in N_{\mathcal{M}}(i)} q_{ij} - \beta_i \sum_{j \in N_{\mathcal{M}}(i)} q_{ij}^2 - \beta_i \sum_{\substack{k \leq j \\ k,j \in N_{\mathcal{M}}(i)}} q_{ij}q_{ik} - \sum_{j \in N_{\mathcal{M}}(i)} \frac{c_j(s_j)}{|N_{\mathcal{F}}(j)|} \right] \quad (1)
$$

$$
\text{subject to} \qquad q_{ij} \geq 0 \ \forall (i,j) \in \mathcal{E}.
$$

Note that in this optimization program we are trying to maximize P^* for a bipartite graph with set of edges $\mathcal{E}$, linear price functions characterized by the pair (α_i, β_i) for each market i, and cost functions c_j for each firm j. This algorithm has a time complexity equal to the time complexity of a convex optimization algorithm with E variables. The best such algorithm has a running time $O(E^3)$ [7].

4 Finding Equilibrium for Cournot Game with General Cost and Inverse Demand Functions

In this section, we focus on a much more general class of price and cost functions. Our approach is based on reducing NCC to a polynomial time solvable class of Nonlinear Complementarity Problem (NLCP). First in 4.1, we introduce our marginal profit function as the vector of partial derivatives of all firms with respect to the quantities they produce. Then in 4.2, we show how this marginal profit function helps in reducing NCC to a general NLCP. We also discuss uniqueness of equilibrium in this situation. Unfortunately, in its most general form, NLCP is computationally intractable. For a large class of functions, though, these problems are polynomial time solvable. In 4.3, we rigorously define the conditions under which NLCP is polynomial time solvable. We then present our algorithm with a theorem, showing it converges in polynomial number of steps. To show the conditions required for quick convergence are not restrictive, we refer the reader to the full version of this paper on arXiv, where we explore a wide range of important price functions that satisfy them.

Assumptions. Throughout the rest of this section we assume that the price functions are decreasing and concave and the cost functions are strongly convex (*to be defined later*). We also assume that for each firm there is a finite quantity at which extra production ceases to be profitable even if that is the only firm operating in the market. Thus, all production hence supply quantities are finite. In addition, we assume Lipschitz continuity and finiteness of the first and the second derivatives of price and cost functions. We note that these Lipschitz continuity assumptions are very common for convergence analysis in convex optimization [7] and finiteness assumptions are implied by Lipschitz continuity. In addition, they are not very restrictive as we do not expect unbounded price/cost fluctuation with supply change. For sake of brevity, we use the terms inverse demand function and price function interchangeably.

4.1 Marginal Profit Function

For the rest of this section, we assume that P_i and c_i are twice differentiable functions of quantities. For a firm j and a market i such that $(i, j) \in \mathcal{E}$, we define $f_{ij} = -\frac{\partial \pi_j}{\partial q_{ij}} = -P_i(D_i) - \frac{\partial P_i(D_i)}{\partial q_{ij}} q_{ij} + \frac{\partial c_j}{\partial q_{ij}}$. Recall that the price function of a market is only a function of the total production in that market and not the individual quantities produced by individual firms. Thus $\frac{\partial P_i(D_i)}{\partial q_{ij}} = \frac{\partial P_i(D_i)}{\partial q_{ik}} \ \forall j, k \in N_{\mathcal{M}}(i)$. Therefore, we replace these terms by $P_i'(D_i)$ to obtain $f_{ij} = -P_i(D_i) - P_i'(D_i)q_{ij} + \frac{\partial c_j}{\partial q_{ij}}$.

Let vector F be the vector of all f_{ij}'s corresponding to the edges of the graph in the same format that we defined the vector q. Note that F is a function of q. Moreover, we separate the part representing marginal revenue from the part representing marginal cost in function F. More formally, we split F into two functions R and S such that $F = R + S$, and the element corresponding to the edge $(i, j) \in \mathcal{E}$ in the *marginal revenue function* $R(q)$ is $r_{ij} = -\frac{\partial \pi_j}{\partial q_{ij}} = -P_i(D_i) - P'(D_i)q_{ij}$, whereas for the *marginal cost function* $S(q)$ is $s_{ij} = \frac{\partial c_j}{\partial q_{ij}}$.

4.2 Non-linear Complementarity Problem

We now formally define NLCP, and prove our problem is an NLCP.

Definition 1. *Let $F : \mathbb{R}^n \to \mathbb{R}^n$ be a continuously differentiable function on $\mathbb{R}_+^n$. The complementarity problem seeks a vector $x \in \mathbb{R}^n$ that satisfies $x \geq 0$, $F(x) \geq 0$, and $x^T F(x) = 0$.*

Theorem 8. *The problem of finding the vector q at equilibrium in the Cournot game is a complementarity problem.*

Definition 2. *$F : \mathcal{K} \to \mathbb{R}^n$ is said to be strictly monotone at x^* if $\langle [F(x) - F(x^*)]^T, x - x^* \rangle \geq 0, \forall x \in \mathcal{K}$. Then, F is said to be strictly monotone if it is strictly monotone at any $x^* \in \mathcal{K}$. Equivalently, F is strictly monotone if its Jacobian matrix is positive definite.*

The following theorem is a well known theorem for Complementarity Problems.

Theorem 9. *[26] Let $F : \mathcal{K} \to \mathbb{R}^n$ be a continuous and strictly monotone function with a point $x \in \mathcal{K}$ such that $F(x) \geq 0$ (i.e., there exists a potential solution to the CP). Then the Complementarity Problem introduced in Definition 1 characterized by function F has a unique solution.*

Hence, the Complementarity Problem characterized by function F has a unique solution under the assumption that the revenue function is strongly monotone (special case of strictly monotone). In the next subsection, we aim to find this unique equilibrium of the NCC problem.

4.3 Designing a Polynomial-Time Algorithm

In this subsection, we present an algorithm to find the equilibrium of NCC, and establish its polynomial time convergence by Theorem 10. This theorem requires the marginal profit function to satisfy Scaled Lipschitz Condition (SLC) and monotonicity. We first introduce SLC, and show how the marginal profit function satisfies SLC and monotonicity by Lemmas 1 to 5. We present in in Lemma 5 the conditions that the cost and price functions should have in order for the marginal profit function to satisfy SLC and monotonicity. Finally, in Theorem 10, we show convergence of our algorithm in polynomial time.

Before introducing the next theorem, we explain what the Jacobians ∇R, ∇S, and ∇F are for the Cournot game. First note that these are $E \times E$ matrices. Let $(i, j) \in \mathcal{E}$ and $(l, k) \in \mathcal{E}$ be two edges of the graph. Let e_1 denote the index of edge (i, j), and e_2 denote the index of edge (l, k) in the vector as we discussed in the first section. Then the element in row e_1 and column e_2 of matrix ∇R, denoted $\nabla R_{e_1 e_2}$, is equal to $\frac{\partial r_{ij}}{\partial q_{lk}}$. We name the corresponding elements in ∇F and ∇S similarly. We have $\nabla F = \nabla R + \nabla S$ as $F = R + S$.

Definition 3 (Scaled Lipschitz Condition (SLC)). *A function $G : D \mapsto \mathbb{R}^n$, $D \subseteq \mathbb{R}^n$ is said to satisfy* Scaled Lipschitz Condition (SLC) *if there exists a scalar $\lambda > 0$ such that $\forall h \in \mathbb{R}^n, \forall x \in D$, such that $\|X^{-1}h\| \leq 1$, we have $\|X[G(x + h) - G(x) - \nabla G(x)h]\|_\infty \leq \lambda |h^T \nabla G(x)h|$, where X is a diagonal matrix with diagonal entries equal to elements of the vector x in the same order, i.e., $X_{ii} = x_i$ for all $i \in \mathcal{M}$.*

Satisfying SLC and monotonicity are essential for marginal profit function in Theorem 10. In Lemma 5 we discuss the assumptions for cost and revenue function under which these conditions hold for our marginal profit function. We use Lemmas 1 to 5 to show F satisfies SLC. More specifically, we demonstrate in Lemma 1, if we can derive an upperbound for LHS of SLC for R and S, then we can derive an upperbound for LHS of SLC for $F = R + S$ too. Then in Lemma 2 and Lemma 3 we show LHS of S and R in SLC definition can be upperbounded. Afterwards, we show monotonicity of S in Lemma 4. In Lemma 5 we aim to prove F satisfies SLC under some assumptions for cost and revenue functions. We use the fact that LHS of SLC for F can be upperbounded using Lemma 3 and Lemma 2 combined with Lemma 1. Then we use the fact that RHS of SLC can be upperbounded using strong monotonicity of R and Lemma 4. Using these two facts, we conclude F satisfies SLC in Lemma 5.

Lemma 1. *Let F, R, S be three $\mathbb{R}^n \rightarrow \mathbb{R}^n$ functions such that $F(q) = R(q) + S(q)$, $\forall q \in \mathbb{R}^n$. Let R and S satisfy the following inequalities for some $C > 0$ and $\forall h$ such that $\|X^{-1}h\| \leq 1$:*

$$\|X[R(q + h) - R(q) - \nabla R(q)h]\|_\infty \leq C\|h\|^2,$$
$$\|X[S(q + h) - S(q) - \nabla S(q)h]\|_\infty \leq C\|h\|^2,$$

where X is the diagonal matrix with $X_{ii} = q_i$. Then we have:

$$\|X[F(q + h) - F(q) - \nabla F(q)h]\|_\infty \leq 2C\|h\|^2.$$

The following lemmas give upper bounds for LHS of the SLC for S and R respectively.

Lemma 2. *Assume X is the diagonal matrix with $X_{ii} = q_i$. $\forall$ h such that $\|X^{-1}h\| \leq$ 1, there exists a constant $C > 0$ satisfying: $\|X[S(q+h) - S(q) - \nabla S(q)h]\|_\infty \leq C\|h\|^2$.*

Lemma 3. *Assume X is the diagonal matrix with $X_{ii} = q_i$. $\forall$ h such that $\|X^{-1}h\| \leq$ 1, $\exists C > 0$ such that $\|X[R(q+h) - R(q) - \nabla R(q)h]\|_\infty \leq C\|h\|^2$.*

If R is assumed to be strongly monotone, we immediately have a lower bound on RHS of the SLC for R. The following lemma gives a lower bound on RHS of the SLC for S.

Lemma 4. *If cost functions are (strongly) convex, S is (strongly) monotone.*

The following lemma combines the results of Lemma 2 and Lemma 3 using Lemma 1 to derive an upper bound for LHS of the SLC for F. We bound RHS of the SLC from below by using strong monotonicity of R and Lemma 4.

Lemma 5. *F satisfies SLC and is monotone if: (1) Cost functions are convex. (2) Marginal revenue function is monotone. (3) Cost functions are strongly convex or marginal revenue function is strongly monotone.*

We wrap up with the description of the algorithm. The algorithm first constructs the vector F of length E. It then finds the initial feasible solution $(F(x_0), x_0)$ for the complementarity problem. (This solution should satisfy $x_0 \geq 0$ and $F(x_0) \geq 0$.) If finally run Algorithm 3.1 from [43] to find the solution $(F(x^*), x^*)$ to the CP characterized by F, which gives the vector q of quantities produced by firms at equilibrium. Lemma 5 guarantees that our problem satisfies the two conditions mentioned in Zhao and Han 1999. Therefore, we can prove the following theorem.

Theorem 10. *The algorithm converges to an equilibrium of Network Cournot Competition in time $O\big(E^2 \log(\mu_0/\epsilon)\big)$ under the following assumptions:*

1. *The cost functions are strongly convex.*
2. *The marginal revenue function is strongly monotone.*
3. *The first derivative of cost functions and price functions and the second derivative of price functions are Lipschitz continuous.*

This algorithm outputs an approximate solution $(F(q^*), q^*)$ satisfying $(q^*)^T F(q^*)/n \leq \epsilon$ where $\mu_0 = (q_0)^T F(q_0)/n$, and $(F(q_0), q_0)$ is the initial feasible point [6].

For a discussion of price functions that satisfy the convergence conditions for our algorithm, we refer the reader to the full version of the paper on arXiv.

5 Algorithm for Cournot Oligopoly

In this section we present a new algorithm for computing the equilibrium in a Cournot oligopoly, i.e., when the firms compete over a single market. Computation of Cournot

---

[6] Initial feasible solution can be trivially found. E.g., it can be the same production quantity along each edge, large enough to ensure losses for all firms. Such quantity can easily be found by binary search between [0, Q].

Equilibrium is an important problem in its own right. A considerable body of literature has been dedicated to this problem [37, 25, 29, 8]. All earlier work computing Cournot equilibrium for a general class of price and cost functions rely on solving a Linear Complementarity Problem or a Variational Inequality which in turn are set up as convex optimization problems of size $O(n)$ where n is the number of firms in oligopoly. Thus, the runtime guarantee of the earlier works is $O(n^3)$ at best. We give a novel combinatorial algorithm for this important problem when the quantities produced are integral. Our algorithm runs in time $n \log^2(Q_{max})$ where Q_{max} is an upper bound on total quantity produced at equilibrium. There is always an upper bound for Q_{max} since if $Q = \sum_{i \in F} q_i$ is large enough the price function would become negative and no firm has any incentive to produce a higher quantity. We note that, for two reasons, the restriction to integral quantities is practically no restriction at all. Firstly, in real-world all commodities and products are traded in integral (or rational) units. Secondly, this algorithm can easily be adapted to compute approximate Cournot-Nash equilibrium for the continuous case and since the quantities at equilibrium may be irrational numbers, this is the best we can hope for.

With only a single market present, we simplify the notation. Let $[n] = \{1, \ldots, n\}$ be the set of firms competing over the single market. Let $\mathbf{q} = (q_1, q_2, \ldots, q_n)$ be the set of all quantities they produce, one quantity for each firm. Let $Q = \sum_{i \in [n]} q_i$. In this case, there is only a single inverse demand function $P : \mathbb{Z} \mapsto \mathbb{R}_{\geq 0}$, which maps total supply, Q, to market price. We assume that, P is a decreasing function of Q. For each firm $i \in [n]$, the function $c_i : \mathbb{Z} \mapsto \mathbb{R}_{\geq 0}$ denotes the cost to firm i for producing quantity q_i of the good. We assume convex cost functions. The profit of firm $i \in [n]$ as a function of q_i and Q, denoted $\pi_i(q_i, Q)$, is $P(Q)q_i - c_i(q_i)$. Also let $f_i(q_i, Q) = \pi_i(q_i + 1, Q + 1) - \pi_i(q_i, Q)$ be the marginal profit for firm i of producing one extra unit. Although the quantities are nonnegative integers, for simplicity we assume the functions c_i, P, π_i and f_i are zero whenever any of their inputs are negative. Also, we refer to the forward difference $P(Q + 1) - P(Q)$ by $P'(Q)$.

Polynomial Time Algorithm. We leverage the supermodularity of price functions and Topkis' Monotonicity Theorem [38] to design a nested binary search algorithm to find the Cournot equilibrium. Intuitively, the algorithm works as follows. At each point we guess Q' to be the total quantity of good produced by all the firms. Then we check how good this guess is by computing for each firm the set of quantities that it can produce at equilibrium if we assume the total quantity is the fixed integer Q'. We prove that for given Q', the set of possible quantities for each firm at equilibrium is a consecutive set of integers. Let $I_i = \{q_i^l, q_i^l + 1, \ldots, q_i^u - 1, q_i^u\}$ be the range of all possible quantities for firm $i \in [n]$ assuming Q' is the total quantity produced in the market. We can conclude Q' was too low a guess if $\sum_{i \in [n]} q_i^l > Q'$. This implies our search should continue among total quantities above Q'. Similarly, if $\sum_{i \in [n]} q_i^u < Q'$, we can conclude our guess was too high, and the search should continues among total quantities below Q'. If neither case happens, then for each firm $i \in [n]$, there exists a $q_i' \in I_i$ such that $Q' = \sum_{i \in [n]} q_i'$ and firm i has no incentive to change this quantity if the total quantity is Q' and we have found an equilibrium. The pseudocode for the algorithm and its correctness is proved in the full version of this paper (http://arxiv.org/abs/1405.1794).

References

[1] Amir, R.: Cournot oligopoly and the theory of supermodular games. Games and Economic Behavior (1996)

[2] Anderson, S.P., Renault, R.: Efficiency and surplus bounds in cournot competition. Journal of Economic Theory (2003)

[3] Babaioff, M., Lucier, B., Nisan, N.: Bertrand networks. In: EC 2013, pp. 33–34 (2013)

[4] Bateni, M., Hajiaghayi, M., Immorlica, N., Mahini, H.: The cooperative game theory foundations of network bargaining games. In: Abramsky, S., Gavoille, C., Kirchner, C., Meyer auf der Heide, F., Spirakis, P.G. (eds.) ICALP 2010, Part II. LNCS, vol. 6198, pp. 67–78. Springer, Heidelberg (2010)

[5] Bertrand, J.: Book review of théorie mathématique de la richesse sociale and of recherches sur les principes mathématiques de la théorie des richesses. Journal de Savants 67, 499–508 (1883)

[6] Bimpikis, K., Ehsani, S., Ilkiliç, R.: Cournot competition in networked markets. In: EC 2014, pp. 733 (2014)

[7] Boyd, S.P., Vandenberghe, L.: Convex optimization. Cambridge University Press (2004)

[8] Campos, F.A., Villar, J., Barquín, J.: Solving cournot equilibriums with variational inequalities algorithms. IET Gener. Transm. Distrib. 4(2), 268–280 (2010)

[9] Chakraborty, T., Judd, S., Kearns, M., Tan, J.: A behavioral study of bargaining in social networks. In: EC 2010, pp. 243–252. ACM (2010)

[10] Daughety, A.F.: Cournot oligopoly: characterization and applications. Cambridge University Press (2005)

[11] Day, C.J., Hobbs, B.F., Pang, J.-S.: Oligopolistic competition in power networks: A conjectured supply function approach. IEEE Trans. Power Syst. 17(3), 597–607 (2002)

[12] Devanur, N.R., Kannan, R.: Market equilibria in polynomial time for fixed number of goods or agents. In: FOCS 2008, pp. 45–53. IEEE (2008)

[13] Devanur, N.R., Papadimitriou, C.H., Saberi, A., Vazirani, V.V.: Market equilibrium via a primal-dual-type algorithm. In: FOCS 2002, pp. 389–395. IEEE (2002)

[14] Eisenberg, E., Gale, D.: Consensus of subjective probabilities: The pari-mutuel method. The Annals of Mathematical Statistics 30(1), 165–168 (1959)

[15] EU Commission Staff Working Document. Annex to the green paper: A European strategy for sustainable, competitive and secure energy. Brussels (2006)

[16] Farczadi, L., Georgiou, K., Könemann, J.: Network bargaining with general capacities. In: Bodlaender, H.L., Italiano, G.F. (eds.) ESA 2013. LNCS, vol. 8125, pp. 433–444. Springer, Heidelberg (2013)

[17] Fiat, A., Koutsoupias, E., Ligett, K., Mansour, Y., Olonetsky, S.: Beyond myopic best response (in cournot competition). In: SODA 2012, pp. 993–1005. SIAM (2012)

[18] Gabriel, S.A., Kiet, S., Zhuang, J.: A mixed complementarity-based equilibrium model of natural gas markets. Oper. Res. 53(5), 799–818 (2005)

[19] Ghiyasvand, M., Orlin, J.B.: A simple approximation algorithm for computing arrow-debreu prices. Oper. Res. 60(5), 1245–1248 (2012)

[20] Häckner, J.: A note on price and quantity competition in differentiated oligopolies. Journal of Economic Theory 93(2), 233–239 (2000)

[21] Hotelling, H.: Stability in competition. Springer (1990)

[22] Immorlica, N., Markakis, E., Piliouras, G.: Coalition formation and price of anarchy in cournot oligopolies. In: Saberi, A. (ed.) WINE 2010. LNCS, vol. 6484, pp. 270–281. Springer, Heidelberg (2010)

[23] Jain, K.: A polynomial time algorithm for computing an arrow-debreu market equilibrium for linear utilities. SIAM Journal on Computing 37(1), 303–318 (2007)

[24] Kanoria, Y., Bayati, M., Borgs, C., Chayes, J., Montanari, A.: Fast convergence of natural bargaining dynamics in exchange networks. In: SODA 2011, pp. 1518–1537. SIAM (2011)

[25] Kolstad, C.D., Mathiesen, L.: Computing cournot-nash equilibria. Oper. Res. 39(5), 739–748 (1991)

[26] Konnov, I.: Equilibrium models and variational inequalities. Elsevier (2007)

[27] Kreps, D.M., Scheinkman, J.A.: Quantity precommitment and Bertrand competition yield Cournot outcomes. Bell J. Econ., 326–337 (1983)

[28] Kukushkin, N.S.: Cournot Oligopoly with "almost" Identical Convex Costs. Instituto Valenciano de Investigaciones Económicas (1993)

[29] Mathiesen, L.: Computation of economic equilibria by a sequence of linear complementarity problems. In: Economic Equilibrium: Model Formulation and Solution, pp. 144–162. Springer (1985)

[30] Milgrom, P., Roberts, J.: Rationalizability, learning, and equilibrium in games with strategic complementarities. Econometrica (1990)

[31] Monderer, D., Shapley, L.S.: Potential games. Games and Economic Behavior 14(1), 124–143 (1996)

[32] Okuguchi, K., Szidarovszky, F.: On the existence and computation of equilibrium points for an oligopoly game with multi-product firms. Annales, Univ. Sci. bud. Roi. Fotvos Nom (1985)

[33] Orlin, J.B.: Improved algorithms for computing fisher's market clearing prices: Computing fisher's market clearing prices. In: STOC 2010, pp. 291–300. ACM (2010)

[34] Osborne, M.J., Pitchik, C.: Price competition in a capacity-constrained duopoly. Journal of Economic Theory 38(2), 238–260 (1986)

[35] Siliverstovs, B., L'Hégaret, G., Neumann, A., von Hirschhausen, C.: International market integration for natural gas? A cointegration analysis of prices in Europe, North America and Japan. Energy Economics 27(4), 603–615 (2005)

[36] Singh, N., Vives, X.: Price and quantity competition in a differentiated duopoly. The RAND Journal of Economics, 546–554 (1984)

[37] Thorlund-Petersen, L.: Iterative computation of cournot equilibrium. Games and Economic Behavior 2(1), 61–75 (1990)

[38] Topkis, D.M.: Minimizing a submodular function on a lattice. Oper. Res. (1978)

[39] Ventosa, M., Baıllo, A., Ramos, A., Rivier, M.: Electricity market modeling trends. Energy Policy 33(7), 897–913 (2005)

[40] Villar, J.A., Joutz, F.L.: The relationship between crude oil and natural gas prices. Energy Information Administration, Office of Oil and Gas (2006)

[41] Vives, X.: Oligopoly pricing: old ideas and new tools. The MIT Press (2001)

[42] Weibull, J.W.: Price competition and convex costs. Technical report. SSE/EFI Working Paper Series in Economics and Finance (2006)

[43] Zhao, Y.B., Han, J.Y.: Two interior-point methods for nonlinear $p_*(\tau)$-complementarity problems. J. Optimiz. Theory App. 102(3), 659–679 (1999)

Bounding the Potential Function in Congestion Games and Approximate Pure Nash Equilibria

Matthias Feldotto[1], Martin Gairing[2], and Alexander Skopalik[1,*]

[1] Heinz Nixdorf Institute & Department of Computer Science,
University of Paderborn, Germany
{feldi,skopalik}@mail.upb.de
[2] University of Liverpool, U.K.
gairing@liverpool.ac.uk

Abstract. In this paper we study the potential function in congestion games. We consider both games with non-decreasing cost functions as well as games with non-increasing utility functions.

We show that the value of the potential function $\Phi(\mathsf{s})$ of any outcome s of a congestion game approximates the optimum potential value $\Phi(\mathsf{s}^*)$ by a factor $\Psi_{\mathcal{F}}$ which only depends on the set of cost/utility functions $\mathcal{F}$, and an additive term which is bounded by the sum of the total possible improvements of the players in the outcome s.

The significance of this result is twofold. On the one hand it provides *Price-of-Anarchy*-like results with respect to the potential function. On the other hand, we show that these approximations can be used to compute $(1 + \varepsilon) \cdot \Psi_{\mathcal{F}}$-approximate pure Nash equilibria for congestion games with non-decreasing cost functions. For the special case of polynomial cost functions, this significantly improves the guarantees from Caragiannis et al. [FOCS 2011]. Moreover, our machinery provides the first guarantees for general latency functions.

1 Introduction

A central problem in large scale networks like the Internet is network congestion, or more generally contention for scarce resources. *Congestion games* were introduced by Rosenthal [22] and provide us with a general model for the non-cooperative sharing of them. In a congestion game, we are given a set of resources and each player selects a subset of them (e.g. a path in a network). Each resource has a cost function that depends on the load induced by the players that use it. Each player aims to minimize the sum of the resources' costs in its strategy given the strategies chosen by the other players. A state in which no player can improve by unilaterally changing its strategy is called a Nash equilibrium [21].

Congestion games always admit a *pure* Nash equilibrium, where players pick a single strategy and do not randomize. Rosenthal [22] showed this by means

---

[*] This work was partially supported by the German Research Foundation (DFG) within the Collaborative Research Centre "On-The-Fly Computing" (SFB 901), by the EU within FET project MULTIPLEX under contract no. 317532 and by EPSRC grants EP/J019399/1 and EP/L011018/1.

T.-Y. Liu et al. (Eds.): WINE 2014, LNCS 8877, pp. 30–43, 2014.

of a *potential function*. Such a function has the following property: if a single player deviates to a different strategy, then the value of the potential changes by the same amount as the cost of the deviating player. Pure Nash equilibria now correspond to local optima of the potential function. Games admitting such a potential function are called potential games and each potential game is isomorphic to a congestion game [20].

Besides establishing the existence of a pure Nash equilibrium, the potential function has played an important role for proving various results in potential games. Its use ranges from bounding the *price of stability* [9,11,13] to tracking the convergence rate of best response dynamics [4,10].

Fabrikant et al. [15] showed that the problem of computing a pure Nash equilibrium in congestion games is PLS-complete, that is, computing a pure Nash equilibrium is as hard as the problem of finding a local optimum. PLS was defined as a class of local search problems where local optimality can be verified in polynomial time [18]. Computing a pure Nash equilibrium in congestion games stays a hard problem even if the cost functions are linear [1]. Efficient algorithms are only known for special cases, e. g. for symmetric network congestion games [15] or when the strategies are restricted to be bases of matroids [1].

The hardness of computing a pure Nash equilibrium in congestion games motivates relaxing the Nash equilibrium conditions and asking for approximations instead. One possible approximation is a ρ-approximate pure Nash equilibrium, a state in which no player can improve by a factor larger than ρ. Without restricting the cost (or utility) functions the problem of computing ρ-approximate pure Nash equilibria in congestion games remains PLS-complete for any fixed ρ [24]. However, the problem becomes tractable for certain subclasses of congestion and potential games with varying approximation guarantees. For *symmetric* congestion games certain best response dynamics converge in polynomial time to a $(1+\varepsilon)$-Nash equilibrium [10]. For *asymmetric* congestion games, it has been shown that for linear resource cost functions a $(2+\varepsilon)$-approximate Nash equilibrium can be computed in polynomial time [7]. More generally, for polynomial resource cost functions with maximum degree d, the best known approximation guarantee is $d^{O(d)}$ [7]. These results have recently been extended to congestion games with weighted players [8]. For linear cost functions it is shown how to compute a $\frac{3+\sqrt{5}}{2} + \varepsilon$-approximate equilibrium. For polynomial cost functions it is proved that $d!$-approximate equilibria always exist and $d^{2d+o(d)}$-approximate equilibria can be computed in polynomial time. The bounds for the existence of approximate equilibria in weighted congestion games were improved by [17] to $d + 1$ for polynomial cost functions and $\frac{3}{2}$ for concave cost functions. Existing approaches [5,7] for computing ρ-approximate pure Nash equilibria (with small ρ) heavily build on the ability to compute intermediate states that approximate the optimum potential value and satisfy certain more local conditions. By focussing on approximating the potential function, our results significantly further this line of research.

Our Contribution. In this paper we show that for any outcome s of a congestion game the value of the potential function $\Phi(\mathsf{s})$ can be bounded by the optimum potential value $\Phi(s^*)$, a factor $\Psi_{\mathcal{F}}$ which only depends on the set of cost/utility functions $\mathcal{F}$, and an additive term $D(s, s^*)$ which is bounded by the sum of the total possible improvements of the players in the outcome s. We consider both games with non-decreasing cost functions (Section 4.2), in which players seek to minimize cost, as well as games with non-increasing utility functions (Section 4.1), in which players seek to maximize utility. As a direct corollary we get that any outcome s provides us with a bound on the optimum potential value. For both cases we also present lower bounds. The lower bound for non-increasing utility functions matches the upper bound. For non-decreasing cost-functions, our lower bound is matching if some technical constraint on the resource functions $\mathcal{F}$ is fulfilled.

To achieve this result we introduce a *transition graph*, which is defined on a pair of outcomes s, s^* and captures how to transform s into s^*. On this transition graph we define an *ordered path-cycle decomposition*. We upper bound the change in the potential for every path and cycle in the decomposition, and lower bound their contribution to the potential $\Phi(s)$. The result then follows by summing up over all paths and cycles.

For games with *non-decreasing cost* functions, our result can be used to obtain ρ-approximate equilibria with small values of $\rho = \Psi_{\mathcal{F}}(1 + \varepsilon)$ with the method of [7]. Our technique significantly improves the approximation [7] for polynomial cost functions. Moreover, our analysis suggests and identifies large and practically relevant classes of cost functions for which ρ-approximate equilibria with small ρ can be computed in polynomial time .

For example, in games where resources have a certain cost offset, e.g., traffic networks, the approximation factor ρ drastically decreases with the increase of offsets or coefficients in delay functions. In particular for congestion games with linear functions with strictly positive offset, ρ is smaller than 2. To the best of our knowledge this is the first work to show that ρ-approximate equilibria with $\rho < 2$ are polynomial time computable without restricting the strategy spaces.

Other Related Work. Our bounds on the spread of the potential function for two outcomes are related to results on the *price of anarchy* (PoA). The PoA was introduced in [19] as the worst case ratio between the value of some global objective function in a Nash equilibrium and its optimum value. Most results on the PoA in congestion games use the *total latency* (i.e., the sum of the players' costs) as the global objective function. For this setting, Christodoulou and Koutsoupias [12] showed that the PoA for non-decreasing affine cost functions is $\frac{5}{2}$. Aland et. al. [2] obtained the exact value on the PoA for polynomial cost functions. Roughgarden's [23] smoothness framework determines the PoA with respect to any set of allowable cost functions. These results have been extended to the more general class of *weighted* congestion games [2,3,6,12].

For congestion games, the total latency and the value of the potential function are related. So, for Nash [2,12,23] and approximate Nash equilibria [14], bounds on the potential function can be derived from the corresponding results on the price of anarchy. However, this approach yields much weaker guarantees than our approach. Congestion games with non-increasing utility functions where the global objective is defined as the potential function are a subclass of *valid utility games* as introduced by Vetta [25]. Thus the bound on the price of anarchy from [25] for such games implies that $\frac{\Phi(s)}{\Phi(s^*)} \leq 2$ for any pair of outcomes s, s^*, where s is a Nash equilibrium. Our result in Theorem 3 refines (as it holds for all outcomes s) and improves (the factor of) this bound.

2   Notation

Congestion Games. A congestion game is a tuple $\Gamma = (\mathcal{N}, E, (S_i)_{i \in \mathcal{N}}, (f_e)_{e \in E})$. Here, $\mathcal{N} = \{1, 2, \ldots, |\mathcal{N}|\}$ is a set of n players and E is a set of resources. Each player chooses as her *strategy* a set $s_i \subseteq E, s_i \in S_i$ from a given *set of available strategies* $S_i \subseteq 2^E$. Associated with each resource $e \in E$ is a non-negative function $f_e : \mathbb{N} \mapsto \mathbb{R}^+$. We consider both *cost minimizing* and *utility maximizing* congestion games, so these functions either describe *costs* or *utilities* to be credited to the players for using resource e. An outcome (or strategy profile) is a choice of strategies $s = (s_1, s_2, \ldots, s_{|\mathcal{N}|})$ by players with $s_i \in S_i$. For an outcome s define $n_e(s) = |i \in \mathcal{N} : e \in s_i|$ as the number of players that use resource e. In cost minimizing games the *cost* for player i is defined by $c_i(s) = \sum_{e \in s_i} f_e(n_e(s))$ (in utility maximizing games $u_i(s) = \sum_{e \in s_i} f_e(n_e(s))$). For two outcomes s and s' define $D(s, s') = \sum_{i \in \mathcal{N}} (c_i(s_{-i}, s'_i) - c_i(s))$ (and analogously for utility maximizing games). Here, (s_{-i}, s'_i) denotes the outcome that results when player i changes its strategy in s from s_i to s'_i.

Pure Nash Equilibria. A *pure Nash equilibrium* is an outcome s where no player has an incentive to deviate from its current strategy. Formally, s is a pure Nash equilibrium if for each player $i \in \mathcal{N}$ and $s'_i \in S_i$, an alternative strategy for player i, we have $c_i(s) \leq c_i(s_{-i}, s'_i)$ (or $u_i(s) \geq u_i(s_{-i}, s'_i)$).

Approximate Pure Nash Equilibria. An outcome s is a ρ-*approximate pure Nash equilibrium* if for each player $i \in \mathcal{N}$ and $s'_i \in S_i$, an alternative strategy for player i, we have $c_i(s) \leq \rho \cdot c_i(s_{-i}, s'_i)$ (or $u_i(s) \geq \rho \cdot u_i(s_{-i}, s'_i)$).

Potential Function. Congestion games admit a potential function $\Phi(s) = \sum_{e \in E} \sum_{j=1}^{n_e(s)} f_e(j)$ which was introduced by Rosenthal [22] and has the following remarkable property: for any two outcomes s and (s_{-i}, s'_i) that differ only in the strategy of player $i \in \mathcal{N}$, we have $\Phi(s) - \Phi(s_{-i}, s'_i) = c_i(s) - c_i(s_{-i}, s'_i)$ (and analogously for utility maximizing games). Thus, the set of pure Nash equilibria corresponds to the set of local optima of the potential function. For any resource $e \in E$ denote $\Phi_e(s) = \sum_{j=1}^{n_e(s)} f_e(j)$ the contribution of e to the potential.

3   Path-Cycle Decomposition

In this section we introduce a directed multigraph G, called *transition graph*, which is defined for two given strategy profiles s, s^* and captures how to transform s into s^*. We then define a path-cycle decomposition of G which will be important for our analysis in the following sections.

Transition Graph. Given a congestion game and two strategy profiles $\mathbf{s}, \mathbf{s}^*$ we construct a directed edge-weighted multi-graph $G = G(\mathbf{s}, \mathbf{s}^*)$. For each player $i \in \mathcal{N}$, denote $E_i^1 := s_i \setminus s_i^*$ and $E_i^2 := s_i^* \setminus s_i$ and augment the smaller of those sets with dummy resources with utility/cost function $f_e(x) = 0$ until $|E_i^1| = |E_i^2|$. The node set of G consists of all resources of the congestion game including the dummy resources. For each player $i \in \mathcal{N}$ construct a perfect matching between E_i^1 and E_i^2 and introduce $|E_i^1| = |E_i^2|$ directed edges from E_i^1 to E_i^2 accordingly. Denote A_i the set of these directed edges and let $A = \cup_{i \in \mathcal{N}} A_i$ be the multiset consisting of all directed edges. We can think of each edge $a \in A_i$ as being a sub-player of player $i \in \mathcal{N}$. For each directed edge $a = (e_1, e_2) \in A$, define $\delta_a = f_{e_2}(n_{e_2}(\mathbf{s}) + 1) - f_{e_1}(n_{e_1}(\mathbf{s}))$ as the weight of a. For any set $B \subseteq A$ of edges denote $D_B = \sum_{a \in B} \delta_a$. This completes the construction of G.

Path-Cycle Decomposition. We now decompose G into directed cycles and paths as follows:

- While there is a directed cycle C in G, remove C from G. Let $\mathcal{C} = \{C_1, C_2, ...\}$ be the set of removed cycles.
- For the remaining directed acyclic multigraph $G' = G - \mathcal{C}$ iteratively find a maximal path P, i.e., one which cannot be augmented further, and remove it from G'. Let $\mathcal{P} = \{P_1, P_2, ...\}$ be the ordered set of removed paths.

We call $(\mathcal{C}, \mathcal{P})$ the *ordered path-cycle decomposition* of G. By construction, reassigning all sub-players $a \in A$ according to the path-cycle decomposition $(\mathcal{C}, \mathcal{P})$ has the same effect on the potential as reassigning all players $i \in \mathcal{N}$ from $\mathbf{s}$ to $\mathbf{s}^*$. However, the ordered path-cycle decomposition has some nice structural properties which we will exploit for our results on approximating the potential.

4   Approximating the Potential

4.1   Non-increasing Utility Functions

Now, we study the difference of potential function values of two strategy profiles $\mathbf{s}$ and $\mathbf{s}^*$. We begin with the easier case of non-increasing utility functions. We show that the ratio of the potential values of $\mathbf{s}$ and $\mathbf{s}^*$ can be bounded by $D(\mathbf{s}, \mathbf{s}^*)$ and a parameter $\Psi_{\mathcal{F}}$ of the class of cost functions which is defined as follows.

Definition 1. *For a class of functions $\mathcal{F}$ define*

$$\Psi_{\mathcal{F}} = \sup \left\{ \frac{n \cdot (f(n) - f(n+1))}{\sum_{j=1}^n f(j)} : f \in \mathcal{F}, n \in \mathbb{N} \right\}.$$

Observe that $\Psi_{\mathcal{F}} \leq 1$. By reorganizing terms we directly get the following lemma.

Lemma 2. *For all $f \in \mathcal{F}$ and $n \in \mathbb{N}$ we have $f(n+1) \geq f(n) - \frac{\Psi_{\mathcal{F}} \cdot \sum_{j=1}^n f(j)}{n}$.*

Theorem 3. *Let $\mathcal{F}$ be a set of non-increasing functions. Consider a congestion game with utility functions in $\mathcal{F}$ and two arbitrary outcomes $\mathbf{s}, \mathbf{s}^*$. Then $\Phi(\mathbf{s}^*) \leq (1 + \Psi_{\mathcal{F}}) \cdot \Phi(\mathbf{s}) + D(\mathbf{s}, \mathbf{s}^*)$.*

Proof. Given s, s^* let $(\mathcal{C}, \mathcal{P})$ be the ordered path-cycle decomposition of the transition graph $G(s, s^*)$ as defined in Section 3. We will now reassign the sub-players corresponding to cycles and paths in order. We upper bound their corresponding change in the potential and lower bound their contribution to the potential $\Phi(s)$. We split $\Phi_e(s)$ equally among all players using e. Therefore, we further subdivide $\Phi_e(s)$ with respect to the path-cycle decomposition $\mathcal{C} \cup \mathcal{P}$ as follows: For every $B \in \mathcal{C} \cup \mathcal{P}$ with $e \in B$, denote $\Phi_{e,B}(s)$ the fraction of e with respect to B of $\Phi_e(s)$ and let $\Phi_B(s) = \sum_{e \in B} \Phi_{e,B}(s)$. Hence,

$$\Phi_{e,B}(s) = \frac{1}{n_e(s)} \cdot \sum_{i=1}^{n_e(s)} f_e(i). \tag{1}$$

Observe that $\Phi_e(s) \geq \sum_{B \in \mathcal{C} \cup \mathcal{P}} \Phi_{e,B}(s)$. For any $B \in \mathcal{C} \cup \mathcal{P}$ denote $\Delta_B(\Phi)$ the change in the potential due to the reassignment of sub-players in B at time of the reassignment.

First consider the cycles in $\mathcal{C}$. Observe that $\Delta_C(\Phi) = 0$ for all $C \in \mathcal{C}$. Consider a directed cycle C of $k \in \mathbb{N}$ nodes $(k, k-1, \ldots, 1, k)$. With a slight abuse of notation denote $\delta_j = \delta_{(j, j-1)}$ for $j \in \{2, \ldots, k\}$ and $\delta_1 = \delta_{(1,k)}$. Then by the definition of δ_j, and by (1) and Lemma 2,

$$D_C = \sum_{j=1}^{k} \delta_j = \sum_{j=1}^{k} f_j(n_j + 1) - \sum_{j=1}^{k} f_j(n_j)$$

$$\geq \sum_{j=1}^{k} \left(-\Psi_{\mathcal{F}} \cdot \Phi_{j,C}(s) + f_j(n_j) \right) - \sum_{j=1}^{k} f_j(n_j) = -\Psi_{\mathcal{F}} \cdot \Phi_C(s). \tag{2}$$

Now consider the paths in $\mathcal{P} = \{P_1, P_2, \ldots\}$. Consider an arbitrary path $P_\ell \in \mathcal{P}$ with k edges and $P_\ell = (k, k-1, \ldots, 1, 0)$. Denote $\delta_j = \delta_{(j, j-1)}$ for $j \in [k]$.

Denote $\tilde{s}$ the strategy profile of the players just before we reassign P_ℓ. By the property that earlier reassigned paths $(P_1, \ldots, P_{\ell-1})$ could not be further extended we know that nodes in the subpath $(k, k-1, \ldots, 1)$ were not the final node of some earlier path, while nodes in $(k-1, \ldots, 1, 0)$ were not the first node of some earlier path. This implies $n_k(\tilde{s}) \leq n_k(s)$, $n_0(\tilde{s}) \geq n_0(s)$, and $n_i(\tilde{s}) = n_i(s)$ for all $i \in \{1, \ldots, k-1\}$. We derive:

$$\Delta_{P_\ell}(\Phi) = f_0(n_0(\tilde{s}) + 1) - f_k(n_k(\tilde{s}))$$
$$\leq f_0(n_0(s) + 1) - f_k(n_k(s)) = f_1(n_1(s)) + \delta_1 - f_k(n_k(s))$$
$$\leq \Psi_{\mathcal{F}} \cdot \Phi_{1,P_\ell}(s) + f_1(n_1(s) + 1) + \delta_1 - f_k(n_k(s))$$
$$= \Psi_{\mathcal{F}} \cdot \Phi_{1,P_\ell}(s) + f_2(n_2(s)) + \sum_{j=1}^{2} \delta_j - f_k(n_k(s))$$

Iterating the last two steps along the path P_ℓ yields

$$\Delta_{P_\ell}(\Phi) \leq \Psi_{\mathcal{F}} \cdot \sum_{j=1}^{k-1} \Phi_{j,P_\ell}(\mathsf{s}) + f_k(n_k(\mathsf{s})) + \sum_{i=1}^{k} \delta_i - f_k(n_k(\mathsf{s}))$$

$$\leq \Psi_{\mathcal{F}} \cdot \Phi_{P_\ell}(\mathsf{s}) + D_{P_\ell} \qquad (3)$$

Combining (2) and (3), we get

$$\Phi(\mathsf{s}^*) - \Phi(\mathsf{s}) = \sum_{P \in \mathcal{P}} \Delta_P(\Phi) \leq \Psi_{\mathcal{F}} \cdot \sum_{P \in \mathcal{P}} \Phi_P(\mathsf{s}) + \sum_{P \in \mathcal{P}} D_P$$

$$\leq \Psi_{\mathcal{F}} \cdot \left(\Phi(\mathsf{s}) - \sum_{C \in \mathcal{C}} \Phi_C(\mathsf{s}) \right) + D(\mathsf{s}, \mathsf{s}^*) - \sum_{C \in \mathcal{C}} D_C$$

$$\leq \Psi_{\mathcal{F}} \cdot \left(\Phi(\mathsf{s}) - \sum_{C \in \mathcal{C}} \Phi_C(\mathsf{s}) \right) + D(\mathsf{s}, \mathsf{s}^*) + \Psi_{\mathcal{F}} \cdot \sum_{C \in \mathcal{C}} \Phi_C(\mathsf{s})$$

$$= \Psi_{\mathcal{F}} \cdot \Phi(\mathsf{s}) + D(\mathsf{s}, \mathsf{s}^*)$$

or equivalently $\Phi(\mathsf{s}^*) \leq (1 + \Psi_{\mathcal{F}}) \cdot \Phi(\mathsf{s}) + D(\mathsf{s}, \mathsf{s}^*)$, as claimed in the theorem.   □

Denote s_i' the best response of player $i \in \mathcal{N}$ to the outcome s. Then we can upper bound $D(\mathsf{s}, \mathsf{s}^*) = \sum_{i \in \mathcal{N}} (u_i(\mathsf{s}_{-i}, s_i^*) - u_i(\mathsf{s})) \leq \sum_{i \in \mathcal{N}} (u_i(\mathsf{s}_{-i}, s_i') - u_i(\mathsf{s}))$ which yields the following corollary:

Corollary 4. *Given any outcome s denote s_i' the best response of player $i \in \mathcal{N}$ to s. Then, $\Phi(\mathsf{s}^*) \leq (1 + \Psi_{\mathcal{F}}) \cdot \Phi(\mathsf{s}) + \sum_{i \in \mathcal{N}} (u_i(\mathsf{s}_{-i}, s_i') - u_i(\mathsf{s}))$. So, any outcome s provides us with an upper bound on the maximum potential value.*

The following theorem provides a matching lower bound, even for the case that s is a Nash equilibrium.

Theorem 5. *Given a class of non-increasing functions $\mathcal{F}$, there is a congestion game $\Gamma_{\mathcal{F}}$ with utility functions in $\mathcal{F}$ and two strategy profiles s and s^* with $\Phi(\mathsf{s}^*) = (1 + \Psi_{\mathcal{F}}) \cdot \Phi(\mathsf{s})$ and $u_i(\mathsf{s}_{-i}, s_i^*) - u_i(\mathsf{s}) = 0$ for all players i.*

4.2   Non-decreasing Cost Functions

We now consider the case of non-decreasing cost functions. As in the previous section we reassign the sub-players corresponding to cycles and paths and upper bound their corresponding change in the potential and lower bound their contribution to the potential. Unlike before, we cannot split the potential of a resource equally among the players using it. We have to differentiate whether a node in the path-cycle decomposition is the start of some path or an intermediate node. For non-decreasing cost functions the crucial parameter $\Psi_{\mathcal{F}}$ is defined as follows.

Definition 6. *For a class of functions $\mathcal{F}$ define*

$$\Psi_{\mathcal{F}} = \sup\left\{\frac{(n-m)\cdot f(n+1) - n\cdot f(n) + \sum_{j=1}^{n} f(j)}{\sum_{j=1}^{n-m} f(j)} : f \in \mathcal{F}, n, m \in \mathbb{N}, n > m\right\}$$

By reorganising terms we derive the following lemma.

Lemma 7. *For all $f \in \mathcal{F}$ and $n, m \in \mathbb{N}$ with $n > m$ we have*

$$f(n+1) \leq (\Psi_{\mathcal{F}} - 1)\cdot\frac{\sum_{j=1}^{n-m} f(j)}{n-m} + \left(1 - \frac{\sum_{j=n-m+1}^{n} f(j)}{m\cdot f(n)}\right)\cdot\frac{m}{n-m}\cdot f(n) + f(n)$$

Theorem 8. *Let $\mathcal{F}$ be a set of non-decreasing cost functions. Consider a congestion game with cost functions in $\mathcal{F}$ and two arbitrary outcomes s, s^*. Then $\Phi(\mathsf{s}) \leq \Psi_{\mathcal{F}} \cdot \Phi(\mathsf{s}^*) - D(\mathsf{s}, \mathsf{s}^*)$.*

Proof. Given s, s^* let $(\mathcal{C}, \mathcal{P})$ be the ordered path-cycle decomposition of the transition graph $G(\mathsf{s}, \mathsf{s}^*)$ as defined in Section 3. As before let denote $\Delta_B(\Phi)$ the change in the potential due to the reassignment of sub-players in $B \in \mathcal{C} \cup \mathcal{P}$ at time of the reassignment and $\Phi_{e,B}(\mathsf{s})$ the contribution of e with respect to B to $\Phi_e(\mathsf{s})$ and $\Phi_B(\mathsf{s}) = \sum_{e \in B} \Phi_{e,B}(\mathsf{s})$. For each resource $e \in E$ denote m_e the number of times e is a start node of some path in $\mathcal{P}$. Observe, that $m_e = \max\{0, n_e(\mathsf{s}) - n_e(\mathsf{s}^*)\}$.

To simplify notation let $n_e := n_e(\mathsf{s})$ and define $\alpha_e = \frac{\sum_{j=n_e-m_e+1}^{n_e} f_e(j)}{m_e \cdot f_e(n_e)}$, for each resource $e \in E$ if $m_e > 0$ and $\alpha_e = 1$ if $m_e = 0$. If $B \in \mathcal{P}$ is a path, e is the start node of B then

$$\Phi_{e,B}(\mathsf{s}) = \alpha_e \cdot f_e(n_e) - \frac{1-\alpha_e}{\Psi_{\mathcal{F}} - 1}\cdot f_e(n_e) = \left(\frac{\Psi_{\mathcal{F}} \cdot \alpha_e - 1}{\Psi_{\mathcal{F}} - 1}\right)\cdot f_e(n_e) \qquad (4)$$

In all other cases this contribution is

$$\Phi_{e,B}(\mathsf{s}) = \frac{\sum_{j=1}^{n_e-m_e} f_e(j)}{n_e - m_e} + \frac{1-\alpha_e}{\Psi_{\mathcal{F}} - 1}\cdot\frac{m_e}{n_e - m_e}\cdot f_e(n_e). \qquad (5)$$

Observe that $\Phi_e(\mathsf{s}) \geq \sum_{B \in \mathcal{C} \cup \mathcal{P}} \Phi_{e,B}(\mathsf{s})$.

First consider the cycles in $\mathcal{C}$. Observe that $\Delta_C(\Phi) = 0$ for all $C \in \mathcal{C}$. Consider a directed cycle C of $k \in \mathbb{N}$ nodes $(k, k-1, \ldots, 1, k)$. With a slight abuse of notation denote $\delta_j = \delta_{(j,j-1)}$ for $j \in \{2, \ldots, k\}$ and $\delta_1 = \delta_{(1,k)}$. Then by the definition of δ_j, and by (5) and Lemma 7,

$$D_C = \sum_{j=1}^{k} \delta_j = \sum_{j=1}^{k} f_j(n_j + 1) - \sum_{j=1}^{k} f_j(n_j)$$

$$\leq \sum_{j=1}^{k}\left((\Psi_{\mathcal{F}} - 1)\cdot\Phi_{j,C}(\mathsf{s}) + f_j(n_j)\right) - \sum_{j=1}^{k} f_j(n_j) = (\Psi_{\mathcal{F}} - 1)\cdot\Phi_C(\mathsf{s}). \qquad (6)$$

Now consider the paths in $\mathcal{P} = \{P_1, P_2, \ldots\}$. Consider an arbitrary path $P_\ell \in \mathcal{P}$ with k edges. Name the nodes so that $P_\ell = (k, k-1, \ldots, 1, 0)$. Similar as before, denote $\delta_j = \delta_{(j,j-1)}$ for $j \in [k]$. Denote $\tilde{s}$ the strategy profile of the players just before we reassign P_ℓ. By the property that earlier reassigned paths $(P_1, \ldots, P_{\ell-1})$ could not be further extended we know that $n_0(\tilde{s}) \geq n_0(s)$. By averaging over all events with node k as start node of some path in $\mathcal{P}$ we get

$$\Delta_{P_\ell}(\Phi) = \alpha_e \cdot f_k(n_k(s)) - f_0(n_0(\tilde{s}) + 1) \leq \alpha_e \cdot f_k(n_k) - f_0(n_0 + 1)$$

$$\overset{(4)}{=} \frac{\Psi_{\mathcal{F}} - 1}{\Psi_{\mathcal{F}}} \cdot \Phi_{k,P_\ell}(s) + \frac{f_k(n_k)}{\Psi_{\mathcal{F}}} - f_0(n_0 + 1)$$

$$= \frac{\Psi_{\mathcal{F}} - 1}{\Psi_{\mathcal{F}}} \cdot \Phi_{k,P_\ell}(s) + \frac{f_{k-1}(n_{k-1} + 1)}{\Psi_{\mathcal{F}}} - \frac{\delta_k}{\Psi_{\mathcal{F}}} - f_0(n_0 + 1)$$

$$\leq \frac{\Psi_{\mathcal{F}} - 1}{\Psi_{\mathcal{F}}} \cdot \Phi_{k,P_\ell}(s) + \frac{\Psi_{\mathcal{F}} - 1}{\Psi_{\mathcal{F}}} \Phi_{k-1,P_\ell}(s) + \frac{f_{k-1}(n_{k-1})}{\Psi_{\mathcal{F}}} - \frac{\delta_k}{\Psi_{\mathcal{F}}} - f_0(n_0 + 1)$$

$$= \frac{\Psi_{\mathcal{F}} - 1}{\Psi_{\mathcal{F}}} \cdot \sum_{j=k-1}^{k} \Phi_{j,P_\ell}(s) + \frac{f_{k-1}(n_{k-1})}{\Psi_{\mathcal{F}}} - \frac{\delta_k}{\Psi_{\mathcal{F}}} - f_0(n_0 + 1),$$

where the last inequality follows with (5) and Lemma 7. Iterating along P_ℓ yields

$$\Delta_{P_\ell}(\Phi) \leq \frac{\Psi_{\mathcal{F}} - 1}{\Psi_{\mathcal{F}}} \cdot \sum_{j=1}^{k} \Phi_{j,P_\ell}(s) - \sum_{j=1}^{k} \frac{\delta_j}{\Psi_{\mathcal{F}}} + \frac{f_0(n_0 + 1)}{\Psi_{\mathcal{F}}} - f_0(n_0 + 1)$$

$$\leq \frac{\Psi_{\mathcal{F}} - 1}{\Psi_{\mathcal{F}}} \cdot \Phi_{P_\ell}(s) - \frac{D_{P_\ell}}{\Psi_{\mathcal{F}}} . \tag{7}$$

Combining (6) and (7), we get

$$\Phi(s) - \Phi(s^*) = \sum_{P \in \mathcal{P}} \Delta_P(\Phi) \leq \frac{\Psi_{\mathcal{F}} - 1}{\Psi_{\mathcal{F}}} \cdot \sum_{P \in \mathcal{P}} \Phi_P(s) - \frac{\sum_{P \in \mathcal{P}} D_P}{\Psi_{\mathcal{F}}}$$

$$\leq \frac{\Psi_{\mathcal{F}} - 1}{\Psi_{\mathcal{F}}} \left(\Phi(s) - \sum_{C \in \mathcal{C}} \Phi_C(s) \right) - \frac{D(s, s^*) - \sum_{C \in \mathcal{C}} D_C}{\Psi_{\mathcal{F}}}$$

$$\leq \frac{\Psi_{\mathcal{F}} - 1}{\Psi_{\mathcal{F}}} \left(\Phi(s) - \sum_{C \in \mathcal{C}} \Phi_C(s) \right) - \frac{D(s, s^*) - (\Psi_{\mathcal{F}} - 1) \cdot \sum_{C \in \mathcal{C}} \Phi_C(s)}{\Psi_{\mathcal{F}}}$$

$$= \frac{\Psi_{\mathcal{F}} - 1}{\Psi_{\mathcal{F}}} \cdot \Phi(s) - \frac{D(s, s^*)}{\Psi_{\mathcal{F}}},$$

or equivalently $\Phi(s) \leq \Psi_{\mathcal{F}} \cdot \Phi(s^*) - D(s, s^*)$, as claimed in the theorem. □

Denote s_i' the best response of player $i \in \mathcal{N}$ to the outcome s. Then we can lower bound $D(s, s^*) = \sum_{i \in \mathcal{N}} (c_i(s_{-i}, s_i^*) - c_i(s)) \geq \sum_{i \in \mathcal{N}} (c_i(s_{-i}, s_i') - c_i(s))$ which yields the following corollary:

Corollary 9. *Given any outcome s denote s_i' the best response of player $i \in \mathcal{N}$ to s. Then, $\Phi(s^*) \geq \frac{1}{\Psi_{\mathcal{F}}} (\Phi(s) + \sum_{i \in \mathcal{N}} (c_i(s_{-i}, s_i') - c_i(s)))$. So, any outcome s provides us with a lower bound on the minimum potential value.*

We have a matching lower bound in the case in which the set of functions $\mathcal{F}$ satisfies a technical condition. Let (f, n, m) be a tuple of parameters that determine $\Psi_{\mathcal{F}}$ in Definition 6 and define $D_{\mathcal{F}} = (n - m)f(n + 1) - nf(n)$.

With these parameters at hand, we are ready to present the matching lower bound for families of functions $\mathcal{F}$ that satisfy $D_{\mathcal{F}} \geq 0$.

Theorem 10. *Given a class of non-decreasing functions $\mathcal{F}$ with $D_{\mathcal{F}} \geq 0$ there is a congestion game $\Gamma_{\mathcal{F}}$ with cost functions in $\mathcal{F}$ and two strategy profiles s and s^* with $\Phi(\mathsf{s}) = \Psi_{\mathcal{F}} \cdot \Phi(\mathsf{s}^*)$ and $c_i(\mathsf{s}_{-i}, s_i^*) - c_i(\mathsf{s}) = 0$ for all players $i \in \mathcal{N}$.*

5   Computing Approximate Pure Nash Equilibria

We use our results to compute approximate Nash equilibria. Our approach is based on the idea of [7] and we improve the analysis of their algorithm.

Input : A congestion game $\mathcal{G} = (\mathcal{N}, E, (\mathsf{s}_i)_{i \in \mathcal{N}}, (f_e)_{e \in E})$ with n players and a constant $c > \max\{1, \log_n \Psi_{\mathcal{F}}\}$

Output: A strategy profile s of $\mathcal{G}$

1 Set $q = 1 + n^{-c}$, $\theta(q) = \frac{\Psi_{\mathcal{F}}}{1 - \frac{1-q}{q}n}$, $p = \left(\frac{1}{\theta(q)} - n^{-c}\right)^{-1}$ and $\Delta = \max_{e \in E} \frac{f_e(n)}{f_e(1)}$;

2 **foreach** $u \in N$ **do** set $\ell_u = c_u\left(\mathcal{BR}_u(0)\right)$ Set $\ell_{\min} = \min_{u \in N} \ell_u$, $\ell_{\max} = \max_{u \in N} \ell_u$, and set $m = 1 + \lceil \log_{2\Delta n^{2c+2}}(\ell_{\max}/\ell_{\min}) \rceil$;

3 (Implicitly) partition players into *blocks* $B_1, B_2, \ldots, B_m$, such that

$u \in B_i \Leftrightarrow \ell_u \in \left(\ell_{\max}\left(2\Delta n^{2c+2}\right)^{-i}, \ell_{\max}\left(2\Delta n^{2c+2}\right)^{-i+1}\right]$;

4 **foreach** $u \in N$ **do** set u to play the strategy $s_u \leftarrow \mathcal{BR}_u(0)$ for *phase* $i \leftarrow 1$ to $m - 1$ *such that* $B_i \neq \emptyset$ **do**

5 | **while** *there exists a player u that either belongs to B_i and has a p-move or belongs to B_{i+1} and has a q-move* **do**

6 | | u deviates to the best-response strategy $s_u \leftarrow \mathcal{BR}_u(s_1, \ldots, s_n)$.

7 **return** s

Algorithm 1. Computing approximate equilibria in congestion games

Algorithm 1 divides the set of players into polynomially many blocks depending on the costs of the players. For any strategy profile s we denote $\mathcal{BR}_u(\mathsf{s})$ the best response of player u to s. Let $\mathcal{BR}_u(\mathbf{0})$ be the best response of a player u if no other player participates in the game. We partition the players into blocks according to their costs in $\mathcal{BR}_u(\mathbf{0})$. The lower and upper bounds of theses blocks are polynomially related in n and Δ, where $\Delta = \max_{e \in E} \frac{f_e(n)}{f_e(1)}$. The algorithm proceeds in phases, starting with the blocks of players with high costs. Each phase the players of two consecutive blocks B_i and B_{i+1} are allowed to make approximate best response moves until they reach an approximate equilibrium. The players in B_i make p-approximate move with p being slightly larger than $\Psi_{\mathcal{F}}$ and the players in Block B_{i+1} do q-approximate moves with q being slightly larger that 1. After polynomially many phases the algorithm terminates.

Theorem 11. *For every constant $c > \max\{1, \log_n \Psi_{\mathcal{F}}\}$, the algorithm computes a $(1+O(n^{-c}))\Psi_{\mathcal{F}}$-approximate equilibrium for every congestion game with cost functions from $\mathcal{F}$ and n players. The algorithm terminates after at most $O\left(\Delta^3 n^{5c+5}\right)$ best-response moves.*

Proof. To prove the theorem we need several additional notations. Let b_i be the boundaries of the different blocks, exactly $b_i = 2\Delta n^{2c+2} b_{i+1}$ with $b_1 = \ell_{\max}$. In addition to the set of players in a block B_i, we define R_i as the set of players who move during the phase i of the algorithm. With s^i we denote the strategy profile after phase i, where s^0 gives the strategy profile after the execution of step 4. For the following proof we will use sub games among a subset of players $F \subseteq \mathcal{N}$. All other players of $\mathcal{N} \setminus F$ are frozen to their strategies. In this sub game $n_e^F(s) = |i \in F : e \in s_i|$ gives the number of players in F which uses resource e in strategy profile s and the latency function is defined as $f_e^F(x) = f_e(x + n_e^{\mathcal{N} \setminus F}(s))$ with $n_e^{\mathcal{N} \setminus F}(s) = |i \in \mathcal{N} \setminus F : e \in s_i|$. Then, the potential is defined as $\Phi_F = \sum_{e \in E} \sum_{j=1}^{n_e^F(s)} f_e^F(j)$.

Firstly, we bound the potential value of an arbitrary q-approximate equilibrium with the minimal potential value:

Lemma 12. *Let s be a q-approximate equilibrium and s^* be a strategy profile with minimal potential then $\Phi_F(s) \le \theta(q)\Phi_F(s^*)$ for every $F \subseteq \mathcal{N}$.*

Proof. Since s is a q-approximate equilibrium, we have $c_i(s) \le qc_i(s_{-i}, s_i^*)$. Thus,

$$c_i(s_{-i}, s_i^*) - c_i(s) \ge \frac{1-q}{q} c_i(s) \ge \frac{1-q}{q} \Phi_F(s).$$

With the definition of $D(s, s^*)$, we get $-D(s, s^*) \le n\frac{1-q}{q}\Phi_F(s)$ and using Theorem 8 gives us

$$\Phi_F(s) \le \Psi_{\mathcal{F}}\Phi_F(s^*) + n\frac{1-q}{q}\Phi_F(s),$$

or equivalently

$$\Phi_F(s) \le \frac{\Psi_{\mathcal{F}}}{1 - \frac{1-q}{q}n}\Phi_F(s^*).$$

Together with our definition of $\theta(q)$ we have shown the lemma.   □

Afterwards we denote the key argument where we show with the help of Lemma 12 that the potential of the sub game is significantly smaller than b_i. Therefore, the costs experienced by players moving in phase i are considerably lower than the costs of any player in blocks $B_1, \ldots, B_{i-1}$:

Lemma 13. *For every phase $i \ge 2$, it holds that $\Phi_{R_i}(s^{i-1}) \le \frac{b_i}{n^c}$.*

Further, we can show that for players in block B_t neither its costs increase considerably nor a deviation to another strategy with considerably lower costs is interesting caused by the movements of the other players in all following rounds:

Lemma 14. *Let u be a player in the block B_t, where $t \leq m - 2$. Let s'_u be a strategy different from the one assigned to u by the algorithm at the end of phase t. Then, for each phase $i \geq t$, it holds that*

$$c_u(s^i) \leq p \cdot c_u(s^i_{-u}, s'_u) + \frac{p+1}{n^c} \sum_{k=t+1}^{i} b_k.$$

Finally, we have to show that in the state s^{m-1}, computed by the algorithm after the last phase, no player has an incentive to deviate to another strategy in order to decrease her costs by a factor of at least $p\left(1 + \frac{4}{n^c}\right)$. The claim is obviously true for the players in the blocks B_{m-1} and B_m by the definition of the last phase of the algorithm. Let u be a player in block B_t with $t \leq m - 2$ and let s'_u be any strategy different from the one assigned to u by the algorithm after phase t. We apply Lemma 14 to player u. By the definition of b_i, we have $\sum_{k=t+1}^{m} b_k \leq 2b_{t+1}$. Also, $c_u(s^{m-1}_{-u}, s'_u) \geq b_{t+1}$, since u belongs to block B_t. Hence, Lemma 14 implies that

$$c_u(s^{m-1}) \leq p \cdot c_u(s^{m-1}_{-u}, s'_u) + \frac{2(p+1)}{n^c} c_u(s^{m-1}_{-u}, s'_u) \leq p\left(1 + \frac{4}{n^c}\right) c_u(s^{m-1}_{-u}, s'_u),$$

as desired. The last inequality follows since $p \geq 1$.

By the definition of the parameters q and p, we obtain that the computed state is a ρ-approximate equilibrium with $\rho \leq \left(\frac{1}{\theta(q)} - \frac{1}{n^c}\right)^{-1}\left(1 + \frac{4}{n^c}\right)$, where $\theta(q) = \frac{\Psi_{\mathcal{F}}}{1 - \frac{1-q}{q}n}$ and $q = 1 + n^{-c}$. By making simple calculations, we obtain

$$\rho \leq \frac{1}{\frac{1 + \frac{n}{n^c+1}}{\Psi_{\mathcal{F}}} - n^{-c}}\left(1 + \frac{4}{n^c}\right) \leq \frac{\Psi_{\mathcal{F}}}{1 + \frac{n}{n^c+1} - \frac{\Psi_{\mathcal{F}}}{n^c}}\left(1 + \frac{4}{n^c}\right) \leq \left(1 + O\left(\frac{1}{n^c}\right)\right)\Psi_{\mathcal{F}}.$$

The last inequality holds as $c > \log_n \Psi_{\mathcal{F}}$.

We will consider the different phases of the algorithm to upper-bound the total number of best-response moves. In line 4, n best-response moves are executed in which each player deviates to her best strategy if there would not be any other player. Afterwards, we have at most n remaining phases. We start by looking at the first phase: Due to the definition of block B_1 and the relation between the cost functions Δ, any player has a latency of at most Δb_1. We can bound the potential with $\Phi_{R_1}(s^0) \leq \sum_{u \in R_1} c_u(s^0) \leq n \Delta b_1$. On the other side no player which moves has a latency smaller than b_3, otherwise she would not change in this phase. Hence, the decrease of the potential caused by each q−move is at least $(q - 1)b_3$. Therefore, we can bound the maximal moves in the first phase with the definition of b_i by $\frac{n \Delta b_1}{(q-1)b_3} = 4\Delta^3 n^{5c+5}$.

For all other phase $i \geq 2$ Lemma 13 implies that $\Phi_{R_i}(s^{i-1}) \leq \frac{b_i}{n^c}$. Equivalently to the first phase, each player in R_i experiences a latency of at least b_{i+2} and each move decreases the potential by at least $(q - 1)b_{i+2}$. As result, the maximal number of moves in each phase is bounded by $\frac{b_i}{n^c(q-1)b_{i+2}} = 4\Delta^2 n^{4c+4}$.

Altogether, we can upper-bound the number of best-response moves during the execution of the algorithm by $O\left(\Delta^3 n^{5c+5}\right)$.   □

6 Conclusions

We presented a novel technique to analyze the value of potential function Φ of an arbitrary strategy profile. This allows for better bounds for computing approximate pure Nash equilibria in congestion games. It would be interesting to see whether our techniques can be extended to other classes of games – most prominently weighted congestion games.

References

1. Ackermann, H., Röglin, H., Vöcking, B.: On the impact of combinatorial structure on congestion games. Journal of the ACM 55(6) (2008)
2. Aland, S., Dumrauf, D., Gairing, M., Monien, B., Schoppmann, F.: Exact Price of Anarchy for Polynomial Congestion Games. SIAM J. Comput. 40(5), 1211–1233 (2011)
3. Awerbuch, B., Azar, Y., Epstein, A.: The Price of Routing Unsplittable Flow. SIAM J. Comput. 42(1), 160–177 (2013)
4. Awerbuch, B., Azar, Y., Epstein, A., Mirrokni, V.S., Skopalik, A.: Fast convergence to nearly optimal solutions in potential games. In: Proceedings of the 9th ACM Conference on Electronic Commerce (EC 2008), pp. 264–273 (2008)
5. Bhalgat, A., Chakraborty, T., Khanna, S.: Approximating pure Nash equilibrium in cut, party affiliation, and satisfiability games. In: Proceedings of the 11th ACM Conference on Electronic Commerce (EC 2010), pp. 73–82 (2010)
6. Bhawalkar, K., Gairing, M., Roughgarden, T.: Weighted Congestion Games: Price of Anarchy, Universal Worst-Case Examples, and Tightness. In: de Berg, M., Meyer, U. (eds.) ESA 2010, Part II. LNCS, vol. 6347, pp. 17–28. Springer, Heidelberg (2010)
7. Caragiannis, I., Fanelli, A., Gravin, N., Skopalik, A.: Efficient Computation of Approximate Pure Nash Equilibria in Congestion Games. In: Proceedings of the 52nd Annual Symposium on Foundations of Computer Science (FOCS 2011), pp. 532–541 (2011)
8. Caragiannis, I., Fanelli, A., Gravin, N., Skopalik, A.: Approximate pure Nash equilibria in weighted congestion games: existence, efficient computation, and structure. In: Proceedings of the 13th ACM Conference on Electronic Commerce (EC 2012), pp. 284–301 (2012)
9. Caragiannis, I., Flammini, M., Kaklamanis, C., Kanellopoulos, P., Moscardelli, L.: Tight Bounds for Selfish and Greedy Load Balancing. In: Bugliesi, M., Preneel, B., Sassone, V., Wegener, I. (eds.) ICALP 2006, Part I. LNCS, vol. 4051, pp. 311–322. Springer, Heidelberg (2006)
10. Chien, S., Sinclair, A.: Convergence to approximate Nash equilibria in congestion games. In: Proceedings of the 18th Annual ACM-SIAM Symposium on Discrete Algorithms (SODA 2007), pp. 169–178 (2007)
11. Christodoulou, G., Gairing, M.: Price of Stability in Polynomial Congestion Games. In: Fomin, F.V., Freivalds, R., Kwiatkowska, M., Peleg, D. (eds.) ICALP 2013, Part II. LNCS, vol. 7966, pp. 496–507. Springer, Heidelberg (2013)
12. Christodoulou, G., Koutsoupias, E.: The price of anarchy of finite congestion games. In: Proceedings of the 37th Annual ACM Symposium on Theory of Computing (STOC 2005), pp. 67–73 (2005)

13. Christodoulou, G., Koutsoupias, E.: On the Price of Anarchy and Stability of Correlated Equilibria of Linear Congestion Games. In: Brodal, G.S., Leonardi, S. (eds.) ESA 2005. LNCS, vol. 3669, pp. 59–70. Springer, Heidelberg (2005)
14. Christodoulou, G., Koutsoupias, E., Spirakis, P.G.: On the Performance of Approximate Equilibria in Congestion Games. Algorithmica 61(1), 116–140 (2011)
15. Fabrikant, A., Papadimitriou, C.H., Talwar, K.: The complexity of pure Nash equilibria. In: Proceedings of the 36th Annual ACM Symposium on Theory of Computing (STOC 2004), pp. 604–612 (2004)
16. Gairing, M.: Covering Games: Approximation through Non-cooperation. In: Leonardi, S. (ed.) WINE 2009. LNCS, vol. 5929, pp. 184–195. Springer, Heidelberg (2009)
17. Hansknecht, C., Klimm, M., Skopalik, A.: Approximate pure Nash equilibria in weighted congestion games. In: Proceedings of the 17th Intl. Workshop on Approximation Algorithms for Combinatorial Optimization Problems (APPROX 2014), pp. 242–257 (2014)
18. Johnson, D.S., Papadimitriou, C.H., Yannakakis, M.: How Easy is Local Search? Journal of Computer and System Sciences 37(1), 79–100 (1988)
19. Koutsoupias, E., Papadimitriou, C.: Worst-case Equilibria. In: Meinel, C., Tison, S. (eds.) STACS 1999. LNCS, vol. 1563, pp. 404–413. Springer, Heidelberg (1999)
20. Monderer, D., Shapley, L.S.: Potential Games. Games and Economic Behavior 14(1), 124–143 (1996)
21. Nash, J.F.: Equilibrium Points in n-Person Games. Proceedings of the National Academy of Sciences of the United States of America 36, 48–49 (1950)
22. Rosenthal, R.W.: A Class of Games Possessing Pure-Strategy Nash Equilibria. International Journal of Game Theory 2, 65–67 (1973)
23. Roughgarden, T.: Intrinsic robustness of the price of anarchy. In: Proceedings of the 41st Annual ACM Symposium on Theory of Computing (STOC 2009), pp. 513–522 (2009)
24. Skopalik, A., Vöcking, B.: Inapproximability of pure Nash equilibria. In: Proceedings of the 40th Annual ACM Symposium on Theory of Computing (STOC 2008), pp. 355–364 (2008)
25. Vetta, A.: Nash Equilibria in Competitive Societies, with Applications to Facility Location, Traffic Routing and Auctions. In: Proceedings of the 43rd Annual Symposium on Foundations of Computer Science (FOCS 2002), pp. 416–425 (2002)

Limiting Price Discrimination when Selling Products with Positive Network Externalities*

Luděk Cigler, Wolfgang Dvořák, Monika Henzinger, and Martin Starnberger

University of Vienna, Faculty of Computer Science, Austria

Abstract. Assume a seller wants to sell a *digital product* in a *social network* where a buyer's valuation of the item has positive network externalities from her neighbors that already have the item. The goal of the seller is to maximize his revenue. Previous work on this problem [7] studies the case where clients are offered the item in sequence and have to pay personalized prices. This is highly infeasible in large scale networks such as the Facebook graph: (1) Offering items to the clients one after the other consumes a large amount of time, and (2) *price-discrimination* of clients could appear unfair to them and result in negative client reaction or could conflict with legal requirements.

We study a setting dealing with these issues. Specifically, the item is offered in parallel to multiple clients at the same time and at the same price. This is called a round. We show that with $O(\log n)$ rounds, where n is the number of clients, a constant factor of the revenue with price discrimination can be achieved and that this is not possible with $o(\log n)$ rounds. Moreover we show that it is APX-hard to maximize the revenue and we give constant factor approximation algorithms for various further settings of limited price discrimination.

1 Introduction

With the appearance of *online social networks* the issue of monetizing network information arises. Many digital products such as music, movies, apps, e-books, and computer games are sold via platforms with social network functionality. Often these products have so called *positive network externalities*: the valuation of a client for a product increases (potentially marginal) when a related client (e.g., a friend) buys the product, i.e., a product appears more valuable for a client if a friend already owns the same product. In the presence of positive network externalities, motivating a client to buy a product by lowering the price he has to pay could incentivize his friends to also buy the product. Consequently, it could increase future revenue. Thus, when trying to maximize revenue there is an interesting trade off between the current and the future revenue.

We follow the work of Hartline et al. [7] for modeling network externalities and (marketing) strategies in social networks with the goal of maximizing the

---

* The research leading to these results has received funding from the European Unions Seventh Framework Programme (FP7/2007-2013) under grant agreement no. 317532.

T.-Y. Liu et al. (Eds.): WINE 2014, LNCS 8877, pp. 44–57, 2014.

seller's revenue. We model the seller's information about the clients' valuations by using a directed weighted graph or, more generally, by using submodular set functions. For our positive results we assume that the seller has only incomplete information about the valuations, i.e., we are in a Bayesian setting where the seller is given a distribution of each client's valuation but not the valuation itself. The seller's *strategy* decides (a) when to offer the product to a client and (b) at which price. Thus each strategy assigns each client a (time, price)-pair.

In [7] a setting with *full price discrimination* is studied where a seller offers a product sequentially for a different price to different clients. (See [2,4,5] for further work on settings with full price discrimination.) While it gives a good baseline to compare with, this approach has multiple drawbacks. First, processing one client after the other and waiting for the earlier client's decision requires too much time if the number of clients is large. Second, price-discrimination could appear unfair to the clients and could result in a negative reaction of some clients [10]; moreover, it might be in conflict with legal requirements. On the other side offering all clients the *same* price (i.e., a *uniform price*) reduces the revenue significantly, namely, by a factor of $\log n$, as we show below.

Hence, we introduce *rounds* such that in a round the product is offered to a set of clients at the *same* time and we consider strategies with a limited number of rounds and/or limited price discrimination. Specifically we study k-round strategies where the product is offered to the clients in k rounds with $1 \leq k \leq n$ such that only clients that have purchased the product in a *previous round* can influence the valuation functions of the clients to whom the product is offered in the current round. Following [7] the strategies offer the product only once to each client to avoid that clients behave strategically, i.e., wait for price decreases in the future. We study two types of k-round strategies: (1) k-$\mathcal{PD}$ *strategies* where each client has a personalized price (*limited number of rounds*), and (2) k-$\mathcal{PR}$ *strategies* where all clients in the same round are offered the same price (*limited number of rounds and limited price discrimination*). Thus, k-$\mathcal{PR}$ strategies generalize the simple uniform price setting, where one might distribute free copies at the beginning and then charge everyone the same price. The setting in [7] corresponds to the n-$\mathcal{PR}$ setting. Throughout the paper we use $\widehat{R}$ to denote the optimal revenue achievable by an n-$\mathcal{PR}$ strategy. To summarize we study the natural question of how many different prices/rounds are necessary and sufficient if we want to achieve a constant factor approximation algorithm.

Our main results are: (1) There is a $\log n$-$\mathcal{PR}$ strategy that achieves a constant factor approximation of $\widehat{R}$ for very general valuation functions, namely probabilistic submodular valuation functions. Thus only $\log n$ different prices are necessary. We show that this result is tight (up to constant factors) in two regards: (a) It cannot be achieved with $o(\log n)$ rounds, even for very limited valuations with deterministic and additive externalities. (b) There exists a constant c such that it is NP-hard to compute a c-approximation of $\widehat{R}$, no matter how many rounds, i.e., maximizing revenue in k-$\mathcal{PR}$ strategies (as well as k-$\mathcal{PD}$ strategies) is APX-hard. (2) There is a 2-$\mathcal{PR}$ strategy that achieves an $O(\log n)$-approximation of $\widehat{R}$. (3) We give (nearly) 1/16-approximation algorithms for the maximum revenue achievable by any k-$\mathcal{PR}$ strategy when compared to the optimal k-$\mathcal{PR}$ strategy (i.e., not compared with $\widehat{R}$).

All algorithms we present are polynomial in the number of clients. Interestingly, all of them make very limited use of the network structure: They only exploit information about the neighbors of a node and not any global properties.

Discussion of Related Work. In the presence of network externalities two main types of revenue maximizing strategies have been used in the literature: strategies *with price discrimination* (each client pays a different price), and strategies *with uniform price* (every paying client pays the same price). We have already mentioned the work of Hartline et al. [7] on price discriminating strategies with n rounds (n-$\mathcal{PD}$). They study so-called *influence-and-exploit* strategies consisting of two steps: (1) the *influence* step, in which the product is given for free to a set of *influence nodes;* and (2) the *exploit* step, in which clients are approached sequentially and each client is offered the product at a personalized price. Hartline et al. give a randomized influence-and-exploit strategy that gives an $\frac{e}{4e-2}$-approximation of the optimal revenue $\widehat{R}$. Note that the revenue of our generalization to k-$\mathcal{PD}$ in Section 3 is quite close to this as it gives an $\frac{e}{4e-2+2/(k-1)}$-approximation. In particular for $k \geq 10$ our strategy k-PD(q) achieves more than 95% of the revenue of their strategy. Moreover with the improvements of Theorem 3 and $k \geq 10$ we get even better constants than [7]. Additionally, Hartline et al. present an algorithm that, together with a novel result on submodular function maximization [3], 0.5-approximates the optimal influence set.

Later, Fotakis and Siminelakis [5] studied a restricted model of client valuations and improved the approximation algorithms of Hartline et al. [7]. Furthermore, they study the ratio between the optimal strategies and the optimal influence-and-exploit strategies. Babaei et al. [2] experimentally evaluated several marketing strategies without an influence step, instead giving the most influential clients *discounts*. They conclude that discounts increase the revenue in the considered artificial and real networks.

Influence-and-exploit strategies with uniform prices have been studied by Mirrokni et al. [9]. They use generic algorithms for submodular function maximization to obtain an influence set with at least $1/2$ of the revenue of the optimal uniform price influence-and-exploit strategy, *not* of $\widehat{R}$. In both, [7] and [9], similar *graph models with concave influences* (CG) are introduced as model for network externalities.

Akhlaghpour et al. [1] study a different scenario with uniform prices, without any price discrimination: The product is offered on k consecutive rounds to all clients for the same price, and a client buys the product when its value exceeds the price for the day. They present an FPTAS for the *Basic* scenario, where a client buying the product immediately influences the valuation of the other clients who then may also buy the product in the same round. A round ends (the price changes) when no client is willing to buy the product for the current price. This model does not fit well to our assumptions of limited time and a large network. In the *Rapid* scenario, where buyers on the same day do not affect each other (like in our setting) they show that no constant factor approximation is possible and give an $O(\log_k n)$ approximation. The main difference to our setting is that in [1] the product has to be offered to every client (not having the product) in each round and thus there is no influence round where clients get the product for free.

For non-digital goods Ehsani et al. [4] study revenue maximizing strategies with both price discrimination and uniform prices with full information about the clients valuations and with *production costs* per unit in a setting where clients arrive randomly. They give an FPTAS for the optimal uniform price. Recall that we are studying digital goods without full information about the valuation functions.

Haghpanah et al. [6] study submodular network externalities for bidders in auctions and provide auctions that give a 0.25-approximation of the optimal revenue. In our models the strategies have to offer items in rounds since the clients are only influenced by clients, who bought the product in a previous round; that is an important difference to the auctions in [6].

Structure of the paper. In Section 2, we present our model for networks externalities as well as the different kinds of marketing strategies we consider in this paper. In Section 3, we study the effect of restricting the number of rounds, i.e., the effect of offering the product to several clients in parallel, but allowing full price discrimination. In Section 4 we compare the optimal revenue achievable with individual prices against the optimal revenue achievable with uniform prices. Efficiently computable k-$\mathcal{PR}$ strategies are studied in Section 5. In Section 6 we discuss several extensions of our model. All omitted proofs are provided in the full version available online.

2   Preliminaries

We are given a network $G = (V, E)$ of n clients V and edges $E \subseteq V \times V$ that represent their relationships. Suppose that we want to offer a digital product (i.e., the unit costs of the product are zero and we can produce an arbitrary number of copies) to each client $i \in V$ for some price $p_i \in \mathbb{R}_{\geq 0}$ and maximize our revenue. We call a client that has bought our product *active client* or *buyer*; otherwise we call him *inactive client*. We define the valuation of client $i \in V$ by $v_i : V \setminus \{i\} \to \mathbb{R}_{\geq 0}$, such that the valuation of i only depends on his neighbors, i.e., for A being the set of active clients and N_i being the set of neighbors of i in G holds $v_i(A) = v_i(A \cap N_i)$. We try to exploit this dependency of the valuation on the status of the neighbors (called *externality*) by offering the product to clients in a certain order, i.e., we want to compute an order on the clients. Furthermore, we restrict ourselves to a single offer to each client. We assume that clients are *individually rational* and have *quasi-linear utilities*. Thus client i buys the product if and only if the price p_i is not larger than the valuation $v_i(A)$.

Valuation Functions. We describe the different models for externalities for a client $i \in V$ and his active neighbors B. Our main focus is on submodular[1]

---

[1] A set function $f : 2^S \to \mathbb{R}$ is called submodular if for all $X \subseteq Y \subseteq S$ and each $x \in S \setminus Y$ it holds that $f(X \cup \{x\}) - f(X) \geq f(Y \cup \{x\}) - f(Y)$.

valuation functions, based on the intuition that the positive influence of a fixed neighbor does not increase when the set of active neighbors grows. Next we define the models we consider in the paper:

- *Simple Additive Model (SA).* There are non-negative weights $w_{i,i}$ and $w_{i,j}$ for $(i, j) \in E$. The valuation of i is given by $v_i(B) = \sum_{j \in B \cup \{i\}} w_{i,j}$.
- *Deterministic Submodular Model (DS).* There are monotone, submodular set functions $g_i : V \setminus \{i\} \to \mathbb{R}_{\geq 0}$. The valuation of i is given by $v_i(B) = g_i(B)$.
- *Probabilistic Submodular Model (SM)* [6]. The valuation of i is given by $v_i(B) = \tilde{v}_i \cdot g_i(B)$ where $g_i : V \setminus \{i\} \to [0, 1]$ is a (publicly known) monotone, submodular function with $g_i(V \setminus \{i\}) = 1$ and the private value $\tilde{v}_i \geq 0$ is drawn from a (publicly known) distribution with the CDF F_i.

In the first two models the seller has full information about the valuation while in the SM-model she only knows the distribution. We have that the DS-model generalizes the SA model and the SM-model generalizes both the SA and the DS-model. To simplify the presentation in this paper we state positive results for the SM-model and hardness results (whenever possible) for the SA-model. For all the models we call $v_i(\emptyset)$ the intrinsic valuation of client $i \in V$. Note that $v_i(V \setminus \{i\})$ is the maximum valuation of client $i \in V$ in each model. We will use this fact for upper bounds on the revenue any strategy can extract from a client.

Seller Information. By the previous definitions the valuation functions model the information of the seller about the real valuation of the clients. If the seller has full information, the seller maximizes her revenue by setting $p_i = v_i(B)$, where B are the active neighbors of $i \in V$. For the case of incomplete information price setting is more challenging. In particular, multiple prices could maximize the expected payment, the so-called myopic prices, and we do not know in general how likely it is that the client accepts one of those myopic prices.

Definition 1. *Given a client $i \in V$, and the set of active clients $B \subseteq V \setminus \{i\}$, the* myopic prices *of client i are defined as $\mathrm{argmax}_{p \in \mathbb{R}_{\geq 0}} \, p \cdot \mathbf{P}\left[v_i(B) \geq p\right]$. If $\mathbf{P}\left[v_i(B) \geq 0\right] = 0$ we define zero as the unique myopic price.*

The frequently used monotone hazard rate condition implies that there is a unique myopic price. The *hazard rate* of a PDF $f_{i,B}$ is defined to be $\frac{f_{i,B}(y)}{1 - F_{i,B}(y)}$ for $y \geq 0$. If the hazard rate of $f_{i,B}$ is a monotone non-decreasing function of $y \geq 0$ where y satisfies $F_{i,B}(y) < 1$ we say that $F_{i,B}$ has a *monotone hazard rate*. In the *SM-model with monotone hazard rates* we assume that for each $i \in V$ the CDF F_i has monotone hazard rate. Note that for full information models, $F_{i,B}(y) = 0$ and $f_{i,B}(y) = 0$ for all $y < v_i(B)$ and $F_{i,B}(y) = 1$ for all $y \geq v_i(B)$.

Lemma 1 ([7]). *In the SM-model with monotone hazard rates each client has a unique myopic price which is accepted with probability at least $\frac{1}{e}$. For a set of active clients B we denote the unique myopic price of client i as $\hat{p}_i(B)$.*

We will also assume that we can compute this myopic price in polynomial time.

(Marketing) Strategies. A marketing strategy determines in each round to which clients and at what prices the product is offered in this round. This choice may depend on the already visited clients, the active clients and the number of rounds remaining.

Definition 2. *A k-round (marketing) strategy is a probabilistic function s that maps (C, B, j) to (V_j, p), where $C \subseteq V$ are the clients visited so far, $B \subseteq C$ are the buyers in the previous rounds, $j \in [k]$ is the current round, $V_j \subseteq V \setminus C$ are the clients in round j, and $p: V_j \to \mathbb{R}_{\geq 0}$ gives the prices for clients in V_j.*[2]

In the following we consider two classes of k-round strategies, (i) one where each client gets an individual price, i.e., the rounds only influence the valuations and place no additional restrictions on the price, and (ii) one where the seller must set uniform prices in each round, and for each of them also the subclass of *Influence and Exploit (IE)*-strategies, where the seller offers the product for free to the clients of the first round, i.e., the price in the first round is fixed to 0. In 1-round strategies the seller has to offer the product to all clients at the same time and thus network externalities do not come into play at all.

Price Discrimination. $[k\text{-}\mathcal{PD}]$ This class contains all k-round strategies. If we set $k = |V|$ we get the class of all possible strategies. For $k \geq 2$ we consider the subclass $[k\text{-}\mathcal{PD}^{\text{IE}}]$ of *k-round influence and exploit strategies*, where the seller gives the product for free to the clients selected in the first round.

Uniform Prices Per Round. $[k\text{-}\mathcal{PR}]$ This class contains all *k-round uniform price strategies*, where all clients visited in the same round are offered the same price. For $k \geq 2$ the *k-round uniform price influence and exploit strategies* $[k\text{-}\mathcal{PR}^{\text{IE}}]$ are the $k\text{-}\mathcal{PR}$ strategies with the first round having uniform price 0.

Given a strategy s we use $R(s)$ to denote the (expected) revenue obtained by s. By $\widehat{R}_{k\text{-}\mathcal{PD}}$, $\widehat{R}^{\text{IE}}_{k\text{-}\mathcal{PD}}$, $\widehat{R}_{k\text{-}\mathcal{PR}}$ and $\widehat{R}^{\text{IE}}_{k\text{-}\mathcal{PR}}$ we denote the *optimal* revenues achievable by the above classes of strategies, where $\widehat{R} = \widehat{R}_{n\text{-}\mathcal{PD}}$ is the optimal revenue achievable by *any* strategy. Restricted to k-rounds and uniform prices, our main goals are to achieve constant factor approximations of $\widehat{R}$ and $\widehat{R}_{k\text{-}\mathcal{PR}}$.

3   Strategies with Individual Prices

In this section we analyze $k\text{-}\mathcal{PD}$ strategies, i.e., k-round strategies with full price discrimination. We first show that maximizing the revenue of such strategies is computationally hard even in the SA-model; in particular, we show that it is NP-hard to approximate better than within a factor of $34k/(1 + 34k)$. The reduction uses the fact that even in the SA-model, the problem of maximizing the revenue of $k\text{-}\mathcal{PD}$ generalizes Maximum k-Cut, and the latter is APX-hard [8].

Theorem 1. *Maximizing the revenue of $k\text{-}\mathcal{PD}$, resp. $k\text{-}\mathcal{PD}^{IE}$, is APX-hard in the SA-model; it is NP-hard to $\frac{34k}{1+34k}$-approximate $\widehat{R}_{k\text{-}\mathcal{PD}}$, resp. $\widehat{R}^{IE}_{k\text{-}\mathcal{PD}}$, for $k \geq 2$.*

---

[2] In principle it suffices that $s(\cdot, \cdot, j)$ is defined on the possible outcomes of round $j-1$. In particular for $j = 1$ it has only to be defined for $s(\emptyset, \emptyset, 1)$.

On the positive side we generalize the result in [7] to the SM-model with monotone hazard rates and to k rounds. Specifically, we show that the following IE strategy gives a constant factor approximation of the optimal k-round revenue as well as of the optimal revenue $\widehat{R}$ and can be computed in polynomial time. We will use these results in the following sections as they imply that any k-$\mathcal{PR}$ strategy that is an α-approximation of $\widehat{R}_{k\text{-}\mathcal{PD}}$ is an $O(\alpha)$-approximation of $\widehat{R}$.

Algorithm 1 (Strategy k-PD(q)). Let q be in $[0, 1]$.

1. Assign clients in V independently with probability q to set V_1. Give the clients in V_1 the product for free.
2. Partition the clients in $V \setminus V_1$ into sets $V_2, \ldots, V_k$ s.t. each client is in V_j independently of the other client with probability $(1 - q)/(k - 1)$.
3. Offer the clients in V_j the product in parallel for their myopic price.

To analyze the strategy we first consider the expected payment $\pi_i(S) = \hat{p}_i(S) \cdot \mathbf{P}\left[v_i(S) \geq \hat{p}_i(S)\right]$ we can extract from a client i given the active clients S. By the definition of the myopic price, we can show that $\hat{p}_i(S) = \hat{p}_i(V \setminus \{i\}) \cdot g_i(S)$. The crucial idea in Lemma 2 is now that we can lower bound the expected revenue $\pi_i(S)$ collected from client i by the maximum revenue that can be collect from i, namely $\pi_i(V \setminus \{i\})$, multiplied by the probability β that a client is in S. Note that β is a function of q. Theorem 2 then determines the value β, which in turn sets q. Finally we use a well-known property of submodular functions [7] to lower bound the revenue of k-PD(q).

Lemma 2. *Let $S \subseteq V \setminus \{i\}$ be the random set of clients and let each client $j \in V \setminus \{i\}$ be in S independently with a probability of at least β. Then it holds that $\mathbf{E}_S\left[\pi_i(S)\right] \geq \beta \cdot \pi_i(V \setminus \{i\})$.*

Theorem 2. *Consider the SM-model with monotone hazard rates. For $q = 1 - \frac{e \cdot (k-1)}{2e(k-1) - k + 2}$ it follows that $R(k\text{-}PD(q)) \geq \frac{e \cdot (k-1)}{4e(k-1) - 2k + 4}\widehat{R}$ and thus also $\widehat{R}_{k\text{-}\mathcal{PD}} \geq \frac{e \cdot (k-1)}{4e(k-1) - 2k + 4}\widehat{R}$.*

For $k = 2$, buyers are only influenced by clients in the influence set and Theorem 2 gives a 2-$\mathcal{PD}$ strategy, i.e., 2-PD(0.5), which achieves at least $\frac{1}{4}$ of the optimal revenue (a similar result was given in [7]). However the main challenge in the above algorithm is to exploit also the externalities from the other preceding rounds. The 2-round case will be crucial for our k-$\mathcal{PR}$-algorithm in Section 5.

Corollary 1. *Given the SM-model with monotone hazard rates, it follows that $\widehat{R}_{k\text{-}\mathcal{PD}} \geq \widehat{R}^{IE}_{k\text{-}\mathcal{PD}} \geq \frac{1}{4} \cdot \widehat{R}$ for $k \geq 2$.*

Fotakis and Siminelakis [5] show that myopic prices are not necessarily optimal for IE-strategies. They provide IE-strategies, using lower prices, that beat those of [7] if the valuations follow the uniform additive model. In the following we generalize this idea to (a) submodular valuations with monotone hazard rates and (b) to the k-round setting. That is, we consider strategies that use different discount factors α_j for different rounds j. To be more precise in each round the seller charges every client only an α_j-fraction of his myopic price. Moreover, we also consider different probabilities q_j for a client being assigned to round j. The next theorem shows that charging less than the myopic price can improve the overall revenue.

Algorithm 2 (Strategy k-PD($\bar{q}, \bar{\alpha}$)). Let $\bar{q}$ and $\bar{\alpha}$ be vectors of length k with entries in $[0, 1]$ and let the entries of $\bar{q}$ sum up to 1.

1. Partition V into sets $V_1, \ldots, V_k$ s.t. each client $i \in V$ is in V_j independently of the others with probability q_j.
2. Offer the clients $i \in V_j$ the product in parallel for price $\alpha_j \cdot \hat{p}_i$ where $\hat{p}_i$ is the myopic price of client i.

Theorem 3. *Given the SM-Model with monotone hazard rates, for each k there exist vectors $\bar{q}, \bar{\alpha}$ such that $R(k$-PD$(\bar{q}, \bar{\alpha})) \geq C_k \cdot \hat{R}$, where $C_3 = 0.279$, $C_5 = 0.298$, $C_8 = 0.308$, and $C_{10} = 0.311$.*

Computing C_k is a multi-parameter optimization problem (with $2k$ parameters) that we solved numerically. More details are provided in the full version. Finally, note that the Algorithms 1 and 2 use the network structure only in the computation of the myopic prices, which only requires to know the active neighbors.

4   Comparing Individual Prices to Uniform Prices

In this section we study k-$\mathcal{PR}$ strategies where there are k rounds and in each round we offer the product to a subset of the clients for a uniform price. We first analyze the impact that restricting the strategies to be uniform price strategies has on the optimal revenue for a constant number of rounds. We show that in the SM-model the optimal revenue can decrease in the worst case by a factor of $\Theta(1/n)$. Thus, if we do not make assumptions on the probability distributions we cannot do better than in each round just selecting the most valuable client and offer the product to him for his myopic price. However, if we consider the SM-model with monotone hazard rates the optimal revenue can decrease in the worst case by a factor of $\Theta(1/\log n)$. As a result we will focus on models with monotone hazard rates in the remainder of the paper.

Theorem 4. *Assume that the valuations of the clients follow the SM-model.*

1. *For every $\varepsilon > 0$ and $k \geq 1$ there exists a network and valuations v_i such that $\hat{R}_{k\text{-}\mathcal{PR}} \leq \frac{k+\varepsilon}{n} \hat{R}_{k\text{-}\mathcal{PD}}$.*
2. *For any network and valuations v_i, $\hat{R}_{1\text{-}\mathcal{PR}} \geq \frac{1}{n} \hat{R}_{1\text{-}\mathcal{PD}}$.*
3. *For any network and valuations v_i, $\hat{R}_{2\text{-}\mathcal{PR}}^{IE} \geq \frac{1}{n} \hat{R}_{2\text{-}\mathcal{PD}}^{IE} \geq \frac{1}{4n} \hat{R}$.*

The next theorem shows three points: (1) Even with monotone hazard rates, no k-$\mathcal{PR}$ strategy can be better than a k/H_n-approximation of $\hat{R}_{k\text{-}\mathcal{PD}}$ and, thus, also of $\hat{R}$. Recall, that the SA-model satisfies the monotone hazard rate condition and is a special case of a DS and an SM-model and thus these negative results also extend to these models. Thus without price discrimination within a round no constant factor approximation of $\hat{R}$ with $o(\log n)$ different rounds exists.

(2) Even with only 2 rounds the *optimal* 2-$\mathcal{PR}$ strategy achieves an $O(\log n)$ approximation of $\widehat{R}^{IE}_{2\text{-}\mathcal{PD}}$, which, by Corollary 1, achieves a 4-approximation of $\widehat{R}$. Thus, the optimal 2-$\mathcal{PR}$ strategy achieves an $O(\log n)$ approximation of $\widehat{R}$. This is a large improvement over the negative result from Theorem 4, which holds for valuations that do not have monotone hazard rates. However, we show in the next section that computing the optimal 2-$\mathcal{PR}$ strategy is NP-hard.

Theorem 5. *Assume that valuations of the clients follow the SM-model with monotone hazard rates.*

1. *For each $k \geq 1$ there exists a network and valuations v_i such that $\widehat{R}_{k\text{-}\mathcal{PR}} \leq \frac{k}{H_n} \widehat{R}_{k\text{-}\mathcal{PD}}$ (even in the SA-model).*
2. *For any network and valuations v_i, $\widehat{R}_{1\text{-}\mathcal{PR}} \geq \frac{1}{e \cdot H_n} \widehat{R}_{1\text{-}\mathcal{PD}}$.*
3. *For any network and valuations v_i, $\widehat{R}^{IE}_{2\text{-}\mathcal{PR}} \geq \frac{1}{e \cdot H_n} \widehat{R}^{IE}_{2\text{-}\mathcal{PD}}$.*

Recall that we want to achieve a constant approximation of $\widehat{R}$ using a uniform price strategy. Thus, in the next section we give a polynomial time computable k-$\mathcal{PR}$ strategy, with $k \in \Theta(\log n)$, that achieves a constant factor approximation.

5   Strategies with Uniform Prices

In the analysis of the algorithms in Section 3 we exploited that the *expected revenue* from a client i was submodular in the set of active neighbors. This is not true in the $\mathcal{PR}$ setting, as we can only extract revenue from a client if his valuation is larger than the uniform price. Still we can show the following: (1) We give a polynomial-time approximation scheme (PTAS) for one round strategies in the SM-model with monotone hazard rates, i.e., for finding the optimal uniform price for one round. (2) We show that finding an optimal 2-$\mathcal{PR}$ strategy is not only NP-hard but also APX-hard, even for the DS-model. (3) We give a constant factor approximation of $\widehat{R}$ with $O(\log n)$ rounds for valuations from the SM-model with monotone hazard rates. (4) From Section 4 we know that k-$\mathcal{PR}$ strategies, where k is a constant, lose a factor of $\log n$ of the optimum revenue when compared to $\widehat{R}$. Thus, in this case the best we can hope for is a constant factor approximation of $\widehat{R}_{k\text{-}\mathcal{PR}}$, *not* of $\widehat{R}$. We have two such results: (4a) We give a $(1/16 - \varepsilon)$ approximation of $\widehat{R}_{k\text{-}\mathcal{PR}}$ for the SM-model with monotone hazard rates. (4b) We show that under certain conditions we can even give a $(1/4 - \varepsilon)$-approximation of $\widehat{R}_{2\text{-}\mathcal{PR}}$. Combined with Theorem 5 this gives an $O(\log(n)/k)$-approximation of $\widehat{R}$ in k rounds.

We first give a PTAS for computing the optimal price for the one round setting. This will be a useful tool for the 2-round setting.

Algorithm 3. Let $c = (1 - \varepsilon)^{-1}$ and $\varepsilon > 0$.

1. Compute $\hat{p}_{\max} = \max_{i \in V} \hat{p}_i$.
2. For all $j \in \{0, \ldots, \lfloor \log_c(e \cdot n) \rfloor\}$:
   Compute the expected revenue R_j for the uniform price $p_j = \frac{\hat{p}_{\max}}{c^j}$.
3. Return p_j with maximal R_j.

Theorem 6. *Given the SM-model with monotone hazard rates, then for each* $\varepsilon > 0$ *Algorithm 3 gives a 1-$\mathcal{PR}$ strategy s (i.e., a uniform price), such that* $R(s) \geq (1 - \varepsilon) \cdot \widehat{R}_{1\text{-}\mathcal{PR}}$ *in polynomial time.*

The basic idea of the proof is that the optimal uniform price p^* cannot be less than $\hat{p}_{\max}/(e \cdot n)$ and if we pick a price within $(1 - \varepsilon)$ of p^* we get a $(1 - \varepsilon)$-approximation of $\widehat{R}_{1\text{-}\mathcal{PR}}$.

Next we show that for two rounds the problem becomes APX-hard. That is it is NP-hard to approximate better than within a factor of $259/260$. The proof is via a reduction from the dominated set problem. In this reduction a client has valuation 1 iff at least one of its neighbors is in the dominating set, and 0 otherwise. This function is not additive and thus the result requires the DS-model (and not the SA-model).

Theorem 7. *Maximizing the revenue of 2-$\mathcal{PR}$, resp. 2-$\mathcal{PR}^{IE}$, is APX-hard for the DS-model (and also for the concave graph models of [7,9]), in particular, it is not approximable within $259/260$.*

Next we present the constant factor approximation of $\widehat{R}$ for $k \in \Omega(\log n)$. In the following strategy the set A of clients for the first round is given. We will then choose A using the 2-$\mathcal{PD}^{IE}$-strategy of Theorem 2 to get the final result.

Algorithm 4 (Strategy k-PR(c, A)). Let $A \subseteq V$ be the influence set and $c > 1$ be a constant.

1. Give the product to all clients in A for free in the first round.
2. Set $(\hat{p}_1, \hat{p}_2, \ldots, \hat{p}_t)$ to the myopic prices of the clients in $V \backslash A$ for the influence set A in descending order.
3. Set $S_j = \left\{ i \mid \frac{\hat{p}_1}{c^{j-1}} \geq \hat{p}_i > \frac{\hat{p}_1}{c^j} \right\}$ and select the first $k - 1$ non-empty sets.
4. Each of these sets S_j becomes a set of clients that is offered the product in one round with uniform price $p(j) = \min_{i \in S_j} \hat{p}_i$.

Our analysis of this strategy only collects revenue for clients in $V \backslash A$ and only exploits externalities induced by clients in A, i.e., from clients in the first round. Thus this algorithm would have the same performance if all nodes in $V \backslash A$ are offered the item in the same round but with $k - 1$ different prices.

We denote by k-PR$^*(c, q)$ the strategy where the influence set A is chosen randomly such that each client is in A with probability q, independently of the other clients. For the clients in the selected sets S_j we extract at least $1/c$ of the revenue the optimal 2-$\mathcal{PD}$ strategy would extract from them. Additional in each set there is one client that gets his myopic price (i.e., an additional $(1 - 1/c)$ factor of his optimal revenue). We show in the proof below that this second contribution can be used to compensate for the optimal revenue of the clients which are not in a selected set, resulting in the bound of the next theorem.

Theorem 8. *Let $c > 1$ be a constant. Given valuations from the SM-model with monotone hazard rates then for every 2-$\mathcal{PD}^{IE}$ strategy s with influence set A the strategy $(k + 1)$-PR(c, A) achieves at least* $\min\{\frac{1}{c}, \frac{(c^k - 1)}{(c^k - 1) + e(n - k)(c - 1)}\}$ *of the revenue $R(s)$ of s.*

Proof. Consider the set $V \setminus A = \{1, \ldots, n\}$ and let $\hat{\mathbf{p}} := (\hat{p}_1, \hat{p}_2, \ldots, \hat{p}_n)$ be the vector of (myopic) prices induced by A. W.l.o.g., we assume that the prices and the corresponding clients are sorted in a descending order. By the definition $R(s) = \sum_{i=1}^{n} \hat{p}_i \cdot \mathbf{P}[v_i \geq \hat{p}_i]$.

For each client i we denote the price charged by the strategy $(k+1)$-PR(c, A) by p_i^*. The uniform price in round j is denoted by $p(j)$. Then the revenue of $(k+1)$-PR(c, A) is given by: $R((k+1)$-PR$(c, A)) = \sum_{i=1}^{n} p_i^* \cdot \mathbf{P}[v_i \geq p_i^*]$

Now, by construction of S_j, either $p_i^* \geq \hat{p}_i/c$ in the case where i is in one of the selected sets (the first k non-empty sets), or $p_i^* = 0$ otherwise.

Let J be the set of the indices of the selected sets and l the largest index among them. Let m be the number of clients that are offered the product, i.e., m is the client with the lowest myopic price in S_l.

Consider suitable chosen $\alpha \leq 1/c$. For each client i in a selected set the algorithm collects at least a revenue of $\alpha \hat{p}_i \cdot \mathbf{P}[v_i \geq \hat{p}_i]$. Additionally for each $j \in J$ there exists at least one client $i_j \in S_j$ who is charged his myopic price and thus the algorithm collects the full revenue $\hat{p}_{i_j} \cdot \mathbf{P}[v_{i_j} \geq \hat{p}_{i_j}]$.

$$R((k+1)\text{-PR}(c, A)) \geq \sum_{1 \leq i \leq m} \alpha \hat{p}_i \cdot \mathbf{P}[v_i \geq \hat{p}_i] + (1 - \alpha) \sum_{j \in J} p(j) \cdot \mathbf{P}[v_{i_j} \geq p(j)]$$

The first term is an α-approximation for the revenue of the first m clients. We next relate the second term to the revenue of the remaining clients and compute an approximation factor α such that:

$$(1 - \alpha) \sum_{j \in J} p(j) \cdot \mathbf{P}[v_{i_j} \geq p(j)] \geq \alpha \sum_{m+1 \leq i \leq n} \hat{p}_i \cdot \mathbf{P}[v_i \geq \hat{p}_i]$$

By the definition of the sets, $p(j) \geq \frac{\hat{p}_1}{c^j}$ and by the monotone hazard rate condition $\mathbf{P}[v_{i_j} \geq p(j)] \geq 1/e$. Thus

$$\sum_{j \in J} p(j) \cdot \mathbf{P}[v_{i_j} \geq p(j)] \geq \sum_{l-k+1 \leq j \leq l} \hat{p}_1 c^{-j} \frac{1}{e} = \frac{c^{k-l}}{e} \cdot \frac{\hat{p}_1(1 - c^{-k})}{(c - 1)} = \frac{\hat{p}_1(c^k - 1)}{(c - 1)c^l e}.$$

Using (a) $m \geq k$, (b) $\mathbf{P}[v_i \geq \hat{p}_i] \leq 1$ and (c) $\hat{p}_i \leq \hat{p}_1 \cdot c^{-l}$ for all $i \geq m + 1$ we get $\sum_{i=m+1}^{n} \hat{p}_i \cdot \mathbf{P}[v_i \geq \hat{p}_i] \leq (n - k)\hat{p}_1 c^{-l}$. When resolving the inequality $\frac{(1-\alpha)\hat{p}_1(c^k - 1)}{(c-1)c^l e} \geq \frac{\alpha(n-k)\hat{p}_1}{c^l}$ we obtain $\alpha \leq \frac{(c^k - 1)}{(c^k - 1) + e \cdot (n - k)(c - 1)} =: \beta$. Now setting $\alpha = \min(\beta, 1/c)$ yields the claim. $\qquad\square$

If the number of rounds is $\Omega(\log n)$ and we are using the influence set from the $2\text{-}\mathcal{PD}^{\text{IE}}$ strategy 2-PD(0.5) in Theorem 2 we get a constant factor approximation.

Corollary 2. *Assuming valuations from the SM-model with monotone hazard rates, $R(((\log_c n) + 1)\text{-PR}^*(c, 1/2)) \geq \widehat{R}/(4c \cdot e)$ for any constant $c > 1$.*

Proof. Consider the $2\text{-}\mathcal{PD}^{\text{IE}}$ strategy s from Theorem 2, i.e., 2-PD(0.5), which is a $1/4$-approximation of $\widehat{R}$, i.e., $R(s) \geq \widehat{R}/4$. Using the influence set A from

s, i.e., randomly picking nodes with probability $1/2$, we get that k-$\text{PR}(c, A)$ is equal to k-$\text{PR}^*(c, 1/2)$. If we set $k = \log_c n + 1$ then Theorem 8 shows that $R(((\log_c n) + 1)\text{-}\text{PR}^*(c, 1/2)) \geq R(S)/(c \cdot e)$. Combining the two results we get a $\frac{1}{4e \cdot c}$-approximation of $\widehat{R}$.   □

To obtain a k-$\mathcal{PR}$ strategy that matches the bound of Theorem 5 one can first construct the $((\log_c n) + 1)\text{-}\text{PR}^*(c, 1/2)$ strategy from above. Then for the k-$\mathcal{PR}$ strategy one uses the same influence set for the first round and for the remaining rounds one picks the $k - 1$ rounds with the highest expected payment in the strategy $((\log_c n) + 1)\text{-}\text{PR}^*(c, 1/2)$.[3]

Now let us consider 2-$\mathcal{PR}$ strategies. Due to the results in Section 4, the best we can hope for is a constant factor approximation of $\widehat{R}_{2\text{-}\mathcal{PR}}$, *not* of $\widehat{R}$ or of $\widehat{R}_{2\text{-}\mathcal{PD}}$. We first show that we can restrict ourselves to approximating the optimal IE strategy, as a revenue optimal IE strategy is within half of the revenue optimal 2-$\mathcal{PR}$ strategies. The proof idea is to design two IE strategies, one for the case that at least half of the revenue of the optimal k-$\mathcal{PR}$ strategy comes from the first round, and one or the case that it does not. In either case, at most half of the revenue is lost.

Lemma 3. *Given valuations v_i from the SM-model, then $\widehat{R}^{IE}_{k\text{-}\mathcal{PR}} \geq \frac{1}{2}\widehat{R}_{k\text{-}\mathcal{PR}}$.*

Thus it suffices to approximate $\widehat{R}^{IE}_{k\text{-}\mathcal{PR}}$. We give a simple 2-round algorithm for the SM-model that is based on our 1-round strategy from Algorithm 3.

Algorithm 5 (Strategy $\text{PR}^{0.5}(\varepsilon)$). Let ε be in $\mathbb{R}_{>0}$.
1. Assign each client in V to an influence set A, s.t. each client is a member of A independently of the others with probability $1/2$. Give the product to the clients in A for free in the first round.
2. Use Algorithm 3 to compute a $(1 - \varepsilon)$-approximation of the optimal revenue for the given influence set A.

In the analysis of Algorithm 5 we first bound the *probability* that the valuation of a client is larger than a fixed uniform price. This is different from the approach in Section 3, where it was sufficient to argue about the expected revenue we collect from a client. Then we use a technique similar to [9] to show that $R(\text{PR}^{0.5}(\varepsilon))$ is a $(1/8 - \varepsilon)$-approximation of $\widehat{R}^{IE}_{2\text{-}\mathcal{PR}}$.

Theorem 9. *Given valuations v_i from the SM-model with monotone hazard rates, then $R(\text{PR}^{0.5}(\varepsilon)) \geq \left(\frac{1}{8} - \varepsilon\right) \cdot \widehat{R}^{IE}_{2\text{-}\mathcal{PR}}$ for every $\varepsilon > 0$.*

Together with Lemma 3 we then obtain that the above algorithm achieves at least $1/16$ of $\widehat{R}_{2\text{-}\mathcal{PR}}$ in the SM-model with monotone hazard rates. By Theorem 5, $\widehat{R}^{IE}_{2\text{-}\mathcal{PR}}$ is a $\frac{1}{eH_n}$-approximation of $\widehat{R}^{IE}_{2\text{-}\mathcal{PD}}$ the above strategy is thus also a $\Theta(\frac{1}{H_n})$-approximation of $\widehat{R}$.

Corollary 3. *Given valuations v_i from the SM-model with monotone hazard rates, then $R(\text{PR}^{0.5}(\varepsilon)) \geq \frac{(1/8 - \varepsilon)}{4H_n} \cdot \widehat{R}^{IE}_{2\text{-}\mathcal{PD}} \geq \frac{(1/8 - \varepsilon)}{16H_n} \cdot \widehat{R}$ for every $\varepsilon > 0$.*

---

[3] The authors are grateful to an anonymous reviewer for pointing this out.

The above results can be generalized to k-$\mathcal{PR}$ strategies.

Theorem 10. *Given valuations v_i from the SM-model with monotone hazard rates, for any $k \geq 2$ and $\varepsilon > 0$ there exists a polynomial-time computable k-$\mathcal{PR}$ strategy s such that $R(s) \geq \left(\frac{1}{8} - \varepsilon\right) \cdot \widehat{R}^{IE}_{k\text{-}\mathcal{PR}}$ and thus $R(s) \geq \left(\frac{1}{16} - \varepsilon\right) \cdot \widehat{R}_{k\text{-}\mathcal{PR}}$.*

The proof of Theorem 10 exploits that (i) we only lose a constant factor when ignoring the influence between the latter rounds and that (ii) when given the influence set and an instance without influence between the other clients we can give an approximation scheme for the optimal uniform prices and compute the corresponding round assignment.

Mirrokni et al. [9] study a different less general model, called concave graph model (CG). They give an algorithm that, under certain assumptions, finds an influence set A which achieves at least $1/2$ of the revenue achieved by the optimal influence set. We extend this result to 2-$\mathcal{PR}^{IE}$ strategies in the SM-model. The key ideas of the proof are that (1) if the seller charges a uniform price sufficiently close to the optimal price then she only loses an ε of the revenue and (2) once the seller has fixed the posted price, under the assumptions of the theorem, the expected revenue is a submodular function of the influence set.

Theorem 11. *Let $\mu > 0$, $M_v \geq 0$ and $M_p \geq 0$ such that $M_p \leq M_v \cdot \mu$. For each client, let their valuations follow the SM-model with the following additional assumptions: $g_i(\emptyset) \geq \mu > 0$, and $\tilde{v}_i$ is drawn from a probability distribution F_i whose probability density function f_i is positive, differentiable, non-decreasing on $(0, M_v)$ and for all $x \in (0, M_v)$, $f_i(x) \leq \bar{f}$ for some constant $\bar{f}$, and $F_i(0) = 0$, $F_i(M_v) = 1$. Let the price be in the interval $0 \leq p \leq M_p$. Then for every $\varepsilon = o(|V|^{-1})$ there is an algorithm finding a 2-$\mathcal{PR}^{IE}$ strategy s, i.e., an influence set A^* and a uniform price p^* for the second round, such that $R(s) \geq \left(\frac{1}{2} - \varepsilon\right) \cdot \widehat{R}^{IE}_{2\text{-}\mathcal{PR}}$.*

By Lemma 3, the algorithm of Theorem 11 achieves at least $(1/4 - \varepsilon)$ of $\widehat{R}_{2\text{-}\mathcal{PR}}$.

6   Extensions of the Model

Our models and results can be extended in several directions.

First, one can consider more general classes of externalities. In the *General Monotone Model (GM)* the valuation $v_i(B)$ of i is drawn from a (known) distribution with the CDF $F_{i,B}$ such that $\mathbf{P}\left[v_i(B) \geq p\right] \geq \mathbf{P}\left[v_i(B') \geq p\right]$ for all $B' \subseteq B$ and $p \in \mathbb{R}_{\geq 0}$. Notice that the proofs of Theorems 4 and 8 do not exploit the fact that the valuations are from the SM-model and thus extend to the GM-model.

Second, the monotone hazard rate condition can be relaxed. For all theorems, except Theorem 3, the crucial part we use is that there is a myopic price with a certain acceptance probability. The exact approximation bound then depends on this acceptance probability. If one can guarantee a higher acceptance probability than $1/e$ also the presented approximation guarantees improve. For instance, if one considers only uniform distributions for $\tilde{v}_i$ then the acceptance probability of the myopic price is $1/2$ and the approximation guarantee of Theorem 1 improves to $(k-1)/(3k-2)$.

Third, one can consider different classes of marketing strategies. For instance strategies where clients are split into k groups and l rounds such that (a) each client belongs to exactly one group and round, (b) all clients in the same group are offered the same price independent of their round and (c) only clients that have purchased the product *in a previous* round can influence the valuation functions of the clients in the current round, but this influence is independent of their group. For instance, a group could model all clients that live in the same country, preferred clients, or an age group. Our results extend to this setting as well. That is, one can get a constant factor of $\widehat{R}$ using $O(\log n)$ different groups/prices, but not with $o(\log n)$ different groups/prices.

References

1. Akhlaghpour, H., Ghodsi, M., Haghpanah, N., Mirrokni, V.S., Mahini, H., Nikzad, A.: Optimal iterative pricing over social networks (Extended abstract). In: Saberi, A. (ed.) WINE 2010. LNCS, vol. 6484, pp. 415–423. Springer, Heidelberg (2010)
2. Babaei, M., Mirzasoleiman, B., Jalili, M., Safari, M.A.: Revenue maximization in social networks through discounting. Social Network Analysis and Mining 3(4), 1249–1262 (2013)
3. Buchbinder, N., Feldman, M., Naor, J.S., Schwartz, R.: A tight linear time (1/2)-approximation for unconstrained submodular maximization. In: 53rd FOCS, pp. 649–658 (2012)
4. Ehsani, S., Ghodsi, M., Khajenezhad, A., Mahini, H., Nikzad, A.: Optimal online pricing with network externalities. Information Processing Letters 112(4), 118–123 (2012)
5. Fotakis, D., Siminelakis, P.: On the efficiency of influence-and-exploit strategies for revenue maximization under positive externalities. In: Goldberg, P.W. (ed.) WINE 2012. LNCS, vol. 7695, pp. 270–283. Springer, Heidelberg (2012)
6. Haghpanah, N., Immorlica, N., Mirrokni, V., Munagala, K.: Optimal auctions with positive network externalities. ACM Transactions on Economics and Computation 1(2), 13:1–13:24 (2013)
7. Hartline, J., Mirrokni, V.S., Sundararajan, M.: Optimal marketing strategies over social networks. In: 17th WWW, pp. 189–198 (2008)
8. Kann, V., Khanna, S., Lagergren, J., Panconesi, A.: On the hardness of approximating max k-cut and its dual. Chicago Journal of Theoretical Computer Science 1997 (1997)
9. Mirrokni, V.S., Roch, S., Sundararajan, M.: On fixed-price marketing for goods with positive network externalities. In: Goldberg, P.W. (ed.) WINE 2012. LNCS, vol. 7695, pp. 532–538. Springer, Heidelberg (2012)
10. Oliver, R.L., Shor, M.: Digital redemption of coupons: satisfying and dissatisfying effects of promotion codes. Journal of Product & Brand Management 12(2), 121–134 (2003)

Computing Approximate Nash Equilibria in Polymatrix Games*

Argyrios Deligkas[1], John Fearnley[1], Rahul Savani[1], and Paul Spirakis[1,2]

[1] Department of Computer Science, University of Liverpool, UK
[2] Research Academic Computer Technology Institute (CTI), Greece

Abstract. In an ϵ-Nash equilibrium, a player can gain at most ϵ by unilaterally changing his behaviour. For two-player (bimatrix) games with payoffs in $[0, 1]$, the best-known ϵ achievable in polynomial time is 0.3393 [23]. In general, for n-player games an ϵ-Nash equilibrium can be computed in polynomial time for an ϵ that is an increasing function of n but does not depend on the number of strategies of the players. For three-player and four-player games the corresponding values of ϵ are 0.6022 and 0.7153, respectively. Polymatrix games are a restriction of general n-player games where a player's payoff is the sum of payoffs from a number of bimatrix games. There exists a very small but constant ϵ such that computing an ϵ-Nash equilibrium of a polymatrix game is **PPAD**-hard. Our main result is that an $(0.5+\delta)$-Nash equilibrium of an n-player polymatrix game can be computed in time polynomial in the input size and $\frac{1}{\delta}$. Inspired by the algorithm of Tsaknakis and Spirakis [23], our algorithm uses gradient descent on the maximum regret of the players.

1 Introduction

Approximate Nash Equilibria. Nash equilibria are the central solution concept in game theory. Since it is known that computing an *exact* Nash equilibrium [9,5] is unlikely to be achievable in polynomial time, a line of work has arisen that studies the computational aspects of approximate Nash equilibria. The most widely studied notion is of an *ϵ-approximate Nash equilibrium* (ϵ-Nash), which requires that all players have an expected payoff that is within ϵ of a best response. This is an *additive* notion of approximate equilibrium; the problem of computing approximate equilibria of bimatrix games using a relative notion of approximation is known to be **PPAD**-hard even for constant approximations [8].

So far, ϵ-Nash equilibria have mainly been studied in the context of two-player *bimatrix* games. A line of work [11,10,2] has investigated the best ϵ that can be guaranteed in polynomial time for bimatrix games. The current best result,

---

* The first author is supported by the Microsoft Research PhD sponsorship program. The second and third author are supported by EPSRC grant EP/L011018/1, and the third author is also supported by ESRC grant ESRC/BSB/09. The work of the fourth author is supported partially by the EU ERC Project ALGAME and by the Greek THALIS action "Algorithmic Game Theory". A full version of this paper, with all missing proofs, is available at http://arxiv.org/abs/1409.3741

T.-Y. Liu et al. (Eds.): WINE 2014, LNCS 8877, pp. 58–71, 2014.
© Springer International Publishing Switzerland 2014

due to Tsaknakis and Spirakis [23], is a polynomial-time algorithm that finds a 0.3393-Nash equilibrium of a bimatrix game with all payoffs in $[0, 1]$.

In this paper, we study ϵ-Nash equilibria in the context of *many-player* games, a topic that has received much less attention. A simple approximation algorithm for many-player games can be obtained by generalising the algorithm of Daskalakis, Mehta and Papadimitriou [11] from the two-player setting to the n-player setting, which provides a guarantee of $\epsilon = 1 - \frac{1}{n}$. This has since been improved independently by three sets of authors [3,18,2]. They provide a method that converts a polynomial-time algorithm that for finding ϵ-Nash equilibria in $(n-1)$-player games into an algorithm that finds a $\frac{1}{2-\epsilon}$-Nash equilibrium in n-player games. Using the polynomial-time 0.3393 algorithm of Tsaknakis and Spirakis [23] for 2-player games as the base case for this recursion, this allows us to provide polynomial-time algorithms with approximation guarantees of 0.6022 in 3-player games, and 0.7153 in 4-player games. These guarantees tend to 1 as n increases, and so far, no constant $\epsilon < 1$ is known such that, for all n, an ϵ-Nash equilibrium of an n-player game can be computed in polynomial time.

For n-player games, we have lower bounds for ϵ-Nash equilibria. More precisely, Rubinstein has shown that when n is not a constant there exists a constant but very small ϵ such that it is PPAD-hard to compute an ϵ-Nash equilibrium [22]. This is quite different from the bimatrix game setting, where the existence of a quasi-polynomial time approximation scheme rules out such a lower bound, unless all of PPAD can be solved in quasi-polynomial time [21].

Polymatrix Games.   In this paper, we focus on a particular class of many-player games called *polymatrix games*. In a polymatrix game, the interaction between the players is specified by an n vertex graph, where each vertex represents one of the players. Each edge of the graph specifies a bimatrix game that will be played by the two respective players, and thus a player with degree d will play d bimatrix games simultaneously. More precisely, each player picks a strategy, and then plays this strategy in *all* of the bimatrix games that he is involved in. His payoff is then the sum of the payoffs that he obtains in each of the games.

Polymatrix games are a class of *succinctly represented* n-player games: a polymatrix game is specified by at most n^2 bimatrix games, each of which can be written down in quadratic space with respect to the number of strategies. This is unlike general n-player strategic form games, which require a representation that is exponential in the number of players.

There has been relatively little work on the approximation of polymatrix games. Obviously, the approximation algorithms for general games can be applied in this setting, but to the best of our knowledge there have been no upper bounds that are specific to polymatrix games. On the other hand, the lower bound of Rubinstein mentioned above is actually proved by constructing polymatrix games. Thus, there is a constant but very small ϵ such that it is PPAD-hard to compute an ϵ-Nash equilibrium [22], and this again indicates that approximating polymatrix games is quite different to approximating bimatrix games.

Our Contribution. Our main result is an algorithm that, for every δ in the range $0 < \delta \leq 0.5$, finds a $(0.5 + \delta)$-Nash equilibrium of a polymatrix game in time polynomial in the input size and $\frac{1}{\delta}$. Note that our approximation guarantee *does not depend on the number of players*, which is a property that was not previously known to be achievable for polymatrix games, and still cannot be achieved for general strategic form games.

We prove this result by adapting the algorithm of Tsaknakis and Spirakis [23] (henceforth referred to as the TS algorithm). They give a gradient descent algorithm for finding a 0.3393-Nash equilibrium in a bimatrix game. We generalise their algorithm to the polymatrix setting, and show that it always arrives at a $(0.5 + \delta)$-Nash equilibrium after a polynomial number of iterations.

In order to generalise the TS algorithm, we had to overcome several issues. Firstly, the TS algorithm makes the regrets of the two players equal in every iteration, but there is no obvious way to achieve this in the polymatrix setting. Instead, we show how gradient descent can be applied to strategy profiles where the regrets are not necessarily equal. Secondly, the output of the TS algorithm is either a point found by gradient descent, or a point obtained by modifying the result of gradient descent. In the polymatrix game setting, it is not immediately obvious how such a modification can be derived with a non-constant number of players (without an exponential blowup). Thus we apply a different analysis, which proves that the point resulting from gradient descent always has our approximation guarantee. It is an interesting open question whether a better approximation can be achieved when there is a constant number of players.

An interesting feature of our algorithm is that it can be applied even when players have differing degrees. Originally, polymatrix games were defined only for complete graphs [19]. Since previous work has only considered lower bounds for polymatrix games, it has been sufficient to restrict the model to only including complete graphs, or in the case of Rubinstein's work [22], regular graphs. However, since this paper is proving an upper bound, we must be more careful. As it turns out, our algorithm will find a 0.5-Nash equilibrium, no matter what graph structure the polymatrix game has.

Related Work. An FPTAS for the problem of computing an ϵ-Nash equilibrium of a bimatrix game does not exist unless every problem in PPAD can be solved in polynomial time [5]. Arguably, the biggest open question in equilibrium computation is whether there exists a PTAS for this problem. As we have mentioned, for any constant $\epsilon > 0$, there does exist a *quasi-polynomial*-time algorithm for computing an ϵ-Nash equilibria of a bimatrix game, or any game with a constant number of players [21,1], with running time $k^{O(\log k)}$ for a $k \times k$ bimatrix game. Consequently, in contrast to the many-player case, it is not believed that there exists a constant ϵ such that the problem of computing an ϵ-Nash equilibrium of a bimatrix game (or any game with a constant number of players) is PPAD-hard, since it seems unlikely that all problems in PPAD have quasi-polynomial-time algorithms. On the other hand, for multi-player games, as mentioned above, there is a small constant ϵ such that it is PPAD-hard to compute an ϵ-Nash equilibrium of an n-player game when n is not constant.

One positive result we do have for multi-player games is that there is a PTAS for *anonymous games* (where the identity of players does not matter) when the number of strategies is constant [12].

Polymatrix games have played a central role in the reductions that have been used to show PPAD-hardness of games and other equilibrium problems [9,5,13,15,6]. Computing an *exact* Nash equilibrium in a polymatrix game is PPAD-hard even when all the bimatrix games played are either zero-sum games or coordination games [4]. Polymatrix games have been used in other contexts too. For example, Govindan and Wilson proposed a (non-polynomial-time) algorithm for computing Nash equilibria of an n-player game, by approximating the game with a sequence of polymatrix games [16]. Later, they presented a (non-polynomial) reduction that reduces n-player games to polymatrix games while preserving approximate Nash equilibria [17]. Their reduction introduces a central coordinator player, who interacts bilaterally with every player.

2 Preliminaries

We start by fixing some notation. We use $[k]$ to denote the set of integers $\{1, 2, \ldots, k\}$, and when a universe $[k]$ is clear, we will use $\bar{S} = \{i \in [k], i \notin S\}$ to denote the complement of $S \subseteq [k]$. For a k-dimensional vector x, we use x_{-S} to denote the elements of x with with indices $\bar{S}$, and in the case where $S = \{i\}$ has only one element, we simply write x_{-i} for x_{-S}.

Polymatrix Games. An n-player polymatrix game is defined by an undirected graph (V, E) with n vertices, where every vertex corresponds to a player. The edges of the graph specify which players interact with each other. For each $i \in [n]$, we use $N(i) = \{j : (i, j) \in E\}$ to denote the neighbours of player i, and we use $d(i) = |N(i)|$ to denote player i's *degree*.

Each edge $(i, j) \in E$ specifies that a bimatrix game will be played between players i and j. Each player $i \in [n]$ has a fixed number of pure strategies m_i, and the bimatrix game on edge $(i, j) \in E$ will therefore be specified by an $m_i \times m_j$ matrix A_{ij}, which gives the payoffs for player i, and an $m_j \times m_i$ matrix A_{ji}, which gives the payoffs for player j. We assume that all payoff lie in the range $[0, 1]$, and therefore each payoff matrix A_{ij} lies in $[0, 1]^{m_i \times m_j}$.

Strategies. A *mixed strategy* for player i is a probability distribution over player i's pure strategies. Formally, for each positive integer k, we denote the $(k-1)$-dimensional simplex by $\Delta_k := \{x : x \in \mathbb{R}^k, x \geq 0, \sum_{i=1}^{k} x_i = 1\}$, and therefore the set of strategies for player i is Δ_{m_i}. For each mixed strategy $x \in \Delta_m$, the *support* of x is defined as $\text{supp}(x) := \{i \in [m] : x_i \neq 0\}$, which is the set of strategies played with positive probability by x.

A *strategy profile* specifies a mixed strategy for every player. We denote the set of mixed strategy profiles as $\Delta := \Delta_{m_1} \times \ldots \times \Delta_{m_n}$. Given a strategy profile $\mathbf{x} = (x_1, \ldots, x_n) \in \Delta$, the payoff of player i under $\mathbf{x}$ is the sum of the payoffs that he obtains in each of the bimatrix games that he plays. Formally, we define:

$$u_i(\mathbf{x}) := x_i^T \sum_{j \in N(i)} A_{ij} x_j. \tag{1}$$

We denote by $u_i(x_i', \mathbf{x})$ the payoff for player i when he plays x_i' and the other players play according to the strategy profile $\mathbf{x}$. In some cases the first argument will be $x_i - x_i'$ which may not correspond to a valid strategy for player i but we still apply the equation as follows:

$$u_i(x_i - x_i', \mathbf{x}) := x_i^T \sum_{j \in N(i)} A_{ij} x_j - x_i'^T \sum_{j \in N(i)} A_{ij} x_j = u_i(x_i, \mathbf{x}) - u_i(x_i', \mathbf{x}).$$

Best Responses. Let $v_i(\mathbf{x})$ be the vector of payoffs for each pure strategy of player i when the rest of players play strategy profile $\mathbf{x}$. Formally,

$$v_i(\mathbf{x}) = \sum_{j \in N(i)} A_{ij} x_j.$$

For each vector $x \in R^m$, we define suppmax(x) to be the set of indices that achieve the maximum of x, that is, we define suppmax$(x) = \{i \in [m] : x_i \geq x_j, \forall j \in [m]\}$. Then the *pure best responses* of player i against a strategy profile $\mathbf{x}$ (where only $\mathbf{x}_{-i}$ is relevant) is given by:

$$\mathrm{Br}_i(\mathbf{x}) = \mathrm{suppmax}\left(\sum_{j \in N(i)} A_{ij} x_j\right) = \mathrm{suppmax}(v_i(\mathbf{x})). \tag{2}$$

The corresponding *best response payoff* is given by:

$$u_i^*(\mathbf{x}) = \max_k \left\{\left(\sum_{j \in N(i)} A_{ij} x_j\right)_k\right\} = \max_k \left\{\left(v_i(\mathbf{x})\right)_k\right\}. \tag{3}$$

Equilibria. In order to define the exact and approximate equilibria of a polymatrix game, we first define the *regret* that is suffered by each player under a given strategy profile. For each player i, we define the regret function $f_i : \Delta \to [0, 1]$ as:

$$f_i(\mathbf{x}) := \frac{1}{d(i)}\left(u_i^*(\mathbf{x}) - u_i(\mathbf{x})\right). \tag{4}$$

Note that here we have taken the standard definition of regret, and divided it by the player's degree. This rescales the regret so that it lies in the range $[0, 1]$, which ensures that our approximation guarantee is comparable with those in the literature. The maximum regret under a strategy profile $\mathbf{x}$ is given by the function $f(\mathbf{x})$ where:

$$f(\mathbf{x}) := \max\{f_1(\mathbf{x}), \ldots, f_n(\mathbf{x})\}. \tag{5}$$

We say that $\mathbf{x}$ is an ϵ-approximate Nash equilibrium (ϵ-NE) if we have $f(\mathbf{x}) \leq \epsilon$, and $\mathbf{x}$ is an *exact* Nash equilibrium if we have $f(\mathbf{x}) = 0$.

3   The Gradient

Our goal is to apply gradient descent to the regret function f. In this section, we formally define the gradient of f in Definition 1, and give a reformulation of that definition in Lemma 3. In order to show that our gradient descent method terminates after a polynomial number of iterations, we actually need to use a slightly modified version of this reformulation, which we describe at the end of this section in Definition 5.

Given a point $\mathbf{x} \in \Delta$, a *feasible direction* from $\mathbf{x}$ is defined by any other point $\mathbf{x}' \in \Delta$. This defines a line between $\mathbf{x}$ and $\mathbf{x}'$, and formally speaking, the direction of this line is $\mathbf{x}' - \mathbf{x}$. In order to define the gradient of this direction, we consider the function $f((1 - \epsilon) \cdot \mathbf{x} + \epsilon \cdot \mathbf{x}') - f(\mathbf{x})$ where ϵ lies in the range $0 \leq \epsilon \leq 1$. The gradient of this direction is given in the following definition.

Definition 1. *Given profiles* $\mathbf{x}, \mathbf{x}' \in \Delta$ *and* $\epsilon \in [0, 1]$, *we define:*

$$Df(\mathbf{x}, \mathbf{x}', \epsilon) := f((1 - \epsilon) \cdot \mathbf{x} + \epsilon \cdot \mathbf{x}') - f(\mathbf{x}).$$

Then, we define the gradient of f *at* $\mathbf{x}$ *in the direction* $\mathbf{x}' - \mathbf{x}$ *as:*

$$Df(\mathbf{x}, \mathbf{x}') = \lim_{\epsilon \to 0} \frac{1}{\epsilon} Df(\mathbf{x}, \mathbf{x}', \epsilon).$$

This is the natural definition of the gradient, but it cannot be used directly in a gradient descent algorithm. We now show how this definition can be reformulated. Firstly, for each $\mathbf{x}, \mathbf{x}' \in \Delta$, and for each player $i \in [n]$, we define:

$$Df_i(\mathbf{x}, \mathbf{x}') := \frac{1}{d(i)} \left(\max_{k \in \mathrm{Br}_i(\mathbf{x})} \left\{ (v_i(\mathbf{x}'))_k \right\} - u_i(x_i, \mathbf{x}') + u_i(x_i - x_i', \mathbf{x}) \right). \quad (6)$$

Next we define $\mathcal{K}(\mathbf{x})$ to be the set of players that have maximum regret under the strategy profile $\mathbf{x}$.

Definition 2. *Given a strategy profile* $\mathbf{x}$, *define* $\mathcal{K}(\mathbf{x})$ *as follows:*

$$\mathcal{K}(\mathbf{x}) := \left\{ i \in [n], f_i(\mathbf{x}) = f(\mathbf{x}) \right\} = \left\{ i \in [n], f_i(\mathbf{x}) = \max_{j \in [n]} f_j(\mathbf{x}) \right\}. \quad (7)$$

The following lemma provides our reformulation.

Lemma 3. *The gradient of* f *at point* $\mathbf{x}$ *along direction* $\mathbf{x}' - \mathbf{x}$ *is:*

$$Df(\mathbf{x}, \mathbf{x}') = \max_{i \in \mathcal{K}(\mathbf{x})} Df_i(\mathbf{x}, \mathbf{x}') - f(\mathbf{x}).$$

In order to show that our gradient descent algorithm terminates after a polynomial number of steps, we have to use a slight modification of the formula given in Lemma 3. More precisely, in the definition of $Df_i(\mathbf{x}, \mathbf{x}')$, we need to take the maximum over the δ-best responses, rather than the best responses.

We begin by providing the definition of the δ-best responses.

Definition 4 (δ-best response). *Let* $\mathbf{x} \in \Delta$, *and let* $\delta \in (0, 0.5]$. *The δ-best response set* $\mathrm{Br}_i^\delta(\mathbf{x})$ *for player* $i \in [n]$ *is defined as:*

$$\mathrm{Br}_i^\delta(\mathbf{x}) := \left\{ j \in [m_i] : (v_i(\mathbf{x}))_j \geq u_i^*(\mathbf{x}) - \delta \cdot d(i) \right\}.$$

Observe that we have multiplied δ by $d(i)$, because $d(i)$ is the maximum possible payoff that player i can obtain. We now define the function $Df_i^\delta(\mathbf{x}, \mathbf{x}')$.

Definition 5. *Let* $\mathbf{x}, \mathbf{x}' \in \Delta$, *let* $\epsilon \in [0, 1]$, *and let* $\delta \in (0, 0.5]$. *We define* $Df_i^\delta(\mathbf{x}, \mathbf{x}')$ *as:*

$$Df_i^\delta(\mathbf{x}, \mathbf{x}') := \frac{1}{d(i)} \left(\max_{k \in \mathrm{Br}_i^\delta(\mathbf{x})} \left\{ (v_i(\mathbf{x}'))_k \right\} - u_i(x_i, \mathbf{x}') - u_i(x_i', \mathbf{x}) + u_i(x_i, \mathbf{x}) \right). \tag{8}$$

Furthermore, we define $Df^\delta(\mathbf{x}, \mathbf{x}')$ *as:*

$$Df^\delta(\mathbf{x}, \mathbf{x}') = \max_{i \in \mathcal{K}(\mathbf{x})} Df_i^\delta(\mathbf{x}, \mathbf{x}') - f(\mathbf{x}). \tag{9}$$

Our algorithm works by performing gradient descent using the function Df^δ as the gradient. Obviously, this is a different function to Df, and so we are not actually performing gradient descent on the gradient of f. It is important to note that all of our proofs are in terms of Df^δ, and so this does not affect the correctness of our algorithm. We gave Lemma 3 in order to explain where our definition of the gradient comes from, but the correctness of our algorithm does not depend on the correctness of Lemma 3.

4   The Algorithm

In this section, we describe our algorithm for finding a $(0.5+\delta)$-Nash equilibrium in a polymatrix game by gradient descent. Each iteration of the algorithm comprises of two steps. First we find the *direction* of steepest descent with respect to Df^δ, and then we determine *how far* we should move in that direction. In this section, we describe these two components, and then we combine them in order to give our algorithm.

The Direction of Steepest Descent. We show that the direction of steepest descent can be found by solving a linear program. Our goal is, for a given strategy profile $\mathbf{x}$, to find another strategy profile $\mathbf{x}'$ so as to minimize the gradient $Df^\delta(\mathbf{x}, \mathbf{x}')$. Recall that Df^δ is defined in Equation (9) to be:

$$Df^\delta(\mathbf{x}, \mathbf{x}') = \max_{i \in \mathcal{K}(\mathbf{x})} Df_i^\delta(\mathbf{x}, \mathbf{x}') - f(\mathbf{x}).$$

Note that the term $f(\mathbf{x})$ is a constant in this expression, because it is the same for all directions $\mathbf{x}'$. Thus, it is sufficient to formulate a linear program in order to find the $\mathbf{x}'$ that minimizes $\max_{i \in \mathcal{K}(\mathbf{x})} Df_i^\delta(\mathbf{x}, \mathbf{x}')$. Using the definition of Df_i^δ in Equation (8), we can do this as follows.

Definition 6 (Steepest descent linear program). *Given a strategy profile* **x**, *the steepest descent linear program is defined as follows. Find* $\mathbf{x}' \in \Delta$, $l_1, l_2, \ldots, l_{|\mathcal{K}(\mathbf{x})|}$, *and* w *such that:*

$$
\begin{aligned}
minimize \quad & w \\
subject\ to \quad & \left(v_i(\mathbf{x}')\right)_k \leq l_i && \forall k \in \mathrm{Br}_i^\delta(\mathbf{x}), && \forall i \in \mathcal{K}(\mathbf{x}) \\
& \frac{1}{d(i)}\left(l_i - u_i(x_i, \mathbf{x}') - u_i(x_i', \mathbf{x}) + u_i(\mathbf{x})\right) \leq w && \forall i \in \mathcal{K}(\mathbf{x}) \\
& \mathbf{x}' \in \Delta.
\end{aligned}
$$

The l_i variables deal with the maximum in the term $\max_{k \in \mathrm{Br}_i^\delta(\mathbf{x})}\left\{\left(v_i(\mathbf{x}')\right)_k\right\}$, while the variable w is used to deal with the maximum over the functions Df_i^δ. Since the constraints of the linear program correspond precisely to the definition of Df^δ, it is clear that, when we minimize w, the resulting $\mathbf{x}'$ specifies the direction of steepest descent. For each profile $\mathbf{x}$, we define $Q(\mathbf{x})$ to be the direction $\mathbf{x}'$ found by the steepest descent LP for $\mathbf{x}$.

The Descent Distance. Once we have found the direction of steepest descent, we then need to know how far we should move in that direction. This can also be formulated as a linear program. Formally, given a strategy profile $\mathbf{x}$ and a descent direction $\mathbf{x}'$, we wish to find the ϵ that minimizes the value of $f(\mathbf{x} + \epsilon(\mathbf{x}' - \mathbf{x}))$. The following definition shows how to write this as a linear program.

Definition 7 (Optimal distance linear program). *Given two strategy profiles* **x** *and* **x**' *we define the following linear program over the variables* ϵ, w, *and* $l_1, l_2, \ldots, l_n$:

$$
\begin{aligned}
min \quad & w \\
& v_i(\mathbf{x} + \epsilon(\mathbf{x}' - \mathbf{x})) \leq l_i && \forall i \in [n] \\
& \frac{1}{d(i)}\left(l_i + u_i(\mathbf{x} + \epsilon(\mathbf{x}' - \mathbf{x}))\right) \leq w && \forall i \in [n] \\
& \epsilon \in [0, 1].
\end{aligned}
$$

To see that this is correct, observe that we have simply expanded $f(\mathbf{x}+\epsilon(\mathbf{x}'-\mathbf{x}))$ using Equations (5) and (4). The l_i variables are used to handle the max used in the definition of $u_i^*(\mathbf{x})$ from Equation (3), and the variable w is used to minimise the overall expression. Thus, in the solution to this LP, we have that the variable ϵ will hold the value that minimises the expression $f(\mathbf{x} + \epsilon(\mathbf{x}' - \mathbf{x}))$.

The Algorithm. We can now formally describe our algorithm. The algorithm takes a parameter $\delta \in (0, 0.5]$, which will be used as a tradeoff between running time and the quality of approximation.

Algorithm 1

1. Choose an arbitrary strategy profile $\mathbf{x} \in \Delta$.

2. Solve the steepest descent LP with input $\mathbf{x}$ to obtain $\mathbf{x}' = Q(\mathbf{x})$.

3. Solve the optimal distance linear program for $\mathbf{x}$ and $\mathbf{x}'$. Let ϵ be the value returned by the LP, and set $\mathbf{x} := \mathbf{x} + \epsilon(\mathbf{x}' - \mathbf{x})$.

4. If $f(\mathbf{x}) \leq 0.5 + \delta$ then stop, otherwise go to step 2.

A single iteration of this algorithm corresponds to executing steps 2, 3, and 4. Since this only involves solving two linear programs, it is clear that each iteration can be completed in polynomial time. The rest of this paper is dedicated to showing the following theorem, which is our main result.

Theorem 8. *Algorithm 1 finds a $(0.5 + \delta)$-NE after at most $O(\frac{1}{\delta^2})$ iterations.*

To prove Theorem 8, we will show two properties. Firstly, in Section 5, we show that our gradient descent algorithm never gets stuck in a stationary point before it finds a $(0.5 + \delta)$-NE. To do so, we define the notion of a δ-*stationary point*, and we show that every δ-stationary point is at least a $(0.5 + \delta)$-NE, which then directly implies that the gradient descent algorithm will not get stuck before it finds a $(0.5 + \delta)$-NE.

Secondly, in Section 6, we prove the upper bound on the number of iterations. To do this we show that, if an iteration of the algorithm starts at a point that is not a δ-stationary point, then that iteration will make a large enough amount of progress. This then allows us to show that the algorithm will find a $(0.5 + \delta)$-NE after $O(\frac{1}{\delta^2})$ many iterations, and therefore the overall running time of the algorithm is polynomial.

5   Stationary Points

Recall that Definition 6 gives a linear program for finding the direction $\mathbf{x}'$ that minimises $Df^\delta(\mathbf{x}, \mathbf{x}')$. Our steepest descent procedure is able to make progress whenever this gradient is negative, and so a stationary point is any point $\mathbf{x}$ for which $Df^\delta(\mathbf{x}, \mathbf{x}') \geq 0$. In fact, our analysis requires us to consider δ-stationary points, which we now define.

Definition 9 (δ-stationary point). *Let $\mathbf{x}^*$ be a mixed strategy profile, and let $\delta > 0$. We have that $\mathbf{x}^*$ is a δ-stationary point if for all $\mathbf{x}' \in \Delta$:*

$$Df^\delta(\mathbf{x}^*, \mathbf{x}') \geq -\delta.$$

We now show that every δ-stationary point of $f(\mathbf{x})$ is a $(0.5 + \delta)$-NE. Recall from Definition 5 that:

$$Df^\delta(\mathbf{x}, \mathbf{x}') = \max_{i \in \mathcal{K}(\mathbf{x})} Df_i^\delta(\mathbf{x}, \mathbf{x}') - f(\mathbf{x}).$$

Therefore, if $\mathbf{x}^*$ is a δ-stationary point, we must have, for every direction $\mathbf{x}'$:

$$f(\mathbf{x}^*) \leq \max_{i \in \mathcal{K}(\mathbf{x})} Df_i^{\delta}(\mathbf{x}^*, \mathbf{x}') + \delta. \tag{10}$$

Since $f(\mathbf{x}^*)$ is the maximum regret under the strategy profile $\mathbf{x}^*$, in order to show that $\mathbf{x}^*$ is a $(0.5 + \delta)$-NE, we only have to find some direction $\mathbf{x}'$ such that that $\max_{i \in \mathcal{K}(\mathbf{x})} Df_i^{\delta}(\mathbf{x}, \mathbf{x}') \leq 0.5$. We do this in the following lemma.

Lemma 10. *In every stationary point $\mathbf{x}^*$, there exists a direction $\mathbf{x}'$ such that:*

$$\max_{i \in \mathcal{K}(\mathbf{x})} Df_i^{\delta}(\mathbf{x}^*, \mathbf{x}') \leq 0.5.$$

Proof. First, define $\bar{\mathbf{x}}$ to be a strategy profile in which each player $i \in [n]$ plays a best response against $\mathbf{x}^*$. We will set $\mathbf{x}' = \frac{\bar{\mathbf{x}} + \mathbf{x}^*}{2}$. Then for each $i \in \mathcal{K}(\mathbf{x})$, we have that $Df_i^{\delta}(\mathbf{x}^*, \mathbf{x}')$, is less than or equal to:

$$\frac{1}{d(i)} \left(\max_{k \in \mathrm{Br}_i^{\delta}(\mathbf{x}^*)} \left\{ \left(v_i\left(\frac{\bar{\mathbf{x}} + \mathbf{x}^*}{2}\right)\right)_k \right\} - u_i\left(x_i^*, \frac{\bar{\mathbf{x}} + \mathbf{x}^*}{2}\right) - u_i\left(\frac{\bar{x}_i + x_i^*}{2}, \mathbf{x}^*\right) + u_i(x_i^*, \mathbf{x}^*) \right)$$

$$= \frac{1}{d(i)} \left(\frac{1}{2} \max_{k \in \mathrm{Br}_i^{\delta}(\mathbf{x}^*)} \left\{ \left(v_i(\bar{\mathbf{x}} + \mathbf{x}^*)\right)_k \right\} - \frac{1}{2} u_i(x_i^*, \bar{\mathbf{x}}) - \frac{1}{2} u_i(\bar{x}_i, \mathbf{x}^*) \right)$$

$$\leq \frac{1}{2d(i)} \left(\max_{k \in \mathrm{Br}_i^{\delta}(\mathbf{x}^*)} \left\{ \left(v_i(\bar{\mathbf{x}})\right)_k \right\} + \max_{k \in \mathrm{Br}_i^{\delta}(\mathbf{x}^*)} \left\{ \left(v_i(\mathbf{x}^*)\right)_k \right\} - u_i(x_i^*, \bar{\mathbf{x}}) - u_i(\bar{x}_i, \mathbf{x}^*) \right)$$

$$= \frac{1}{2d(i)} \left(\max_{k \in \mathrm{Br}_i^{\delta}(\mathbf{x}^*)} \left\{ \left(v_i(\bar{\mathbf{x}})\right)_k \right\} - u_i(x_i^*, \bar{\mathbf{x}}) \right) \quad \text{because } \bar{x}_i \text{ is a b.r. to } x^*$$

$$\leq \frac{1}{2d(i)} \left(\max_{k \in \mathrm{Br}_i^{\delta}(\mathbf{x}^*)} \left\{ \left(v_i(\bar{\mathbf{x}})\right)_k \right\} \right)$$

$$\leq \frac{1}{2d(i)} \cdot d(i) = \frac{1}{2}.$$

Thus, the point $\mathbf{x}'$ satisfies $\max_{i \in \mathcal{K}(\mathbf{x})} Df_i^{\delta}(\mathbf{x}^*, \mathbf{x}') \leq 0.5$. $\qquad\square$

We can sum up the results of the section in the following lemma.

Lemma 11. *Every δ-stationary point $\mathbf{x}^*$ is a $(0.5 + \delta)$-Nash equilibrium.*

6   The Time Complexity of the Algorithm

In this section, we show that Algorithm 1 terminates after a polynomial number of iterations. Let $\mathbf{x}$ be a strategy profile that is considered by Algorithm 1, and let $\mathbf{x}' = Q(\mathbf{x})$ be the solution of the steepest descent LP for $\mathbf{x}$. These two profiles will be fixed throughout this section. Recall that Algorithm 1 moves from $\mathbf{x}$ to the point $\bar{\mathbf{x}} := \mathbf{x} + \epsilon(\mathbf{x}' - \mathbf{x})$, where ϵ is found by solving the optimal distance linear program. In this section, we show a lower bound on $f(\mathbf{x} + \epsilon(\mathbf{x}' - \mathbf{x})) - f(\mathbf{x})$, which corresponds to showing a lower bound on the amount of progress made by each iteration of the algorithm.

To simplify our analysis, we show our lower bound for $\epsilon = \frac{\delta}{\delta+2}$, which will be fixed throughout the rest of this section. Since $\epsilon = \frac{\delta}{\delta+2}$ gives a feasible point in the optimal distance linear program, a lower bound for the case where $\epsilon = \frac{\delta}{\delta+2}$ is also a lower bound for the case where ϵ solves the optimal distance LP.

We first prove a lemma that will be used to show our bound on the number of iterations. To simplify our notation, throughout this section we define $f_{new} := f(\mathbf{x} + \epsilon(\mathbf{x}' - \mathbf{x}))$ and $f := f(\mathbf{x})$. Furthermore, we define $\mathcal{D} = \max_{i \in [n]} Df_i^{\delta}(\mathbf{x}, \mathbf{x}')$. The following lemma gives a relationship between f and f_{new}.

Lemma 12. *In every iteration of Algorithm 1 we have:*

$$f_{new} - f \leq \epsilon(\mathcal{D} - f) + \epsilon^2(1 - \mathcal{D}). \tag{11}$$

In the next lemma we prove that, if we are not in a δ-stationary point, then we have a bound on the amount of progress made in each iteration. We use this in order to bound the number of iterations needed before we reach a point $\mathbf{x}$ where $f(\mathbf{x}) \leq 0.5 + \delta$.

Lemma 13. *Fix* $\epsilon = \frac{\delta}{\delta+2}$, *where* $0 < \delta \leq 0.5$. *Either* $\mathbf{x}$ *is a* δ-*stationary point or:*

$$f_{new} \leq \left(1 - \left(\frac{\delta}{\delta + 2}\right)^2\right) f. \tag{12}$$

Proof. Recall from Lemma 12 the gain in each iteration of the steepest descent is:

$$f_{new} - f \leq \epsilon(\mathcal{D} - f) + \epsilon^2(1 - \mathcal{D}). \tag{13}$$

We consider the following two cases:

a) $\mathcal{D} - f > -\delta$. Then, by definition, we are in a δ-stationary point.
b) $\mathcal{D} - f \leq -\delta$. We have set $\epsilon = \frac{\delta}{\delta+2}$. If we solve for δ we get that $\delta = \frac{2\epsilon}{1-\epsilon}$. Since $\mathcal{D} - f \leq -\delta$, we have that $(\mathcal{D} - f)(1 - \epsilon) \leq -2\epsilon$. Thus we have:

$$(\mathcal{D} - f)(\epsilon - 1) \geq 2\epsilon$$
$$0 \geq (\mathcal{D} - f)(1 - \epsilon) + 2\epsilon$$
$$0 \geq (\mathcal{D} - f) + \epsilon(2 - \mathcal{D} + f)$$
$$-\epsilon f - \epsilon \geq (\mathcal{D} - f) + \epsilon(1 - \mathcal{D}) \qquad (\epsilon \geq 0)$$
$$-\epsilon^2 f - \epsilon^2 \geq \epsilon(\mathcal{D} - f) + \epsilon^2(1 - \mathcal{D}).$$

Thus, since $\epsilon^2 \geq 0$ we get:

$$-\epsilon^2 f \geq \epsilon(\mathcal{D} - f) + \epsilon^2(1 - \mathcal{D})$$
$$\geq f_{new} - f \qquad \qquad \text{According to (13).}$$

Thus we have shown that:

$$f_{new} - f \leq -\epsilon^2 f$$
$$f_{new} \leq (1 - \epsilon^2)f.$$

Finally, using the fact that $\epsilon = \frac{\delta}{\delta+2}$, we get that

$$f_{new} \leq \left(1 - \left(\frac{\delta}{\delta+2}\right)^2\right)f.$$

$\square$

So, when the algorithm has not reached yet a δ-stationary point, there is a decrease on the value of f that is at least as large as the bound specified in (12) in every iteration of the gradient descent procedure. In the following lemma we prove that after $O(\frac{1}{\delta^2})$ iterations of the steepest descent procedure the algorithm finds a point $\mathbf{x}$ where $f(\mathbf{x}) \leq 0.5 + \delta$.

Lemma 14. *After $O(\frac{1}{\delta^2})$ iterations of the steepest descent procedure the algorithm finds a point $\mathbf{x}$ where $f(\mathbf{x}) \leq 0.5 + \delta$.*

Proof. Let $\mathbf{x}_1, \mathbf{x}_2, \ldots, \mathbf{x}_k$ be the sequence of strategy profiles that are considered by Algorithm 1. Since the algorithm terminates as soon as it finds a $(0.5+\delta)$-NE, we have $f(\mathbf{x}_i) > 0.5 + \delta$ for every $i < k$. Therefore, for each $i < k$ we we can apply Lemma 11 to argue that $\mathbf{x}_i$ is not a δ-stationary point, which then allows us to apply Lemma 13 to obtain:

$$f(\mathbf{x}_{i+1}) \leq \left(1 - \left(\frac{\delta}{\delta+2}\right)^2\right)f(\mathbf{x}_i).$$

So, the amount of progress made by the algorithm in iteration i is:

$$f(\mathbf{x}_i) - f(\mathbf{x}_{i+1}) \geq f(\mathbf{x}_i) - \left(1 - \left(\frac{\delta}{\delta+2}\right)^2\right)f(\mathbf{x}_i)$$
$$= \left(\frac{\delta}{\delta+2}\right)^2 f(\mathbf{x}_i)$$
$$\geq \left(\frac{\delta}{\delta+2}\right)^2 \cdot 0.5.$$

Thus, each iteration of the algorithm decreases the regret by at least $(\frac{\delta}{\delta+2})^2 \cdot 0.5$. The algorithm starts at a point $\mathbf{x}_1$ with $f(\mathbf{x}_1) \leq 1$, and terminates when it reaches a point $\mathbf{x}_k$ with $f(\mathbf{x}_k) \leq 0.5 + \delta$. Thus the total amount of progress made over all iterations of the algorithm can be at most $1 - (0.5+\delta)$. Therefore, the number of iterations used by the algorithm can be at most:

$$\frac{1 - (0.5 + \delta)}{\left(\frac{\delta}{\delta+2}\right)^2 \cdot 0.5} \leq \frac{1 - 0.5}{\left(\frac{\delta}{\delta+2}\right)^2 \cdot 0.5}$$
$$= \frac{(\delta+2)^2}{\delta^2} = \frac{\delta^2}{\delta^2} + \frac{4\delta}{\delta^2} + \frac{4}{\delta^2}.$$

Since $\delta < 1$, we have that the algorithm terminates after at most $O(\frac{1}{\delta^2})$ iterations.   □

Lemma 14 implies that that after polynomially many iterations the algorithm finds a point such that $f(\mathbf{x}) \leq 0.5 + \delta$, and by definition such a point is a $(0.5 + \delta)$-NE. Thus we have completed the proof of Theorem 8.

7 Conclusions and Open Questions

We have presented a polynomial-time algorithm that finds a 0.5-Nash equilibrium of a polymatrix game. Though we do not have examples that show that the approximation guarantee is tight for our algorithm, we do not see an obvious approach to prove a better guarantee. The initial choice of strategy profile affects our algorithm, and it is conceivable that one may be able to start the algorithm from an efficiently computable profile with certain properties that allow a better approximation guarantee. One natural special case is when there is a constant number of players, which may allow one to derive new strategy profiles from a stationary point as done by Tsaknakis and Sprirakis [23]. It may also be possible to develop new techniques when the number of pure strategies available to the players is constant, or when the structure of the graph is restricted in some way.

This paper has considered ϵ-Nash equilibria, which are the most well-studied type of approximate equilibria. However, ϵ-Nash equilibria have a drawback: since they only require that the expected payoff is within ϵ of a pure best response, it is possible that a player could be required to place probability on a strategy that is arbitrarily far from being a best response. An alternative, stronger, notion is an ϵ-*well supported approximate Nash equilibrium* (ϵ-WSNE). It requires that players only place probability on strategies that have payoff within ϵ of a pure best response. Every ϵ-WSNE is an ϵ-Nash, but the converse is not true. For bimatrix games, the best-known additive approximation that is achievable in polynomial time gives a $\left(\frac{2}{3} - 0.0047\right)$-WSNE [14]. It builds on the algorithm given by Kontogiannis and Spirakis that achieves a $\frac{2}{3}$-WSNE in polynomial time [20]. Recently a polynomial-time algorithm with a better approximation guarantee have been given for *symmetric* bimatrix games [7]. Note, it has been shown that there is a PTAS for finding ϵ-WSNE of bimatrix games if and only if there is a PTAS for ϵ-Nash [9,5]. For n-player games with $n > 2$ there has been very little work on developing algorithms for finding ϵ-WSNE. This is a very interesting direction, both in general and when $n > 2$ is a constant.

References

1. Babichenko, Y., Barman, S., Peretz, R.: Simple approximate equilibria in large games. In: EC, pp. 753–770 (2014)
2. Bosse, H., Byrka, J., Markakis, E.: New algorithms for approximate Nash equilibria in bimatrix games. Theoretical Computer Science 411(1), 164–173 (2010)
3. Briest, P., Goldberg, P., Röglin, H.: Approximate equilibria in games with few players. CoRR, abs/0804.4524 (2008)

4. Cai, Y., Daskalakis, C.: On minmax theorems for multiplayer games. In: SODA, pp. 217–234 (2011)
5. Chen, X., Deng, X., Teng, S.-H.: Settling the complexity of computing two-player Nash equilibria. Journal of the ACM 56(3), 14:1–14:57 (2009)
6. Chen, X., Paparas, D., Yannakakis, M.: The complexity of non-monotone markets. In: STOC, pp. 181–190 (2013)
7. Czumaj, A., Fasoulakis, M., Jurdziński, M.: Approximate well-supported nash equilibria in symmetric bimatrix games. In: Lavi, R. (ed.) SAGT 2014. LNCS, vol. 8768, pp. 244–254. Springer, Heidelberg (2014)
8. Daskalakis, C.: On the complexity of approximating a Nash equilibrium. ACM Transactions on Algorithms 9(3), 23 (2013)
9. Daskalakis, C., Goldberg, P.W., Papadimitriou, C.H.: The complexity of computing a Nash equilibrium. SIAM Journal on Computing 39(1), 195–259 (2009)
10. Daskalakis, C., Mehta, A., Papadimitriou, C.H.: Progress in approximate Nash equilibria. In: Proceedings of ACM-EC, pp. 355–358 (2007)
11. Daskalakis, C., Mehta, A., Papadimitriou, C.H.: A note on approximate Nash equilibria. Theoretical Computer Science 410(17), 1581–1588 (2009)
12. Daskalakis, C., Papadimitriou, C.H.: Approximate Nash equilibria in anonymous games. Journal of Economic Theory (to appear, 2014), http://dx.doi.org/10.1016/j.jet.2014.02.002
13. Etessami, K., Yannakakis, M.: On the complexity of nash equilibria and other fixed points. SIAM J. Comput. 39(6), 2531–2597 (2010)
14. Fearnley, J., Goldberg, P.W., Savani, R., Sørensen, T.B.: Approximate well-supported Nash equilibria below two-thirds. In: Serna, M. (ed.) SAGT 2012. LNCS, vol. 7615, pp. 108–119. Springer, Heidelberg (2012)
15. Feige, U., Talgam-Cohen, I.: A direct reduction from k-player to 2-player approximate Nash equilibrium. In: Kontogiannis, S., Koutsoupias, E., Spirakis, P.G. (eds.) SAGT 2010. LNCS, vol. 6386, pp. 138–149. Springer, Heidelberg (2010)
16. Govindan, S., Wilson, R.: Computing nash equilibria by iterated polymatrix approximation. Journal of Economic Dynamics and Control 28(7), 1229–1241 (2004)
17. Govindan, S., Wilson, R.: A decomposition algorithm for n-player games. Economic Theory 42(1), 97–117 (2010)
18. Hémon, S., de Rougemont, M., Santha, M.: Approximate Nash equilibria for multiplayer games. In: Monien, B., Schroeder, U.-P. (eds.) SAGT 2008. LNCS, vol. 4997, pp. 267–278. Springer, Heidelberg (2008)
19. Howson Jr., J.T.: Equilibria of polymatrix games. Management Science 18(5), 312–318 (1972)
20. Kontogiannis, S.C., Spirakis, P.G.: Well supported approximate equilibria in bimatrix games. Algorithmica 57(4), 653–667 (2010)
21. Lipton, R.J., Markakis, E., Mehta, A.: Playing large games using simple strategies. In: EC, pp. 36–41 (2003)
22. Rubinstein, A.: Inapproximability of Nash equilibrium. CoRR, abs/1405.3322 (2014)
23. Tsaknakis, H., Spirakis, P.G.: An optimization approach for approximate Nash equilibria. Internet Mathematics 5(4), 365–382 (2008)

Optimal Cost-Sharing in Weighted Congestion Games

Vasilis Gkatzelis, Konstantinos Kollias, and Tim Roughgarden

Stanford University, Stanford CA 94305, USA

Abstract. We identify how to share costs locally in weighted congestion games with polynomial cost functions in order to minimize the worst-case price of anarchy (PoA). First, we prove that among all cost-sharing methods that guarantee the existence of pure Nash equilibria, the Shapley value minimizes the worst-case PoA. Second, if the guaranteed existence condition is dropped, then the proportional cost-sharing method minimizes the worst-case PoA over all cost-sharing methods. As a byproduct of our results, we obtain the first PoA analysis of the simple marginal contribution cost-sharing rule, and prove that marginal cost taxes are ineffective for improving equilibria in (atomic) congestion games.

Keywords: cost-sharing, selfish routing, congestion games.

1 Introduction

Sharing Costs to Optimize Equilibria. Weighted congestion games [35] are a simple class of competitive games that are flexible enough to model diverse settings (e.g., routing [38], network design [3], and scheduling [26]). These games consist of a ground set of resources E and a set of players N who are competing for the use of these resources. Every player $i \in N$ is associated with a weight w_i, and has a set of strategies $\mathcal{P}_i \subseteq 2^E$, each of which corresponds to a subset of the resources. Given a strategy profile $P = (P_i)_{i \in N}$, where $P_i \in \mathcal{P}_i$. The set of players $S_j = \{i : j \in P_i\}$ using some resource $j \in E$ generates a social cost $C_j(f_j)$ on this resource (e.g., $C_j(f_j) = \alpha \cdot f_j^d$), which is a function of their total weight $f_j = \sum_{i \in S_j} w_i$; this joint cost could represent monetary cost, or a physical cost such as aggregate queueing delay [40]. The social cost of every resource can be distributed among the players using it. As a result, each player i suffers some cost $c_{ij}(P)$ from each of the resources $j \in P_i$, and its goal is to choose a strategy that minimizes the cost $\sum_{j \in P_i} c_{ij}(P)$ that it suffers across all the resources that it uses.

How can a system designer minimize the sum of the players' costs

$$\sum_{i \in N} \sum_{j \in P_i} c_{ij}(P) = \sum_{j \in E} C_j(f_j) \tag{1}$$

over all possible outcomes P? The answer depends on what the designer can do. We are interested in settings where centralized optimization is infeasible, and

T.-Y. Liu et al. (Eds.): WINE 2014, LNCS 8877, pp. 72–88, 2014.
© Springer International Publishing Switzerland 2014

the designer can only influence players' behavior through local design decisions. Precisely, we allow a designer to choose a *cost-sharing* rule that defines what share $\xi_j(i, S_j)$ of the joint cost $C_j(f_j)$ each player $i \in S_j$ is responsible for (so $c_{ij}(P) = \xi_j(i, S_j)$). Such cost-sharing rules are "local" in the sense that they depend only on the set of players using the resource, and not on the users of other resources. Given a choice of a cost-sharing rule, we can quantify the inefficiency in the resulting game via the price of anarchy (PoA) — the ratio of the total cost at the worst equilibrium and the optimal cost. The set of equilibria and hence the PoA are a complex function of the chosen cost-sharing rule.

The goal of this paper is to answer the following question.

> *Which cost-sharing rule minimizes the worst-case PoA in polynomial weighted congestion games?*

In other words, when a system designer can only indirectly influence the game outcome through local design decisions, what should he or she do?

The present work is the first to study this question. Previous work on the PoA in weighted congestion games, reviewed next, has focused exclusively on evaluating the worst-case PoA with respect to a single cost-sharing rule. Previous work on how to best locally influence game outcomes in other models is discussed in Section 1.2.

Example: Proportional Cost Sharing. Almost all previous work on weighted congestion games has studied the proportional cost-sharing rule [4, 6, 18, 20, 21, 29, 30, 36]. According to this rule, at each resource j, each player $i \in S_j$ is responsible for a w_i/f_j fraction of the joint cost, i.e., a fraction proportional to its weight. The worst-case PoA is well understood in games with proportional cost sharing. For polynomial cost functions $C_j(f_j)$ of maximum degree d, the worst-case PoA is ϕ_d^d, where $\phi_d = \Theta(d/\ln d)$ is the positive root of $f_d(x) = x^d - (x+1)^{d-1}$ [2]. One of the main disadvantages of this cost-sharing rule is that it does not guarantee the existence of a pure Nash equilibrium (PNE), but the upper bounds are still meaningful since they apply to much more general equilibrium concepts, like coarse correlated equilibria, which do exist [37].

Example: Shapley Cost Sharing. The only other cost-sharing rule for which the worst-case PoA of weighted congestion games is known is the Shapley cost sharing rule. The cost shares defined by the Shapley value can be derived in the following manner: given an ordering over the users of a resource, these users are introduced to the resource in that order and each user is responsible for the marginal increase of the cost caused by its arrival. The Shapley cost share of each user is then defined as its average marginal increase over all orderings. Unlike proportional cost sharing, this cost-sharing rule guarantees the existence of a PNE in weighted congestion games [25]. The worst-case PoA of this rule for polynomials of maximum degree d is χ_d^d, where $\chi_d \approx 0.9 \cdot d$ is the root of $g_d(x) = 3 \cdot x^d - (x+1)^d - 1$ [25].

Other Cost-Sharing Rules. Without the condition of guaranteed PNE existence, there is obviously a wide range of possible cost-sharing rules. The space of rules that guarantee the existence of PNE is much more limited but still quite rich. [19] showed that the space of such rules correspond exactly to the weighted Shapley values. This class of cost-sharing rules generalizes the Shapley cost sharing rule by assigning a sampling weight λ_i to each player i. The cost shares of the players are then defined to be an appropriately *weighted* average of their marginal increases over different orderings (see Section 2.1); hence the "design space" is $(k-1)$-dimensional, where k is the number of players.[1]

1.1   Our Results

Our two main results resolve the question of how to optimally share cost in weighted congestion games to minimize the worst-case PoA.

Main Result 1 (Informal): Among all cost-sharing rules that guarantee the existence of PNE, the worst-case PoA of weighted congestion games is minimized by the Shapley cost sharing rule.

For example, the plot of Figure 1 shows how the worst-case PoA varies for a well-motivated subclass of the weighted Shapley rules parameterized by a variable γ (details are in Section 2.1). The PoA of these cost-sharing rules varies and it exhibits discontinuous behavior, but in all cases it is at least as large as the PoA when the parameter value is $\gamma = 0$, which corresponds to the (unweighted) Shapley cost-sharing rule.

Main Result 2 (Informal): Among all cost-sharing rules, the worst-case PoA of weighted congestion games is minimized by the proportional cost sharing rule.

In the second result, we generously measure the PoA of pure Nash equilibria only in instances where such equilibria exist. That is, our lower bounds construct games that have a PNE that is far from optimal. For the optimal rule (proportional cost-sharing), however, the PoA upper bound applies more generally to equilibrium concepts that are guaranteed to exist, including coarse correlated equilibria.

As a byproduct of our results, we also obtain tight bounds for the worst-case PoA of the marginal contribution cost-sharing rule (see Section 2.2). The marginal contribution rule defines individual cost shares that may in general add up to more than the total joint costs, but we show that, even if any additional costs are disregarded, which reduces this policy to marginal cost taxes, the worst-case PoA remains high.

---

[1] The sampling weights λ_i can be chosen to be related to the players' weights w_i, or not. The joint cost is a function of players' weights w_i; the sampling weights only affect how this joint cost is shared amongst them.

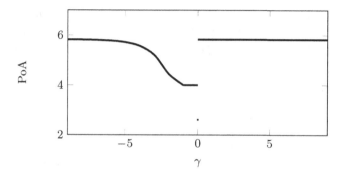

Fig. 1. PoA of parameterized weighted Shapley values for quadratic resource costs

1.2   Further Related Work

This paper contributes to the literature on how to design and modify games to minimize the inefficiency of equilibria. Several previous works consider how the choice of a cost-sharing rule affects this inefficiency in other models: [33] in participation games; [11, 15] in the network cost-sharing games of [3]; [32, 31, 22] in queueing games; and [28] in distributed welfare games. Closely related in spirit is previous work on coordination mechanisms, beginning with [12] and more recently in [23, 5, 24, 8, 13, 1, 14]. Most work on coordination mechanisms concerns scheduling games, and how the price of anarchy varies with the choice of local machine policies (i.e., the order in which to process jobs assigned to the same machine). Some of the recent work comparing the price of anarchy of different auction formats, such as [27, 7, 41], also has a similar flavor.

1.3   Organization of the Paper

In Section 2, we restrict ourselves to cost-sharing rules that guarantee the existence of PNE and we prove worst-case PoA bounds for such policies. In Section 3, we remove this restriction and we provide lower bounds for the worst-case PoA of arbitrary cost-sharing rules.

2   Cost-Sharing Rules That Guarantee PNE Existence

In this section we restrict our attention to cost-sharing rules that guarantee the existence of a PNE. This class of cost-sharing rules corresponds to weighted Shapley values, parameterized by a set of sampling weights λ_i, one for each player i [19]. We focus on congestion games with resource cost functions $C_j(f_j)$ that are polynomials with positive coefficients and maximum degree $d \geq 1$, and we provide worst-case PoA bounds parameterized by d. Note that every game with such cost functions has an equivalent game such that all cost functions have the form $\alpha \cdot x^k$ for $\alpha \geq 0$ and $k \in [1, d]$ (each resource is decomposed into many resources of this form that can only be used as a group). Hence, we will

be assuming that all games studied in what follows have cost functions of the
form $C_j(x) = \alpha_j \cdot x^{k_j}$. We conclude this section with a byproduct of our results:
tight worst-case PoA bounds for the marginal contribution cost-sharing rule.

2.1   Weighted Shapley Values

We first describe how a weighted Shapley value defines payments for the players
S that share a cost given by function $C(\cdot)$. For a given ordering π of the players
in S, the marginal cost increase caused by player i is $C(f_i^\pi + w_i) - C(f_i^\pi)$, where
f_i^π denotes the total weight of the players preceding i in π. Given a distribution
over orderings, the cost share of player i is given by

$$\mathrm{E}_\pi \left[C(f_i^\pi + w_i) - C(f_i^\pi) \right]. \tag{2}$$

A weighted Shapley value then defines a distribution over orderings by assigning
to each player i a sampling parameter $\lambda_i > 0$: the last player of the ordering is
picked with probability proportional to its λ_i; given this choice, the penultimate
player is chosen randomly from the remaining ones, again with probability proportional to its λ_i, and so on. Below we present an example of how the values
of the λ_i's lead to the distribution over orderings of the players.

Example 1. Consider players a, b, c, with sampling parameters $1, 2, 3$, respectively. The probability that a is the last in the ordering is $1/(1+2+3)$. Similarly
we get $2/(1+2+3)$ for player b and $3/(1+2+3)$ for player c. Also, suppose c
was chosen to be the last, then the probability that b is the second is $2/(1+2)$,
while the probability that a is the second is $1/(1+2)$. This yields the following
distribution over orderings: $1/3$ probability for ordering (a, b, c), $1/4$ for (a, c, b),
$1/6$ for (b, a, c), $1/10$ for (b, c, a), $1/12$ for (c, a, b), and $1/15$ for (c, b, a).

Defining a weighted Shapley value reduces to choosing a λ_i value for each
player i. In weighted congestion games the weight w_i of each player fully defines
the impact that this player has on the social cost of the resources it uses. Hence,
this is the only pertinent attribute of the player and it would be natural to
assume that λ_i depends only on the value of w_i. Nevertheless, our results hold
even if we allow the value of λ_i to also depend on the ID of player i, which enables
treating players with the same weight w_i differently in an arbitrary fashion.

We first focus on an interesting subclass of weighted Shapley values for which
λ_i is a function of w_i parameterized by a real number γ. In particular, we let the
sampling parameter λ_i of each player i be $\lambda_i = \lambda(w_i) = w_i^\gamma$. Within this class,
which contains all the previously studied weighted Shapley value variants, we
prove that the unweighted Shapley value is optimal with respect to the PoA. We
then extend this result, proving that the optimality of the unweighted Shapley
value remains true even if we let λ_i be an arbitrary continuous function.

A parameterized class of weighted Shapley values. For the weighted Shapley
values induced by a function of the form $\lambda(w_i) = w_i^\gamma$, we show that their PoA
lies between that of the (unweighted) Shapley value, i.e., approximately $(0.9 \cdot d)^d$,

and $(1.4 \cdot d)^d$. This class of λ_i values is interesting because it contains all the well-known weighted Shapley values: If $\gamma = 0$, then the induced cost-sharing rule is equivalent to the (unweighted) Shapley value. With $\gamma = -1$, we recover the most common weighted Shapley value [39]. For $\gamma \to +\infty$ (resp. $\gamma \to -\infty$) we get the order-based cost-sharing rule that introduces players to the resource from smallest to largest (resp. largest to smallest) and charges them the increase they cause to the joint cost when they are introduced. Also, as we show with Lemma 1, this class of λ_i values is natural because these are the only ones that induce scale-independent cost-sharing rules when the cost functions of the resources are homogeneous (e.g., in our setting which has $C_j(x) = \alpha_j \cdot x_j^k$).

Lemma 1. *For any homogeneous cost function, the weighted Shapley value cost-sharing rule is scale-independent if and only if $\lambda(w) = w^\gamma$ for some $\gamma \in \mathbb{R}$.*

The parameter γ fully determines our cost-sharing rule. Higher values of λ_i for some player i imply higher cost shares so, if $\gamma > 0$, this benefits lower weight players, and if $\gamma < 0$, this benefits higher weight players. We therefore use γ in order to parameterize the PoA that the cost-sharing rules of this class yield. The following theorem, which follows directly from Lemma 2 and Lemma 3, shows that, for any value of γ other than 0, the PoA of the induced cost-sharing rule is strictly worse. Figure 1 plots the PoA for $d = 2$.

Theorem 1. *The optimal PoA among weighted Shapley values of the form $\lambda(w_i) = w_i^\gamma$ is achieved for $\gamma = 0$, which recovers the (unweighted) Shapley value. Hence, the optimal PoA is approximately $(0.9 \cdot d)^d$.*

Before presenting our lower bounds in Lemma 2 and Lemma 3, we begin with an upper bound on the PoA of any weighted Shapley value, for polynomials with maximum degree d.

Theorem 2. *The PoA of any weighted Shapley value is at most*

$$\left(2^{\frac{1}{d}} - 1\right)^{-d} \approx (1.4 \cdot d)^d.$$

Proof. Let P be a PNE and P^* the optimal profile. We get

$$\sum_{j \in E} C_j(f_j) = \sum_{j \in E} \sum_{i \in N} \xi_j(i, S_j) = \sum_{i \in N} \sum_{j \in P_i} \xi_j(i, S_j) \leq \sum_{i \in N} \sum_{j \in P_i^*} \xi_j(i, S_j \cup \{i\}). \quad (3)$$

The inequality follows from the equilibrium condition on P. Note that, when the cost-sharing method is a weighted Shapley value and the resource costs are convex, the cost share of any player on any resource is upper bounded by the increase that would be caused to the joint resource cost if that player was be the last in the ordering. This means that for every $j \in P_i^*$ we get

$$\xi_j(i, S_j \cup \{i\}) \leq C_j(f_j + w_i) - C_j(f_j). \quad (4)$$

Combining (3) with (4), we get

$$\sum_{j \in E} C_j(f_j) \leq \sum_{i \in N} \sum_{j \in P_i^*} C_j(f_j + w_i) - C_j(f_j) \tag{5}$$

$$= \sum_{j \in E} \sum_{i: j \in P_i^*} C_j(f_j + w_i) - C_j(f_j) \tag{6}$$

$$\leq \sum_{j \in E} C_j(f_j + f_j^*) - C_j(f_j), \tag{7}$$

where f_j^* is the total weight on j in P^*. The last inequality follows by convexity of the expression as a function of w_i. We now claim that the following is true, for any $x, y > 0$, and $d \geq 1$:

$$(x + y)^d - x^d \leq \hat{\lambda} \cdot y^d + \hat{\mu} \cdot x^d, \tag{8}$$

with

$$\hat{\lambda} = 2^{(d-1)/d} \cdot \left(2^{1/d} - 1\right)^{-(d-1)} \quad \text{and} \quad \hat{\mu} = 2^{(d-1)/d} - 1. \tag{9}$$

We can verify this as follows. Note that, without loss of generality, we can set $y = 1$ (equivalent to dividing both sides of (8) with y^d and renaming x/y to q). We can then see that the value of q that maximizes $(q + 1)^d - (\hat{\mu} + 1) \cdot q^d$, and, hence, is the worst case for (8), is $q = 1/(2^{1/d} - 1)$, for which inequality (8) is tight. Also, note that the expressions for $\hat{\lambda}$ and $\hat{\mu}$ are increasing as functions of d, which implies that the given values for degree d, satisfy (8) for smaller degrees as well. This means we can combine (7), (8), and (9), to get

$$\sum_{j \in E} C_j(f_j) \leq \sum_{j \in E} \hat{\lambda} \cdot C_j(f_j^*) + \hat{\mu} \cdot C_j(f_j). \tag{10}$$

Rearranging, we get $\sum_{j \in E} C_j(f_j) / \sum_{j \in E} C_j(f_j^*) \leq \hat{\lambda}/(\hat{\mu} + 1) = \left(2^{1/d} - 1\right)^{-d}$, which completes the proof. $\qquad \square$

We now proceed with our lower bounds for $\gamma \neq 0$.

Lemma 2. *The PoA of any weighted Shapley value of the form* $\lambda(w_i) = w_i^\gamma$, *for* $\gamma > 0$ *is at least*

$$\left(2^{\frac{1}{d}} - 1\right)^{-d} \approx (1.4 \cdot d)^d.$$

Proof. Define $\rho = (2^{1/d} - 1)^{-1}$ and let T be a set of ρ/ϵ players with weight ϵ each, where $\epsilon > 0$ is an arbitrarily small parameter. Consider a player i with weight $w_i = 1$ and suppose she uses a resource j with cost function $C_j(x) = x^d$ with the players in T, for our weighted Shapley value with $\gamma > 0$. We now argue that, as we let $\epsilon \to 0$, the cost share of i in j becomes $(\rho + 1)^d - \rho^d$. Consider the probability p that i is not among the last $\delta \cdot |T|$ players of the random ordering generated by our sampling weights (i.e., i is not among the first $\delta \cdot |T|$ players sampled), for some $\delta < 1$. This probability is upper bounded by the probability that i is not drawn, using our sampling weights, among everyone in $T \cup \{i\}$, $\delta \cdot |T| = \delta \cdot \rho/\epsilon$ times. Note that the sampling weight of i is 1 and the total sampling weight of the players in T is $\rho \cdot \epsilon^{\gamma-1}$. Hence, if $\gamma \geq 1$, we get:

$$p \leq \left(1 - \frac{1}{1 + \rho \cdot \epsilon^{\gamma-1}}\right)^{\delta \cdot \rho/\epsilon} \leq \left(1 - \frac{1}{1 + \rho}\right)^{\delta \cdot \rho/\epsilon}, \tag{11}$$

which goes to 0 as $\epsilon \to 0$. Similarly, if $\gamma < 1$, we get:

$$p \leq \left(1 - \frac{1}{1 + \rho \cdot \epsilon^{\gamma-1}}\right)^{\delta \cdot \rho/\epsilon} \leq \exp\left(-\delta \cdot \frac{\rho}{\epsilon} \cdot \frac{1}{1 + \rho \cdot \epsilon^{\gamma-1}}\right), \tag{12}$$

which always goes to 0 as $\epsilon \to 0$, for any arbitrarily small $\delta > 0$. Then, by letting $\delta \to 0$, our claim that the cost share of i is $(\rho+1)^d - \rho^d$ follows by the definition of the weighted Shapley value. Similarly, it follows that if a player with weight w shares a resource with cost function $a \cdot x^d$ with ρ/ϵ players with weight $w \cdot \epsilon$ each, her cost share will be $a \cdot w^d \cdot ((\rho+1)^d - \rho^d)$ (since scaling the cost function and the player weights does not change the fractions of the cost that are assigned to the players), which, for our choice of ρ is equal to $a \cdot w^d \cdot \rho^d$.

Using facts from the previous paragraph as building blocks, we construct a game such that the total cost in the worst equilibrium is ρ^d times the optimal. Suppose our resources are organized in a tree graph $G = (E, A)$, where each vertex corresponds to a resource. There is a one-to-one mapping between the set of edges of the tree, A, and the set of players of the game, N. The player i, that corresponds to edge (j, j'), has strategy set $\{\{j\}, \{j'\}\}$, i.e., she must choose one of the two endpoints of her designated edge. Tree G has branching factor ρ/ϵ and l levels, with the root positioned at level 1.

Player weight. The weight of every player (edge) between resources (vertices) at levels j and $j + 1$ of the tree is ϵ^{j-1}.

Cost functions. The cost function of any resource (vertex) at level $j = 1, 2, \ldots, l-1$, is:

$$C^j(x) = \left(\frac{1}{\rho \cdot \epsilon^{d-1}}\right)^{j-1} \cdot x^d. \tag{13}$$

The cost functions of any resource (vertex) at level l is equal to:

$$C^l(x) = \frac{\rho^{d-l+1}}{\epsilon^{(d-1)\cdot(l-1)}} \cdot x^d. \tag{14}$$

Pure Nash equilibrium. Let P be the outcome that has all players play the resource closer to the root. We claim that this outcome is a PNE. The cost of every player, using a resource at level $j < l$, in P, is $(\rho/\epsilon)^{d-j}$. If one of the players that are adjacent to the leaves were to switch to her other strategy (play the leaf resource), she would incur a cost equal to $(\rho/\epsilon)^{d-l+1}$, which is the same as the one she has in P. Consider any other player and her potential deviation from the resource at level j, to the resource at level $j + 1$. By the analysis in the first paragraph of this proof (she would be a player with weight ϵ^{j-1} sharing a resource with ρ/ϵ players with weight ϵ^j), her cost would be $(\rho \cdot \epsilon^{d-1})^j \cdot \epsilon^{d \cdot (j-1)} \cdot \rho^d = (\rho/\epsilon)^{d-j}$, which is her current cost in P. This proves that the equilibrium condition holds for all players in P.

Price of anarchy. As we have shown, every player using a resource at level j has cost $(\rho/\epsilon)^{d-j}$ in P. There are $(\rho/\epsilon)^j$ such players, which implies the total cost of P is $(l - 1) \cdot (\rho/\epsilon)^d$, since there are $l - 1$ levels of nonempty resources, and every level has the same total cost, $(\rho/\epsilon)^d$. Now, let P^* be the outcome that has all players play the resource further from the root. In this outcome, every player using a resource at level $j = 2, \ldots, l - 1$, has cost $\rho^{-j+1}/\epsilon^{d-j+1}$. There are $(\rho/\epsilon)^{j-1}$ such players, hence, the total cost at level j is $(1/\epsilon)^d$. Similarly, we get that the total cost at level l is $(\rho/\epsilon)^d$. In total, the cost of P^* is $(l - 2) \cdot (1/\epsilon)^d + (\rho/\epsilon)^d$. We can then see that, as $l \to +\infty$, the ratio between the cost of P and the cost of P^* becomes ρ^d. □

Lemma 3. *The PoA of any weighted Shapley value of the form* $\lambda(w_i) = w_i^\gamma$, *for* $\gamma < 0$ *is at least* d^d.

Proof. We construct a game such that the total cost in the worst equilibrium is d^d times the optimal. Suppose our resources are organized in a tree graph $G = (E, A)$, where each vertex corresponds to a resource. There is a one-to-one mapping between the set of edges of the tree, A, and the set of players of the game, N. The player i, that corresponds to edge (j, j'), has strategy set $\{\{j\}, \{j'\}\}$, i.e., she must choose one of the two endpoints of her designated edge. Tree G has branching factor $1/(d \cdot \epsilon)$, with $\epsilon > 0$ an arbitrarily small parameter, and l levels.

Player weights. The weight of every player (edge) between resources (vertices) at levels j and $j + 1$ of the tree is ϵ^{j-1}.

Cost functions. The cost function of any resource (vertex) at level $j = 2, 3, \ldots, l$, is:

$$C^j(x) = \left(\frac{d}{\epsilon^{d-1}}\right)^{j-2} \cdot x^d. \tag{15}$$

The cost functions of the root is:

$$C^1(x) = x^d. \tag{16}$$

PNE. Let P be the outcome that has all players play the resource further from the root. We prove that this outcome is a PNE. The cost of every player that has played a resource at level j is $(d \cdot \epsilon)^{j-2}$. If one of the players that are adjacent to the root were to switch to her other strategy (play the root), she would incur a cost equal to 1, which is the same as the one she has in P. Consider any other player and her potential deviation from the resource at level j, to the resource at level $j-1$. Since our construction considers ϵ arbitrarily close to 0, the deviating player will go last with probability 1 in the Shapley ordering (since $\gamma < 0$) and her cost will be equal to $(d/\epsilon^{d-1})^{j-3} \cdot \left((\epsilon^{j-1} + \epsilon^{j-2})^d - \epsilon^{(j-1) \cdot d}\right) = (d \cdot \epsilon)^{j-2}$, which is equal to her current cost in P. Hence, the equilibrium condition holds for all players.

PoA. As we have shown, every player playing a resource at level j has cost $(d \cdot \epsilon)^{j-2}$ in P. There are $1/(d \cdot \epsilon)^{j-1}$ such players, hence, the total cost at level j is $1/(d \cdot \epsilon)$. Then, it follows that the total cost of P is $(l-1)/(d \cdot \epsilon)$. Now let P^* be the outcome that has all players play the resource closer to the root. Then the joint cost at the root is $1/(d \cdot \epsilon)^d$. The joint cost of every other resource at level j is $(d \cdot \epsilon)^{j-2}/d^d$, and the number of resources at level j is $1/(d \cdot \epsilon)^{j-1}$. Hence, we get in total, that the cost of P^* is $(l-2)/(d^{d+1} \cdot \epsilon) + 1/(d \cdot \epsilon)^d$. We can then see that, as $l \to +\infty$, the ratio of the cost of P to the cost of P^* becomes d^d.   □

We defer details on deriving the plot in Figure 1 to our full version.

Main result. We now state the main result of the section. The proof applies arguments similar to the ones we used for Lemma 2 and Lemma 3 but on a more technical level. We defer the details to the full version.

Theorem 3. *The optimal PoA among weighted Shapley values induced by a collection of continuous functions $\lambda_i(\cdot)$ is achieved by the (unweighted) Shapley value.*

2.2   Marginal Contribution

We now focus on the marginal contribution cost-sharing rule which dictates that every player i is responsible for the marginal increase it causes to the joint resource cost. Namely, the cost share of player $i \in S_j$ on resource j is equal to $C_j(f_j) - C_j(f_j - w_i)$. Although the marginal contribution rule does induce games that always possess PNE, the total cost suffered by the players will, in general, be greater than the total cost that they generate, something that places the marginal contribution rule outside the scope of our model. To see this, note that in (1) the left hand side can be larger than the right hand side when the marginal contribution rule is used. In fact, for polynomial cost functions of maximum degree d the total cost suffered can be up to d times the generated cost. The following theorem, which is a byproduct of our previous results, provides the exact worst-case PoA of this cost-sharing rule.

Theorem 4. *The PoA of the marginal contribution rule is*

$$\left(2^{\frac{1}{d}} - 1\right)^{-d} \approx (1.4 \cdot d)^d.$$

Theorem 4, shows that the worst-case PoA of marginal contribution is equal to that of the worst weighted Shapley value (see Theorem 2). In fact, this holds even if the equilibrium cost on each resource j is measured as $\sum_{i \in S_j} \xi_j(i, S_j)$ instead of $C_j(f_j)$, i.e., even if the additional costs that the marginal contribution rule enforces are disregarded when evaluating the quality of the outcome. Measuring the PoA with respect to the cost generated by the players (instead of the cost that they actually suffer) can be motivated by thinking of the costs suffered by the players as tolls that the system uses in order to affect the incentives of the players. There has been a sequence of results focusing on designing tolls of this form in order to optimize this PoA measure for atomic congestion games [10, 17, 9, 16], and the marginal contribution rule is known as *marginal cost pricing* tolls in this literature. In this context, Theorem 4 leads to the following corollary.

Corollary 1. *There exists a weighted congestion game with marginal cost pricing tolls that has a PNE with joint cost* $(2^{1/d} - 1)^{-d}$ *times the optimal joint cost.*

3   Unrestricted Cost-Sharing Rules

In this section we consider any possible cost-sharing rule and show that the price of anarchy is always at least $\Theta(d/\ln d)^d$. In fact, our lower bound is approximately $(1.3 \cdot d/\ln d)^d$, which is also the approximate value of the PoA of proportional sharing. Before presenting this main result, we provide, as a warm-up, the proof of a weaker, but still exponential in d, lower bound for all cost-sharing rules; this simpler proof carries some of the ideas used in the more elaborate proof of Theorem 5. A key idea in the proof is to define a tournament amongst the players, with the winner of a match of players i, j corresponding to the player with the larger cost share when i and j are together. This tournament admits a Hamiltonian path [34], which we use to construct a bad example.

Proposition 1. *The PoA of any cost-sharing rule is at least* 2^{d-1}.

Proof. The structure of this proof resembles the proof structure of the main theorem of this section: we begin by partly defining the elements of the problem instance (the number of players and resources, as well as the cost functions of the resources), and then, using any given cost-sharing rule as input, we come up with a set of strategies for each player. This way, even though the cost-sharing rule may not be anonymous, we can still ensure that we "place" each players in a role such that some inefficient strategy profile is a PNE for the given cost-sharing rule.

Instance initialization: Our resources are organized as a line graph $G = (E, A)$. The edge between resources i and $i+1$ is a player that has to pick one of the two resources. All players have unit weight. Call vertex (resource) 1, which has cost $C_1(x) = x^d$, the root. As we move along the path, resources are getting better by a factor of 2^{d-1}, which means $C_i(x) = x^d/2^{(i-1)\cdot(d-1)}$. Resource n is the only exception and has the same cost function as its neighbor. For the instance to be complete, we now also need to define what the strategy set of each player is.

We are given identities of $n - 1$ players and we must decide how to place them on the edges of G, i.e., determine who will be player i, the one that must choose between resources i and $i + 1$.

Player placement: To determine the strategy sets of the players, we will first define a permutation π and then we will let player $\pi(i)$ be the $\pi(i)$-th edge of G. In choosing this permutation, we seek that the following property is satisfied for all $i = 1, 2, \ldots, n - 1$: when players $\pi(i)$ and $\pi(i + 1)$ share one of the resources in E, the cost-sharing rule[2] distributes at least half of the induced cost to player $\pi(i)$. We now show that a permutation satisfying this property always exists.

Consider a directed graph whose vertices correspond to the players of our instance and a directed edge from i to i' exists if and only if player i suffers at least half of the cost induced when it shares a resource with player i'. This is a tournament graph and hence it has at least one Hamiltonian path; starting from its first vertex and following this Hamiltonian path implies a desired permutation.

Now that we have established existence of such a permutation π, we let each player $\pi(i)$ pick between resources $\pi(i)$ and $\pi(i + 1)$. Given the property that is guaranteed by the permutation, it is not hard to verify that the strategy profile P, which has total cost C, and according to which every player $\pi(i)$ chooses resource $\pi(i)$, is a PNE, while the strategy profile P^* according to which every player $\pi(i)$ chooses resource $\pi(i + 1)$ is the one that achieves the optimal total cost. The corresponding total costs are

$$\sum_{j=1}^{n} 2^{-(d-1)\cdot(j-1)} \quad \text{and} \quad 2^{-(d-1)\cdot(j-1)} + \sum_{j=1}^{n-1} 2^{-(d-1)\cdot j}.$$

The ratio of the two approaches 2^{d-1} as $n \to +\infty$.   □

The main result of this section strengthens this, more intuitive, lower bound further. Let

$$\Upsilon(d) = \frac{(\lfloor \phi_d \rfloor + 1)^{2\cdot(d-1)+1} - \lfloor \phi_d \rfloor^d \cdot (\lfloor \phi_d \rfloor + 2)^{d-1}}{(\lfloor \phi_d \rfloor + 1)^d - (\lfloor \phi_d \rfloor + 2)^{d-1} + (\lfloor \phi_d \rfloor + 1)^{d-1} - \lfloor \phi_d \rfloor^d},$$

where ϕ_d corresponds to the solution of $x^d = (x + 1)^{d-1}$. The following theorem shows that the PoA of any cost-sharing rule that may depend on the weights and IDs of the players in an arbitrary fashion has a PoA of at least $\Upsilon(d)$, which is approximately $(1.3 \cdot d/\ln d)^d$ and, in fact, is at least $\lfloor \phi_d \rfloor^d$.

Theorem 5. *The PoA of any cost-sharing rule is at least $\Upsilon(d)$.*

---

[2] Even though it is not necessary for our results we assume for simplicity that if $C_{j'}(x) = \alpha \cdot C_j(x)$, then for every $i \in T$ we have $\xi_{j'}(i, T) = \alpha \cdot \xi_j(i, T)$. To see why this is not necessary note that in any game we can substitute a resource with cost function $\alpha \cdot C(x)$ with $\alpha \cdot M$ resources with cost functions $C(x)$ which can only be used as a group. Here M is a very large number and the incentive structure remains unaltered.

Proof. Our resources are organized in a graph $G = (E, A)$, which we describe below. A vertex of the tree corresponds to a resource, and an edge in A corresponds to a specific player, who must select one of the two endpoints of the edge as her strategy. All but one of the vertices of G are part of a tree as follows. At the root there is a complete d-ary tree with $k + 1$ levels. The leaves of this tree are roots for complete $(d - 1)$-ary trees with $k + 1$ levels, and so on until the final stage with unary trees with $k + 1$ levels. The final vertex of G is isolated and will have only self-loops (i.e., players that will only have this resource as their possible strategy). The main idea is that in the optimal profile P^*, all tree players move away from the root and are alone, while in the worst PNE P all tree players move towards the root and are congested. The purpose of the isolated resource is to cancel out any benefit the cost-sharing rule could extract by introducing major asymmetries on the players (using their IDs) as we will see in what follows. The construction of our lower bound is a three-stage process. During the first stage, we initialize our instance and set temporary cost functions for the resources that yield the required PoA. During the second stage we start with a very large number of players $|N|$, place a subset of them on the tree, and fix the rest on the isolated resource. This placement of players will happen in a way that will allow us to turn P into a PNE in the next stage. During the final stage we tweak the cost functions on the tree in order to maintain the fact that the profile with everyone moving towards the root is a PNE while, at the same time, we manage to keep the total costs of the PNE and the optimal profile intact.

Instance initialization: The cost function of resource j at level $(d - i) \cdot k + j$ of the tree is initialized as $(\prod_{l=i+1}^{d} l/(l + 1))^{(d-1)\cdot(k-1)} \cdot (i/(i + 1))^{(d-1)\cdot j} \cdot x^d$. The constant multipliers of x^d on the resources are not finalized yet and will be altered during Stage 3 of our construction. The cost function of the extra resource is constant $\delta \cdot x^d$, with δ arbitrarily small. With P and P^* as above we get a ratio of $\Upsilon(d)$ between the two total costs (see [18] for the detailed calculation).

Player placement: Suppose the game has a very large number of players $|N|$. Some of these players will be used to fill all slots of the tree and the rest will be fixed on the 0-cost resource. The players on the 0-cost resource will clearly have no impact on the PNE and optimal costs and their only purpose is to cancel out any benefit the cost-sharing rule could extract by using the player IDs in order to introduce asymmetry. Focus on a single resource of the tree. The structure of the tree clearly dictates how many players should have that resource as the top endpoint of the corresponding edge (we will call them the children players of the resource) and that one player should have that resource as the bottom endpoint of its corresponding edge (we will call this the parent player of the resource). Our claim is that given a large enough number of players, we can always find a subset of them to place on the tree such that for every vertex, the parent player covers for at least its proportional share when all children and the parent are on the resource. We will call this the *parent property*. Once we prove this fact, we will be ready to finalize the cost functions and prove our result.

Here we describe how the placement of players on the tree is performed. Let S be the set of available players which is initialized to all players N and is updated at each iteration. We will fill the edges of the tree in a bottom-up fashion. At each iteration we select a resource j that has not been assigned children players and has the maximum depth among such resources. We will select its children players from S simultaneously. Suppose j must have t children players. We must find a group T of t players, use them on these edges, and delete them from S. Then we look at each player i left in S. If i pays at least its proportional share when using j with the players in T, then i remains in S, otherwise i is assigned a unique possible strategy, which is the 0-cost resource and is removed from S. This way we ensure that no matter what our future choices are, the parent property will hold on resource j. We will pick the set T that maximizes the size of S after its placement.

The key question is how much smaller does S become at each iteration? The candidate sets of size t are $\binom{|S|}{t}$. The number of times a $t+1$-th player pays its fair share and can be a parent of a t-sized group is at least the number of groups of size $t+1$, i.e., $\binom{|S|}{t+1}$. This means there is a set T for which there exist at least $\binom{|S|}{t+1}/\binom{|S|}{t} = (|S|-t)/(t+1)$ players that can be used as its corresponding parent. So the set S is getting smaller by a factor that is a function of d at each iteration and the number of iterations is a function of d and k. This means we can take the initial $|N|$ large enough so that we can complete the process.

Cost function update: Recall P is the strategy profile such that every player on the tree picks the resource closer to the root. We want this to be a PNE. We know that, because of Stage 2, the parent property holds on every resource, hence every deviation has a player pay at least its proportional share on its new resource. We can also see that the initial cost functions are such that if a player pays its proportional share in P, then the deviation is at least tight (possibly the deviation costs more depending on what the cost-sharing rule does, but it is at least tight due to the parent property). To ensure that P is a PNE in our construction we make the following update on the cost functions. We start from the root and move towards the leaves examining every player i. If player i pays γ_i times its proportional share on its resource in P, then the cost function of the resource j it can deviate to, and the cost functions of the resources of the whole subtree rooted at j, are multiplied by γ_i. Given the facts described above with respect to the parent property and the cost functions, it follows that P is a PNE in our game.

Recall P^* is the profile such that every player picks the resource that is further from the root. At this point, all that is left to show is that the total cost of P and P^* do not change after we update the cost functions. Since, both in P and in P^*, at every level the total weight on every resource is the same, the initial multipliers of every resource cost function were identical, and the sum of the scaling factors we applied is equal to 1, it follows that the total costs remain unchanged. $\qquad\square$

References

[1] Abed, F., Huang, C.-C.: Preemptive coordination mechanisms for unrelated machines. In: Epstein, L., Ferragina, P. (eds.) ESA 2012. LNCS, vol. 7501, pp. 12–23. Springer, Heidelberg (2012)

[2] Aland, S., Dumrauf, D., Gairing, M., Monien, B., Schoppmann, F.: Exact price of anarchy for polynomial congestion games. SIAM J. Comput. 40(5), 1211–1233 (2011)

[3] Anshelevich, E., Dasgupta, A., Kleinberg, J., Tardos, É., Wexler, T., Roughgarden, T.: The price of stability for network design with fair cost allocation. SIAM Journal on Computing 38(4), 1602–1623 (2008)

[4] Awerbuch, B., Azar, Y., Epstein, L.: The price of routing unsplittable flow. In: Proceedings of the 37th Annual ACM Symposium on Theory of Computing (STOC), pp. 57–66 (2005)

[5] Azar, Y., Jain, K., Mirrokni, V.: (almost) optimal coordination mechanisms for unrelated machine scheduling. In: Proceedings of the Nineteenth Annual ACM-SIAM Symposium on Discrete Algorithms, SODA 2008, pp. 323–332. Society for Industrial and Applied Mathematics, Philadelphia (2008)

[6] Bhawalkar, K., Gairing, M., Roughgarden, T.: Weighted congestion games: Price of anarchy, universal worst-case examples, and tightness. In: de Berg, M., Meyer, U. (eds.) ESA 2010, Part II. LNCS, vol. 6347, pp. 17–28. Springer, Heidelberg (2010)

[7] Bhawalkar, K., Roughgarden, T.: Simultaneous single-item auctions. In: Goldberg, P.W. (ed.) WINE 2012. LNCS, vol. 7695, pp. 337–349. Springer, Heidelberg (2012)

[8] Caragiannis, I.: Efficient coordination mechanisms for unrelated machine scheduling. In: Proceedings of the Twentieth Annual ACM-SIAM Symposium on Discrete Algorithms, SODA 2009, pp. 815–824. Society for Industrial and Applied Mathematics, Philadelphia (2009)

[9] Caragiannis, I., Kaklamanis, C., Kanellopoulos, P.: Improving the efficiency of load balancing games through taxes. In: Papadimitriou, C., Zhang, S. (eds.) WINE 2008. LNCS, vol. 5385, pp. 374–385. Springer, Heidelberg (2008)

[10] Caragiannis, I., Kaklamanis, C., Kanellopoulos, P.: Taxes for linear atomic congestion games. ACM Transactions on Algorithms 7(1), 13 (2010)

[11] Chen, H., Roughgarden, T., Valiant, G.: Designing network protocols for good equilibria. SIAM Journal on Computing 39(5), 1799–1832 (2010)

[12] Christodoulou, G., Koutsoupias, E., Nanavati, A.: Coordination mechanisms. Theor. Comput. Sci. 410(36), 3327–3336 (2009)

[13] Christodoulou, G., Mehlhorn, K., Pyrga, E.: Improving the price of anarchy for selfish routing via coordination mechanisms. In: Demetrescu, C., Halldórsson, M.M. (eds.) ESA 2011. LNCS, vol. 6942, pp. 119–130. Springer, Heidelberg (2011)

[14] Cole, R., Correa, J.R., Gkatzelis, V., Mirrokni, V., Olver, N.: Decentralized utilitarian mechanisms for scheduling games. Games and Economic Behavior (2013)

[15] von Falkenhausen, P., Harks, T.: Optimal cost sharing for resource selection games. Math. Oper. Res. 38(1), 184–208 (2013)

[16] Fotakis, D., Karakostas, G., Kolliopoulos, S.G.: On the existence of optimal taxes for network congestion games with heterogeneous users. In: Kontogiannis, S., Koutsoupias, E., Spirakis, P.G. (eds.) SAGT 2010. LNCS, vol. 6386, pp. 162–173. Springer, Heidelberg (2010)

[17] Fotakis, D., Spirakis, P.G.: Cost-balancing tolls for atomic network congestion games. Internet Mathematics 5(4), 343–363 (2008)
[18] Gairing, M., Schoppmann, F.: Total latency in singleton congestion games. In: Deng, X., Graham, F.C. (eds.) WINE 2007. LNCS, vol. 4858, pp. 381–387. Springer, Heidelberg (2007)
[19] Gopalakrishnan, R., Marden, J.R., Wierman, A.: Potential games are necessary to ensure pure nash equilibria in cost sharing games. In: Proceedings of the Fourteenth ACM Conference on Electronic Commerce, EC 2013, pp. 563–564. ACM, New York (2013)
[20] Harks, T., Klimm, M.: On the existence of pure Nash equilibria in weighted congestion games. Mathematics of Operations Research 37(3), 419–436 (2012)
[21] Harks, T., Klimm, M., Möhring, R.H.: Characterizing the existence of potential functions in weighted congestion games. Theory of Computing Systems 49(1), 46–70 (2011)
[22] Harks, T., Miller, K.: The worst-case efficiency of cost sharing methods in resource allocation games. Operations Research 59(6), 1491–1503 (2011)
[23] Immorlica, N., Li, L.E., Mirrokni, V.S., Schulz, A.S.: Coordination mechanisms for selfish scheduling. Theor. Comput. Sci. 410(17), 1589–1598 (2009)
[24] Kollias, K.: Nonpreemptive coordination mechanisms for identical machines. Theory of Computing Systems 53(3), 424–440 (2013)
[25] Kollias, K., Roughgarden, T.: Restoring pure equilibria to weighted congestion games. In: Aceto, L., Henzinger, M., Sgall, J. (eds.) ICALP 2011, Part II. LNCS, vol. 6756, pp. 539–551. Springer, Heidelberg (2011)
[26] Koutsoupias, E., Papadimitriou, C.H.: Worst-case equilibria. Computer Science Review 3(2), 65–69 (2009)
[27] Lucier, B., Borodin, A.: Price of anarchy for greedy auctions. In: SODA, pp. 537–553 (2010)
[28] Marden, J.R., Wierman, A.: Distributed welfare games. Operations Research 61(1), 155–168 (2013)
[29] Milchtaich, I.: Congestion games with player-specific payoff functions. Games and Economic Behavior 13(1), 111–124 (1996)
[30] Monderer, D., Shapley, L.S.: Potential games. Games and Economic Behavior 14(1), 124–143 (1996)
[31] Mosk-Aoyama, D., Roughgarden, T.: Worst-case efficiency analysis of queueing disciplines. In: Albers, S., Marchetti-Spaccamela, A., Matias, Y., Nikoletseas, S., Thomas, W. (eds.) ICALP 2009, Part II. LNCS, vol. 5556, pp. 546–557. Springer, Heidelberg (2009)
[32] Moulin, H.: The price of anarchy of serial, average and incremental cost sharing. Economic Theory 36(3), 379–405 (2008)
[33] Moulin, H., Shenker, S.: Strategyproof sharing of submodular costs: Budget balance versus efficiency. Economic Theory 18(3), 511–533 (2001)
[34] Redei, L.: Ein kombinatorischer satz. Acta Litteraria Szeged 7, 39–43 (1934)
[35] Rosenthal, R.W.: A class of games possessing pure-strategy Nash equilibria. International Journal of Game Theory 2(1), 65–67 (1973)
[36] Rosenthal, R.W.: The network equilibrium problem in integers. Networks 3(1), 53–59 (1973)

[37] Roughgarden, T.: Intrinsic robustness of the price of anarchy. In: 41st ACM Symposium on Theory of Computing (STOC), pp. 513–522 (2009)

[38] Roughgarden, T., Tardos, É.: How bad is selfish routing? Journal of the ACM 49(2), 236–259 (2002)

[39] Shapley, L.S.: Additive and Non-Additive Set Functions. Ph.D. thesis, Department of Mathematics, Princeton University (1953)

[40] Shenker, S.J.: Making greed work in networks: A game-theoretic analysis of switch service disciplines. IEEE/ACM Transactions on Networking 3(6), 819–831 (1995)

[41] Syrgkanis, V., Tardos, É.: Composable and efficient mechanisms. In: STOC, pp. 211–220 (2013)

Truthful Multi-unit Procurements with Budgets

Hau Chan and Jing Chen

Department of Computer Science, Stony Brook University,
Stony Brook, NY 11794, USA
{hauchan,jingchen}@cs.stonybrook.edu

Abstract. We study procurement games where each seller supplies multiple units of his item, with a cost per unit known only to him. The buyer can purchase any number of units from each seller, values different combinations of the items differently, and has a budget for his total payment. For a special class of procurement games, the *bounded knapsack* problem, we show that no universally truthful budget-feasible mechanism can approximate the optimal value of the buyer within $\ln n$, where n is the total number of units of all items available. We then construct a polynomial-time mechanism that gives a $4(1 + \ln n)$-approximation for procurement games with *concave additive valuations*, which include bounded knapsack as a special case. Our mechanism is thus optimal up to a constant factor. Moreover, for the bounded knapsack problem, given the well-known FPTAS, our results imply there is a provable gap between the optimization domain and the mechanism design domain. Finally, for procurement games with *sub-additive valuations*, we construct a universally truthful budget-feasible mechanism that gives an $O(\frac{\log^2 n}{\log \log n})$-approximation in polynomial time with a demand oracle.

Keywords: procurement auction, budget-feasible mechanism, optimal mechanism, approximation.

1 Introduction

In a procurement game/auction, m sellers compete for providing their items (referred to as products or services in some scenarios) to the buyer. Each seller i has one item and can provide at most n_i units of it, with a fixed cost c_i per unit which is known only to him. The buyer may purchase any number of units from each seller. For example, a local government may buy 50 displays from Dell, 20 laptops from Lenovo, and 30 printers from HP.[1] The buyer has a valuation function for possible combinations of the items, and a budget B for the total payment he can make. We consider universally truthful mechanisms that (approximately) maximize the buyer's value subject to the budget constraint.

Procurement games with budgets have been studied in the framework of budget-feasible mechanisms (see, e.g., [35, 19, 17, 10]). Yet most studies focus

---

[1] In reality Dell also sells laptops and Lenovo also sells displays. But for the purpose of this paper we consider settings where each seller has one item to supply, but has many units of it. However, we allow cases where different sellers have the same item, just as one can buy the same laptops from Best Buy and/or Walmart.

T.-Y. Liu et al. (Eds.): WINE 2014, LNCS 8877, pp. 89–105, 2014.
© Springer International Publishing Switzerland 2014

on settings where each seller has only one unit of his item. Thus there are only two possible allocations for a seller: either his item is taken or it is not.[2] When a seller has multiple units and may benefit from selling any number of them, there are more possibilities for him to deviate into and it becomes harder to provide incentives for him to be truthful. To the best of our knowledge, this is the first time where multi-unit budget-feasible mechanisms are systematically studied.

Multi-unit procurements with budgets can be used to model many interesting problems. For example, in the classic *bounded knapsack* problem the buyer has a value v_i for one unit of item i, and his total value is the sum of his value for each unit he buys. In job scheduling, the planner may assign multiple jobs to a machine, with different values for different assignments. As another example, in the Provision-after-Wait problem in healthcare [11], the government needs to serve n patients at m hospitals. Each patient has his own value for being served at each hospital, and the value of the government is the social welfare.

1.1 Our Main Results

We present our main results in three parts. Due to lack of space, most of the proofs are provided in the full version of this paper [14].

An impossibility result. Although budget-feasible mechanisms with constant approximation ratios have been constructed for single-unit procurements [35, 17], our first result, formally stated and proved in Section 3, shows that this is impossible in multi-unit settings, even for the special case of bounded knapsack.

THEOREM 1. (rephrased) *No universally truthful, budget-feasible mechanism can do better than a* $\ln n$*-approximation for bounded knapsack, where n is the total number of units of all items available.*

This theorem applies to all classes of multi-unit procurement games considered in this paper, since they all contain bounded knapsack as a special case.

An optimal mechanism for concave additive valuations. A concave additive valuation function is specified by the buyer's marginal values for getting the j-th unit of each item i, v_{ij}, which are non-increasing in j. The following theorem is formally stated in Section 4.

THEOREM 2. (rephrased) *There is a polynomial-time mechanism which is a* $4(1 + \ln n)$*-approximation for concave additive valuations.*

Our mechanism is very simple. The central part is a greedy algorithm, which yields a monotone allocation rule. However, one needs to be careful about how to compute the payments, and new ideas are needed for proving budget-feasibility.

Since bounded knapsack is a special case of concave additive valuations, our mechanism is optimal within a constant factor. More interestingly, given that bounded knapsack has an FPTAS when there is no strategic considerations, our results show that there is a gap between the optimization domain and the mechanism design domain for what one can expect when solving bounded knapsack.

---

[2] In the coverage problem a player has a set of elements, but still the allocation is bimodal for him: either his whole set is taken or none of the elements is taken.

Beyond concave additive valuations. We do not know how to use greedy algorithms to construct budget-feasible mechanisms for larger classes of valuations. The reason is that *they may not be monotone:* if a player lowers his cost, he might actually sell fewer units. This is demonstrated by our example in Section 5.1. Thus we turn to a different approach, *random sampling* [10, 24, 18, 16, 6, 7]. The following theorem is formally stated in Section 5.3.

THEOREM 5. (rephrased) *Given a demand oracle, there is a polynomial-time mechanism which is an $O(\frac{\log^2 n}{\log\log n})$-approximation for sub-additive valuations.*

A demand oracle is a standard assumption for handling sub-additive valuations [19, 10, 8], since such a valuation function takes exponentially many numbers to specify. Notice that for bounded knapsack and concave additive valuations our results are presented using the natural logarithm, since those are the precise bounds we achieve; while for sub-additive valuations we present our asymptotic bound under base-2 logarithm, to be consistent with the literature.

Our mechanism generalizes that of [10], which gives an $O(\frac{\log n}{\log\log n})$-approximation for single-unit sub-additive valuations. Several new issues arise in the multi-unit setting. For example, we must distinguish between an item and a unit of that item, and in both our mechanism and our analysis we need to be careful about which one to deal with. Also, we have constructed, as a sub-routine, a mechanism for approximating the optimal *single-item outcome*: namely, an outcome that only takes units from a single seller. We believe that this mechanism will be a useful building block for budget-feasible mechanisms in multi-unit settings.

1.2   Related Work

Various procurement games have been studied [30, 33, 32, 21, 22], but without budget considerations. In particular, frugal mechanisms [5, 13, 20, 27, 36, 15, 28] aim at finding mechanisms that minimize the total payment. As a "dual" problem to procurement games, auctions where the buyers have budget constraints have also been studied [2, 23], but the models are very different from ours.

Single-unit budget-feasible mechanisms were introduced by [35], where the author achieved a constant approximation for sub-modular valuations. In [17] the approximation ratio was improved and variants of knapsack problems were studied, but still in single-unit settings. In [19] the authors considered single-unit sub-additive valuations and constructed a randomized mechanism that is an $O(\log^2 n)$-approximation and a deterministic mechanism that is an $O(\log^3 n)$-approximation. We notice that their randomized mechanism can be generalized to multi-unit settings, resulting in an $O(\log^3 n)$-approximation. In [10] the authors consider both prior-free and Bayesian models. For the former, they provide a constant approximation for XOS valuations and an $O(\frac{\log n}{\log\log n})$-approximation for sub-additive valuations; and for the latter, they provide a constant approximation for the sub-additive case. As mentioned we generalize their prior-free mechanism, but we need to give up a $\log n$ factor in the approximation ratio. It is nice to see that the framework of budget-feasible mechanism design generalizes to multi-unit settings.

In [25] the author considered settings where each seller has multiple items. Although it was discussed why such settings are harder than single-item settings, no explicit upper bound on the approximation ratio was given. Instead, the focus there was a different benchmark. The author provided a constant approximation of his benchmark for sub-modular valuations, but the mechanism does not run in polynomial time. Also, budget-feasible mechanisms where each seller has one unit of an infinitely divisible item have been considered in [3], under the *large-market* assumption: that is, the cost of buying each item completely is much smaller than the budget. The authors constructed a deterministic mechanism which is a $1 - 1/e$ approximation for additive valuations and which they also prove to be optimal. In our study we do not impose any assumption about the sellers costs, and the cost of buying all units of an item may or may not exceed the budget. Moreover, in [9] the authors studied online procurements and provided a randomized posted-price mechanism that is an $O(\log n)$-approximation for sub-modular valuations under the random ordering assumption.

Finally, knapsack auctions have been studied by [1], where the underlying optimization problem is the knapsack problem, but a seller's private information is the value of his item, instead of the cost. Thus the model is very different from ours and from those studied in the budget-feasibility framework in general.

1.3   Open Problems

Many questions can be asked about multi-unit procurements with budgets and are worth studying in the future. Below we mention a few of them.

First, it would be interesting to close the gap between the upper bound in Theorem 1 and the lower bound in Theorem 5, even for subclasses such as sub-modular or diminishing-return valuations, as defined in Section 2. A related problem is whether the upper bound can be bypassed under other solution concepts. For example, is there a mechanism with price of anarchy [29, 34] better than $\ln n$? How about a mechanism with a *unique* equilibrium? Solution concepts that are not equilibrium-based are also worth considering, such as undominated strategies and iterated elimination of dominated strategies. Another problem is whether a better approximation can be achieved for other benchmarks, such as the one considered in [25], by truthful mechanisms that run in polynomial time.

Second, online procurements with budget constraints have been studied in both optimization settings [26] and strategic settings [9]. But only single-unit scenarios are considered in the latter. It is natural to ask, what if a seller with multiple units of the same item can show up at different time points, and the buyer needs to decide how many units he wants to buy each time.

Finally, the buyer may have different budgets for different sellers, a seller's cost for one unit of his item may decrease as he sells more, or the number of units each seller has may not be publicly known[3]. However, the last two cases are not single-parameter settings and presumably need very different approaches.

2 Procurement Games

Now let us define our model. In a procurement game there are m *sellers* who are the players, and one *buyer*. There are m *items* and they *may or may not be different*. Each player i can provide n_i *units* of item i, where each unit is indivisible. The total number of units of all the items is $n \triangleq \sum_i n_i$. The *true cost* for providing one unit of item i is $c_i \geq 0$, and $c = (c_1, \ldots, c_m)$. The value of c_i is player i's private information. All other information is public.

An *allocation* A is a profile of integers, $A = (a_1, \ldots, a_m)$. For each $i \in [m]$, $a_i \in \{0, 1, \ldots, n_i\}$ and a_i denotes the number of units bought from player i. An *outcome* ω is a pair, $\omega = (A, P)$, where A is an allocation and P is the *payment profile*: a profile of non-negative reals with P_i being the payment to player i. Player i's *utility* at ω is $u_i(\omega) = P_i - a_i c_i$.

The buyer has a *valuation function* V, mapping allocations to non-negative reals, such that $V(0, \ldots, 0) = 0$. For allocations $A = (a_1, \ldots, a_m)$ and $A' = (a'_1, \ldots, a'_m)$ with $a_i \leq a'_i$ for each i, $V(A) \leq V(A')$ —namely, V is *monotone*.[4] The buyer has a *budget* B and wants to implement an *optimal allocation*,

$$A^* \in \underset{A : \sum_{i \in [m]} c_i a_i \leq B}{\mathrm{argmax}} \ V(A),$$

while keeping the *total payment* within the budget. An outcome $\omega = (A, P)$ is *budget-feasible* if $\sum_{i \in [m]} P_i \leq B$.

The solution concept. A deterministic revealing mechanism is *dominant-strategy truthful (DST)* if for each player i, announcing c_i is a dominant strategy:

$$u_i(c_i, c'_{-i}) \geq u_i(c'_i, c'_{-i}) \ \forall c'_i, c'_{-i}.$$

A deterministic mechanism is *individually rational* if $u_i(c) \geq 0$ for each i. A randomized mechanism is *universally truthful* (respectively, *individually rational*) if it is a probabilistic distribution over deterministic mechanisms that are DST (respectively, individually rational).

A deterministic DST mechanism is *budget-feasible* if its outcome under c is budget-feasible. A universally truthful mechanism is *budget-feasible (in expectation)* if the expected payment under c is at most B.

---

[3] In many real-life scenarios the numbers of available units are public information, including procurements of digital products, procurements of cars, some arms trades, etc. Here procurement auctions are powerful tools and may result in big differences in prices, just like in the car market. However, there are also scenarios where the sellers can hide the numbers of units they have, particularly in a seller's market. In such cases they may manipulate the supply level, hoping to affect the prices.

[4] Monotonicity is a standard assumption for single-unit budget-feasible mechanisms.

Definition 1. *Let C be a class of procurement games and $f(n) \geq 0$. A universally truthful mechanism is an $f(n)$-approximation for class C if, for any game in C, the mechanism is individually rational and budget-feasible, and the outcome under the true cost profile c has expected value at least $\frac{V(A^*)}{f(n)}$.*

Remark 1. One can trade truthfulness for budget-feasibility: given a universally truthful budget-feasible mechanism, by paying each player the expected payment he would have received, we get a mechanism that is *truthful in expectation* and meets the budget constraint *with probability 1*. As implied by Theorem 1, no universally truthful mechanism that meets the budget constraint with probability 1 can do better than a $\ln n$-approximation. Thus there has to be some trade-off.

Remark 2. We allow different players to have identical items, just like different dealers may carry the same products, with or without the same cost. But we require the same player's units have the same cost. In the future, one may consider cases where one player has units of different items with different costs: that is, a multi-parameter setting instead of single-parameter.

Below we define several classes of valuation functions for procurement games.

Concave additive valuations and the bounded knapsack problem. An important class of valuation functions are the *additive* ones. For such a function V, there exists a value v_{ik} for each item i and each $k \in [n_i]$ such that, $V(A) = \sum_{i \in [m]} \sum_{k \in [a_i]} v_{ik}$ for any $A = (a_1, \ldots, a_m)$. Indeed, v_{ik} is the marginal value from the k-th unit of item i given that the buyer has already gotten $k-1$ units, no matter how many units he has gotten for other items. V is *concave* if for each i, $v_{i1} \geq v_{i2} \geq \cdots \geq v_{in_i}$; namely, the margins for the same item are non-increasing.

A special case of concave additive valuations is the *bounded knapsack* problem, one of the most classical problems in computational complexity. Here, all units of an item i have the same value v_i: that is, $v_{i1} = v_{i2} = \cdots = v_{in_i} = v_i$.

Sub-additive valuations. A much larger class is the *sub-additive* valuations. Here a valuation V is such that, for any $A = (a_1, \ldots, a_m)$ and $A' = (a'_1, \ldots, a'_m)$,

$$V(A \vee A') \leq V(A) + V(A'),$$

where $\vee$ is the item-wise max operation: $A \vee A' = (\max\{a_1, a'_1\}, \ldots, \max\{a_m, a'_m\})$.

Notice that the requirement of sub-additivity is imposed only across different players, and values can change arbitrarily across units of the same player. Indeed, when A and A' differ at a single player, sub-additivity *does not impose any constraint* on $V(A)$ and $V(A')$, not even that there are decreasing margins. Thus this definition is more general than requiring sub-additivity also across units of the same player. Following the literature, we stick to the more general notion.

Between concave additivity and sub-additivity, two classes of valuations have been defined, as recalled below.[5] To the best of our knowledge, no budget-feasible mechanisms were considered for either of them in multi-unit settings.

- *Diminishing return*: for any A and A' such that $a_i \leq a'_i$ for each i, and for any item j, $V(A + e_j) - V(A) \geq V(A' + e_j) - V(A')$, where $A + e_j$ means adding one extra unit of item j to A unless $a_j = n_j$, in which case $A + e_j = A$.
- *Sub-modularity*: for any A and A', $V(A \vee A') + V(A \wedge A') \leq V(A) + V(A')$, where $\wedge$ is the item-wise min operation.[6]

Diminishing return implies sub-modularity, and both collapse to sub-modularity in single-unit settings. The reason for diminishing return to be considered separately is that multi-unit sub-modularity is a very weak condition: when A and A' differ at a single player, it does not impose any constraint, as sub-additivity. Diminishing return better reflects the idea behind single-unit sub-modularity: the buyer's value for one extra unit of any item gets smaller as he buys more.

Since the valuation classes defined above are nested:

$$\text{bounded knapsack} \subseteq \text{concave additivity} \subseteq \text{diminishing return}$$
$$\subseteq \text{sub-modularity} \subseteq \text{sub-additivity},$$

any impossibility result for one class applies to all classes above it, and any positive result for one class applies to all classes below it. Moreover, since sub-additivity contains additivity, any positive result for the former also applies to the latter.

Demand oracle. A sub-additive valuation function V may take exponentially many numbers to specify. Thus following the studies of single-unit sub-additive valuations [35, 10], we consider a *demand oracle*, which takes as input a set of players $\{1, \ldots, m\}$, a profile of costs $(p_1, \ldots, p_m)$ and a profile of numbers of units $(n_1, \ldots, n_m)$,[7] and returns, regardless of the budget, an allocation

$$\hat{A} \in \operatorname*{argmax}_{A = (a_1, \ldots, a_m) : a_i \leq n_i \forall i} V(A) - \sum_{i \in [m]} a_i p_i.$$

It is well known that a demand oracle can simulate in polynomial time a value oracle, which returns $V(A)$ given A. Thus we also have access to a value oracle.

---

[5] The literature of multi-unit procurements has been particularly interested in valuations with some forms of "non-increasing margins", thus has considered classes that contain all concave additive valuations but not necessarily all additive ones.

[6] The item-wise max and min operations when defining sub-additivity and submodularity follow directly from the set-union and set-intersection operations when defining them in general settings, and have been widely adopted in the literature (see, e.g., [12] and [26]). One may consider alternative definitions where, for example, $\vee$ represents item-wise sum rather than item-wise max. However, we are not aware of existing studies where the alternative definitions are used.

[7] In single-unit settings a demand oracle takes as input a set of players and the costs. For multi-unit settings it is natural to also include the numbers of units.

Our goal. We shall construct universally truthful mechanisms that are individually rational, budget-feasible, and approximate the optimal value of the buyer. Our mechanisms run in polynomial time for concave additive valuations, and in polynomial time given the demand oracle for sub-additive valuations.

Single-parameter settings with budgets. Since the cost c_i is player i's only private information, we are considering single-parameter settings [4]. Following Myerson's lemma [31] or the characterization in [4], the only truthful mechanisms are those with a monotone allocation rule and threshold payments. In multi-unit settings, each unit of an item i has its own threshold and the total payment to i will be the sum of the thresholds for all of his units bought by the mechanism.

With a budget constraint, this characterization still holds, but the problem becomes harder: the monotone allocation rule must be such that, not only (1) it provides good approximation to the optimal value, but also (2) the unique total payment that it induces must satisfy the budget constraint. Therefore, similar to single-unit budget-feasible mechanisms, we shall construct monotone allocation rules while keeping an eye on the structure of the threshold payments. We need to make sure that when the two are combined, both (1) and (2) are satisfied.

3   Impossibility Results for Bounded Knapsack

The following observation for bounded knapsack is immediate.

Observation 1. *No deterministic DST budget-feasible mechanism can be an n-approximation for bounded knapsack.*

Proof. When $m = 1$, $n_1 = n$, $v_1 = 1$ and $c_1 = B$, a DST mechanism, being an n-approximation, must buy 1 unit and pay the player B. When $c_1 = B/n$, the mechanism must still buy 1 unit and pay B, otherwise the player will bid B instead. Thus the mechanism's value is 1, while the optimal value is n.   □

Clearly, buying 1 unit from a player $i \in \text{argmax}_j v_j$ and paying him B is an n-approximation. For randomized mechanisms we have the following.

Theorem 1. *No universally truthful mechanism can be an $f(n)$-approximation for bounded knapsack with $f(n) < \ln n$.*

Proof. Consider the case where $m = 1$, $n_1 = n$, and $v_1 = 1$. For any $b, c \in [0, B]$, let $u_1(b; c)$ be the player's expected utility by bidding b when $c_1 = c$. For each $k \in [n]$, consider the bid $\frac{B}{k}$: let P^k be the expected payment and, for each $j \in [n]$, let p_j^k be the probability for the mechanism to buy j units. When $c_1 = \frac{B}{k}$, the optimal value is k and

$$\sum_{j \in [n]} p_j^k \cdot j \geq \frac{k}{f(n)} \quad \forall k \in [n], \tag{1}$$

as the mechanism is an $f(n)$-approximation. By universal truthfulness and individual rationality, $u_1(\frac{B}{k}; \frac{B}{k}) \geq u_1(\frac{B}{k-1}; \frac{B}{k}) \ \forall k > 1$ and $u_1(B; B) \geq 0$. Namely,

$$P^k - \frac{B}{k} \sum_{j\in[n]} p_j^k \cdot j \geq P^{k-1} - \frac{B}{k} \sum_{j\in[n]} p_j^{k-1} \cdot j \quad \forall k > 1, \quad \text{and}$$

$$P^1 - B \sum_{j\in[n]} p_j^1 \cdot j \geq 0.$$

Summing up these n inequalities, we have

$$\sum_{k\in[n]} P^k - \sum_{k\in[n]} \frac{B}{k} \sum_{j\in[n]} p_j^k \cdot j \geq \sum_{1\leq k<n} P^k - \sum_{1\leq k<n} \frac{B}{k+1} \sum_{j\in[n]} p_j^k \cdot j,$$

which implies

$$P^n \geq \frac{B}{n} \sum_{j\in[n]} p_j^n \cdot j + \sum_{1\leq k<n} \frac{B}{k(k+1)} \sum_{j\in[n]} p_j^k \cdot j.$$

By Equation 1, we have

$$P^n \geq \frac{B}{f(n)} + \sum_{1\leq k<n} \frac{B}{(k+1)f(n)} = \frac{B}{f(n)} \sum_{k\in[n]} \frac{1}{k} \geq \frac{B \ln n}{f(n)}.$$

By budget-feasibility, $P^n \leq B$. Thus $f(n) \geq \ln n$, implying Theorem 1. $\square$

Remark 3. Notice that as long as the mechanism is truthful *in expectation* and individually rational *in expectation* (namely, with respect to the players' expected utilities), the analysis of Theorem 1 implies that it cannot do better than a $\ln n$-approximation. Also notice that the impossibility result does not impose any constraint on the running time of the mechanism.

Remark 4. When there is a single player, that player has a monopoly and it is not too surprising that no mechanism can do better than a $\ln n$-approximation. For example, in frugality mechanism design in procurement games, it has been explicitly assumed that there is no monopoly. However, when monopoly might actually exist, it is interesting to see that there is a tight bound (by Theorems 1 and 2) on the power of budget-feasible mechanisms in multi-unit settings.

4 An Optimal Mechanism for Concave Additive Valuations

We construct a polynomial-time universally truthful mechanism M_{Add} that is a $4(1 + \ln n)$-approximation for procurement games with concave additive valuations. Our mechanism is very simple, and the basic idea is a greedy algorithm with proportional cost sharing, as has been used for single-unit settings [17, 35]. However, the key here is to understand the structure of the threshold payments and to show that the mechanism is budget-feasible, which requires ideas not seen before. Moreover, given our impossibility result, this mechanism is optimal up to a constant factor. In particular, it achieves the optimal approximation ratio for bounded knapsack. The simplicity and the optimality of our mechanism make it attractive to be actually implemented in real-life scenarios.

Notations and Conventions. Without loss of generality, we assume $v_{ij} > 0$ for each item i and $j \in [n_i]$, since otherwise the mechanism can first remove the units with value 0 from consideration. Because we shall show that M_{Add} is universally truthful, we describe it only with respect to the truthful bid $(c_1, \ldots, c_n)$. Also, we describe the allocation rule only, since it uniquely determines the threshold payments. An algorithm for computing the thresholds will be given in the analysis. Finally, let $i^* \in \text{argmax}_i\, v_{i1}$ be the player with the highest marginal value, e_{i^*} be the allocation with 1 unit of item i^* and 0 unit of others, and $A_\perp = (0, \ldots, 0)$ be the allocation where nothing is bought. We have the following.

Mechanism M_{Add} for Concave Additive Valuations

1. With probability $\frac{1}{2(1+\ln n)}$, go to Step 2; with probability $\frac{1}{2}$, output e_{i^*} and stop; and with the remaining probability, output $A_\perp$ and stop.
2. For each $i \in [m]$ and $j \in [n_i]$, let the *value-rate* $r_{ij} = v_{ij}/c_i$.
   (a) Order the n pairs (i, j) according to r_{ij} decreasingly, with ties broken lexicographically, first by i and then by j.
       For any $\ell \in [n]$, denote by (i_ℓ, j_ℓ) the ℓ-th pair in the ordered list.
   (b) Let k be the largest number in $[n]$ satisfying $\frac{c_{i_k}}{v_{i_k j_k}} \leq \frac{B}{\sum_{\ell \leq k} v_{i_\ell j_\ell}}$.
   (c) Pick up the first k pairs in the list: that is, output allocation $A = (a_1, \ldots, a_n)$ where $a_i = |\{\ell : \ell \leq k \text{ and } i_\ell = i\}|$.

Theorem 2. *Mechanism M_{Add} runs in polynomial time, is universally truthful, and is a $4(1 + \ln n)$-approximation for procurement games with concave additive valuations.*

Combining Theorems 1 and 2 we immediately have the following.

Corollary 1. *Mechanism M_{Add} is optimal up to a constant factor among all universally truthful, individually rational, and budget-feasible mechanisms for multi-unit procurement games with concave additive valuations.*

Remark 5. Theorems 1 and 2 show that multi-unit settings are very different from single-unit settings. In single-unit settings various constant-approximation mechanisms have been constructed, while in multi-unit settings an $O(\log n)$-approximation is the best, and our mechanism provides such an approximation.

Furthermore, for bounded knapsack, without strategic considerations there is an FPTAS, while with strategic considerations the best is a $\ln n$-approximation. Thus we have shown that bound knapsack is a problem for which *provably* there is a gap between the optimization domain and the mechanism design domain.

Finally, it would be interesting to see how the constant gap between Theorems 1 and 2 can be closed, and whether there is a mechanism that meets the budget constraint with probability 1 and achieves an $O(\log n)$-approximation.

An optimal mechanism for symmetric valuations. A closely related class of valuations are the *symmetric* ones: there exists $v_1, \ldots, v_n$ such that, for any allocation

A with k units, $V(A) = \sum_{\ell \le k} v_\ell$. In general, symmetric valuations are not concave additive, nor are concave additive valuations necessarily symmetric. But they are equivalent with a single seller. Thus the proof of Theorem 1 implies no mechanism can do better than a $\ln n$-approximation for symmetric valuations, as stated in the first part of the theorem below. Similar to our analysis of Theorem 2, one can verify that the following mechanism is a $4(1 + \ln n)$-approximation for symmetric valuations: it is the same as M_{Add} except in Step 2, where k is set to be the largest number in $[n]$ satisfying $c_{i_k} \le \frac{B}{k}$. We omit the analysis since it is very similar to that of M_{Add}, and only present the following theorem.

Theorem 3. *For symmetric valuations, no universally truthful mechanism can be an $f(n)$-approximation with $f(n) < \ln n$, and there exists a polynomial-time universally truthful mechanism which is a $4(1 + \ln n)$-approximation.*

5   Truthful Mechanisms for Sub-additive Valuations

5.1   The Non-monotonicity of the Greedy Algorithm

Although the greedy algorithm with proportional cost-sharing played an important role in budget-feasible mechanisms, we do not know how to use it for multi-unit sub-additive valuations, since *it is not monotone*. Indeed, by lowering his cost, a player i will still sell his first unit as in the old allocation. But once the rank of his first unit changes, all units after that will be re-ranked according to their new marginal value-rates. Under the new ordering there is no guarantee whether player i will sell any of his remaining units. Below we give an example demonstrating this phenomenon in settings with diminishing returns.

Example 1. There are 3 players, $n_1 = 1$, $n_2 = n_3 = 2$, $c_1 = c_3 = 1$, $c_2 = 1 + \epsilon$ for some arbitrarily small $\epsilon > 0$, and $B = 3 + 2\epsilon$. To highlight the non-monotonicity of the greedy algorithm, we work through the algorithm and define the marginal values on the way. The valuation function will be defined accordingly.

Given any allocation A and player i, denote by $V(i|A)$ the marginal value of item i, namely, $V(A + e_i) - V(A)$. The greedy algorithm works as follows.

- At the beginning, the allocation is $A_0 = (0, 0, 0)$.
- $V(1|A_0) = 10$, $V(2|A_0) = 10 + \epsilon$, and $V(3|A_0) = 10 - \epsilon$. Item 1 has the largest marginal value-rate, thus $A_1 = (1, 0, 0)$.
- $V(1|A_1) = 0$ (item 1 is unavailable now), $V(2|A_1) = 5 + 5\epsilon$, and $V(3|A_1) = 5 - \epsilon$. Item 2 has the largest marginal value-rate, thus $A_2 = (1, 1, 0)$.
- $V(1|A_2) = 0$, $V(2|A_2) = 1 + \epsilon$, and $V(3|A_2) = 1 - \epsilon$. Item 2 has the largest marginal value-rate, thus $A_3 = (1, 2, 0)$.
- The budget is used up, the final allocation is A_3, and player 2 sells 2 units.

Now let $c_2' = 1 - \epsilon < c_2$. The greedy algorithm works as follows.

- $A_0 = (0, 0, 0)$.
- $V(1|A_0) = 10$, $V(2|A_0) = 10 + \epsilon$, and $V(3|A_0) = 10 - \epsilon$. Item 2 has the largest marginal value-rate, thus $A_1' = (0, 1, 0)$.
- Notice that player 2 sells his first unit earlier than before.

- $V(1|A_1') = 5 + 4\epsilon$, $V(2|A_1') = 5 - 5\epsilon$, and $V(3|A_1') = 5 + 5\epsilon$. Item 3 has the largest marginal value-rate, thus $A_2' = (0, 1, 1)$.
- $V(1|A_2') = 1 - 2\epsilon$, $V(2|A_2') = 1 - \epsilon$, and $V(3|A_2') = 1 + \epsilon$, thus $A_3' = (0, 1, 2)$.
- The remaining budget is 3ϵ, no further unit can be added, and the final allocation is A_3'. But player 2 only sells one unit, violating monotonicity.

Given the marginal values, the valuation function is defined as follows:

$V(0, 0, 0) = 0, V(1, 0, 0) = 10, V(0, 1, 0) = 10 + \epsilon, V(0, 0, 1) = 10 - \epsilon,$

$V(1, 1, 0) = 15 + 5\epsilon, V(1, 0, 1) = 15 - \epsilon, V(0, 2, 0) = 15 - 4\epsilon, V(0, 1, 1) = 15 + 6\epsilon,$

$V(0, 0, 2) = 15,$

$V(1, 2, 0) = 16 + 6\epsilon, V(1, 1, 1) = 16 + 4\epsilon, V(1, 0, 2) = 16, V(0, 2, 1) = 16 + 5\epsilon,$

$V(0, 1, 2) = 16 + 7\epsilon,$

$V(0, 2, 2) = V(1, 2, 1) = V(1, 1, 2) = 16 + 7\epsilon, V(1, 2, 2) = 16 + 7\epsilon.$

One can verify that V is consistent with the marginal values and has diminishing returns. Indeed, for any allocation with k units for k from 0 to 4, the marginal value of adding 1 more unit is roughly $10, 5, 1, \epsilon, 0$, and thus diminishing.

Given the non-monotonicity of the greedy algorithm, we turn to another approach for constructing truthful mechanisms, namely, *random sampling*. We provide our main mechanism in Section 5.3. In Section 5.2 we first construct a mechanism that will be used as a subroutine.

5.2   Approximating the Optimal Single-Item Allocation

From the analysis of Theorem 1, we notice that part of the hardness in designing mechanisms for multi-unit settings comes from cases where a single player's item contributes a lot to the optimal solution. In order to obtain a good approximation, we need to identify such a player and buy *as many units as possible from him*. More precisely, given the true cost profile $(c_1, \ldots, c_n)$, let

$$i^{**} \in \operatorname*{argmax}_i V(\min\{n_i, \lfloor \frac{B}{c_i} \rfloor\} \cdot e_i),$$

where for any $\lambda \in [n_i]$, λe_i is the allocation with λ units of item i and 0 unit of others. Ideally we want to buy $\lambda^{**} \triangleq \min\{n_{i^{**}}, \lfloor \frac{B}{c_{i^{**}}} \rfloor\}$ units from i^{**} and pay him (at most) B. We shall refer to (i^{**}, λ^{**}) as the *optimal single-item allocation*.

Notice that a similar scenario occurs in single-unit settings: part of the value approximation comes from a single player i^* with the highest marginal value. The problem is, although the identity of player i^* is publicly known, both i^{**} and λ^{**} depend on the players' true costs and have to be solved from their bids. Below we construct a universally truthful mechanism, M_{One}, which is budget-feasible and approximates $V(\lambda^{**}e_{i^{**}})$ within a $1 + \ln n$ factor. We have the following theorem.

Theorem 4. *Mechanism M_{One} is universally truthful, individually rational, budget-feasible, and is a $(1 + \ln n)$-approximation for $V(\lambda^{**}e_{i^{**}})$.*

Mechanism M_{One} for Approximating the Optimal Single-item Allocation

With probability $\frac{1}{1+\ln n}$, do the following.

1. Let $v_i = V(\min\{n_i, \lfloor \frac{B}{c_i} \rfloor\} \cdot e_i)$ and order the players according to the v_i's decreasingly, with ties broken lexicographically.
   Let i^{**} be the first player in the list and $\lambda^{**} = \min\{n_{i^{**}}, \lfloor \frac{B}{c_{i^{**}}} \rfloor\}$.
2. Let $k \in [\lambda^{**}]$ be the smallest number such that player i^{**} is still ordered the first with cost $c'_{i^{**}} = \frac{B}{k}$.
3. Set $\theta_\ell = \frac{B}{k}$ for each $\ell \leq k$ and $\theta_\ell = \frac{B}{\ell}$ for each $k+1 \leq \ell \leq \lambda^{**}$.
4. Output allocation $\lambda^{**}e_{i^{**}}$ and pay $\sum_{\ell \leq \lambda^{**}} \theta_\ell$ to player i^{**}.

Since the impossibility result in Theorem 1 applies to settings with a single item, we have the following corollary.

Corollary 2. *Mechanism M_{One} is optimal for approximating $V(\lambda^{**}e_{i^{**}})$ among all universally truthful, individually rational, and budget-feasible mechanisms.*

Remark 6. As it will become clear from the analysis, M_{One} does not require the valuation to be sub-additive. The only thing it requires is that, for each player i, $V(\lambda e_i)$ is non-decreasing in λ. Thus it can be used for valuations that are not even monotone, as long as they are monotone across units of the same item.

Furthermore, given that (i^{**}, λ^{**}) is the multi-unit counterpart of player i^* in single-unit settings, and given the important role i^* has played in single-unit budget-feasible mechanisms, we believe mechanism M_{One} will be a useful building block in the design of budget-feasible mechanisms for multi-unit settings.

5.3   A Truthful Mechanism for Sub-additive Valuations

Our mechanism for sub-additive valuations generalizes that of [10]. In particular, the algorithm A_{Max} and the mechanism M_{Rand} below are respectively variants of their algorithm SA-ALG-MAX and mechanism SA-RANDOM-SAMPLE. Several new issues arise in multi-unit settings. For example, we must now distinguish between an item and a unit of that item. In the mechanism and its analysis, we sometimes deal with an item —thus all of its units at the same time— and sometimes deal with a single unit. Also, as discussed in Section 5.2, the role of player i^* with the highest marginal value is replaced by player i^{**}, and the way i^{**} contributes to the value approximation has changed a lot —this is where the extra $\log n$ factor comes. Indeed, to construct and analyze our mechanism one need good understanding of the problem in multi-unit settings. Our mechanism M_{Sub} is a uniform distribution between M_{Rand} and the mechanism M_{One} of Section 5.2. We have the following theorem.

Theorem 5. *Mechanism M_{Sub} runs in polynomial time, is universally truthful, and is an $O(\frac{(\log n)^2}{\log \log n})$-approximation for procurement games with sub-additive valuations.*

Algorithm A_{Max}

Since this algorithm will be used multiple times with different inputs, we specify the inputs explicitly to avoid confusion. Given players $1, \ldots, m$, numbers of units $n_1, \ldots, n_m$, costs $c_1, \ldots, c_m$, budget B, and a demand oracle for the valuation function V, do the following.

1. Let $n_i' = \min\{n_i, \lfloor \frac{B}{c_i} \rfloor\}$ for each i, $i^{**} = \arg\max_i V(n_i' e_i)$, $v^* = V(n_{i^{**}}' e_{i^{**}})$, and $\mathcal{V} = \{v^*, 2v^*, \ldots, mv^*\}$.
2. For $v \in \mathcal{V}$ from mv^* to v^*,
   (a) Set $p_i = \frac{v}{2B} \cdot c_i$ for each player i. Query the oracle with m players, number of units n_i' and cost p_i for each i, to find
   $S = (s_1, \ldots, s_m) \in \arg\max_{A=(a_1, \ldots, a_m): a_i \leq n_i' \forall i} V(A) - \sum_{i \in [m]} a_i p_i$.
   (When there are multiple optimal solutions, the oracle always returns the same one whenever queried with the same instance.)
   (b) Set allocation $S_v = A_\perp$. (Recall $A_\perp = (0, \ldots, 0)$ represents buying nothing.)
   (c) If $V(S) < \frac{v}{2}$, then continue to the next v.
   (d) Else, order the players according to $s_i c_i$ decreasingly with ties broken lexicographically, and denote them by $i_1, \ldots, i_m$.
   Let k be the largest number in $[m]$ satisfying $\sum_{\ell \leq k} s_{i_\ell} c_{i_\ell} \leq B$, and let S_v be S projected on $\{i_1, \ldots, i_k\}$: $S_v = \bigvee_{\ell \leq k} s_{i_\ell} e_{i_\ell}$, namely, S_v consists of taking s_{i_ℓ} units of item i_ℓ for each $\ell \leq k$, and taking 0 unit of others.
3. Output $S_{Max} \in \arg\max_{v \in \mathcal{V}} V(S_v)$.
   (When there are several choices, the algorithm chooses one arbitrarily, but always outputs the same one when executed multiple times with the same input.)

Mechanism M_{Rand}

1. Put each player independently at random with probability $1/2$ into group T, and let $T' = [m] \setminus T$.
2. Run A_{Max} with the set of players T, number of units n_i and cost c_i for each $i \in T$, budget B, and the demand oracle for valuation function V. Let v be the value of the returned allocation.
3. For k from 1 to $\sum_{i \in T'} n_i$,
   (a) Run A_{Max} with the set of players $T_k = \{i : i \in T', c_i \leq \frac{B}{k}\}$, number of units n_i and cost $\frac{B}{k}$ for each $i \in T_k$, budget B, and the demand oracle for V. Denote the returned allocation by $X = (x_1, \ldots, x_m)$, where $x_i = 0$ for each $i \notin T_k$.
   (b) If $V(X) \geq \frac{\log \log n}{64 \log n} \cdot v$, then output allocation X, pay $x_i \cdot \frac{B}{k}$ to each player i, and stop.
4. Output $A_\perp$ and pay 0 to each player.

Since diminishing return, sub-modularity, and additivity all imply sub-additivity, we immediately have the following.

Corollary 3. M_{Sub} *is an* $O(\frac{(\log n)^2}{\log\log n})$-*approximation for procurement games with diminishing returns, those with sub-modular valuations, and those with additive valuations.*

Remark 7. The worst case of the approximation above comes from cases where $V(\lambda^{**}e_{i^{**}})$ (and thus M_{One}) is the main contribution to the final value. Unlike single-unit settings, we need an additional $\log n$ factor because the optimal approximation ratio for $V(\lambda^{**}e_{i^{**}})$ is $O(\log n)$. For scenarios where the players' costs are very small, in particular, where $n_i c_i \leq B$ for each i, the optimal single-item allocation (i^{**}, λ^{**}) is publicly known, just as the player i^* in single-unit settings. In such a *small-cost* setting, which is very similar to the *large-market* setting considered by [3] except that the items here are not infinitely divisible, the subroutine M_{One} in M_{Sub} can be replaced by "allocating $n_{i^{**}}$ units of item i^{**} and paying him B", and the $\log n$ factor is avoided, resulting in an $O(\frac{\log n}{\log\log n})$-approximation.

A small-cost setting is possible in some markets, but it is not realistic in many others. For example, in the Provision-after-Wait problem in healthcare [11], it is very unlikely that all patients can be served at the most expensive hospital within the government's budget. Also, in many procurement games, a seller, as the manufacture of his product, can be considered as having infinite supply, and the total cost of all units he has will always exceed the buyer's budget. Thus one need to be careful about where the small-cost condition applies.

Acknowledgements. We thank several anonymous reviewers for their comments. The first author is supported by the NSF Graduate Research Fellowship.

References

[1] Aggarwal, G., Hartline, J.D.: Knapsack auctions. In: SODA, pp. 1083–1092 (2006)

[2] Aggarwal, G., Muthukrishnan, S., Pál, D., Pál, M.: General auction mechanism for search advertising. In: Proceedings of the 18th International Conference on World Wide Web, pp. 241–250 (2009)

[3] Anari, N., Goel, G., Nikzad, A.: Mechanisms design for crowdsourcing: An optimal $1-1/e$ approximate budget-feasible mechanism for large markets. In: FOCS (2014)

[4] Archer, A., Tardos, E.: Truthful mechanisms for one-parameter agents. In: Proceedings of the 42nd IEEE Symposium on Foundations of Computer Science, pp. 482–491 (2001)

[5] Archer, A., Tardos, É.: Frugal path mechanisms. ACM Trans. Algorithms 3(1), 1–22 (2007)

[6] Babaioff, M., Dinitz, M., Gupta, A., Immorlica, N., Talwar, K.: Secretary problems: Weights and discounts. In: Proceedings of the Twentieth Annual ACM-SIAM Symposium on Discrete Algorithms, pp. 1245–1254 (2009)

[7] Babaioff, M., Immorlica, N., Kleinberg, R.: Matroids, secretary problems, and online mechanisms. In: Proceedings of the Eighteenth Annual ACM-SIAM Symposium on Discrete Algorithms, pp. 434–443 (2007)

[8] Badanidiyuru, A., Dobzinski, S., Oren, S.: Optimization with demand oracles. In: EC, pp. 110–127 (2012)

[9] Badanidiyuru, A., Kleinberg, R., Singer, Y.: Learning on a budget: Posted price mechanisms for online procurement. In: Proceedings of the 13th ACM Conference on Electronic Commerce, pp. 128–145 (2012)

[10] Bei, X., Chen, N., Gravin, N., Lu, P.: Budget feasible mechanism design: From prior-free to Bayesian. In: Proceedings of the Forty-fourth Annual ACM Symposium on Theory of Computing, pp. 449–458 (2012)

[11] Braverman, M., Chen, J., Kannan, S.: Optimal provision-after-wait in healthcare. In: Proceedings of the 5th Conference on Innovations in Theoretical Computer Science, pp. 541–542 (2014)

[12] Calinescu, G., Chekuri, C., Pál, M., Vondrák, J.: Maximizing a monotone submodular function subject to a matroid constraint. SICOMP, Special Section on STOC 2008 40(6), 1740–1766 (2011)

[13] Cary, M.C., Flaxman, A.D., Hartline, J.D., Karlin, A.R.: Auctions for structured procurement. In: Proceedings of the Nineteenth Annual ACM-SIAM Symposium on Discrete Algorithms, pp. 304–313 (2008)

[14] Chan, H., Chen, J.: Truthful multi-unit procurements with budgets (2014), full version http://arxiv.org/abs/1409.7595

[15] Chen, N., Elkind, E., Gravin, N., Petrov, F.: Frugal mechanism design via spectral techniques. In: FOCS, pp. 755–764 (2010)

[16] Chen, N., Gravin, N., Lu, P.: Mechanism design without money via stable matching. CoRR abs/1104.2872 (2011)

[17] Chen, N., Gravin, N., Lu, P.: On the approximability of budget feasible mechanisms. In: Proceedings of the Twenty-second Annual ACM-SIAM Symposium on Discrete Algorithms, pp. 685–699 (2011)

[18] Dobzinski, S.: Two randomized mechanisms for combinatorial auctions. In: Charikar, M., Jansen, K., Reingold, O., Rolim, J.D.P. (eds.) APPROX and RANDOM 2007. LNCS, vol. 4627, pp. 89–103. Springer, Heidelberg (2007)

[19] Dobzinski, S., Papadimitriou, C.H., Singer, Y.: Mechanisms for complement-free procurement. In: Proceedings of the 12th ACM Conference on Electronic Commerce, pp. 273–282 (2011)

[20] Elkind, E., Sahai, A., Steiglitz, K.: Frugality in path auctions. In: Proceedings of the Fifteenth Annual ACM-SIAM Symposium on Discrete Algorithms, pp. 701–709 (2004)

[21] Feigenbaum, J., Papadimitriou, C.H., Sami, R., Shenker, S.: A BGP-based mechanism for lowest-cost routing. In: PODC, pp. 173–182 (2002)

[22] Feigenbaum, J., Sami, R., Shenker, S.: Mechanism design for policy routing. In: PODC, pp. 11–20 (2004)

[23] Goel, G., Mirrokni, V., Leme, R.P.: Clinching auctions beyond hard budget constraints. In: EC, pp. 167–184 (2014)

[24] Goldberg, A.V., Hartline, J.D., Karlin, A.R., Wright, A., Saks, M.: Competitive auctions. In: Games and Economic Behavior, pp. 72–81 (2002)

[25] Gravin, N.: Incentive Compatible Design of Reverse Auctions, Section 5.2. Ph.D. thesis, Nanyang Technological University (2013)

[26] Kapralov, M., Post, I., Vondrák, J.: Online submodular welfare maximization: Greedy is optimal. In: Proceedings of SODA 2013, pp. 1216–1225 (2013)

[27] Karlin, A.R., Kempe, D., Tamir, T.: Beyond VCG: Frugality of truthful mechanisms. In: Proceedings of the 46th Annual IEEE Symposium on Foundations of Computer Science, pp. 615–626 (2005)

[28] Kempe, D., Salek, M., Moore, C.: Frugal and truthful auctions for vertex covers, flows and cuts. In: FOCS, pp. 745–754 (2010)

[29] Koutsoupias, E., Papadimitriou, C.: Worst-case equilibria. In: Meinel, C., Tison, S. (eds.) STACS 1999. LNCS, vol. 1563, pp. 404–413. Springer, Heidelberg (1999)

[30] Mishra, D., Veeramani, D.: Vickrey-Dutch procurement auction for multiple items. European Journal of Operational Research 180, 617–629 (2006)

[31] Myerson, R.B.: Optimal auction design. Mathematics of Operations Research 6(1), 58–73 (1981)

[32] Nisan, N., Ronen, A.: Algorithmic mechanism design. Games and Economic Behavior 35, 166–196 (2001)

[33] Parkes, D.C., Kalagnanam, J.: Models for iterative multiattribute procurement auctions. Management Science (Special Issue on Electronic Markets) 51, 435–451 (2005)

[34] Roughgarden, T., Tardos, E.: How bad is selfish routing? Journal of the ACM 49(2), 236–259 (2002)

[35] Singer, Y.: Budget feasible mechanisms. In: Proceedings of the 2010 IEEE 51st Annual Symposium on Foundations of Computer Science, pp. 765–774 (2010)

[36] Talwar, K.: The price of truth: Frugality in truthful mechanisms. In: Alt, H., Habib, M. (eds.) STACS 2003. LNCS, vol. 2607, pp. 608–619. Springer, Heidelberg (2003)

The Shapley Value in Knapsack Budgeted Games

Smriti Bhagat[1], Anthony Kim[2,*], S. Muthukrishnan[3], and Udi Weinsberg[1]

[1] Technicolor Research, Los Altos, CA, USA
{smriti.bhagat,udi.weinsberg}@technicolor.com
[2] Department of Computer Science, Stanford University, Stanford, CA, USA
tonyekim@stanford.edu
[3] Department of Computer Science, Rutgers University, Piscataway, NJ, USA
muthu@cs.rutgers.edu

Abstract. We propose the study of computing the Shapley value for a new class of cooperative games that we call budgeted games, and investigate in particular knapsack budgeted games, a version modeled after the classical knapsack problem. In these games, the "value" of a set S of agents is determined only by a critical subset $T \subseteq S$ of the agents and not the entirety of S due to a budget constraint that limits how large T can be. We show that the Shapley value can be computed in time faster than by the naïve exponential time algorithm when there are sufficiently many agents, and also provide an algorithm that approximates the Shapley value within an additive error. For a related budgeted game associated with a greedy heuristic, we show that the Shapley value can be computed in pseudo-polynomial time. Furthermore, we generalize our proof techniques and propose what we term algorithmic representation framework that captures a broad class of cooperative games with the property of efficient computation of the Shapley value. The main idea is that the problem of determining the efficient computation can be reduced to that of finding an alternative representation of the games and an associated algorithm for computing the underlying value function with small time and space complexities in the representation size.

1 Introduction

The Shapley value is a well-studied solution concept for fair distribution of profit among agents in cooperative game theory. Given a coalition of agents that collectively generate some profit, fair distribution is important to maintain a stable coalition such that no subgroup of agents has an incentive to unilaterally deviate and form its own coalition. While the Shapley value is not a stability concept, it uniquely satisfies a set of desirable properties for fair profit distribution based on individual contributions. It has been shown useful on a wide range of cooperative games and, more recently, applied beyond the game-theoretic setting in problems related to social networks [19, 17] and computer networks [14, 18].

---

* This work was done while the author was an intern at Technicolor Research Lab. Supported in part by an NSF Graduate Research Fellowship.

T.-Y. Liu et al. (Eds.): WINE 2014, LNCS 8877, pp. 106–119, 2014.
© Springer International Publishing Switzerland 2014

Efficient — (pseudo) polynomial time — computation of the Shapley value has been studied for many classes of cooperative games. One such example is weighted voting games that model parliamentary voting where agents are parties, the weight of each party is the number of the same party representatives, and a coalition of parties is winning (has value 1) if its total weight is at least some quota, or losing (has value 0) otherwise. It was shown that computing the Shapley value in the weighted majority games, where the quota is half the total weight of all the agents, is #P-complete [8] and NP-hard [16]. Note, however, that there is a pseudo-polynomial time algorithm using dynamic programming [15].

In another line of research, representation schemes for cooperative games have been proposed in [7, 11, 12, 1]; if a given cooperative game has a small alternative representation in one of these schemes, then the Shapley value can be computed efficiently in time polynomial in the size of the alternative representation. For example, we can represent a given cooperative game as a collection of smaller cooperative games in multi-issue representation [7], or in terms of logic rules in marginal contribution net representation [11].

We propose a new class of cooperative games that we call *budgeted games* and study the Shapley value computation in these games. In cooperative games, the value function $v(S)$ for a coalition S is determined by all the agents in S, but may explicitly depend on a sub-coalition in some domains (e.g., [3, 5, 2]). We study value functions conditioned on a budget B where $v(S)$ may be totally determined by a potentially strict subset $T \subset S$ of agents. That is, budget B models a physical or budget constraint that may limit the actual value of a coalition to be less than simply the total aggregate value of all the individual contributions and, hence, the profit generation of a coalition is determined only by a sub-coalition of the agents. There are many examples we can readily formulate as budgeted games to model real-life scenarios:

- *(Graph Problems)* Consider a network of nodes that correspond to facilities and edges between them that correspond to communication links. This can be modeled as a graph G with weights on nodes. For any subset S of nodes, $v_B(S)$, the value created by set S under budget B, may be the maximum weight of an independent set of at most B nodes.
- *(Set Problems)* Let each agent be a sales agent targeting a specific set of customers. Then $v_B(S)$ may be the maximum number of customers that can be targeted by a subset of size at most B of sales agents from S.
- *(Packing Problems)* Consider creating a task force from a pool S of available agents where each agent is associated with some value and cost. Then $v_B(S)$ may be the largest total aggregate value from a subset of the agents with total cost at most B.
- *(Data Mining Problems[1])* Let each agent represent a document with some quality measure with respect to a fixed search query. We may approximate the total value of an ordered list of documents S, ordered by the quality

---

[1] This is the Shapley value computation problem for what is commonly known as the Top-k problem.

measure, by those that appear at the top of the list. Then, the corresponding $v_B(S)$ is the sum of the top B quality scores of documents in S.

For the Shapley value to be useful in value division problems modeled as budgeted games, we cannot simply apply the formula for the Shapley value as it would lead to an exponential time algorithm. Hence, it is important to understand its computational complexity in these games, and we study the knapsack version (equivalently, Packing Problems) in this paper. As far as we know, the budgeted games have not been studied previously. A related class of games called bin-packing games [9, 13, 20] has been studied for different solution concepts of core and ϵ-core.[2]

Our Contributions. First, we propose a new class of cooperative games, *budgeted games*, and investigate the computational complexity of the Shapley value in a particular version of budgeted games. Second, we generalize our proof techniques and propose a general framework, *algorithmic representation*, for cooperative games. We note that all our algorithms have running times with a polynomial dependence on the number of agents. More specifically, our contributions are as follows:

- We study the knapsack version of budgeted games and show that computing the Shapley value in these games is NP-hard. On the other hand, we show that the Shapley value can be computed in time faster than by the naïve exponential time algorithm when there are sufficiently many agents.
- We provide an additive approximation scheme for the Shapley value via rounding; our approach does not use the standard sampling and normal distribution techniques [4, 10] in estimating the Shapley value.
- We consider the value function obtained by a 2-approximation greedy algorithm for the classical knapsack problem and show that for this function, the Shapley value can be computed in pseudo-polynomial time.
- We provide generalizations and present the algorithmic representation framework that captures a broad class of cooperative games with the property of efficient computation of the Shapley value. This includes many known classes of cooperative games in [8, 15, 17] and those with concise representations using schemes in [7, 11, 1].

Due to space constraints, we refer to the long version of this paper [6] for more details.

2   Preliminaries

We represent the profit distribution problem as a *cooperative game* (N, v) where N is the set of agents and $v : 2^N \to \mathbb{R}$ is the *characteristic function* that assigns

---

[2] While items and bins separate and bins model linear constraints in knapsack budgeted games, both items and bins are treated as agents and the goal is to share profit among them in a fair way in bin-packing games.

a value to each subset of agents, with $v(\emptyset) = 0$. We also call v the *value function* and use both characteristic and value functions interchangeably. For a subset of agents $S \subseteq N$, we interpret $v(S)$ as the value that these agents can generate collectively; $v(N)$ is the total value that the whole group generates.

The *Shapley value* [21] is a solution concept based on marginal contributions that divides the total value $v(N)$ into individual shares $\phi_1, \ldots, \phi_{|N|}$ satisfying an intuitive notion of fairness. For $i \in N$ and $S \subseteq N \setminus \{i\}$, we define agent i's *marginal contribution to S* to be $v(S \cup \{i\}) - v(S)$. The Shapley value is the unique profit distribution solution that satisfies the following properties:

1. (Efficiency) $\sum_{i \in N} \phi_i(v) = v(N)$;
2. (Symmetry) If $v(S \cup \{i\}) - v(S) = v(S \cup \{j\}) - v(S)$ for all $S \subseteq N \setminus \{i, j\}$, then $\phi_i(v) = \phi_j(v)$;
3. (Null Player) If $v(S \cup \{i\}) - v(S) = 0$ for all $S \subseteq N \setminus \{i\}$, then $\phi_i(v) = 0$;
4. (Linearity) For any two cooperative games (N, v) and (N, w) and their combined game $(N, v + w)$, $\phi_i(v) + \phi_i(w) = \phi_i(v + w)$ for all $i \in N$.

The Shapley value for each agent i is computed as

$$\phi_i(v) = \sum_{S \subseteq N \setminus \{i\}} \frac{|S|!(|N| - |S| - 1)!}{|N|!} (v(S \cup \{i\}) - v(S)). \tag{1}$$

Note the Shapley value is a weighted average of agent i's marginal contributions. Equivalently, it can also be computed as $\phi_i(v) = \frac{1}{|N|!} \sum_{\pi \in \Pi} v(P_\pi^i \cup \{i\}) - v(P_\pi^i)$, where Π is the set of all $|N|!$ permutations of the agents and P_π^i is the set of agents preceding agent i in the order represented by permutation π.

There are two sources of computational complexity in the Shapley value: an exponential number of terms in the summation and individual evaluations of the characteristic function v. Directly applying the above equations leads to a naïve algorithm with running time at least exponential in the number of agents, $\Omega(2^{|N|})$; furthermore, each individual evaluation of v can be expensive.

3   Knapsack Budgeted Games

A *knapsack budgeted game* (N, v) is a cooperative game with the alternative representation given by a nonnegative integer tuple $(\{(l_1, w_1), \ldots, (l_{|N|}, w_{|N|})\}, l_{\text{bin}})$ such that $v(S) = \max_{S' \subseteq S : l(S') \leq l_{\text{bin}}} w(S')$ for all $S \subseteq N$, where $l(S') = \sum_{k \in S'} l_k$ and $w(S') = \sum_{k \in S'} w_k$. Each agent i is described by (l_i, w_i) where l_i and w_i are the agent's length and weight, respectively. The variable l_{bin} is the bin size that restricts which set of agents can directly determine the value function v. For a set of agents S, the value $v(S)$ is determined by solving an optimization problem where the total value of selected agents, possibly a strict subset of S, is optimized subject to a budget constraint; the other unselected agents do not contribute explicitly. Note the similarities with the classical knapsack problem in which the objective is to find the maximum total value of items that can be packed into a fixed size bin.

Knapsack budgeted games are useful when the characteristic function v of a cooperative game can be modeled as the objective value of an optimization problem subject to linear constraints. In this paper, we only consider the games with a single linear constraint, but our results extend to knapsack budgeted games with multiple linear constraints. In a knapsack budgeted game with multiple budget constraints, each agent is associated with a length vector $l = (l^1, \ldots, l^d)$ and a weight and there is a budget constraint on each coordinate, i.e., $l^1_{\text{bin}}, \ldots, l^d_{\text{bin}}$, assuming d budget constraints.

For an application, we can use knapsack budgeted games and the Shapley value to model value division in a sport team. We would like to give out bonuses proportional to the Shapley value solution. Assume each player i is associated with a skill level w_i and, in a game of the sport, at most B players from each team can play. We model the value of the team as the total aggregate skill level of its best B players, since they usually start and play the majority of the games. Then, this is a knapsack budgeted game with skill levels as weights, unit lengths, and $l_{\text{bin}} = B$. Note the Shapley value of a player not in the top B may be positive. Since he is still contributing to the team as a reserve player and might be one of the top B players in a subset of the team, say available players in an event of injury, he should be compensated accordingly.

In the following sections, we assume that the knapsack budgeted game (N, v) has the representation $(\{(l_1, w_1), \ldots, (l_{|N|}, w_{|N|})\}, l_{\text{bin}})$. We define $w_{\max} = \lceil l_{\text{bin}} \cdot \max_i w_i/l_i \rceil$, which is an upper bound on the value $v(N)$. We use shorthand notations $l(S) = \sum_{k \in S} l_k$ and $w(S) = \sum_{k \in S} w_k$ for any subset S. The set of agents are ordered and labeled with $1, \ldots, |N|$. For a set of agents X and two integers a and b, we use $X_{a,b}$ to denote the subset $\{i \in X : a \leq i \leq b\}$. To avoid degenerate cases, we further assume $0 < l_i \leq l_{\text{bin}}$ for all i. We use the indicator function Id that equals to 1 if all the input conditions hold, or 0 otherwise.

4   The Shapley Value in Knapsack Budgeted Games

We present a hardness result, an algorithm for computing the Shapley value exactly, and a deterministic approximation scheme that approximates within an additive error.

4.1   Exact Computation

By the NP-completeness of the classical knapsack problem and the efficiency property of the Shapley value, it follows that (see [6] for details):

Theorem 1. *The problem of computing the Shapley value in the knapsack budgeted games is NP-hard.*

While a polynomial time algorithm for computing the Shapley value may or may not exist, the naïve exponential time algorithm is too slow when $|N|$ is large. When $|N|$ is sufficiently large, especially when $|N| \gg l_{\text{bin}}$, we show that a faster algorithm exists:

Theorem 2. *In the knapsack budgeted games, the Shapley value can be computed in time $O(l_{bin}(w_{max} + 1)^{l_{bin}+1}|N|^2)$ for each agent.*

To prove Theorem 2, we associate each subset $S \subseteq N$ with a vector from a finite-sized vector space that completely determines an agent's marginal contribution to S. If the cardinality of the vector space is small and the partitions of the $2^{|N|}$ subsets corresponding to the vectors can be found efficiently, we can evaluate v once for each vector instead of once for each subset, reducing the overall computation time. Note that the well-known dynamic programming algorithm, call it $\mathcal{A}$, for the classical knapsack problem can be used to compute v; for a given S, the algorithm iteratively updates an integer array of length $l_{bin} + 1$ holding the optimal values for the sub-problems with smaller bin sizes and returns a final value determined by the array at termination.[3] We associate with each subset S the final state of the array when $\mathcal{A}$ runs on S and determine the cardinalities of resulting partitions using a dynamic program, different but related to $\mathcal{A}$; the dynamic program counts the number of optimal solutions to the sub-problems grouped by objective value while $\mathcal{A}$ simply computes the optimal solutions to the sub-problems.

We use the following lemma to prove Theorem 2; it shows that if the set of possible marginal contribution values for agent i is small, then we can reduce the number of evaluations of v by grouping subsets of $N \setminus \{i\}$ by marginal contribution value and evaluating v once for each group (see [6] for a proof).

Lemma 1. *Assume there exist positive integers p_i and partition functions P_i : $2^{N\setminus\{i\}} \to \{1, \ldots, p_i\}$, for $i = 1, \ldots, |N|$, such that if $P_i(S) = P_i(S')$ for two different $S, S' \subseteq N \setminus \{i\}$, then $v(S \cup \{i\}) - v(S) = v(S' \cup \{i\}) - v(S')$. Let $m_i(p)$ be agent i's marginal contribution to S for all S satisfying $P_i(S) = p$, and $c(i, s, p) = \#\{S \subseteq N \setminus \{i\} : |S| = s, P_i(S) = p\}$ for $i \in N$, $0 \leq s \leq |N| - 1$, and $1 \leq p \leq p_i$. Then, the Shapley value for agent i can be computed as*

$$\phi_i = \sum_{p=1}^{p_i} \sum_{s=0}^{|N|-1} c(i, s, p) \frac{s!(|N|-s-1)!}{|N|!} m_i(p)$$

in time $O(p_{max}(t + q)|N|)$, where $p_{max} = \max_i p_i$, t is an upper bound on the computation time of the coefficients c, and q is the evaluation time of v.

We now prove Theorem 2 by applying Lemma 1:

Proof. (of Theorem 2) We compute the Shapley value for some fixed agent i. We define $V_{A,b} = \max_{S' \subseteq A : l(S') \leq b} w(S')$, for $A \subseteq N$ and $0 \leq b \leq l_{bin}$, and vector $\mathbf{V}_S = (V_{S,0}, \ldots, V_{S,l_{bin}})$, for subsets $S \subseteq N$. Let $\mathcal{V}$ be the finite vector space $\{0, \ldots, w_{max}\}^{l_{bin}+1}$ that contains vectors $\mathbf{V}_S$. We use the 0-based index to indicate coordinates of a vector in $\mathcal{V}$; so, $v(S) = V_{S,l_{bin}} = \mathbf{V}_S(l_{bin})$ for all S. Given $\mathbf{V}_S$, agent i's marginal contribution to S can be computed in constant time

---

[3] Assume the agents in S are labeled $1, \ldots, |S|$ for simplicity. For $1 \leq j \leq |S|$, we define $c(j, b) = \max_{S' \subseteq S_{1,j} : l(S') \leq b} w(S')$. It has the recurrence relation $c(j, b) = \max\{c(j - 1, b), c(j - 1, b - l_j) + w_j\}$. We compute $c(j, b)$'s and, hence, $v(S) = c(|S|, l_{bin})$ in $O(|S|l_{bin})$ time.

as $v(S \cup \{i\}) - v(S) = \max\{\mathbf{V}_S(l_{\text{bin}} - l_i) + w_i - \mathbf{V}_S(l_{\text{bin}}), 0\}$. Let this expression be defined more generally as $m_i(\mathbf{v}) = \max\{\mathbf{v}(l_{\text{bin}} - l_i) + w_i - \mathbf{v}(l_{\text{bin}}), 0\}$ for $\mathbf{v} \in \mathcal{V}$.

We partition $2^{N \setminus \{i\}}$ by the pair $(|S|, \mathbf{V}_S)$ so that for each possible $(s, \mathbf{v})$ pair, all subsets S satisfying $|S| = s$ and $\mathbf{V}_S = \mathbf{v}$ are grouped together. Clearly, the marginal contribution of agent i is the same within each partition. To compute the cardinality of each partition, we use dynamic programming. Let $N' = N \setminus \{i\}$, ordered and relabeled $1, \ldots, |N| - 1$. For $0 \leq j \leq |N| - 1$, $0 \leq s \leq j$, and $\mathbf{v} \in \mathcal{V}$, we define $\hat{c}(j, s, \mathbf{v}) = \#\{S \subseteq N'_{1,j} : |S| = s, \mathbf{V}_S = \mathbf{v}\}$. Note $\hat{c}$ has the recurrence relation

$$\hat{c}(j, s, \mathbf{v}) = \hat{c}(j - 1, s, \mathbf{v}) + \sum_{\mathbf{u}: \text{UPDATE}(\mathbf{u}, l'_j, w'_j) = \mathbf{v}} \hat{c}(j - 1, s - 1, \mathbf{u}),$$

with the base case $\hat{c}(0, 0, \mathbf{0}) = 1$, where l'_j and w'_j correspond to the j-th agent in order in N' and UPDATE is an $O(l_{\text{bin}})$ algorithm that updates $\mathbf{u}$ with the additional agent: 1) Initialize $\mathbf{v} = \mathbf{u}$; 2) For $j = l'_j, \ldots, l_{\text{bin}}$, $\mathbf{v}(j) = \max\{\mathbf{v}(j), \mathbf{u}(j - l'_j) + w'_j\}$; and 3) Return $\mathbf{v}$.

Using the recurrence relation, we compute $\hat{c}(j, s, \mathbf{v})$ for all j, s, and $\mathbf{v}$ in time $O(l_{\text{bin}}(w_{\text{max}} + 1)^{l_{\text{bin}}+1}|N|^2)$. By Lemma 1,

$$\phi_i = \sum_{\mathbf{v} \in \mathcal{V}} \sum_{s=0}^{|N|-1} \hat{c}(|N| - 1, s, \mathbf{v}) \frac{s!(|N|-s-1)!}{|N|!} m_i(\mathbf{v}),$$

and the Shapley value can be calculated in time $O((w_{\text{max}} + 1)^{l_{\text{bin}}+1}|N|)$ using the precomputed values of $\hat{c}$. The computation of $\hat{c}$ dominates the application of the Shapley value equation, and the overall running time is $O(l_{\text{bin}}(w_{\text{max}} + 1)^{l_{\text{bin}}+1}|N|^2)$ per agent. □

4.2   Additive Approximation

Similar to the fully polynomial time approximation scheme for the classical knapsack problem (see [22]), we show an approximation scheme for the Shapley value by rounding down the weights w_i's and computing the Shapley value of the cooperative game (N, v') where v' is an approximation of v. Our technique of computing the Shapley value by approximating the characteristic function v is deterministic and does not require concentration inequalities like the standard statistical methods of sampling and normal distribution techniques in [4, 10].

The following lemma formalizes how an approximation of the characteristic function v leads to an additive error in the Shapley value computation (see [6] for a proof):

Lemma 2. *If v' is an α-additive approximation of v, i.e., $v'(S) \leq v(S) \leq v'(S) + \alpha$ for all $S \subseteq N$, then the Shapley value ϕ'_i computed with respect to v' is within an α-additive error of the Shapley value ϕ_i computed with respect to v, for all i.*

When w_{max} is sufficiently larger than l_{bin}, the approximation scheme's running time is faster than that of the exact algorithm of Theorem 2:

Theorem 3. *In the knapsack budgeted games, the Shapley value can be computed within an $\epsilon w_{\max}$-additive error in $O((l_{\mathrm{bin}}^2/\epsilon+1)^{l_{\mathrm{bin}}+1}|N|^2)$ for each agent, where $\epsilon > 0$.*[4]

Proof. We construct an approximate characteristic function v' of v as follows. Let $\epsilon > 0$ and $k = \epsilon w_{\max}/l_{\mathrm{bin}}$. Note that when $l_{\mathrm{bin}}^2/\epsilon < w_{\max}$, $k > 1$. For each agent i, let the rounded weight w_i' be $\lfloor \frac{w_i}{k} \rfloor$. The lengths do not change. To compute $v'(S)$, we compute the optimal set $S' \subseteq S$, using dynamic programming, with respect to the rounded weights $w_1', \ldots, w_{|N|}'$ and let $v'(S) = k \sum_{i \in S'} w_i'$. In other words, $v'(S) = k \cdot \max_{S' \subseteq S: l(S') \leq l_{\mathrm{bin}}} w'(S)$ for all $S \subseteq N$, where we use the shorthand notation $w'(S) = \sum_{k \in S} w_k'$.

We show $v(S) \geq v'(S) \geq v(S) - \epsilon w_{\max}$, for all $S \subseteq N$. Let S be a subset and $T_O, T' \subseteq S$ be the optimal subsets using original and rounded weights, respectively, such that $v(S) = w(T_O)$ and $v'(S) = k \cdot w'(T')$. Note that both optimal sets have cardinality at most l_{bin}. Because of rounding down, $w_i - kw_i' \leq k$ and $\sum_{j \in T_O} w_j - k\sum_{j \in T_O} w_j' \leq kl_{\mathrm{bin}}$. Since T' is optimal with respect to the rounded weights, $\sum_{j \in T'} w_j' \geq \sum_{j \in T_O} w_j'$. Then, $v'(S) = k\sum_{j \in T'} w_j' \geq k\sum_{j \in T_O} w_j' \geq \sum_{j \in T_O} w_j - kl_{\mathrm{bin}} = v(S) - \epsilon w_{\max}$. Since $w_i \geq kw_i'$ for all i, $v(S) = w(T_O) \geq w(T') \geq kw'(T') = v'(S)$. Hence, v' is an $\epsilon w_{\max}$-additive approximation of v. Then, the Shapley value computed with respect to v' is within $\epsilon w_{\max}$ of the original Shapley value by Lemma 2.

We now compute the Shapley value with respect to v'. For $A \subseteq N, 0 \leq b \leq l_{\mathrm{bin}}$, we define $V_{A,b}' = \max_{S' \subseteq A: l(S') \leq b} w'(S')$. For a subset $S \subseteq N$, we define vector $\mathbf{V}_S' = (V_{S,0}', \ldots, V_{S,l_{\mathrm{bin}}}')$. Note that $w_i' = \lfloor \frac{w_i}{k} \rfloor \leq \lfloor \frac{w_{\max}}{k} \rfloor = \lfloor \frac{l_{\mathrm{bin}}}{\epsilon} \rfloor$. Then, we can upper bound $w'(S) \leq l_{\mathrm{bin}} \lfloor \frac{l_{\mathrm{bin}}}{\epsilon} \rfloor$, for all S. Let $\mathcal{V}' = \{0, \ldots, l_{\mathrm{bin}} \lfloor \frac{l_{\mathrm{bin}}}{\epsilon} \rfloor\}^{l_{\mathrm{bin}}+1}$ that vectors $\mathbf{V}_S'$ are contained in. Note $v'(S) = k \cdot \mathbf{V}_S'(l_{\mathrm{bin}})$ for all S. From vector $\mathbf{V}_S'$, we can compute agent i's marginal contribution to S with respect to v' in constant time: $v'(S \cup \{i\}) - v'(S) = k \cdot \max\{\mathbf{V}_S'(l_{\mathrm{bin}} - l_i) + w_i' - \mathbf{V}_S'(l_{\mathrm{bin}}), 0\}$.

From here, we follow the proof of Theorem 2. We compute the analogue of $\hat{c}$ in $O((l_{\mathrm{bin}}^2/\epsilon + 1)^{l_{\mathrm{bin}}+1}|N|^2)$, and this is the dominating term in the Shapley value computation with respect to v'. $\qquad\square$

5   Greedy Knapsack Budgeted Games

Motivated by the approximation scheme in Theorem 3, we investigate *greedy knapsack budgeted games*, a variant of knapsack budgeted games, and show the Shapley value in these games can be computed in pseudo-polynomial time. A greedy knapsack budgeted game has the same representation as the knapsack budgeted games, but its characteristic function is computed by a 2-approximation heuristic for the classical knapsack problem. We defer proofs to [6].

---

[4] For agent i, its Shapley value ϕ_i is clearly in $[0, w_{\max}]$. Using the approximation scheme, we can compute ϕ_i within $\frac{1}{7}w_{\max}$ for instance. As long as $\epsilon > l_{\mathrm{bin}}^2/w_{\max}$, the approximation scheme has a faster running time than the exact algorithm in Theorem 2; this observation about ϵ is also true for the fully polynomial time approximation scheme for the classical knapsack problem (see [22]).

Algorithm 1. Greedy Heuristic $\mathcal{A}'(S, l_{\text{bin}})$

1: Let $a = \text{argmax}_{k \in S} \, w_k$.
2: Select agents in S in decreasing order of $\frac{w_i}{l_i}$ and stop when the next agent does not fit into the bin of size l_{bin}; let S' be the selected agents.
3: Return S' if $w(S') \geq w_a$, or $\{a\}$ otherwise.

Theorem 4. *In the greedy knapsack budgeted games (N, v) with $v(S) = \mathcal{A}'(S, l_{\text{bin}})$ for all S, the Shapley value can be computed in $O(l_{\text{bin}}{}^5 w_{\text{max}}{}^5 |N|^8)$ for each agent, where the greedy heuristic $\mathcal{A}'(S, l_{\text{bin}})$ is computed as in Algorithm 1.*

While motivated by knapsack budgeted games, we use a different proof technique using the following lemma to prove Theorem 4. It generalizes the observation that in the simple cooperative game (N, v) where the agents have weights $w_1, \ldots, w_{|N|}$ and the characteristic function v is additive, i.e., $v(S) = \sum_{k \in S} w_k$, the Shapley value ϕ_i is exactly w_i for all i.

Lemma 3. *Assume that the cooperative game (N, v) has a representation (M, w, A) where M is a set, $w : M \to \mathbb{R}$ is a weight function, and $A : 2^N \to 2^M$ is a mapping such that $v(S) = \sum_{e \in A(S)} w(e), \forall S \subseteq N$. Let $c_+(i, s, e) = \#\{S \subseteq N \setminus \{i\} : |S| = s, e \in A(S \cup \{i\})\}$ and $c_-(i, s, e) = \#\{S \subseteq N \setminus \{i\} : |S| = s, e \in A(S)\}$, for $i \in N$, $e \in M$, and $0 \leq s \leq |N| - 1$. Then, the Shapley value for agent i can be computed as*

$$\phi_i = \sum_{e \in M} \sum_{s=0}^{|N|-1} (c_+(i, s, e) - c_-(i, s, e)) \frac{s!(|N|-s-1)!}{|N|!} w(e).$$

in time $O(t|M||N|)$ where t is an upper bound on the computation time of the coefficients c_+ and c_-.

6   Generalizations

We present generalizations of our proof techniques and propose an unifying framework that captures a broad class of cooperative games in which computing the Shapley value is tractable, including many known classes of cooperative games in [8, 15, 17] and those with concise representations using schemes in [7, 11, 1]. The main idea is that the problem of computing the Shapley value reduces to that of finding an efficient algorithm for the cooperative game's characteristic function. More precisely, if a cooperative game (N, v) is described in terms of an alternative representation I and an algorithm A with low time and space complexities that computes v, formalized in terms of *decomposition*, then we can compute the Shapley value efficiently. To illustrate the generalizations' applicability, we use them to give examples of cooperative games in which the Shapley value can be computed efficiently.

For each generalization, we consider two cases: the order-agnostic case in which A processes agents in an arbitrary order, and the order-specific case in which A processes in a specific order, like the greedy heuristic in Theorem 4.

Algorithm 2. Computing $A(I, S)$ with a decomposition $(A_{\text{setup}}, A_{\text{update}}, A_{\text{final}})$

1: $A_{\text{setup}}(I)$ outputs I', $\mathbf{x}$
2: **for** $i \in S$ **do**
3:     $\mathbf{x} = A_{\text{update}}(I', i, \mathbf{x})$
4: **end for**
5: Return $A_{\text{final}}(I', \mathbf{x})$

Definition 1. *Assume a cooperative game (N, v) has an alternative representation I and a deterministic algorithm A such that $v(S) = A(I, S)$ for all $S \subseteq N$. Algorithm A has a decomposition $(A_{\text{setup}}, A_{\text{update}}, A_{\text{final}})$ if $A(I, S)$ can be computed as in Algorithm 2. We denote the the running times of the sub-algorithms of the decomposition t_{setup}, t_{update} and t_{final}, respectively.*

In Algorithm 2, $\mathbf{x} = (x_1, x_2, \ldots)$ is a vector of variables that is initialized to some values independent of subset S and determines the algorithm A's final return value. I' is an auxiliary data structure or states that only depend on the representation I and is used in subsequent steps for ease of computation; I' can be simply I if no such preprocessing is necessary. Theorem 2 can be generalized as follows:

Theorem 5. *Assume a cooperative game (N, v) has an alternative representation I and a deterministic algorithm A that computes v. If A has a decomposition $(A_{\text{setup}}, A_{\text{update}}, A_{\text{final}})$ such that at most $n(I)$ variables $\mathbf{x}$ are used with each taking at most $m(I)$ possible values as S ranges over all subsets of N, then the Shapley value can be computed in $O(t_{\text{setup}} + t_{\text{update}} m^n |N|^2 + t_{\text{final}} m^n |N|)$ for each agent. In order-specific cases, for Steps 2-4 of Algorithm 2, the running time is $O(t_{\text{setup}} + t_{\text{update}} m^{2n} |N|^2 + t_{\text{final}} m^{2n} |N|)$. Note that n and m are representation-dependent numbers and the argument I has been omitted.*

Proof. Given the alternative representation I, we compute the Shapley value of agent i. We associate $v(S)$ with the final values, $\mathbf{x}_{S,\text{final}}$, of $n(I)$ variables $\mathbf{x}$ in $A(I, S)$, for all $S \subseteq N \setminus \{i\}$. We partition $2^{N \setminus \{i\}}$ by the pair $(|S|, \mathbf{x}_{S,\text{final}})$ into at most $m^n |N|$ partitions, omitting the argument I from n and m. Let $\mathcal{X}$ be the set of all possible final values of the variables $\mathbf{x}$; note that its cardinality is at most m^n. We compute the cardinalities of the partitions using dynamic programming. Let $N' = N \setminus \{i\}$, ordered and relabeled $1, \ldots, |N| - 1$, and $i = |N|$. For $0 \leq j \leq |N| - 1$, $0 \leq s \leq j$, and $\mathbf{v} \in \mathcal{X}$, we define $\hat{c}(j, s, \mathbf{v}) = \#\{S \subseteq N'_{1,j} : |S| = s, \mathbf{x}_{S,\text{final}} = \mathbf{v}\}$. Then, $\hat{c}$ has the recurrence relation

$$\hat{c}(j, s, \mathbf{v}) = \hat{c}(j - 1, s, \mathbf{v}) + \sum_{\mathbf{u}: A_{\text{update}}(I', j, \mathbf{u}) = \mathbf{v}} \hat{c}(j - 1, s - 1, \mathbf{u})$$

with the base case $\hat{c}(0, 0, \mathbf{s}) = 1$, where $\mathbf{s}$ is the initial states of variables $\mathbf{x}$. Using A_{setup}, we compute I' and the initial values $\mathbf{s}$ in $O(t_{\text{setup}})$. Using the recurrence relation and A_{update}, we compute $\hat{c}(j, s, \mathbf{v})$ for all j, s, and $\mathbf{v}$ in time $O(t_{\text{update}} m^n |N|^2)$. Note that for a subset $S \subseteq N \setminus \{i\}$, we can compute agent i's marginal contribution to S, i.e., $v(S \cup \{i\}) - v(S)$, in $O(t_{\text{update}} + t_{\text{final}})$ from the

---

Algorithm 3. Computing $A(S)$ with a per-element decomposition $\{(A^e_{\text{setup}}, A^e_{\text{update}}, A^e_{\text{final}})\}_{e \in M}$

1: Initialize $S' = \emptyset$
2: **for** $e \in M$ **do**
3:     $A^e_{\text{setup}}(M, w)$ outputs I', $\mathbf{x}$
4:     For $i \in S$: $\mathbf{x} = A^e_{\text{update}}(I', i, \mathbf{x})$
5:     If $A_{\text{final}}(I', \mathbf{x}) = 1$, $S' = S' \cup \{e\}$
6: **end for**
7: Return S'

---

final values of $\mathbf{x}$ associated with the partition that S belongs to, i.e., $\mathbf{x}_{S,\text{final}}$; let $m_i(\mathbf{v})$ be the agent i's marginal contribution to subsets associated with $\mathbf{v} \in \mathcal{X}$. By Lemma 1,

$$\phi_i = \sum_{\mathbf{v} \in \mathcal{X}} \sum_{s=0}^{|N|-1} \hat{c}(|N| - 1, s, \mathbf{v}) \frac{s!(|N|-s-1)!}{|N|!} m_i(\mathbf{v}),$$

and the Shapley value can be calculated in time $O((t_{\text{update}} + t_{\text{final}})m^n|N|)$ using the precomputed values of $\hat{c}$. The overall running time is $O(t_{\text{setup}} + t_{\text{update}}m^n|N|^2 + (t_{\text{update}} + t_{\text{final}})m^n|N|)$.

Now assume that the agents have to be processed in a specific order determined by representation I. For a given S and its final values $\mathbf{x}_{S,\text{final}}$, we cannot compute $\mathbf{x}_{S \cup \{i\},\text{final}}$ as $\mathcal{A}_{\text{update}}(I', i, \mathbf{x}_{S,\text{final}})$ and compute agent i's marginal contribution to S, because it would violate the order if some agents in S have to be processed after i. Instead, we associate S with the final values $\mathbf{x}_{S,\text{final}}$ and $\mathbf{x}_{S \cup \{i\},\text{final}}$ and partition $2^{N \setminus \{i\}}$ by the tuple $(|S|, \mathbf{x}_{S,\text{final}}, \mathbf{x}_{S \cup \{i\},\text{final}})$ into at most $m^{2n}|N|$ partitions, omitting the argument I. Following the same argument as before, we get the running time $O(t_{\text{setup}} + t_{\text{update}}m^{2n}|N|^2 + t_{\text{final}}m^{2n}|N|)$. □

The following definition and theorem generalize Theorem 4 and can also be considered a specialization of Theorem 5. See [6] for proof details.

Definition 2. *Assume a cooperative game (N, v) has an alternative representation (M, w, A) as described in Lemma 3 such that $v(S) = \sum_{e \in A(S)} w(e)$, for all $S \subseteq N$. Algorithm A has a* per-element decomposition $(A^e_{\text{setup}}, A^e_{\text{update}}, A^e_{\text{final}})$ *for all $e \in M$ if $A(S)$ can be computed as in Algorithm 3. We denote the upper bounds, over all $e \in M$, on running times of the sub-algorithms of the per-element decomposition t_{setup}, t_{update} and t_{final}, respectively.*

Theorem 6. *Assume a cooperative game (N, v) has an alternative representation (M, w, A), as given in Lemma 3. If A has a per-element decomposition $(A^e_{\text{setup}}, A^e_{\text{update}}, A^e_{\text{final}})$ for all $e \in M$ such that at most $n(M, w)$ variables $\mathbf{x}$ are used with each taking at most $m(M, w)$ possible values as S ranges over all subsets of N and e over M, the Shapley value can be computed in $O((t_{\text{setup}} + t_{\text{update}}m^n|N|^2 + t_{\text{final}}m^n|N|)|M|)$ for each agent. In order-specific cases, for Step 4 of Algorithm 3, the running time is $O((t_{\text{setup}} + t_{\text{update}}m^{2n}|N|^2 + t_{\text{final}}m^{2n}|N|)|M|)$. Note that n and m are representation-dependent numbers and the argument (M, w) has been omitted.*

The above definitions apply broadly and suggest the following framework for cooperative games that we term *algorithmic representation*; we represent each cooperative game (N, v) in terms of an alternative representation I and an accompanying algorithm A that computes v. As we can represent any cooperative game by a table with exponentially many entries for v values and a simple lookup algorithm, the algorithmic representation always exist. The main challenge is to determine an "efficient" algorithmic representation for cooperative games in general. The algorithmic representation framework subsumes the concise representation schemes in [7, 11, 1] as these assume specific structures on the alternative representation I. It also captures the notion of classes of cooperative games for we can represent a class of cooperative games by a set of alternative representations corresponding to those games in the class. In this framework, Theorems 5 and 6 show that if the algorithms for computing v satisfy the decomposability properties outlined in Definitions 1 and 2, then the Shapley value can be computed efficiently as long as these algorithms are efficient.

Using the generalizations, we can reproduce many previous results on efficient computation of the Shapley value up to a (pseudo) polynomial factor in the running time.[5] As concrete examples, we prove several such results (and a new one on the Data Mining Problem in Section 1). We defer proofs to [6]:

Corollary 1. *(Weighted Majority Games) Assume a cooperative game (N, v) has a representation given by $|N| + 1$ nonnegative integers $q, w_1, \ldots, w_{|N|}$ such that $v(S)$ is 1 if $\sum_{i \in S} w_i \geq q$, or 0 otherwise. Then, the Shapley value can be computed in pseudo-polynomial time $O(q|N|^2)$ for each agent. (Identical to [15])*

Corollary 2. *(MC-net Representation) Assume a cooperative game (N, v) has a marginal-contribution (MC) net representation with boolean rules $R = \{r_1, \ldots, r_m\}$ with each r_i having value v_i and of the form $(p_1 \wedge \ldots \wedge p_a \wedge \neg n_1 \wedge \ldots \wedge \neg n_b)$ such that $v(S) = \sum_{r_i : S \, satisfies \, r_i} v_i$ for all $S \subseteq N$.[6] Then, the Shapley value can be computed in $O(m|N|^2(\max_i |r_i|)^2)$ for each agent, where $|r|$ is the number of literals in rule r. (Compare to $O(m \max_i |r_i|)$, linear time in the representation size, in [11])*

Corollary 3. *(Multi-Issue Representation) Assume a cooperative game (N, v) has a multi-issue representation with subsets $C_1, \ldots, C_t \subseteq N$ and characteristic functions $v_i : 2^{C_i} \to \mathbb{R}$ for all i such that $v(S) = \sum_{i=1}^{t} v_i(S \cap C_i)$ for all $S \subseteq N$. Then, the Shapley value can be computed in $O(t 2^{\max_i |C_i|} |N|^2 \max_i |C_i|)$ for each agent. (Compare to $O(t 2^{\max_i |C_i|})$ in [7])*

Corollary 4. *(Data Mining Problem) Assume a cooperative game (N, v) has a representation given by $|N| + 1$ nonnegative integers $k, w_1, \ldots, w_{|N|}$ such that*

---

[5] The slightly slower running times can be attributed to our generalizations' inability to derive closed form expressions on a game-by-game basis; for instance, evaluating the sum $\sum_{i=1}^{n} i$ in $O(n)$ instead of using the identity $\frac{n(n+1)}{2} = \sum_{i=1}^{n} i$ in $O(1)$. As generalizations apply in a black-box manner, we argue the loss in running time is reasonable for (pseudo) polynomial time computation.

[6] If $r = (1 \wedge 2 \wedge \neg 3)$, then $S = \{1, 2\}$ satisfies r, but $S = \{1, 3\}$ does not.

$v(S) = \max_{S' \subseteq S : |S'| \leq k} w(S')$. *Then, the Shapley value can be computed in polynomial time* $O(|N|^3)$ *for each agent.* (*This is our own problem.*)

7   Further Discussion

We have introduced a class of cooperative games called budgeted games and investigated the computational complexity of the Shapley value in the knapsack version, knapsack budgeted games, in particular. We presented exact and approximation algorithms for knapsack budgeted games and a pseudo-polynomial time algorithm for closely related greedy knapsack budgeted games. These algorithms have only polynomial dependence on $|N|$, the number of agents, and are more efficient than the naïve exponential time algorithm when $|N|$ is large. Our results extend to knapsack budgeted games with multiple budget constraints. We believe knapsack budgeted games are useful in modeling value division problems in real-life scenarios and our algorithms applicable; for example, when finding a profit distribution solution for a joint venture of, say, 100-plus agents.

We also provided generalizations and proposed the algorithmic representation framework in which we represent each cooperative game in terms of an alternative representation and an accompanying algorithm that computes the underlying value function. We formalized efficient algorithmic representations and used the generalizations to show that computing the Shapley value in those cooperative games with efficient algorithmic representations can be done efficiently. To demonstrate the generalizations' applicability, we proved old and new results on the efficient computation of the Shapley value.

We note that further improvement to our algorithmic results might be possible. While the exact algorithm in Theorem 2 has polynomial time dependence on $|N|$, it is not a pseudo-polynomial time algorithm and the hardness result in Theorem 1 does not preclude the existence of a polynomial time algorithm for the Shapley value computation in the restricted case of $|N| \gg l_{\mathrm{bin}}$.[7] Similarly, we do not know if the results in Theorems 3 and 4 are the best possible. We pose these as open problems.

Finally, we believe our techniques can have applications beyond the games considered in this paper and to other economic concepts such as the Banzhaf index. It would be also interesting to investigate the computational complexity of the Shapley value in other kinds of budgeted games.

Acknowledgements. We would like to thank Vasilis Gkatzelis for his helpful comments.

---

[7] In this case, the $O(|N| l_{\mathrm{bin}})$ dynamic programming time algorithm for the classical knapsack problem algorithm in Footnote 3 becomes an $O(|N|^2)$ algorithm, and the classical knapsack problem can be solved in polynomial time.

References

[1] Aadithya, K.V., Michalak, T.P., Jennings, N.R.: Representation of coalitional games with algebraic decision diagrams. In: AAMAS 2011 (2011)

[2] Aziz, H., Sorensen, T.B.: Path coalitional games. In: CoopMAS 2011 (2011)

[3] Bachrach, Y., Lev, O., Lovett, S., Rosenschein, J.S., Zadimoghaddam, M.: Cooperative weakest link games. In: AAMAS 2014 (to appear, 2014)

[4] Bachrach, Y., Markakis, E., Resnick, E., Procaccia, A.D., Rosenschein, J.S., Saberi, A.: Approximating power indices: Theoretical and empirical analysis. In: Autonomous Agents and Multi-Agent Systems (March 2010)

[5] Bachrach, Y., Porat, E.: Path disruption games. In: AAMAS 2010 (2010)

[6] Bhagat, S., Kim, A., Muthukrishnan, S., Weinsberg, U.: The shapley value in knapsack budgeted games. arXiv:1409.5200 (2014)

[7] Conitzer, V., Sandholm, T.: Computing shapley values, manipulating value division schemes, and checking core membership in multi-issue domains. In: AAAI 2004 (2004)

[8] Deng, X., Papadimitriou, C.H.: On the complexity of cooperative solution concepts. Mathematics of Operations Research 19(2) (1994)

[9] Faigle, U., Kern, W.: On some approximately balanced combinatorial cooperative games. Zeitschrift für Operations Research 38(2) (1993)

[10] Fatima, S.S., Wooldridge, M., Jennings, N.R.: A linear approximation method for the shapley value. Artificial Intelligence 172(14) (2008)

[11] Ieong, S., Shoham, Y.: Marginal contribution nets: A compact representation scheme for coalitional games. In: EC 2005 (2005)

[12] Ieong, S., Shoham, Y.: Multi-attribute coalitional games. In: EC 2006 (2006)

[13] Kuipers, J.: Bin packing games. Mathematical Methods of Operations Research 47(3) (1998)

[14] Ma, R.T., Chiu, D., Lui, J.C., Misra, V., Rubenstein, D.: Internet economics: The use of shapley value for isp settlement. In: CoNEXT 2007 (2007)

[15] Matsui, T., Matsui, Y.: A survey of algorithms for calculating power indices of weighted majority games. J. Oper. Res. Soc. Japan (2000)

[16] Matsui, Y., Matsui, T.: Np-completeness for calculating power indices of weighted majority games. Theoretical Computer Science (2001)

[17] Michalak, T.P., Aadithya, K.V., Szczepanski, P.L., Ravindran, B., Jennings, N.R.: Efficient computation of the shapley value for game-theoretic network centrality. J. Artif. Int. Res. (January 2013)

[18] Misra, V., Ioannidis, S., Chaintreau, A., Massoulié, L.: Incentivizing peer-assisted services: A fluid shapley value approach. In: SIGMETRICS 2010 (2010)

[19] Narayanam, R., Narahari, Y.: A shapley value-based approach to discover influential nodes in social networks. IEEE Transactions on Automation Science and Engineering 8(1), 130–147 (2011)

[20] Qiu, X.: Bin packing games. Master's thesis, University of Twente (2010)

[21] Shapley, L.S.: A value for n-person games. Contributions to the Theory of Games 2, 307–317 (1953)

[22] Vazirani, V.V.: Approximation Algorithms. Springer-Verlag New York, Inc., New York (2001)

Fast Convex Decomposition for Truthful Social Welfare Approximation

Dennis Kraft, Salman Fadaei, and Martin Bichler

Department of Informatics, TU München, Munich, Germany
{dennis.kraft,salman.fadaei,bichler}@in.tum.de

Abstract. Approximating the optimal social welfare while preserving truthfulness is a well studied problem in algorithmic mechanism design. Assuming that the social welfare of a given mechanism design problem can be optimized by an integer program whose integrality gap is at most α, Lavi and Swamy [1] propose a general approach to designing a randomized α-approximation mechanism which is truthful in expectation. Their method is based on decomposing an optimal solution for the relaxed linear program into a convex combination of integer solutions. Unfortunately, Lavi and Swamy's decomposition technique relies heavily on the ellipsoid method, which is notorious for its poor practical performance. To overcome this problem, we present an alternative decomposition technique which yields an $\alpha(1 + \epsilon)$ approximation and only requires a quadratic number of calls to an integrality gap verifier.

Keywords: Convex decomposition, Truthful in expectation, Mechanism design, Approximation algorithms.

1   Introduction

Optimizing the social welfare in the presence of self-interested players poses two main challenges to algorithmic mechanism design. On the one hand, the social welfare consists of the player's valuations for possible outcomes of the mechanism. However, since these valuations are private information, they can be misrepresented for personal advantage. To avoid strategic manipulation, which may harm the social welfare, it is important to encourage truthful participation. In mechanism design, this is achieved through additional payments which offer each player a monetary incentive to reveal his true valuation. Assuming that the mechanism returns an optimal outcome with respect to the reported valuations, the well known Vickrey, Clarke and Groves (VCG) principle [2–4] provides a general method to design payments such that each player maximizes his utility if he reports his valuation truthfully. On the other hand, even if the player's valuations are known, optimizing the social welfare is NP-hard for many combinatorial mechanism design problems. Since an exact optimization is intractable under these circumstances, the use of approximation algorithms becomes necessary. Unfortunately, VCG payments are generally not compatible with approximation algorithms.

T.-Y. Liu et al. (Eds.): WINE 2014, LNCS 8877, pp. 120–132, 2014.

To preserve truthfulness, so called maximal-in-range (MIR) approximation algorithms must be used [5]. This means there must exist a fixed subset of outcomes, such that the approximation algorithm performs optimally with respect to this subset. Given that the players are risk-neutral, the concept of MIR algorithms can be generalized to distributions over outcomes. Together with VCG payments, these maximal-in-distribution-range (MIDR) algorithms allow for the design of randomized approximation mechanisms such that each player maximizes his expected utility if he reveals his true valuation [6]. This property, which is slightly weaker than truthfulness in its deterministic sense, is also referred to as truthfulness in expectation.

A well-known method to convert general approximation algorithms which verify an integrality gap of α into MIDR algorithms is the linear programing approach of Lavi and Swamy [1]. Conceptually, their method is based on the observation that scaling down a packing polytope by its integrality gap yields a new polytope which is completely contained in the convex hull of the original polytope's integer points. Considering that the social welfare of many combinatorial mechanism design problems can be expressed naturally as an integer program, this scaled polytope corresponds to a set of distributions over the outcomes of the mechanism. Thus, by decomposing a scaled solution of the relaxed linear program into a convex combination of integer solutions, Lavi and Swamy obtain an α-approximation mechanism which is MIDR.

Algorithmically, Lavi and Swamy's work builds on a decomposition technique by Carr and Vempala [7], which uses a linear program to decompose the scaled relaxed solution. However, since this linear program might have an exponential number of variables, one for every outcome of the mechanism, it can not be solved directly. Instead, Carr and Vempala use the ellipsoid method in combination with an integrality gap verifier to identify a more practical, but still sufficient, subset of outcomes for the decomposition. Although this approach only requires a polynomial number of calls to the integrality gap verifier in theory, the ellipsoid method is notoriously inefficient in practice [8].

In this work, we propose an alternative decomposition technique which does not rely on the ellipsoid method and is general enough to substitute Carr and Vempala's [7] decomposition technique. The main component of our decomposition technique is an algorithm which is based on a simple geometric idea and computes a convex combination within an arbitrarily small distance ϵ to the scaled relaxed solution. However, since an exact decomposition is necessary to guarantee truthfulness, we slightly increase the scaling factor of the relaxed solution and apply a post-processing step to match the convex combination with the relaxed solution. Assuming that ϵ is positive and fixed, our technique yields an $\alpha(1 + \epsilon)$ approximation of the optimal social welfare but uses only a quadratic number of calls to the integrality gap verifier, with respect to the number of positive components in the relaxed solution vector.

It turns out that our method has interesting connections to an old algorithm of Von Neumann reproduced by Dantzig [9] [1]. At first sight, similarities in the

---

[1] We thank the anonymous referee of WINE 2014 who pointed us to this paper.

sampling and geometric techniques used in both algorithms can be observed. However, Von Neumann's algorithm may sample fractional points whereas our setting requires integral points. Due to these more involved constraints, a direct usage of Von Neumann's technique in our setting is impossible.

2   Setting

Integer programming is a powerful tool in combinatorial optimization. Using binary variables to indicate whether certain goods are allocated to a player, the outcomes of various NP-hard mechanism design problems, such as combinatorial auctions or generalized assignment problems [1, 10], can be modeled as integer points of an n-dimensional packing polytope $X \subseteq [0, 1]^n$.

Definition 1. *(Packing Polytope) Polytope X satisfies the packing property if all points y which are dominated by some point x from X are also contained in X*

$$\forall x, y \in \mathbb{R}_{\geq 0}^n : \ x \in X \wedge x \geq y \Rightarrow y \in X.$$

Together with a vector $\mu \in \mathbb{R}_{\geq 0}^n$ which denotes the accumulated valuations of the players, it is possible to express the social welfare as an integer program of the form $\max_{x \in \mathbb{Z}(X)} \sum_{k=1}^n \mu_k x_k$, where $\mathbb{Z}(X)$ denotes the set of integer points in X. Using the simplex method, or other standard linear programming techniques, an optimal solution $x^* \in X$ of the relaxed linear program $\max_{x \in X} \sum_{k=1}^n \mu_k x_k$ can be computed efficiently for most mechanism design problems. Note that for combinatorial auctions, where the dimension of X grows exponentially with the number of available goods, special attention is necessary to preserve computational feasibility. One possible approach is the use of demand queries which yields an optimal solution in polynomial time and with a polynomial number of positive components [1].

The maximum ratio between the original program and its relaxation is called the integrality gap of X. Assuming this gap is at most $\alpha \in \mathbb{R}_{\geq 1}$, Lavi and Swamy [1] observe that the scaled fractional solution $\frac{x^*}{\alpha}$ can be decomposed into a convex combination of integer solutions. More formally, there exists a convex combination λ from the set $\Lambda = \{\lambda \in \mathbb{R}_{\geq 0}^{\mathbb{Z}(X)} \mid \sum_{x \in \mathbb{Z}(X)} \lambda_x = 1\}$ such that the point $\sigma(\lambda)$, which is defined as $\sigma(\lambda) = \sum_{x \in \mathbb{Z}(X)} \lambda_x x$, is equal to $\frac{x^*}{\alpha}$. Regarding λ as a probability distribution over the feasible integer solutions, the MIDR principle allows for the construction of a randomized α-approximation mechanism which is truthful in expectation.

From an algorithmic point of view, the main challenge in decomposing $\frac{x^*}{\alpha}$ is the computation of suitable integer points. Since the size of $\mathbb{Z}(X)$ is typically exponential in n, it is intractable to consider the entire polytope. Instead, Carr and Vempala [7] propose the use of an approximation algorithm $\mathcal{A} : \mathbb{R}_{\geq 0}^n \to \mathbb{Z}(X)$ which verifies an integrality gap of α to sample a more practical, but still sufficient, subset of integer points.

Definition 2. (Integrality Gap Verifier) *Approximation algorithm $\mathcal{A}$ verifies an integrality gap of α if the integer solution which is computed by $\mathcal{A}$ is at least α times the optimal relaxed solution for all non-negative vectors μ*

$$\forall \mu \in \mathbb{R}_{\geq 0}^n : \quad \alpha \sum_{k=1}^n \mu_k \mathcal{A}(\mu)_k \geq \max_{x \in X} \sum_{k=1}^n \mu_k x_k.$$

As it turns out, Carr and Vempala's approach only requires a polynomial number of calls to to $\mathcal{A}$ with respect to n. In particular, this implies that the number of integer points in λ, which is defined as $\psi(\lambda) = |\{x \in \mathbb{Z}(X) \mid \lambda_x > 0\}|$, is polynomial as well. Observe that for sparse x^*, which are common in the case of combinatorial auctions, it is only necessary to consider the subspace of positive components in x^*. This is possible since no point in $\mathbb{Z}(X)$ which has a positive component k can contribute to λ if x_k^* is 0. In either case, the fact that Carr and Vempala strongly rely on the ellipsoid method indicates that their results are more of theoretical importance than of practical use.

3   Decomposition with Epsilon Precision

The first part of our decomposition technique is to construct a convex combination λ such that the point $\sigma(\lambda)$ is within an arbitrarily small distance $\epsilon \in \mathbb{R}_{>0}$ to the scaled relaxed solution $\frac{x^*}{\alpha}$. Similar to Carr and Vempala's approach, our technique requires an approximation algorithm $\mathcal{A}' : \mathbb{R}^n \to \mathbb{Z}(X)$ to sample integer points from X. It is important to note that $\mathcal{A}'$ must verify an integrality gap of α for arbitrary vectors $\mu \in \mathbb{R}^n$ whereas $\mathcal{A}$, only accepts non-negative vectors. However, since X satisfies the packing property, it is easy to extend the domain of $\mathcal{A}$ while preserving an approximation ratio of α.

Lemma 1. *Approximation algorithm $\mathcal{A}$ can be extended to a new approximation algorithm $\mathcal{A}'$ which verifies an integrality gap of α for arbitrary vectors μ.*

Proof. The basic idea of $\mathcal{A}'$ is to replace all negative components of μ by 0 and run the original integrality gap verifier $\mathcal{A}$ on the resulting non-negative vector, which is defined as $\xi(\mu)_k = \max(\{\mu_k, 0\})$. Exploiting the fact that X is a packing polytope, the output of $\mathcal{A}$ is then set to 0 for all negative components of μ. More formally, $\mathcal{A}'$ is defined as

$$\mathcal{A}'(\mu)_k = \begin{cases} \mathcal{A}(\xi(\mu))_k & \text{if } \mu_k \geq 0 \\ 0 & \text{if } \mu_k < 0. \end{cases}$$

Since $\mathcal{A}'(\mu)_k$ is equal to 0 if μ_k is negative and otherwise corresponds to $\mathcal{A}(\xi(\mu))_k$, it holds that

$$\sum_{k=1}^n \mu_k \mathcal{A}'(\mu)_k = \sum_{k=1}^n \xi(\mu)_k \mathcal{A}'(\mu)_k = \sum_{k=1}^n \xi(\mu)_k \mathcal{A}(\xi(\mu))_k.$$

Furthermore, since X only contains non-negative points, $\max_{x \in X} \sum_{k=1}^{n} \xi(\mu)_k x_k$ must be greater or equal to $\max_{x \in X} \sum_{k=1}^{n} \mu_k x_k$. Together with the fact that $\mathcal{A}$ verifies an integrality gap of α for $\xi(\mu)$ this proves that $\mathcal{A}'$ verifies the same integrality gap for μ

$$\alpha \sum_{k=1}^{n} \mu_k \mathcal{A}'(\mu)_k = \alpha \sum_{k=1}^{n} \xi(\mu)_k \mathcal{A}(\xi(\mu))_k \geq \max_{x \in X} \sum_{k=1}^{n} \xi(\mu)_k x_k \geq \max_{x \in X} \sum_{k=1}^{n} \mu_k x_k.$$

$\square$

Once $\mathcal{A}'$ is specified, algorithm 1 is used to decompose $\frac{x^*}{\alpha}$. Starting at the origin, which can be expressed trivially as a convex combination from Λ due to the packing property of X, the algorithm gradually improves $\sigma(\lambda^i)$ until it is sufficiently close to $\frac{x^*}{\alpha}$. For each iteration of the algorithm, μ^i denotes the vector which points from $\sigma(\lambda^i)$ to $\frac{x^*}{\alpha}$. If the length of μ^i is less or equal to ϵ, then $\sigma(\lambda^i)$ must be within an ϵ-distance to $\frac{x^*}{\alpha}$ and the algorithm terminates. Otherwise, $\mathcal{A}'$ samples a new integer point x^{i+1} based on the direction of μ^i. It is important to observe that all points on the line segment between $\sigma(\lambda^i)$ and x^{i+1} can be expressed as a convex combination of the form $\delta \lambda^i + (1-\delta)\tau(x^{i+1})$, where δ is a value between 0 and 1 and $\tau(x^{i+1})$ denotes a convex combination such that the coefficient $\tau(x^{i+1})_{x^{i+1}}$ is equal to 1 while all other coefficients are 0. Thus, by choosing λ^{i+1} as the convex combination which minimizes the distance between the line segment and $\frac{x^*}{\alpha}$, an improvement over the current convex combination is possible. As theorem 1 shows, at most $\lceil n\epsilon^{-2} \rceil - 1$ iterations are necessary to obtain the desired ϵ-precision.

Algorithm 1. Decomposition with Epsilon Precision

Input: an optimal relaxed solution x^*, an approximation algorithm $\mathcal{A}'$, a precision ϵ
Output: a convex combination λ which is within an ϵ-distance to $\frac{x^*}{\alpha}$

$x^0 \leftarrow 0$, $\lambda^0 \leftarrow \tau(x^0)$, $\mu^0 \leftarrow \frac{x^*}{\alpha} - \sigma(\lambda^0)$, $i \leftarrow 0$
while $\|\mu^i\|_2 > \epsilon$ **do**
    $x^{i+1} \leftarrow \mathcal{A}'(\mu^i)$
    $\delta \leftarrow \arg\min_{\delta \in [0,1]} \|\frac{x^*}{\alpha} - (\delta\sigma(\lambda^i) + (1-\delta)x^{i+1})\|_2$
    $\lambda^{i+1} \leftarrow \delta\lambda^i + (1-\delta)\tau(x^{i+1})$
    $\mu^{i+1} \leftarrow \frac{x^*}{\alpha} - \sigma(\lambda^{i+1})$
    $i \leftarrow i+1$
end while
return λ^i

Theorem 1. *Algorithm 1 returns a convex combination within an ϵ-distance to the scaled relaxed solution $\frac{x^*}{\alpha}$ after at most $\lceil n\epsilon^{-2} \rceil - 1$ iterations.*

Proof. Clearly, algorithm 1 terminates if and only if the distance between $\sigma(\lambda^i)$ and $\frac{x^*}{\alpha}$ becomes less or equal to ϵ. Thus, suppose the length of vector μ^i is still greater than ϵ. Consequently, approximation algorithm $\mathcal{A}'$ is deployed to sample

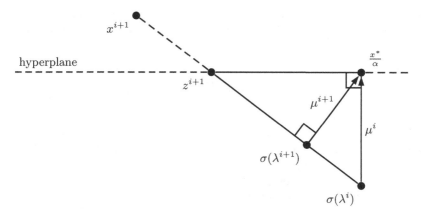

Fig. 1. Right triangle between the points $\frac{x^*}{\alpha}$, $\sigma(\lambda^i_x)$ and z^{i+1}

a new integer point x^{i+1}. Keeping in mind that $\mathcal{A}'$ verifies an integrality gap of α, the value of x^{i+1} must be greater or equal to the value of $\frac{x^*}{\alpha}$ with respect to vector μ^i

$$\sum_{k=1}^{n} \mu_k^i x_k^{i+1} = \sum_{k=1}^{n} \mu_k^i \mathcal{A}'(\mu^i)_k \geq \max_{x \in X} \sum_{k=1}^{n} \mu_k^i \frac{x_k}{\alpha} \geq \sum_{k=1}^{n} \mu_k^i \frac{x^*}{\alpha}.$$

Conversely, since the squared distance between $\sigma(\lambda^i)$ and $\frac{x^*}{\alpha}$ is greater than ϵ^2, and therefore also greater than 0, it holds that the value of $\sigma(\mu^i)$ is less than the value of $\frac{x^*}{\alpha}$ with respect to vector μ^i

$$0 < \sum_{k=1}^{n} \left(\frac{x_k^*}{\alpha} - \sigma(\lambda^i)_k \right)^2$$

$$\Longleftrightarrow \qquad 0 < \sum_{k=1}^{n} \left(\left(\frac{x_k^*}{\alpha} \right)^2 - 2 \frac{x_k^*}{\alpha} \sigma(\lambda^i)_k + \sigma(\lambda^i)_k^2 \right)$$

$$\Longleftrightarrow \quad \sum_{k=1}^{n} \left(\frac{x_k^*}{\alpha} \sigma(\lambda^i)_k - \sigma(\lambda^i)_k^2 \right) < \sum_{k=1}^{n} \left(\left(\frac{x_k^*}{\alpha} \right)^2 - \frac{x_k^*}{\alpha} \sigma(\lambda^i)_k \right)$$

$$\Longleftrightarrow \qquad \sum_{k=1}^{n} \mu_k^i \sigma(\lambda^i)_k < \sum_{k=1}^{n} \mu_k^i \frac{x_k^*}{\alpha}.$$

As a result, the hyper plane $\{x \in \mathbb{R}^n \mid \sum_{k=1}^{n} \mu_k^i x_k = \sum_{k=1}^{n} \mu_k^i \frac{x_k^*}{\alpha}\}$ separates $\sigma(\lambda^i)$ from x^{i+1}, which in turn implies that the line segment $\mathrm{conv}(\{\sigma(\lambda^i), x^{i+1}\})$ intersects the hyperplane at a unique point z^{i+1}.

Since the hyperplane is orthogonal to μ^i, the points $\frac{x^*}{\alpha}$, $\sigma(\lambda^i_x)$ and z^{i+1} form a right triangle, as figure 1 illustrates. Furthermore, the altitude of this triangle minimizes the distance from the line segment $\mathrm{conv}(\{\sigma(\lambda^i), x^{i+1}\})$ to $\frac{x^*}{\alpha}$ and therefore corresponds to the length of new vector μ^{i+1}. According to the basic relations between the sides in a right triangle, the length of μ^{i+1} can be expressed as

$$\left\|\mu^{i+1}\right\|_2 = \sqrt{\frac{\left\|\mu^i\right\|_2^2 \left\|\frac{x^*}{\alpha} - z^{i+1}\right\|_2^2}{\left\|\mu^i\right\|_2^2 + \left\|\frac{x^*}{\alpha} - z^{i+1}\right\|_2^2}}.$$

Unfortunately, the exact position of z^{i+1}, depends on the implementation $\mathcal{A}'$. To obtain an upper bound on the length μ^{i+1} which does not rely on z^{i+1}, it is helpful to observe that the altitude of the triangle grows as the distance between z^{i+1} and $\frac{x^*}{\alpha}$ increases. However, since both points are contained in the standard hyper cube $[0,1]^n$, the square of this distance is at most n

$$\left\|\frac{x^*}{\alpha} - z^{i+1}\right\|_2^2 = \sum_{k=1}^n \left(\frac{x_k^*}{\alpha} - z_k^{i+1}\right)^2 \le \sum_{k=1}^n 1 = n,$$

which means that the maximum length of μ^{i+1} is given by

$$\left\|\frac{x^*}{\alpha} - z^{i+1}\right\|_2^2 \le n$$

$$\Longleftrightarrow \quad \frac{\left\|\frac{x^*}{\alpha} - z^{i+1}\right\|_2^2}{\left\|\mu^i\right\|_2^2 + \left\|\frac{x^*}{\alpha} - z^{i+1}\right\|_2^2} \le \frac{n}{\left\|\mu^i\right\|_2^2 + n}$$

$$\Longleftrightarrow \quad \frac{\left\|\mu^i\right\|_2^2 \left\|\frac{x^*}{\alpha} - z^{i+1}\right\|_2^2}{\left\|\mu^i\right\|_2^2 + \left\|\frac{x^*}{\alpha} - z^{i+1}\right\|_2^2} \le \frac{\left\|\mu^i\right\|_2^2 n}{\left\|\mu^i\right\|_2^2 + n}$$

$$\Longleftrightarrow \quad \sqrt{\frac{\left\|\mu^i\right\|_2^2 \left\|\frac{x^*}{\alpha} - z^{i+1}\right\|_2^2}{\left\|\mu^i\right\|_2^2 + \left\|\frac{x^*}{\alpha} - z^{i+1}\right\|_2^2}} \le \sqrt{\frac{\left\|\mu^i\right\|_2^2 n}{\left\|\mu^i\right\|_2^2 + n}}.$$

It is important to note that this upper bound on the length of μ^{i+1}, which is illustrated in figure 2, only depends on the previous vector μ^i and the dimension n. Solving the recurrence inequality yields yet another upper bound which is based on the initial vector μ^0 and the number of iterations i

$$\left\|\mu^i\right\|_2^2 \le \frac{\left\|\mu^{i-1}\right\|_2^2 n}{\left\|\mu^{i-1}\right\|_2^2 + n}$$

$$\Longleftrightarrow \quad \frac{\left\|\mu^i\right\|_2^2}{n} \le \frac{\left\|\mu^{i-1}\right\|_2^2}{\left\|\mu^{i-1}\right\|_2^2 + n}$$

$$\Longleftrightarrow \quad \frac{n}{\left\|\mu^i\right\|_2^2} \ge \frac{n}{\left\|\mu^{i-1}\right\|_2^2} + 1 \ldots$$

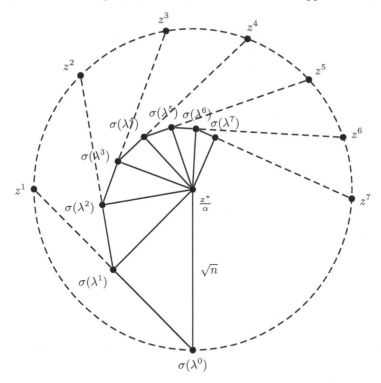

Fig. 2. Upper bound on the distance between $\sigma(\lambda^i)$ and $\frac{x^*}{\alpha}$ for the first 7 iterations

$$\Longrightarrow \qquad \frac{n}{\left\|\mu^i\right\|_2^2} \geq \frac{n}{\left\|\mu^0\right\|_2^2} + i$$

$$\Longleftrightarrow \qquad \frac{\left\|\mu^i\right\|_2^2}{n} \leq \frac{\left\|\mu^0\right\|_2^2}{\left\|\mu^0\right\|_2^2 i + n}$$

$$\Longleftrightarrow \qquad \left\|\mu^i\right\|_2 \leq \sqrt{\frac{\left\|\mu^0\right\|_2^2 n}{\left\|\mu^0\right\|_2^2 i + n}}.$$

Considering that the squared length of vector μ^0, which corresponds to the distance between $\frac{x^*}{\alpha}$ and the origin, is at most n

$$\left\|\mu^0\right\|_2^2 = \sum_{k=1}^{n} \left(\frac{x_k^*}{\alpha}\right)^2 \leq \sum_{k=1}^{n} 1 = n,$$

it follows that

$$\|\mu^i\|_2 \le \sqrt{\frac{\|\mu^0\|_2^2 n}{\|\mu^0\|_2^2 i + n}} \le \sqrt{\frac{n^2}{ni + n}} = \sqrt{\frac{n}{i+1}}.$$

Finally, this proves that the distance between $\sigma(\lambda^i)$ and $\frac{x^*}{\alpha}$ must be less or equal to ϵ after not more than $\lceil n\epsilon^{-2} \rceil - 1$ iterations, at which point the algorithm terminates

$$\left\|\mu^{\lceil n\epsilon^{-2}\rceil-1}\right\|_2 \le \sqrt{\frac{n}{1 + (\lceil n\epsilon^{-2}\rceil - 1)}} \le \epsilon.$$

$\square$

At this point, it should be mentioned that the upper bound on the number of iterations given in theorem 1 can be further refined with a simple modification of $\mathcal{A}'$. Due to the packing property of X it is possible to set all components of $\mathcal{A}'(\mu^i)$ which correspond to a component of value 0 in x^* to 0 as well. Given that μ^0 is equal to $\frac{x^*}{\alpha}$ and all other μ^{i+1} are defined recursively as the difference between $\frac{x^*}{\alpha}$ and a convex combination of $\frac{x^*}{\alpha} - \mu^i$ and $\mathcal{A}'(\mu^i)$, every vector μ^{i+1} must share the 0 components of x^*. As a result, the new $\mathcal{A}'$ preserves the approximation ratio and algorithm 1 still works as expected. Furthermore, only integer points from the subspace of positive components in x^* are considered, which means that the convergence of algorithm 1 depends on the number of positive components in x^* rather than n.

4 Exact Decomposition

Although the convex combination λ which is returned by algorithm 1 is within an ϵ-distance to $\frac{x^*}{\alpha}$, an exact decomposition of the relaxed solution is necessary to guarantee truthfulness. Assuming that an additional scaling factor of $\sqrt{n}\epsilon$ is admissible, the second part of our decomposition technique shows how to convert λ into a new convex combination λ'' such that $\sigma(\lambda'')$ is equal to $\frac{x^*}{\alpha(1+\sqrt{n}\epsilon)}$. Note that this additional scaling factor depends on ϵ, which means that it can still be made arbitrarily small. In particular, running algorithm 1 with a precision of $\frac{\epsilon}{\sqrt{n}}$, instead of ϵ, reduces the factor to ϵ and yields a decomposition which is equal to $\frac{x^*}{\alpha(1+\epsilon)}$. However, since this new precision is not independent of n anymore, the maximum number of iterations is increased to $\lceil n(\frac{\epsilon}{\sqrt{n}})^{-2}\rceil - 1$, which is quadratic in n. It is helpful to observe that the techniques which are introduced in this chapter can be adapted easily to the subspace of positive components in x^*. Hence, all complexity results carry over directly from n to the number of positive components in x^*.

To adjust $\sigma(\lambda)$ component-wisely, it is helpful to consider the integer points $e^k \in \{0,1\}^n$. For every dimension k, the kth component of e^k is defined to be 1 while all other components are 0. Since X has a finite integrality gap and also satisfies the packing property, all points e^k must be contained in X.

Lemma 2. *The polytope X contains all points e^k.*

Proof. For the sake of contradiction, assume there exists a dimension k for which e^k is not contained in X. Since X satisfies the packing property, this implies that there exists no point in X whose kth component is 1, in particular no integer point. As a result, the optimal solution for the integer program with respect to the vector e^k must be 0

$$\max_{x \in \mathbb{Z}(X)} \sum_{l}^{n} e_l^k x_l = \max_{x \in \mathbb{Z}(X)} x_k = 0.$$

Keeping in mind that X has an integrality gap of at most α, it immediately follows that the optimal solution for the relaxed linear program with respect to e^k must also be 0

$$\max_{x \in X} \sum_{l}^{n} e_l^k x_l = \max_{x \in X} x_k = 0.$$

However, this implies that the kth component of every point in X is 0, which contradicts the fact that X is n-dimensional.   □

Applying theorem 2, our decomposition technique uses the points e^k to construct an intermediate convex combination λ' such that $\sigma(\lambda')$ dominates $\frac{x^*}{\alpha(1+\sqrt{n}\epsilon)}$.

Theorem 2. *Convex combination λ can be converted into a new convex combination λ' which dominates $\frac{x^*}{\alpha(1+\sqrt{n}\epsilon)}$.*

Proof. According to lemma 2, the points e^k are contained in $\mathbb{Z}(X)$. Thus, they can be added to λ to construct a positive combination $\lambda + \sum_{k=1}^{n} |\frac{x_k^*}{\alpha} - \sigma(\lambda)_k| \tau(e^k)$ which dominates $\frac{x^*}{\alpha}$

$$\sigma\left(\lambda + \sum_{k=1}^{n} \left|\frac{x_k^*}{\alpha} - \sigma(\lambda)_k\right| \tau(e^k)\right) = \sigma(\lambda) + \left(\sum_{k=1}^{n} \left|\frac{x_k^*}{\alpha} - \sigma(\lambda)_k\right| e^k\right)$$

$$\geq \sigma(\lambda) + \left(\sum_{k=1}^{n} \left(\frac{x_k^*}{\alpha} - \sigma(\lambda)_k\right) e^k\right)$$

$$= \sigma(\lambda) + \frac{x^*}{\alpha} - \sigma(\lambda)$$

$$= \frac{x^*}{\alpha}.$$

Since the sum over the additional coefficients $\sum_{k=1}^{n} |\frac{x_k^*}{\alpha} - \sigma(\lambda)_k|$ is equivalent to the L1 distance between $\sigma(\lambda)$ and $\frac{x^*}{\alpha}$, it is bounded by the Hölder inequality

$$\sum_{k=1}^{n} \left|\frac{x_k^*}{\alpha} - \sigma(\lambda)_k\right| = \left\|\frac{x^*}{\alpha} - \sigma(\lambda)\right\|_1 \leq \left\|1\right\|_2 \left\|\frac{x^*}{\alpha} - \sigma(\lambda)\right\|_2 \leq \sqrt{n}\epsilon.$$

As a result, scaling down the positive combination by a factor of $1 + \sqrt{n}\epsilon$ yields a new positive combination which dominates $\frac{x^*}{\alpha(1+\sqrt{n}\epsilon)}$ and whose coefficients sum up to a value less or equal to 1. To ensure that this sum becomes exactly 1, the coefficients must be increased by an additional value of $\sqrt{n}\epsilon - \sum_{k=1}^n |\frac{x_k^*}{\alpha} - \sigma(\lambda)_k|$. An easy way to achieve this is by adding the origin, which is trivially contained in $\mathbb{Z}(X)$ due to the packing property of X, to the positive combination. Thus, the desired convex combination λ' corresponds to

$$\frac{\lambda + \sum_{k=1}^n |\frac{x_k^*}{\alpha} - \sigma(\lambda)_k|\tau(e^k) + \left(\sqrt{n}\epsilon - \sum_{k=1}^n |\frac{x_k^*}{\alpha} - \sigma(\lambda)_k|\right)\tau(0)}{1 + \sqrt{n}\epsilon}.$$

□

In the final step, our decomposition technique exploits the packing property of X to convert λ' into an exact decomposition of $\frac{x^*}{\alpha(1+\sqrt{n}\epsilon)}$. A simple but general approach to this problem is provided by algorithm 2. Given a point $x \in X$ which is dominated by $\sigma(\lambda')$, the basic idea of the algorithm is to iteratively weaken the integer points which comprise λ' until the desired convex combination λ'' is reached. As theorem 3 shows, this computation requires at most $|\psi(\lambda)|n + \frac{n^2+n}{2}$ iterations.

Algorithm 2. From a Dominating to an Exact Decomposition

Input: a convex combination λ', a point x which is dominated by $\sigma(\lambda')$
Output: a convex combination λ'' which is an exact decomposition of x
  $\lambda^0 \leftarrow \lambda'$, $i \leftarrow 0$
  for all $1 \le k \le n$ **do**
    while $\sigma(\lambda^i)_k > x_k$ **do**
      $y \leftarrow$ pick some y from $\mathbb{Z}(X)$ such that $\lambda_y^i > 0$ and $y_k = 1$
      if $\lambda_y^i \ge \sigma(\lambda^i)_k - x_k$ **then**
        $\lambda^{i+1} \leftarrow \lambda^i - (\sigma(\lambda^i)_k - x_k)\tau(y) + (\sigma(\lambda^i)_k - x_k)\tau(y - e^k)$
      else
        $\lambda^{i+1} \leftarrow \lambda^i - \lambda_y^i\tau(y) + \lambda_y^i\tau(y - e^k)$
      end if
      $i \leftarrow i + 1$
    end while
  end for
  return λ^i

Theorem 3. *Assuming that $\sigma(\lambda')$ dominates the point x, algorithm 2 converts λ' into a new convex combination λ'' such that $\sigma(\lambda'')$ is equal to x. Furthermore, the required number of iterations is at most $|\psi(\lambda')|n + \frac{n^2+n}{2}$.*

Proof. In order to match $\sigma(\lambda')$ with x, algorithm 2 considers each dimension k separately. Clearly, while $\sigma(\lambda^i)_k$ is still greater than x_k, there must exist at least one point y in λ^i which has a value of 1 in component k. If λ_y^i is greater or equal to the difference between $\sigma(\lambda^i)_k$ and x_k, it is reduced by the value of this difference. To compensate for this operation, the coefficient of the point $y - e^k$, which is trivially contained in X due to its packing property, is increased by the same value. Thus, the value of $\sigma(\lambda^{i+1})_k$ is equal to x_k

$$
\begin{aligned}
\sigma(\lambda^{i+1})_k &= \sigma(\lambda^i)_k - (\sigma(\lambda^i)_k - x_k)\tau(y)_k + (\sigma(\lambda^i)_k - x_k)\tau(y - e^k)_k \\
&= \sigma(\lambda^i)_k - (\sigma(\lambda^i)_k - x_k) \\
&= x_k,
\end{aligned}
$$

which means that the algorithm succeeded at computing a matching convex combination for x at component k. It should be noted that the other components of λ^{i+1} are unaffected by this update.

Conversely, if λ_y^i is less than the remaining difference between $\sigma(\lambda^i)_k$ and x_k, the point y can be replaced completely by $y - e^k$. In this case the value of $\sigma(\lambda^{i+1})_k$ remains greater than x_k

$$
\sigma(\lambda^{i+1})_k = \sigma(\lambda^i)_k - \lambda_y^i \tau(y)_k + \lambda_y^i \tau(y - e^k)_k = \sigma(\lambda^i)_k - \lambda_y^i > x_k
$$

Furthermore, the number of points in λ^{i+1} which have a value of 1 at component k is reduced by one with respect to λ^i. Considering that the number of points in λ^i is finite, this implies that the algorithm must eventually compute a convex combination λ'' which matches x at component k.

To determine an upper bound on the number of iterations, it is helpful to observe that the size of the convex combination can only increase by 1 for every iteration of the for loop, namely if λ_y^i is greater than the difference between $\sigma(\lambda^i)_k$ and x_k. As a result, the number of points which comprise a convex combination during the kth iteration of the for loop is at most $\psi(\lambda') + k$. Since this number also gives an upper bound on the number of iterations performed by the while loop, the total number of iterations is at most

$$
\sum_{k=1}^{n}(|\psi(\lambda')| + k) = n|\psi(\lambda')| + \sum_{k=1}^{n} k = n|\psi(\lambda')| + \frac{n^2 + n}{2}.
$$

$\square$

Acknowledgments. The authors would like to thank the anonymous referees for the their insightful comments and suggestions. Furthermore, we gratefully acknowledge support of the Deutsche Forschungsgemeinschaft (DFG) (BI 1057/7-1).

References

1. Lavi, R., Swamy, C.: Truthful and near-optimal mechanism design via linear programming. Journal of the ACM (JACM) 58(6), 25 (2011)
2. Vickrey, W.: Counterspeculation, auctions, and competitive sealed tenders. Journal of Finance (3), 8–37 (1961)

 3. Clarke, E.: Multipart pricing of public goods. Public Choice XI, 17–33 (1971)
 4. Groves, T.: Incentives in teams. Econometrica 41, 617–631 (1973)
 5. Nisan, N., Ronen, A.: Computationally feasible vcg mechanisms. In: Electronic Commerce: Proceedings of the 2nd ACM Conference on Electronic Commerce, vol. 17, pp. 242–252 (2000)
 6. Dobzinski, S., Dughmi, S.: On the power of randomization in algorithmic mechanism design. In: 50th Annual IEEE Symposium on Foundations of Computer Science, FOCS 2009, pp. 505–514. IEEE (2009)
 7. Carr, R., Vempala, S.: Randomized metarounding. In: Proceedings of the Thirty-second Annual ACM Symposium on Theory of Computing, pp. 58–62. ACM (2000)
 8. Bland, R.G., Goldfarb, D., Todd, M.J.: The ellipsoid method: A survey. Operations Research 29(6), 1039–1091 (1981)
 9. Dantzig, G.B.: An epsilon precise feasible solution to a linear program with a convexity constraint in 1 over epsilon squared iterations independent of problem size (1992)
10. Dughmi, S., Ghosh, A.: Truthful assignment without money. In: Proceedings of the 11th ACM Conference on Electronic Commerce, pp. 325–334. ACM (2010)

A Near-Optimal Mechanism for Impartial Selection

Nicolas Bousquet[1,3], Sergey Norin[1], and Adrian Vetta[1,2]

[1] Department of Mathematics and Statistics, McGill University
[2] School of Computer Science, McGill University
[3] Group for Research in Decision Analysis (GERAD), HEC Montréal

Abstract. We examine strategy-proof elections to select a winner amongst a set of agents, each of whom cares only about winning. This *impartial selection* problem was introduced independently by Holzman and Moulin [5] and Alon et al. [1]. Fischer and Klimm [4] showed that the permutation mechanism is impartial and $\frac{1}{2}$-optimal, that is, it selects an agent who gains, in expectation, at least half the number of votes of the most popular agent. Furthermore, they showed the mechanism is $\frac{7}{12}$-optimal if agents cannot abstain in the election. We show that a better guarantee is possible, provided the most popular agent receives at least a large enough, but constant, number of votes. Specifically, we prove that, for any $\epsilon > 0$, there is a constant N_ϵ (independent of the number n of voters) such that, if the maximum number of votes of the most popular agent is at least N_ϵ then the permutation mechanism is $(\frac{3}{4} - \epsilon)$-optimal. This result is tight.

Furthermore, in our main result, we prove that near-optimal impartial mechanisms exist. In particular, there is an impartial mechanism that is $(1 - \epsilon)$-optimal, for any $\epsilon > 0$, provided that the maximum number of votes of the most popular agent is at least a constant M_ϵ.

1 Introduction

Imagine an election where the voters are the candidates and each voter is allowed to vote for as many of the other candidates as she wishes. Now suppose each voter cares only about winning. The goal of the mechanism is to elect the candidate with the maximum support. To achieve this, we desire that the election mechanism be strategy-proof. Thus, we want an *impartial mechanism*, where voting truthfully cannot affect an agent's own chances of election.

This problem, called the *impartial selection problem*, was introduced independently by Holzman and Moulin [5] and Alon et al. [1]. In addition to elections, they were motivated by nomination mechanisms for prestigious prizes and committees, hyperlink formations, and reputation systems in social networks. Fischer and Klimm [4] also proposed the use of such mechanisms for peer review evaluation processes.

The impartial selection problem can be formalized via a directed graph $G = (V, A)$. There is a vertex $v \in V$ for each voter (candidate) v, and there is an arc $(u, v) \in A$ if u votes for v. The aim is to maximize the in-degree of the selected vertex, and we say that an impartial mechanism is α-optimal, for $\alpha \leq 1$, if the in-degree of the vertex it selects is always at least α times the in-degree of the most popular vertex.

Unfortunately, Holzman and Moulin [5] and Alon et al. [1] observed that a *deterministic* impartial mechanism must have an arbitrarily poor approximation guarantee α.

T.-Y. Liu et al. (Eds.): WINE 2014, LNCS 8877, pp. 133–146, 2014.

Specifically, a deterministic mechanism may have to select a vertex with zero in-degree even when other vertices receive votes; or it may be forced to select a vertex with in-degree one whilst another vertex receives $n - 1$ votes! This negative result motivated Alon et al. [1] to study *randomized* impartial mechanisms. In particular, they examined a simple mechanism dubbed the *2-partition mechanism*. This mechanism independently assigns each vertex to one of two groups $\{V_1, V_2\}$. Then, only the arcs from vertices in V_1 to vertices in V_2 are counted as votes. The vertex with the maximum number of *counted* votes in V_2 is selected (breaking ties arbitrarily). It is straight-forward to verify that this mechanism is impartial and is $\frac{1}{4}$-optimal. They further conjectured the existence of an $\frac{1}{2}$-optimal impartial randomized mechanism.

This conjecture was recently proven by Fischer and Klimm [4]. Specifically, they proved that the *permutation mechanism* is impartial and $\frac{1}{2}$-optimal. This election mechanism examines the vertices in a random order, and can only count the votes of a vertex that go to vertices behind it in the ordering. (See Section 3 for a detailed description of the mechanism and a short proof of Fischer and Klimm's result.) Interestingly, the factor $\frac{1}{2}$-approximation guarantee is tight. Consider an n-vertex graph containing only a single arc (u, v). Then, unless u is before v in the random permutation the mechanism will select a vertex with in-degree zero. Thus the expected in-degree of the vector is at most one half.

Observe that this tight example is rather unsatisfactory. It is extremely unnatural and relies on the fact that every vertex bar one abstains from voting. Indeed, Fischer and Klimm [4] showed that without abstentions the permutation mechanism is at least $\frac{7}{12}$-optimal. They leave open the possibility that the permutation mechanism actually proffers a better approximation guarantee than $\frac{7}{12}$. They do prove, however, that without abstentions the permutation mechanism can be no better than $\frac{2}{3}$-optimal. Moreover, Fischer and Klimm [4] provide an even stronger inapproximation bound: **no** impartial mechanism can be better than $\frac{3}{4}$-optimal, even without abstentions.

This appears to severely limit the potential for progress. But, again, the lower bounds are somewhat unsatisfactory. The issue now is not low out-degrees (that is, abstentions) but rather low in-degrees. The lower bounds are all based on instances with extremely small maximum in-degree Δ^-. Specifically, the factor $\frac{1}{2}$ optimal example [1] for the permutation mechanism with abstentions has $\Delta^- = 1$; the factor $\frac{2}{3}$ optimal example [4] for the permutation mechanism without abstentions has $\Delta^- = 3$; the factor $\frac{3}{4}$ optimal example [4] for any randomized mechanism without abstentions has $\Delta^- = 2$. Of course, in applications with a large number n of voters, we would anticipate that the most popular agent receives a moderate number of votes. Do these inapproximability bounds still apply for these more realistic settings? Interestingly, the answer is no, even for cases where the most popular agent receives only a (large enough) constant number of votes. Specifically, we first prove that the permutation mechanism is nearly $\frac{3}{4}$-optimal in such instances.

Theorem 1. *For any $\epsilon > 0$, there is a constant N_ϵ such that if $\Delta^- \geq N_\epsilon$ then the permutation mechanism is $(\frac{3}{4} - \epsilon)$-optimal.*

This result is tight. We show that the permutation mechanism cannot produce a guarantee better than $\frac{3}{4}$ regardless of the magnitude of Δ^-.

This result suggests that it may be possible to find a mechanism that beats the $\frac{3}{4}$-inapproximability bound of [4], even for constant maximum in-degree. This is indeed the case and spectacularly so. There is an impartial mechanism, which we call the *slicing mechanism*, that produces a near optimal approximation guarantee.

Theorem 2. *For any $\epsilon > 0$, there is a constant M_ϵ such that if $\Delta^- \geq M_\epsilon$ then the slicing mechanism is $(1 - \epsilon)$-optimal.*

The slicing mechanism differs from previous mechanisms in that it adds an initial sampling phase. In this first phase, it samples a small fraction of the vertices. It then uses the votes of these vertices to build a non-random ordering of the other vertices. This specific ordering is exploited in the second phase to elect a vertex with very high expected in-degree.

These results, as in previous works [1,4,5], relate to single-winner elections. Some of the motivating applications, however, involve multiple-winner elections. We remark that our main result can be generalized to multiple-winner elections via small modifications to the mechanism.

2   The Model

We begin by formalizing the impartial selection problem and introducing some necessary notation. An election is represented via a directed graph $G = (V, A)$. The number of vertices of G is denoted by n, and each vertex represents an agent (voter/candidate). An agent can make multiple votes, but cannot vote for herself nor vote more than once for any other agent. Thus, the graph G is loopless and contains no multiple arcs.

A vertex u is an *in-neighbor of v* (resp. *out-neighbor of v*) if there is an arc $uv \in A$ (resp. $vu \in A$). In this case, we say that u votes for v. Given a subset $Y \subseteq V$ and $v \in V$, the *in-degree of v in Y*, denoted by $d_Y^-(v)$, is the number of in-neighbors of v in Y. For simplicity, we denote $d_V^-(v)$, the *in-degree of v*, by $d^-(v)$. The maximum in-degree of any vertex in G is denoted in by $\Delta^-(G)$, or simply by Δ when there is no ambiguity.

A mechanism is *impartial* if, for every vertex v, the probability of selecting v is not modified when the out-neighborhood of v is modified. That is, if v changes its votes then this does not affect the probability of v being elected. More formally, take any pair of graphs G and G' on the same vertex set V. Let v be a vertex. Then we require that the probability that v is elected in G is equal to the probability that v is elected in G', whenever the sets of out-neighbors of u and v are equal for every $u \neq v$.

Given $1 \geq \alpha \geq 0$, an impartial mechanism is *α-optimal* if for any graph G, the expected degree of the winner differs from the maximum degree by a factor of at most α, that is,

$$\frac{\sum_{v \in V} d^-(v) \cdot \Pr(v \text{ is the winner})}{\Delta} \geq \alpha$$

3   The Permutation Mechanism

In this section, we analyze the permutation mechanism of Fischer and Klimm [4]. This election mechanism examines the vertices in a random order $\{\pi_1, \pi_2, \ldots, \pi_n\}$. At time

t, the mechanism selects a *provisional leader* y_t amongst the set $\Pi_t = \{\pi_1, \ldots \pi_t\}$. At time $t + 1$ the mechanism then examines π_{t+1}. If π_{t+1} receives at least as many votes from $\Pi_t \setminus y_t$ as y_t from the set of voters before him then π_{t+1} is declared the provisional leader y_{t+1}. Otherwise $y_{t+1} := y_t$. The winner of the election is y_n. A formal description of the permutation mechanism is given in Procedure 1 (where d_i denotes the in-degree of the provisional leader). Given an integer n, the set $\{1, 2, \ldots, n\}$ is denoted by $[n]$.

Procedure 1. The Permutation Mechanism

> **Input:** A directed graph $G = (V, A)$.
> Let π be a random permutation of $V = [n]$.
> $y_1 \leftarrow \pi_1$;
> $d_1 \leftarrow 0$;
> **for** $i = 1$ to $n - 1$ **do**
>   **if** $d^-_{\Pi_i \setminus \{y_i\}}(\pi_{i+1}) \geq d_i$ **then**
> $y_{i+1} \leftarrow \pi_{i+1}$;
> $d_{i+1} \leftarrow d^-_{\Pi_i}(\pi_{i+1})$
>   **else**
> $y_{i+1} \leftarrow y_i$;
> $d_{i+1} \leftarrow d_i$
>   **end if**
> **end for**
> **output** y_n

Observe that the permutation mechanism is impartial because it has the following property: the votes of a vertex are only considered after it has been eliminated. Specifically, the votes of π_t are considered at time $\tau > t$ only if π_t is not the provisional leader at time $\tau - 1$. But, if π_t is not the provisional leader at time $\tau > t$ then it cannot be elected. This ensures that eliminated agents have no interest to lie, *i.e.* the mechanism is impartial. Fischer and Klimm [4] proved this mechanism is $\frac{1}{2}$-optimal using an intricate analysis based upon viewing the permutation mechanism as a generalization of the 2-partition mechanism. First, we present a simpler proof of their result.

Theorem 3. *[4] The permutation mechanism is $\frac{1}{2}$-optimal.*

Proof. Let v be a vertex with maximum in-degree Δ. Now suppose exactly j of its in-neighbors appear before v in the random ordering π. In this case, at the time v is considered it has received at least $j - 1$ valid votes (one of the j votes may not be counted if it comes from the provisional leader).

Suppose v is now declared the provisional leader. Then all j of these votes become valid. (Indeed, if one of the in-neighbors of v was the provisional leader, this is no longer the case.) On the other-hand, suppose v is now declared a loser. Then, because ties are broken in favor of newly examined vertices, the provisional leader must already be receiving at least j valid votes. Thus in either case, the final winner y_n must also receive at least j valid votes (the in-degree of the provisional leader is non-decreasing).

Now with probability $\frac{1}{\Delta+1}$, exactly j of its in-neighbors appear before v, for any $0 \leq j \leq \Delta$. Thus, in expectation, the winner receives at least $\frac{1}{\Delta+1} \cdot \sum_{j=0}^{\Delta} j = \frac{1}{2}\Delta$ votes. $\qquad\square$

As discussed in the introduction, the factor $\frac{1}{2}$-approximation guarantee in Theorem 3 is tight. This tightness is slightly misleading, though. Recall that the tight example was a graph with just a single arc. Under a natural assumption that the maximum in-degree is large enough, the permutation mechanism is $\frac{3}{4}$-optimal. Specifically,

Theorem 1. *For any $\epsilon > 0$, there is a constant N_ϵ such that if $\Delta^- \geq N_\epsilon$ then the permutation mechanism is $(\frac{3}{4} - \epsilon)$-optimal.*

The $\frac{3}{4}$ bound in Theorem 1 is tight in a very strong sense. There are tight examples for any choice of Δ, no matter how large; see Theorem 4. The proof of Theorem 1 has two basic components. The first is the basic observation, used above in the proof of Theorem 3, that the mechanism will perform well if the vertex v of highest in-degree has many in-neighbors before it in the random permutation. The second is the observation that if the mechanism does well when v does not participate then it will do at least as well when v does participate. In order to be able to apply these two observations simultaneously, however, we must show random permutations are "well-behaved". Specifically, we say that a permutation π of $[n]$ is (Δ, ϵ)-*balanced* if, for every $0 \leq k \leq n$,

$$|[\Delta] \cap \Pi_k| \geq \left(\frac{k}{n} - \epsilon\right) \cdot \Delta$$

and we want to show that a random permutation is typically balanced.

To do this, we need the following result, which provides a large deviation bound for the size of intersection of two sets of fixed cardinalities.

Lemma 1. *For every $\epsilon_1 > 0$, there exists N_1 such that for all positive integers $N_1 < \Delta \leq n$ and $k \leq n$ the following holds. If $X \subseteq [n]$ are chosen uniformly at random subject to $|X| = \Delta$, then*

$$\Pr\left[\left||X \cap [k]| - \frac{k\Delta}{n}\right| \geq \epsilon_1 \cdot \Delta\right] < \epsilon_1 \tag{1}$$

Due to space restriction, the proof of the following lemma is not included in this extended abstract [1].

Lemma 2. *For every $0 < \epsilon_2 < 1$, there exists N_2 such that, for all $n \geq \Delta > N_2$, at least $(1 - \epsilon_2) \cdot n!$ permutations of $[n]$ are (Δ, ϵ_2)-balanced.*

Proof. Let N_1 be chosen to satisfy Lemma 1 with $\epsilon_1 := \frac{\epsilon_2^2}{4}$. We choose $N_2 \geq \max(N_1, \frac{12}{\epsilon_2})$. Let $k_1, k_2, \ldots, k_l \in [n]$ be a collection of integers such that for every $k \in [n]$ there exists $i \in [l]$ satisfying $0 \leq k - k_i \leq \epsilon_2 \cdot \frac{n}{3}$. Clearly such a collection can be chosen with $l \leq \frac{n}{\lceil \epsilon_2 \cdot n/3 \rceil} \leq \frac{4}{\epsilon_2}$, where the last inequality holds as $n \geq \frac{12}{\epsilon_2}$.

---

[1] A complete version of this paper can be found at http://arxiv.org/abs/1407.8535

Let π be a permutation of $[n]$ chosen uniformly at random. By Lemma 1 and the choice of N_2 we have

$$\Pr\left[|[\Delta] \cap \Pi_{k_i}| \leq \left(\frac{k_i}{n} - \epsilon_1\right) \cdot \Delta\right] < \epsilon_1 \tag{2}$$

for every $1 \leq i \leq l$.

We claim that if $|[\Delta] \cap \Pi_{k_i}| \geq \left(\frac{k_i}{n} - \epsilon_1\right) \cdot \Delta$ for every $0 \leq i \leq l$ then $|[\Delta] \cap \Pi_k| \geq \left(\frac{k}{n} - \epsilon_2\right) \cdot \Delta$ for every $0 \leq k \leq n$. Indeed, given k let $i \in [l]$ satisfy $0 \leq k - k_i \leq \epsilon_2 \cdot \frac{n}{3}$. Then

$$|[\Delta] \cap \Pi_k| \geq |[\Delta] \cap \Pi_{k_i}| \geq \left(\frac{k_i}{n} - \epsilon_1\right) \cdot \Delta$$

$$\geq \left(\frac{k}{n} - \frac{\epsilon_2}{3} - \epsilon_1\right) \cdot \Delta = \left(\frac{k}{n} - \frac{\epsilon_2}{3} - \frac{\epsilon_2^2}{4}\right) \cdot \Delta$$

$$\geq \left(\frac{k}{n} - \epsilon_2\right) \cdot \Delta$$

as claimed. By the union bound applied to (2) we have

$$\Pr\left[\forall i : i \leq l : |[\Delta] \cap \Pi_{k_i}| \geq \left(\frac{k_i}{n} - \epsilon_1\right) \cdot \Delta\right] \geq 1 - l \cdot \epsilon_1 \geq 1 - \frac{4}{\epsilon_2} \cdot \frac{\epsilon_2^2}{4}$$

$$= 1 - \epsilon_2 \tag{3}$$

The lemma immediately follows from (3) and the claim above. $\square$

We are now ready to prove Theorem 1.

Proof of Theorem 1. Let N_2 be chosen to satisfy Lemma 2 with $\epsilon_2 := \frac{\epsilon}{3}$. We show that $N_\epsilon := \max(N_2, \lceil \frac{6}{\epsilon_2} \rceil)$ satisfies the theorem. Let v be a vertex of G with in-degree $\Delta := \Delta^-(G)$. We assume that $V(G) = [n]$, where v is vertex n, and $[\Delta]$ is the set of in-neighbors of v. For a permutation π, let $d(\pi)$ denote the in-degree of the winner determined by the mechanism.

Let π' be a fixed (Δ, ϵ_2)-balanced permutation of $[n-1]$. We claim that

$$\mathrm{E}[d(\pi) \mid \pi|_{[n-1]} = \pi'] \geq \left(\frac{3}{4} - \epsilon/2\right) \cdot \Delta \tag{4}$$

Note that the theorem follows from (4), as the probability that $\pi|_{[n-1]}$ is not (Δ, ϵ_2)-balanced is at most ϵ_2 by the choice of N_ϵ, and thus

$$\mathrm{E}[d(\pi)] \geq (1 - \epsilon_2) \cdot \left(\frac{3}{4} - \epsilon/2\right) \cdot \Delta \geq \left(\frac{3}{4} - \epsilon\right) \cdot \Delta$$

It remains to prove (4). Let w be the winner when the permutation mechanism is applied to $G \setminus v$ and π', and let x be the number of votes w receives from its left (*i.e.* from vertices before it in the permutation). Let π be a permutation of $[n]$ such that $\pi|_{[n-1]} = \pi'$. It is not hard to check that if at least $(x+1)$ in-neighbors of v precede v in π then v wins the election. Moreover, whilst the addition of vertex v can change the winner (and, indeed, produce a less popular winner), it cannot decrease the "left" degree of any vertex. Thus, the (new) winner has still in-degree at least x after the addition of v. So, as π' is (Δ, ϵ_2)-balanced, we have $|[\Delta] \cap \Pi_{cn}| \geq c\Delta - \epsilon_2\Delta \geq x + 1$, whenever $c \geq \frac{x+1}{\Delta} + \epsilon_2$. Furthermore, $\Pr[\pi(v) > cn] \geq 1 - c$. Thus the probability that v wins the election is at least $1 - (x+1)/\Delta - \epsilon_2$. It follows that

$$
\begin{aligned}
\mathrm{E}[d(\pi) \mid \pi|_{[n-1]} = \pi'] &\geq \left(\frac{x+1}{\Delta} + \epsilon_2\right) \cdot x + \left(1 - \frac{x+1}{\Delta} - \epsilon_2\right) \cdot \Delta \\
&\geq \frac{\Delta^2 - (x+1)\Delta + (x+1)x}{\Delta} - \epsilon_2\Delta \\
&\geq \left(\frac{3}{4} - \epsilon_2 - \frac{1}{\Delta}\right) \cdot \Delta + \frac{(x - \Delta/2)^2}{\Delta} \geq \left(\frac{3}{4} - \frac{\epsilon}{2}\right) \cdot \Delta \quad \square
\end{aligned}
$$

The $\frac{3}{4}$ bound provided in Theorem 1 is tight for any Δ.

Theorem 4. *For every $0 < \epsilon < 1/4$ and every $N > 0$, there exists a directed graph G such that $\Delta^-(G) \geq N$ and the expected degree of the winner selected by the permutation mechanism is at most $(\frac{3}{4} + \epsilon)\Delta^-(G)$.*

Proof. Without loss of generality we assume that $N \geq 1/\epsilon$. Let G' be a directed graph such that $n := |V(G')| \geq (N+1)(N^2 + N + 1) \cdot \ln\frac{1}{\epsilon}$, and $d^-(v) = d^+(v) = N$ for every $v \in V(G')$. Let G be obtained from G' by adding a new vertex v_0 and $2N - 1$ directed edges from arbitrary vertices in $V(G')$ to v_0. Thus $\Delta := \Delta^-(G) = d^-(v_0) = 2N - 1$.

Now, in G' one can greedily construct a set Z of at least $n/(N^2 + N + 1)$ vertices, such that no two vertices of Z have common in-neighbors and no two vertices of Z are joined by an edge. After a vertex $z \in Z$ is chosen, simply remove z, the in-neighbors and out-neighbors of z, and the out-neighbors of z's in-neighbors (the inequality is satisfied since the in-neighbors have a common out-neighbor). Then recurse. Let π be a permutation of $V(G)$ chosen uniformly at random. Let X_v denote the event that a vertex $v \in V(G')$ is preceded by all of its in-neighbors in π. Clearly $\Pr[X_v] = \frac{1}{N+1}$ for every $v \in V(G')$, and moreover, by construction of Z, the events $\{X_v\}_{v \in Z}$ are mutually independent. Hence

$$
\Pr[\cup_{v \in V(G')} X_v] \geq 1 - \left(1 - \frac{1}{N+1}\right)^{\frac{n}{N^2 + N}} \geq 1 - \left(1 - \frac{1}{N+1}\right)^{(N+1) \cdot \ln\frac{1}{\epsilon}}
$$
$$
\geq 1 - \epsilon.
$$

Note that if the event $\cup_{v \in V(G')} X_v$ occurs then one of the vertices of G' receives N votes in the permutation mechanism. By symmetry the probability that v_0 is preceded by at most $(N-1)$ of its in-neighbors in π is equal to $1/2$. Thus v_0 is not selected as a winner with probability at least $1/2 - \epsilon$. We deduce that the expected in-degree of the winner is at most

$$
\left(\frac{1}{2} - \epsilon\right) \cdot \frac{\Delta + 1}{2} + \left(\frac{1}{2} + \epsilon\right) \cdot \Delta = \left(\frac{3}{4} + \epsilon\right) \cdot \Delta - \epsilon N + \frac{1}{4} \leq \left(\frac{3}{4} + \epsilon\right) \cdot \Delta. \quad \square
$$

Procedure 2. The Slicing Mechanism

SAMPLING PHASE

[Sample] Draw a random sample $\mathcal{X}$, where each vertex is sampled with probability ϵ.

for all $v \in V \setminus \mathcal{X}$ **do**

  [Estimated-Degree.] $d_e(v) \leftarrow \frac{1}{\epsilon} \cdot d_{\mathcal{X}}^-(v)$

end for

SLICING PHASE

[Slices] Create $\tau = \lceil \frac{1}{\epsilon^2} \rceil$ sets $\{S_1, \ldots, S_\tau\}$ initialized to empty sets.

$\Delta_e \leftarrow \max_{v \in V \setminus \mathcal{X}}(d_e(v))$

for all $v \in V \setminus \mathcal{X}$ **do**

  for $i = 1$ to τ **do**

    if $(i-1)\epsilon^2 \cdot \Delta_e \leq d_e(v) \leq i\epsilon^2 \cdot \Delta_e$ **then**

      $S_i \leftarrow S_i \cup \{v\}$

    end if

  end for

end for

ELECTION PHASE

[Revealed Set] $\mathcal{R} \leftarrow \mathcal{X}$

[Provisional Winner] $y_0 \leftarrow \text{argmax}_{u \in V \setminus \mathcal{R}}(d_{\mathcal{R}}^-(u))$ [Break ties arbitrarily.]

for $i = 1$ to τ **do**

  for all $v \in S_i \setminus \{y_{i-1}\}$ **do**

    $\mathcal{R} \leftarrow \mathcal{R} \cup \{v\}$ with probability $(1 - \epsilon)$.

  end for

  $y_i' \leftarrow \text{argmax}_{u \in V \setminus \mathcal{R}}(d_{\mathcal{R}}^-(u))$ [Break ties arbitrarily.]

  $\mathcal{R} \leftarrow (\mathcal{R} \cup \bigcup_{j \leq i} S_j) \setminus \{y_i'\}$ [Only y_{i-1} can be in S_j with $j < i$]

  [Provisional Winner] $y_i \leftarrow \text{argmax}_{u \in V \setminus \mathcal{R}}(d_{\mathcal{R}}^-(u))$ [Break ties arbitrarily.]

  $\mathcal{R} \leftarrow (\mathcal{R} \cup \bigcup_{j \leq i} S_j) \setminus \{y_i\}$ [Only y_i' can be in $\cup_{j \leq i} S_j$]

end for

The elected vertex is y_τ.

---

4   The Slicing Mechanism

In this section, we present the *slicing mechanism* and prove that it outputs a vertex whose expected in-degree is near optimal.

Theorem 2. *For any $\epsilon > 0$, there is a constant M_ϵ such that if $\Delta^- \geq M_\epsilon$ then the slicing mechanism is $(1 - \epsilon)$-optimal.*

The constant M_ϵ is independent of the number of vertices and is a polynomial function of $\frac{1}{\epsilon}$. We remark that we have made no attempt to optimize this constant. The *slicing mechanism* is formalized in Procedure 2.

This mechanism consists of three parts which we now informally discuss. In the first part, the *sampling phase*, we independently at random collect a sample $\mathcal{X}$ of the vertices. We use arcs incident to $\mathcal{X}$ to estimate the in-degree of every other vertex in the graph. In the second part, the *slicing phase*, we partition the unsampled vertices into slices, where each slice consists of vertices with roughly the same *estimated-degree*.

The third part, the *election phase*, selects the winning vertex. It does this by considering each slice in increasing order (of estimated-degrees). After the i-th slice is examined the mechanism selects as *provisional leader*, y_i, the vertex that has the largest number of in-neighbors amongst the set of vertices $\mathcal{R}$ that have currently been eliminated. The winning vertex is the provisional leader after the final slice has been examined.

We emphasize, again, that the impartiality of the mechanisms follows from the fact that the votes of a vertex are only revealed when it has been eliminated, that is, added to $\mathcal{R}$. Observe that at any stage we have one provisional leader; if this leader changes when we examine a slice then the votes of the previous leader are revealed if its slice has already been examined.

4.1   Analysis of the Sampling Phase

Observe that the sampling phase is used to estimate the in-degree of each unsampled vertex v. Since each in-neighbor of v is sampled in $\mathcal{X}$ with probability ϵ, we anticipate that an ϵ-fraction of the in-neighbors of v are sampled. Thus, we have an *estimated in-degree* $d_e(v) := \frac{1}{\epsilon} \cdot d_{\mathcal{X}}^-(v)$, for each vertex $v \in V \setminus \mathcal{X}$. It will be important to know how often these estimates are (roughly) accurate. In particular, we say that a vertex u is $\hat{\epsilon}$-*well-estimated* if $|d_e(u) - d(u)| \leq \hat{\epsilon} d(u)$.

We will be interested in the case where $\hat{\epsilon} \ll \epsilon$. (In particular, we will later select $\hat{\epsilon} = \frac{\epsilon^2}{4}$.) Before analyzing the probability that a vertex is $\hat{\epsilon}$-well-estimated, recall the classical Chernoff bound.

Theorem 5. [Chernoff bound]
Let $(X_i)_{i \leq n}$ be n independent Bernouilli variables each having probability p. Then

$$\Pr[|\sum X_i - pn| \geq \delta pn] \leq e^{-\frac{\delta^2 pn}{3}}.$$

Corollary 1. *For any vertex v of in-degree at least $\Delta_0 = \max(2109, \frac{9\epsilon^2}{\hat{\epsilon}^4})$, the probability that v is not $\hat{\epsilon}$-well-estimated is at most $\frac{1}{d(v)^6}$.*

Proof. The proof is an application of Theorem 5. For every in-neighbor u_i of v, the vertex u_i is sampled with probability ϵ. Denote by X_i the Bernoulli variable corresponding to "u_i is in $\mathcal{X}$" which has value 1 if $u_i \in \mathcal{X}$ and 0 otherwise. The variables X_i are obviously independent and identically distributed. Note that $\sum X_i = \epsilon \cdot d_e(u)$ and its expectation is $\epsilon \cdot d(u)$.

$$\Pr\left(|d_e(u) - d(u)| \geq \frac{\hat{\epsilon}}{\epsilon} \cdot d(u)\right) = \Pr\left(|\epsilon \cdot d_e(u) - \epsilon \cdot d(u)| \geq \hat{\epsilon} \cdot d(u)\right)$$
$$\leq e^{-\frac{\hat{\epsilon}^2 d(u)}{3\epsilon}} \leq e^{-\frac{\hat{\epsilon}^2 \sqrt{\Delta_0}}{3\epsilon} \cdot \sqrt{d(u)}} \leq e^{-\sqrt{d(u)}}$$
$$\leq \frac{1}{d(u)^6}$$

Here the first inequality is an application of Theorem 5 with $\delta = \frac{\hat{\epsilon}}{\epsilon}$. The second inequality holds because $d(u) \geq \Delta_0$. The third inequality follows as $\Delta_0 \geq \frac{9\epsilon^2}{\hat{\epsilon}^4}$. Finally, the fourth inequality holds since $\sqrt{d(u)} \geq 6\ln(d(u))$ when $d(u) \geq \Delta_0 \geq 2109$. □

Let $\hat{\epsilon} := \frac{\epsilon^2}{4}$. We will be interested in the probability that every vertex of high degree in a local region is $\hat{\epsilon}$-well-estimated. Specifically, let x be a vertex of maximum in-degree Δ. Denote by $N^{-k}(x)$ the set of vertices which can reach x with an oriented path of length at most k. For instance, $N^{-1}(x)$ is the in-neighborhood of x plus x. Applying the union bound with Corollary 1, we obtain:

Corollary 2. *Let x be a vertex of in-degree Δ. If $\Delta \geq \Delta_1 = \max(\frac{\Delta_0}{\epsilon^2}, \frac{3}{\epsilon^5})$ then, with probability $(1-\epsilon)$, any vertex of $N^{-3}(x)$ of in-degree at least $\epsilon^2 \cdot \Delta$ is $\hat{\epsilon}$-well-estimated.*

Proof. Since $\epsilon^2 \cdot \Delta \geq \Delta_0$, Corollary 1 ensures that a vertex of in-degree at least $\epsilon^2 \cdot \Delta$ is not $\hat{\epsilon}$-well-estimated with probability at most $\frac{1}{(\epsilon^2 \Delta)^6}$. There are at most $1 + \Delta + \Delta^2 + \Delta^3 \leq 3 \cdot \Delta^3$ vertices in $N^{-3}(x)$ since $\Delta \geq 2$. The union bound implies that every vertex in $N^{-3}(x)$ with in-degree at least $\epsilon^2 \Delta$ is $\hat{\epsilon}$-well-estimated with probability at least $(1 - \frac{3\Delta^3}{\epsilon^{12}\Delta^6})$. As $\Delta \geq \frac{3}{\epsilon^5}$, the conclusion holds. □

It the rest of this section we will make a set of assumptions. Given these assumptions, we will prove that the mechanism outputs a vertex of high expected in-degree. We will say that the mechanism "fails" if these assumptions do not hold. We will then show that the probability that the mechanism fails is very small. The two assumptions we make are:

(A1) Vertex x is not sampled. This assumption fails with probability ϵ.

(A2) Every vertex in $N^{-2}(x)$ with in-degree at least $\epsilon^2 \cdot \Delta$ is regionally well-estimated. Here, we say a vertex is *regionally well-estimated* if its degree is $\hat{\epsilon}$-well-estimated and all its in-neighbors of in-degree at least $\epsilon^2 \Delta$ are also $\hat{\epsilon}$-well-estimated. Corollary 2 ensures that all the vertices of $N^{-2}(x)$ of degree at least $\epsilon^2 \cdot \Delta$ are regionally well-estimated with probability $(1 - \epsilon)$. Thus, this assumption also fails with probability at most ϵ.

4.2 Analysis of the Slicing Phase

Now we consider the slicing phase. In this phase we partition the unsampled vertices into groups (slices) according to their estimated degrees. The *width* of a slice is the difference between the upper and lower estimated-degree requirements for vertices in that group. We will need the following bounds on the width of a slice.

Lemma 3. *The width of any slice is at least $(1 - \hat{\epsilon})\epsilon^2 \cdot \Delta$ and at most $\epsilon \cdot \Delta$.*

Proof. By assumption, the vertex x of maximum degree is $\hat{\epsilon}$-well-estimated. Thus, $\Delta_e \geq (1 - \hat{\epsilon}) \cdot \Delta$. Therefore the width of any slice is at least $(1 - \hat{\epsilon})\epsilon^2 \cdot \Delta$.

On the other-hand, take any vertex u. At most Δ of u's in-neighbors can be sampled because it has degree at most Δ. It follows that $d_e(u) \leq \frac{\Delta}{\epsilon}$. Thus, $\Delta_e \leq \frac{\Delta}{\epsilon}$, and the width of any slice is at most $\epsilon \cdot \Delta$. □

4.3   Analysis of the Election Phase

We are now ready to analyze the election phase. Initially we reveal every vertex in the sample $\mathcal{X}$. The vertex y_0 with largest estimated-degree is then the provisional winner. We then treat the slices in increasing order of estimated-degree. When we the slice S_i has been considered, all the vertices in S_i except at most one (if it is the provisional winner y_i) have been revealed. For technical reasons, we will denote by S_0 the set $\mathcal{X}$. Observe that the set $\mathcal{R}$ is the set of already revealed (eliminated) vertices.

Now let $S_{\leq \ell} = \cup_{j=0}^{\ell} S_j$, and denote by $d_\ell(u) = |\{v \in S_{\leq \ell} : vu \in A\}|$ the number of in-neighbors of v that are in S_j, for $j \leq \ell$. Then we begin by proving two lemmas. The first, Lemma 4, states that if a vertex $u \in S_\ell$ has a large $d_{\ell-1}(u)$ then the elected vertex has large in-degree. The second, Lemma 5, guarantees that the elected vertex has a large in-degree (with high probability) if there are many regionally well-estimated vertices in S_ℓ with large $d_\ell(u)$. These lemmas will be applied to a vertex x of in-degree Δ: either many in-neighbors of x are in slices before x and Lemma 4 will apply, or many in-neighbors of x are in its slice and we will apply Lemma 5 to this set of in-neighbors.

Lemma 4. *Take $u \in S_{\ell+1}$. If $d_\ell(u) = d$, the elected vertex has in-degree at least $d - 1$.*

Proof. When we select the provisional winner y_ℓ all vertices of $S_{\leq \ell} = \cup_{j=0}^{\ell} S_j$ (but at most one, y'_ℓ, if it is in this set) have been revealed. Now $u \in S_{\ell+1}$ is an eligible candidate for y_ℓ. Thus, at that time, $d_{\mathcal{R}}^-(y_\ell) \geq d_{\mathcal{R}}^-(u) \geq d_\ell(u) - 1 = d - 1$. Since the in-degrees of the provisional winners can only increase, the elected vertex y_τ has is in-degree at least $d - 1$. Note that the minus one comes from the fact that y'_ℓ can be an in-neighbor of u. $\square$

Lemma 5. *Let $\Delta \geq \Delta_2 = \frac{12^2}{\epsilon^4}$. If there exists an integer ℓ and a set $Z \subseteq S_\ell$ of size at least $\epsilon \Delta$ of regionally well-estimated vertices with $d_\ell(z) \geq (1 - 3\epsilon)\Delta + 1$ for every $z \in Z$, then with probability at least $(1 - \epsilon)$ we have $d(y'_\ell) \geq (1 - 5\epsilon)\Delta$.*

Proof. First, by selecting a subset of Z if necessary, we may assume that $Z = \lceil \epsilon \Delta \rceil$. Now we define a collection of bad events and show that $d(y_\ell) \geq (1 - 5\epsilon)\Delta$ if none of these events arise. We then show the probability that any of these bad events occurs is small.

Let $\mathbf{B}_0$ be the event that every vertex in Z is placed in $\mathcal{R}$ when we sample the vertices of slice ℓ. We may assume the provisional leader $y_{\ell-1}$ is not in Z. Thus, since $|Z| \geq \epsilon \Delta$, the probability of event $\mathbf{B}_0$ is at most

$$(1 - \epsilon)^{\epsilon \Delta} = e^{\epsilon \Delta \cdot \ln(1-\epsilon)} \leq e^{-\epsilon^2 \Delta} \leq \frac{\epsilon}{2}$$

Here the first inequality holds since $\ln(1 - \epsilon) \leq -\epsilon$. The second inequality holds as $\Delta \geq \frac{2}{\epsilon^4} \geq \frac{12^2}{\epsilon^4}$.

Now take any $z \in Z$ and let U_z be the set of in-neighbors of z in $S_{\leq \ell} \setminus \{y_{\ell-1}\}$. We have $|U_z| \geq (1 - 3\epsilon) \cdot \Delta$. Let $\mathbf{B}_z$ be the event that less than $(1 - 5\epsilon) \cdot \Delta$ vertices of $|U_z|$ are in $\mathcal{R}$ at the time we sample the vertices of slice ℓ.

To analyze the probability of this event consider any $u_i \in U_z$. Now, if $u_i \in S_j$ for $j < \ell$ then u_i is already in $\mathcal{R}$. Otherwise, if $u_i \in S_\ell$ then it is now added to $\mathcal{R}$ with probability $(1 - \epsilon)$. So consider a random variable Y_i which has value 1 if $u_i \in \mathcal{R}$ after this sampling and 0 otherwise. Note the Y_i are not identically distributed. So let X_i be variables which are independent and identically distributed and such that $X_i = Y_i$ if $u_i \in S_\ell$ and X_i has value 1 with probability $(1 - \epsilon)$ otherwise. We have

$$\Pr[\sum_i Y_i \leq (1 - \epsilon - \hat{\epsilon}) \cdot |U_z|] \leq \Pr[\sum_i X_i \leq (1 - \epsilon - \hat{\epsilon}) \cdot |U_z|]$$

$$\leq e^{-\hat{\epsilon}^2(1-\epsilon) \cdot |U_z|/3} \leq e^{-\frac{1}{3}\hat{\epsilon}^2(1-\epsilon)(1-3\epsilon)\Delta}$$

$$\leq e^{-2\sqrt{\Delta}} \leq \frac{1}{3\Delta}$$

Here the first inequality follows from Theorem 5. The second inequality holds as $|U_z| \geq (1 - 3\epsilon)\Delta$. The third inequality holds by the choice $\sqrt{\Delta} \geq \frac{12}{\hat{\epsilon}^2} \geq \frac{6}{\hat{\epsilon}^2(1-\epsilon)(1-3\epsilon)}$. The fourth one is satisfied since $\Delta \geq 100$.

We now apply the union bound to the events $\mathbf{B}_0 \cup \bigcup_{z \in Z} \mathbf{B}_z$. Since $Z = \lceil \epsilon\Delta \rceil$, none of these events occur with probability at least $1 - \frac{\epsilon\Delta+1}{3\Delta} - \frac{\epsilon}{2} \geq 1 - \epsilon$. Thus, with probability at least $1 - \epsilon$, after the sampling of the slice S_ℓ, there is a vertex $z \in Z$ that is not in $\mathcal{R}$ but that has at least $(1 - 5\epsilon) \cdot \Delta$ in-neighbors in $\mathcal{R}$. The new provisional leader y'_ℓ must then satisfy $d^-_{\mathcal{R}}(y'_\ell) \geq d^-_{\mathcal{R}}(z) \geq (1 - 5\epsilon)\Delta$, as required, since $(1 - 5\epsilon) \cdot \Delta \leq (1 - \epsilon - \hat{\epsilon}) \cdot |U_z|$.   □

Proof of Theorem 2. We may now prove that the slicing mechanism is nearly optimal. We assume that $\Delta \geq M_\epsilon = \max(\Delta_1, \Delta_2)$ and that $\epsilon \leq \frac{1}{8}$. Let x be a vertex of in-degree Δ. We assume that x is not selected in $\mathcal{X}$ during the sampling phase and that all the vertices of $N^{-2}(x)$ with in-degree at least $\epsilon^2\Delta$ are regionally well-estimated. We need the following claim, where k denotes the integer such that the vertex x of maximum in-degree is in S_k.

Claim. Let u be a vertex in $N^{-3}(x)$ that is not in $S_{\leq k}$. Then $u \in S_{k+1}$.

Proof. Take a vertex $u \in N^{-3}(x)$. If $d^-(u) \leq \epsilon^2\Delta$, then its estimated degree is at most $\epsilon\Delta \leq d_e(x)$. Thus now we can assume that $d^-(u) \geq \epsilon^2\Delta$ and then u is $\hat{\epsilon}$-well-estimated by assumption on x. First observe that the set of possible estimated degrees of u intersects at most two slices. To see this note that the range of $d_e(u)$ is less than $2\hat{\epsilon} \cdot \Delta$ as u is $\hat{\epsilon}$-well-estimated. On the other-hand, by Lemma 3, the width of a slice is at least $(1 - \hat{\epsilon})\epsilon^2 \cdot \Delta$. Since $\hat{\epsilon} = \frac{\epsilon^2}{4}$ we have

$$2\hat{\epsilon}\Delta \leq \frac{1}{2}\epsilon^2\Delta < (1 - \hat{\epsilon})\epsilon^2\Delta$$

Since the range is less than the width, the observation follows.

The vertex x of maximum degree is $\hat{\epsilon}$-well-estimated and is in the slice k. Therefore, because u is $\hat{\epsilon}$-well-estimated (and necessarily $d(u) \leq d(x)$), there must be a slice smaller than or equal to k in its range of u. Thus u cannot be in a slice with index exceeding $k + 1$.   □

Assume first that there exists a set Z_1 of at least $\epsilon\Delta$ vertices of $N^{-2}(x)$ such that $Z_1 \cap S_i = \emptyset$ for $i \leq k$. The claim ensures that $Z_1 \subseteq S_{k+1}$. By considering a subset of

Z_1, we may assume that $|Z_1| = \epsilon\Delta$. (We assume that $\epsilon\Delta$ is an integer, for simplicity.) Then, for any $z \in Z_1$, we have $d_e(z) \geq d_e(x)$ since z is in the slice after x. Moreover, as x and z are $\hat{\epsilon}$-well-estimated, the facts that $|d_e(z) - d(z)| \leq \hat{\epsilon}\Delta$ and $|d_e(x) - d(x)| \leq \hat{\epsilon}\Delta$ imply that

$$d(z) \geq (1 - 2\hat{\epsilon})\Delta \geq (1 - \epsilon)\Delta$$

Furthermore, by the above claim, we must have that $d_{k+1}(z) = d(z)$. Consequently, we may apply Lemma 5 to the set Z_1. This ensures that the in-degree of the elected vertex is at least $(1 - 5\epsilon)\Delta$ with probability at least $(1 - \epsilon)$.

On the other hand, assume that now less than $\epsilon\Delta$ vertices of $N^{-2}(x)$ are in S_{k+1}. In particular, we have $d_k(x) \geq (1 - \epsilon)\Delta$. If $d_{k-1}(x) \geq (1 - 4\epsilon) \cdot \Delta + 1$ then the elected vertex has degree at least $(1 - 4\epsilon)\Delta$ by Lemma 4.

So, assume that $d_{k-1}(x) \leq (1 - 4\epsilon)\Delta$. Then at least $3\epsilon\Delta$ in-neighbors of x are in S_k. Denote by Z_2 a set of $\epsilon\Delta$ in-neighbors of x in S_k. Every vertex $z \in Z_2$ has in-degree at least $(1 - \epsilon - 2\hat{\epsilon})\Delta \geq (1 - 2\epsilon)\Delta + 1$; this follows because both x and z are $\hat{\epsilon}$-well-estimated and because the width of a slice is at most $\epsilon\Delta$ (Lemma 3). For any $z \in Z_2$, since at most $\epsilon\Delta$ of the in-neighbors of z are in S_{k+1}, we have $d_k(z) \geq (1 - 3\epsilon)\Delta + 1$. Moreover, by assumption all the vertices of Z_2 are regionally well-estimated. Hence, by Lemma 5, with probability at least $(1 - \epsilon)$, the degree of the elected vertex is at least $(1 - 5\epsilon)\Delta$, as desired.

Consequently, the slicing mechanism typically outputs a near-optimal vertex. So what is the probability that assumptions made during the proof fail to hold? Recall that Assumptions (A1) and (A2) fail to hold with probability at most 2ϵ. Given these two assumptions, Lemma 5 fails to output a provisional leader with in-degree at least $(1 - 5\epsilon) \cdot \Delta$ with probability at most ϵ. Thus the total failure probability is at most 3ϵ. Consequently, the expected in-degree of the elected vertex is at least $(1 - 3\epsilon)(1 - 5\epsilon) \cdot \Delta \geq (1 - 8\epsilon)\Delta$, which concludes the proof of Theorem 2. □

We conclude with some remarks. Here $M_\epsilon = \mathcal{O}(\frac{1}{\epsilon^8})$; the degree of this polynomial can certainly be improved as we did not attempt to optimize it.

The slicing mechanism can be adapted to select a fixed number c of winners rather than one. Let us briefly explain how. Instead of selecting only one provisional winner y during each iteration of the election phase, we can select a set of size c containing unrevealed vertices maximizing $d_{\mathcal{R}}^-$.

Let $x_1, \ldots, x_c$ be the c vertices of highest in-degree. With high probability all the vertices of $N^{-2}(x_i)$ are regionally well-estimated for every $i \leq c$ and with high probability none of them are selected during the sampling phase. Now consider two cases: either $N^{-2}(x_1)$ contains many vertices of degree almost Δ, and then an adaptation of Lemma 5 ensures that with high probability c vertices are not sampled during the sampling of the election phase and the c elected vertices have large degree. Or $N^{-2}(x_1)$ has few vertices of degree almost Δ and then when the slice of x_1 is considered, if x_1 is not selected, then all the selected vertices have degree almost Δ by Lemma 4. A similar argument can be repeated for every vertex x_i.

Acknowledgements. The authors are extremely grateful to Felix Fischer for introducing them to the impartial selection problem and for discussions. The authors also want to thanks the anonymous reviewers for their careful reading and relevant suggestions.

References

1. Alon, N., Fischer, F., Procaccia, A., Tennenholtz, M.: Sum of us: Strategyproof selection from the selectors. In: Proceedings of 13th Conference on Theoretical Aspects of Rationality and Knowledge (TARK), pp. 101–110 (2011)
2. de Clippel, G., Moulin, H., Tideman, N.: Impartial division of a dollar. Journal of Economic Theory 139, 176–191 (2008)
3. Dekel, O., Fischer, F., Procaccia, A.: Incentive compatible regression learning. Journal of Computer and System Sciences 76(8), 759–777 (2013)
4. Fischer, F., Klimm, M.: Optimal impartial selection. In: Proceedings of the 15th Conference on Economics and Computation (EC), pp. 803–820 (2014)
5. Holzman, R., Moulin, H.: Impartial nominations for a prize. Econometrica 81(1), 173–196 (2013)
6. Procaccia, A., Tennenholtz, M.: Approximate mechanism design without money. ACM Transcactions on Economics and Computing (to appear, 2014)

Value-Based Network Externalities
and Optimal Auction Design

Kamesh Munagala* and Xiaoming Xu**

Department of Computer Science, Duke University, Durham, NC 27708-0129
kamesh@cs.duke.edu, xiaomingnatexu@gmail.com

Abstract. We study revenue maximization in settings where agents' valuations exhibit positive network externalities. In our model, items have unlimited supply, and agents are unit demand. In a departure from previous literature, we assume agents have *value based* externalities, meaning that their valuation depends not only on their own signal, but also on the signals of other agents in their neighborhood who win the item. We give a complete characterization of ex-post incentive compatible and individually rational auctions in this setting. Using this characterization, we show that the optimal auction is in fact deterministic, and can be computed in polynomial time when the agents' signals are independent. We further show a constant factor approximation when the signals of agents are correlated, and an optimal mechanism in this case for a constant number of bidders.

1 Introduction

There are many goods and services for which the utility of an individual consumer increases with the number of consumers using the same good or service. This phenomenon is called *positive externalities* in the economics literature. There have been extensive studies on various settings of positive externalities in both the economics and computer science communities. Most of the literature so far has focused on the *cardinality based* utility model given by Katz *et al.* [11], where the utility of an agent is of the form $r + v(y) - p$. Here r is the agent's intrinsic *type*, *i.e.*, her private information about the good. The quantity y is the number of agents using the good; v is an non-decreasing function that measures the externalities by the number of agents using the good; p is the price for the good. Such a model of externality is motivated by several factors:

- The physical effect of the number of buyers on the quality of the good. For example choosing a telephone network over other competing brands depends on the number of users each network has.

* Supported by an award from Cisco, and by NSF grants CCF-0745761, CCF-1008065, CCF-1348696, and IIS-1447554; and by grant W911NF-14-1- 0366 from the Army Research Office (ARO).
** Supported by NSF Awards CCF-1008065.

T.-Y. Liu et al. (Eds.): WINE 2014, LNCS 8877, pp. 147–160, 2014.

- An indirect effect that gives rise to consumption externalities. For example the amount of software available in different operating systems is a function of the number of people using them.
- The availability and quality of post-purchase services depend on the size of the community using the good.

1.1   Value Based Externality Model

The cardinality based externality model discussed above assumes the externality leads to an additive increase in value depending on the number of users who obtain service. This implicitly assumes agents are identical in terms of how much they use the service. In several scenarios, the extent to which agents use the service is itself a function of their intrinsic value for the good. This motivates us to introduce the value based externality model. Agents are unit demand. Given the agents' intrinsic types $\{s_i\}$, suppose the set of agents winning the item is W. Then, the valuation for agent $i \in W$ is $v_i(s_i, W) = h_i(s_i) + \sum_{j \in W \ j \neq i} g_{ij}(s_j)$. On the other hand, for $i \notin W$, we have $v_i(s_i, W) = 0$. Since we consider positive externalities, we assume the functions h_i and g_{ij} are non-negative and non-decreasing.

As an example to illustrate the usefulness of this model, suppose agent i is deciding to adopt a social network. The agent's type is her signal s_i. This signal stands for how much she plans to use social networks. Furthermore, the agent receives externalities if her friend j also uses the same social network. The amount of externality received by i from j is determined by how much j plans to use the same network ($g_{ij}(s_j)$). Therefore, under the value based utility model, the agent's utility depends linearly on her friends' private information about how much they use the social network.

Note that the value based utility model naturally captures the *network externality* case, where the agents are located in a network $G(V, E)$, and receive externality only from neighbors in the network. Our valuation function is not only a generalization of cardinality based externality functions, but also of the *weighted sum values* model introduced in [15,12], generalized to the setting with network externalities.

1.2   Summary of Results

In this paper, we consider the Bayesian setting, where the agents' intrinsic types are assumed to be drawn from a known distribution. We assume there is unlimited supply of the item, and agents are unit demand. The goal of the auctioneer is to design an incentive compatible and individually rational mechanism that optimizes expected revenue, where the expectation is over the distribution of types, as well as the randomness introduced by the mechanism. Our solution concept will be ex-post, meaning that even when agents know the signals of the other agents, truthfulness and rationality hold in expectation over the randomness introduced by the mechanism. For formal definitions, see Section 2.

We present a characterization of ex-post (randomized) mechanisms in Section 3. Using this characterization, we show in Section 4 that when the intrinsic types of the agents are drawn from a regular product distribution, the optimal auction can be computed in polynomial time. Our characterization allows us to define a *virtual value* on each agent's private signal in a standard way. However, the winning set can have agents to have negative virtual values if they produce enough externalities. We show that despite this difficulty, we can modify the densest subgraph algorithm [5] in an interesting way to compute the minimal densest subgraph, and this allows us to design the optimal, polynomial time computable mechanism.

In Section 5 we show how to achieve near optimal ex post revenue when the distributions are correlated. Our mechanism takes the better of two deterministic mechanisms. One mechanism focuses on extracting revenue from the intrinsic value, the other one from the externalities. We show that the better of these two mechanisms produces at least $\frac{1}{4}$ of the optimal revenue.

We finally show an LP formulation whose size is polynomial in the size of the support of the joint distribution of the signal space. We round the solution to this LP to obtain an optimal mechanism when there a constant number of agents with correlated signals. More interestingly, this algorithm shows that the optimal ex-post incentive compatible and individually rational mechanism is always deterministic, *i.e.*, there is no gap between the revenues of the optimal deterministic and randomized mechanisms.

1.3 Related Work

The seminal work by Myerson [13] pioneered the study of optimal auctions in the *Bayesian* setting, where the bidders' values are assumed to be drawn from known distributions. In this setting, Myerson showed that any incentive compatible and rational mechanism satisfies monotonicity of the expected allocations of a bidder, and a relation between price and allocation. However with value-based externalities, a bidder's value also depends on her neighbor's private information. We therefore assume an agent's *type* (a.k.a. signal) is drawn from a known distribution, and her value is determined by her own signal, together with her neighbors' signals. The common approach when an agent's value depends not only on her own type but also on others' types is called the *interdependent values* setting. The key difference between the interdependent value model and the externalities model is that, in the interdependent value model, an agent can influence another agent even when she does not win the auction. However in the externalities model, an agent can influence another agent only if both of them win the items. Nevertheless our study is closely related to the literature of interdependent values, here we mention the most relevant works [15,12,6]. Roughgarden *et al.* [15] develop an analog to the Myerson's characterization for interdependent values under a matroid constraint. We show a similar characterization in the value based utility model. In terms of approximation algorithms, Li [12] showed a constant approximation for MHR distributions with interdependent values under a matroid constraint and Chawla et al. [6] generalized this result to arbitrary distributions building on a result due to Ronen [14]. We show a constant approximation to the externality model when the signals are correlated using the result in [6] as a subroutine.

Network externalities effects received much attention in recent years. These models generalize the classical model of Katz et al. [11], the value of player is her intrinsic value plus a function of the total number of winners. The work of [10,3,1,8,9] extends this model to the setting where agents are located in a network, and derive utility from the set of winners in their neighborhood. However, in all this work, the externality function only takes the identity of the winners into account, and does not take the types (signals) of the neighbors into account. In particular, the work of Haghpanah et al. [9] considered two interesting valuation functions which they call *concave externalities* and *step-function externalities*. In concave externalities, the value of an agent is a function of the set of the neighboring winners; in step-function externalities, the value of an agent is her own type if she and one of her neighbors win at the same time. Under their valuation model they studied the near optimal Bayesian incentive compatible mechanisms. We depart from this literature in considering the setting where the externality depends on the *signals* of the winning agents, and not just their identities. As mentioned before, with type-dependent externality, the valuation of an agent becomes multi-dimensional (depending on the types of other agents).

We finally note that in the ex-interim setting, the Bayesian optimal mechanism can be designed in polynomial time using the techniques in [4,2], even when the agents' signals are correlated. Similarly, for independent signals, it is not too hard to compute a constant approximation using techniques such as [10,9]; the hard part is to obtain an optimal auction.

2   Preliminaries

In this paper, we consider *unconstrained environments*, where the auctioneer can serve any subset of the agents simultaneously. As mentioned before, in our setting there are n unit-demand agents, and an unlimited supply of a homogeneous item.

Player types. An agent's type stands for all the private information about the good that is available to the agent. We denote bidder i's type by s_i. We call $s = (s_1, s_2, \ldots, s_n)$ the *signal profile* of all the bidders. And we denote (s_i', s_{-i}) as the signal profile when we change bidder i's signal from s_i to s_i' and keep signals of all other bidders the same.

As in the optimal auction design literature, we assume that the signals s is drawn from a known distribution with probability density function (PDF) f. In Section 4 the distribution is a product distribution over the bidders, and is regular. In Section 5 we allow the distribution to be general and possibly correlated across bidders. We denote the marginal PDF and CDF of bidder i as $f_i(s_i|s_{-i})$ and $F_i(s_i|s_{-i})$ respectively, where we drop s_{-i} if the marginals are independent. For analytic convenience, we assume the type space is continuous unless otherwise stated; our results easily extend to discrete type spaces.

Player values. As mentioned in the introduction, given an unconstrained environment and a signal profile s, when the winning set is W the valuation for a winning agent $i \in W$ is $v_i(s_i, W) = h_i(s_i) + \sum_{j \in W \; j \neq i} g_{ij}(s_j)$. If i does not win, $i \notin W$, we have $v_i(s_i, W) = 0$. The functions h_i and g_{ij} are non-negative and non-decreasing.

Auction. An auction or a mechanism is specified by an allocation rule x and a payment rule p. We allow the mechanisms to be randomized, so that when the reported signal profile is s, we denote $x_i(s)$ the probability that agent i wins. Denote $p_i(s)$ as the payment of agent i. The utility of an agent is her value minus her payment. An auction is *deterministic* if $x_i(s)$ only takes value 0 or 1. Denote $y_{i,j}(s)$ the probability that both agent i and j win.

Solution Concepts. In this paper we focus on *ex post incentive compatible (IC)* and *ex post individual rational (IR)* auctions. There are three popular notions of equilibria. In this paper we focus on ex post IC and IR mechanisms. We denote W_1 the winning set when agent i tells the truth s_i, and W_2 is the winning set when she misreports s_i'. An auction is *Ex post IC* if for all agents i, reported signal profiles s,

$$x_i(s)v(s, W_1) - p_i(s) \geq x(s_i', s_{-i})v(s, W_2) - p_i(s_i', s_{-i})$$

Note that this solution concept is defined agnostic to the prior distribution, which may not even be common knowledge. Ex post individually rational (IR) means that the agents do not receive negative utility, so that the condition $x_i(s)v(s, W_1) - p_i(s) \geq 0$ always holds.

Optimal Auction Design. The total expected revenue of an auction is $E_s[\sum_i p_i(s)]$. The expectation is taken over all the possible signal profile s, according to the distribution with PDF f, as well as the randomness introduced by the mechanis. In this paper we focus on achieving optimal expected revenue when s is drawn from independent regular distributions and near optimal expected revenue when s is drawn from correlated distributions.

3   Characterization of Ex-Post Mechanisms

In this section we develop a characterization of ex post IC and IR mechanisms for the value based utility model. We note that this characterization holds for both independent and correlated distributions over the signal profile.

Theorem 1 (characterization). *A (possibly randomized) mechanism is ex Post IC IR if and only if it satisfies the following two conditions:*

1. *(**Monotonicity**) $x_i(s) \leq x_i(s')$ for all $s = (s_i, s_{-i})$ and $s' = (s_i', s_{-i})$ where $s_i < s_i'$;*

2. (**Payment Identity**) *Fixing the signals of the other agents, the expected payment of agent i is*

$$p_i(s) = h(s_i)x_i(s) - \int_0^{s_i} h'(z)(x_i(z, s_{-i}))dz + \sum_{j \neq i} g(s_j)y_{ij}(s)$$

Proof. We focus on agent i and drop the subscripts in $h_i(s_i)$ and $g_{ij}(s_j)$. Consider any ex-post IC and IR mechanism. The IC conditions imply:

$$h(s_i) \cdot x_i(s) + \sum_{j \neq i} g(s_j) \cdot y_{ij}(s) - p_i(s) \geq h(s_i) \cdot x_i(s') + \sum_{j \neq i} g(s_j) \cdot y_{ij}(s') - p_i(s')$$

$$h(s_i') \cdot x_i(s') + \sum_{j \neq i} g(s_j) \cdot y_{ij}(s') - p_i(s') \geq h(s_i') \cdot x_i(s) + \sum_{j \neq i} g(s_j) \cdot y_{ij}(s) - p_i(s)$$

From these two inequalities it is easy to derive that:

$$x_i(s)(h(s_i)) - h(s_i')) \geq x_i(s')(h(s_i) - h(s_i'))$$

Therefore $x_i(s) \leq x_i(s')$ since $s_i \leq s_i'$, showing monotonicity.

The above two inequalities imply:

$$\sum_{j \neq i}(y_{ij}(s') - y_{ij}(s))g(s_j) + (x_i(s') - x_i(s))h(s_i)$$

$$\leq p_i(s') - p_i(s) \leq \sum_{j \neq i}(y_{ij}(s') - y_{ij}(s))g(s_j) + (x_i(s') - x_i(s))h(s_i')$$

Since we assumed the type space is continuous, we have:

$$\frac{dp_i(s)}{ds_i} = \frac{d\sum_{j \neq i} g(s_j)y_{ij}(s)}{ds_i} + h(s_i)\frac{dx_i(s)}{ds_i}$$

Taking the integral, we have:

$$p_i(s) = p_i(0, s_{-i}) + \int_0^{s_i} g(s_j) \, d\sum_{j \neq i} y_{ij}(z, s_{-i}) + \int_0^{s_i} h(z) \, dx_i(z, s_{-i})$$

$$= h(s_i)x_i(s)) - \int_0^{s_i} h'(z)x_i(z, s_{-i}))dz + \sum_{j \neq i} g(s_j)y_{ij}(s)$$

The second equality is true because we assume i pays 0 when she reports 0. This shows that the payment identity holds.

Suppose a mechanism satisfies monotonicity and the payment identity. Plugging in the payment identity into the ex post IC condition, we need to show:

$$x_i(s_i', s_{-i})(h(s_i') - h(s_i)) \geq \int_{s_i}^{s_i'} h'(z)x_i(z, s_{-i})dz$$

The monotonicity condition now implies the above inequality directly. This shows that any mechanism that satisfies monotonicity and the payment identity is ex-post IC and IR.

4 Optimal Mechanism for Independent, Regular Signals

Using the characterization developed so far, we design an optimal auction when the distributions of the agents' signals are independent and regular. We show that the payment identity implies we can perform optimization for each signal profile individually. For each signal profile, the resulting problem is a densest subgraph problem, which has an optimal solution computable in polynomial time [5]. However, in order to preserve monotonicity, we need a densest subgraph with a specific property, that we term the minimum densest subgraph. We show that even this solution is poly-time computable, which yields the desired mechanism.

Definition 1. *Let f_i and F_i denote the PDF and CDF of the distribution of s_i, which are assumed to be independent for different i. We define $\varphi_i(s_i) = h_i(s_i) - \frac{1-F_i(s_i)}{f_i(s_i)}h_i'(s_i)$. We say $\varphi_i(s_i)$ is the virtual value for agent i when she reports s_i. A distribution is said to be* regular *if when $s_i \geq s_i'$, then $\varphi_i(s_i) \geq \varphi_i(s_i')$.*

4.1 Revenue Expression

Lemma 1. *Fixing s_{-i}, the expected payment of agent i is $E_{s_i}[p_i(s)] = E_{s_i}[\varphi_i(s_i)x_i(s) + \sum_{i\neq j} y_{ij}(s)g_{ij}(s_j)]$.*

Proof. Since we fix s_{-i} we replace $x_i(s)$, $p_i(s)$ and $y_{ij}(s)$ by $x_i(s_i)$, $p_i(s_i)$ and $y_{ij}(s_i)$ in this proof. By Theorem 1,

$$E_{s_i}[p_i(s_i)] = \int_{z=0}^{h} p_i(z)f(z)dz$$

$$= \int_{z=0}^{h} (x_i(z)h_i(z) - \int_{b=0}^{z} h_i'(b)x(b)db + \sum_{i\neq j} y_{ij}(s_z)g_{ij}(s_j))f(z)dz$$

By integration by parts and changing the order of integration of the second term:

$$\int_{z=0}^{h} x_i(z)h_i(z)f(z)dz - \int_{b=0}^{h} x_i(b)\int_{z=b}^{h} f(z)dzh_i'(b)db + \int_{z=0}^{h} \sum_{i\neq j} y_{ij}(s_z)g_{ij}(s_j)f(z)dz$$

Renaming the variables, we get:

$$E_{s_i}[p_i(s_i)] = \int_{z=0}^{h} x_i(z)h_i(z)f(z)dz - \int_{z=0}^{h} x_i(z)[1 - F(z)]h_i'(z)dz$$

$$+ \int_{z=0}^{h} \sum_{i\neq j} y_{ij}(s_z)g_{ij}(s_j)f(z)dz$$

$$= \int_{z=0}^{h} \varphi_i(s_i)x_i(z)f(z)dz + \int_{z=0}^{h} \sum_{i\neq j} y_{ij}(s_z)g_{ij}(s_j)f(z)dz$$

$$= E_{s_i}[\varphi_i(s_i)x_i(s) + \sum_{i\neq j} y_{ij}(s)g_{ij}(s_j)]$$

Corollary 1. *The expected revenue of an ex post IC and IR mechanism is*
$E_s[Rev] = E_s[\sum_i^n \varphi_i(s_i)x_i(s) + \sum_{i \neq j}(g_{ij}(s_j) + g_{ji}(s_i))y_{ij}(s)]$

We call the sum in the expectation *virtual surplus*.

4.2   Linear Program

We call following linear program as the linear program for signal profile s.

$$\text{maximize} \sum_{i=1}^n \varphi_i(s_i)x_i + \sum_{i \neq j}(g_{ji}(s_i) + g_{ij}(s_j))y_{ij}$$

$$\begin{aligned}
\text{subject to } x_i &\geq y_{ij} & , i \neq j \\
x_j &\geq y_{ij} & , i \neq j \\
0 \leq x_i &\leq 1 & , \forall i
\end{aligned}$$

Lemma 2. *The optimal value of the linear program for signal profile s is an upper bound on the optimal expected revenue from any ex post IC IR mechanism.*

Proof. Take any ex post IC IR mechanism and set the linear program variables according to the allocation rules of the mechanism. We can easily see the linear program constraints are satisfied. By Corollary 1 we have that objective of the linear program is the expected revenue of the mechanism. Therefore the optimal value of the linear program for signal profile s is an upper bound for the optimal expected revenue from any ex post IC IR mechanisms.

The linear program for signal profile s encodes a relaxation of the densest subgraph problem (see [5]), which we define below.

Densest Subgraph Problem. Let $G = (V, E)$ be an weighted undirected graph, and let $S = (V_S, E_S)$ be a subgraph of G. We define the density to be the sum of the weights induced by S. The densest subgraph problem asks to find the subgraph S which maximizes the density. Note that there are different definitions of density in the literature. In a LP relaxation of the densest subgraph problem, we have a variable x_i for vertex i, which is 1 if i belongs to the solution, and a variable y_{ij} for edge (i, j) if both i and j are in the solution. The constraints are exactly those in the LP written above. We can therefore view the LP for signal profile s as solving a densest subgraph problem on the agents.

Lemma 3. *[5] The linear program relaxation for densest subgraph problem has an optimal integral solution which can be found in polynomial time.*

Proof. Take an fractional optimal solution to the above linear program $\hat{x}_i, \hat{y}_{ij}$ with optimal value v. Choose a number $r \in [0, 1]$. We call $V_r = \{i : x_i \geq r\}$ and $E_r = \{(ij) : y_{ij} \geq r\}$. Round x_i for all $i \in V_r$ to 1, and set all other x_i to 0. It is easy to see that $y_{ij} = 1$ if and only if $(ij) \in E_r$, since $y_{ij} = \min\{x_i, x_j\}$.

Define function $f(r) = \sum_{i \in V_r} \varphi_i(s_i) + \sum_{(i,j) \in E_r} (g_{ji}(s_i) + g_{ij}(s_j))$. We have that $\int_{r=0}^{1} f(r) dr = \sum_{i=1}^{n} \varphi_i(s_i)\hat{x}_i + \sum_{i \neq j} (g_{ji}(s_i) + g_{ij}(s_j))\hat{y}_{ij} = v$. Therefore there must be at least one r such that $f(r) \geq v$. In other words the LP has an integral optimal solution. To find the right r one need only to look for all distinct V_r sets. Note that there are at most n such sets. For details please see [5].

Definition 2. *We call the winning set found by the integral optimal solution (with optimal value v) found in Lemma 3 as a* densest subgraph. *Among all densest subgraphs let V_r be the set that has the smallest cardinality. We say that $V_r(s)$ is the* minimum densest subgraph *with density v for signal profile s.*

Lemma 4. *The minimum densest subgraph can be computed in polynomial time.*

Proof. Let G denote the original problem instance. Denote d be any number that is smaller than the difference between the optimal solution to G, and the solution with next highest density. Add a term $-\epsilon \sum_{i=1}^{n} x_i$ to the objective function in the linear program, where $\epsilon = d/n^2$. Modify this instance to G' where we subtract ϵ from the weights on all the vertices. By our choice of ϵ, it is easy to see that the densest subgraphs for G and G' differs at most d/n. Therefore the densest subgraph for instance G' can only be selected from the integral solutions for G. The modified LP finds the optimal integral solution for G', hence it computes the minimum cardinality solution to instance G.

Lemma 5. *For any signal profile s and agent i, if agent i belong to the minimum densest subgraph $V_r(s)$, fixing s_{-i}, if agent i increases her signal to $s_i' > s_i$, and denote the new signal profile s'. Then in the new instance, $i \in V_r(s')$.*

Proof. First, the minimum densest subgraph $V_r(s)$ is unique for any signal profile s. Suppose not. Let there be $V_r \neq V_r'$, and denote the induced edge sets E_r and E_r'. Suppose that

$$\sum_{i \in V_r} \varphi_i(s_i) + \sum_{(i,j) \in E_r} (g_{ji}(s_i) + g_{ij}(s_j)) = \sum_{i \in V_r'} \varphi_i(s_i) + \sum_{(i,j) \in E_r'} (g_{ji}(s_i) + g_{ij}(s_j)) = v$$

It is easy to see that since $g_{ji}(s_i) \geq 0 \; \forall i, j$, we have

$$\sum_{i \in V_r \cup V_r'} \varphi_i(s_i) + \sum_{(i,j) \in E_r \cup E_r'} (g_{ji}(s_i) + g_{ij}(s_j)) > v$$

unless

$$\sum_{i \in V_r - V_r'} \varphi_i(s_i) + \sum_{(i,j) \in E_r - E_r'} (g_{ji}(s_i) + g_{ij}(s_j)) = 0$$

However it contradicts the fact that both V_r and V_r' are minimum densest subgraphs.

Next, denote $\varphi_j'(s_j)$ the new virtual value for agent j when i increased her signal. Note that $\varphi_j'(s_j) = \varphi_j(s_j) \; \forall j \neq i$ since the signals are independent, and $\varphi_i(s_i) \leq \varphi_i'(s_i)$ by regularity. Suppose $i \in V_r(s)$ but $i \notin V_r(s')$, we have that:

$$\sum_{j \in V_r(s')} \varphi'_j(s_j) + \sum_{(j,k) \in E_r(s')} (g_{kj}(s_j) + g_{jk}(s_k))$$

$$\geq \sum_{j \in V_r(s)} \varphi'_j(s_j) + \sum_{(j,k) \in E_r(s)} (g_{kj}(s_j) + g_{jk}(s_k))$$

$$\geq \sum_{j \in V_r(s)} \varphi_j(s_j) + \sum_{(j,k) \in E_r(s)} (g_{kj}(s_j) + g_{jk}(s_k))$$

$$\geq \sum_{j \in V_r(s')} \varphi_j(s_j) + \sum_{(j,k) \in E_r(s')} (g_{kj}(s_j) + g_{jk}(s_k))$$

$$= \sum_{j \in V_r(s')} \varphi'_j(s_j) + \sum_{(j,k) \in E_r(s')} (g_{kj}(s_j) + g_{jk}(s_k))$$

The last equality holds because by our assumption, $i \notin V_r(s')$ and the fact that $\varphi'_j(s_j) = \varphi_j(s_j) \ \forall j \neq i$. This implies $V_r(s)$ and $V_r(s')$ are two distinct minimum densest subgraphs for signal profile s. This contradicts the fact that the minimum densest subgraph is unique for any input s. This completes the proof.

Algorithm 1. Mechanism 1 for Independent Signals

---

1. Ask for the signal profile $s = (s_1, s_2, \ldots, s_n)$.
2. Compute the φ virtual values based on s.
3. Solve the linear program for signal profile s. Calculate the threshold signals(corollary 4.2).
4. Allocate according to the minimal densest subgraph $V_r(s)$, and make payments $p_i = v_i((s_i^*, s_{-i}), V_r(s))$ where s_i^* is the threshold signal and $V_r(s)$ is the minimum densest subgraph for signal profile s.

Our mechanism is illustrated in Mechanism 1. We now show several properties of this mechanism. First, as a corollary of Lemma 5, we have that if we maximize the objective in the above linear program by choosing the minimum densest subgraph for all signal profiles s, then if an agent i increases her signal, her allocation is non-decreasing. Therefore, the allocation rule in Mechanism 1 satisfies the monotonicity condition in Theorem 1.

Fixing the signal profile s_{-i}, to calculate the correct payment for agent i we have to compute the minimum signal s_i^* for agent i for her to be selected by the minimum densest subgraph. As a direct consequence of Lemma 5, we have the following corollary.

Claim. Fixing s_{-i} the threshold signal s_i^* for which agent i remains in the minimum densest subgraph can be computed in polynomial time.

Proof. By lemma 5 we can use binary search to find the minimum s_i^* so that agent i remains in the minimum densest subgraph in at most $O(\log h)$ linear programming computations where h is the maximum possible value for any signals.

Putting all this together, we have the following theorem. As a corollary, we also observe that the optimal mechanism is also deterministic.

Theorem 2. *Mechanism 1 is ex post IC and IR, polynomial time computable, and it achieves optimal expected revenue among all ex post mechanisms when the signal profile s is drawn from a regular product distribution.*

5   Mechanisms for Correlated Signals

In this section we present ex post mechanisms when the signals of the agents are correlated. For small type spaces, this mechanism is optimal, while it is an approximation algorithm for implicitly specified type spaces. We use the *conditional virtual values* as defined in [15].

Definition 3. *[15] For correlated signals, we define*

$$\varphi_i(s_i|s_{-i}) = h_i(s_i) - \frac{1 - F_i(s_i|s_{-i})}{f_i(s_i|s_{-i})} h_i'(s_i)$$

as the conditional virtual value for agent i when she reports s_i. As before, we call the sum of the conditional virtual values together with the externalities the virtual surplus.

Using Theorem 1, we have the following lemma, whose proof is identical to Lemma 1.

Lemma 6. *Fixing s_{-i} the expected payment of agent i is*

$$E_{(s_i|s_{-i})}[p_i(s|s_{-i})] = E_{(s_i|s_{-i})}[\varphi_i(s_i|s_{-i})x_i(s) + \sum_{j \neq i} y_{ij}(s)g_{ij}(s_j)]$$

Here, $x_i(s)$ is the probability that agent i gets the item when the signal profile is s; and $y_{ij}(s)$ is the corresponding probability that both agents i and j get the item. Therefore, the expected revenue of an ex post IC and IR mechanism with correlated signals is

$$E[Rev] = E[\sum_i^n \varphi_i(s_i|s_{-i})x_i(s) + \sum_{i \neq j}(g_{ij}(s_j) + g_{ji}(s_i))y_{ij}(s)]$$

The approach in the previous section does not extend to correlated signals. Since when a winning agent increases her signal, the conditional virtual values for the other agents in the winning set also change. As a result, the agent can be rule out from the new optimal winning set. Nevertheless we can develop optimal and near optimal ex post IC IR mechanisms below.

Definition 4. *For signal profile s we define the auction H(s) to be the auction in which each agent's value is simply $h_i(s_i)$. We denote $Rev(H(s))$ the optimal expected ex post revenue for auction H(s). Let $G(s) = \sum_{i \neq j}(g_{ij}(s_j) + g_{ji}(s_i))$.*

5.1   Optimal Mechanism for Constant Number of Bidders

We now present an optimal mechanism that runs in polynomial time under the following assumptions. Bidder i's signal $s_i \in Q_i = \{0, 1, 2, \ldots, R_i\}$, and let $T = \times_{i=1}^{n} Q_i$ denote the joint type space, that has size $O(R^n)$, where $R = \max_i R_i$. We assume n is constant, so that $|T| = O(R^n)$ is poly-bounded. We assume $f(s) > 0$ for all $s \in T$. The definition of conditional virtual value (Def. 3) easily extends to such discrete spaces. Using the revenue formula, Lemma 6, and the monotonicity characterization Theorem 1, it is easy to check that the following integer program encodes the optimal mechanism.

$$\text{Maximize } E_{s \in T} \left[\sum_i \varphi_i(s_i | s_{-i}) x_i(s) + \sum_{(ij), i \neq j} y_{ij}(s)(g_{ij}(s_j) + g_{ji}(s_i)) \right]$$

$$
\begin{aligned}
x_i(s) &\geq y_{ij}(s) & \forall i, j, s \in T \\
x_j(s) &\geq y_{ij}(s) & \forall i, j, s \in T \\
x_i(s_i, s_{-i}) &\geq x_i(s_i', s_{-i}) & \forall i, s_{-i}, R \geq s_i \geq s_i' \geq 0 \\
x_i(s), y_{ij}(s) &\in \{0, 1\} & \forall i, j, s \in T
\end{aligned}
$$

Here, the third set of constraints encodes monotonicity; the first and second set of constraints simply encodes that agents obtain externality from each other only if they both receive the item. We relax the final constraints so that the variables are real values in $[0, 1]$. Since the support of the signals, $|T|$, is polynomial size, the above LP has polynomial size and can be solved in polynomial time. Using the same technique as in the proof of Lemma 3, we choose an r uniformly at random in $[0, 1]$. For every variable, if its value is at least r, we set that variable to 1, else we set it to 0. It is easy to check that the resulting integer solution satisfies all the constraints, and its objective is the same as the LP in expectation. Hence, we have a valid mechanism that satisfies monotonicity, and whose expected revenue has the same as the LP solution. We omit the details, and note that with some technical work, this result also extends to arbitrary discrete type spaces with poly-bounded support.

As a consequence, since the above LP has an integral optimum solution, we have the following.

Theorem 3. *For the value based utility model, there is no gap between the expected revenue of the optimal deterministic and randomized mechanisms.*

5.2   Approximation Algorithm for the General Case

We now present an approximation algorithm when there are polynomially many bidders, and the type space of the signals is continuous. We use the VCG-L mechanism of Chawla *et al.* [6] as a subroutine.

Note that for items with unlimited supply, the $VCG - L$ auction simply offers each agent a posted price which is the conditional monopoly price for that agents' marginal distribution, given the signals of the other agents. For the sake of completeness, we state the result of Chawla *et al.* [6].

Algorithm 2. Mechanism 2 for Correlated Signals

---

1. Run the mechanism that yields higher expected revenue (over all signal profiles).
2. **Either** allocate to all agents and charge each agent i $\sum_{j\neq i} g_{ij}(s_j)$; **or**
3. Run the $VCG - L$ [6] auction for correlated private values on $H(s)$.

Theorem 4. *[6] The $VCG - L$ auction with conditional monopoly reserves obtains at least half of the optimal revenue under a matroid feasibility constraint when the agent have correlated private values.*

Lemma 7. *The optimal expected ex post revenue for correlated signal profile s is at most $Rev(H(s)) + G(s)$.*

Proof. For any signal profile s, let M be any ex post IC IR mechanism for valuations which externalities. Denote M's allocation rule and payment rule by (x, p). We can construct a mechanism for auction $H(s)$ by keeping the allocation rule of M exactly the same and let the winning set be W. Subtract the externalities from the payments of all winning agents in M, that is the new payment for any winning agent i in $H(s)$ is $p'_i = p_i - \sum_{j\neq i,\ j\in W} g_{i,j}(s_j)$. We call the new mechanism M'. By Theorem 1, $p'_i = h(s^*_i) \leq h(s_i)$. Therefore M' is ex post IR for $H(s)$. On the other hand it is also easy to see M' is ex post IC for $H(s)$ since M' satisfies the two conditions in Theorem 1 for the auction $H(s)$ with zero externality. We denote the expected payment from M' by $E_s[\sum_i p'_i(s)]$ and the expected payment from M by $E_s[\sum_i p_i(s)]$. Therefore by definition of $Rev(H(s))$, we have $E_s[\sum_i p_i(s)] - G(s) \leq E_s[\sum_i p_i(s)] - \sum_{(i,j),j\neq i,i,j\in W}(g_{i,j}(s_j) + g_{j,i}(s_i)) = E_s[\sum_i p'_i(s)] \leq Rev(H(s))$ since $G(s)$ is an upper bound on the amount of externality subtracted. Therefore we have $E_s[\sum_i p_i(s)] - G(s) \leq Rev(H(s))$.

Theorem 5. *Mechanism 2 is ex post IC IR, and a 4 approximation to the expectation of the optimal ex post revenue.*

Proof. We first observe that mechanism 2 is ex post IC and IR. It takes the better of two deterministic ex post IC IR mechanisms. By Lemma 7, the optimal expected revenue is upper bounded $Rev(H(s)) + G(s)$. If step 2 is used, the revenue is $REV_1 = \sum_{i\neq j}(g_{i,j}(s_j) + g_{j,i}(s_i)) = G(s)$. If step 3 is used, by Theorem 4 we have the revenue $REV_2 \geq Rev(H(s))$. Overall we have the expected revenue $REV = \max(REV_1, REV_2) \geq 1/4 E_s[(G(s) + Rev(H(s)))]$.

References

1. Akhlaghpour, H., Ghodsi, M., Haghpanah, N., Mirrokni, V.S., Mahini, H., Nikzad, A.: Optimal iterative pricing over social networks (Extended abstract). In: Saberi, A. (ed.) WINE 2010. LNCS, vol. 6484, pp. 415–423. Springer, Heidelberg (2010)
2. Bhalgat, A., Gollapudi, S., Munagala, K.: Optimal auctions via the multiplicative weight method. In: EC, pp. 73–90 (2013)

3. Bhalgat, A., Gollapudi, S., Munagala, K.: Mechanisms and allocations with positive network externalities. In: Proceedings of the 13th ACM Conference on Electronic Commerce, pp. 179–196. ACM (2012)
4. Cai, Y., Daskalakis, C., Matthew Weinberg, S.: Optimal multi-dimensional mechanism design: Reducing revenue to welfare maximization. In: FOCS (2012)
5. Charikar, M.: Greedy approximation algorithms for finding dense components in a graph. In: Jansen, K., Khuller, S. (eds.) APPROX 2000. LNCS, vol. 1913, pp. 84–95. Springer, Heidelberg (2000)
6. Chawla, S., Fu, H., Karlin, A.: Approximate revenue maximization in interdependent value settings. Manuscript (2013)
7. Dobzinski, S., Fu, H., Kleinberg, R.D.: Optimal auctions with correlated bidders are easy. In: Proceedings of the Forty-third Annual ACM Symposium on Theory of Computing, pp. 129–138 (2011)
8. Feldman, M., Kempe, D., Lucier, B., Leme, R.P.: Pricing public goods for private sale. In: Proceedings of the Fourteenth ACM Conference on Electronic Commerce, pp. 417–434. ACM (2013)
9. Haghpanah, N., Immorlica, N., Mirrokni, V., Munagala, K.: Optimal auctions with positive network externalities. ACM Transactions on Economics and Computation 1(2), 13 (2013)
10. Hartline, J., Mirrokni, V., Sundararajan, M.: Optimal marketing strategies over social networks. In: Proceedings of the 17th International Conference on World Wide Web, WWW 2008, pp. 189–198. ACM, New York (2008)
11. Katz, M.L., Shapiro, C.: Network externalities, competition, and compatibility. The American Economic Review, 424–440 (1985)
12. Li, Y.: Approximation in mechanism design with interdependent values. In: ACM Conference on Electronic Commerce, pp. 675–676 (2013)
13. Myerson, R.B.: Optimal auction design. Mathematics of Operations Research 6(1), 58–73 (1981)
14. Ronen, A.: On approximating optimal auctions. In: Proceedings of the 3rd ACM Conference on Electronic Commerce, EC 2001, pp. 11–17. ACM, New York (2001)
15. Roughgarden, T., Talgam-Cohen, I.: Optimal and near-optimal mechanism design with interdependent values. In: Proceedings of the Fourteenth ACM Conference on Electronic Commerce, pp. 767–784. ACM (2013)

Matching Dynamics with Constraints*

Martin Hoefer[1] and Lisa Wagner[2]

[1] Max-Planck-Institut für Informatik and Saarland University, Germany
mhoefer@mpi-inf.mpg.de
[2] Dept. of Computer Science, RWTH Aachen University, Germany
lwagner@cs.rwth-aachen.de

Abstract. We study uncoordinated matching markets with additional local constraints that capture, e.g., restricted information, visibility, or externalities in markets. Each agent is a node in a fixed matching network and strives to be matched to another agent. Each agent has a complete preference list over all other agents it can be matched with. However, depending on the constraints and the current state of the game, not all possible partners are available for matching at all times.

For correlated preferences, we propose and study a general class of hedonic coalition formation games that we call coalition formation games with constraints. This class includes and extends many recently studied variants of stable matching, such as locally stable matching, socially stable matching, or friendship matching. Perhaps surprisingly, we show that all these variants are encompassed in a class of "consistent" instances that always allow a polynomial improvement sequence to a stable state. In addition, we show that for consistent instances there always exists a polynomial sequence to every reachable state. Our characterization is tight in the sense that we provide exponential lower bounds when each of the requirements for consistency is violated.

We also analyze matching with uncorrelated preferences, where we obtain a larger variety of results. While socially stable matching always allows a polynomial sequence to a stable state, for other classes different additional assumptions are sufficient to guarantee the same results. For the problem of reaching a *given* stable state, we show NP-hardness in almost all considered classes of matching games.

1 Introduction

Matching problems are at the basis of many important assignment and allocation tasks in computer science, operations research, and economics. A classic approach in all these areas is *stable matching*, as it captures distributed control and rationality of participants that arise in many assignment markets. In the standard two-sided variant, there is a set of men and a set of women. Each man (woman) has a preference list over all women (men) and strives to be matched to one woman (man). A (partial) matching M has a blocking pair (m, w) if both m and w prefer each other to their current partner in M (if any). A matching

---

* Supported by DFG Cluster of Excellence MMCI and grant Ho 3831/3-1.

T.-Y. Liu et al. (Eds.): WINE 2014, LNCS 8877, pp. 161–174, 2014.

M is stable if it has no blocking pair. A large variety of allocation problems in markets can be analyzed using variants and extensions of stable matching, e.g., the assignment of jobs to workers, organs to patients, students to dormitory rooms, buyers to sellers, etc. In addition, stable matching problems arise in the study of distributed resource allocation problems in networks.

In this paper, we study uncoordinated matching markets with dynamic matching constraints. An underlying assumption in the vast majority of works on stable matching is that matching possibilities are always available – deviations of agents are only restricted by their preferences. In contrast, many assignment markets in reality are subject to additional (dynamic) constraints in terms of information, visibility, or externalities that prohibit the formation of certain matches (in certain states). Agents might have restricted information about the population and learn about other agents only dynamically through a matching process. For example, in scientific publishing we would not expect any person to be able to write a joint paper with a possible collaborator instantaneously. Instead, agents first have to get to know about each other to engage in a cooperation. Alternatively, agents might have full information but exhibit externalities that restrict the possibility to form certain matches. For example, an agent might be more reluctant to accept a proposal from the current partner of a close friend knowing that this would leave the friend unmatched.

Recent work has started to formalize some of these intuitions in generalized matching models with dynamic restrictions. For example, the lack of information motivates *socially* [5] or *locally stable matching* [4], externalities between agents have been addressed in *friendship matching* [3]. On a formal level, these are matching models where the definition of blocking pair is restricted beyond the condition of mutual improvement and satisfies additional constraints depending on the current matching M (expressing visibility/externalities/...). Consequently, the resulting stable states are supersets of stable matchings. Our main interest in this paper are convergence properties of dynamics that evolve from iterative resolution of such restricted blocking pairs. Can a stable state be reached from every initial state? Can we reach it in a polynomial number of steps? Will randomized dynamics converge (with probability 1 and/or in expected polynomial time)? Is it possible to obtain a particular stable state from an initial state (quickly)? These questions are prominent also in the economics literature (for a small survey see below) and provide valuable insights under which conditions stable matchings will evolve (quickly) in uncoordinated markets. Also, they highlight interesting structural and algorithmic aspects of matching markets.

Perhaps surprisingly, there is a unified approach to study these questions in all the above mentioned scenarios (and additional ones) via a novel class of coalition formation games with constraints. In these games, the coalitions available for deviation in a state are specified by the interplay of generation and domination rules. We provide a tight characterization of the rules that allow to show polynomial-time convergence results. They encompass all above mentioned matching models and additional ones proposed in this paper. In addition, we provide lower bounds in each model.

Contribution and Outline. A formal definition of stable matching games, socially stable, locally stable, and friendship matching can be found in Section 1.1. In addition, we describe a novel scenario that we term *considerate matching*.

In Section 2 we concentrate on stable matching with correlated preferences, in which each matched pair generates a single number that represents the utility of the match to both agents. Blocking pair dynamics in stable matching with correlated preferences give rise to a lexicographical potential function [1, 2]. In Section 2.1 we present a general approach on *coalition formation games with constraints*. These games are hedonic coalition formation games, where deviating coalitions are characterized by sets of generation and domination rules. We concentrate on classes of rules that we term *consistent*. For correlated preferences all matching scenarios introduced in Section 1.1 can be formulated as coalition formation games with constraints and consistent rules. For games with consistent rules we show that from every initial coalition structure a stable state can be reached by a sequence of polynomially many iterative deviations. This shows that for every initial state there is always *some* stable state that can be reached efficiently. In other words, there are polynomial "paths to stability" for all consistent games. Consistency relies on three structural assumptions, and we show that if either one of them is relaxed, the result breaks down and exponentially many deviations become necessary. This also implies that in consistent games random dynamics converge with probability 1 in the limit. While it is easy to observe convergence in expected polynomial time for socially stable matching, such a result is impossible for all consistent games due to exponential lower bounds for locally stable matching. The question for considerate and friendship matching remains an interesting open problem.

In Section 2.2 we study the same question for a given initial state and a *given stable state*. We first show that if there is a sequence leading to a given stable state, then there is also another sequence to that state with polynomial length. Hence, there is a polynomial-size certificate to decide if a given (stable) state can be reached from an initial state or not. Consequently, this problem is in NP for consistent games. We also provide a generic reduction in Section 2.2 to show that it is NP-complete for all, socially stable, locally stable, considerate, and friendship matching, even with strict correlated preferences in the two-sided case. Our reduction also works for traditional two-sided stable matching with either correlated preferences and ties, or strict (non-correlated) preferences.

In Section 3 we study general preferences with incomplete lists and ties that are not necessarily correlated. We show that for socially and classes of considerate and friendship matching we can construct for every initial state a polynomial sequence of deviations to a stable state. Known results for locally stable matching show that such a result cannot hold for all consistent games.

Related Work. For a general introduction to stable matching and variants of the model we refer to textbooks in the area [26]. Over the last decade, there has been significant interest in dynamics, especially in economics, but usually there is no consideration of worst-case convergence times or computational complexity. While the literature is too broad to survey here, a few directly related works are as follows. If agents iteratively resolve blocking pairs in the two-sided stable marriage problem, dynamics can cycle [25]. On the other hand, there is always a "path to stability", i.e., a sequence of (polynomially many) resolutions converging to a stable matching [28]. If blocking pairs are chosen uniformly at random at each step, the worst-case convergence time is exponential. In the case of weighted or correlated matching, however, random dynamics converge in expected polynomial time [2,27]. More recently, several works studied convergence time of random dynamics using combinatorial properties of preferences [20], or the probabilities of reaching certain stable matchings via random dynamics [8].

In the roommates problem, where every pair of players is allowed to match, stable matchings can be absent, but deciding existence can be done in polynomial time [23]. If there exists a stable matching, there are also paths to stability [13]. Similar results hold for more general concepts like P-stable matchings that always exist [21]. Ergodic sets of the underlying Markov chain have been studied [22] and related to random dynamics [24]. Alternatively, several works have studied the computation of (variants of) stable matchings using iterative entry dynamics [7,9,10], or in scenarios with payments or profit sharing [3,6,18].

Locally stable matching was introduced by [4] in a two-sided job-market model, in which links exist only among one partition. More recently, we studied locally stable matching with correlated preferences in the roommates case [16], and with strict preferences in the two-sided case [19]. For correlated preferences, we can always reach a locally stable matching using polynomially many resolutions of local blocking pairs. The expected convergence time of random dynamics, however, is exponential. For strict non-correlated preferences, no converging sequence might exist, and existence becomes NP-hard to decide. Even if they exist, the shortest sequence might require an exponential number of steps. These convergence properties improve drastically if agents have random memory.

Friendship and other-regarding preferences in stable matching games have been addressed by [3] in a model with pairwise externalities. They study existence of friendship matchings and bound prices of anarchy and stability in correlated games as well as games with unequal sharing of matching benefits. In friendship matching, agents strive to maximize a weighted linear combination of all agent benefits. In addition, we here propose and study considerate matching based on a friendship graph, where no agent accepts a deviation that deteriorates a friend. Such ordinal externalities have been considered before in the context of resource selection games [17].

Our general model of coalition formation games with constraints is related to hedonic coalition formation games [11,12,14]. A prominent question in the literature is the existence and computational complexity of stable states (for details and references see, e.g., a recent survey [29]).

1.1   Preliminaries

A *matching game* consists of a graph $G = (V, E)$ where V is a set of vertices representing *agents* and $E \subseteq \{\{u, v\} \mid u, v \in V, u \neq v\}$ defines the *potential matching edges*. A *state* is a matching $M \subseteq E$ such that for each $v \in V$ we have $|\{e \mid e \in M, v \in e\}| \leq 1$. An edge $e = \{u, v\} \in M$ provides *utilities* $b_u(e), b_v(e) > 0$ for u and v, respectively. If for every $e \in E$ we have some $b_u(e) = b_v(e) = b(e) > 0$, we speak of *correlated preferences*. If no explicit values are given, we will assume that each agent has an order $\succeq$ over its possible matching partners, and for every agent the utility of matching edges is given according to this ranking. In this case we speak of *general preferences*. Note that in general, the ranking is allowed to be an incomplete list or to have ties. We define $B(M, u)$ to be $b_u(e)$ if $u \in e \in M$ and 0 otherwise. A *blocking pair* for matching M is a pair of agents $\{u, v\} \notin M$ such that each agent u and v is either unmatched or strictly prefers the other over its current partner (if any). A *stable matching* M is a matching without blocking pair.

Unless otherwise stated, we consider the *roommates case* without assumptions on the topology of G. In contrast, the *two-sided* or *bipartite* case is often referred to as the *stable marriage problem*. Here V is divided into two disjoint sets U and W such that $E \subseteq \{\{u, w\} \mid u \in U, w \in W\}$. Further we will consider matchings when each agent can match with up to k different agents at the same time.

In this paper, we consider broad classes of matching games, in which additional constraints restrict the set of available blocking pairs. Let us outline a number of examples that fall into this class and will be of special interest.

Socially Stable Matching. In addition to the graph G, there is a (social) *network of links* (V, L) which models static visibility. A state M has a *social blocking pair* $e = \{u, v\} \in E$ if e is blocking pair and $e \in L$. Thus, in a social blocking pair both agents can strictly increase their utility by generating e (and possibly dismissing some other edge thereby). A state M that has no social blocking pair is a *socially stable matching*. A *social improvement step* is the resolution of such a social blocking pair, that is, the blocking pair is added to M and all conflicting edges are removed.

Locally Stable Matching. In addition to G, there is a network (V, L) that models dynamic visibility by taking the current matching into account. To describe stability, we assume the pair $\{u, v\}$ is *accessible* in state M if u and v have hop-distance at most 2 in the graph $(V, L \cup M)$, that is, the shortest path between u and v in $(V, L \cup M)$ is of length at most 2 (where we define the shortest path to be of length ∞, if u and v are not in the same connected component). A state M has a *local blocking pair* $e = \{u, v\} \in E$ if e is blocking pair and u and v are accessible. Consequently, a *locally stable matching* is a matching without local blocking pair. A *local improvement step* is the resolution of such a local blocking pair, that is, the blocking pair is added to M and all conflicting edges are removed.

Considerate Matching. In this case, the (social) network (V, L) symbolizes friendships and consideration. We assume the pair $\{u, v'\}$ is *not accessible* in state M if there is agent v such that $\{u, v\} \in M$, and (a) $\{u, v\} \in L$ or (b) $\{v, v'\} \in L$. Otherwise, the pair is called accessible in M. Intuitively, this implies a form of consideration – formation of $\{u, v'\}$ would leave a friend v unmatched, so (a) u will not propose to v' or (b) v' will not accept u's proposal. A state

M has a *considerate blocking pair* $e = \{u, v\} \in E$ if e is blocking pair and it is accessible. A state M that has no considerate blocking pair is a *considerate stable matching*. A *considerate improvement step* is the resolution of such a considerate blocking pair.

Friendship Matching. In this scenario, there are numerical values $\alpha_{u,v} \geq 0$ for every unordered pair $u, v \in V$, $u \neq v$, representing how much u and v care for each other's well-being. Thus, instead of the utility gain through its direct matching partner, u now receives a *perceived utility* $B_p(M, u) = B(M, u) + \sum_{v \in V \setminus \{u\}} \alpha_{u,v} B(M, v)$. In contrast to all other examples listed above, this definition requires cardinal matching utilities and cannot be applied directly on ordinal preferences. A state M has a *perceived blocking pair* $e = \{u, v\} \in E$ if $B_p(M, u) < B_p((M \setminus \{e' \mid e \cap e' \neq \emptyset\}) \cup \{e\}, u)$ and $B_p(M, v) < B_p((M \setminus \{e' \mid e \cap e' \neq \emptyset\}) \cup \{e\}, v)$. A state M that has no perceived blocking pair is a *perceived* or *friendship stable matching*. A *perceived improvement step* is the resolution of such a perceived blocking pair.

2 Correlated Preferences

2.1 Coalition Formation Games with Constraints

In this section, we consider correlated matching where agent preferences are correlated via edge benefits $b(e)$. In fact, we will prove our results for a straightforward generalization of correlated matching – in correlated coalition formation games that involve coalitions of size larger than 2. In such a *coalition formation game* there is a set N of agents, and a set $\mathcal{C} \subseteq 2^N$ of hyper-edges, the *possible coalitions*. We denote $n = |N|$ and $m = |\mathcal{C}|$. A *state* is a *coalition structure* $\mathcal{S} \subseteq \mathcal{C}$ such that for each $v \in N$ we have $|\{C \mid C \in \mathcal{S}, v \in C\}| \leq 1$. That is, each agent is involved in at most one coalition. Each coalition C has a weight or benefit $w(C) > 0$, which is the profit given to each agent $v \in C$. For a coalition structure $\mathcal{S}$, a *blocking coalition* is a coalition $C \in \mathcal{C} \setminus \mathcal{S}$ with $w(C) > w(C_v)$ where $v \in C_v \in \mathcal{S}$ for every $v \in C$ which is part of a coalition in $\mathcal{S}$. Again, the resolution of such a blocking coalition is called an improvement step. A stable state or *stable coalition structure* $\mathcal{S}$ does not have any blocking coalitions. Correlated matching games are a special case of coalition formation games where $\mathcal{C}$ is restricted to pairs of agents and thereby defines the edge set E.

To embed the classes of matching games detailed above into a more general framework, we define *coalition formation games with constraints*. For each state $\mathcal{S}$ we consider two sets of rules – generation rules that determine candidate coalitions, and *domination rules* that forbid some of the candidate coalitions. The set of undominated candidate coalitions then forms the blocking coalitions for state $\mathcal{S}$. Using suitable generation and domination rules, this allows to describe socially, locally, considerate and friendship matching in this scenario.

More formally, there is a set $T \subseteq \{(\mathcal{T}, C) \mid \mathcal{T} \subset \mathcal{C}, C \in \mathcal{C}\}$ of *generation rules*. If in the current state $\mathcal{S}$ we have $\mathcal{T} \subseteq \mathcal{S}$ and $C \notin \mathcal{S}$, then C becomes a candidate coalition. For convenience, we exclude generation rules of the form $(\emptyset, C)$ from T

and capture these rules by a set $\mathcal{C}_g \subseteq \mathcal{C}$ of self-generating coalitions. A coalition $C \in \mathcal{C}_g$ is a candidate coalition for all states $\mathcal{S}$ with $C \notin \mathcal{S}$. In addition, there is a set $D \subseteq \{(\mathcal{T}, C) \mid \mathcal{T} \subset \mathcal{C}, C \in \mathcal{C}\}$ of *domination rules*. If $\mathcal{T} \subseteq \mathcal{S}$ for the current state $\mathcal{S}$, then C must not be inserted. To capture the underlying preferences of the agents, we assume that D always includes at least the set $D_w = \{(\{C_1\}, C_2) \mid w(C_1) \geq w(C_2), C_1 \cap C_2 \neq \emptyset, C_1 \neq C_2\}$ of all weight domination rules.

The undominated candidate coalitions represent the blocking coalitions for $\mathcal{S}$. In particular, the latter assumption on D implies that a blocking coalition must at least yield strictly better profit for every involved agent. Note that in an improvement step, one of these coalitions is inserted, and every coalition that is dominated in the resulting state is removed. By assumption on D, we remove at least every overlapping coalition with smaller weight. A coalition structure is stable if the set of blocking coalitions is empty.

Note that we could also define coalition formation games with constraints for general preferences. Then $D_w = \{(\{C_1\}, C_2) \mid C_1 \cap C_2 \neq \emptyset, C_1 \neq C_2, \exists v \in C_1 : w_v(C_1) \geq w_v(C_2)\}$. However, a crucial point in our proofs is that in a chain of succeeding deletions no coalition can appear twice. This is guaranteed for correlated preferences as coalitions can only be deleted by more worthy ones. For general preferences on the other hand there is no such argument.

In the following we define *consistency* for generation and for domination rules. This encompasses many classes of matching cases described above and is key for reaching stable states (quickly).

Definition 1. *The generation rules of a coalition formation game with constraints are called* consistent *if $T \subseteq \{(\{C_1\}, C_2) \mid C_1 \cap C_2 \neq \emptyset\}$, that is, all generation rules have only a single coalition in their precondition and the candidate coalition shares at least one agent.*

Definition 2. *The domination rules of a coalition formation game with constraints are called* consistent *if $D \subseteq \{(\mathcal{S}, C) \mid \mathcal{S} \subset \mathcal{C}, C \in \mathcal{C}, C \notin \mathcal{S}, \exists S \in \mathcal{S} : S \cap C \neq \emptyset\}$, that is, at least one of the coalitions in $\mathcal{S}$ overlaps with the dominated coalition. Note that weight domination rules are always consistent.*

Theorem 1. *In every correlated coalition formation game with constraints and consistent generation and domination rules, for every initial structure $\mathcal{S}$ there is a sequence of polynomially many improvement steps that results in a stable coalition structure. The sequence can be computed in polynomial time.*

Proof. At first we analyze the consequences of consistency in generation and domination rules. For generation rules we demand that there is only a single precondition coalition and that this coalition overlaps with the candidate coalition. Thus if we apply such a generation rule we essentially replace the precondition with the candidate. The agents in the intersection of the two coalitions would not approve such a resolution if they would not improve. Therefore, the only applicable generation rules are those where the precondition is of smaller value than the candidate.

Now for domination rules we allow an arbitrary number of coalitions in the precondition, but at least one of them has to overlap with the dominated coalition. In consequence a larger set of coalitions might dominate a non-existing coalition, but to remove a coalition they can only use the rules in D_w. That is due to the fact that when a coalition C already exists, the overlapping coalition of the precondition cannot exist at the same time. But this coalition can only be created if C does not dominate it. Especially C has to be less worthy than the precondition. Thus the overlapping precondition alone can dominate C via weight.

The proof is inspired by the idea of the edge movement graph [15]. Given a coalition formation game with consistent constraints and some initial coalition structure $\mathcal{S}_0$, we define an object movement hypergraph

$$G_{mov} = (V, V_g, T_{mov}, D_{mov}).$$

A coalition structure corresponds to a marking of the vertices in G_{mov}. The vertex set is $V = \{v_C \mid C \in \mathcal{C}\}$, and $V_g = \{v_C \mid C \in \mathcal{C}_g\}$ the set of vertices which can generate a marking by themselves. The directed exchange edges are $T_{mov} = \{(v_{C_1}, v_{C_2}) \mid (\{C_1\}, C_2) \in E, w(C_1) < w(C_2)\}$. The directed domination hyperedges are given by $D_{mov} = D_1 \cup D_w$, where $D_1 = \{(\{v_S \mid S \in \mathcal{S}\}, v_C) \mid (\mathcal{S}, C) \in D\}$. This covers the rule that a newly inserted coalition must represent a strict improvement for all involved agents. The initial structure is represented by a marking of the vertices $V_0 = \{v_C \mid C \in \mathcal{S}_0\}$.

We represent improvement steps by adding, deleting, and moving markings over exchange edges to undominated vertices of the object movement graph. Suppose we are given a state $\mathcal{S}$ and assume we have a marking at every v_C with $C \in \mathcal{S}$. We call a vertex v in G_{mov} currently *undominated* if for every hyperedge $(U, v) \in D_{mov}$ at least one vertex in U is currently unmarked. An improvement step that inserts coalition C is represented by marking v_C. For this v_C must be unmarked and undominated. We can create a new marking if $v_C \in V_g$. Otherwise, we must move a marking along an exchange edge to v_C. Note that this maps the generation rules correctly as we have seen, that we exchange the precondition for the candidate. To implement the resulting deletion of conflicting coalitions from the current state, we delete markings at all vertices which are now dominated through a rule in D_{mov}. That is, we delete markings at all vertices v with $(U, v) \in D$ and every vertex in U marked.

Observe that T_{mov} forms a DAG as the generation of the candidate coalition deletes its overlapping precondition coalition and thus the rule will only be applied if the candidate coalition yields strictly more profit for every agent in the coalition.

Lemma 1. *The transformation of markings in the object movement graph correctly mirrors the improvement dynamics in the coalition formation game with constraints.*

Proof. Let $\mathcal{S}$ be a state of the coalition formation game and let C be a blocking coalition for $\mathcal{S}$. Then C can be generated either by itself (that is, $C \in \mathcal{C}_g$) or through some generation rule with fulfilled precondition $C' \in \mathcal{S}$, and is not dominated by any subset of $\mathcal{S}$ via D. Hence, for the set of marked vertices $V_{\mathcal{S}} = \{v_C \mid C \in \mathcal{S}\}$ it holds that v_C can be generated either because $v_C \in V_g$ or because there is a marking on some $v_{C'}$ with $(v_{C'}, v_C) \in T_{mov}$, and is further not dominated via D. Hence, we can generate a marking on v_C. It is straightforward to verify that if v_C gets marked, then in the resulting deletion step only domination rules of the form $\{(\{v_S\}, v_T) \mid S, T \in \mathcal{C}, S \cap T \neq \emptyset$ and $w(S) \geq w(T)\}$ are relevant. Thus, deletion of markings is based only on overlap with the newly inserted coalition C. These are exactly the coalitions we lose when inserting C in $\mathcal{S}$.

Conversely, let $V_{\mathcal{S}}$ be a set of marked vertices of G_{mov} such that $\mathcal{S} = \{C \mid v_C \in V_{\mathcal{S}}\}$ does not violate any domination rule (i.e., for every $(\mathcal{U}, C) \in D$, we have $\mathcal{U} \not\subseteq \mathcal{S}$ or $C \notin \mathcal{S}$). Then $\mathcal{S}$ is a feasible coalition structure. Now if v_C is an unmarked vertex in G_{mov}, then $C \notin \mathcal{S}$. Furthermore, assume v_C is undominated and can be marked, because $v_C \in V_g$ or because some marking can be moved to v_C via an edge in T_{mov}. Thus for every $\{\mathcal{S}_C, C\} \in D$ v_C being undominated implies $\mathcal{S}_C \not\subseteq \mathcal{S}$. The property that v_C can be marked implies that C is self-generating or can be formed from $\mathcal{S}$ using a generation rule. Hence C is a blocking coalition in $\mathcal{S}$. The insertion C again causes the deletion of exactly the coalitions whose markings get deleted when v_C is marked. □

To show the existence of a short sequence of improvement steps we consider two phases.

Phase 1. In each round we check whether there is an exchange edge from a marked vertex to an undominated one. If this is the case, we move the marking along the exchange edge and start the next round. Otherwise for each unmarked, undominated $v \in V_g$ we compute the set of reachable positions. This can be done by doing a forward search along the exchange edges that lead to an unmarked undominated vertex. Note that the vertex has to remain undominated when there are the existing markings and a marking on the source of the exchange edge. If we find a reachable position that dominates an existing marking, we create a marking at the associated $v \in V_g$ and move it along the exchange edges to the dominating position. Then we start the next round. If we cannot find a reachable position which dominates an existing marking, we switch to Phase 2.

Phase 2. Again we compute all reachable positions from $v \in V_g$. We iteratively find a reachable vertex v_C with highest weight $w(C)$, generate a marking at the corresponding $v \in V_g$ and move it along the path of exchange edges to v_C. We repeat this phase until no reachable vertex remains.

To prove termination and bound the length, we consider each phase separately. In Phase 1 in each round we replace an existing marking by a marking of higher value either by using an exchange edge or by deleting it through domination by weight. Further the remaining markings either stay untouched or get deleted. Now the number of improvements that can be made per marking is limited by m and the number of markings is limited by n. Hence, there can be at most

mn rounds in Phase 1. Additionally, the number of steps we need per round is limited m again, as we move the marking along the DAG structure of exchange edges. Thus, phase 1 generates a total of $O(n \cdot m^2)$ steps.

If in Phase 1 we cannot come up with an improvement, there is no way to (re)move the existing markings, no matter which other steps are made in subsequent iterations. This relies on the fact that the presence of additional markings can only restrict the subgraph of reachable positions. For the same reason, iteratively generating the reachable marking of highest weight results in markings that cannot be deleted in subsequent steps. Thus, at the end of every iteration in Phase 3, the number of markings is increased by one, and all markings are un(re)movable. Consequently, in Phase 2 there are $O(m \cdot n)$ steps.

For computation of the sequence, the relevant tasks are constructing the graph G_{mov}, checking edges in T_{mov} for possible improvement of markings, or constructing subgraphs and checking connectivity of single vertices to V_g. Obviously, all these tasks can be executed in time polynomial in n, m, $|T|$ and $|D|$ using standard algorithmic techniques.   □

Next, we want to analyze whether consistency of generation and domination rules is necessary for the existence of short sequences or can be further relaxed.

Proposition 1. *If the generation rules contain more than one coalition in the precondition-set, there are instances and initial states such that every sequence to a stable state requires an exponential number of improvement steps.*

The proof uses a coalition formation game with constraints and inconsistent generation rules obtained from locally stable matching, when agents are allowed to match with partners at a hop distance of at most $\ell = 3$ in $(V, L \cup M)$. For this setting in [16, Theorem 3] we have given an instance such that every sequence to a stable state requires an exponential number of improvement steps. Note that the example is minimal in the sense that now we have at most 2 coalitions in the precondition-set. The detailed proof can be found in the full version.

Proposition 2. *If the generation rules have non-overlapping precondition- and target-coalitions, there are instances and initial states such that every sequence to a stable state requires an exponential number of improvement steps.*

The construction used for the proof exploits the fact that if precondition- and target-coalition do not overlap the precondition can remain when the target-coalition is formed. Then the dynamics require additional steps to clean up the leftover precondition-coalitions which results in an exponential blow-up. The entire proof as well as a sketch of the resulting movement graph can be found in the full version.

Proposition 3. *If the domination rules include target-coalitions that do not overlap with any coalition in the precondition, there are instances and starting states such that every sequence cycles.*

Consistent generation and domination rules arise in a large variety of settings, not only in basic matching games but also in some interesting extensions.

Corollary 1. *Consistent generation and domination rules are present in*

- *locally stable matching if agents can create $k = 1$ matching edges and have lookahead $\ell = 2$ in $G = (V, M \cup L)$.*
- *socially stable matching, even if agents can create $k \geq 1$ matching edges.*
- *considerate matching, even if agents can create $k \geq 1$ matching edges.*
- *friendship matching, even if agents can create $k \geq 1$ matching edges.*

Due to space restrictions we cannot give a detailed description of the embedding into coalition formation games with constraints. In most cases the embedding is quite straightforward. Agents and edge set are kept as well as the benefits. The generation and domination rules often follow directly from the definitions. The exact embedding for every type of game can be found in the full version. Additionally an exemplar proof for correctness is stated.

Unlike for the other cases, for locally stable matching we cannot guarantee consistent generation rules if we increase the number of matching edges. The same holds for lookahead > 2. In both cases the accessibility of an edge might depend on more than one matching edge. There are exponential lower bounds in [16, 19] for those extensions which proves that it is impossible to find an embedding with consistent rules even with the help of auxiliary constructions.

2.2 Reaching a Given Matching

In this section we consider the problem of deciding reachability of a *given* stable matching from a given initial state. We first show that for correlated coalition formation games with constraints and consistent rules, this problem is in NP. If we can reach it and there exists a sequence, then there always exists a polynomial-size certificate due to the following result.

Theorem 2. *In a correlated coalition formation game with constraints and consistent generation and domination rules, for every coalition structure S^* that is reachable from an initial state S_0 through a sequence of improvement steps, there is also a sequence of polynomially many improvement steps from S_0 to S^*.*

For the proof we analyze an arbitrary sequence of improvement steps from S_0 to S^* and show that, if the sequence is too long, there are unnecessary steps, that is, coalitions are created and deleted without making a difference for the final outcome. By identifying and removing those superfluous steps we can reduce every sequence to one of polynomial length. The detailed proof can be found in the full version.

For locally stable matching, the problem of reaching a given locally stable matching from a given initial matching is known to be NP-complete [19]. Here we provide a generic reduction that shows NP-completeness for socially, locally, considerate, and friendship matching, even in the two-sided case. Surprisingly, it also applies to ordinary two-sided stable matching games that have either correlated preferences with ties, or non-correlated strict preferences. Observe that the problem is trivially solvable for ordinary stable matching and correlated preferences without ties, as in this case there is a unique stable matching that can always be reached using the greedy construction algorithm [2].

Theorem 3. *It is* NP-*complete to decide if for a given matching game, initial matching M_0 and stable matching M^*, there is a sequence of improvement steps leading form M_0 to M^*. This holds even for bipartite games with strict correlated preferences in the case of*

1. *socially stable matching and locally stable matching,*
2. *considerate matching, and*
3. *friendship matching for symmetric α-values in $[0, 1]$.*

In addition, it holds for ordinary bipartite stable matching in the case of

4. *correlated preferences with ties,*
5. *strict preferences.*

3   General Preferences

In this section we consider convergence to stable matchings in the two-sided case with general preferences that may be incomplete and have ties. For locally stable matching it is known that in this case there are instances and initial states such that no locally stable matching can be reached using local blocking pair resolutions. Moreover, deciding the existence of a converging sequence of resolutions is NP-hard [19].

We here study the problem for socially, considerate, and friendship matching. Our positive results are based on the following procedure from [2] that is known to construct a sequence of polynomial length for unconstrained stable matching. The only modification of the algorithm for the respective scenarios is to resolve "social", "considerate" or "perceived blocking pairs" in both phases.

Phase 1. Iteratively resolve only blocking pairs involving a matched vertex $w \in W$. Phase 1 ends when for all blocking pairs $\{u, w\}$ we have $w \in W$ unmatched.

Phase 2. Choose an unmatched $w \in W$ that is involved in a blocking pair. Resolve one of the blocking pairs $\{u, w\}$ that is most preferred by w. Repeat until there are no blocking pairs.

It is rather straightforward to see that the algorithm can be applied directly to build a sequence for socially stable matching.

Theorem 4. *In every bipartite instance of socially stable matching $G = (V = U \dot\cup W, E)$ with general preference lists and social network L, for every initial matching M_0 there is a sequence of polynomially many improvement steps that results in a socially stable matching. The sequence can be computed in polynomial time.*

For extended settings the algorithm still works for somewhat restricted social networks. For considerate matching we assume that the link set is only within $L \subseteq (U \times U) \cup (U \times W)$, i.e., no links within partition W.

Theorem 5. *In every bipartite instance of considerate matching $G = (V = U \dot{\cup} W, E)$ with general preference lists and social network L such that $\{w, w'\} \notin L$ for all $w, w' \in W$, for every initial matching M_0 there is a sequence of polynomially many improvement steps that results in a considerate matching. The sequence can be computed in polynomial time.*

We also apply the algorithm to friendship matching in case there can be arbitrary friendship relations $\alpha_{u,u'}, \alpha_{u',u} \geq 0$ for each pair $u, u' \in U$. Here we allow asymmetry with $\alpha_{u,u'} \neq \alpha_{u',u}$. Otherwise, for all $u \in U, w, w' \in W$ we assume that $\alpha_{u,w} = \alpha_{w,u} = \alpha_{w,w'} = 0$, i.e., friendship only exists within U.

Theorem 6. *In every bipartite instance of friendship matching $G = (V = U \dot{\cup} W, E)$ with benefits b and friendship values α such that $\alpha_{u,u'} > 0$ only for $u, u' \in U$, for every initial matching M_0 there is a sequence of polynomially many improvement steps that results in a friendship matching. The sequence can be computed in polynomial time.*

The algorithm works fine with links between partitions U and W for the considerate setting, but it fails for positive α between partitions in the friendship case. We defer a discussion to the full version of the paper.

Acknowledgment. Part of this research was done at the Institute for Mathematical Sciences of NUS Singapore, and at NTU Singapore. The authors thank Edith Elkind for suggesting to study considerate matching.

References

1. Abraham, D., Levavi, A., Manlove, D., O'Malley, G.: The stable roommates problem with globally ranked pairs. Internet Math. 5(4), 493–515 (2008)
2. Ackermann, H., Goldberg, P., Mirrokni, V., Röglin, H., Vöcking, B.: Uncoordinated two-sided matching markets. SIAM J. Comput. 40(1), 92–106 (2011)
3. Anshelevich, E., Bhardwaj, O., Hoefer, M.: Friendship and stable matching. In: Bodlaender, H.L., Italiano, G.F. (eds.) ESA 2013. LNCS, vol. 8125, pp. 49–60. Springer, Heidelberg (2013)
4. Arcaute, E., Vassilvitskii, S.: Social networks and stable matchings in the job market. In: Leonardi, S. (ed.) WINE 2009. LNCS, vol. 5929, pp. 220–231. Springer, Heidelberg (2009)
5. Askalidis, G., Immorlica, N., Kwanashie, A., Manlove, D.F., Pountourakis, E.: Socially stable matchings in the hospitals/Residents problem. In: Dehne, F., Solis-Oba, R., Sack, J.-R. (eds.) WADS 2013. LNCS, vol. 8037, pp. 85–96. Springer, Heidelberg (2013)
6. Biró, P., Bomhoff, M., Golovach, P.A., Kern, W., Paulusma, D.: Solutions for the stable roommates problem with payments. Theoret. Comput. Sci. 540, 53–61 (2014)

7. Biró, P., Cechlárová, K., Fleiner, T.: The dynamics of stable matchings and half-matchings for the stable marriage and roommates problems. Int. J. Game Theory 36(3-4), 333–352 (2008)
8. Biró, P., Norman, G.: Analysis of stochastic matching markets. Int. J. Game Theory 42(4), 1021–1040 (2013)
9. Blum, Y., Roth, A., Rothblum, U.: Vacancy chains and equilibration in senior-level labor markets. J. Econom. Theory 76, 362–411 (1997)
10. Blum, Y., Rothblum, U.: "Timing is everything" and martial bliss. J. Econom. Theory 103, 429–442 (2002)
11. Bogomolnaia, A., Jackson, M.: The stability of hedonic coalition structures. Games Econom. Behav. 38, 201–230 (2002)
12. Cechlárová, K.: Stable partition problem. In: Encyclopedia of Algorithms (2008)
13. Diamantoudi, E., Miyagawa, E., Xue, L.: Random paths to stability in the roommates problem. Games Econom. Behav. 48(1), 18–28 (2004)
14. Hajduková, J.: Coalition formation games: A survey. Intl. Game Theory Rev. 8(4), 613–641 (2006)
15. Hoefer, M.: Local matching dynamics in social networks. In: Aceto, L., Henzinger, M., Sgall, J. (eds.) ICALP 2011, Part II. LNCS, vol. 6756, pp. 113–124. Springer, Heidelberg (2011)
16. Hoefer, M.: Local matching dynamics in social networks. Inf. Comput. 222, 20–35 (2013)
17. Hoefer, M., Penn, M., Polukarov, M., Skopalik, A., Vöcking, B.: Considerate equilibrium. In: Proc. 22nd Intl. Joint Conf. Artif. Intell. (IJCAI), pp. 234–239 (2011)
18. Hoefer, M., Wagner, L.: Designing profit shares in matching and coalition formation games. In: Chen, Y., Immorlica, N. (eds.) WINE 2013. LNCS, vol. 8289, pp. 249–262. Springer, Heidelberg (2013)
19. Hoefer, M., Wagner, L.: Locally stable marriage with strict preferences. In: Fomin, F.V., Freivalds, R., Kwiatkowska, M., Peleg, D. (eds.) ICALP 2013, Part II. LNCS, vol. 7966, pp. 620–631. Springer, Heidelberg (2013)
20. Hoffman, M., Moeller, D., Paturi, R.: Jealousy graphs: Structure and complexity of decentralized stable matching. In: Chen, Y., Immorlica, N. (eds.) WINE 2013. LNCS, vol. 8289, pp. 263–276. Springer, Heidelberg (2013)
21. Inarra, E., Larrea, C., Moris, E.: Random paths to P-stability in the roommates problem. Int. J. Game Theory 36(3-4), 461–471 (2008)
22. Inarra, E., Larrea, C., Moris, E.: The stability of the roommate problem revisited. Core Discussion Paper 2010/7 (2010)
23. Irving, R.: An efficient algorithm for the "stable roommates" problem. J. Algorithms 6(4), 577–595 (1985)
24. Klaus, B., Klijn, F., Walzl, M.: Stochastic stability for roommate markets. J. Econom. Theory 145, 2218–2240 (2010)
25. Knuth, D.: Marriages stables et leurs relations avec d'autres problemes combinatoires. Les Presses de l'Université de Montréal (1976)
26. Manlove, D.: Algorithmics of Matching Under Preferences. World Scientific (2013)
27. Mathieu, F.: Acyclic preference-based systems. In: Shen, X., Yu, H., Buford, J., Akon, M. (eds.) Handbook of Peer-to-Peer Networking. Springer (2010)
28. Roth, A., Vate, J.V.: Random paths to stability in two-sided matching. Econometrica 58(6), 1475–1480 (1990)
29. Woeginger, G.J.: Core stability in hedonic coalition formation. In: van Emde Boas, P., Groen, F.C.A., Italiano, G.F., Nawrocki, J., Sack, H. (eds.) SOFSEM 2013. LNCS, vol. 7741, pp. 33–50. Springer, Heidelberg (2013)

Truthful Approximations to Range Voting

Aris Filos-Ratsikas and Peter Bro Miltersen*

Department of Computer Science, Aarhus University, Aarhus, Denmark
{filosra,bromille}@cs.au.dk

Abstract. We consider the fundamental mechanism design problem of *approximate social welfare maximization* under *general cardinal preferences* on a finite number of alternatives and *without money*. The well-known *range voting* scheme can be thought of as a non-truthful mechanism for exact social welfare maximization in this setting. With m being the number of alternatives, we exhibit a randomized truthful-in-expectation ordinal mechanism with approximation ratio $\Omega(m^{-3/4})$. On the other hand, we show that for sufficiently many agents, the approximation ratio of any truthful-in-expectation ordinal mechanism is $O(m^{-2/3})$. We supplement our results with an upper bound for any truthful-in-expectation mechanism. We get tighter bounds for the natural special case of $m = 3$, and in that case furthermore obtain separation results concerning the approximation ratios achievable by natural restricted classes of truthful-in-expectation mechanisms. In particular, we show that the best cardinal truthful mechanism strictly outperforms all ordinal ones.

1 Introduction

We consider the fundamental mechanism design problem of *approximate social welfare maximization* under *general cardinal preferences* and *without money*. In this setting, there is a finite set of agents (or *voters*) $N = \{1, \ldots, n\}$ and a finite set of alternatives (or *candidates*) $M = \{1, \ldots, m\}$. Each voter i has a private valuation function $u_i : M \to \mathbb{R}$ that can be arbitrary, except that it is injective, i.e., it induces a total order on candidates. Standardly, the function u_i is considered well-defined only up to positive affine transformations. That is, $x \to a u_i(x) + b$, for $a > 0$ and any b, is considered to be a different representation of u_i. Given this, we fix a canonical representation of u_i. The two most widely used cannonical representations in literature are *unit-range* (i.e. $\forall j, u_i(j) \in [0, 1]$ and $\max_j u_i(j) = 1$, $\min_j u_i(j) = 0$) [1–4, 6, 8, 9] and *unit-sum* (i.e. $\forall j, u_i(j) \in [0, 1]$ and $\sum_j u_i(j) = 1$) [7, 8, 13]. In this paper we will assume that all u_i are

---
* The authors acknowledge support from the Danish National Research Foundation and The National Science Foundation of China (under the grant 61061130540) for the Sino-Danish Center for the Theory of Interactive Computation, within which this work was performed. The authors also acknowledge support from the Center for Research in Foundations of Electronic Markets (CFEM), supported by the Danish Strategic Research Council. Author's addresses: Department of Computer Science, Aarhus University, Aabogade 34, DK-8200 Aarhus N, Denmark.

T.-Y. Liu et al. (Eds.): WINE 2014, LNCS 8877, pp. 175–188, 2014.

canonically represented using the unit-sum representation, because it is arguably more suited for social welfare maximization. Intuitively, agents should not be "punished" for liking a lot of different outcomes. We shall let V_m denote the set of all unit-range canonically represented valuation functions.

We shall be interested in *direct revelation mechanisms without money* that elicit the *valuation profile* $\mathbf{u} = (u_1, u_2, \ldots, u_n)$ from the voters and based on this elect a candidate $J(\mathbf{u}) \in M$. We shall allow mechanisms to be randomized and $J(\mathbf{u})$ is therefore in general a random map. In fact, we shall define a mechanism simply to be a random map $J : V_m{}^n \to M$. We prefer mechanisms that are *truthful-in-expectation*, by which we mean that the following condition is satisfied: For each voter i, and all $\mathbf{u} = (u_i, u_{-i}) \in V_m{}^n$ and $\tilde{u}_i \in V_m$, we have $E[u_i(J(u_i, u_{-i})] \geq E[u_i(J(\tilde{u}_i, u_{-i})]$. That is, if voters are assumed to be expected utility maximizers, the optimal behavior of each voter is always to reveal their true valuation function to the mechanism. As truthfulness-in-expectation is the only notion of truthfulness of interest to us in this paper, we shall use "truthful" as a synonym for "truthful-in-expectation" from now on. Furthermore, we are interested in mechanisms for which the expected *social welfare*, i.e., $E[\sum_{i=1}^{n} u_i(J(\mathbf{u}))]$, is as high as possible, and we shall in particular be interested in the *approximation ratio* of the mechanism, trying to achieve mechanisms with as high an approximation ratio as possible. Note that for $m = 2$, the problem is easy; a majority vote is a truthful mechanism that achieves optimal social welfare, i.e., it has approximation ratio 1, so we only consider the problem for $m \geq 3$.

A mechanism without money for general cardinal preferences can be naturally interpreted as a *cardinal voting scheme* in which each voter provides a *ballot* giving each candidate $j \in M$ a numerical score between 0 and 1. A winning candidate is then determined based on the set of ballots. With this interpretation, the well-known *range voting scheme* is simply the determinstic mechanism that elects the socially optimal candidate $\text{argmax}_{j \in M} \sum_{i=1}^{n} u_i(j)$, or, more precisely, elects this candidate *if* ballots are reflecting the true valuation functions u_i. In particular, range voting has by construction an approximation ratio of 1. However, range voting is not a truthful mechanism.

As our first main result, we exhibit a randomized truthful mechanism with an approximation ratio of $0.37m^{-3/4}$. The mechanism is *ordinal*: Its behavior depends only on the *rankings* of the candidates on the ballots, not on their numerical scores. We also show a negative result: For sufficiently many voters and any truthful ordinal mechanism, there is a valuation profile where the mechanism achieves at most an $O(m^{-2/3})$ fraction of the optimal social welfare in expectation. The negative result also holds for non-ordinal mechanisms that are *mixed-unilateral*, by which we mean mechanisms that elect a candidate based on the ballot of a single randomly chosen voter. Finally, we prove that no truthful mechanism can achieve an approximation ratio of 0.94.

We get tighter bounds for the natural case of $m = 3$ candidates and for this case, we also obtain separation results concerning the approximation ratios achievable by natural restricted classes of truthful mechanisms. In particular, the best mixed-unilateral mechanism strictly outperforms all ordinal ones, even the non-unilateral ordinal ones. The mixed-unilateral mechanism that establishes this is a convex combination of *quadratic-lottery*, a mechanism presented by Freixas [9] and Feige and Tennenholtz [6] and *random-favorite*, the mechanism that picks a voter uniformly at random and elects his favorite candidate.

1.1   Background, Related Research and Discussion

Characterizing strategy-proof social choice functions (a.k.a., truthful direct revelation mechanisms without money) under general preferences is a classical topic of mechanism design and social choice theory. The class of truthful deterministic mechanisms is limited to *dictatorships*, as proven by the celebrated Gibbard-Satterthwaite theorem [10, 20]. On the other hand, the class of randomized truthful mechanisms is much richer [2], as suggested by the following characterization for randomized ordinal mechanisms:

Theorem 1. *[11] The ordinal mechanisms without money that are truthful under general cardinal preferences[1] are exactly the convex combinations of truthful* unilateral *ordinal mechanisms and truthful* duple *mechanisms.*

Here, a *unilateral* mechanism is a randomized mechanism whose output depends on the ballot of a single distinguished voter i^* only. A *duple* mechanism is an ordinal mechanism for which there are two distinguished candidates so that all other candidates are elected with probability 0, for all valuation profiles.

One of the main conceptual contributions from computer science to mechanism design is the suggestion of a measure for comparing mechanisms and finding the best one, namely the notion of worst case approximation ratio [16, 18] relative to some objective function. Following this research program, and using Gibbard's characterization, Procaccia [17] gave in a paper conceptually very closely related to the present one but he only considered objective functions that can be defined ordinally (such as, e.g., Borda count), and did in particular not consider approximating the optimal social welfare, as we do in the present paper.

Social welfare maximization is indeed a very standard objective in mechanism design. In particular, it is very widespread in *quasi-linear* settings (where valuations are measured in monetary terms)(see [15, 19]). On the other hand, in the setting of social choice theory, the valuation functions are to be interpreted as von Neumann-Morgenstern utilities (i.e, they are meant to encode orderings on lotteries), and in particular are only well-defined up to affine transformations. In this setting, the social welfare has to be defined as above, as the result of adding up the valuations of all players, *after* these are normalized by scaling to, say, the interval [0,1]. A significant amount of work considers social welfare maximization in the von Neumann-Morgenstern setting. [5, 7, 8, 13].

---

[1] without ties, i.e., valuation functions must be injective, as we require throughout this paper, except in Theorem 6. If ties were allowed, the characterization would be much more complicated.

It is often argued that while an underlying cardinal utility structure exists, it is more reasonable to only ask individuals to only provide a *ranking* of the candidates, rather than exact numerical values. This makes ordinal mechanisms particularly appealing. The limitations of this class of mechanisms were considered recently by Boutilier *et al.* [5] in a very interesting paper closely related to the present one, but crucially, they did not require truthfulness of the mechanisms in their investigations. On the other hand, truthfulness is the pivotal property in our approach. Perhaps the most interesting question to ask is whether truthful cardinal mechanisms [4, 9, 22], can outperform truthful ordinal ones, in terms of social welfare. We answer this in the positive for the case of three alternatives. Exploring the limitations of truthful cardinal mechanisms is impaired by the lack of a characterization similar to the one of Theorem 1 for the general case. Obtaining such a characterization is a major open problem in social choice theory and several attempts have been made throughout the years [3, 4, 9, 12]. Our results imply that one could be able to sidestep the need for such a characterization and use direct manipulation arguments to obtain upper bounds and at the same time highlight what to look for and what to avoid, when trying to come up with "good" cardinal truthful mechanisms.

Our investigations are very much helped by the work of Feige and Tennenholtz [6] and Freixas [9]. In particular, our construction establishing the gap between the approximation ratios for cardinal and ordinal mechanisms for three candidates is based on the *quadratic lottery*, first presented in [9] and later in [6]. Most of the proofs are omitted due to lack of space but appear in the full version.

2   Preliminaries

We let V_m denote the set of canonically represented valuation functions on $M = \{1, 2, \ldots, m\}$. That is, V_m is the set of injective functions $u : M \to [0, 1]$ with the property that 0 as well as 1 are contained in the image of u.

We let $\mathrm{Mech}_{m,n}$ denote the set of truthful mechanisms for n voters and m candidates. That is, $\mathrm{Mech}_{m,n}$ is the set of random maps $J : V_m{}^n \to M$ with the property that for voter $i \in \{1, \ldots, n\}$, and all $\mathbf{u} = (u_i, u_{-i}) \in V_m{}^n$ and $\tilde{u}_i \in V_m$, we have $E[u_i(J(u_i, u_{-i}))] \geq E[u_i(J(\tilde{u}_i, u_{-i}))]$. Alternatively, instead of viewing a mechanism as a random map, we can view it as a map from $V_m{}^n$ to Δ_m, the set of probability density functions on $\{1, \ldots, m\}$. With this interpretation, note that $\mathrm{Mech}_{m,n}$ is a convex subset of the vector space of all maps from $V_m{}^n$ to $\mathbb{R}^m$. We shall be interested in certain special classes of mechanisms. In the following definitions, we throughout view a mechanism J as a map from $V_m{}^n$ to Δ_m.

An *ordinal* mechanism J is a mechanism with the property: $J(u_i, u_{-i}) = J(u'_i, u_{-i})$, for any voter i, any preference profile $\mathbf{u} = (u_i, u_{-i})$, and any valuation function u'_i with the property that for all pairs of candidates j, j', it is the case that $u_i(j) < u_i(j')$ if and only if $u'_i(j) < u'_i(j')$. Informally, the behavior of an ordinal mechanism only depends on the ranking of candidates on each ballot; not on the numerical valuations. We let $\mathrm{Mech}^{\mathrm{o}}_{m,n}$ denote those mechanisms in $\mathrm{Mech}_{m,n}$ that are ordinal.

Following Barbera [2], we define an *anonymous* mechanism J as one that does not depend on the names of voters. Formally, given any permutation π on N, and any $\mathbf{u} \in (V_m)^n$, we have $J(\mathbf{u}) = J(\pi \cdot \mathbf{u})$, where $\pi \cdot \mathbf{u}$ denotes the vector $(u_{\pi(i)})_{i=1}^n$. Similarly following Barbera [2], we define a *neutral* mechanism J as one that does not depend on the names of candidates. Formally, given any permutation σ on M, any $\mathbf{u} \in (V_m)^n$, and any candidate j, we have $J(\mathbf{u})_{\sigma(j)} = J(u_1 \circ \sigma, u_2 \circ \sigma, \dots, u_n \circ \sigma)_j$.

Following [4, 11], a *unilateral* mechanism is a mechanism for which there exists a single voter i^* so that for all valuation profiles (u_{i^*}, u_{-i^*}) and any alternative valuation profile u'_{-i^*} for the voters except i^*, we have $J(u_{i^*}, u_{-i^*}) = J(u_{i^*}, u'_{-i^*})$. Note that i^* is *not* allowed to be chosen at random in the definition of a unilateral mechanism. In this paper, we shall say that a mechanism is *mixed-unilateral* if it is a convex combination of unilateral truthful mechanisms. Mixed-unilateral mechanisms are quite attractive seen through the "computer science lens": They are mechanisms of *low query complexity*, consulting only a single randomly chosen voter, and therefore deserve special attention in their own right. We let $\mathrm{Mech}_{m,n}^{\mathsf{U}}$ denote those mechanisms in $\mathrm{Mech}_{m,n}$ that are mixed-unilateral. Also, we let $\mathrm{Mech}_{m,n}^{\mathsf{OU}}$ denote those mechanisms in $\mathrm{Mech}_{m,n}$ that are ordinal as well as mixed-unilateral.

Following Gibbard [11], a *duple* mechanism J is an ordinal[2] mechanism for which there exist two candidates j_1^* and j_2^* so that for all valuation profiles, J elects all other candidates with probability 0.

We next give names to some specific important mechanisms. We let $U_{m,n}^q \in \mathrm{Mech}_{m,n}^{\mathsf{OU}}$ be the mechanism for m candidates and n voters that picks a voter uniformly at random, and elects uniformly at random a candidate among his q most preferred candidates. We let *random-favorite* be a nickname for $U_{m,n}^1$ and *random-candidate* be a nickname for $U_{m,n}^m$. We let $D_{m,n}^q \in \mathrm{Mech}_{m,n}^{\mathsf{O}}$, for $\lfloor n/2 \rfloor + 1 \leq q \leq n + 1$, be the mechanism for m candidates and n voters that picks two candidates uniformly at random and eliminates all other candidates. It then checks for each voter which of the two candidates he prefers and gives that candidate a "vote". If a candidate gets at least q votes, she is elected. Otherwise, a coin is flipped to decide which of the two candidates is elected. We let *random-majority* be a nickname for $D_{m,n}^{\lfloor n/2 \rfloor + 1}$. Note also that $D_{m,n}^{n+1}$ is just another name for *random-candidate*. Finally, we shall be interested in the following mechanism Q_n for three candidates shown to be in $\mathrm{Mech}_{3,n}^{\mathsf{U}}$ by Feige and Tennenholtz [6]: Select a voter uniformly at random, and let α be the valuation of his second most preferred candidate. Elect his most preferred candidate with probability $(4 - \alpha^2)/6$, his second most preferred candidate with probability $(1 + 2\alpha)/6$ and his least preferred candidate with probability $(1 - 2\alpha + \alpha^2)/6$. We let *quadratic-lottery* be a nickname for Q_n. Note that *quadratic-lottery* is not ordinal. Feige and Tennenholtz [6] in fact presented several explicitly given non-ordinal one-voter truthful mechanisms, but *quadratic-lottery* is particularly amenable to an

---

[2] Barbera *et al.* [4] gave a much more general definition of duple mechanism; their duple mechanisms are not restricted to be ordinal. In this paper, "duple" refers exclusively to Gibbard's original notion.

approximation ratio analysis due to the fact that the election probabilities are quadratic polynomials.

We let ratio(J) denote the approximation ratio of a mechanism $J \in \mathrm{Mech}_{m,n}$, when the objective is social welfare. That is,

$$\mathrm{ratio}(J) = \inf_{\mathbf{u} \in V_m{}^n} \frac{E[\sum_{i=1}^n u_i(J(\mathbf{u}))]}{\max_{j \in M} \sum_{i=1}^n u_i(j)}.$$

We let $r_{m,n}$ denote the best possible approximation ratio when there are n voters and m candidates. That is, $r_{m,n} = \sup_{J \in \mathrm{Mech}_{m,n}} \mathrm{ratio}(J)$. Similarly, we let $r^C_{m,n} = \sup_{J \in \mathrm{Mech}^C_{m,n}} \mathrm{ratio}(J)$, for C being either $\mathbf{O}$, $\mathbf{U}$ or $\mathbf{OU}$. We let r_m denote the asymptotically best possible approximation ratio when the number of voters approaches infinity. That is, $r_m = \liminf_{n \to \infty} r_{m,n}$, and we also extend this notation to the restricted classes of mechanisms with the obvious notation $r^{\mathbf{O}}_m, r^{\mathbf{U}}_m$ and $r^{\mathbf{OU}}_m$.

The importance of neutral and anonymous mechanisms is apparent from the following simple lemma:

Lemma 1. *For all $J \in \mathrm{Mech}_{m,n}$, there is a $J' \in \mathrm{Mech}_{m,n}$ such that J' is anonymous and neutral and so that $\mathrm{ratio}(J') \geq \mathrm{ratio}(J)$. Similarly, for all $J \in \mathrm{Mech}^C_{m,n}$, there is $J' \in \mathrm{Mech}^C_{m,n}$ so that J' is anonymous and neutral and so that $\mathrm{ratio}(J') \geq \mathrm{ratio}(J)$, for C being either $\mathbf{O}$, $\mathbf{U}$ or $\mathbf{OU}$.*

Lemma 1 makes the characterizations of the following theorem very useful.

Theorem 2. *The set of anonymous and neutral mechanisms in $\mathrm{Mech}^{\mathbf{OU}}_{m,n}$ is equal to the set of convex combinations of mechanisms $U^q_{m,n}$, for $q \in \{1, \ldots, m\}$. Also, the set of anonymous and neutral mechanisms in $\mathrm{Mech}_{m,n}$ that can be obtained as convex combinations of duple mechanisms is equal to the set of convex combinations of the mechanisms $D^q_{m,n}$, for $q \in \{\lfloor n/2 \rfloor + 1, \lfloor n/2 \rfloor + 2, \ldots, n, n+1\}$.*

The following corollary is immediate from Theorem 1 and Theorem 2.

Corollary 1. *The ordinal, anonymous and neutral mechanisms in $\mathrm{Mech}_{m,n}$ are exactly the convex combinations of the mechanisms $U^q_{m,n}$, for $q \in \{1, \ldots, m\}$ and $D^q_{m,n}$, for $q \in \{\lfloor n/2 \rfloor + 1, \lfloor n/2 \rfloor + 2, \ldots, n\}$.*

We next present some lemmas that allow us to understand the asymptotic behavior of $r_{m,n}$ and $r^C_{m,n}$ for fixed m and large n, for C being either $\mathbf{O}$, $\mathbf{U}$ or $\mathbf{OU}$.

Lemma 2. *For any positive integers n, m, k, we have $r_{m,kn} \leq r_{m,n}$ and $r^C_{m,kn} \leq r^C_{m,n}$, for C being either $\mathbf{O}$, $\mathbf{U}$ or $\mathbf{OU}$.*

Lemma 3. *For any $m, n \geq 2, \epsilon > 0$ and all $n' \geq (n-1)m/\epsilon$, we have $r_{m,n'} \leq r_{m,n} + \epsilon$ and $r^C_{m,n'} \leq r^C_{m,n} + \epsilon$, for C being either $\mathbf{O}$, $\mathbf{U}$, or $\mathbf{OU}$.*

In particular, Lemma 3 implies that $r_{m,n}$ converges to a limit as $n \to \infty$.

2.1 Quasi-Combinatorial Valuation Profiles

It will sometimes be useful to restrict the set of valuation functions to a certain finite domain $R_{m,k}$ for an integer parameter $k \geq m$. Specifically, we define:

$$R_{m,k} = \left\{ u \in V_m | u(M) \subseteq \{0, \frac{1}{k}, \frac{2}{k}, \ldots, \frac{k-1}{k}, 1\} \right\}$$

where $u(M)$ denotes the image of u. Given a valuation function $u \in R_{m,k}$, we define its *alternation number* $a(u)$ as

$$a(u) = \#\{j \in \{0, \ldots, k-1\} | [\frac{j}{k} \in u(M)] \oplus [\frac{j+1}{k} \in u(M)]\},$$

where $\oplus$ denotes exclusive-or. That is, the alternation number of u is the number of indices j for which exactly one of j/k and $(j+1)/k$ is in the image of u. Since $k \geq m$ and $\{0, 1\} \subseteq u(M)$, we have that the alternation number of u is at least 2. We shall be interested in the class of valuation functions $C_{m,k}$ with minimal alternation number. Specifically, we define:

$$C_{m,k} = \{u \in R_{m,k} | a(u) = 2\}$$

and shall refer to such valuation functions as *quasi-combinatorial valuation functions*. Informally, the quasi-combinatorial valuation functions with sufficiently small k, have all valuations as close to 0 or 1 as possible.

The following lemma will be very useful in later sections. It formalizes the intuition that for ordinal mechanisms, the worst approximation ratio is achieved in extreme profiles, when all valuations are either very close to 1 or very close to 0.

Lemma 4. *Let $J \in \mathrm{Mech}_{m,n}$ be ordinal and neutral. Then*

$$\mathrm{ratio}(J) = \liminf_{k \to \infty} \min_{\mathbf{u} \in (C_{m,k})^n} \frac{E[\sum_{i=1}^{n} u_i(J(\mathbf{u}))]}{\sum_{i=1}^{n} u_i(1)}.$$

The idea of the proof is that starting from a valuation profile, we can iductively "shift" blocks of valuations towards 0 or 1, without increasing the approximation ratio and this way transform the profile into a quasi-combinatorial profile. This is possible because since the mechanism is ordinal, this "shift" leaves the outcome unchanged. See the full version for the full proof.

3   Mechanisms and Negative Results for the Case of Many Candidates

We can now analyze the approximation ratio of the mechanism $J \in \mathrm{Mech}_{m,n}^{\mathrm{OU}}$ that with probability 3/4 elects a uniformly random candidate and with probability 1/4 uniformly at random picks a voter and elects a candidate uniformly at random from the set of his $\lfloor m^{1/2} \rfloor$ most preferred candidates.

Theorem 3. Let $n \geq 2, m \geq 3$. Let $J = \frac{3}{4}U_{m,n}^m + \frac{1}{4}U_{m,n}^{\lfloor m^{1/2} \rfloor}$. Then, ratio$(J) \geq 0.37m^{-3/4}$.

Proof. For a valuation profile $\mathbf{u} = (u_i)$, we define $g(\mathbf{u}) = \frac{E[\sum_{i=1}^n u_i(J(\mathbf{u}))]}{\sum_{i=1}^n u_i(1)}$. By Lemma 4, since J is ordinal, it is enough to bound from below $g(\mathbf{u})$ for all $\mathbf{u} \in (C_{m,k})^n$ with $k \geq 1000(nm)^2$. Let $\epsilon = 1/k$. Let $\delta = m\epsilon$. Note that all functions of $\mathbf{u}$ map each alternative either to a valuation smaller than δ or a valuation larger than $1 - \delta$.

Since each voter assigns valuation 1 to at least one candidate, and since J with probability 3/4 picks a candidate uniformly at random from the set of all candidates, we have $E[\sum_{i=1}^n u_i(J(\mathbf{u}))] \geq 3n/(4m)$. Suppose $\sum_{i=1}^n u_i(1) \leq 2m^{-1/4}n$. Then $g(\mathbf{u}) \geq \frac{3}{8}m^{-3/4}$, and we are done. So we shall assume from now on that

$$\sum_{i=1}^n u_i(1) > 2m^{-1/4}n. \tag{1}$$

Obviously, $\sum_{i=1}^n u_i(1) \leq n$. Since J with probability 3/4 picks a candidate uniformly at random from the set of all candidates, we have $E[\sum_{i=1}^n u_i(J(\mathbf{u}))] \geq \frac{3}{4m}\sum_{i,j} u_i(j)$. So if $\sum_{i,j} u_i(j) \geq \frac{1}{2}nm^{1/4}$, we have $g(\mathbf{u}) \geq \frac{3}{8}m^{-3/4}$, and we are done. So we shall assume from now on that

$$\sum_{i,j} u_i(j) < \frac{1}{2}nm^{1/4}. \tag{2}$$

Still looking at the fixed quasi-combinatorial $\mathbf{u}$, let a voter i be called *generous* if his $\lfloor m^{1/2} \rfloor + 1$ most preferred candidates are all assigned valuation greater than $1 - \delta$. Also, let a voter i be called *friendly* if he has candidate 1 among his $\lfloor m^{1/2} \rfloor$ most preferred candidates. Note that if a voter is neither generous nor friendly, he assigns to candidate 1 valuation at most δ. This means that the total contribution to $\sum_{i=1}^n u_i(1)$ from such voters is less than $n\delta < 0.001/m$. Therefore, by equation (1), the union of friendly and generous voters must be a set of size at least $1.99m^{-1/4}n$.

If we let g denote the number of generous voters, we have $\sum_{i,j} u_i(j) \geq gm^{1/2}(1 - \delta) \geq 0.999gm^{1/2}$, so by equation (2), we have that $0.999gm^{1/2} < \frac{1}{2}nm^{1/4}$. In particular $g < 0.51m^{-1/4}n$. So since the union of friendly and generous voters must be a set of size at least a $1.99m^{-1/4}n$ voters, we conclude that there are at least $1.48m^{-1/4}n$ friendly voters, i.e. the friendly voters is at least a $1.48m^{-1/4}$ fraction of the set of all voters. But this ensures that $U_{m,n}^{\lfloor m^{1/2} \rfloor}$ elects candidate 1 with probability at least $1.48m^{-1/4}/m^{1/2} \geq 1.48m^{-3/4}$. Then, J elects candidate 1 with probability at least $0.37m^{-3/4}$ which means that $g(\mathbf{u}) \geq 0.37m^{-3/4}$, as desired. This completes the proof. $\square$

We next state our negative result. We show that any convex combination of (not necessarily ordinal) unilateral and duple mechanisms performs poorly. The proof is omitted due to lack of space, but can be found in the full version of the paper.

Theorem 4. *Let $m \geq 20$ and let $n = m - 1 + g$ where $g = \lfloor m^{2/3} \rfloor$. For any mechanism J that is a convex combination of unilateral and duple mechanisms in $\mathrm{Mech}_{m,n}$, we have $\mathrm{ratio}(J) \leq 5m^{-2/3}$.*

Corollary 2. *For all m, and all sufficiently large n compared to m, any mechanism J in $\mathrm{Mech}_{m,n}^{\mathrm{o}} \cup \mathrm{Mech}_{m,n}^{\mathrm{U}}$ has approximation ratio $O(m^{-2/3})$.*

Proof. Combine Theorem 1, Lemma 3 and Theorem 4. □

As followup work to the present paper, in a working manuscript, Lee [14] states a lower bound of $\Omega(m^{-2/3})$ that closes the gap between our upper and lower bounds. The mechanism achieving this bound is a convex combination of random-favorite and the mixed unilateral mechanism that uniformly at random elects one of the $m^{1/3}$ most preferred candidates of a uniformly chosen voter. The main question that we would like to answer is how well one can do with (general) cardinal mechanisms. The next theorem provides a weak upper bound.

Theorem 5. *All mechanisms $J \in \mathrm{Mech}_{m,n}$ with $m, n \geq 3$ have $\mathrm{ratio}(J) < 0.94$.*

Recall that in the definition of valuation functions u_i, we required u_i to be injective, i.e. no ties are not allowed. This requirement is made primarily for convenience, and all results of this paper can also be proved for the setting with ties. In contrast, allowing ties seems crucial for the proof of the follwing theorem, yielding a much stronger upper bound on the approximation ratio of any truthful mechanism than Theorem 5:

Theorem 6. *Any voting mechanism in the settting with ties, for m alternatives and n agents with $m \geq n^{\lfloor \sqrt{n} \rfloor + 2}$, has approximation ratio $O(\log \log m / \log m)$.*

The proof uses a black-box reduction from the *one-sided matchings problem* for which Filos-Ratsikas et al. [8] proved a $O(1/\sqrt{n})$ upper bound. Ideally, we want all negative result to hold for the setting without ties and the positive ones to hold for the setting with ties. We leave a "no-ties" version of Theorem 6 for future work.

4   Mechanisms and Negative Results for the Case of Three Candidates

In this section, we consider the special case of three candidates $m = 3$. To improve readability, we shall denote the three candidates by A, B and C, rather than by 1,2 and 3. When the number of candidates m as well as the number of voters n are small constants, the exact values of $r_{m,n}^{\mathrm{o}}$ and $r_{m,n}^{\mathrm{OU}}$ can be determined. We describe a general method for how to exactly and mechanically compute $r_{m,n}^{\mathrm{o}}$ and $r_{m,n}^{\mathrm{OU}}$ and the associated optimal mechanisms for small values of m and n. The key is to apply *Yao's principle* [21] and view the construction of a randomized mechanism as devising a strategy for Player I in a two-player zero-sum game G played between Player I, the mechanism designer, who picks a mechanism J and

Player II, the adversary, who picks an input profile $\mathbf{u}$ for the mechanism, i.e., an element of $(V_m)^n$. The payoff to Player I is the approximation ratio of J on $\mathbf{u}$. Then, the value of G is exactly the approximation ratio of the best possible randomized mechanism. In order to apply the principle, the computation of the value of G has to be tractable. In our case, Theorem 2 allows us to reduce the strategy set of Player I to be finite while Lemma 4 allows us to reduce the strategy set of Player II to be finite. This makes the game into a matrix game, which can be solved to optimality using linear programming. The details follow.

For fixed m, n and $k > 2m$, recall that the set of quasi-combinatorial valuation functions $C_{m,k}$ is the set of valuation functions u for which there is a j so that $\Im(u) = \{0, \frac{1}{k}, \frac{2}{k}, \ldots, \frac{m-j-1}{k}\} \cup \{\frac{k-j+1}{k}, \frac{k-j+2}{k}, \ldots, \frac{k-1}{k}, 1\}$. Note that a quasi-combinatorial valuation function u is fully described by the value of k, together with a partition of M into two sets M_0 and M_1, with M_0 being those candidates close to 0 and M_1 being those sets close to 1 together with a ranking of the candidates (i.e., a total ordering $<$ on M), so that all elements of M_1 are greater than all elements of M_0 in this ordering. Let the *type* of a quasi-combinatorial valuation function be the partition and the total ordering $(M_0, M_1, <)$. Then, a quasi-combinatorial valuation function is given by its type and the value of k. For instance, if $m = 3$, one possible type is $(\{B\}, \{A, C\}, \{B < A < C\})$, and the quasi-combinatorial valuation function u corresponding to this type for $k = 1000$ is $u(A) = 0.999$, $u(B) = 0$, $u(C) = 1$. We see that for any fixed value of m, there is a finite set T_m of possible types. In particular, we have $|T_3| = 12$. Let $\eta : T_m \times \mathbb{N} \to C_{m,k}$ be the map that maps a type and an integer k into the corresponding quasi-combinatorial valuation function.

For fixed m, n, consider the following matrices G and H. The matrix G has a row for each of the mechanisms $U_{m,n}^q$ for $q = 1, \ldots, m$, while the matrix H has a row for each of the mechanisms $U_{m,n}^q$ for $q = 1, \ldots, m$ as well as for each of the mechanisms $D_{m,n}^q$, for $q = \lfloor n/2 \rfloor + 1, \lfloor n/2 \rfloor + 2, \ldots, n$. Both matrices have a column for each element of $(T_m)^n$. The entries of the matrices are as follows: Each entry is indexed by a mechanism $J \in \text{Mech}_{m,n}$ (the row index) and by a type profile $\mathbf{t} \in (T_m)^n$ (the column index). We let that entry be

$$c_{J,\mathbf{t}} = \lim_{k \to \infty} \frac{E[\sum_{i=1}^n u_i(J(\mathbf{u}^k))]}{\max_{j \in M} \sum_{i=1}^n u_i^k(j)},$$

where $u_i^k = \eta(t_i, k)$. Informally, we let the entry be the approximation ratio of the mechanism on the quasi-combinatorial profile of the type profile indicated in the column and with $1/k$ being "infinitisimally small". Note that for the mechanisms at hand, despite the fact that the entries are defined as a limit, it is straightforward to compute the entries symbolically, and they are rational numbers. We now have the following lemma.

Lemma 5. *The value of G, viewed as a matrix game with the row player being the maximizer, is equal to $r_{m,n}^{\text{OU}}$. The value of H is equal to $r_{m,n}^{\text{O}}$. Also, the optimal strategies for the row players in the two matrices, viewed as convex combinations of the mechanisms corresponding to the rows, achieve those ratios.*

When applying Lemma 5 for concrete values of m, n, one can take advantage of the fact that all mechanisms corresponding to rows are anonymous and neutral. This means that two different columns will have identical entries if they correspond to two type profiles that can be obtained from one another by permuting voters and/or candidates. This makes it possible to reduce the number of columns drastically. After such reduction, we have applied the theorem to $m = 3$ and $n = 2, 3, 4$ and 5, computing the corresponding optimal approximation ratios and optimal mechanisms. We leave the details for the full version and instead now turn our attention to the case of three candidates and arbitrarily many voters. In particular, we shall be interested in $r_3^{\text{O}} = \liminf_{n \to \infty} r_{3,n}^{\text{O}}$ and $r_3^{\text{OU}} = \liminf_{n \to \infty} r_{3,n}^{\text{OU}}$. By Lemma 3, we in fact have $r_3^{\text{O}} = \lim_{n \to \infty} r_{3,n}^{\text{O}}$ and $r_3^{\text{OU}} = \lim_{n \to \infty} r_{3,n}^{\text{OU}}$. We present a family of ordinal and mixed-unilateral mechanisms J_n with $\text{ratio}(J_n) > 0.610$. In particular, $r_3^{\text{OU}} > 0.610$. The coefficents c_1 and c_2 were found by trial-and-error; we present more information about how in the full version.

Theorem 7. *Let* $c_1 = \frac{77066611}{157737759} \approx 0.489$ *and* $c_2 = \frac{80671148}{157737759} \approx 0.511$. *Let* $J_n = c_1 \cdot U_{m,n}^1 + c_2 \cdot U_{m,n}^2$. *For all* n, *we have* $\text{ratio}(J_n) > 0.610$.

Proof. By Lemma 4, we have that

$$\text{ratio}(J_n) = \liminf_{k \to \infty} \min_{\mathbf{u} \in (C_{3,k})^n} \frac{E[\sum_{i=1}^n u_i(J_n(\mathbf{u}))]}{\sum_{i=1}^n u_i(A)}.$$

Recall the definition of the set of *types* T_3 of quasi-combinatorial valuation functions on three candidates and the definintion of η preceding the proof of Lemma 5. From that discussion, we have $\liminf_{k \to \infty} \min_{\mathbf{u} \in (C_{m,k})^n} \frac{E[\sum_{i=1}^n u_i(J_n(\mathbf{u}))]}{\sum_{i=1}^n u_i(A)} = \min_{\mathbf{t} \in (T_3)^n} \liminf_{k \to \infty} \frac{E[\sum_{i=1}^n u_i(J_n(\mathbf{u}))]}{\sum_{i=1}^n u_i(A)}$, where $u_i = \eta(t_i, k)$. Recall that $|T_3| = 12$. Since J_n is anonymous, to determine the approximation ratio of J_n on $\mathbf{u} \in (C_{m,k})^n$, we observe that we only need to know the value of k and the *fraction* of voters of each of the possible 12 types. In particular, fixing a type profile $\mathbf{t} \in (C_{m,k})^n$, for each type $k \in T_3$, let x_k be the fraction of voters in $\mathbf{u}$ of type k. For convenience of notation, we identify T_3 with $\{1, 2, \ldots, 12\}$ using the scheme depicted in Table 1. Let $w_j = \lim_{k \to \infty} \sum_{i=1}^n u_i(i)$, where $u_i = \eta(t_i, k)$, and let $p_j = \lim_{k \to \infty} \Pr[E_j]$, where E_j is the event that candidate j is elected by J_n in an election with valuation profile $\mathbf{u}$ where $u_i = \eta(t_i, k)$. We then have $\liminf_{k \to \infty} \frac{E[\sum_{i=1}^n u_i(J_n(\mathbf{u}))]}{\sum_{i=1}^n u_i(A)} = (p_A \cdot w_A + p_B \cdot w_B + p_C \cdot w_C)/w_A$. Also, from Table 1 and the definition of J_n, we see:

$$w_A = n(x_1 + x_2 + x_3 + x_4 + x_5 + x_9)$$
$$w_B = n(x_1 + x_5 + x_6 + x_7 + x_8 + x_{11})$$
$$w_C = n(x_4 + x_7 + x_9 + x_{10} + x_{11} + x_{12})$$
$$p_A = (c_1 + c_2/2)(x_1 + x_2 + x_3 + x_4) + (c_2/2)(x_5 + x_6 + x_9 + x_{10})$$
$$p_B = (c_1 + c_2/2)(x_5 + x_6 + x_7 + x_8) + (c_2/2)(x_1 + x_2 + x_{11} + x_{12})$$
$$p_C = (c_1 + c_2/2)(x_9 + x_{10} + x_{11} + x_{12}) + (c_2/2)(x_3 + x_4 + x_7 + x_8)$$

Table 1. Variables for types of quasi-combinatorial valuation functions with ϵ denoting $1/k$

Candidate/Variable	x_1	x_2	x_3	x_4	x_5	x_6	x_7	x_8	x_9	x_{10}	x_{11}	x_{12}
A		1	1	1	1	$1-\epsilon$	ϵ	0	0	$1-\epsilon$	ϵ	0	0
B	$1-\epsilon$	ϵ	0	0	1	1	1	1	0	0	$1-\epsilon$	ϵ
C	0	0	ϵ	$1-\epsilon$	0	0	$1-\epsilon$	ϵ	1	1	1	1

Thus we can establish that ratio(J_n) > 0.610 for all n, by showing that the quadratic program "*Minimize* $(p_A \cdot w_A + p_B \cdot w_B + p_C \cdot w_C) - 0.610 w_A$ *subject to* $x_1 + x_2 + \cdots + x_{12} = 1, x_1, x_2, \ldots, x_{12} \geq 0$", where $w_A, w_B, w_C, p_A, p_B, p_C$ have been replaced with the above formulae using the variables x_i, has a strictly positive minimum (note that the parameter n appears as a multiplicative constant in the objective function and can be removed, so there is only one program, not one for each n). This was established rigorously by solving the program symbolically in Maple by a facet enumeration approach (the program being non-convex), which is easily feasible for quadratic programs of this relatively small size.   □

We next present a family of ordinal mechanisms J'_n with ratio(J'_n) > 0.616. In particular, $r_3^o > 0.616$. The proof idea is the same as in the proof of Theorem 7 althought the existence of duple mechanisms requires some additional care. The details are left for the full version.

Theorem 8. *Let* $c'_1 = 0.476, c'_2 = 0.467$ *and* $d = 0.057$ *and let* $J_n = c'_1 \cdot U^1_{3,n} + c'_2 U^2_{3,n} + d \cdot D^{\lfloor n/2 \rfloor + 1}_{m,n}$. *Then* ratio($J_n$) > 0.616 *for all* n.

We next show that $r_3^{ou} \leq 0.611$ and $r_4^o \leq 0.641$. By Lemma 3, it is enough to show that $r_{3,n^*}^{ou} \leq 0.611$ and $r_{3,n^*}^o \leq 0.641$ for some fixed n^*. Therefore, the statements follow from the following theorem. We leave the proof for the full version.

Theorem 9. $r_{3,23000}^{ou} \leq \frac{32093343}{52579253} < 0.611$ *and* $r_{3,23000}^o \leq \frac{41}{64} < 0.641$.

We finally show that r_3^u is between 0.660 and 0.750. The upper bound follows from the following proposition and Lemma 3.

Proposition 1. $r_{3,2}^u \leq 0.75$.

The lower bound follows from an analysis of the *quadratic-lottery* [6, 9]. The main reason that we focus on this particular cardinal mechanism is given by the following lemma. The proof is a simple modification of the proof of Lemma 4 and is omitted here.

Lemma 6. *Let* $J \in \text{Mech}_{3,n}$ *be a convex combination of* Q_n *and any ordinal and neutral mechanism. Then*

$$\text{ratio}(J) = \liminf_{k \to \infty} \min_{\mathbf{u} \in (C_{m,k})^n} \frac{E[\sum_{i=1}^n u_i(J(\mathbf{u}))]}{\sum_{i=1}^n u_i(1)}.$$

Theorem 10. *The limit of the approximation ratio of Q_n as n approaches infinity, is exactly the golden ratio, i.e., $(\sqrt{5} - 1)/2 \approx 0.618$. Also, let J_n be the mechanism for n voters that selects* random-favorite *with probability $29/100$ and* quadratic-lottery *with probability $71/100$. Then,* $\mathrm{ratio}(J_n) > \frac{33}{50} = 0.660$.

Proof. (sketch) Lemma 6 allows us to proceed completely as in the proof of Theorem 7, by constructing and solving appropriate quadratic programs. As the proof is a straightforward adaptation, we leave out the details. □

Mechanism J_n of Theorem 10 achieves an approximation ratio strictly better than 0.641. In other words, the best truthful cardinal mechanism for three candidates strictly outperforms all ordinal ones.

5 Conclusion

By the statement of Lee [14], mixed-unilateral mechanisms are asymptotically no better than ordinal mechanisms. Can a cardinal mechanism which is not mixed-unilateral beat this approximation barrier? Getting upper bounds on the performance of general cardinal mechanisms is impaired by the lack of a characterization of cardinal mechanisms a la Gibbard's. Can we adapt the proof of Theorem 6 to work in the general setting without ties? For the case of $m = 3$, can we close the gaps for ordinal mechanisms and for mixed-unilateral mechanisms? How well can cardinal mechanisms do for $m = 3$? Theorem 5 holds for $m = 3$ as well, but perhaps we could prove a tighter upper bound for cardinal mechanisms in this case.

References

1. Barbera, S.: Nice decision schemes. In: Leinfellner, Gottinger (eds.) Decision Theory and Social Ethics. Reidel (1978)
2. Barbera, S.: Majority and positional voting in a probabilistic framework. The Review of Economic Studies 46(2), 379–389 (1979)
3. Barbera, S.: Strategy-proof social choice. In: Arrow, K.J., Sen, A.K., Suzumura, K. (eds.) Handbook of Social Choice and Welfare, vol. 2, ch. 25. North-Holland, Amsterdam (2010)
4. Barbera, S., Bogomolnaia, A., van der Stel, H.: Strategy-proof probabilistic rules for expected utility maximizers. Mathematical Social Sciences 35(2), 89–103 (1998)
5. Boutilier, C., Caragiannis, I., Haber, S., Lu, T., Procaccia, A.D., Sheffet, O.: Optimal social choice functions: A utilitarian view. In: Proceedings of the 13th ACM Conference on Electronic Commerce, pp. 197–214. ACM (2012)
6. Feige, U., Tennenholtz, M.: Responsive lotteries. In: Kontogiannis, S., Koutsoupias, E., Spirakis, P.G. (eds.) SAGT 2010. LNCS, vol. 6386, pp. 150–161. Springer, Heidelberg (2010)
7. Feldman, M., Lai, K., Zhang, L.: The proportional-share allocation market for computational resources. IEEE Transactions on Parallel and Distributed Systems 20(8), 1075–1088 (2009)

8. Filos-Ratsikas, A., Frederiksen, S.K.S., Zhang, J.: Social welfare in one-sided matchings: Random priority and beyond. In: Lavi, R. (ed.) SAGT 2014. LNCS, vol. 8768, pp. 1–12. Springer, Heidelberg (2014)
9. Freixas, X.: A cardinal approach to straightforward probabilistic mechanisms. Journal of Economic Theory 34(2), 227–251 (1984)
10. Gibbard, A.: Manipulation of voting schemes: A general result. Econometrica 41(4), 587–601 (1973)
11. Gibbard, A.: Manipulation of schemes that mix voting with chance. Econometrica 45(3), 665–681 (1977)
12. Gibbard, A.: Straightforwardness of game forms with lotteries as outcomes. Econometrica 46(3), 595–614 (1978)
13. Guo, M., Conitzer, V.: Strategy-proof allocation of multiple items between two agents without payments or priors. In: Proceedings of the 9th International Conference on Autonomous Agents and Multiagent Systems, vol. 1, pp. 881–888 (2010)
14. Lee, A.S.: Maximization of relative social welfare on truthful voting scheme with cardinal preferences. Working Manuscript (2014)
15. Nisa, N.: Introduction to Mechanism Design (for Computer Scientists). In: Algorithmic Game Theory, ch. 9, pp. 209–241. Cambridge University Press, New York (2007)
16. Nisan, N., Ronen, A.: Algorithmic mechanism design (extended abstract). In: Proceedings of the Thirty-first Annual ACM Symposium on Theory of Computing, pp. 129–140. ACM (1999)
17. Procaccia, A.D.: Can approximation circumvent Gibbard-Satterthwaite? In: AAAI 2010, Proceedings. AAAI Press (2010)
18. Procaccia, A.D., Tennenholtz, M.: Approximate mechanism design without money. In: Proceedings of the 10th ACM Conference on Electronic Commerce, pp. 177–186. ACM (2009)
19. Roberts, K.: The characterization of implementable choice rules. In: Laffont, J.-J. (ed.) Aggregation and Revelation of Preferences. Papers presented at the 1st European Summer Workshop of the Econometric Society, pp. 321–349. North-Holland (1979)
20. Satterthwaite, M.A.: Strategy-proofness and Arrow's conditions: Existence and correspondence theorems for voting procedures and social welfare functions. Journal of Economic Theory 10(2), 187–217 (1975)
21. Yao, A.C.-C.: Probabilistic computations: Toward a unified measure of complexity. In: 18th Annual Symposium on Foundations of Computer Science, pp. 222–227. IEEE (1977)
22. Zeckhauser, R.: Voting systems, honest preferences and Pareto optimality. The American Political Science Review 67, 934–946 (1973)

Resource Competition on Integral Polymatroids

Tobias Harks[1,*], Max Klimm[2,**], and Britta Peis[3]

[1] Department of Quantitative Economics, Maastricht University, The Netherlands
t.harks@maastrichtuniversity.nl
[2] Department of Mathematics, Technische Universität Berlin, Germany
klimm@math.tu-berlin.de
[3] School of Business and Economics, RWTH Aachen University, Germany
britta.peis@oms.rwth-aachen.de

Abstract. We study competitive resource allocation problems in which players distribute their demands integrally over a set of resources subject to player-specific submodular capacity constraints. Each player has to pay for each unit of demand a cost that is a non-decreasing and convex function of the total allocation of that resource. This general model of resource allocation generalizes both singleton congestion games with integer-splittable demands and matroid congestion games with player-specific costs. As our main result, we show that in such general resource allocation problems a pure Nash equilibrium is guaranteed to exist by giving a pseudo-polynomial algorithm computing a pure Nash equilibrium.

1 Introduction

In an influential paper, Rosenthal [23] introduced *congestion games*, a class of strategic games, where a finite set of players competes over a finite set of resources. Each player is associated with a set of allowable subsets of resources and a pure strategy of a player consists of an allowable subset. In the context of *network games*, the resources may correspond to edges of a graph and the allowable subsets correspond to the paths connecting a source and a sink. The utility a player receives by using a resource depends only on the number of players choosing the same resource and each player wants to maximize (minimize) the utility (cost) of the sum of the resources contained in the selected subset. Rosenthal proved the existence of a pure Nash equilibrium. Up to day congestion games have been used as reference models for describing decentralized systems involving the selfish allocation of congestible resources (e.g., selfish route choices in traffic networks [4,25,29] and flow control in telecommunication networks [17,18,27]) and for decades they have been a focal point of research in (algorithmic) game theory, operations research and theoretical computer science.

* The research of the first author was supported by the Marie-Curie grant "Protocol Design" (nr. 327546) funded within FP7-PEOPLE-2012-IEF.
** The research of the second author was carried out in the framework of MATHEON supported by the Einstein Foundation Berlin.

T.-Y. Liu et al. (Eds.): WINE 2014, LNCS 8877, pp. 189–202, 2014.

In the past, the existence of pure Nash equilibria has been analyzed in many variants of congestion games such as singleton congestion games with player-specific cost functions (cf. [11,16,21,22]), congestion games with weighted players (cf. [1,2,5,10,13]), nonatomic and atomic splittable congestion games (cf. [4,14,18,29]) and congestion games with player- and resource-specific and variable demands (cf. [12]).

Most of these previous works can be classified according to the following two categories: (i) the demand of each player is unsplittable and must be completely assigned to exactly one subset of the allowable subsets; (ii) the demand of a player may be fractionally split over the set of allowable subsets. While these assumptions and the resulting models are obviously important (and also realistic for some applications), they do not allow for the requirement that only *integral fractions* of the demand may be assigned to allowable subsets of resources. This requirement is clearly important in many applications, where the demand represents a collection of indivisible items or tasks that need to be placed on subsets of resources. Examples include the scheduling of integer-splittable tasks in the context of load balancing on server farms (cf. [19]) or in logistics where a player controls a fleet of vehicles and each must be assigned to a single route.

Although Rosenthal proposed congestion games with integer-splittable demands as an important and meaningful model already back in 1973 – in his first work on congestion games [24] even published prior to his more famous work [23] – not much is known regarding existence and computability of pure Nash equilibria. Rosenthal gave an example showing that in general, pure Nash equilibria need not exist. Dunkel and Schulz [7] strengthened this result showing that the existence of a pure Nash equilibrium in integer-splittable congestion games is NP-complete to decide. Meyers [20] proved that in games with linear cost functions, a pure Nash equilibrium is always guaranteed to exist. For singleton strategy spaces and non-negative and convex cost functions, Tran-Thanh et al. [28] showed the existence of pure Nash equilibria. They also showed that pure Nash equilibria need not exist (even for the restricted strategy spaces) if cost functions are semi-convex.

Our Results. We introduce congestion games on *integral polymatroids*, where each player may fractionally assign the demand in integral units among the allowable subsets of resources subject to player-specific submodular capacity constraints. This way, the resulting strategy space for each player forms an integral polymatroid base polyhedron (truncated at the player-specific demand). As our main result, we devise an algorithm that computes a pure Nash equilibrium for congestion games on integral polymatroids with player-specific non-negative, non-decreasing and *strongly semi-convex* cost functions. The class of strongly semi-convex functions strictly includes convex functions but is included in the class of semi-convex functions (see Section 2.2 for a formal definition). The runtime of our algorithm is bounded by $n^{\delta+1} \cdot m^\delta \delta^{\delta+1}$, where n is the number of players, m the number of resources, and δ is an upper bound on the maximum demand. Thus, for constant δ, the algorithm is polynomial.

Our existence result generalizes that of Tran-Thanh et al. [28] for singleton congestion games with integer-splittable demands and convex cost functions and that of Ackermann et al. [1] for matroid congestion games with unit demands and player-specific non-decreasing costs. For the important class of network design games, where players need to allocate bandwidth in integral units across multiple spanning trees of a player-specific communication graph (cf. [3,6,9]), our result shows for the first time the existence of pure Nash equilibria provided that the cost on each edge is a strongly semi-convex function of total bandwidth allocated.

Techniques. Our algorithm for computing pure Nash equilibria maintains data structures for *preliminary demands, strategy spaces, and strategies* of the players that all are set to zero initially. Then, it iteratively increases the demand of a player by one unit and recomputes a preliminary pure Nash equilibrium (with respect to the current demands) by following a sequence of best response moves of players. The key insight to prove the correctness of the algorithm is based on two invariants that are fulfilled during the course of the algorithm. As a first invariant, we show that, whenever the demand of a player is increased by one unit, there is a best response that assigns the new unit to some resource *without* changing the allocation of previously assigned demand units. As second invariant, we obtain that, after assigning this new unit to some resource, only those players that use this particular resource with increased load may have an incentive to deviate. Moreover, there is a best response that has the property that at most a single unit of demand is shifted to some other resource. Given the above two invariants, we prove that during the sequence of best response moves a carefully defined vector of *marginal costs* lexicographically decreases, thus, ensuring that the sequence is finite.

The first invariant follows by reducing an integral polymatroid to an ordinary matroid (cf. Helgason [15]) and the fact that for a matroid, a minimum independent set I_d with rank d can be extended to a minimum independent set I_{d+1} with rank $d+1$ by adding a single element to I_d. The second invariant, however, is significantly more complex since a change of the load of one resource results (when using the matroid construction in the spirit of Helgason) in changed element weights for several elements simultaneously. To prove the second invariant we use several exchange and uncrossing arguments that make use of the submodularity of the rank functions and the fact that a non-optimal basis of a matroid can be improved locally. This is the technically most involved part of our paper.

We note that the above invariants have also been used by Tran-Thanh et al. [28] for showing the existence of pure Nash equilibria in singleton integer-splittable congestion games. For singleton games, however, these invariants follow almost directly. The algorithmic idea to incrementally increase the total demand by one unit is similar to the (inductive) existence proof of Milchtaich [21] for singleton congestion games with player-specific cost functions (see also Ackerman et al. [1] for a similar proof for matroid congestion games). The convergence proof for our algorithm and the above mentioned invariants, however, are considerably more involved for general integral polymatroids.

Besides providing new existence results for an important and large class of games, the main contribution of this paper is to propose a unified approach to prove the existence of pure Nash equilibria that connects the seemingly unrelated existence results of Milchtaich [21] and Ackerman et al. [1] on the one hand, and Tran-Thanh et al. [28] on the other hand.

2   Preliminaries

In this section, we introduce polymatroids, strong semi-convexity, and congestion games on integral polymatroids.

2.1   Polymatroids

Let $\mathbb{N}$ denote the set of non-negative integers and let R be a finite and non-empty set of resources. We write $\mathbb{N}^R$ shorthand for $\mathbb{N}^{|R|}$. Throughout this paper, vectors $\mathbf{x} = (x_r)_{r \in R}$ will be denoted with bold face. An integral (set) function $f : 2^R \to \mathbb{N}$ is *submodular* if $f(U) + f(V) \geq f(U \cup V) + f(U \cap V)$ for all $U, V \in 2^R$. Function f is *monotone* if $U \subseteq V$ implies $f(U) \leq f(V)$, and *normalized* if $f(\emptyset) = 0$. An integral submodular, monotone and normalized function $f : 2^R \to \mathbb{N}$ is called an *integral polymatroid rank function*. The associated *integral polyhedron* is defined as

$$\mathbb{P}_f = \Big\{ \mathbf{x} \in \mathbb{N}^R : \sum_{r \in U} x_r \leq f(U) \text{ for each } U \subseteq R \Big\}.$$

Given the integral polyhedron $\mathbb{P}_f$ and some integer $d \in \mathbb{N}$ with $d \leq f(R)$, the *d-truncated integral polymatroid* $\mathbb{P}_f(d)$ is defined as

$$\mathbb{P}_f(d) = \Big\{ \mathbf{x} \in \mathbb{N}^R : \sum_{r \in U} x_r \leq f(U) \text{ for each } U \subseteq R, \sum_{r \in R} x_r \leq d \Big\}.$$

The corresponding *integral polymatroid base polyhedron* is

$$\mathcal{B}_f(d) = \Big\{ \mathbf{x} \in \mathbb{N}^R : \sum_{r \in U} x_r \leq f(U) \text{ for each } U \subseteq R, \sum_{r \in R} x_r = d \Big\}.$$

2.2   Strongly Semi-convex Functions

Recall that a function $c : \mathbb{N} \to \mathbb{N}$ is *convex* if $c(x+1) - c(x) \leq c(x+2) - c(x+1)$ for all $x \in \mathbb{N}$. A function c is called *semi-convex* if the function $x \cdot c(x)$ is convex, i.e.,

$$(x+1)c(x+1) - xc(x) \leq (x+2)c(x+2) - (x+1)c(x+1)$$

for all $x \in \mathbb{N}$.

For the main existence result of this paper, we require a property of each cost function that we call *strong semi-convexity*, which is weaker than convexity but stronger than semi-convexity. Roughly speaking, it states that the marginal difference $c(a + x)x - c(a + x - 1)(x - 1)$ does not decrease as a or x increase. We also introduce a slightly weaker notion, termed u-truncated strong semi-convexity, where strong semi-convexity is only required for values of x not larger than u.

Definition 1 (Strong Semi-Convexity). *A function* $c : \mathbb{N} \to \mathbb{N}$ *is strongly semi-convex if*

$$c(a + x)x - c(a + x - 1)(x - 1) \leq c(b + y)y - c(b + y - 1)(y - 1) \qquad (1)$$

for all $x, y \in \mathbb{N}$ *with* $1 \leq x \leq y$ *and all* $a, b \in \mathbb{N}$ *with* $a \leq b$. *For an integer* $u \geq 1$, *c is* u-*truncated strongly semi-convex, if the above inequality is only required to be satisfied for all* $x, y \in \mathbb{N}$ *with* $1 \leq x \leq y \leq u$ *and all* $a, b \in \mathbb{N}$ *with* $a \leq b$.

We note that a similar definition is also given in Tran-Thanh et al. [28]. It is not hard to show that strong semi-convexity is indeed strictly weaker than convexity. In the interest of space, we defer a formal proof to the full version of the paper.

Proposition 1. *Every convex and non-decreasing function* $c : \mathbb{N} \to \mathbb{N}$ *is also strongly semi-convex, but not vice versa.*

Finally, we remark that every non-decreasing function is 1-truncated strongly semi-convex.

Remark 1. A function is 1-truncated strongly semi-convex if and only if it is non-decreasing.

2.3   Congestion Games on Integral Polymatroids

In a congestion game on integral polymatroids, there is a non-empty and finite set N of players and a non-empty and finite set R of resources. Each resource is endowed with a player-specific cost function $c_{i,r} : \mathbb{N} \to \mathbb{N}$, $r \in R, i \in N$ and each player i is associated with a demand $d_i \in \mathbb{N}$, $d_i \geq 1$ and an integral poly-matroid rank function $f^{(i)} : 2^R \to \mathbb{N}$ that together define a d_i-truncated integral polymatroid $\mathbb{P}_{f^{(i)}}(d_i)$ with base polyhedron $\mathcal{B}_{f^{(i)}}(d_i)$ on the set of resources. A strategy of player $i \in N$ is to choose a vector $\mathbf{x}_i = (x_{i,r})_{r \in R} \in \mathcal{B}_{f^{(i)}}(d_i)$, i.e., player i chooses an integral resource consumption $x_{i,r} \in \mathbb{N}$ for each resource r such that the demand d_i is exactly distributed among the resources and for each $U \subseteq R$ not more than $f^{(i)}(U)$ units of demand are distributed to the resources contained in U. Using the notation $\mathbf{x}_i = (x_{i,r})_{r \in R}$, the set X_i of feasible strategies of player i is defined as

$$X_i = \mathcal{B}_{f^{(i)}}(d_i) = \left\{ \mathbf{x}_i \in \mathbb{N}^R : \sum_{r \in U} x_{i,r} \leq f^{(i)}(U) \text{ for each } U \subseteq R, \sum_{r \in R} x_{i,r} = d_i \right\}.$$

The Cartesian product $X = \times_{i \in N} X_i$ of the players' sets of feasible strategies is the joint strategy space. An element $\mathbf{x} = (\mathbf{x}_i)_{i \in N} \in X$ is a strategy profile.

For a resource r, and a strategy profile $\mathbf{x} \in X$, we write $x_r = \sum_{i \in N} x_{i,r}$. The private cost of player i under strategy profile $\mathbf{x} \in X$ is defined as $\pi_i(\mathbf{x}) = \sum_{r \in R} c_{i,r}(x_r) x_{i,r}$. In the remainder of the paper, we will compactly represent the strategic game by the tuple $G = (N, X, (d_i)_{i \in N}, (c_{i,r})_{i \in N, r \in R})$.

We use standard game theory notation. For a player $i \in N$ and a strategy profile $\mathbf{x} \in X$, we write $\mathbf{x}$ as $(\mathbf{x}_i, \mathbf{x}_{-i})$. A *best response* of player i to $\mathbf{x}_{-i}$ is a strategy $\mathbf{x}_i \in X_i$ with $\pi_i(\mathbf{x}_i, \mathbf{x}_{-i}) \leq \pi_i(\mathbf{y}_i, \mathbf{x}_{-i})$ for all $\mathbf{y}_i \in X_i$. A pure Nash equilibrium is a strategy profile $\mathbf{x} \in X$ such that for each player i the strategy $\mathbf{x}_i$ is a best response to $\mathbf{x}_{-i}$.

Throughout this paper, we assume that the player-specific cost function $c_{i,r}$ of each player i on each resource r is $u_{i,r}$-truncated strongly semi-convex, where $u_{i,r} = f^{(i)}(\{r\})$. Note that $u_{i,r}$ is a natural upper bound on the units of demand player i can allocate to resource r in any strategy $\mathbf{x}_i \in X_i$.

Assumption. For all $i \in N, r \in R$, the cost function $c_{i,r} : \mathbb{N} \to \mathbb{N}$ is non-negative, non-decreasing and $u_{i,r}$-truncated strongly semi-convex, where $u_{i,r} = f^{(i)}(\{r\})$.

2.4   Examples

We proceed to illustrate that we obtain the well known classes of integer-splittable singleton congestion games and matroid congestion games as special cases of congestion games on integer polymatroids.

Example 1 (Singleton integer-splittable congestion games). For the special case that, for each player i, there is a player-specific subset $R_i \subseteq R$ of resources such that $f^{(i)}(\{r\}) = d_i$, if $r \in R_i$, and $f^{(i)}(\{r\}) = 0$, otherwise, we obtain integer-splittable singleton congestion games previously studied by Tran-Thanh et al. [28]. While they consider the special case of convex and *player-independent* cost functions, our general existence result implies existence of a pure Nash equilibrium even for *player-specific* and strongly semi-convex cost functions.

Example 2 (Matroid congestion games with player-specific costs). For the special case, that for each player i, $f^{(i)}$ is the rank function of a player-specific matroid defined on R, and $d_i = f^{(i)}(R)$, we obtain ordinary matroid congestion games with player-specific costs and unit demands studied by Ackermann et al. [1] as a special case.

Note that the rank function $\text{rk} : 2^R \to \mathbb{N}$ of a matroid is always subcardinal, i.e., $\text{rk}(U) \leq |U|$ for all $U \subseteq R$. Thus, we obtain in particular that $\text{rk}(\{r\}) \leq 1$ for all $r \in R$. This implies that our existence result continues to hold if we only require that the player-specific cost functions are 1-truncated strongly semi-convex, which is equivalent to requiring that cost functions are non-decreasing as in [1]. Like this, we obtain the existence result of [1] as a special case of our existence result for congestion games on integer polymatroids. As a strict generalization, our model includes the case in which players have a demand $d_i \in \mathbb{N}$ that can be distributed in integer units over bases (or even arbitrary independent sets) of a given player-specific matroid. A prominent application arises in network design (cf. [3,6,9]), where a player needs to allocate bandwidth along several spanning trees and the cost function for installing enough capacity on an edge is a convex function of the total bandwidth allocated.

3   Equilibrium Existence

In this section, we give an algorithm that computes a pure Nash equilibrium for congestion games on integral polymatroids. Our algorithm relies on two key sensitivity properties of optimal solutions minimizing a linear function over an integral polymatroid base polyhedron (see Lemma 1 and Lemma 2 below). After reducing the usual reduction of integer polymatroids to ordinary matroids (cf. [15]), Lemma 1 follows more or less directly from the respective property for matroids. The proof of Lemma 2 is considerably more involved and relies heavily on uncrossing arguments. The two lemmata will be proven formally in Section 4.

3.1   Key Sensitivity Results

For two vectors $\mathbf{x}_i, \mathbf{y}_i \in \mathbb{N}^R$, we denote their Hamming distance by $H(\mathbf{x}_i, \mathbf{y}_i) = \sum_{r \in R} |x_{i,r} - y_{i,r}|$. Lemma 1 shows that, whenever a strategy $\mathbf{x}_i$ minimizes the cost of player i over the base polyhedron $\mathcal{B}_{f(i)}(d_i)$, then we only need to increase $x_{i,r}$ for some $r \in R$ by one unit to obtain a strategy $\mathbf{y}_i$ minimizing the player's cost over the base polyhedron $\mathcal{B}_{f(i)}(d_i + 1)$.

Lemma 1 (Demand Increase). *Let $\mathbf{x}_i \in \mathcal{B}_{f(i)}(d_i)$ be a best response of player i to $\mathbf{x}_{-i} \in X_{-i}$. Then there exists a best response $\mathbf{y}_i \in \mathcal{B}_{f(i)}(d_i + 1)$ to $\mathbf{x}_{-i}$ such that $H(\mathbf{x}_i, \mathbf{y}_i) = 1$.*

The second result shows that, when some other player $j \neq i$ increases her demand for some resource r that is also used by player i with at least one unit, then player i can simply shift one unit from resource r to some resource $s \in R$ in order to retain minimal costs.

Lemma 2 (Load Increase). *Let $\mathbf{x}_i \in \mathcal{B}_{f(i)}(d_i)$ be a best response of player i to $\mathbf{x}_{-i} \in X_{-i}$ and for each resource r let $a_r = \sum_{j \neq i} x_{j,r}$ be the induced allocation. If for a resource r, the value a_r is increased by 1, then there exists a best response $\mathbf{y}_i \in \mathcal{B}_{f(i)}(d_i)$ towards the new profile with $H(\mathbf{x}_i, \mathbf{y}_i) \in \{0, 2\}$.*

3.2   The Algorithm

Both sensitivity results are used as the main building blocks for Algorithm 1 that computes a pure Nash equilibrium for congestion games on integral polymatroids. Algorithm 1 maintains *preliminary demands, strategy spaces, and strategies* of the players denoted by $\bar{d}_i \leq d_i$, $\bar{X}_i = X_i(\bar{d}_i)$, and $\mathbf{x}_i \in \bar{X}_i$, respectively. Initially, the preliminary demand $\bar{d}_i$ of each player i is set to zero. Trivially, for this game the strategy profile where the strategy of each player equals the zero vector is a pure Nash equilibrium.

Then, in each round, for some player i, the demand is increased from $\bar{d}_i$ to $\bar{d}_i + 1$, and a best response $\mathbf{y}_i \in X(\bar{d}_i + 1)$ with $H(\mathbf{x}_i, \mathbf{y}_i) = 1$ is computed, see Line 5 in Algorithm 1. By Lemma 1, such a best response always exists. In effect, the load on exactly one resource r increases and only those players j with $x_{j,r} > 0$ on this resource can potentially decrease their private cost by a unilateral deviation. By Lemma 2, it is without loss of generality to assume that a best response of such players consists of moving a single unit from this resource to another resource, see Line 8 of Algorithm 1. As a consequence, during the while-loop (Lines 7-10), only one additional unit (compared to the previous iteration) is moved preserving the invariant that only players using a resource to which this additional unit is assigned may have an incentive to profitably deviate. Thus, if the while-loop is left, the current strategy profile $\mathbf{x}$ is a pure Nash equilibrium for the reduced game $\bar{G} = (N, \bar{X}, \bar{d}, (c_{i,r})_{i \in N, r \in R})$. Now we are ready to prove the main existence result.

ALGORITHM 1. Compute PNE

> **Input:** $G = (N, X, (d_i)_{i \in N}, (c_{i,r})_{i \in N, r \in R})$
> **Output:** pure Nash equilibrium $\mathbf{x}$
> 1 $\bar{d}_i \leftarrow 0, \bar{X}_i \leftarrow X_i(0)$ and $\mathbf{x}_i \leftarrow \mathbf{0}$ for all $i \in N$;
> 2 **for** $k = 1, \ldots, \sum_{i \in N} d_i$ **do**
> 3 $\quad$ Choose $i \in N$ with $\bar{d}_i < d_i$;
> 4 $\quad$ $\bar{d}_i \leftarrow \bar{d}_i + 1$; $\bar{X}_i \leftarrow X_i(\bar{d}_i)$;
> 5 $\quad$ Choose a best response $y_i \in \bar{X}_i$ with $H(y_i, x_i) = 1$;
> 6 $\quad$ $\mathbf{x}_i \leftarrow \mathbf{y}_i$;
> 7 $\quad$ **while** $\exists i \in N$ *who can improve in* $\bar{G} = (N, \bar{X}, \bar{d}, (c_{i,r})_{i \in N, r \in R})$ **do**
> 8 $\quad\quad$ Compute a best response $\mathbf{y}_i \in \bar{X}_i$ with $H(\mathbf{y}_i, \mathbf{x}_i) = 2$;
> 9 $\quad\quad$ $\mathbf{x}_i \leftarrow \mathbf{y}_i$;
> 10 $\quad$ **end**
> 11 **end**
> 12 Return $\mathbf{x}$;

Theorem 1. *Congestion games on integral polymatroids with player-specific non-negative, non-decreasing, and strongly semi-convex cost functions possess a pure Nash equilibrium.*

Proof. We prove by induction on the total demand $d = \sum_{i \in N} d_i$ of the input game $G = (N, X, (d_i)_{i \in N}, (c_{i,r})_{i \in N, r \in R})$ that Algorithm 1 computes a pure Nash equilibrium of G.

For $d = 0$, this is trivial. Suppose that the algorithm works correctly for games with total demand $d - 1$ for some $d \geq 1$ and consider a game G with total demand d. Let us assume that in Line 3, the algorithm always chooses a player with minimum index. Consider the game $G' = (N, X, (d_i')_{i \in N}, (c_{i,r})_{i \in N, r \in R})$ that differs from G only in the fact that the demand of the last player n is reduced by one, i.e. $d_i' = d_i$ for all $i < n$ and $d_n' = d_n - 1$. Then, when running the algorithm with G' as input, the $d - 1$ iterations (of the for-loop) are equal to the first $d - 1$ iterations when running the algorithm with G as input. Thus, with G as input, we may assume that after the first $d - 1$ iterations, the preliminary strategy profile that we denote by $\mathbf{x}'$ is a pure Nash equilibrium of G'.

We analyze the final iteration $k = d$ of the algorithm in which the demand of player n is increased by 1 (see Line 4). In Line 5, a best reply $\mathbf{y}_n$ with $H(\mathbf{x}_n, \mathbf{y}_n) = 1$ is computed which exists by Lemma 1. Then, as long as there is a player i that can improve unilaterally, in Line 8, a best response $\mathbf{y}_i$ with $H(\mathbf{y}_i, \mathbf{x}_i) = 2$ is computed which exists by Lemma 2.

It remains to show that the while-loop in Lines 7–10 terminates. To prove this, we give each unit of demand of each player $i \in N$ an identity denoted by $i_j, j = 1, \ldots, d_i$. For a strategy profile $\mathbf{x}$, we define $r(i_j, \mathbf{x}) \in R$ to be the resource to which unit i_j is assigned in strategy profile $\mathbf{x}$. Let $\mathbf{x}^l$ be the strategy profile after Line 8 of the algorithm has been executed the l-th time, where we use the convention that $\mathbf{x}^0$ denotes the preliminary strategy profile when entering the while-loop. As we chose in Line 5 a strategy of player n with Hamming distance one, there is a unique resource r_0 such that $x_{r_0}^0 = x_{r_0}' + 1$ and $x_r^0 = x_r'$ for all $r \in R \setminus \{r_0\}$. Furthermore, because we choose in Line 8 a best response with Hamming distance two, a simple inductive claim shows that after each iteration l of the while-loop, there is a unique resource $r_l \in R$ such that $x_{r_l}^l = x_{r_l}' + 1$ and $x_r^l = x_r'$ for all $r \in R \setminus \{r_l\}$.

For any $\mathbf{x}^l$ during the course of the algorithm, we define the *marginal cost* of unit i_j under strategy profile $\mathbf{x}^l$ as

$$\Delta_{i_j}(\mathbf{x}^l) = \begin{cases} c_{i,r}(x_r^l)\, x_{i,r}^l - c_{i,r}(x_r^l - 1)\,(x_{i,r}^l - 1), & \text{if } r = r(i_j, \mathbf{x}) = r_l \\ c_{i,r}(x_r^l + 1)\, x_{i,r}^l - c_{i,r}(x_r^l)\,(x_{i,r}^l - 1), & \text{if } r = r(i_j, \mathbf{x}) \neq r_l. \end{cases} \quad (2)$$

Intuitively, if $r(i_j, \mathbf{x}) = r_l$, the value $\Delta_{i_j}(\mathbf{x})$ measures the *cost saving* on resource $r(i_j, \mathbf{x})$ if i_j (or any other unit of player i on resource $r(i_j, \mathbf{x})$) is removed from $r(i_j, \mathbf{x})$. If $r(i_j, \mathbf{x}) \neq r_l$, the value $\Delta_{i_j}(\mathbf{x})$ measures the cost saving if i_j is removed from $r(i_j, \mathbf{x})$ after the total allocation has been increased by one unit by some other player. For a strategy profile $\mathbf{x}$ we define $\Delta(\mathbf{x}) = (\Delta_{i_j}(\mathbf{x}))_{i=1,\ldots,n, j=1,\ldots,d_i}$ to be the vector of marginal costs and let $\bar{\Delta}(\mathbf{x})$ be the vector of marginal costs sorted in non-increasing order. We claim that $\bar{\Delta}(\mathbf{x})$ decreases lexicographically during the while-loop. To see this, consider an iteration l in which some unit i_j of player i is moved from resource r_{l-1} to resource r_l.

For proving $\bar{\Delta}(\mathbf{x}^l) <_{\text{lex}} \bar{\Delta}(\mathbf{x}^{l-1})$, we first observe that we only have to care for Δ-values that correspond to units i_j of the deviating player i, because for all players $h \neq i$ we obtain $\Delta_{h_j}(\mathbf{x}^{l-1}) = \Delta_{h_j}(\mathbf{x}^l)$ for all $j = 1, \ldots, d_h$. This follows immediately if h_j is neither assigned to r_{l-1} nor to r_l. If h_j is assigned to r_{l-1} or r_l, then we switch the case in (2), and the claimed equality still holds. It remains to consider the Δ-values corresponding to the units of the deviating player i. Recall that the deviation of player i consists of moving unit i_j from resource r_{l-1} to resource r_l. We obtain

$$\begin{aligned} \Delta_{i_j}(\mathbf{x}^{l-1}) &= c_{i,r_{l-1}}(x_{r_{l-1}}^l)\, x_{i,r_{l-1}}^l - c_{i,r_{l-1}}(x_{r_{l-1}}^l - 1)\,(x_{i,r_{l-1}}^l - 1) \\ &> c_{i,r_l}(x_{r_l}^l + 1)\,(x_{i,r_l}^l + 1) - c_{i,r_l}(x_{r_l}^l)\, x_{i,r_l}^l = \Delta_{i_j}(\mathbf{x}^l), \end{aligned}$$

where the inequality follows since player i strictly improves. For every unit i_m of player i that is assigned to resource r_l as well, i.e, $r(i_m, \mathbf{x}^l) = r(i_j, \mathbf{x}^l) = r_l$, we have $\Delta_{i_j}(\mathbf{x}^l) = \Delta_{i_m}(\mathbf{x}^l)$ since the Δ-value is the same for all units of a single player assigned to the same resource. The Δ-values of such units i_m might have increased, but only to the Δ-value of unit i_j.

Next, consider the Δ-values of a unit i_m assigned to resource r_{l-1}, i.e., $r(i_m, \mathbf{x}^l) = r(i_j, \mathbf{x}^l) = r_{l-1}$. We obtain

$$\Delta_{i_m}(\mathbf{x}^l) = c_{i,r_l}(x^l_{i,r_{l-1}})\,(x^l_{i,r_{l-1}} - 1) - c_{i,r_{l-1}}(x^l_{i,r_{l-1}} - 1)\,(x^l_{i,r_{l-1}} - 2)$$
$$\leq c_{i,r_{l-1}}(x^l_{i,r_{l-1}})\,x^l_{i,r_{l-1}} - c_{i,r_{l-1}}(x^l_{i,r_{l-1}} - 1)\,(x^l_{i,r_{l-1}} - 1) = \Delta_{i_m}(\mathbf{x}^{l-1}),$$

where for the inequality we used that $c_{i,r}(x_{r_{l-1}}) \geq c_{i,r}(x_{r_{l-1}} - 1)$ as $c_{i,r}$ is non-decreasing.

Altogether, the Δ-values of all units of all players $h \neq i$ have not changed, for player i, the Δ-values of remaining units assigned to resource r_{l-1} decreased, and the Δ-values assigned to resource r_l increased exactly to $\Delta_{i_j}(\mathbf{x}^l)$ which is strictly smaller than $\Delta_{i_j}(\mathbf{x}^{l-1})$. Thus, $\bar{\Delta}(\mathbf{x}^l) <_{\text{lex}} \bar{\Delta}(\mathbf{x}^{l-1})$ follows.   □

The following corollary states an upper bound on the number of iterations of the algorithm in terms of $\delta = \max_{i \in N} d_i$.

Corollary 1. *The number of iterations is at most $n^{\delta+1} m^\delta \delta^{\delta+1}$, which yields a polynomial algorithm computing a pure Nash equilibrium for constant δ.*

Proof. We analyze the worst-case runtime of Algorithm 1. To this end, let us fix an iteration of the for-loop. In the proof of Theorem 1, we showed that during this iteratioe, for each player, the sorted vector of marginal costs as defined in (2) decreases lexicographically during the while-loop. Moreover, the marginal cost of a particular unit of demand i_j of player i assigned to a resource r does not depend on the aggregated demand $\sum_{j \in N} x_{j,r}$ of all players for resource r, but only on the number of units of demand $x_{i,r}$ assigned to r by player i. We derive that for each player i and each resource r at most d_i different marginal cost values can occur. This observation bounds the number of different marginal cost vectors of player i by $(m \cdot d_i)^{d_i}$, where $m = |R|$. Since the marginal cost vectors lexicographically decrease, the total number of iterations of the while-loop for each iteration of the for-loop is bounded by $\sum_{i \in N}(m \cdot d_i)^{d_i}$. Setting $\delta = \max_{i \in N} d_i$, this expression is bounded by $(n \cdot m \cdot \delta)^\delta$, where $n = |N|$. Using that there are $\sum_{i \in N} d_i \leq n \cdot \delta$ iterations of the for-loop, one for each unit of demand in the game, we obtain the following corollary.   □

4   Sensitivity Analysis for Integral Polymatroids

It remains to show the key sensitivity results of Lemma 1 and Lemma 2. For ease of notation, let us drop the index i form the statements of the lemmata and let us consider a fixed integral polymatroid base polyhedron

$$\mathcal{B}_f(d) = \left\{ \mathbf{x} \in \mathbb{N}^R : \sum_{r \in U} x_r \leq f(U) \text{ for each } U \subseteq R, \sum_{r \in R} x_r = d \right\}.$$

w.r.t. some submodular, monotone, and normalized function $f : 2^R \to \mathbb{N}$, and some demand value $d \in \mathbb{N}$.

We identify the points in $\mathcal{B}_f(d)$ with a set family $\mathcal{F}(d)$ on a largely extended ground set E as follows: For each resource $r \in R$, let $u_r = f(\{r\})$ and let $K_r = \{r_1 \prec \ldots \prec r_{u_r}\}$ be a totally ordered set (chain) with $|u_r|$ distinct elements $r_1, \ldots, r_{u_r}$. Let further $E = \bigcup_{r \in R} K_r$ be the disjoint union of these chains. Then, $P = (E, \preceq)$ is a partially ordered set (poset) where two elements e, e' are comparable if and only if they are contained in the same chain K_r for some $r \in R$. Furthermore, let $\mathcal{D}(P)$ denote the set of *ideals* of P, i.e., $\mathcal{D}(P)$ consists of all subsets $I \subseteq E$ such that for each $e \in I$ all elements $g \prec e$ also belong to I. Note that there is a one-to-one correspondence between the sets in $\mathcal{D}(P)$ and the integral points in $\{\mathbf{x} \in \mathbb{N}^R : x_r \leq f(\{r\}) \; \forall r \in R\}$. As a consequence, the feasible points in the integral polymatroid $\mathbb{P}_f$ can be identified with the set family

$$\mathcal{F} = \left\{ F \in \mathcal{D}(P) : \left| \bigcup_{r \in U} K_r \cap F \right| \leq f(U) \text{ for each } U \subseteq R \right\}. \tag{3}$$

Accordingly, the vectors contained in the polymatroid base polyhedron $\mathcal{B}_f(d)$ for $d \in \mathbb{N}$ can be identified with the set family

$$\mathcal{F}(d) = \left\{ F \in \mathcal{F} : |F| = d \right\}. \tag{4}$$

In fact, it is known (see, e.g., [26] and [15]) that any integral polymatroid $\mathbb{P}_f$ can be reduced to an ordinary matroid $\mathcal{M} = (E, r)$ on ground set E with rank function $r : 2^E \to \mathbb{N}$ defined via

$$r(U) = \min_{T \subseteq R} \left(\left| U \setminus \bigcup_{r \in T} K_r \right| + f(T) \right)$$

for all $U \subseteq E$. It turns out that the independent sets in $\mathcal{M}$ of cardinality d are exactly the ideals in $\mathcal{F}(d)$ as defined above. Applying this kind of transformation for each player i, we can identify the strategy set $\mathcal{B}_{f^{(i)}}(d_i)$ of each player i with the set family $\mathcal{F}_i(d_i)$, and this set family, in turn, with the matroid $\mathcal{M}_i = (E_i, r_i)$.

With this notation, let us now return to the problem of finding a best response $\mathbf{x}_i$ of player i towards a strategy profile $\mathbf{a} = \mathbf{x}_{-i} \in \mathbb{N}^R$ of the remaining players. Note that, for $\mathbf{a} \in \mathbb{N}^R$, the player-specific strongly semi-convex cost functions $c_{i,r} : \mathbb{N} \to \mathbb{N}$ induce weight functions $w_i^{\mathbf{a}} : E \to \mathbb{N}$ on the ground set E constructed above via

$$w_i^{\mathbf{a}}(r_t) = t c_{i,r}(a_r + t) - (t-1) c_{i,r}(a_r + t - 1) \quad \text{for all } r \in R, t \in \{1, \ldots, d_i\}.$$

Hence, finding a best response $\mathbf{x}_i \in \mathcal{B}_{f^{(i)}}(d_i)$ reduces to the problem of minimizing a linear function over the independent sets of cardinality d_i of the matroid $\mathcal{M}_i = (E_i, r_i)$ associated with the submodular function $f^{(i)}$.

However, the ground set E_i can be of exponential size, so that it is not a priori clear whether the matroid greedy algorithm minimizes a linear weight function over the base polyhedron $\mathcal{B}_{f^{(i)}}(d_i)$ in strongly polynomial time. Still, since we assume that the cost functions $c_{i,r} : \mathbb{N} \to \mathbb{N}$ are strongly semi-convex, it follows that the induced weight functions $w_i^{\mathrm{a}} : E \to \mathbb{N}$ are *admissible* in the sense that $e \prec g$ implies $w_i(e) \leq w_i(g)$.

Given an ideal $F \in \mathcal{D}(P)$, we denote by F^+ the set of $\preceq$-maximal elements in F, and by $(E \setminus F)^-$ the set of $\preceq$-minimal elements in $E \setminus F$. For $\mathcal{F}(d)$ as defined in (4), and any admissible weight functions $w : E \to \mathbb{N}$, Faigle [8] showed that the following *ordered greedy algorithm* determines an ideal of minimal weight in $\mathcal{F}(d)$ (provided $\mathcal{F}(d) \neq \emptyset$):

ALGORITHM 2. Ordered Greedy Algorithm

1 $F \leftarrow \emptyset$;
2 **for** $k = 1, \ldots, d$ **do**
3 $\quad$ Let $e_k \leftarrow \arg\min\{w(e) : e \in (E \setminus F)^- \text{ and } F + e \in \mathcal{F}\}$;
4 $\quad$ $F \leftarrow F + e_k$;
5 **end**
6 Return $\mathcal{F}$;

In fact, the greedy algorithm determines in each iteration $k \leq d$ an ideal of minimal weight in $\mathcal{F}(k)$. The following proposition arises as a consequence of the discussion above and implies Lemma 1.

Proposition 2. *Let $\mathcal{F} \subseteq \mathcal{D}(P)$ as defined in (3), $k \in \mathbb{N}$, and $w : E \to \mathbb{R}$ admissible. Suppose F is of minimal w-weight in $\mathcal{F}(k)$. Then there exists $e \in E \setminus F$ such that $F + e$ is of minimal w-weight in $\mathcal{F}(k+1)$*

Due to the reduction of integral polymatroids to ordinary matroids, most of the structural properties of matroids carry over to integral polymatroids. For example, the following proposition follows as a consequence of the well-known fact, that for any basis B of an ordinary matroid $\mathcal{M}$ which is not of minimal weight, there exists a local improvement step towards a basis $B - e + f$ of smaller weight.

Proposition 3. *Suppose $F \in \mathcal{F}(k)$ is not of minimal w-weight for some admissible function $w : E \to \mathbb{R}$. Then there exists some local improvement step $F \to F - e + g \in \mathcal{F}(k)$ such that $w(e) > w(g)$.*

The possibility to improve a non-optimal basis by local steps, as well as the possibility to uncross tight constraints due to the submodularity of the rank functions, are the main ingredients of the proof of the following theorem, which implies Lemma 2. We defer the proof to the full version of the paper.

Theorem 2. *Let $F \in \mathcal{F}(k)$ be of minimal weight w.r.t. the admissible weight function w. If the weight function $\bar{w}$ differs from w only on chain K_{r^*} such that*

$$\bar{w}(r_k) = \begin{cases} w(r_k), & \text{if } r \neq r^*, \\ w(r_{k+1}), & \text{else}, \end{cases}$$

then there exists $F' = F - e + g \in \mathcal{F}(k)$ of minimal weight w.r.t. $\bar{w}$.

References

1. Ackermann, H., Röglin, H., Vöcking, B.: Pure Nash equilibria in player-specific and weighted congestion games. Theoret. Comput. Sci. 410(17), 1552–1563 (2009)
2. Anshelevich, E., Dasgupta, A., Kleinberg, J., Tardos, É., Wexler, T., Roughgarden, T.: The price of stability for network design with fair cost allocation. SIAM J. Comput. 38(4), 1602–1623 (2008)
3. Antonakopoulos, S., Chekuri, C., Shepherd, F.B., Zhang, L.: Buy-at-bulk network design with protection. Math. Oper. Res. 36(1), 71–87 (2011)
4. Beckmann, M., McGuire, C., Winsten, C.: Studies in the Economics and Transportation. Yale University Press, New Haven (1956)
5. Chen, H., Roughgarden, T.: Network design with weighted players. Theory Comput. Syst. 45(2), 302–324 (2009)
6. Chen, H.L., Roughgarden, T., Valiant, G.: Designing network protocols for good equilibria. SIAM J. Comput. 39(5), 1799–1832 (2010)
7. Dunkel, J., Schulz, A.: On the complexity of pure-strategy Nash equilibria in congestion and local-effect games. Math. Oper. Res. 33(4), 851–868 (2008)
8. Faigle, U.: The greedy algorithm for partially ordered sets. Discrete Math. 28(2), 153–159 (1979)
9. von Falkenhausen, P., Harks, T.: Optimal cost sharing for resource selection games. Math. Oper. Res. 38(1), 184–208 (2013)
10. Fotakis, D., Kontogiannis, S., Spirakis, P.: Selfish unsplittable flows. Theoret. Comput. Sci. 348(2-3), 226–239 (2005)
11. Gairing, M., Monien, B., Tiemann, K.: Routing (un-)splittable flow in games with player-specific linear latency functions. ACM Trans. Algorithms 7(3), 1–31 (2011)
12. Harks, T., Klimm, M.: Congestion games with variable demands. In: Apt, K. (ed.) Proc. 13th Conf. Theoret. Aspects of Rationality and Knowledge, pp. 111–120 (2011)
13. Harks, T., Klimm, M.: On the existence of pure Nash equilibria in weighted congestion games. Math. Oper. Res. 37(3), 419–436 (2012)
14. Haurie, A., Marcotte, P.: On the relationship between Nash-Cournot and Wardrop equilibria. Networks 15, 295–308 (1985)
15. Helgason, T.: Aspects of the theory of hypermatroids. In: Hypergraph Seminar, pp. 191–213. Springer (1974)
16. Ieong, S., McGrew, R., Nudelman, E., Shoham, Y., Sun, Q.: Fast and compact: A simple class of congestion games. In: Proc. 20th Natl. Conf. Artificial Intelligence and the 17th Innovative Appl. Artificial Intelligence Conf., pp. 489–494 (2005)
17. Johari, R., Tsitsiklis, J.N.: A scalable network resource allocation mechanism with bounded efficiency loss. IEEE J. Sel. Area Commun. 24(5), 992–999 (2006)
18. Kelly, F., Maulloo, A., Tan, D.: Rate control in communication networks: Shadow prices, proportional fairness, and stability. J. Oper. Res. Soc. 49, 237–252 (1998)
19. Krysta, P., Sanders, P., Vöcking, B.: Scheduling and traffic allocation for tasks with bounded splittability. In: Rovan, B., Vojtáš, P. (eds.) MFCS 2003. LNCS, vol. 2747, pp. 500–510. Springer, Heidelberg (2003)
20. Meyers, C.: Network Flow Problems and Congestion Games: Complexity and Approximation Results. Ph.D. thesis, MIT, Operations Research Center (2006)
21. Milchtaich, I.: Congestion games with player-specific payoff functions. Games Econom. Behav. 13(1), 111–124 (1996)
22. Milchtaich, I.: The equilibrium existence problem in finite network congestion games. In: Spirakis, P., Mavronicolas, M., Kontogiannis, S. (eds.) WINE 2006. LNCS, vol. 4286, pp. 87–98. Springer, Heidelberg (2006)

23. Rosenthal, R.: A class of games possessing pure-strategy Nash equilibria. Internat. J. Game Theory 2(1), 65–67 (1973)
24. Rosenthal, R.: The network equilibrium problem in integers. Networks 3, 53–59 (1973)
25. Roughgarden, T.: Selfish Routing and the Price of Anarchy. MIT Press, Cambridge (2005)
26. Schrijver, A.: Combinatorial optimization: Polyhedra and efficiency, vol. 24. Springer (2003)
27. Srikant, R.: The Mathematics of Internet Congestion Control. Birkhäuser, Basel (2003)
28. Tran-Thanh, L., Polukarov, M., Chapman, A., Rogers, A., Jennings, N.R.: On the existence of pure strategy Nash equilibria in integer–splittable weighted congestion games. In: Persiano, G. (ed.) SAGT 2011. LNCS, vol. 6982, pp. 236–253. Springer, Heidelberg (2011)
29. Wardrop, J.: Some theoretical aspects of road traffic research. Proc. Inst. Civil Engineers 1(Part II), 325–378 (1952)

PTAS for Minimax Approval Voting

Jarosław Byrka and Krzysztof Sornat

Institute of Computer Science, University of Wrocław
Joliot-Curie 15
50-383 Wrocław, Poland
{jby,krzysztof.sornat}@cs.uni.wroc.pl

Abstract. We consider Approval Voting systems where each voter decides on a subset of candidates he/she approves. We focus on the optimization problem of finding the committee of fixed size k, minimizing the maximal Hamming distance from a vote. In this paper we give a PTAS for this problem and hence resolve the open question raised by Carragianis et al. [AAAI'10]. The result is obtained by adapting the techniques developed by Li et al. [JACM'02] originally used for the less constrained Closest String problem. The technique relies on extracting information and structural properties of constant size subsets of votes.

1 Introduction

Approval Voting systems are widely considered [2] as an alternative to traditional elections, where each voter may select and support at most some small number of candidates. In Approval Voting each voter decides about every single candidate if he approves the candidate or does not approve him/her. A result is obtained by applying a predefined election rule to the set of collected votes.

In this paper we study the problem of implementing an appropriate election rule and focus on the Minimax objective [3]: we minimize the biggest dissatisfaction over voters. The resulting optimization problem is denoted MAV, and it is to select a committee composed of exactly k candidates, and minimizing the maximal symmetric difference between the committee and the set of approved candidates by a single voter.

Using the string terminology, votes are encoded as strings, and the goal is to find a string encoding a committee minimizing the maximal Hamming distance to an input string. Unlike in the related Closest String problem, in MAV there is also a constraint: the selected committee must be of fixed size k, and hence in the string terminology there must be exactly k ones in the string.

1.1 Related Work and Our Results

Many different objective functions have been proposed and studied in the context of selecting the committee based on the set of votes collected in an Approval Voting system [1,2]. Clearly, optimizing the sum of Hamming distances to all votes is an easy task and can be done by simply selecting the k candidates approved by

T.-Y. Liu et al. (Eds.): WINE 2014, LNCS 8877, pp. 203–217, 2014.

the largest number of voters. By contrast, Minimax Approval Voting was shown by LeGrand [6] to be NP-hard. LeGrand et al. [7] obtained 3-approximation by a very simple k-completion algorithm. Next, Carragianis et al. [5] gave the currently best 2-approximation algorithm. The algorithm was obtained by rounding a fractional solution to the natural LP relaxation of the problem, and obtained approximation ratio essentially matches the integrality gap of the LP.

In this paper we give a PTAS for the Minimax Approval Voting problem. Our work is based on the PTAS for Closest String [8], which is a similar problem to MAV but there we do not have the restriction on the number of 1's in the result. Technically, our contribution is the method of handling the number of 1's in the output. We also believe that our presentation is somewhat more intuitive.

Approval Voting systems are also analyzed in respect of manipulability, see e.g., [1] or [5]. In particular, [5] proved that each strategy-proof algorithm for MAV must have approximation ratio at least $2 - \frac{2}{k+1}$, which implies that our PTAS cannot be strategy-proof.

1.2   Definitions

We will use the following notation:
n – number of voters,
m – number of candidates,
$s_i \in \{0,1\}^m$ – a vote of voter i,
$s_i[j] = 1$ if voter i approves candidate j,
$s_i[j] = 0$ if voter i does not approve candidate j,
$S = \{s_1, s_2, \ldots, s_n\}$ – the set of collected votes,
$s^{(1)} = \left|\{j : s[j] = 1\}\right|$ – the number of 1's in s.
For $x, y \in [0,1]^m$ we define a distance $d(x,y) = \sum_{j=1}^{m} |x[j] - y[j]| = \|x - y\|_1$.
For $x, y \in \{0,1\}^m$, $d(x,y)$ is called the Hamming distance.

Definition 1
$$OPT = \min_{\substack{x \in \{0,1\}^m \\ x^{(1)} = k}} \max_{i \in \{1,2,\ldots,n\}} d(x, s_i)$$

Let s_{OPT} be an optimal solution, i.e., $\max_{i \in \{1,2,\ldots,n\}} d(s_{OPT}, s_i) = OPT$.

WLOG we assume that $n > k$. If not, we copy the first string $k - n + 1$ times.

1.3   The Main Idea Behind Our Algorithm

The general idea behind our PTAS is to find a small enough subset X of votes that is a "good representation" of the whole set of votes S. Then the candidates are partitioned into those for which voters in X agree and the rest of candidates. For the "consensus candidates" we fix our decision to the decision induced by votes in X (additionally correcting the number of selected candidates in the "consensus" set). Next, we consider the optimization problem of finding a proper subset of the remaining candidates to join the committee. The key insight is that there exists a small enough subset X such that the induced decision for the "consensus candidates" will not be a big mistake.

1.4   Organization of the Paper

First, in Section 2 we formalize the information we may extract from subset of votes, and introduce a measure of inaccuracy of such a subset. Next, in Section 3 we prove the existence of a small subset of votes with stable inaccuracy. In Section 4 we show that the optimization problem of deciding the part of the committee not induced by the subset of votes can be approximated with only a small additional loss in the objective function. Finally, in Section 5 we give an algorithm considering all subsets of a fixed size and show that, in the iteration when the algorithm happens to consider a subset with stable inaccuracy, it will produce a $(1 + \epsilon)$-approximate solution to MAV.

2   Extracting Information from Subsets

We consider subsets of votes and analyze the information they carry. We measure the inaccuracy of this information with respect to the set of all votes. We show that there exists a small subset with stable inaccuracy, i.e., the drop of inaccuracy after including one more vote is small.

Let us define an inaccuracy function $ina : 2^S \mapsto \mathbb{R}_{\geq 0}$ that measures the inaccuracy if we will consider subset $Y \subseteq S$ instead of S. The smaller the $ina(Y)$ is the better the common parts of strings in Y represent s_{OPT}.

Definition 2. *For all* $Y \subseteq S, Y \neq \emptyset$ *we define functions* $t(Y) \in \{0,1\}^m$ *and* $ina(Y) \in \mathbb{R}_{\geq 0}$ *as follows:*

$$(t(Y))[j] = \begin{cases} 0 & \text{if } \forall_{y \in Y} \quad y[j] = 0 \\ 1 & \text{if } \forall_{y \in Y} \quad y[j] = 1 \\ s_{OPT}[j] & \text{otherwise,} \end{cases}$$

$$ina(Y) = d(t(Y), s_{OPT}).$$

Intuitively $t(Y)$ is the optimal solution s_{OPT} changed at positions where all strings from Y agree. Also we define the pattern of a subset of votes.

Definition 3. *For all* $Y \subseteq S, Y \neq \emptyset$ *we define pattern* $p(Y) \in \{0, 1, *\}^m$ *as:*

$$(p(Y))[j] = \begin{cases} 0 & \text{if } \forall_{y \in Y} \quad y[j] = 0 \\ 1 & \text{if } \forall_{y \in Y} \quad y[j] = 1 \\ * & \text{otherwise.} \end{cases}$$

It represents positions that all strings in Y agree. "$*$" encodes a mismatch.

Note that (from Definitions 2 and 3) $t(Y)$ is an optimal solution s_{OPT} overwritten by a pattern p_r on no-star positions:

$$(t(Y))[j] = \begin{cases} s_{OPT}[j] & \text{if } (p(Y))[j] = * \\ (p(Y))[j] & \text{otherwise.} \end{cases}$$

The inaccuracy function has the following properties:

Lemma 1. $\forall_{s_{i_1} \in S}$, for all sequences $\{s_{i_1}\} = Y_1 \subseteq Y_2 \subseteq \cdots \subseteq Y_n = S$ we have

$$OPT \geqslant ina(Y_1) \geqslant ina(Y_2) \geqslant \cdots \geqslant ina(Y_n) = 0$$

Proof. It is easy to see that

$$ina(Y_1) \stackrel{\text{def.}}{=} d\big(t(Y_1), s_{OPT}\big) = d\big(t(\{s_{i_1}\}), s_{OPT}\big) = d\big(s_{i_1}, s_{OPT}\big) \leqslant OPT,$$

$$ina(Y_n) = ina(S) = d(s_{OPT}, s_{OPT}) = 0.$$

Still we need to prove $ina(Y_i) \geqslant ina(Y_{i+1})$. Pattern $p(Y_{i+1})$ is built on strings from $Y_i \subseteq Y_{i+1}$ and strings from $Y_{i+1} \setminus Y_i$. So $p(Y_{i+1})$ has at least as many $*$ as $p(Y_i)$ has. Therefore $t(Y_{i+1})$ has at least as many positions as $t(Y_i)$ has that agree with optimal solution s_{OPT}, so $d\big(t(Y_i), s_{OPT}\big) \geqslant d\big(t(Y_{i+1}), s_{OPT}\big)$. Using definition of the inaccuracy function (Definition 2) we prove the lemma.   ■

Intuitively $ina(Y) - ina(Y \cup \{y\})$ is the decrease of the inaccuracy from adding element y to set Y. We will show that, when adding one more element y to sets Y, Z such that $Y \subseteq Z$, the inaccuracy decrease more in a case of adding y to the smaller set Y than adding y to the bigger set Z.

Lemma 2. *If we artificially extend the $ina(\cdot)$ function for the empty set: $ina(\emptyset) = 2 \cdot OPT$, then function $ina(\cdot)$ is supermodular[1], i.e.,*

$$\forall_{Y \subseteq Z \subseteq S} \quad \forall_{s \in S} \quad ina(Z) - ina(Z \cup \{s\}) \leqslant ina(Y) - ina(Y \cup \{s\}) \qquad (1)$$

Proof. Let fix Y, Z and s such that $Y \subseteq Z \subseteq S$ and $s \in S$.

Case 1: $Z = \emptyset$:
   Then also $Y = \emptyset$, and inequality (1) holds obviously.

Case 2: $Z \neq \emptyset, Y = \emptyset$:
   We have:

$$ina(Z) - ina(Z \cup \{s\}) \leqslant OPT =$$

$$= 2 \cdot OPT - OPT \leqslant ina(\emptyset) - ina(\{s\}) = ina(Y) - ina(Y \cup \{s\}), \qquad (2)$$

because we use respectively: Lemma 1 and the fact that Z has at least one element; definition of $ina(\cdot)$ for empty set and upperbound for $ina(\cdot)$ function; assumption that $Y = \emptyset$.

---

[1] According to [11], $f : 2^S \mapsto \mathbb{R}$ is supermodular iff
   $\forall_{Y,Z \subseteq S} \quad f(Y) + f(Z) \leqslant f(Y \cup Z) + f(Y \cap Z)$ which is equivalent with
   $\forall_{Y \subseteq Z \subseteq S} \quad \forall_{s \in S} \quad f(Z) - f(Z \cup \{s\}) \leqslant f(Y) - f(Y \cup \{s\})$.

Case 3: $Z \neq \emptyset, Y \neq \emptyset$:

From definition of $ina(\cdot)$ we have:

$$ina(Z) - ina(Z \cup \{s\}) = d\big(t(Z), s_{OPT}\big) - d\big(t(Z \cup \{s\}), s_{OPT}\big) =$$

counting a difference by considering two cases for value of s_{OPT} we obtain

$$= \Big|\{j : s_{OPT}[j] = 1 \wedge t(Z \cup \{s\})[j] = 1 \wedge t(Z)[j] = 0\}\Big| +$$

$$+ \Big|\{j : s_{OPT}[j] = 0 \wedge t(Z \cup \{s\})[j] = 0 \wedge t(Z)[j] = 1\}\Big| =$$

using definition of function $t(\cdot)$:

$$= \Big|\{j : s_{OPT}[j] = 1 \wedge s[j] = 1 \wedge \forall_{z \in Z} \, z[j] = 0\}\Big| +$$

$$+ \Big|\{j : s_{OPT}[j] = 0 \wedge s[j] = 0 \wedge \forall_{z \in Z} \, z[j] = 1\}\Big| \leqslant$$

taking an universal quantifier over a smaller subset we obtain:

$$\leqslant \Big|\{j : s_{OPT}[j] = 1 \wedge s[j] = 1 \wedge \forall_{y \in Y} \, y[j] = 0\}\Big| +$$

$$+ \Big|\{j : s_{OPT}[j] = 0 \wedge s[j] = 0 \wedge \forall_{y \in Y} \, y[j] = 1\}\Big| =$$

reversing all previous transformations finally we obtain:

$$= ina(Y) - ina(Y \cup \{s\}).$$

∎

3   Existence of a Stable Subset

Lemma 3. *For any fixed $R \in \mathbb{N}_{\geqslant 1}$ there exists a subset $X \subseteq S, |X| = R$ such that*

$$\forall_{s \in S \setminus X} \quad ina(X) - ina(X \cup \{s\}) \leqslant \frac{OPT}{R}. \tag{3}$$

We say such X is $\frac{OPT}{R}$-stable.

It means that there exists such a subset of votes X that adding one more vote into X the inaccuracy decreases by at most $\frac{OPT}{R}$.

Proof. First, we construct $S_{\underline{r}}$ satisfying (3) with at most R elements.

Let us construct a sequence of subsets $S_1 \subset S_2 \subset \ldots \subset S_n = S, |S_i| = i$. We take $S_1 = \{s_{i_1}\}$, where s_{i_1} is any element of S and for $r \in \{2, 3, \ldots, n\}$ we take $S_r = S_{r-1} \cup \{s_{i_r}\}$ where s_{i_r} is such a vote that after adding it the inaccuracy function decreases the most, i.e.,

$$s_{i_r} = \arg\max_{s \in S \setminus S_{r-1}} \big(ina(S_{r-1}) - ina(S_{r-1} \cup \{s\})\big). \tag{4}$$

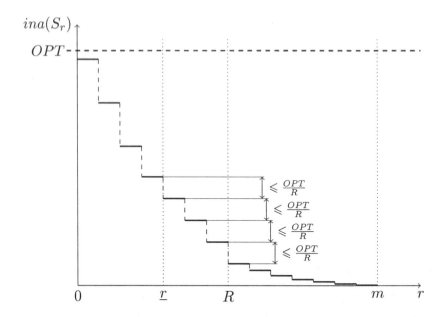

Fig. 1. The $ina(\cdot)$ function for the sequence of subsets $S_1 \subset S_2 \subset \ldots \subset S_n = S$

We have

$$\min_{r \in \{1,2,\ldots,R\}} ina(S_r) - ina(S_{r+1}) \leqslant \frac{1}{R}\left(\sum_{r=1}^{R} ina(S_r) - ina(S_{r+1})\right) =$$

$$= \frac{1}{R}\big(ina(S_1) - ina(S_{R+1})\big) \leqslant \frac{OPT}{R}, \qquad (5)$$

because (from Lemma 1) we know that $ina(S_1) \leqslant OPT$ and $ina(S_{R+1}) \geqslant 0$. Let $\underline{r}$ be a minimizer for the left-hand side of (5), then (by the choice of $s_{i_{\underline{r}}}$ in (4)) we have:

$$\max_{s \in S \setminus S_{\underline{r}}} \big(ina(S_{\underline{r}}) - ina(S_{\underline{r}} \cup \{s\})\big) \leqslant \frac{OPT}{R}, \qquad (6)$$

thus $S_{\underline{r}}$ satisfies (3), see Figure 1. If $S_{\underline{r}}$ has less elements than R we can extend $S_{\underline{r}}$ to an R-elements subset X by adding any elements of S. It follows from the supermodularity of $ina(\cdot)$. From Lemma 2 we have:

$$\forall_{s \in S \setminus S_{\underline{r}}} \quad ina(X) - ina(X \cup \{s\}) \leqslant ina(S_{\underline{r}}) - ina(S_{\underline{r}} \cup \{s\}),$$

and hence also:

$$\max_{s \in S \setminus S_{\underline{r}}} \big(ina(X) - ina(X \cup \{s\})\big) \leqslant \max_{s \in S \setminus S_{\underline{r}}} \big(ina(S_{\underline{r}}) - ina(S_{\underline{r}} \cup \{s\})\big). \qquad (7)$$

Finally, taking (6) and (7) we obtain:

$$\max_{s \in S \setminus X} \left(ina(X) - ina(X \cup \{s\}) \right) \leqslant \frac{OPT}{R}.$$

∎

Of course we cannot construct such a subset efficiently if we do not know s_{OPT}. How to find a proper subset X? For constructing our PTAS we will fix $R \in \mathbb{N}_{>1}$ and consider all subsets $Y \subseteq S$ with cardinality R. There is less than $n^R \in Poly(n)$ such subsets. For clarity, we will use $Y \subseteq S$ in arguments valid for all subsets considered by the algorithm, and $X \subseteq S$ for a $\frac{OPT}{R}$-stable subset of votes.

For a fixed $Y \subseteq S, Y \neq \emptyset$, WLOG we reorder candidates in such a way that $p(Y)$ is a lexicographically smallest permutation:

$$p(Y) = **\ldots*00\ldots011\ldots1.$$

The first part (from the left) is called "star positions" or "star part". The remaining part is called "no-star part". We define $p^{(*)}(Y)$ as the number of $*$ in $p(Y)$ and we denote it β:

$$\beta = p^{(*)}(Y) = \left| \left\{ j : (p(Y))[j] = * \right\} \right|.$$

In our PTAS we essentially fix the "no-star part" of the answer to the pattern $p(Y)$ and optimize over the choices for the "star part" of the outcome. If the number of stars or number of 1's on star positions of s_{OPT} is small enough, then there is only $Poly(m, n)$ possible solutions and we can consider all of them. Let us analyze the size of the "star part".

Lemma 4. *For all $Y \subseteq S$ we have*

$$\beta = p^{(*)}(Y) \leqslant |Y| \cdot OPT$$

The proof is easy and you can find it in arXiv version of the paper [4].

Note that for X from Lemma 3 we have

$$p^{(*)}(X) \leqslant |X| \cdot OPT = R \cdot OPT. \tag{8}$$

Let us now introduce some more notation. Assuming $Y \subseteq S$ and hence also $\beta = p^{(*)}(Y)$ are fixed, we will use the following notation to denote the "star part" and the "no-star part" of a string $x \in \{0,1\}^m$:

$$x' = x[1] \cdot x[2] \cdot \ldots \cdot x[\beta],$$

$$x'' = x[\beta + 1] \cdot x[\beta + 2] \cdot \ldots \cdot x[m],$$

where "·" is a concatenation of strings (letters). So we divide x into two parts: $x = x' \cdot x''$.

Let us now define a k-completion of $x \in \{0,1\}^m$ (definition from [7]) to be a $y \in \{0,1\}^m$ such that $y^{(1)} = k$ and $d(y, x)$ is the minimum possible Hamming distance between x and any vector with k of 1's. To obtain a k-completion we only add or only delete a proper number of 1's. To be more specific in this paper we assume the k-completion is always obtained by changing bits at positions with the smallest possible index[2].

In the following lemma we will show that for the pattern from a stable subset X we can change the number of 1's in the "no-star part" to the properly guessed number of 1's loosing only twice the stability constant.

Lemma 5. *If $X \subseteq S$ is $(\epsilon_1 \cdot OPT)$-stable, z'' is a k''-completion of $\big(p(X)\big)''$, where $k'' = (s''_{OPT})^{(1)}$, then*

$$\forall_{i \in \{1, 2, \cdots, n\}} \quad d(s'_{OPT} \cdot z'', s_i) \leqslant (1 + 2\epsilon_1) \cdot OPT \tag{9}$$

Proof. WLOG there is insufficient number of 1's in no-star part of pattern $p(X)$, i.e., $k'' \geqslant \big((p(X))''\big)^{(1)}$. The other case is symmetric.

Let us fix $s_i \in S$ and consider all combinations of values in strings $\big(p(X)\big)''$, z'', s''_i, s''_{OPT} at the same position j. $\alpha_a \in \mathbb{N}$, for $a \in \{1, 2, \cdots, 12\}$, counts the number of positions j with combination a, see Table 1:

Table 1. Combinations of values in strings $(p(X))'', z'', s''_i, s''_{OPT}$. There is only 12 combinations (no $2^4 = 16$), because by the assumption $k'' \geqslant ((p(X))'')^{(1)}$ we never change from 1 in $((p(X))'')^{(1)}$ to 0 in z''.

	combinations											
index of a combination	1	2	3	4	5	6	7	8	9	10	11	12
$(p(X))''[j]$	0	0	0	0	0	0	0	0	1	1	1	1
$z''[j]$	0	0	0	0	1	1	1	1	1	1	1	1
$s''_i[j]$	0	1	0	1	0	1	0	1	0	1	0	1
$s''_{OPT}[j]$	0	0	1	1	0	0	1	1	0	0	1	1
number of occurrences	α_1	α_2	α_3	α_4	α_5	α_6	α_7	α_8	α_9	α_{10}	α_{11}	α_{12}
$d(z''[j], s''_i[j])$	0	1	0	1	1	0	1	0	1	0	1	0
$d(s''_{OPT}[j], s''_i[j])$	0	1	1	0	0	1	1	0	0	1	1	0

We have:

$$d(z'', s''_i) = \big|\{j : z''[j] \neq s''_i[j]\}\big| =$$

we consider two cases for value of s_{OPT} at position j:

$$= \big|\{j : z''[j] \neq s''_i[j] \wedge (z''[j] = s_{OPT} \vee z''[j] \neq s_{OPT})\}\big| =$$

we divide it into two components:

$$= \big|\{j : s_{OPT} = z''[j] \neq s''_i[j] \qquad\quad \}\big| +$$
$$+ \big|\{j : \qquad\quad z''[j] \neq s''_i[j] = s_{OPT})\}\big| =$$

---

[2] Any other deterministic rule would work for us just as well.

we use case counts from Table 1 to count positions in both components:

$$= \underbrace{(\alpha_2 + \alpha_7 + \alpha_{11}}_{\text{first component}} + \underbrace{\alpha_3 + \alpha_6 + \alpha_{10} - \alpha_3 - \alpha_6 - \alpha_{10})}_{=0} + \underbrace{(\alpha_4 + \alpha_5 + \alpha_9)}_{\text{second component}} =$$

and we use the definition of the Hamming distance:

$$= \left(d(s''_{OPT}, s''_i) - \alpha_3 - \alpha_6 - \alpha_{10}\right) + (\alpha_4 + \alpha_5 + \alpha_9). \tag{10}$$

Since $(z'')^{(1)} = k'' = (s''_{OPT})^{(1)}$,

$$\sum_{k=5}^{12} \alpha_k = \alpha_3 + \alpha_4 + \alpha_7 + \alpha_8 + \alpha_{11} + \alpha_{12}$$

$$\alpha_5 = \alpha_3 + \alpha_4 - \alpha_6 - \alpha_9 - \alpha_{10}. \tag{11}$$

Also

$$\alpha_4 + \alpha_8 + \alpha_9 \leqslant \epsilon_1 \cdot OPT, \tag{12}$$

because X is $\epsilon_1 \cdot OPT$-stable. Now we are ready to prove equation (9).

$$d(s'_{OPT} \cdot z'', s_i) \stackrel{\text{def.}}{=} d(s'_{OPT}, s'_i) + d(z'', s''_i) \stackrel{(10)}{=}$$

$$\stackrel{(10)}{=} d(s'_{OPT}, s'_i) + d(s''_{OPT}, s''_i) - \alpha_3 - \alpha_6 - \alpha_{10} + \alpha_4 + \alpha_5 + \alpha_9 \stackrel{(11)}{=}$$

$$\stackrel{(11)}{=} \underbrace{d(s_{OPT}, s_i)}_{\leqslant OPT} + 2(\underbrace{\alpha_4}_{\substack{(12) \\ \leqslant \epsilon_1 \cdot OPT}} - \alpha_6 - \alpha_{10}) \stackrel{(12)}{\leqslant} (1 + 2\epsilon_1) \cdot OPT.$$

∎

4   An Auxiliary Optimization Problem

In this section we will consider the optimization problem obtained after guessing the number of 1's in the two parts and fixing the "no-star part" of the outcome. It has variables for all the positions of the "star part" and constraints for all the original votes $s_i \in S$.

Let us define the optimization problem in terms of the integer program $IP_{(13)-(17)}(Y, k')$ by (13)-(17):

$$\min q \tag{13}$$

$$(s')^{(1)} = k' \tag{14}$$

$$\forall_{i \in \{1,2,\ldots,n\}} \quad d(s', s'_i) \leqslant q - d(s''_{ALG}, s''_i) \tag{15}$$

$$q \geqslant 0 \tag{16}$$

$$\forall_{j \in \{1,2,\ldots,\beta\}} \quad s'[j] \in \{0,1\} \tag{17}$$

where $Y \subseteq S, k = k' + k''$, and s''_{ALG} is the k''-completion of $(p(Y))''$. Recall that $\beta = p^{(*)}(Y)$ and $(p(Y))''$ is the "no-star part" of the pattern $p(Y)$.

In the LP relaxation (17) is replaced with:

$$\forall_{j \in \{1,2,\ldots,\beta\}} \quad s'[j] \in [0,1] \tag{18}$$

Lemma 6. $\forall_{R \in \mathbb{N}_{\geqslant 1}, Y \subseteq S, |Y| \leqslant R, k' \in \mathbb{N}, \epsilon_2 > 0}$ we can find $(1 + 2\epsilon_2)$-approximation solution for $IP_{(13)-(17)}(Y,k')$ by solving the LP and considering at most

$$(3n)^{\frac{3R\ln(2)}{(\epsilon_2)^2}} + m^{\frac{3R^2\ln(6)}{(\epsilon_2)^2}} \quad cases.$$

Proof. Let us fix constants $\epsilon_2 \in (0, \frac{1}{2})$ (for $\epsilon_2 \geqslant \frac{1}{2}$ we could use 2-approximation from [5]). Consider three cases:

Case 1: $\beta \leqslant \frac{3R\ln(3n)}{(\epsilon_2)^2}$
There is 2^β possibilities for s'.

$$2^\beta \leqslant 2^{\frac{3R\ln(3n)}{(\epsilon_2)^2}} = e^{\ln(3n)\frac{3R\ln(2)}{(\epsilon_2)^2}} = (3n)^{\frac{3R\ln(2)}{(\epsilon_2)^2}} \in Poly(n),$$

because ϵ_2 and R are fixed constants. So we will check (in polynomial time) all possibilities for s' and we will find optimal solution for the integer program.

Case 2: $k' \leqslant \frac{3R^2\ln(6)}{(\epsilon_2)^2}$
There is $Poly(m)$ possibilities for s' because we can upperbound the number of possibilities of setting 1's into β positions by:

$$\binom{\beta}{k'} \leqslant \beta^{k'} \leqslant \beta^{\frac{3R^2\ln(6)}{(\epsilon_2)^2}} \leqslant m^{\frac{3R^2\ln(6)}{(\epsilon_2)^2}} \in Poly(m),$$

because ϵ_2 and R are fixed constants.

Case 3: $\beta > \frac{3R\ln(3n)}{(\epsilon_2)^2} \wedge k' > \frac{3R^2\ln(6)}{(\epsilon_2)^2}$
We denote an optimal solution of the $IP_{(13)-(17)}(Y,k')$ by $((s')^{IP}, q^{IP})$. Let us use LP relaxation and denote an optimal solution of the LP by $((s')^{LP}, q^{LP})$. Obviously we have $q^{LP} \leqslant q^{IP}$. We can solve the LP in polynomial time but we may obtain a fractional solution. We want to round it independently. We will use a randomized rounding defined by distributions on each position $j \in \{1,2,\ldots,\beta\}$:

$$P(s'[j] = 1) = (s')^{LP}[j], \quad P(s'[j] = 0) = 1 - (s')^{LP}[j]. \tag{19}$$

We can estimate the expected value of a distance to such a random solution s':

$$\forall_{i \in \{1,2,\cdots,n\}} \quad \mathbb{E}\big[d(s',s'_i)\big] \overset{\text{def.}}{=} \mathbb{E}\left[\sum_{j=1}^{\beta} \big|s'[j] - s'_i[j]\big|\right] =$$

$$= \mathbb{E}\left[\sum_{j=1}^{\beta} \Big(\chi(s'_i[j]=0) \cdot s'[j] \quad + \quad \chi(s'_i[j]=1) \cdot (1-s'[j]) \quad \Big)\right] \overset{\text{lin. of } \mathbb{E}}{=}$$

$$\overset{\text{lin. of } \mathbb{E}}{=} \sum_{j=1}^{\beta} \Big(\chi(s'_i[j]=0) \cdot \mathbb{E}\big[s'[j]\big] \quad + \quad \chi(s'_i[j]=1) \cdot \mathbb{E}\big[1-s'[j]\big] \quad \Big) \overset{(19)}{=}$$

$$\overset{(19)}{=} \sum_{j=1}^{\beta} \Big(\chi(s'_i[j]=0) \cdot (s')^{LP}[j] \quad + \quad \chi(s'_i[j]=1) \cdot \big(1-(s')^{LP}[j]\big) \Big) \overset{\text{def.}}{=}$$

$$\overset{\text{def.}}{=} d\big((s')^{LP}, s'_i\big) \overset{(15)}{\leqslant} q^{LP} - d(s''_{ALG}, s''_i). \tag{20}$$

$d(s',s'_i)$ is a sum of β independent 0-1 variables. For $\epsilon' \in (0,1)$ using Chernoff's bound [9] we have:

$$P\Big(d(s',s'_i) \geqslant (1+\epsilon') \cdot \mathbb{E}\big[d(s',s'_i)\big]\Big) \leqslant \exp\left(-\frac{1}{3}(\epsilon')^2 \cdot \mathbb{E}\big[d(s',s'_i)\big]\right).$$

If we take $\epsilon' = \frac{\epsilon_2 \cdot q^{IP}}{\mathbb{E}[d(s',s'_i)]}$ then we obtain:

$$\exp\left(-\frac{1}{3} \cdot \frac{(\epsilon_2)^2 \cdot (q^{IP})^2}{\mathbb{E}\big[d(s',s'_i)\big]}\right) \geqslant P\Big(d(s',s'_i) \geqslant \mathbb{E}\big[d(s',s'_i)\big] + \epsilon_2 \cdot q^{IP}\Big) \overset{(20)}{\geqslant}$$

$$\overset{(20)}{\geqslant} P\Big(d(s',s'_i) \geqslant q^{LP} - d(s''_{ALG},s''_i) + \epsilon_2 \cdot q^{IP}\Big). \tag{21}$$

We want to know an upperbound for the probability that we make an error greater than $\epsilon_2 \cdot q^{IP}$ for at least one vote:

$$P\Big(\exists_{i \in \{1,2,\ldots,n\}} : d(s',s'_i) \geqslant q^{LP} - d(s''_{ALG},s''_i) + \epsilon_2 \cdot q^{IP}\Big) \overset{(21)}{\leqslant}$$

$$\overset{(21)}{\leqslant} n \cdot \exp\left(-\frac{1}{3} \cdot \frac{(\epsilon_2)^2 \cdot (q^{IP})^2}{\mathbb{E}\big[d(s',s'_i)\big]}\right) \leqslant n \cdot \exp\left(-\frac{1}{3}(\epsilon_2)^2 \cdot q^{IP}\right), \tag{22}$$

where the last inequality is because of:

$$\mathbb{E}\big[d(s',s'_i)\big] \overset{(20)}{\leqslant} q^{LP} - d(s''_{ALG},s''_i) \leqslant q^{IP}.$$

We want to further upperbound the probability in (22). From the assumption about β and from Lemma 4 we have:

$$\frac{3R\ln(3n)}{(\epsilon_2)^2} < \beta \overset{\text{Lem.4}}{\leqslant} |Y| \cdot OPT \leqslant R \cdot OPT \leqslant R \cdot q^{IP}, \quad \text{equivalently}$$

$$\frac{1}{3} > n \cdot \exp\left(-\frac{1}{3}(\epsilon_2)^2 \cdot q^{IP}\right). \tag{23}$$

So, finally we have:

$$P\left(\exists_{i \in \{1,2,\ldots,n\}} : d(s', s_i') \geqslant q^{LP} - d(s''_{ALG}, s_i'') + \epsilon_2 \cdot q^{IP}\right) \overset{(22),(23)}{<} \frac{1}{3}. \tag{24}$$

So with probability at least $\frac{2}{3}$ we obtain:

$$\forall_{i \in \{1,2,\ldots,n\}} \quad d(s' \cdot s''_{ALG}, s_i) = d(s', s_i') + d(s''_{ALG}, s_i'') \overset{(24)}{<}$$

$$\overset{(24)}{<} q^{LP} - d(s''_{ALG}, s_i'') + \epsilon_2 \cdot q^{IP} + d(s''_{ALG}, s_i'') \leqslant (1 + \epsilon_2) \cdot q^{IP}. \tag{25}$$

We can also obtain a wrong number o 1's. The solution s'_{ALG} for that is to take the k'-completion of s'. We will show that the additional error for such operation is not so big. Expected number of 1's in s' is equal k':

$$\mathbb{E}\left[(s')^{(1)}\right] \overset{\text{def.}}{=} \mathbb{E}\left[\sum_{j=1}^{\beta} s'[j]\right] \overset{\text{lin. of }\mathbb{E}}{=} \sum_{j=1}^{\beta} (s')^{LP}[j] \overset{\text{def.}}{=} ((s')^{LP})^{(1)} \overset{(14)}{=} k'.$$

We want to know how much we lose taking the k'-completion. Similar as before, $(s')^{(1)} = \sum_{j=1}^{\beta} s'[j]$ is a sum of β independent 0-1 variables. For $\epsilon'' \in (0,1)$ using Chernoff's bound [9] we have:

$$P\left((s')^{(1)} \geqslant (1 + \epsilon'') \cdot k'\right) \leqslant \exp\left(-\frac{1}{3}(\epsilon'')^2 \cdot k'\right),$$

$$P\left((s')^{(1)} \leqslant (1 - \epsilon'') \cdot k'\right) \leqslant \exp\left(-\frac{1}{2}(\epsilon'')^2 \cdot k'\right).$$

Taking both inequalities together, $\epsilon'' = \frac{\epsilon_2}{R}$ and using assumption $k' > \frac{3R^2 \ln(6)}{(\epsilon_2)^2}$ we have:

$$P\left(\left|(s')^{(1)} - k'\right| \geqslant \epsilon'' \cdot k'\right) \leqslant 2 \cdot \exp\left(-\frac{1}{3}(\epsilon'')^2 \cdot k'\right) \leqslant$$

$$\leqslant 2 \cdot \exp\left(-\frac{1}{3}\frac{(\epsilon_2)^2}{R^2} \cdot k'\right) < \frac{1}{3}.$$

So with probability at least $\frac{2}{3}$ the error from taking the k'-completion is not greater than $\epsilon'' \cdot k' = \frac{\epsilon_2}{R} \cdot k' \leqslant \frac{\epsilon_2}{R} \cdot \beta \overset{\text{Lem.4}}{\leqslant} \frac{\epsilon_2}{R} \cdot |Y| \cdot OPT \leqslant \epsilon_2 \cdot OPT \leqslant \epsilon_2 \cdot q^{IP}$.

Combining the above with (25) we obtain a $(1 + 2\epsilon_2)$-approximate solution with probability at least $\frac{1}{3}$. We may derandomize the algorithm analogously to how it was done in the PTAS for the Closest String problem [8]. For more on derandomization techniques see [10]. ∎

5   Algorithm and Its Complexity Analysis

Now we are ready to combine the ideas into a single algorithm.

Algorithm. ALG(R)

Input: $S = \{s_1, s_2, \ldots, s_n\} \in (\{0, 1\}^m)^n, 0 \leqslant k \leqslant m, R \in \mathbb{N}_{\geqslant 1}$
Output: $s_{ALG} \in \{0, 1\}^m$
1: **for** each R-element subset $Y = \{s_{i_1}, s_{i_2}, \ldots, s_{i_R}\} \subseteq S$ **do**
2:     **for** each division k into two parts $k = k' + k''$ **do**
3:         $s''_{ALG} \leftarrow k''$-completion of $(p(Y))''$
            (if not possible, then skip this inner iteration)
4:         $s'_{ALG} \leftarrow$ approximation solution of $IP_{(13)-(17)}(Y, k')$ using Lemma 6
            (if $LP_{(13)-(16),(18)}(Y, k')$ infeasible, then skip this inner iteration)
5:         evaluate $s'_{ALG} \cdot s''_{ALG}$ by computing $\max_{i \in \{1,2,\ldots,n\}} d(s_i, s'_{ALG} \cdot s''_{ALG})$
6:     **end for**
7: **end for**
8: $s_{ALG} \leftarrow$ the best solution from a loop in lines 1-7

It remains to argue that for a large enough parameter R the above algorithm will at some point consider a subset of votes X that leads to an accurate enough approximation of the Minimax objective function of our problem.

Theorem 1. $\forall_{\epsilon \in (0,1)}$ we may compute a $(1 + \epsilon)$-approximate solution to Minimax Approval Voting in $O(Poly(n, m))$ time.

Proof. Let $\epsilon_0 = \frac{\epsilon}{3} < \frac{1}{3}$.

By Lemma 3, there exists an $\frac{\epsilon_0 \cdot OPT}{2}$-stable set of votes $X \subseteq S$ of cardinality $|X| = R = \lceil \frac{2}{\epsilon_0} \rceil$.

Consider algorithm ALG(R). In one iteration it will consider X and k', k'' such that $(s'_{OPT})^{(1)} = k'$. Recall that s''_{ALG} is the specific k''-completion of $(p(X))''$. By Lemma 5 we have:

$$d(s'_{OPT} \cdot s''_{ALG}, s_i) \leqslant (1 + \epsilon_0) \cdot OPT,$$

hence $(s' = s'_{OPT}, q = (1 + \epsilon_0) \cdot OPT)$ is a feasible solution to $IP_{(13-17)}(X, k')$ and the optimal value of $IP_{(13-17)}(X, k')$ is at most $(1 + \epsilon_0) \cdot OPT$.

By Lemma 6 with $\epsilon_2 = \frac{\epsilon_0}{2}$ we find a $(1+\epsilon_0)$-approximate solution (s'_{ALG}, q_{ALG}) to $IP_{(13-17)}(X, k')$. So we have:

$$q_{ALG} \leqslant (1 + \epsilon_0) \cdot (1 + \epsilon_0) \cdot OPT \overset{\epsilon_0 < 1}{\leqslant} (1 + 3\epsilon_0) \cdot OPT = (1 + \epsilon) \cdot OPT.$$

It remains to observe, that $s_{ALG} = s'_{ALG} \cdot s''_{ALG}$ is a solution to MAV of cost $q_{ALG} \leqslant (1 + \epsilon) \cdot OPT$.

The algorithm examined $O(n^R) = O\left(n^{\lceil \frac{6}{\epsilon} \rceil}\right) \in O(Poly(n))$ subsets Y, $O(m)$ choices of k' and each time considered

$$O\left((3n)^{\frac{108 \cdot \lceil \frac{6}{\epsilon} \rceil \cdot \ln(2)}{\epsilon^2}} + m^{\frac{108 \cdot \lceil \frac{6}{\epsilon} \rceil^2 \cdot \ln(6)}{\epsilon^2}}\right) \in O(Poly(n, m)) \text{ cases.}$$

■

6 Concluding Remarks

We showed the existence of a PTAS for Minimax Approval Voting by considering all subsets of a fixed size R. If not the discovered supermodularity for the inaccuracy function $ina(\cdot)$, we would simply consider all subsets of size at most R. Although the supermodularity was not essential for our result, it shows that larger subsets of votes are generally more stable (in the sense of definition in Lemma 3). It seems to suggest that an algorithm considering a smaller number of larger subsets of votes would potentially be more efficient in practice. Perhaps the most interesting open question is whether by randomly sampling a number of subsets of votes to examine, one could obtain a more practical FPRAS for the problem.

Another interesting direction is the optimization of the Minimax objective function subject to a restriction that the voting system must be incentive compatible. According to [5] the best possible approximation ratio in this setting is between $2 - \frac{2}{k+1}$ and $3 - \frac{2}{k+1}$, and a natural challenge is to narrow this gap.

Finally, we know the complexity of the two extreme objectives, i.e., Minimax and Minisum. The latter is easily optimized by selecting the k most often approved candidates. The optimization problem for intermediate objectives such as optimizing the sum of squares of the Hamming distances remains unexplored, and it would be interesting to learn which objective functions are more difficult to approximate than Minimax in the context of Approval Voting systems.

Acknowledgments. We want to thank Katarzyna Staniewicz for many helpful proofreading comments. Also we want to thank reviewers for their valuable suggestions. Krzysztof Sornat was supported by local grant 2139/M/II/14.

References

1. Aziz, H., Gaspers, S., Gudmundsson, J., Mackenzie, S., Mattei, N., Walsh, T.: Computational Aspects of Multi-Winner Approval Voting. arXiv preprint arXiv:1407.3247v1 (2014)
2. Brams, S.J., Fishburn, P.C.: Approval Voting, 2nd edn. Springer (2007)
3. Brams, S.J., Kilgour, D.M., Sanver, M.R.: A minimax procedure for electing committees. Public Choice 132(3-4), 401–420 (2007)

4. Byrka, J., Sornat, K.: PTAS for Minimax Approval Voting. arXiv preprint arXiv:1407.7216v2 (2014)
5. Caragiannis, I., Kalaitzis, D., Markakis, E.: Approximation algorithms and mechanism design for minimax approval voting. In: Proceedings of the 24th AAAI Conference on Artificial Intelligence, pp. 737–742 (2010)
6. LeGrand, R.: Analysis of the minimax procedure. Technical Report WUCSE-2004-67. Department of Computer Science and Engineering, Washington University, St. Louis, Missouri (2004)
7. LeGrand, R., Markakis, E., Mehta, A.: Some results on approximating the minimax solution in approval voting. In: Proceedings of 6th AAMAS, pp. 1193–1195 (2007)
8. Li, M., Ma, B., Wang, L.: On the closest string and substring problems. Journal of the ACM 49, 157–171 (2002)
9. Motvani, R., Raghavan, P.: Randomized Algorithms, ch. 4.1. Cambridge University Press (1995)
10. Raghavan, P.: Probabilistic construction of deterministic algorithms: Approximate packing integer programs. Journal of Computer and System Sciences 37(2), 130–143 (1988)
11. Schrijver, A.: Combinatorial Optimization: Polyhedra and efficiency, p. 766. Springer (2003)

Biobjective Online Bipartite Matching

Gagan Aggarwal[1], Yang Cai[2,*], Aranyak Mehta[1], and George Pierrakos[3]

[1] Google Research, Mountain View, CA
{gagana,aranyak}@google.com
[2] McGill University, Montreal, QC
cai@cs.mcgill.edu
[3] UC Berkeley, Berkeley, CA
georgios@cs.berkeley.edu

Abstract. Online Matching has been a problem of considerable interest recently, particularly due to its applicability in Online Ad Allocation. In practice, there are usually multiple objectives which need to be simultaneously optimized, e.g., revenue and quality. We capture this motivation by introducing the problem of Biobjective Online Bipartite Matching. This is a strict generalization of the standard setting. In our problem, the graph has edges of two colors, Red and Blue. The goal is to find a single matching that contains a large number of edges of each color.

We first show how this problem is a departure from previous settings: In all previous problems, the Greedy algorithm gives a non-trivial ratio, typically $1/2$. In the biobjective problem, we show that the competitive ratio of Greedy is 0, and in fact, any reasonable algorithm would have to *skip* vertices, i.e., not match some incoming vertices even though they have an edge available.

As our main result, we introduce an algorithm which randomly discards some edges of the graph in a particular manner – thus enabling the necessary skipping of vertices – and simultaneously runs the color-oblivious algorithm RANKING. We prove that this algorithm achieves a competitive ratio of $3 - 4/\sqrt{e} \simeq 0.573$ for graphs which have a perfect matching of each color. This beats the upper bound of $1/2$ for deterministic algorithms, and comes close to the upper bound of $1 - 1/e \simeq 0.63$ for randomized algorithms, both of which we prove carry over to the bicriteria setting, even with the perfect matching restriction. The technical difficulty lies in analyzing the expected minimum number of blue and red edges in the matching (rather than the minimum of the two expectations). To achieve this, we introduce a charging technique which has a new locality property, i.e., misses are charged to nearby hits, according to a certain metric.

Along the way we develop and analyze simpler algorithms for the problem: a deterministic algorithm which achieves a ratio of 0.343, and a simpler randomized algorithm, which achieves, intriguingly, precisely the same ratio.

---

* Part of the work was done while the second and fourth coauthors were visiting Google Research.

T.-Y. Liu et al. (Eds.): WINE 2014, LNCS 8877, pp. 218–231, 2014.
© Springer International Publishing Switzerland 2014

1 Introduction

Online Matching and Allocation is a topic that has received considerable interest in the recent past, both due to its practical importance in Internet Ad allocation, and also due to purely theoretical interest and advances that it has generated. The classic problem was introduced in [10]: There is a graph $G(U, V, E)$, with only U known in advance, and vertices from V arriving online in an adversarial order. As a vertex $v \in V$ arrives, its incident edges are revealed. The online algorithm can match v to some neighbor $u \in U$ which has not yet been matched (if any such exist), or choose to leave v unmatched. Each match made is irrevocable, and the goal is to maximize the size of the matching obtained.

Several simple ideas, such as an arbitrary choice of available neighbor (Greedy) or a random choice (Random) provide a competitive ratio of $1/2$, but no greater. The algorithm provided in [10], called RANKING, first permutes the vertices of U in a random permutation, and then matches each arriving vertex to that available neighbor which is highest according to the permutation. This algorithm is optimal, providing a ratio of $1 - 1/e$.

Motivated by applications in Internet advertising – in which U corresponds to advertisers, and V to arriving ad slots – many different variations of this problem have been studied recently, which includes different matching constraints, as well as different input models (we describe some of this related work in Section 2).

In this paper, we introduce a new direction in this literature. In all the variants studied so far, the constraints of the problem vary, but there is one objective function, namely the weight of the matching. However, in practice, there are typically multiple objective functions which an algorithm designer needs to consider, e.g. quality, ROI, revenue, efficiency, etc. These objective functions may not always be well-aligned, and the designer needs to achieve a good balance among them as prescribed by business needs. Sometimes, the different objective functions correspond to the value provided to different agents; in which case, fairness motivates balancing of the different objectives. In this paper, we introduce a new problem which captures this motivation.

1.1 Model and Problem Definition

We consider the basic setting of online bipartite matching, to which we introduce the most natural notion of multiple objectives, as follows: There is a bipartite graph $G(U, V, E)$ with $|U| = |V| = n$, where each edge is colored either Red or Blue. As before, U is known in advance, and the vertices of V arrive online together with their incident edges. The goal is to find a large matching that "balances" the two colors, as described next.

Given a matching in G, let RIM be the number of Red edges in the matching and let BIM be the number of Blue edges in the matching. Also let $\mathcal{R}$ be the size of the maximum matching in the graph G restricted to its Red edges and let $\mathcal{B}$ be the size of the maximum matching on the Blue edges of G. Then, we define the objective function value for this matching as

$$\min\left\{\frac{\text{BIM}}{\mathcal{B}}, \frac{\text{RIM}}{\mathcal{R}}\right\}$$

The competitive ratio of an online algorithm is defined as the minimum over all inputs, of the ratio of the objective value of the matching generated by the algorithm to the optimal offline objective value (i.e., of the best matching for this objective function).

For **randomized algorithms**, the objective function is an expectation-over-min formulation, where the expectation is over the internal randomness of the algorithm:

$$\text{Exp}\left[\min\left\{\frac{\text{BIM}}{\mathcal{B}}, \frac{\text{RIM}}{\mathcal{R}}\right\}\right] \tag{1}$$

Note that we do not define it as the minimum of the two expectations: This is an easier objective, and is not appropriate for our motivation. Indeed, to optimize the Min-of-Exps objective, one could simply flip a coin in the beginning to choose one of the two colors to optimize, and run the single-color algorithm for edges of that color. This would give a Min-of-Exps ratio of $(1 - 1/e)/2$. Clearly, the Exp-of-Mins objective is 0 for this algorithm.

The Perfect-Matching Restriction. We next describe a restriction on problem instances, which we call the perfect-matching restriction. In this, input instances contain a perfect matching on Red edges as well as a perfect matching on Blue edges, i.e. $\mathcal{B} = \mathcal{R} = n$. With this assumption, optimizing the objective function reduces to optimizing

$$\text{Exp}\left[\min\{\text{BIM}, \text{RIM}\}\right]$$

Also, with this assumption, it is not hard to show that there exists a matching with $n/2 - o(n)$ Red as well Blue edges, giving us the following Proposition (proof can be found in the full paper).

Proposition 1. *When $\mathcal{R} = \mathcal{B} = n$, the optimal offline value of $\min\{BIM, RIM\}$ is between $n/2 - O(\sqrt{n})$ and $n/2$.*

Note: We will work with this restriction in this paper[1]. When working under the restriction, for the given instance, we pick a perfect matching on Red edges, and a perfect matching on Blue edges, which we will refer to as the (canonical) Red and Blue perfect matchings in the graph. For $w \in U \cup V$ we define $N_b(w)$ as the match of w in the Blue perfect matching, and $N_r(w)$ as the match of w in the Red perfect matching.

A General Open Problem: The above formulation is the simplest one that captures the essence of the bi-objective motivation. The following weighted generalization, called *online bi-weighted bipartite matching problem*, captures the

---

[1] In the full paper, we describe the results without the restriction.

full extent of the motivation. Each edge e has two weights: $w_1(e)$ and $w_2(e)$. A matching M also has two weights: $w_1(M)$ and $w_2(M)$, which are the sums of the respective edge weights in the matching. The goal is to output a matching M which maximizes $\min\{w_1(M), w_2(M)\}$. This problem immediately inherits the impossibility results for the classic edge-weighted matching problem in the adversarial arrival model, in which deterministic hardness follows from instances where a large weight edge may or may not arrive at the end (for randomized hardness, see [1]). In fact, the general problem has to be considered either in the random arrival [13] or the free-disposal model [7], and we leave this as an interesting future direction.

1.2   Results and Key Ideas

Our main result is a randomized algorithm that achieves a factor of $3 - 4/\sqrt{e} \simeq 0.573$ under the perfect-matching restriction (we show a hardness of $1 - 1/e \simeq 0.63$). This algorithm, called LEFTSUBGRAPHRANKING randomly drops some arriving edges, and runs RANKING ([10], defined in Section 3) on the remaining graph in a color-oblivious manner.

Algorithm. LEFTSUBGRAPHRANKING

---
1. Each vertex in U picks a color uar, and throws away incident edges of that color.
2. Run RANKING on the resulting subgraph.

This artificial dropping of edges is essential – simply running RANKING gives a ratio of 0. The particular manner in which the edges are dropped is also important, and not all natural methods perform well. We also describe two other algorithms, c-BALANCE and p-PROBGREEDY (these are defined formally in the later sections). The former is deterministic, and aims explicitly to balance the colors. It achieves a ratio of 0.343, under the perfect-matching restriction (against a hardness result of 0.5). The latter is a simple randomized algorithm which, intriguingly, achieves the same ratio.

We also study the problem without the perfect-matching restriction. We show in the full paper that no randomized algorithm can do better than 0.43, and describe an algorithm, called DISJOINTRANKING, which achieves a ratio of $\frac{(1-1/e)}{4} \simeq 0.158$. No determimistic algorithm can achieve a non-trivial ratio (better than 0).

We highlight a few key ideas behind the algorithm design and analysis:

1. **Need to Skip:** The biobjective problem is a departure from previous versions of online matching in the following way: In all previous problems, the Greedy algorithm gives a non-trivial ratio, typically $1/2$ (due to some sort of a maximal matching argument). In the biobjective problem, we show that the competitive ratio of Greedy is 0. In fact, for an algorithm to do better than 0, it has to sometimes artificially *skip* vertices, i.e., not match an incoming vertex even though it has an edge available. This is true even under the perfect-matching restriction for deterministic algorithms (proof in Section 3.1). Under the restriction, a randomized algorithm which does not skip

can do no better than $1/2$. This is therefore a new constraint on algorithm design, which leads us to understand the question of when and how should the algorithm skip vertices.

2. **Locality of Charging:** For the analysis of our main algorithm (in Section 4), we use a charging argument (similar to the analysis in [10]). With 2 colors, we are able to charge each miss to $2n$ hits, instead of just n, giving a factor of $3 - 4/\sqrt{e}$ for the minimum of the expectations of the two colors. However, when we try to bound the expectation of the minimum color, even with this augmented charging map, some of the hits get charged twice (once each from misses of Red and Blue). This will lead to a factor of $1-2/e \simeq 0.26$. To overcome this problem, we introduce the notion of *locality of charging*, whereby misses in a given event map to hits in "nearby" events (according to an appropriately-defined metric). This lets us show that the number of hits that get double-charged are small, giving us a nearly identical competitive ratio of $3 - 4/\sqrt{e} - o(1)$ for the expectation of the minimum.

3. **Unchargeable Hits:** We analyze c-BALANCE (can be found in the full paper) using a charging argument that starts off as usual – for every miss, we can point to a hit, namely its perfect matching neighbor (of the appropriate color) that must have been matched. This, by itself, gives a very weak bound; the new idea is that, instead of allowing every hit to be charged by a miss, we identify a set of *unchargeable hits* that cannot be charged by misses. Thus the misses are upper bounded by a subset of hits, leading to a better bound on the competitive ratio.

Figure 1 summarizes our results.

	With perfect-matching restriction		Without perfect-matching restriction	
	Lower Bound	Upper Bound	Lower Bound	Upper Bound
Det. w/o Skips	0	0	0	0
Deterministic	0.343	0.5	0	0
Rand. w/o Skips	?	0.5	0	0
Randomized	$3 - 4/\sqrt{e} \simeq 0.573$	$1 - 1/e \simeq 0.63$	$\frac{(1-1/e)}{4} \simeq 0.158$	0.43

Fig. 1. Table of Results

2   Related Work

Motivated by applications in Internet advertising, several variants and generalizations of Online Matching have been studied recently, starting with the "Adwords" problem ([15], [4]), which generalized the setting to that with bids and budgets. Further generalizations included the Weighted-Vertex Matching problem [1], weighted edges with free-disposal ("Display Ads") [7], among many others. There have also been variants which study stochastic inputs for all these settings, as well as stochastic rewards (we do not mention all the references, since this literature is quite extensive by now, see [14] for a survey). Ours is an orthogonal direction, in introducing multiple objectives to this set of problems. We have started with the basic matching problem, but the question extends to the entire set of variants. In a recent paper, [12] also studied a bi-objective version of online (weighted) matching. In that paper, the goal is to maximize the cardinality of the matching along with its weight. Similar to ours, their model is also motivated by internet advertising, but besides the motivation, the two papers have pursued two drastically different directions and have used orthogonal techniques. One major difference from our setting is that their two objectives are in alignment, rather than in conflict, since adding an edge to the matching contributes both to the cardinality and the weight objective.

In another thread of work, there is a long research tradition of studying combinatorial optimization problems with multiple objectives, initiated by the paper of Papadimitriou and Yannakakis [17], which identifies a relaxed notion of *Pareto set* (the set of all solutions that are not dominated by any other in all objectives). Our problem fits only loosely in this literature: being an online problem, we are interested in implementing one balanced solution as the vertices arrive, not the entire Pareto set of trade-offs.

A similar motivation to ours can be found in a series of papers [5,6,2], which study the problem of designing an auction to balance revenue and efficiency. From a practical view, the importance of multiple objectives like quality, ROI and revenue in budgeted ad allocation, were described in [9].

An unrelated set of online problems with two objectives were studied in [8]. A related offline problem of exact matchings, i.e. finding a matching with exactly k Red edges was studied in [16,11,18], and the problem of approximately sampling and counting exact matchings was studied in [3].

3   Algorithm Evolution

In this section, we present a natural progression of algorithms, leading up to our main randomized algorithm. This sequence is ordered in increasing complexity of ideas employed by the algorithms, and is intended to provide intuition building towards the final algorithm. We start by showing that the simplest idea of Greedy does not give any non-trivial ratio.

3.1   Greedy Does Not Work, and the Need to Skip

As for any matching problem, we start by trying a greedy algorithm. However, we quickly note that any algorithm that always matches an incoming vertex if at least one incident edge is available (i.e., its other end point in U is not yet matched), has a competitive ratio no better than 0.

Similarly, one can prove that a randomized algorithm which does not skip will achieve a ratio no more than $1/2$.

Thus our first important observation is that any online algorithm has to sometimes *skip*, i.e., keep the arriving vertex unmatched even though it has an available neighbor. Note that this is very different from all previous settings in online matching and allocation problems, where greedy algorithms (which do not skip) achieve a competitive ratio of $1/2$.

Consider the instance on the left. Any algorithm, deterministic orrandomized, which never skips matching an incoming vertex, is forced to pick all the Blue edges, and no Red edges. The instance on the right has one extra edge and satisfies the perfect-matching restriction. Note that any deterministic algorithm which does not skip will again pick only blue edges (wlog assume it picks the blue edge for the first arriving vertex).

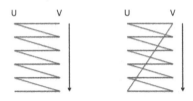

Proposition 2. *An algorithm that always matches an arriving vertex with an available edge cannot achieve a competitive ratio better than 0. This also holds for deterministic algorithms under the perfect-matching restriction, while a randomized algorithm that always matches an arriving vertex with an available edge cannot achieve a competitive ratio better than* $1/2$ *under the restriction.*

3.2   Algorithm c-Balance

The observation that we need to skip leads us to our first algorithm, called c-BALANCE, which skips in order to keep the two colors nearly balanced at all times.

We define *CurrentBlue* (resp. *CurrentRed*) as the number of Blue (resp. Red) edges in the current matching produced during the algorithm. We also define the following operations:

- **NoPreference**: Match the arriving vertex to any available neighbor (irre-spective of color).
- **OnlyBlue** (resp. **OnlyRed**): Match the arriving vertex via an available Blue (resp. Red) edge. If only Red (resp. Blue) edges are available then leave the vertex unmatched.

A natural approach is to do **OnlyRed** when the current matching has more blue edges than red, do **OnlyBlue** when it has more red edges and **NoPreference** otherwise. We will show that this achieves a competitive ratio of $1/3$.

We observe that this algorithm attempts to keep the two colors *perfectly* balanced, and *skips* an arriving vertex whenever the colors are unbalanced and no edge of the lagging color is available. We next try to give the algorithm some leeway in how balanced the two colors need to be during its run. To do that we introduce two new operations:

- **PreferBlue** (resp. **PreferRed**): If a Blue (resp. Red) edge is available, match the arriving vertex via one of them. Else match it via a Red (resp. Blue) edge, if one is available.

We are now ready to describe c-BALANCE[2].

Algorithm. c-BALANCE

For each arriving vertex v, switch case:

1. *CurrentBlue = CurrentRed*: `NoPreference`
2. *CurrentBlue > c · CurrentRed*: `OnlyRed`
3. *CurrentRed > c · CurrentBlue*: `OnlyBlue`
4. *CurrentRed < CurrentBlue ≤ c · CurrentRed*: `PreferRed`
5. *CurrentBlue < CurrentRed ≤ c · CurrentBlue*: `PreferBlue`

This algorithm tries to pick up some extra edges of the leading color (in case the arrival of edges of the leading colors slows down in the future), but not too many (as picking edges now reduces available vertices on the left, reducing the opportunity to pick lagging-color edges in the future). We present the result here, but postpone the full analysis to the full paper.

Proposition 3. c-BALANCE *achieves a competitive ratio of* $\frac{2c}{(1+c)(2+c)}$, *for* $1 \leq c \leq 2$, *and this analysis is tight.*

The competitive ratio is maximized at $c = \sqrt{2}$, giving the algorithm a competitive ratio of 0.343. We note that while c-BALANCE seems more flexible than simple balancing (and its analysis is *much* more difficult), it does not perform significantly better.

We note the following hardness result here, discussed in greater detail in the full paper.

Proposition 4. *Even under the perfect-matching restriction, no deterministic algorithm can achieve a competitive ratio better than* $1/2$.

It seems hard to reduce the performance gap for deterministic algorithms, and we shift our attention to randomized algorithms.

3.3   A Simple Randomized Algorithm

A natural first attempt to balance the two colors using randomness is the following: for each arriving vertex, match via a Red edge w.p. $1/2$ and match via a Blue edge w.p. $1/2$. Note that this algorithm skips a vertex when it has available edges of a single color, but it chooses the other color. This achieves a competitive ratio of $1/3$, with probability almost 1. Next, we consider a generalization of the above algorithm:

This algorithm sometimes skips vertices even when edges of both colors are available. Surprisingly, it does better for some values of p.

---

[2] Note that in the existing literature, *balance* typically refers to balancing the spend or the load on different vertices – here it refers to balancing the two colors in the current matching.

Algorithm. p-PROBGREEDY

For each arriving vertex v:
   w.p. p, match v via an available Red edge, if any.
   w.p. p, match v via an available Blue edge, if any.
   w.p. $1 - 2p$, leave v unmatched.

Proposition 5. p-PROBGREEDY *has a competitive ratio of* $\frac{2p(1-p)}{1+p}$ *with probability almost* 1. *This is maximized at* $p = \sqrt{2} - 1$, *giving* p-PROBGREEDY *a competitive ratio of* 0.343.

We postpone the proof to the full paper. Amazingly, this is the same bound as that achieved by c-BALANCE for $p = \frac{1}{1+c}$. We do not know if there is a deeper connection between the two algorithms, and we leave this possibility as an intriguing **open question**. Although p-PROBGREEDY did not achieve a better competitive ratio than c-BALANCE, it is simpler in that is does not need to keep any state. Also, the analysis for p-PROBGREEDYis significantly simpler than that of c-BALANCE. The next question to ask is whether there is another randomized algorithm that actually improves the competitive ratio.

3.4   Our Final Algorithm

We recall the classic randomized algorithm for online bipartite matching (without colors), namely RANKING [10], defined below. This algorithm by itself has

Algorithm. RANKING

1. Pick a permutation σ of the vertices in U uniformly at random.
2. For each arriving vertex:
   Match it to the highest available neighbor (according to σ).

a competitive ratio of 0, which can be seen again from the instance in the figure in Section 3.1. With probability almost 1, one of the first few arriving vertices will pick its Blue neighbor, and after that, every vertex is forced to pick its Blue neighbor. Is there a way to extend RANKING for our biobjective problem?

In our first attempt, DISJOINTRANKING, we do precisely this, by removing edges from the graph in order to break up the biobjective instance into two disjoint instances, one of each color, and then use RANKING on each instance independently. It is easy to see that this algorithm can be run online.

Algorithm. DISJOINTRANKING

1. Each vertex in $U \cup V$ picks a color uar, and throws away incident edges of that color. Note that only those edges that are not thrown away by either endpoint survive.
2. Run Algorithm RANKING on the resulting subgraph.

Proposition 6. DISJOINTRANKING *achieves a competitive ratio of* $\frac{1-1/e}{2} \simeq$ 0.316.

To see this, observe that the first step creates a subgraph with two vertex partitions, such that no edges go from one part to the other, the edges within one part are all Blue, while the edges within the other part are all Red. Since each edge survives with probability $1/4$, the Blue (resp. Red) part will contain a Blue (resp. Red) matching of size $n/4 - O(\sqrt{n})$. Also, running RANKING on the subgraph is equivalent to running it on each part separately. Hence, we will obtain a matching with $\approx (1 - 1/e)\frac{n}{4}$ Blue edges and Red edges each, giving a competitive ratio of $\frac{1-1/e}{2} \simeq 0.316$.

Thus DISJOINTRANKING is even worse than our previous algorithms, and this is because it throws away $3/4$ of the edges and loses a factor of $1/2$ immediately (since the size of the guaranteed matching drops to $n/4$ and OPT is $n/2$). So one can try and throw away fewer edges. One way to do this is to let vertices of only one side (either U or V) pick a color at random and throw away incident edges of that color. This gives us two algorithms, namely LEFTSUBGRAPHRANKING and RIGHTSUBGRAPHRANKING, defined below:

Algorithm. LEFTSUBGRAPHRANKING (resp. RIGHTSUBGRAPHRANKING)

---

1. Each vertex in U (resp. V) picks a color uar, and throws away incident edges of that color.
2. Run Algorithm RANKING on the resulting subgraph.

These algorithms throw away fewer edges than DISJOINTRANKING, thereby ensuring a matching having $\approx n/2$ edges of each color in the resulting subgraph. So we can hope for an online algorithm that gets a matching with $\approx (1-1/e)n/2$ edges of each color, achieving a ratio of $1 - 1/e$. However, we have lost the partition into a Red and a Blue instance and the analysis needs to take into account the interaction between edges of different colors in the resulting subgraph. This interaction results in some loss. We prove the following in Section 4.

Proposition 7. *The competitive ratio of* LEFTSUBGRAPHRANKING *is* $3 - 4/\sqrt{e} \simeq 0.573$, *and this analysis is tight.*

Although RIGHTSUBGRAPHRANKING is very similar, our analysis does not carry over immediately. The reason is that the analysis of LEFTSUBGRAPHRANK-ING (just like the analysis of RANKING) maps a miss of vertex u on the permuted side to the hit of $N_r(u)$ or $N_b(u)$. Since in RIGHTSUBGRAPHRANKING, the non-permuted side picks the colors to throw away, this charging does not work any more – a vertex u on the permuted side might have a miss even when neither of $N_r(u)$ or $N_b(u)$ was a hit, if $N_r(u)$ chooses to throw away its Red edges and $N_b(u)$ chooses to throw away Blue edges. We leave the analysis of RIGHT-SUBGRAPHRANKING as an interesting **open question**, as also the analysis of these algorithms without the perfect-matching restriction.

We show the following hardness bound in the full paper.

Proposition 8. *Even under the perfect-matching restriction, no randomized algorithm can achieve a competitive ratio greater than* $1 - 1/e$.

So an obvious **open question** is to close the gap for randomized algorithms. If there is a better algorithm, is it a different generalization of RANKING? Another **open question** is how do the algorithms extend to $k > 2$ colors? We believe that the ratio of LEFTSUBGRAPHRANKING only improves as k increases; we can prove that the Min-of-Exps objective improves, but it remains open to analyze the Exp-of-Mins objective.

4   Analysis of LeftSubgraphRanking

In this section we prove the main result of this paper on the performance of LEFTSUBGRAPHRANKING.

Theorem 1. *For any constant* $\epsilon > 0$, *and sufficiently large* n, *the competitive ratio of* LEFTSUBGRAPHRANKING *is at least* $3 - \frac{4}{\sqrt{e}} - 4\epsilon - \frac{10}{\sqrt{n}}$.

We will begin by showing that for each color, the expected number of edges of that color in the matching produced by the algorithm is at least $(3 - \frac{4}{\sqrt{e}})\frac{n}{2}$. Note that this, by itself, does not imply a competitive ratio of $3 - \frac{4}{\sqrt{e}}$, as we need to bound the expectation of the minimum color's edges. However, this is clearly necessary. We will later show (in Section 4.2) how to use *locality of charging* to prove an almost identical ratio for the expectation of the minimum color's edges, giving Theorem 1.

4.1   Bounding the Minimum of the two Expectations

To prove a bound on the expected number of edges of a given color, we use a charging argument, which builds upon the charging argument for RANKING (see [1] for one such proof). We consider the (offline) misses of a particular color, say Red, and charge them to hits of both colors. First we try to use the same charging map as for RANKING – charge each miss to n hits in permutations obtained by moving the (perfect-matching) neighbor of the neighbor of the missed vertex. This does not quite work: Note that each vertex throws away its Red edges with probability $1/2$, so only $n/2$ vertices are trying to pick up a Red edge. Since there could be as many as as $n/2$ Blue hits, we do not get anything non-trivial from this argument. In order to make it work, we map each miss to $2n$ hits in permutations obtained not only by moving the vertex but also by changing its color preference. For this map, a given hit might get charged by two misses, but it gets charged only once by the misses of a given color.

We now dive into the proof. The probability space of the algorithm consists of all tuples (σ, λ), where σ is a permutation of U and $\lambda \in \{r, b\}^n$ is the vector of colors chosen by vertices in U (in this section, we will use r and b to denote color Red and Blue respectively). In order to describe the charging argument, we make the following definitions.

Definition 1. *For any permutation σ, $u \in U$ and $i \in [n]$, let σ_u^i be the permutation obtained by removing u from σ and inserting it back into σ at position i. Likewise, for any λ, $u \in U$ and $d \in \{r, b\}$, let λ_u^d be such that $\lambda_u^d(u) = d$ and $\lambda_u^d(v) = \lambda(v)$ for all $v \neq u$.*

Definition 2 (Set of Misses and Hits). *Define Q_t^d (resp. R_t^d) as the set of all event–position triples (σ, λ, t), s.t. the vertex in position t in σ (say u) has $\lambda(u) = d$, and was matched (resp. unmatched) under (σ, λ). Formally:*

$$Q_t^d = \{(\sigma, \lambda, t) : \sigma(u) = t, \ \lambda(u) = d \text{ and } u \text{ is matched in the event } (\sigma, \lambda)\}$$

$$R_t^d = \{(\sigma, \lambda, t) : \sigma(u) = t, \ \lambda(u) = d \text{ and } u \text{ is unmatched in the event } (\sigma, \lambda)\}$$

Recall that $N_d(u)$ denotes the partner of u in the perfect matching of color d. We are now ready to define the main charging map ψ from a miss to a set of hits.

Consider a triple (σ, λ, t) s.t. that vertex u at position t in σ is unmatched and let $d = \lambda(u)$. Then, we define the d-ChargingMap of the triple (σ, λ, t) as the set of all triples (σ', λ', s), such that $\sigma' = \sigma_u^i$ for some $i \in [n]$ and $\lambda' = \lambda_u^{d'}$ for some $d' \in \{r, b\}$, and s is the rank of the vertex to which $N_d(u)$ is matched in the event (σ', λ').

Definition 3 (Charging Map). *For every $(\sigma, \lambda, t) \in R_t^d$, define the map*

$$\psi_d(\sigma, \lambda, t) = \{(\sigma_u^i, \lambda_u^{d'}, s) : 1 \leq i \leq n, \ d' \in \{r, b\}, \ \sigma(u) = t,$$

$$\text{and } N_d(u) \text{ is matched to } u' \text{ with } \sigma_u^i(u') = s \text{ in the event } (\sigma_u^i, \lambda_u^{d'})\}$$

The following lemma proves that the above charging maps are well-defined (i.e. s always exists) and that $s \leq t$ for all such mappings. This essentially follows the standard alternating path argument for RANKING (see e.g. [1]), except that we also need to argue that the same holds even when u flips its color and throws away a different set of edges. The proof can be found in the full paper.

Lemma 1. *For any permutation σ and coloring λ, if vertex u has rank t in σ and is left unmatched in the event (σ, λ), then $N_{\lambda(u)}(u)$ is matched to some node u' in the event $(\sigma_u^i, \lambda_u^b)$ and some node u'' in the event $(\sigma_u^i, \lambda_u^r)$, for any $1 \leq i \leq n$. Moreover, $\sigma_u^i(u') \leq t$ and $\sigma_u^i(u'') \leq t$.*

We next show that for a fixed t, the set-values $\psi_d(\sigma, \lambda, t)$ are disjoint for different σ or λ. The proof is in the full paper.

Lemma 2. *If $(\sigma, \lambda, s) \in \psi_d(\sigma', \lambda', t)$ and $(\sigma, \lambda, s) \in \psi_d(\sigma'', \lambda'', t)$, then $\sigma' = \sigma''$ and $\lambda' = \lambda''$.*

With Lemma 1 and 2, we are now ready to prove the bound on the expectation of each color. The full proof is postpone to the full paper.

Lemma 3. *Both the number of red matches and the number of blue matches are at least $(\frac{3}{2} - \frac{2}{\sqrt{e}})n$.*

4.2 Bounding the Expectation of the Minimum Color

In order to bound the expectation of the number of matches of the minimum color, we need to consider two parts of the probability space – the events for which Red is the trailing color (where we need to count the number of Red matches) and the events for which Blue is the trailing color (where we need to count the number of Blue matches), breaking ties arbitrarily. However in doing so, a new difficulty arises – when we were bounding the expected number of matches of one color, we were guaranteed that the charging maps for all misses of that color are disjoint. However, this is no longer true when we look at the charging maps for Red misses for some of the events and the charging map for Blue misses for the remaining events – the same hit might appear in the charging map for some Blue miss and for some Red miss. Simply allowing hits to be double-charged will lead to a large loss in competitive ratio, giving a ratio of $1 - 2/e \simeq 0.26$.

The key insight that helps us overcome this problem and show essentially the same bound for expectation of the minimum color, with a loss of only lower order terms, is that our charging map has the property of *locality*, i.e. misses in a given event map to hits in "nearby" events.

To be more concrete, let $\Delta(\sigma, \lambda)$ be the difference between the number of Red matches and Blue matches in the matching produced by the algorithm for the event (σ, λ). We observe that our charging map is local w.r.t. Δ, i.e. misses in an event (σ, λ) map to hits in events whose Δ value is within 2 of $\Delta(\sigma, \lambda)$, as shown in a lemma in the full paper. If we partition the events by their Δ value, we want to count the number of Blue misses for events whose Δ value is positive and the number of Red misses for the rest. By the lemma, we know that Blue misses of interest charge to events whose Δ value is at least -1, while the Red misses of interest charge to events whose Δ value is at most 2. So the only events whose hits get double-charged are those whose Δ value is in $\{-1, 0, 1, 2\}$. If we could show that the number of hits in such events is small, we will be done.

Unfortunately, we do not know how to show this. What we can show, instead, is that there is some $k \in [1, 4\sqrt{n}]$ s.t. the probability mass of hits in events with Δ value in $\{k, k+1, k+2, k+3\}$ is no more than $\frac{1}{\sqrt{n}}$, as shown in the full paper. So if we look at the charges from Blue misses in events with Δ value greater

Tight example: Interestingly, our analysis is tight. Consider the following family of graphs. Let the upper triangular entries (without the diagonal) and the bottom left entry of the adjacency matrix filled with Red edges, and the rest filled with Blue edges. This guarantees two perfect matchings. But running LEFTSUBGRAPHRANKING on this graph gives no more than $(\frac{3}{2} - \frac{2}{\sqrt{e}})n$ red matches; details can be found in the full paper).

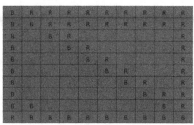

than $k + 1$, and the charges from Red misses from the remaining events, we will double charge only a small number of the hits, thereby giving us the required bound. The full proof can be found in the full paper.

References

1. Aggarwal, G., Goel, G., Karande, C., Mehta, A.: Online vertex-weighted bipartite matching and single-bid budgeted allocations. In: SODA (2010)
2. Azar, P.D., Daskalakis, C., Micali, S., Matthew Weinberg, S.: Optimal and efficient parametric auctions. In: Proceedings of the Twenty-Fourth Annual ACM-SIAM Symposium on Discrete Algorithms, SODA 2013, New Orleans, Louisiana, USA, January 6-8, pp. 596–604 (2013)
3. Bhatnagar, N., Randall, D., Vazirani, V.V., Vigoda, E.: Random bichromatic matchings. Algorithmica 50(4), 418–445 (2008)
4. Buchbinder, N., Jain, K., Naor, J(S.): Online Primal-Dual Algorithms for Maximizing Ad-Auctions Revenue. In: Arge, L., Hoffmann, M., Welzl, E. (eds.) ESA 2007. LNCS, vol. 4698, pp. 253–264. Springer, Heidelberg (2007)
5. Daskalakis, C., Pierrakos, G.: Simple, optimal and efficient auctions. In: Chen, N., Elkind, E., Koutsoupias, E. (eds.) WINE 2011. LNCS, vol. 7090, pp. 109–121. Springer, Heidelberg (2011)
6. Diakonikolas, I., Papadimitriou, C., Pierrakos, G., Singer, Y.: Efficiency-revenue trade-offs in auctions. In: Czumaj, A., Mehlhorn, K., Pitts, A., Wattenhofer, R. (eds.) ICALP 2012, Part II. LNCS, vol. 7392, pp. 488–499. Springer, Heidelberg (2012)
7. Feldman, J., Korula, N., Mirrokni, V., Muthukrishnan, S., Pál, M.: Online ad assignment with free disposal. In: Leonardi, S. (ed.) WINE 2009. LNCS, vol. 5929, pp. 374–385. Springer, Heidelberg (2009)
8. Flammini, M., Nicosia, G.: On multicriteria online problems. In: Paterson, M. (ed.) ESA 2000. LNCS, vol. 1879, pp. 191–201. Springer, Heidelberg (2000)
9. Karande, C., Mehta, A., Srikant, R.: Optimizing budget constrained spend in search advertising. In: WSDM (2013)
10. Karp, R.M., Vazirani, U.V., Vazirani, V.V.: An optimal algorithm for online bipartite matching. In: STOC (1990)
11. Karzanov, A.V.: Maximum matching of given weight in complete and complete bipartite graphs. In: Cybernetics and Systems Analysis (1987)
12. Korula, N., Mirrokni, V.S., Zadimoghaddam, M.: Bicriteria online matching: Maximizing weight and cardinality. In: Chen, Y., Immorlica, N. (eds.) WINE 2013. LNCS, vol. 8289, pp. 305–318. Springer, Heidelberg (2013)
13. Korula, N., Pál, M.: Algorithms for secretary problems on graphs and hypergraphs. In: Albers, S., Marchetti-Spaccamela, A., Matias, Y., Nikoletseas, S., Thomas, W. (eds.) ICALP 2009, Part II. LNCS, vol. 5556, pp. 508–520. Springer, Heidelberg (2009)
14. Mehta, A.: Online matching and ad allocation. Foundations and Trends in Theoretical Computer Science 8(4), 265–368 (2013)
15. Mehta, A., Saberi, A., Vazirani, U., Vazirani, V.: Adwords and generalized online matching. In: FOCS (2005)
16. Mulmuley, K., Vazirani, U.V., Vazirani, V.V.: Matching is as easy as matrix inversion. In: STOC (1987)
17. Papadimitriou, C.H., Yannakakis, M.: On the approximability of trade-offs and optimal access of web sources. In: FOCS (2000)
18. Yi, T., Murty, K.G., Spera, C.: Matchings in colored bipartite networks. Discrete Applied Mathematics 121(1), 261–277 (2002)

Dynamic Reserve Prices for Repeated Auctions: Learning from Bids*
Working Paper

Yash Kanoria[1] and Hamid Nazerzadeh[2]

[1] Columbia Business School
[2] University of Southern California

A large fraction of online advertisement is sold via repeated second price auctions. In these auctions, the reserve price is the main tool for the auctioneer to boost revenues. In this work, we investigate the following question: Can changing the reserve prices based on the previous bids improve the revenue of the auction, taking into account the long-term incentives and strategic behavior of the bidders?

In order to set the reserve price effectively, the auctioneer requires information about distribution of the valuations of the bidders. A natural idea, which is widely used in practice, is to construct these distributions using the history of the bids. This approach, though intuitive, raises a major concern with regards to long-term (dynamic) incentives of the advertisers. Because the bid of an advertiser may determine the price he or she pays in future auctions, this approach may result in the advertisers shading their bids and ultimately in a loss of revenue for the auctioneer.

To understand the effects of changing reserve prices based on the previous bids, we study a setting where the auctioneer sells impressions (advertisements space) via repeated second price auctions. We demonstrate that the long-term incentives of advertisers plays an important role in the performance of these repeated auctions by showing that under standard symmetry and regularity assumptions (i.e., when the valuations of advertisers are independently and identically distributed according to a regular distribution), the optimal mechanism is running a second price auction with a *constant* reserve and changing the reserve prices over time is not beneficial. However, when there is *uncertainty* in the distribution of the valuations and competition among the bidders, we show that there can be substantial benefit in learning the reserve prices using the previous bids. To this end, we propose a simple dynamic reserve mechanism called the *threshold* mechanism that achieves near optimal revenue, while retaining (approximate) incentive compatibility.

---

* A complete version is available at http://papers.ssrn.com/sol3/papers.cfm? abstract_id=2444495. We would like to thank Brendan Lucier, Mohammad Mahdian, Mukund Sundararajan and the anonymous referees for their insightful comments and suggestions. This work was supported in part by Microsoft Research New England. The work of the second author was supported in part by a Google Faculty Research Award.

T.-Y. Liu et al. (Eds.): WINE 2014, LNCS 8877, p. 232, 2014.

Revenue Maximizing Envy-Free Fixed-Price Auctions with Budgets[*]

Riccardo Colini-Baldeschi[1], Stefano Leonardi[1],
Piotr Sankowski[2], and Qiang Zhang[2]

[1] Sapienza University of Rome, Italy
{colini,leonardi}@dis.uniroma1.it
[2] Institute of Informatics, University of Warsaw, Poland
{sank,qzhang}@mimuw.edu.pl

Abstract. Traditional incentive-compatible auctions [6,16] for selling multiple goods to unconstrained and budgeted bidders can discriminate between bidders by selling identical goods at different prices. For this reason, Feldman et al. [7] dropped incentive compatibility and turned the attention to revenue maximizing envy-free item-pricing allocations for budgeted bidders. *Envy-free* allocations were suggested by classical papers [9,15]. The key property of such allocations is that no one envies the allocation and the price charged to anyone else. In this paper we consider this classical notion of envy-freeness and study *fixed-price* mechanisms which use nondiscriminatory uniform prices for all goods. Feldman et al. [7] gave an item-pricing mechanism that obtains 1/2 of the revenue obtained from any envy-free fixed-price mechanism for identical goods. We improve over this result by presenting an FPTAS for the problem that returns an $(1 - \epsilon)$-approximation of the revenue obtained by any envy-free fixed-price mechanism for any $\epsilon > 0$ and runs in polynomial time in the number of bidders n and $1/\epsilon$ even for exponential supply of goods m. Next, we consider the case of budgeted bidders with matching-type preferences on the set of goods, i.e., the valuation of each bidder for each item is either v_i or 0. In this more general case, we prove that it is impossible to approximate the optimum revenue within $O(\min(n, m)^{1/2-\epsilon})$ for any $\epsilon > 0$ unless $P = NP$. On the positive side, we are able to extend the FPTAS for identical goods to budgeted bidders in the case of constant number of different types of goods. Our FPTAS gives also a constant approximation with respect to the general envy-free auction.

1 Introduction

In this paper we address the problem of selling m identical goods to a set of n bidders. Bidder $i \in \{1, \ldots, n\}$ has his own valuation per good v_i and a total budget b_i that he can spent. This setting was introduced in the context of designing

---

[*] This work was partially supported by Google Focused Award "Algorithms for Large-scale Data Analysis", ERC StG project PAAl 259515, and FET IP project MULTIPEX 317532.

T.-Y. Liu et al. (Eds.): WINE 2014, LNCS 8877, pp. 233–246, 2014.

truthful auctions to sell multiple ad slots [6]. In a later paper [7] a serious short-coming of previous mechanisms was observed. Many of the auctions, e.g., the VCG mechanism [5,11,16] (for bidders with unlimited budgets) or the ascending auction [6,14] (for bidders with budgets), sell the same product at different prices. Moreover, this is strictly needed if we insist on incentive-compatible auctions as shown in [6]. Usage of nonuniform prices is called price discrimination [3]. Price discrimination is problematic as pointed out by economic literature [1,2], and in some cases also forbidden by international commerce law [10].

The approach suggested in [7] was to turn the attention to revenue maximizing auctions that are envy-free rather than incentive compatible. Here, we take a next step in this direction. We consider auctions that are as nondiscriminatory as possible by being envy-free and by using uniform prices. We note that in recent studies (e.g., [12] and much subsequent work) envy-freeness has been defined in a much more restrictive manner than the classical notion from economic theory [9,15]. It requires that goods are given prices, and that the allocation to a bidder is a set of goods that maximizes the bidder's utility, subject to these good prices. The reason why the classical notion of envy-freeness was abandoned is probably due to its immanent hardness. For example, if we need to maximize bidders' utilities then given the prices of goods finding envy-free allocation becomes a maximum matching problem. On the other hand, without this restriction, we prove that it is impossible to get a $\Omega(\min(n,m)^{1/2-\epsilon})$-fraction of the optimum revenue, for any $\epsilon > 0$ unless P=NP.

Envy-free allocations are defined in the most intuitive way as suggested by classical papers [9,15]. The key property of such allocations is that no one envies anyone else. Bidder i is allocated a set of goods X_i and is asked to pay some amount p_i, with the restriction that $p_i \leq b_i$. Bidder i utility is defined as $u_i(X_i, p_i) = v_i|X_i| - p_i$. This is called *multi-unit* auction, whereas we assume that $|X_i| \leq 1$ when bidders have *unit demands*. We say that bidder i *envies* bidder i' if $p_{i'} \leq b_i$ and $u_i(X_{i'}, p_{i'}) > u_i(X_i, p_i)$, i.e., bidder i could be allocated bundle of i' and in such a case the utility of bidder i would increase.

The results of [7] when casted to our setting imply that it is possible to construct an efficient *envy-free fixed-price* auction that approximates maximum revenue of general envy-free auction. The *fixed-price* auction assumes that $p_i = p|X_i|$ for some fixed p. Quite surprisingly, such a restricted auction, can extract $1/2$ of the revenue of the optimum envy-free auction. These results rise an interesting question whether such efficient, and nondiscriminatory auctions, can actually be constructed in an optimal or nearly optimal way? We answer this question affirmatively and present an FPTAS for multi-unit auctions, i.e., we compute price p and allocation X_i for each bidder so that selling at a fixed-price p gives revenue no less than an $(1-\epsilon)$-fraction of the revenue of *any* envy-free fixed-price *outcome*. The running time of the algorithm is polynomial in both n and $1/\epsilon$ and it does not depend on the total supply of goods on sale.

We extend the basic setting also to the case of non-identical goods, thus addressing one limitation of previous works [6,7,14] which considered only identical goods. In our generalized *multi-good* setting, we consider the case that there are

c types of goods and the supply of good i is m_i. Here, we use $m = \sum_i m_i$. Denote by S_i the types of goods of interest for bidder i, i.e., his valuation for items of types S_i is v_i, whereas other items have value 0 for him. Such valuations are called *matching-type* preferences and were for example considered in [8]. Let us denote by $\mathbf{X_i}$ a multiset of S_i that is allocated to bidder i. We say that an allocation $\mathbf{X_i}$ is *rational* at price p for bidder i if $\mathbf{X_i}$ only contains goods that are in the preference set of bidder i, and utility of bidder i is nonnegative. The notion of envy-freeness is extended to the multi-good case by defining that bidder i envies bidder i' if allocating $X_{i'}$ to i is rational and increases the utility of bidder i. In the unit demand case, we present the following results for the revenue maximizing envy-free fixed-price outcomes in the multi-good setting:

1. We prove that the problem can be solved optimally in polynomial time.
2. We observe that our solution gives $O(\log n)$-approximation with respect to the optimum envy-free allocation, and this essentially is the best possible.

In the non-unit-demand case, we prove the following:

1. For a non-constant number of different types of goods, we prove that it is NP-hard to approximate the optimum revenue with a factor better than $\Omega(\min(n, m)^{1/2-\epsilon})$. This statement holds even for general non-fixed-price envy-free auctions.
2. We extend the FPTAS for identical goods to the case of a constant number of different types of goods. This holds even when the supply of goods of each type is exponential.
3. We observe that the FPTAS gives $\Theta(c)$-approximation with respect to the optimum envy-free revenue where there are c different types of goods.

While we present the first positive results for the multi-good setting with a constant number of goods, it is quite interesting to observe that our hardness result is not restricted to fixed-price auctions. Hence, even in this restricted case we are coping with the hard core of the problem, what means that even without this assumption it is impossible to obtain qualitatively better results. On the positive side our $O(c)$-approximation algorithm for c types of goods works independently from the number of bidders and goods.

2   Preliminaries

An auction with budgets is denoted by $\mathcal{A} =< n, c, \mathbf{M}, \mathbf{S}, \mathbf{v}, \mathbf{b} >$. There are n bidders and c different goods. Throughout the paper, we use the notation $[n]$ and $[c]$ to denote the sets $\{1, \ldots, n\}$ and $\{1, \ldots, c\}$ respectively. $\mathbf{M} =< m_1, \ldots, m_c >$ indicates the amount of supply of each good. For every $j \in [c]$, there are m_j copies of good j. The total supply of all goods is denoted by $m = \sum_{j \in [c]} m_j$. $\mathbf{S} =< S_1, \ldots, S_n >$ indicates the *preference set* of each bidder. For every $i \in [n]$, S_i is the subset of goods in which bidder i is interested. Finally, $\mathbf{v} =< v_1, \ldots, v_n >$ indicates the valuation and $\mathbf{b} =< b_1, \ldots, b_n >$ indicates the budget of each bidder. For every $i \in [n]$, bidder i has a valuation of v_i for each copy of goods in his preference set S_i and a budget b_i. Given price p, the demand of a bidder i is defined as:

$$D_i(p) = \begin{cases} \min(\lfloor \frac{b_i}{p} \rfloor, \sum_{j \in S_i} m_j), & \text{if } v_i \geq p \\ 0, & \text{if } v_i < p \end{cases}$$

When there is no ambiguity on the price, we simply use D_i instead of $D_i(p)$.

A mechanism maps every auction $\mathcal{A}$ to an outcome $< \mathbf{X}, p >$, where $\mathbf{X} =< \mathbf{X_1}, \ldots, \mathbf{X_n} >$ is an allocation mapping goods to bidders and $p \in \mathbb{R}$ is a fixed price for every goods. Note that for every $i \in [n]$, $\mathbf{X_i} =< x_i^1, \ldots, x_i^c >$ where bidder i gets x_i^j copies of good j. Let X_i be the set of goods allocated to bidder i, i.e., $X_i = \{j \in [c] | x_i^j > 0\}$. An outcome $< \mathbf{X}, p >$ must satisfy all the following conditions:

1. *limited supply:* for every $j \in [c]$, it holds $\sum_{i \in [n]} x_i^j \leq m_j$;
2. *bidder rationality:* for every $i \in [n]$, and every $j \in [c]$, if $x_i^j > 0$ then $j \in S_i$ and $v_i \geq p$;
3. *budget constraint:* for every $i \in [n]$, it holds $p \cdot \sum_{j \in [c]} x_i^j \leq b_i$.

Given outcome $< \mathbf{X}, p >$, the utility of bidder i is defined as: $u_i(\mathbf{X_i}, p) = (v_i - p) \sum_{j \in S_i} x_i^j$. The revenue $r(\mathbf{X}, p)$ of the auction is the sum of payments of all the bidders, i.e., $r(\mathbf{X}, p) = p \sum_{i \in [n]} \sum_{j \in S_i} x_i^j$. When the price and allocation are clear from the context, the revenue is simply denoted by r.

Given price p, we partition bidders as follows. Bidders with $v_i = p$ are called *value-limited* bidders, and are denoted by $VL_p = \{i \in [n] | v_i = p\}$. Similarly, bidders with $v_i > p$ are called *non-value-limited* bidders, and are denoted by $NVL_p = \{i \in [n] | v_i > p\}$. Finally, bidders with $v_i < p$ are called *exited* bidders, and are denoted by $E_p = \{i \in [n] | v_i < p\}$. When there is no ambiguity on the price, we will remove the subscript from the sets.

We consider the following notion of envy-freeness. Given an outcome $< \mathbf{X}, p >$, we say bidder i *envies* bidder i' if all following conditions hold: i) $\mathbf{X_{i'}}$ is a *rational* allocation to bidder i, i.e., $X_{i'} \subseteq S_i$; ii) bidder i has enough budget for the bundle $\mathbf{X_{i'}}$, i.e., $b_i \geq p \sum_{j \in S_{i'}} x_{i'}^j$; iii) $u_i(\mathbf{X_{i'}}, p) > u_i(\mathbf{X_i}, p)$.

An outcome is *envy-free* if for every pair of bidders $i, i' \in [n]$, bidder i does not envy bidder i'.

Definition 1. *The revenue maximizing envy-free fixed-price auction with budgets: given $< n, c, \mathbf{M}, \mathbf{S}, \mathbf{v}, \mathbf{b} >$, design an algorithm to compute an envy-free outcome $< \mathbf{X}, p >$ that maximizes auctioneer's revenue $r(\mathbf{X}, p)$.*

3 Envy-Free Revenue Maximizing Fixed-Price Multi-good Auctions for Unit-Demand Bidders

In this section, we consider envy-free fixed-price auction with budgets when all bidders have unit demands, that is, bidders are only interested in obtaining at most one copy of a good in their preference sets. Here, envy-freeness implies that bidder i will be allocated one good if another bidder i' gets some good $j \in S_i$ and the price is not higher than $\min\{v_i, b_i\}$. We present an algorithm optimizing the revenue among all fixed-price outcomes. Despite the fact that our auction is fixed-price, we prove that it is able to extract $O(\log n)$ of the optimum envy-free revenue. We assume in this section for all $i \in [c]$ we have $m_i \leq n$, as higher supply of goods is not needed in the unit demand case.

We model auctions for the unit-demand case as bipartite graphs. Specifically, given a price p, the demand graph G_p is a bipartite graph $(V = \{1, \ldots, n\}, U = \{1, \ldots, m\}, E)$, where $\{1, \ldots, m\}$ contains m_j identical vertices for good j and E contains an edge (i, j) if and only if $j \in S_i$ and $\min\{v_i, b_i\} \geq p$. We identify vertices in V with bidders. We define non-value-limited subgraph G'_p of G_p to contain only bidders that are non-value-limited.

Denote for a set $S \subseteq V(G)$, $\nu_G(S) = \{v : (u, v) \in E(G) \text{ and } u \in S\}$. A set of vertices $S \subseteq V$ is said to be *tight* in G if and only if $|\nu_G(S)| \geq |S|$. We observe that we cannot sell goods to all bidders in S if S is not tight in G'_p, because we will not be able to satisfy the demand of everybody in S. On the other hand, it is not necessarily true that we can satisfy all bidders in a given tight set S, because S can contain subsets that are not tight. Using the tools from matching theory we will prove the existence of canonical tight sets in G'_p, that can be fully satisfied. We define *surplus* of $S \subseteq V \cup U$ in G as $\min_{T \subseteq S} |\nu_G(T)| - |T|$. By Hall's marriage theorem a set $S \subseteq V$ that has positive surplus in G has a perfect matching onto $\nu_G(S)$. The following is a consequence of Gallai-Edmonds decomposition theorem in the case of bipartite graphs.

Theorem 1 (Theorem 3.2.4 from [13]). *Let $G = (V, U, E)$ be a bipartite graph. V can be partitioned into three subsets C_V, A_V, D_V and U can be partitioned into three subsets C_U, A_U, D_U such that:*

- *$\nu_G(D_V) = A_U$ and $\nu_G(D_U) = A_V$,*
- *surplus of C_V in $G[C_V \cup C_U]$ is 0,*
- *surplus of A_V in $G[A_V \cup D_U]$ is positive,*
- *surplus of A_U in $G[A_U \cup D_V]$ is positive.*

We observe the following. Due to lack of space, We defer the proofs of some theorems, lemmas or corollaries to the full version of the paper.

Corollary 1. *Let A_U be given by Theorem 1 for G'_p. No good from A_U can be sold in any envy-free allocation at price p.*

By Hall's marriage theorem we know that the matching M that is needed in the following observation always exists.

Corollary 2. *Let C_V and A_V be given by Theorem 1 for G'_p. Let M be a matching in G'_p that matches C_V with C_U and A_V with D_U then M induces an envy-free allocation at price p.*

In other words M is the maximum size matching in $G'_p \setminus A_U$. So far we have considered only non-value-limited bidders in G'_p. Adding value-limited bidders can increase the number of goods we can sell and can lead to higher revenue. Still no good in A_U can be sold. Potentially, in $G_p \setminus A_U$ there can be a maximum size matching such that it does not induce an envy-free allocation. However, this can be countered using the following well known fact.

Corollary 3 (Corollary 3.1.6 from [13]). *If a set of vertices is covered by some matching then it is also covered by some maximum matching.*

By applying this corollary to M in G_p, we know that there exits a maximum size matching M' in $G'_p \setminus A_U$ that matches all vertices in C_V and A_V. Hence, M' induces the maximum revenue envy-free allocation at price p. We note that the constructions of Theorem 1 and Corollary 3 can be executed in polynomial time. Now, we can observe that the set of candidate fixed-prices is small.

Lemma 1. *The set of candidate fixed-prices for the unit-demand case is given by $\cup_{i \in [n]} \min(v_i, b_i)$.*

Algorithm 1. Optimal Revenue Maximizing Envy-free Fixed-price for Unit-Demanded Bidders

---

Input: $< n, c, \mathbf{M}, \mathbf{S}, \mathbf{v}, \mathbf{b} >$.
Output: a price p, an allocation $\mathbf{X} = < \mathbf{X_1}, \ldots, \mathbf{X_n} >$, the optimum revenue r.
1 Let $\mathbf{p}$ be the set containing $\{\min(v_i, b_i)\}$, $r = 0$;
2 **while** $\mathbf{p} \neq \emptyset$ **do**
3 | Choose some $y \in \mathbf{p}$, $\mathbf{p} = \mathbf{p} \setminus \{y\}$;
4 | Construct the demand graphs G_y and G'_y with respect to y;
5 | Use Theorem 1 to find A_U in G'_y;
6 | Find maximum size matching M of $G'_y \setminus A_U$;
7 | Extend M to maximum matching M' in $G_y \setminus A_U$ using Corollary 3;
8 | **if** $y|M'| > r$ **then**
9 | | Set $p = y$, $r = y|M'|$;
10 | | **for** $i \in \{1, \ldots, n\}$ **do**
11 | | | **if** $j \in \mathcal{M}'$ **then**
12 | | | | Set $x_i^j = 1$ if $(i, j) \in M'$;

The main result in this section is the following theorem, which directly follows lemmas and corollaries above.

Theorem 2. *Algorithm 1 outputs, in polynomial time, an envy-free outcome which optimizes auctioneer's revenue among all envy-free fixed-price outcomes.*

Next theorem shows that our auction is $O(\log n)$-approximate with respect to the general envy-free auction. This is essentially best possible by the $\log^{1-\epsilon}(n + m)$-inapproximability [4].

Theorem 3. *Algorithm 1 outputs, in polynomial time, an envy-free outcome which is $O(\log n)$-approximate with respect to the optimum envy-free revenue.*

Proof. Consider the optimal allocation $\bar{X}_i$ and optimal pricing $\bar{p}_i$. Assume that in this allocation bidders are sorted in descending order by $\bar{p}_i$. Consider a random number l that is selected uniformly at random form the set $[1, \ldots, 2\log(n)]$, and consider price $p_l = \frac{\bar{p}_1}{2^l}$. Let us denote by $\bar{n}(p)$ the number of bidders who pay in optimum allocation no less then p. We observe that

$$OPT = \sum_{i=1}^{n} \bar{n}(\bar{p}_i)(\bar{p}_i - \bar{p}_{i+1}) \leq 2 \sum_{l=1}^{2\log(n)} \bar{n}(p_l)p_l + n\frac{p_l}{2^{2\log(n)}} < 2 \sum_{l=1}^{2\log(n)} \bar{n}(p_l)p_l + \frac{OPT}{n}$$

Additionally note that for each p_l selling goods to bidders with $p_i \geq p_l$ at fixed price p_l is envy-free. Hence, choosing random p_l gives fixed-price $O(\log n)$-approximation in expectation with respect to the optimal envy-free pricing. By the optimality of our algorithm this bound in expectation is turned into worst-case bound. □

4 Envy-Free Fixed-Price Multi-unit Auctions with Budgets

We now turn to envy-free fixed-price auction with budgets when bidders are not unit-demand, that is, bidders are interested in obtaining goods in their preference sets as much as possible within their budgets. In this section, we present a Fully Polynomial Time Approximation Scheme (FPTAS) for the case when only single type of good is available in a limited supply of m copies. This setting is often referred to as *multi-unit auction*. Note that in the indivisible environment the easier approaches that are usually used for divisible goods do not work any more. The presence of discontinuity points that produce discrete jumps in the demand functions force us to carefully analyze the prices. In particular, when the number of goods is small a rough analysis can blemish the approximation ratio. We denote by $< \mathbf{X^{OPT}}, p^{OPT} >$ the revenue maximizing envy-free outcome. In this section the allocation is described by a vector of natural numbers that represents how many copies each bidder gets, i.e., $\mathbf{X^{OPT}} = < x_1^{OPT}, \ldots, x_n^{OPT} >$. Bidder i gets x_i^{OPT} copies of the good and pays $p^{OPT}x_i^{OPT}$. For the optimum revenue we have $r^{OPT} = p^{OPT} \sum_{i=1}^{n} x_i^{OPT}$. The proposed FPTAS considers the following two cases with regard to $\mathbf{X^{OPT}}$: i) more than $\frac{n^2}{\epsilon}$ goods are allocated in the revenue maximizing envy-free outcome, that is $m \geq \sum_{i=1}^{n} x_i^{OPT} > \frac{n^2}{\epsilon}$; ii) at most $\frac{n^2}{\epsilon}$ copies are allocated in the revenue maximizing envy-free outcome, that is $\sum_{i=1}^{n} x_i^{OPT} \leq \frac{n^2}{\epsilon}$. The distinction between these two cases is important. In the first case, when the number of copies is not polynomial in n, the proposed FPTAS achieves a revenue at least $(1 - \epsilon)r^{OPT}$ by restricting attention to a polynomial number of prices. On the other hand, in the second case, a dynamic programming is used to extract a revenue of r^{OPT} through the enumeration of all possible outcomes.

4.1 The Case of $m \geq \sum_{i=1}^{n} x_i^{OPT} > \frac{n^2}{\epsilon}$

In this case, the number of copies sold can be non-polynomial.. Hence, we cannot enumerate all possible sensible prices, i.e., prices that match a discontinuity point in a demand function. The proposed algorithm overcomes this problem by finding a polynomial number of prices that could extract an $(1-\epsilon)$ fraction of the optimum revenue. We assume for convenience $0 \leq v_1 \leq v_2 \leq \ldots \leq v_n$. It is easy to see that $p^{OPT} \in [0, v_n]$. Set $v_0 = 0$, and let us define $\Pi_i = (v_{i-1}, v_i]$. There exists exactly one Π_i such that $p^{OPT} \in \Pi_i$. Denote by $A_i = \{i' \in [n] | v_{i'} > v_{i-1}\}$ the set of bidders with valuations higher than v_{i-1}.

Furthermore, for each interval Π_i, we define a price

$$\bar{p}_i = \begin{cases} \min\{v_i, \frac{\epsilon \cdot \sum_{j \in A_i} b_j}{n^2}\}, & \text{if } \frac{\epsilon \cdot \sum_{j \in A_i} b_j}{n^2} > v_{i-1} \\ v_i, & \text{if } \frac{\epsilon \cdot \sum_{j \in A_i} b_j}{n^2} \leq v_{i-1} \end{cases}$$

Note that price $\bar{p}_i \in \Pi_i$ and $\bar{p}_i = v_i$ if $v_{i-1} = v_i$. Algorithm 2 computes the revenue obtained for each price in $\{\bar{p}_i\}_{i=1}^n$. Given a price in $\{\bar{p}_i\}_{i=1}^n$ the Algorithm 2 checks if the cumulative demand of the bidders is greater than the available supply or not. If the cumulative demand is less than the available supply (lines 6-7), all the bidders receive their demands. If the cumulative demand is greater than the available supply (lines 8-10), the algorithm computes an upper bound on the number of goods that each bidder can obtain in order to keep the allocation envy-free. Then a bidder receives number of items equal to the minimum between his demand and the computed upper bound. Algorithm 2 computes the revenue obtained this way for all candidate prices, and the maximum revenue is returned as output.

We show that the revenue r produced by Algorithm 2 is an $(1-\epsilon)$ approximation to the optimum revenue r^{OPT}. The proof is split into two parts: i) we first consider the case of $p^{OPT} \in \Pi_i$ and $\bar{p}_i = \frac{\epsilon \cdot \sum_{j \in A_i} b_j}{n^2}$; ii) we later address the case of $p^{OPT} \in \Pi_i$ and $\bar{p}_i = v_i$.

We use the following lemma as a tool to prove the first case.

Lemma 2. If $\bar{p}_i = \frac{\epsilon \cdot \sum_{j \in A_i} b_j}{n^2}$ and $p^{OPT} \in \Pi_i$, then $r^{OPT} \geq \frac{\sum_{j \in A_i} b_j}{n}$.

Proof. If $\bar{p}_i = \frac{\epsilon \cdot \sum_{j \in A_i} b_j}{n^2}$ then there is enough copies to satisfy the demands of all bidders in A_i, those with $v_{i'} > \bar{p}_i$:

$$\sum_{i \in A_i} D_i(\bar{p}_i) = \sum_{i \in A_i} \lfloor \frac{b_i}{\bar{p}_i} \rfloor \leq \sum_{i \in A_i} \frac{b_i}{\bar{p}_i} = \frac{n^2}{\epsilon}.$$

Note that essentially those bidders are the ones in A_i. Thus, we have $r^{OPT} \geq$
$\sum_{j \in A_i} \lfloor \frac{b_j}{\bar{p}_i} \rfloor \cdot \bar{p}_i \geq \sum_{j \in A_i} (\frac{b_j}{\bar{p}_i} - 1) \cdot \bar{p}_i \geq \sum_{j \in A_i} b_j - n \cdot \bar{p}_i = \sum_{j \in A_i} b_j - \frac{\epsilon \cdot \sum_{j \in A_i} b_j}{n} =$
$\sum_{j \in A_i} \frac{b_j}{n}(n - \epsilon)$. From $n \geq 2$ we have $n - \epsilon > 1$ and the lemma follows. $\qquad \square$

Lemma 3. If $p^{OPT} \in \Pi_i$ and $\bar{p}_i = \frac{\epsilon \cdot \sum_{j \in A_i} b_j}{n^2}$, then $r^{ALG} \geq (1 - \epsilon)r^{OPT}$.

Algorithm 2. Envy-free Fixed-price Multi-unit Auction with Budgets ($\sum_{i=1}^{n} x_i^{OPT} > \frac{n^2}{\epsilon}$)

Input: $< n, c = 1, \mathbf{M} = < m_1 = m >, \mathbf{S} = < S_1 = \ldots = S_n = \{1\} >, \mathbf{v}, \mathbf{b} >$.
Output: a price p^{ALG}, an allocation $\mathbf{X^{ALG}} = < x_1^{ALG}, \ldots, x_n^{ALG} >$, the revenue r^{ALG}.

1 Set $p^{ALG} = 0$, $\mathbf{X^{ALG}} = < 0, \ldots, 0 >$ and $r^{ALG} = 0$;
2 Let $\bar{p} = \{\bar{p}_1, \ldots, \bar{p}_n\}$ be the set of candidate prices;
3 **while** $\bar{p} \neq \emptyset$ **do**
4 $\quad$ Pick a price $p \in \bar{p}$;
5 $\quad$ Set $\mathbf{X} = < x_1 = 0, \ldots, x_n = 0 >, r = 0$;
6 $\quad$ **if** $\sum_{i \in A} D_i(p) \leq m$ **then**
7 $\quad\quad$ For each $i \in A$, set $x_i = D_i(p)$, and set $r = p \sum_{i \in A} D_i(p)$;
8 $\quad$ **else**
9 $\quad\quad$ For any $k \in \{1, \ldots, m\}$, let $t_k^p = \{i \in A | D_i(p) \geq k\}$;
10 $\quad\quad$ Let $l = \max\{z | \sum_{j=1}^{z} |t_j^p| \leq m$ and $|t_z^p| > 0\}$;
11 $\quad\quad$ For each $j \in A$, set $x_j = \min\{l, D_j(p)\}$, and set $r = p \sum_{j \in A} x_j$;
12 $\quad$ **if** $r > r^{ALG}$ **then**
13 $\quad\quad$ Set $< p^{ALG}, \mathbf{X^{ALG}}, r^{ALG} > = < p, \mathbf{X}, r >$;
14 $\quad$ Set $\bar{p} = \bar{p} \setminus p$;

Proof. $r^{OPT} \leq \sum_{j \in A_i} b_j = \sum_{j \in A_i} \frac{b_j}{\bar{p}_i} \cdot \bar{p}_i \leq \sum_{j \in A_i} (\lfloor \frac{b_j}{\bar{p}_i} \rfloor + 1) \cdot \bar{p}_i \leq \sum_{j \in A_i} x_j^{ALG}$.

$\bar{p}_i + \sum_{j \in A_i} \bar{p}_i = r^{ALG} + \sum_{j \in A_i} \bar{p}_i \leq r^{ALG} + n \cdot \frac{\epsilon \cdot \sum_{j \in A_i} b_j}{n^2} \leq r^{ALG} + \epsilon \cdot r^{OPT}$.

The first inequality comes from the assumption that $p^{OPT} \in \Pi_i$, and the last inequality is implied by Lemma 2. Hence, we have $r^{ALG} \geq (1 - \epsilon) r^{OPT}$. $\square$

Now we move to the second part of the proof. This is the case that $p^{OPT} \in \Pi_i$ and $\bar{p}_i = v_i$. We first observe the following:

Lemma 4. *The optimal price* $p^{OPT} \notin \Pi_i$ *if* $\frac{\epsilon \cdot \sum_{j \in A_i} b_j}{n^2} < v_{i-1}$.

Proof. Assume that $\frac{\epsilon \cdot \sum_{j \in A_i} b_j}{n^2} < v_{i-1} < p^{OPT}$, it implies that there is less than $\frac{n^2}{\epsilon}$ copies sold in the optimal allocation. It contradicts the assumption that at least $\frac{n^2}{\epsilon}$ goods are allocated in the optimal revenue maximizing envy-free outcome. $\square$

Lemma 4 allows us to only prove the revenue guarantee of Algorithm 2 in the case when $p^{OPT} \in \Pi_i$, $\bar{p}_i = v_i$ and $\frac{\epsilon \cdot \sum_{j \in A_i} b_j}{n^2} \geq v_i$. In this case, it could be that the total demand of bidders in A_i exceeds the number of copies, that is $\sum_{j \in A_i} D_j(\bar{p}_i) \geq \frac{n^2}{\epsilon} > m$. Denote by $t_k^{\bar{p}} = \{i \in \{1, \ldots, n\} | D_i(\bar{p}) \geq k\}$ the set of bidders with demand at least k and $l = \max\{z | \sum_{j=1}^{z} |t_j^{\bar{p}}| \leq m$ and $|t_z^{\bar{p}}| > 0, \}$. Algorithm 2 allocates to each bidder $i \in A_i$ a supply of $\min\{l, D_i(\bar{p})\}$ copies at price $\bar{p}$.

Lemma 5. *If $p^{OPT} \in \Pi_i$ and $\bar{p}_i = v_i$, $r^{ALG} > (1 - \epsilon)r^{OPT}$.*

Proof. Consider the following cases:

- $\sum_{i \in N} D_i(v_i) > m$. In this case, the Algorithm 2 sells at least $m - n$ items at price $\bar{p}_i$. The revenue from Algorithm 2 is given by

$$r^{ALG} \geq (m - n) \cdot \bar{p}_i \geq (m - n) \cdot p^{OPT} = m \cdot p^{OPT} - n \cdot p^{OPT} \geq (1 - \epsilon) \cdot r^{OPT}$$

  Recall that the revenue maximizing outcome allocates at least $\frac{n^2}{\epsilon}$ items. Hence, the last inequality follows from $r^{OPT} < m \cdot p^{OPT}$ and $n \cdot p^{OPT} \leq \epsilon \cdot \frac{n^2}{\epsilon} \cdot p^{OPT} < \epsilon \cdot r^{OPT}$.

- $\sum_{i \in N} D_i(v_i) \leq m$. In this case, we have enough copies to satisfy the demand of all bidders at price v_i. Algorithm 2 sells at least $\frac{n^2}{\epsilon} - n$ copies at price v_i. Now, we can bound the r^{OPT} as follows:
$r^{OPT} \leq \sum_{j \in A_i} b_j = \sum_{j \in A_i} \frac{b_j}{\bar{p}_i} \cdot \bar{p}_i \leq \sum_{j \in A_i} (\lfloor \frac{b_j}{\bar{p}_i} \rfloor + 1) \cdot \bar{p}_i \leq \sum_{j \in A_i} x_j^{ALG} \cdot$
$\bar{p}_i + \sum_{j \in A_i} \bar{p}_i = r^{ALG} + \sum_{j \in A_i} v_i \leq r^{ALG} + n \cdot v_i \leq r^{ALG} + \epsilon \cdot r^{OPT}$. The first inequality comes from the assumption that $p^{OPT} \in \Pi_i$, and the last inequality is implied by $r^{OPT} \geq \frac{n}{\epsilon} \cdot v_i$.

Above two cases conclude that setting $\bar{p}_i = v_i$ when $\frac{\epsilon \cdot \sum_{j \in A_i} b_j}{n^2} \geq v_i$ could achieves a $(1 - \epsilon)$-approximation to the optimal revenue.   □

Lemma 6. $< \mathbf{X}^{ALG}, p^{ALG} >$ *is envy-free.*

Proof. When price $\bar{p}_i$ produces a total demand less than the number of available items, i.e., $\sum_{i \in A_i} D_i(\bar{p}_i) \leq m$, we satisfy all the demands. Hence, no bidder envies anyone. When $\sum_{i \in A_i} D_i(\bar{p}_i) > m$, for every $i \in A_i$, it holds that either bidder i obtains $D_i(\bar{p}_i)$ items or bidder i receives the maximum number of items among all bidders. It concludes that allocation $< X^{ALG}, p^{ALG} >$ is envy-free.

□

Now we present the main theorem that follows from previous lemmas.

Theorem 4. *When there are more than $\frac{n^2}{\epsilon}$ copies sold in the revenue maximizing envy-free outcome in multi-unit auctions, Algorithm 2 outputs, in polynomial time, an envy-free outcome that achieves an $(1 - \epsilon)$-approximation to the optimum envy-free fixed-price revenue.*

4.2   The Case of $\sum_{i=1}^{n} x_i^{OPT} \leq \frac{n^2}{\epsilon}$

Now we consider the other case when at most $\frac{n^2}{\epsilon}$ copies of the good are allocated in $< \mathbf{X}^{OPT}, p^{OPT} >$. We first present a dynamic programming that maximizes the revenue when a price is given. Since there is only a polynomial number of possible prices for p^{OPT}, i.e., $p^{OPT} \in \bigcup_{i=1}^{n} (\{ \frac{b_i}{j} \}_{j=1}^{\frac{n^2}{\epsilon}} \cup \{ v_i \})$, one can simply run the dynamic programming for every possible price and output the optimum revenue. Now let us concentrate on the problem of computing the maximum revenue when a price is given. We first sort bidders by their demands. Without loss of generality, we assume $D_1(p) \leq \ldots \leq D_n(p)$. Recall that VL is the set of value-limited bidders, and NVL is the set of non-value-limited bidders. Both sets VL and NVL are also sorted by non-decreasing demand at price p. Let $VL(i)$ be the ith value-limited bidder, and $NVL(i)$ be the ith non-value-limited bidder. The dynamic programming fills a 4-dimensional table $t[i][j][k][h]$ of boolean values representing the existence of an envy-free allocation where exactly h copies are allocated among the first i value-limited bidders plus the first j non-value-limited bidders, and the maximum number of copies allocated to a bidder is k. The correctness of the dynamic programming relies on the following claim.

Claim 1. *There exits a revenue maximizing envy-free allocation* $\mathbf{X^{OPT}}$ *such that the following conditions hold: i)* $x_1^{OPT} \leq x_2^{OPT} \leq \ldots \leq x_n^{OPT}$*; ii)* $x_{VL(1)}^{OPT} \leq x_{VL(2)}^{OPT} \leq \ldots \leq x_{VL(|VL|)}^{OPT}$*; iii)* $x_{NVL(1)}^{OPT} \leq x_{NVL(2)}^{OPT} \leq \ldots \leq x_{NVL(|NVL|)}^{OPT}$*.*

The dynamic programming proceeds in rounds. In the current round either the next value-limited or the next non-value-limited bidder is considered:

– The bidder considered in the current round is value-limited. If the maximum number of copies already allocated to value limited bidders $[1, \ldots, i-1]$ and non-value-limited bidders $[1, \ldots, j]$ is k and $t[i-1][j][k][h-k]$ is true, then we can allocate k copies to value-limited bidder j. The resulting allocation is still envy-free. On the other hand, if the maximum number of copies allocated is less than k then we must ensure that giving k copies to value-limited bidder j does not violate envy-freeness. That implies that all non-value-limited bidders $[1, \ldots, j]$ have budgets less than kp.
– The bidder considered in the current round is non-value-limited. Similar to the previous case, if the maximum number of copies already allocated to a bidder is k and $t[i][j-i][k][h-k]$ is true, then we can allocate k copies to this bidder. The resulting allocation is still envy-free. On the other hand, if the maximum number of copies allocated to a bidder is less than k, we must ensure that giving k copies to this value-limited bidder does not affect envy-freeness. This essentially means that the already allocated non-value-limited bidders have budgets less than kp.

The recursive formula is given as follows.

$$t[i][j][k][h] = \Big[(i > 0) \wedge (k \leq D_{VL(i)}) \wedge (h > k) \wedge$$
$$\Big(t[i-1][j][k][h-k] \vee \big(\bigvee_{k' < k} t[i-1][j][k'][h-k] \wedge (k > D_{NVL(j)})\big)\Big)\Big] \vee$$
$$\Big[(j > 0) \wedge (k \leq D_{NVL(j)}) \wedge (h > k) \wedge$$
$$\Big(t[i][j-1][k][h-k] \vee \big(\bigvee_{k' < k} t[i][j-1][k'][h-k] \wedge (k > D_{NVL(j-1)})\big)\Big)\Big]$$

Finally, the revenue maximizing envy-free allocation on the given price is the entry of the table with $TRUE$ value in $t[|VL|][|NVL|][\cdot][h]$ that maximizes the total number of allocated copies of the good $h \leq m$. By using this dynamic programing, one could achieve the optimum envy-free fixed-price revenue.

Theorem 5. *When there are at most $\frac{n^2}{\epsilon}$ copies sold in the revenue maximizing envy-free outcome in multi-unit auctions, running dynamic programming on prices in $\bigcup_{i=1}^{n}(\{\frac{b_i}{j}\}_{j=1}^{\frac{n^2}{\epsilon}} \cup \{v_i\})$ and outputting the maximum revenue, achieves the optimum envy-free fixed-price revenue, in polynomial time in terms of n and ϵ.*

5   Envy-Free Revenue Maximizing Fixed-Price Multi-good Auctions with Budgets and Matching Preferences

In previous section we presented encouraging results for the case when there is only a single type of good in the auction. Here, we extend these results to the setting when there are different types of goods and bidders have *matching-type* preferences, i.e., the valuation of bidder i for all copies of goods in $S_i \subseteq [c]$ is v_i and 0 for goods not in S_i. We start with the hardness result for this case.

Theorem 6. *When there are non-constant number of types of goods, the optimum revenue in any envy-free multi-good auctions with budgets cannot be approximated within $O(\min(n, m)^{1/2-\epsilon})$ for any $\epsilon > 0$ unless $P = NP$.*

5.1   An FPTAS for a Constant Number of Types of Goods

The main result in this section is the following theorem.

Theorem 7. *When the number of types of goods is a constant, there exists an algorithm outputs, in polynomial time in terms of n and ϵ, an envy-free fixed-price outcome that achieves an $(1 - \epsilon)$-approximation to the optimum envy-free fixed-price revenue.*

The algorithm could be seen as a generalization of the results in Section 4. Due to the space limit, we only discuss the ideas of how to extend our techniques in Section 4 to obtain an FPTAS in this setting. As before, the proposed FPTAS considers two cases regarding $\mathbf{X^{OPT}}$.

OPT Allocates More Than $\frac{n^2}{\epsilon}$ Copies of Goods. An important difference with respect to the multi-unit case is the following. When $\bar{p}_i$ equals to $\frac{\epsilon \cdot \sum_{j \in A_i} b_j}{n^2}$, it is possible that there is no feasible allocation that sells $\frac{n^2}{\epsilon}$ copies of goods at price $\bar{p}_i$. This is because the cumulative demand for a subset of goods could be greater than the number of copies of the goods. Hence, in order to find a price at which $\frac{n^2}{\epsilon}$ can be sold and to keep the envy-freeness of the allocation, we transfer the problem to a min-cost max-flow problem. When the maximum flow is not equal to $\frac{n^2}{\epsilon}$, the solution of min-cost max-flow identifies the subset of bidders who do not obtain $\frac{b_{i'}}{\bar{p}_i}$ copies of goods. Then, the algorithm iteratively updates $\bar{p}_i$ by decreasing a particular amount until $\bar{p}_i$ is out of the range of Π_i or $\frac{n^2}{\epsilon}$ copies of goods can be sold.

OPT Allocates at Most $\frac{n^2}{\epsilon}$ Copies of Goods In order to cope with this setting, the dynamic programming needs to ensure envy-freeness between different types of bidders. Bidders belongs to the same type if their preference sets are the same. Envy-freeness implies that, when bidder i is allocated to a copy of good $j \in S_i$, bidder i' must also be allocated a copies of $j' \in S_{i'}$ if $j \in S_{i'}$. To achieve it, the dynamic programming considers different type bidders whose preference sets intersect. To be more specific, to guarantee that the allocation is envy-free, when bidder i is assigned a bundle of goods, the dynamic programming checks envy-freeness in the way that all those bidders with preference sets including the bundle, i.e., preference sets are the supersets of the bundle, prefer their bundles to the bundle assigned to bidder i or they cannot afford to buy bidder i's bundle. Therefore, the dynamic programming has $2^c - 1$ parameters to indicate the largest bundles assigned to each type of bidders.

5.2   A c-Approximation for a Constant Number of Types of Goods

Finally, by the results in [7], we complement our study with the following corollary.

Corollary 4. *The optimal envy-free fixed price auction is $\Theta(c)$-approximate with respect to the optimal envy-free auction.*

6   Open Problems

Here, we rise several interesting open problems for further investigation:

- First of all, we have not yet been able to prove NP-hardness of revenue maximizing fixed-price envy-free auctions with budgets in the multi-unit case.
- Second, it is left open to find any approximation for the case of a non-constant number of types of goods.
- Third, we do not know the ratio between the revenue that is extracted from a fixed-price and a non-fixed price auction for the case of a non-constant number of types of goods. Despite the inapproximability result, the ratio might even be $O(\log n)$ as in the unit-demand case, since even for fixed-price it can be NP-hard to decide whether there exists an envy-free allocation.

References

1. Anderson, E.T., Simester, D.I.: Price stickiness and customer antagonism. The Quarterly Journal of Economics 125(2), 729–765 (2010)
2. Avi-Itzhak, B., Levy, H., Raz, D.: A resource allocation queueing fairness measure: Properties and bounds. Queueing Systems 56(2), 65–71 (2007)
3. Carlton, D.W., Perloff, J.M.: Modern industrial organization (2005)

4. Chalermsook, P., Chuzhoy, J., Kannan, S., Khanna, S.: Improved hardness results for profit maximization pricing problems with unlimited supply. In: Gupta, A., Jansen, K., Rolim, J., Servedio, R. (eds.) APPROX/RANDOM 2012. LNCS, vol. 7408, pp. 73–84. Springer, Heidelberg (2012)
5. Clarke, E.H.: Multipart pricing of public goods. Public Choice 11(1), 17–33 (1971)
6. Dobzinski, S., Lavi, R., Nisan, N.: Multi-unit Auctions with Budget Limits. In: Proceedings of the 49th Annual Symposium on Foundations of Computer Science (FOCS), pp. 260–269 (2008)
7. Feldman, M., Fiat, A., Leonardi, S., Sankowski, P.: Revenue maximizing envy-free multi-unit auctions with budgets. In: Proceedings of the 13th ACM Conference on Electronic Commerce, pp. 532–549 (2012)
8. Fiat, A., Leonardi, S., Saia, J., Sankowski, P.: Single valued combinatorial auctions with budgets. In: Proceedings of the 12th ACM Conference on Electronic Commerce, pp. 223–232 (2011)
9. Foley, D.K.: Resource allocation and the public sector. Yale Econ. Essays 7(1), 45–98 (1967)
10. Geradin, D., Petit, N.: Price Discrimination Under EC Competition Law: Another Antitrust Doctrine in Search of Limiting Principles? Journal of Competition Law and Economics 2(3), 479–531 (2006)
11. Groves, T.: Incentives in teams. Econometrica: Journal of the Econometric Society, 617–631 (1973)
12. Guruswami, V., Hartline, J.D., Karlin, A.R., Kempe, D., Kenyon, C., McSherry, F.: On profit-maximizing envy-free pricing. In: Proceedings of the 16th Annual ACM-SIAM Symposium on Discrete Algorithms (SODA), pp. 1164–1173 (2005)
13. Lovsz, L., Plummer, M.D.: Matching Theory (2009)
14. Nisan, N., et al.: Google's auction for TV ads. In: Albers, S., Marchetti-Spaccamela, A., Matias, Y., Nikoletseas, S., Thomas, W. (eds.) ICALP 2009, Part II. LNCS, vol. 5556, pp. 309–327. Springer, Heidelberg (2009)
15. Varian, H.R.: Equity, envy, and efficiency. Journal of Economic Theory 9(1), 63–91 (1974)
16. Vickrey, W.: Counterspeculation, auctions, and competitive sealed tenders. The Journal of Finance 16(1), 8–37 (1961)

A Truthful-in-Expectation Mechanism
for the Generalized Assignment Problem

Salman Fadaei and Martin Bichler

Department of Informatics, TU München, Munich, Germany
{salman.fadaei,bichler}@in.tum.de

Abstract. We propose a truthful-in-expectation, $(1-\frac{1}{e})$-approximation mechanism for the generalized assignment auction. In such an auction, each bidder has a knapsack valuation function and bidders' values for items are private. We present a novel convex optimization program for the auction which results in a maximal-in-distributional-range (MIDR) allocation rule. The presented program contains at least a $(1 - \frac{1}{e})$ ratio of the optimal social welfare. We show how to implement the convex program in polynomial time using a fractional local search algorithm which approximates the optimal solution within an arbitrarily small error. This leads to an approximately MIDR allocation rule which in turn can be transformed to an approximately truthful-in-expectation mechanism. Our contribution has algorithmic importance, as well; it simplifies the existing optimization algorithms for the GAP while the approximation ratio is comparable to the best given approximation.[1]

Keywords: Generalized assignment problem, Truthful-in-expectation, Mechanism design, Convex optimization.

In *algorithmic mechanism design*, a mechanism designer wishes to solve an optimization problem, but the inputs to this problem are the private information of self-interested players. The mechanism designer must thus design a mechanism that solves the optimization problem while encouraging the agents to reveal their information truthfully. The game-theoretic solution concept of truthfulness guarantees that an agent is better off truthfully interacting with the mechanism regardless of what the other agents do.

We consider the generalized assignment problem as a combinatorial auction. In the generalized assignment problem (GAP), a set of items should be assigned to a set of bidders in order to maximize total valuation. Each bidder associates a different value and weight to each item and has a limited capacity. We can assign each bidder any subset of items that does not exceed the bidder's capacity. For every such subset, the bidder's valuation is additive in the values of items in the subset. We assume bidders' valuations for items to be private while weights and capacities are publicly known. Our goal is to find an allocation and payment rule which constitute a truthful-in-expectation mechanism for the GAP.

---

[1] A full version at
http://dss.in.tum.de/files/bichler-research/wine-gaptie.pdf.

T.-Y. Liu et al. (Eds.): WINE 2014, LNCS 8877, pp. 247–248, 2014.

The well-known *Vickrey-Clarke-Groves* (VCG) technique provides truthfulness as well as social welfare maximization in every combinatorial auction. The VCG technique, however, is applicable only when the optimal social welfare can be computed efficiently. Yet, in many cases, including our problem, optimizing social welfare is computationally intractable which makes the VCG technique inapplicable.

From an algorithmic point of view, the generalized assignment problem has been studied extensively in the literature. An approximation factor of $(1 - \frac{1}{e}) + \rho$ with $\rho > 0$, is the best given approximation ratio for the GAP. The presented algorithms, however, are not directly applicable for mechanism design as they rely on non-monotone rounding procedures.

MIDR or maximal-in-distributional-range is the only known general approach for designing randomized truthful mechanisms. An MIDR algorithm fixes a set of distributions over feasible solutions (the distributional range) independently of the valuations reported by the self-interested players, and outputs a random sample from the distribution that maximizes expected (reported) welfare.

In order to achieve a MIDR, we directly optimize over the outcome of the rounding procedure, rather than over the outcome of the relaxation algorithm. To this end, we formulate the GAP as a convex optimization problem where the objective function equals the expected value of the rounding procedure. This is similar to the technique used in [1] for finding a truthful-in-expectation mechanism for players whose valuations are of a special type of submodular functions. We notice that our technique allows to guarantee *non-negativity of payments* and *individual rationality*, *ex post*, while in [1], these important properties are provided only *ex ante*.

We are able to approximate the proposed convex optimization problem within an arbitrarily small error, in the sense of an FPTAS. This in fact leads to an approximate MIDR. Taking into account the black box transformation of an approximately MIDR allocation rule to an approximately truthful-in-expectation mechanism known in the literature, we immediately achieve a $(1 - \epsilon)$-truthful-in-expectation mechanism for the GAP.

We also emphasize the algorithmic importance of our result. Our algorithm has advantages over the existing optimization algorithms in terms of runtime and simplicity. It does not employ the ellipsoid method or any other LP solving algorithms. Additionally, the exact specification of the proposed objective function enables to calculate the gradient of the objective function explicitly which helps in designing a simpler algorithm for the problem.

Acknowledgement. The authors gratefully acknowledge support of the Deutsche Forschungsgemeinschaft (DFG) (BI 1057/7-1).

References

1. Dughmi, S., Roughgarden, T., Yan, Q.: From convex optimization to randomized mechanisms: toward optimal combinatorial auctions. In: Proceedings of the 43rd Annual ACM Symposium on Theory of Computing, pp. 149–158. ACM (2011)

Not Just an Empty Threat: Subgame-Perfect Equilibrium in Repeated Games Played by Computationally Bounded Players

Joseph Y. Halpern, Rafael Pass, and Lior Seeman*

Department of Computer Science, Cornell University, Ithaca, NY, USA
{halpern,rafael,lseeman}@cs.cornell.edu

Abstract. We study the problem of finding a subgame-perfect equilibrium in repeated games. In earlier work [Halpern, Pass and Seeman 2014], we showed how to efficiently find an (approximate) Nash equilibrium if assuming that players are computationally bounded (and making standard cryptographic hardness assumptions); in contrast, as demonstrated in the work of Borgs et al. [2010], unless we restrict to computationally bounded players, the problem is PPAD-hard. But it is well-known that for extensive-form games (such as repeated games), Nash equilibrium is a weak solution concept. In this work, we define and study an appropriate notion of a subgame-perfect equilibrium for computationally bounded players, and show how to efficiently find such an equilibrium in repeated games (again, making standard cryptographic hardness assumptions). As we show in the full paper, our algorithm works not only for games with a finite number of players, but also for constant-degree graphical games.

1 Introduction

Computing a Nash equilibrium (NE) (or even an ϵ-NE) in a (one-shot) game with only two players is believed to be computationally intractable (formally, it is PPAD-Hard) [3, 4]. However, in real life, games are often played repeatedly. In infinitely repeated games, the *Folk Theorem* (see [12] for a review), which shows that the set of NE is large, gives hopes that it might be easier to find one. In two-player repeated games, Littman and Stone [11] show that this is indeed the case, and describe an efficient algorithm for finding a NE, which uses the ideas of the folk theorem. Unfortunately, Borgs et al. [2] show that if the game has three or more players, then even in the infinitely repeated version it is PPAD-Hard to find even an ϵ-NE for an inverse-polynomial ϵ.

* Joseph Halpern and Lior Seeman are supported in part by NSF grants IIS-0911036 and CCF-1214844, by AFOSR grant FA9550-08-1-0266, by ARO grant W911NF-14-1-0017, and by the Multidisciplinary University Research Initiative (MURI) program administered by the AFOSR under grant FA9550-12-1-0040. Lior Seeman is partially supported by a grant from the Simons Foundation #315783. Rafael Pass is supported in part by an Alfred P. Sloan Fellowship, a Microsoft Research Faculty Fellowship, NSF Awards CNS-1217821 and CCF-1214844, NSF CAREER Award CCF-0746990, AFOSR YIP Award FA9550-10-1-0093, and DARPA and AFRL under contract FA8750-11-2-0211. The views and conclusions contained in this document are those of the authors and should not be interpreted as representing the official policies, either expressed or implied, of the Defense Advanced Research Projects Agency or the US Government.

T.-Y. Liu et al. (Eds.): WINE 2014, LNCS 8877, pp. 249–262, 2014.

If we take seriously the importance of being able to find an ϵ-NE efficiently, it is partly because we have computationally bounded players in mind. But then it seems reasonable to see what happens if we assume that the players in the game are themselves computationally bounded. As we show in a recent paper [8], this makes a big difference. Specifically, we show that if we assume that players are resource bounded, which we model as probabilistic polynomial-time Turing machines (PPT TMs) with memory, and restrict the equilibrium deviations strategies to those that can be implemented by such players, then there exist an efficient algorithm for computing an ϵ-NE in an infinitely repeated game. Our equilibrium strategy uses threats and punishment much in the same way that they are used in the Folk Theorem. However, since the players are computationally bounded we can use cryptography (we assume the existence of a secure public key encryption scheme) to secretly correlate the punishing players. This allows us to overcome the difficulties raised by Borgs et al. [2].

While NE has some attractive features, it allows some unreasonable solutions. In particular, the equilibrium might be obtained by what are arguably empty threats. This actually happens in our solution (and in the basic version of the folk theorem). Specifically, players are required to punish a deviating player, even though that might hurt their payoff. Thus, if a deviation occurs, it might not be the best response of the players to follow their strategy and punish; thus, such a punishment is actually an empty threat.

To deal with this (well known) problem, a number of refinements of NE have been considered. The one typically used in dynamic games of perfect information is *subgame-perfect equilibrium*, suggested by Selten [14]. A strategy profile is a subgame-perfect equilibrium if it is a NE at every subgame of the original game. Informally, this means that at any history of the game (even those that are not on any equilibrium path), if all the players follow their strategy from that point on, then no player has an incentive to deviate. In the context of repeated games where players' moves are observed (so that it is a game of perfect information), the folk theorem continues to hold even if the solution concept used is subgame-perfect equilibrium [1, 5, 13].

In this paper, we show that we can efficiently compute a *computational subgame-perfect ϵ-equilibrium*. (The "computational" here means that we restrict deviating players to using polynomial-time strategies.) There are a number of subtleties that arise in making this precise. While we assume that all actions in the underlying repeated game are observable, we allow our TMs to also have memory, which means their action does not depend only on the public history. Like subgame-perfect equilibrium, we would like our solution concept to capture the intuition that the strategies are in equilibrium after any possible deviation. This means that in a computational subgame-perfect equilibrium, at each history for player i, player i must make a (possibly approximate) best response, no matter what his and the other players' memory states are.

Another point of view is to say that the players do not in fact have perfect information in our setting, since we allow the TMs to have memory that is not observed by the other players, and thus the game should be understood as a game of imperfect information. Subgame perfection is still defined in games of imperfect information, but in many cases does not have much bite (see [10] for a discussion on this point). For the games that we consider, subgame-perfect equilibrium typically reduces to NE. An arguably more natural generalization of subgame-perfect equilibrium in imperfect-information games would require that if an information set for player i off the equilibrium path is reached, then player i's strategy is a best response to the other players' strategies *no matter how that information set is reached*. This is quite a strong requirement. (see [12][pp. 219–221] for a discussion of this issue); such equilibria do not in general exist in games of imperfect information.[1] In our setting, a "situation" includes the players' state of memory; after a deviation, players have no idea how the state of memory of other players may have changed. Thus, the nodes in a player's information set are characterized by the possible memory states of the other players. Since in a computational subgame-perfect equilibrium, at each history for player i, player i must make a best response no matter what the memory states of the other players are, it captures the strong requirement mentioned above. Despite this, we show that in a repeated game, a computational subgame-perfect ϵ-eqilibrium exists and can be found efficiently.

To achieve this we use the same basic strategy as in [8], but, as often done to get a subgame-perfect equilibrium (for example see [5]), we limit the punishment phase length, so that the players are not incentivized not to punish deviations. However, to prove our result, we need to overcome a significant hurdle. When using cryptographic protocols, it is often the case (and, specifically is the case in the protocol used in [8]) that player i chooses a secret (e.g., a secret key for a public-key encryption scheme) as the result of some randomization, and then releases some public information which is a function of it (e.g., a public key). After that public information has been released, another party j typically has a profitable deviation by switching to the TM M that can break the protocol—for every valid public information, there always *exists* some TM M that has the secret "hardwired" into it (although there may not be an efficient way of finding M given the information). We deal with this problem by doing what is often done in practice: we do not use any key for too long, so that j cannot gain too much by knowing any one key.

A second challenge we face is that in order to prove that our proposed strategies are even an ϵ-NE, we need to show that the payoff of the *best response* to this strategy is not much greater than that of playing the strategy. However, since for any polynomial-time TM there is always a better polynomial-time TM that has just a slightly longer running time, this natural approach fails. This instead leads us to characterize a class of TMs we can analyze, and show that any other TM can be converted to a TM in this class that has at least the same payoff. While such an argument might seem simple in the traditional setting, since we only allow for polynomial time TMs, in our setting this turns out to require a surprisingly delicate construction and analysis to make sure this converted TM does indeed has the correct size and running time.

There are a few recent papers that investigate solution concepts for extensive-form games involving computationally bounded player [9, 6, 7]; some of these focus on cryptographic protocols [9, 6]. Kol and Naor [9] discuss refinements of NE in the context of cryptographic protocols, but their solution concept requires only that on each history on the equilibrium path, the strategies from that point on form a NE. Our requirement is much stronger. Gradwohl, Livne and Rosen [6] also consider this scenario and offer a solution concept different from ours; they try to define when an empty threat occurs,

---

[1] Indeed, that is part of why notions like *sequential equilibrium* [10] are typically considered in games of imperfect information.

and look for strategy profiles where no empty threats are made. Again, our solution concept is much stronger.

2 Preliminaries

We briefly review some relevant material regarding games and subgame-perfect equilibrium. This material largely repeats definitions from [8]. For a more detailed description and for the definition of the cryptographic primitives we use, see the full paper.

2.1 One-Shot games

We define a game G to be a triple $([c], A, \vec{u})$, where $[c] = \{1, \ldots, c\}$ is the set of players, A_i is the set of possible actions for player i, $A = A_1 \times \ldots \times A_c$ is the set of action profiles, and $\vec{u} : A \to \mathbb{R}^c$ is the utility function ($\vec{u}_i(\vec{a})$ is the utility of player i). A (mixed) *strategy* σ_i for player i is a probability distribution over A_i, that is, an element of $\Delta(A_i)$ (where, as usual, we denote by $\Delta(X)$ the set of probability distributions over the set X). We use the standard notation $\vec{x}_{-i}$ to denote vector $\vec{x}$ with its ith element removed, and $(x', \vec{x}_{-i})$ to denote $\vec{x}$ with its ith element replaced by x'.

Definition 1. *(Nash Equilibrium)* $\sigma = (\sigma_1, \ldots, \sigma_c)$ *is an ϵ-NE of G if, for all players* $i \in [c]$ *and all actions* $a_i' \in A_i$, $E_{\sigma_{-i}}[u_i(a_i', \vec{a}_{-i})] \leq E_\sigma[u_i(\vec{a})] + \epsilon$.

A *correlated strategy* of a game G is an element $\sigma \in \Delta(A)$. It is a *correlated equilibrium* if, for all players i, they have no temptation to play a different action, given that the action profile was chosen according to σ. That is, for all players i for all $a_i \in A_i$ such that $\sigma_i(a_i) > 0$, $E_{\sigma|a_i} u_i(a_i, \vec{a}_{-i}) \geq E_{\sigma|a_i} u_i(a_i', \vec{a}_{-i})$.

Player i's minimax value in a game G is the highest payoff i can guarantee himself if the other players are trying to push his payoff as low as possible. We call the strategy i plays in this case a minimax strategy for i; the strategy that the other players use is i's (correlated) punishment strategy. (Of course, there could be more than one minimax strategy or punishment strategy for player i.) Note that a correlated punishment strategy can be computed using linear programming.

Definition 2. *Given a game $G = ([c], A, \vec{u})$, the strategies $\vec{\sigma}_{-i} \in \Delta(A_{-i})$ that minimize $\max_{\sigma' \in \Delta(A_i)} E_{(\sigma', \vec{\sigma}_{-i})}[u_i(\vec{a})]$ are the* punishment strategies *against player i in G. If $\vec{\sigma}_{-i}$ is a punishment strategy against player i, then $mm_i(G) = \max_{a \in A_i} E_{\vec{\sigma}_{-i}}[u_i(a, a_{-i})]$ is player i's* minimax value *in G*

To simplify the presentation, we assume all payoffs are normalized so that each player's minimax value is 0. Since, in an equilibrium, all players get at least their minimax value, this guarantees that all players get at least 0 in a NE.

2.2 Infinitely Repeated Games

Given a normal-form game G, we define the repeated game $G^t(\delta)$ as the game in which G is played repeatedly t times (in this context, G is called the *stage game*) and $1 - \delta$

is the discount factor (see below). Let $G^\infty(\delta)$ be the game where G is played infinitely many times. An infinite history h in this game is an infinite sequence $\langle \vec{a}^0, \vec{a}^1, \ldots \rangle$ of action profiles. Intuitively, we can think of $\vec{a}^t$ as the action profile played in the tth stage game. We often omit the δ in $G^\infty(\delta)$ if it is not relevant to the discussion. Let H_{G^∞} be the set of all possible histories of G^∞. For a history $h \in H_{G^\infty}$ let $G^\infty(h)$ the subgame that starts at history h (after $|h|$ one-shot games have been played where all players played according to h). We assume that G^∞ is *fully observable*, in the sense that, after each stage game, the players observe exactly what actions the other players played.

A (behavioral) strategy for player i in a repeated game is a function σ from histories of the games to $\Delta(A_i)$. Note that a profile $\vec{\sigma}$ induces a distribution $\rho_{\vec{\sigma}}$ on infinite histories of play. Let $\rho_{\vec{\sigma}}^t$ denote the induced distribution on H^t, the set of histories of length t. (If $t = 0$, we take H^0 to consist of the unique history of length 0, namely $\langle \rangle$.) Player i's utility if $\vec{\sigma}$ is played, denoted $p_i(\vec{\sigma})$, is defined as follows:

$$p_i(\vec{\sigma}) = \delta \sum_{t=0}^{\infty} (1 - \delta)^t \sum_{h \in H^t, \vec{a} \in A} \rho_{\vec{\sigma}}^{t+1}(h \cdot \vec{a})[u_i(\vec{a})].$$

Thus, the discount factor is $1 - \delta$. Note that the initial δ is a normalization factor. It guarantees that if $u_i(\vec{a}) \in [b_1, b_2]$ for all joint actions $\vec{a}$ in G, then i's utility is in $[b_1, b_2]$, no matter which strategy profile $\vec{\sigma}$ is played.

In these game, a more robust solution concept is subgame-perfect equilibrium [14], which requires that the strategies form an ϵ-NE at every history of the game.

Definition 3. *A strategy profile $\vec{\sigma} = (\sigma_1, \ldots, \sigma_c)$, is a subgame-perfect ϵ-equilibrium of a repeated game G^∞, if, for all players $i \in [c]$, all histories $h \in H_{G^\infty}$ where player i moves, and all strategies σ' for player i, $p_i^h((\sigma')^h, \vec{\sigma}_{-i}^h) \le p_i^h(\vec{\sigma}^h) + \epsilon$, where p_i^h is the utility function for player i in game $G^\infty(h)$, and σ^h is the restriction of σ to $G^\infty(h)$.*

3   Computational Subgame-Perfect Equilibrium

In this section we define our solution concept, and show that it can be computed efficiently in a repeated game. We capture computational boundedness by considering only (possibly probabilistic) polynomial time TMs, which at round t use only polynomial in nt many steps to compute the next action, where n is the size of G (the max of the number of actions and the number of players in G). The TM gets as input the history of play so far and can also use internal memory that persists from round to round. A strategy for player i is then a TM M_i. Given a strategy profile $\vec{M}$, as above, we can define the induced distribution $\rho_{\vec{M}}$ and player i's payoff $p_i(\vec{M})$.

We would like to define a notion similar to subgame-perfect equilibrium, where for all histories h in the game tree (even ones not on the equilibrium path), playing $\vec{\sigma}$ restricted to the subtree starting at h forms a NE. This means that a player does not have any incentive to deviate, no matter where he finds himself in the game tree.

As we suggested in the introduction, there are a number of issues that need to be addressed in formalizing this intuition in our computational setting. First, since we consider stateful TMs, there is more to a description of a situation than just the history;

we need to know the memory state of the TM. That is, if we take a history to be just a sequence of actions, then the analogue of history for us is really a pair $(h, \vec{m})$ consisting of a sequence h of actions, and a profile of memory states, one for each player. Thus, to be a computational subgame-perfect equilibrium the strategies should be a NE at every history and no matter what the memory states are.

Since a player's TM cannot observe the memory state of the other players' TMs, the computational game is best thought of as a game of imperfect information, where, in a given history h where i moves, i's information set consists of all situations where the history is h and the states of memory of the other players are arbitrary. While subgame-perfect equilibrium extends to imperfect information games it usually doesn't have much bite. In our setting it reduces to just a NE.

Instead, in games of imperfect information, the solution concept most commonly used is *sequential equilibrium* [10]. A sequential equilibrium is a pair $(\vec{\sigma}, \mu)$ consisting of a strategy profile $\vec{\sigma}$ and a *belief system* μ, where μ associates with each information set I a probability $\mu(I)$ on the nodes in I. Intuitively, if I is an information set for player i, $\mu(I)$ describes i's beliefs about the likelihood of being in each of the nodes in I. Then $(\vec{\sigma}, \mu)$ is a sequential equilibrium if, for each player i and each information set I for player i, σ_i is a best response to $\vec{\sigma}_{-i}$ given i's beliefs $\mu(I)$. However, a common criticism of this solution concept is that it is unclear what these beliefs should be and how players create these beliefs. Instead, our notion of computational subgame-perfection can be viewed as a strong version of a sequential equilibrium, where, for each player i and each information set I for i, σ_i is a best response to $\vec{\sigma}_{-i}$ conditional on reaching I (up to ϵ) no matter what i's beliefs are at I.

As a deviating TM can change its memory state in arbitrary ways, when we argue that a strategy profile is an ϵ-NE at a history, we must also consider all possible states that the TM might start with at that history. Since there exists a deviation that just rewrites the memory in the round just before the history we are considering, any memory state (of polynomial length) is possible. Thus, in the computational setting, we require that the TM's strategies are an ϵ-NE at every history, no matter what the states of the TMs are at that history. This solution concept is in the spirit of subgame-perfect equilibrium, as we require that the strategies are a NE after every possible deviation, although the player might not have complete information as to what the deviation is.

Intuitively, a profile $\vec{M}$ of TMs is a computational subgame-perfect equilibrium if for all players i, all histories h where i moves, and all memory profiles $\vec{m}$ of the players, there is no polynomial-time TM $\bar{M}$ such that player i can gain more than ϵ by switching from M_i to $\bar{M}$. Unfortunately, what we have just said is meaningless if we consider only a single game. The notion of "polynomial-time TM" does not make sense for a single game. To make it precise, we must consider an infinite sequence of games of increasing size (just as was done in [8], although our current definition is more complicated since we must consider memory states).

For a memory state m and a TM M let $M(m)$, stand for running M with initial memory state m. We use $\vec{M}(\vec{m})$ to denote $(M_1(m_1), \ldots, M_c(m_c))$. Let $p_i^{G,\delta}(\vec{M})$ denote player i's payoff in $G^\infty(\delta)$ when $\vec{M}$ is played.

Definition 4. *An infinite sequence of strategy profiles* $\vec{M}^1, \vec{M}^2, \ldots$, *where* $\vec{M}^k = (M_1^k, \ldots, M_c^k)$, *is a computational subgame-perfect ϵ-equilibrium of an* *infinite sequence $G_1^\infty, G_2^\infty, \ldots$ of repeated games where the size of G_k is k, if, for all players $i \in [c]$, all sequences $h_1 \in H_{G_1^\infty}, h_2 \in H_{G_2^\infty}, \ldots$ of histories, all sequences $\vec{m}^1, \vec{m}^2, \ldots$ of polynomial-length memory-state profiles, where $\vec{m}^k = (m_1^k, \ldots, m_c^k)$, and all non-uniform PPT adversaries $\bar{M}$ (polynomial in k and t, as discussed above), there exists k_0 such that, for all $k \geq k_0$,*

$$p_i^{G_k^\infty(h_k),\delta}(\bar{M}(m_i^k), \vec{\bar{M}}_{-i}^k(\vec{m}_{-i}^k)) \leq p_i^{G_k^\infty(h_k),\delta}(\vec{\bar{M}}^k(\vec{m}^k)) + \epsilon(k).$$

We stress that our equilibrium notion considers only deviations that can be implemented by polynomial-time TMs. This differs from the standard definition of NE (and from the definition considered in [2]). But this difference is exactly what allows us to use cryptographic techniques. It is also the reason that we need to consider a sequence of games of growing sizes instead of a single game. We allow the deviation to be a *non-uniform PPT*, which can be viewed as a sequence of TMs whose running time is bounded by some common polynomial (see the full paper for a formal definition).

3.1 Computing a Subgame-Perfect ϵ-NE

Let $A_i^0 \subset A_i$ be a non-empty set and let $A_i^1 = A_i \setminus A_i^0$.[2] A player can broadcast an m-bit string by using his actions for m rounds, by treating actions from A_i^0 as 0 and actions from A_i^1 as 1. Given a polynomial ϕ (with natural coefficients), let (Gen, Enc, Dec) be a multi-message multi-key secure ϕ-bit (see the full paper for the definition), if the security parameter is k, the length of an encrypted message is $z(k)$ for some polynomial z. Let $sq = (s_1, s_2 \ldots, s_m)$ be a fixed sequence of action profiles. Fix a polynomial-time pseudorandom function ensemble $\{PS_s : s \in \{0,1\}^*\}$ (again, see the full paper for the definition).

For a game G such that $|G| = n$, and a polynomial ℓ, consider the following strategy $\sigma^{NE,\ell}$, and let $\vec{M}^{\sigma^{NE,\ell}}$ be the TM that implements this strategy. This strategy is similar in spirit to that proposed in [8]; indeed, the first two phases are identical. Phase 1 explains what to do if no deviation occurs: play sq. Phase 2 gives the preliminaries of what to do if a deviation does occur: roughly, compute a random seed that is shared with all the non-deviating players. Phase 3 explains how to use the random seed to produce a correlated punishment strategy that punishes the deviating player. The key difference between the strategy here and that in [8] is that this punishment phase is played for only $\ell(n)$ rounds. After that, players return to phase 1. As we show, this limited punishment is effective since it is not played long enough to make it an empty threat (if ℓ is chosen appropriately). Phase 4 takes care of one minor issue: The fact that we can start in any memory state means that a player might be called on to do something that, in fact, he cannot do (because he doesn't have the information required to do it). For example, he might be called upon to play the correlated punishment strategy in a state where he has forgotten the random seed, so he cannot play it. In this case, a default action is played.

1. Play according to sq (with wraparound) as long as all players played according to sq in the previous round.

---

[2] We assume that each player has at least two actions in G. This assumption is without loss of generality—we can essentially ignore players for whom it does not hold.

2. After detecting a deviation by player $j \neq i$ in round t_0:[3]

   (a) Generate a pair (pk_i, sk_i) using $Gen(1^n)$. Store sk_i in memory and use the next $l(n)$ rounds to broadcast pk_i, as discussed above.

   (b) If $i = j + 1$ (with wraparound), player i does the following:
       - i records $pk_{j'}$ for all players $j' \notin \{i, j\}$;
       - i generates a random n-bit seed $seed$;
       - for each player $j' \notin \{i, j\}$, i computes $m = Enc_{pk_{j'}}(seed)$, and uses the next $(c-2)z(n)$ rounds to communicate these strings to the players other than i and j (in some predefined order).

   (c) If $i \neq j + 1$, player i does the following:
       - i records the actions played by $j+1$ at time slots designated for i to retrieve $Enc_{Pk_i}(seed)$;
       - i decrypts to obtain $seed$, using Dec and sk_i.

3. Phase 2 ends after $\phi(n) + (c-2)z(n)$ rounds. The players other than j then compute $PS_{seed}(t)$ and use it to determine which action profile to play according to the distribution defined by a fixed (correlated) punishment strategy against j. Player j plays his best response to the correlated punishment strategy throughout this phase. After $\ell(n)$ rounds, they return to phase 1, playing the sequence sq from the point at which the deviation occurred (which can easily be inferred from the history).

4. If at any point less than or equal to $\phi(n) + (c-2)z(n)$ time steps from the last deviation from phase 1 the situation is incompatible with phase 2 as described above (perhaps because further deviations have occurred), or at any point between $\phi(n) + (c-2)z(n)$ and $\phi(n) + (c-2)z(n) + \ell(n)$ steps since the last deviation from phase 1 the situation is incompatible with phase 3 as described above, play a fixed action for the number of rounds left to complete phases 2 and 3 (i.e., up to $\phi(n) + (c-2)z(n) + \ell(n)$ steps from the last deviation from phase 1). Then return to phase 1.

Note that with this strategy a deviation made during the punishment phase is not punished. Phase 2 and 3 are always played to their full length (which is fixed and predefined by ℓ and z). We say that a history h is a phase 1 history if it is a history where an honest player should play according to sq. History h is a phase 2 history if it is a history where at most $\phi(n)+(c-2)z(n)$ rounds have passed since the last deviation from phase 1; h is a phase 3 history if more than $\phi(n)+(c-2)z(n)$ but at most $\phi(n)+(c-2)z(n)+\ell(n)$ rounds have passed since the last deviation from phase 1. No matter what happens in phase 2 and 3, a history in which exactly $\phi(n) + (c-2)z(n) + \ell(n)$ round have passed since the last deviation from phase 1 is also a phase 1 history (even if the players deviate from phase 2 and 3 in arbitrary ways). Thus, no matter how many deviations occur, we can uniquely identify the phase of each round.

We next show that by selecting the right parameters, these strategies are easy to compute and are a subgame-perfect ϵ-equilibrium for all inverse polynomials ϵ.

---

[3] If more than one player deviates while playing sq, the players punish the one with the smaller index. The punished player plays his best response to what the other players are doing in this phase.

Definition 5. *Let $\mathcal{G}_{a,b,c,n}$ be the set of all games with c players, at most n actions per player, integral payoffs,[4] maximum payoff a, and minimum payoff b.[5]*

Our proof uses the following three lemmas proved in [8]. The first lemma shows that, given a correlated strategy σ in a game G, players can get an average payoff that is arbitrarily close to their payoff in σ by playing a fixed sequence of action profiles repeatedly.

Lemma 1. *For all a, b, c, all polynomials q, all n, all games $G \in \mathcal{G}_{a,b,c,n}$, and all correlated strategies σ in G, if the expected payoff vector of playing σ is ξ, then there exists a sequence sq of action profiles of length $w(n) = 2((a-b)q(n)+1)n^c$, such that for all $\delta \leq 1/f(n)$, where $f(n) = 2(a-b)w(n)q(n)$, if sq is played infinitely often, then player i's payoff in $G^\infty(\delta)$ is at least $\xi_i - 1/q(n)$, no matter at which point of the sequence play is started.*

To explain what we mean by the phrase "no matter at which point of the sequence play is started", suppose that the sequence sq has the form $(\vec{a}_1, \ldots, \vec{a}_5)$. Then the result holds if we start by playing $\vec{a}_1$ or if we start by playing $\vec{a}_4$ (and then continue with $\vec{a}_5$, $\vec{a}_1$, $\vec{a}_2$, and so on).

The next lemma shows that, for every inverse polynomial, if we "cut off" the game after some appropriately large polynomial p number of rounds (and compute the discounted utility for the finitely repeated game considering only $p(n)$ repetitions), the difference between a player's utility in the infinitely repeated and the finitely repeated game is negligible; that is, the finitely repeated game is a "good" approximation of the infinitely repeated game.

Lemma 2. *For all a, b, c, all polynomials q, all n, all games $G \in \mathcal{G}_{a,b,c,n}$, all $0 < \delta < 1$, all strategy profiles $\vec{M}$, and all players i, the difference between i's expected utility $p_i[\vec{M}]$ in game $G^{\lceil n/\delta \rceil}(\delta)$ and $p_i[\vec{M}]$ in game $G^\infty(\delta)$ is at most $a/2^n$.*

The last lemma shows that the punished player's expected payoff is negligible.

Lemma 3. *For all a, b, c, all polynomials t and f, all sequences of games $G_1, G_2, \ldots$ such that $G_n \in \mathcal{G}_{a,b,c,n}$, and all players i, if the players other than i play $\vec{M}_{-i}^{\sigma^{NE,\ell}}$, then for all non-uniform polynomial time TMs M, there exists a negligible function ϵ such that if i uses M and M deviates from the phase 1 sequence before round $t(n)$, then i's expected payoff during phase 3 is less then $\epsilon(n)$.*

We first show that for any strategy that deviates while phase 1 is played, there is a strategy whose payoff is at least as good and either does not deviate in the first polynomially many rounds, or after its first deviation, deviates every time phase 1 is played. (Recall that after every deviation in phase 1, the other players play the punishment phase for $\ell(n)$ rounds and then play phase 1 again.)

---

[4] Our result also hold for rational payoffs, except then the size of the game needs to take into account the bits needed to represent the payoffs.

[5] By our assumption that the minimax payoff is 0 for all players, we can assume $a \geq 0$, $b \leq 0$, and $a - b > 0$ (otherwise $a = b = 0$, which makes the game uninteresting).

We do this by showing that if player i has a profitable deviation at some round t of phase 1, then it must be the case that every time this round of phase 1 is played, i has a profitable deviation there. (That is, the strategy of deviating every time this round of phase 1 is played is at least as good as a strategy where player i correlates his plays in different instantiations of phase 1.) While this is trivial in traditional game-theoretic analyses, naively applying it in the computational setting does not necessarily work. It requires us to formally show how we reduce a polynomial time TM M to a different TM M' of the desired form without blowing up the running time and size of the TM.

For a game G, let $H_{G^\infty}^{1,n,f}$ be the set of histories h of G^∞ of length at most $nf(n)$ such that at (the last node of) h, $\sigma_{-i}^{NE,\ell}$ is in phase 1. Let $R(M)$ be the polynomial that bounds the running time of TM M.

Definition 6. *Given a game G, a deterministic TM M is said to be (G, f, n)-well-behaved if, when $(M, \sigma_{-i}^{NE,\ell})$ is played, then either M does not deviate for the first $nf(n)$ rounds or, after M first deviates, M continues to deviate from sq every time phase 1 is played in the next $nf(n)$ rounds.*

Lemma 4. *For all a, b, c, and all polynomials f, there exists a polynomial g such that for all n, all games $G \in \mathcal{G}_{a,b,c,n}$, all $h \in H_{G^\infty}^{1,n,f}$, all players i, and all TMs M, there exists a $(G(h), f, n)$-well-behaved TM M' such that $p_i^{G^h, 1/f(n)}(M', \vec{M}_{-i}^{\sigma^{NE,\ell}}) \geq p_i^{G^h, 1/f(n)}(M, \vec{M}_{-i}^{\sigma^{NE,\ell}})$, and $R(M'), |M'| \leq g(R(M))$.*

Proof. Suppose that we are given $G \in \mathcal{G}_{a,b,c,n}$, $h \in H_{G^\infty}^{1,n,f}$, and a TM M. We can assume without loss of generality that M is deterministic (we can always just use the best random tape). If M does not deviate in the first $nf(n)$ rounds of $G(h)^\infty$ then M' is just M, and we are done. Otherwise, we construct a sequence of TMs starting with M that are, in a precise sense, more and more well behaved, until eventually we get the desired TM M'.

For $t_1 < t_2$, say that M is (t_1, t_2)-(G, f, n)-well-behaved if M does not deviate from sq until round t_1, and then deviates from sq every time phase 1 is played up to (but not including) round t_2 (by which we mean there exists some history in which M does not deviate at round t_2 and this is the shortest such history over all possible random tapes of $\vec{M}_{-i}^{\sigma^{NE,\ell}}$). We construct a sequence $M_1, M_2, \ldots$ of TMs such that (a) $M_1 = M$, (b) M_i is (t_1^i, t_2^i)-(G, f, n)-well-behaved, (c) either $t_1^{i+1} > t_i$ or $t_1^{i+1} = t_1^i$ and $t_2^{i+1} > t_2^i$, and (d) $p_i^{G^h, 1/f(n)}(M_{i+1}, \vec{M}_{-i}^{\sigma^{NE,\ell}}) \geq p_i^{G^h, 1/f(n)}(M_i, \vec{M}_{-i}^{\sigma^{NE,\ell}})$. Note that if $t_1 \geq nf(n)$ or $t_2 \geq t_1 + nf(n)$, then a (t_1, t_2)-(G, f, n)-well-behaved TM is (G, f, n)-well-behaved.

Let $t < nf(n)$ be the first round at which M deviates. (This is well defined since the play up to t is deterministic.) Let the history up to time t be h^t. If M deviates every time that phase 1 is played for the $nf(n)$ rounds after round t, then again we can take $M' = M$, and we are done. If not, let t' be the first round after t at which phase 1 is played and there exists some history of length t' at which M does not deviate. By definition, M is (t, t')-(G, f, n)-well behaved. We take $M_1 = M$ and $(t_1^1, t_2^1) = (t, t')$. (Note that since $\vec{M}_{-i}^{\sigma^{NE,\ell}}$ are randomized during phase 2, the first time after t at which M returns to playing phase 1 and does not deviate may depend on the results of their coin tosses. We take t' to be the first time this happens with positive probability.)

Let s^{h^*} be M's memory state at a history h^*. We assume for ease of exposition that M encodes the history in its memory state. (This can be done, since the memory state at time t is of size polynomial in t.) Consider the TM M'' that acts like M up to round t, and copies M's memory state at that round (i.e., s^{h^t}). M'' continues to plays like M up to the first round t' with $t < t' < t + nf(n)$ at which $\sigma^{NE,\ell}$ would be about to return to phase 1 and M does not deviate (which means that M plays an action in the sequence sq at round t'). At round t', M'' sets its state to s^{h^t} and simulates M from history h^t with states $s^{h(t)}$; so, in particular, M'' does deviate at time t'. (Again, the time t' may depend on random choices made by $\vec{M}_{-i}^{\sigma^{NE,\ell}}$. We assume that M'' deviates the first time M is about to play phase 1 after round t and does not deviate, no matter what the outcome of the coin tosses.) This means, in particular, that M'' deviates at any such t'. We call M'' a *type 1 deviation from M*.

If $p_i^{G^{h^t},1/f(n)}(M'', \vec{M}_{-i}^{\sigma^{NE,\ell}}) > p_i^{G^{h^t},1/f(n)}(M, \vec{M}_{-i}^{\sigma^{NE,\ell}})$, then we take $M_2 = M''$. Note that $t_1^2 = t_1^1 = t$, while $t_2^2 > t_2^1 = t'$, since M'' deviates at t'. If $p_i^{G^{h^t},1/f(n)}(M'', \vec{M}_{-i}^{\sigma^{NE,\ell}}) < p_i^{G^{h^t},1/f(n)}(M, \vec{M}_{-i}^{\sigma^{NE,\ell}})$, then there exists some history h^* of both M and M'' such that $t < |h^*| < t + nf(n)$, M'' deviates at h^*, M does not, and M has a better expected payoff than M'' at h^*. (This is a history where the type 1 deviation failed to improve the payoff.) Take M_2 to be the TM that plays like $\vec{M}_i^{\sigma^{NE,\ell}}$ up to time t, then sets its state to s^{h^*}, and then plays like M with state s^{h^*} in history h^*. We call M_2 a *type 2 deviation from M*. Note that M_2 does not deviate at h^t (since M did not deviate at history h^*). Let $\delta' = (1 - \delta)^{|h^*|-|h^t|}$. Clearly $\delta' p_i^{G^{h^t},1/f(n)}(M_2, \vec{M}_{-i}^{\sigma^{NE,\ell}}) = p_i^{G^{h^*},1/f(n)}(M, \vec{M}_{-i}^{\sigma^{NE,\ell}})$, since $\vec{M}_{-i}^{\sigma^{NE,\ell}}$ acts the same in G^{h^t} and G^{h^*}. Since M'' plays like $M(s^{h_t})$ at h^*, $p_i^{G^{h^*},1/f(n)}(M'', \vec{M}_{-i}^{\sigma^{NE,\ell}}) = \delta' p_i^{G^{h^t},1/f(n)}(M, \vec{M}_{-i}^{\sigma^{NE,\ell}})$. Combining this with the previous observations, we get that $p_i^{G^{h^t},1/f(n)}(M_2, \vec{M}_{-i}^{\sigma^{NE,\ell}}) \geq p_i^{G^{h^t},1/f(n)}(M, \vec{M}_{-i}^{\sigma^{NE,\ell}})$. Also note that $t_1^2 > t_1^1$. This completes the construction of M_2. We inductively construct M_{i+1}, $i = 2, 3, \ldots$, just as we did M_2, letting M_i play the role of M.

Next observe that, without loss of generality, we can assume that this sequence arises from a sequnce of type 2 deviations, followed by a sequence of type 1 deviations: For let j_1 be the first point in the sequence at which a type 1 deviation is made. We claim that we can assume without loss of generality that all further deviations are type 1 deviations. By assumption, since M_{j_1} gives i higher utility than M_{j_1-1}, it is better to deviate the first time M_{j_1-1} wants to play phase 1 again after an initial deviation. This means that when M_{j_1} wants to play phase 1 again after an initial deviation it must be better to deviate again, since the future play of the $\vec{M}_{-i}^{\sigma^{NE,\ell}}$ is the same in both of these situations. This means that once a type 1 deviation occurs, we can assume that all further deviations are type 1 deviations.

Let M_j be the first TM in the sequence that is well behaved. (As we observed earlier, there must be such a TM.) Using the fact that the sequence consists of a sequence of type 2 deviations followed by a sequence of type 1 deviations, it is not hard to show that M_j can be implemented efficiently. First notice that M_{j_1} is a TM that plays like $\vec{M}_i^{\sigma^{NE,\ell}}$ until some round, and then plays M starting with its state at a history which is at most $(nf(n))^2$ longer than the real history at this point. This is because its initial history becomes longer by at most $nf(n)$ at each round and we iterate this construction at most $nf(n)$ times. This means that its running time is obviously polynomially related to the running time of the original M. The same is true of the size of M_{j_1}, since we need to encode only the state at this initial history and the history at which we switch, which is polynomially related to $R(M)(n)$.

To construct M_j, we need to modify M_{j_1} only slightly, since only type 1 deviations occur. Specifically, we need to know only $t_{j_1}^1$ and to encode its state at this round. At every history after that, we run M_{J_1} (which is essentially running M on a longer history) on a fixed history, with a potential additional step of copying the state. It is easy to see that the resulting TM has running time and size at most $O(R(M))$. □

We now state and prove our theorem, which shows that there exists a polynomial-time algorithm for computing a subgame-perfect ϵ-equilibrium by showing that, for all inverse polynomials ϵ, there exists a polynomial function ℓ of ϵ such that $\sigma^{NE^*, \ell}$ is a subgame-perfect ϵ-equilibrium of the game. The main idea of the proof is to show that the players can't gain much from deviating while the sequence is being played, and also that, since the punishment is relatively short, deviating while a player is being punished is also not very profitable.

Theorem 1. *For all a, b, c, and all polynomials q, there is a polynomial f and a polynomial-time algorithm F such that, for all sequences $G_1, G_2, \ldots$ of games with $G^j \in G_{a,b,c,j}$ and for all inverse polynomials $\delta \leq 1/f$, the sequence of outputs of F given the sequence $G_1, G_2, \ldots$ of inputs is a subgame-perfect $\frac{1}{q}$-equilibrium for $G_1^\infty(\delta_1), G_2^\infty(\delta_2), \ldots$.*

Proof. Given a game $G^n \in \mathcal{G}(a, b, c, n)$, the algorithm finds a correlated equilibrium σ of G^n, which can be done in polynomial time using linear programming. Each player's expected payoff is at least 0 when playing σ, since we assumed that the minimax value of the game is 0. Let $r = a - b$. By Lemma 1, we can construct a sequence sq of length $w(n) = 4(rnq(n) + 1)n^c$ and set $f'(n) = 4rw(n)q(n)$, so that if the players play sq infinitely often and $\delta < 1/f'(n)$, then all the players get at least $-1/2q(n)$. The correlated punishment strategy against each player can also be found in polynomial time using linear programming.

Let $m(n)$ be the length of phase 2, including the round where the deviation occurred. (Note that $m(n)$ is a polynomial that depends only on the choice of encryption scheme—that is, it depends on ϕ, where a ϕ-bit public-key encryption scheme is used, and on z, where $z(k)$ is the length of encrypted messages.) Let $\ell(n) = nq(n)(m(n)a + 1)$, let σ_n^* be the strategy $\vec{M}^{\sigma^{NE^*, \ell}}$ described above, and let $f(n) = \max(3rq(n)(\ell(n) + m(n)), f'(n))$.

We now show that $\sigma_1^*, \sigma_2^*, \ldots$ is a subgame-perfect $(1/q)$-equilibrium for every inverse polynomial discount factor $\delta \leq 1/f$. We focus on deviations at histories of length $< \frac{n}{\delta(n)}$, since, by Lemma 2, the sum of payoffs received after that is negligible. Thus, there exists some n_0 such that, for all $n > n_0$, the payoff achieved after that history is less than $1/q(n)$, which does not justify deviating.

We first show that no player has an incentive to deviate in subgames starting from phase 1 histories. By Lemma 4, it suffices to consider only a deviating strategy that after its first deviation deviates every time phase 1 is played; for every deviating strategy, either not deviating does at least as well or there is a deviating strategy of this form that does at least as well. Let h_1 be the history in which the deviation occurs and let M be the deviating strategy. Notice that $\vec{M}\sigma^{NE,\ell}$ can always act as intended at such histories; it can detect it is in such a history and can use the history to compute the next move (i.e., it does not need to maintain memory to figure out what to do next).

The player's payoff from $(M, \vec{M}\sigma^{NE,\ell}_{-i})$ during one cycle of deviation and punishment can be at most a at each round of phase 2 and, by Lemma 3, is negligible throughout phase 3. (We use ϵ_{neg} to denote the negligible payoff to a deviator in phase 3.) Thus, the payoff of the deviating player from $(M, \vec{M}\sigma^{NE,\ell}_{-i})$ from the point of deviation onwards is at most

$$((1 - \delta(n)^{|h_1|})\big(\delta(n)(m(n)a + \epsilon_{neg}) \sum_{t=0}^{\lceil \frac{nf(n)-|h_1|}{m(n)+\ell(n)}\rceil} (1 - \delta(n))^{(m(n)+\ell(n))t} + \epsilon'_{neg}\big)$$

$$\leq ((1 - \delta(n)^{|h_1|})\big(\delta(n)(m(n)a + \epsilon_{neg}) \sum_{t=0}^{\infty} (1 - \delta(n))^{(m(n)+\ell(n))t} + \epsilon'_{neg}\big),$$

where ϵ'_{neg} is the expected payoff after round $nf(n)$. By Lemma 1, no matter where in the sequence the players are, the average discounted payoff at that point from playing honestly is at least $-1/2q(n)$. Thus, the payoff from playing $(\vec{M}\sigma^{NE,\ell})$ from this point onwards is at least $-(1 - \delta(n))^{|h_1|})1/2q(n)$. We can ignore any payoff before the deviation since it is the same whether or not the player deviates. and also divide both sides by $(1 - \delta(n))^{|h_1|})$; thus, it suffices to prove that

$$\delta(n)(m(n)a + \epsilon_{neg}) \sum_{t=0}^{\infty} (1 - \delta(n))^{(m(n)+\ell(n))t} + \epsilon'_{neg} \leq \frac{1}{2q(n)}.$$

The term on the left side is bounded by $O\big(\frac{m(n)a+\epsilon_{neg}}{nq(n)(m(n)a+1)}\big)$, and thus there exists n_1 such that, for all $n > n_1$, the term on the left side is smaller than $\frac{1}{2q(n)}$ (In fact, for all constants c, there exists n_c such that the left-hand side is at most $\frac{1}{cq(n)}$ for any $n > n_c$.)

We next show that no player wants to deviate in phase 2 or 3 histories. Notice that since these phases are carried out to completion even if the players deviate while in these phases (we do not punish them for that), and the honest strategy can easily detect whether it is in such a phase by looking at when the last deviation from phase 1 occurred. First consider a punishing player. By not following the strategy, he can gain at most r for at most $\ell(n)+m(n)$ rounds over the payoff he gets with the original strategy (this is true even if his memory state is such that he just plays a fixed action, or even if another player deviates while the phase is played). Once the players start playing phase 1 again, our previous claim shows that no matter what the actual history is at that point, a strategy that does not follow the sequence does not gain much. It is easy to verify that, given the discount factor, a deviation can increase his discounted payoff by at most $\frac{1}{q(n)}$ in this case. (Notice that the previous claim works for any constant fraction of $1/q(n)$, which is what we are using here since the deviation in the punishment phase gains $1/cq(n)$ for some c.)

The punished player can deviate to a TM that correctly guessed the keys chosen (or the current TM's memory state might contain the actual keys and he defects to a TM that uses these keys) , in which case he would know exactly what the players are going to do while they are punishing him. Such a deviation exists once the keys have been played and are part of the history. Another deviation might be a result of the other TMs being in an inconsistent memory state, so that they play a fixed action, one which the deviating player might be able to take advantage of. However, these deviations work (or any other possible deviation) only for the current punishment phase. Once the players go back to playing phase 1, this player can not gain much by deviating from the sequence again. For if he deviates again, the other players will choose new random keys and a new random seed (and will have a consistent memory state); from our previous claims, this means that no strategy can gain much over a strategy that follows the sequence. Moreover, he can also gain at most r for at most $\ell(n) + m(n)$ rounds which, as claimed before, means that his discounted payoff difference is less than $\frac{1}{q(n)}$ in this case.

This shows that, for n sufficiently large, no player can gain more than $1/q(n)$ from deviating at any history. Thus, this strategy is a subgame-perfect $1/q$-equilibrium. □

References

[1] Aumann, R.J., Shapley, L.S.: Long-term competition: A game-theoretic analysis. In: Megiddo, N. (ed.) Essays in Game Theory, pp. 1–15. Springer (1994)

[2] Borgs, C., Chayes, J.T., Immorlica, N., Kalai, A.T., Mirrokni, V.S., Papadimitriou, C.H.: The myth of the folk theorem. Games and Economic Behavior 70(1), 34–43 (2010)

[3] Chen, X., Deng, X., Teng, S.-H.: Settling the complexity of two-player Nash equilibrium. Journal of the ACM 53(3) (2009)

[4] Daskalis, C., Goldberg, P.W., Papadimitriou, C.H.: The complexity of computing a Nash equilibrium. In: Proc. 38th ACM Symposium on Theory of Computing (STOC 2006), pp. 71–78 (2006)

[5] Fudenberg, D., Maskin, E.: The folk theorem in repeated games with discounting or with incomplete information. Econometrica 54(3), 533–554 (1986)

[6] Gradwohl, R., Livne, N., Rosen, A.: Sequential rationality in cryptographic protocols. ACM Trans. Econ. Comput. 1(1), 2:1–2:38 (2013)

[7] Halpern, J.Y., Pass, R.: Sequential equilibrium in computational games. In: Proc. 23rd International Joint Conference on Artificial Intelligence (IJCAI 2013), pp. 171–176 (2013)

[8] Halpern, J.Y., Pass, R., Seeman, L.: The truth behind the myth of the folk theorem. In: Proc. 5th Conference on Innovations in Theoretical Computer Science (ITCS 2014), pp. 543–554 (2014)

[9] Kol, G., Naor, M.: Games for exchanging information. In: Proc. 40th Annual ACM Symposium on Theory of Computing (STOC 2008), pp. 423–432 (2008)

[10] Kreps, D.M., Wilson, R.B.: Sequential equilibria. Econometrica 50, 863–894 (1982)

[11] Littman, M.L., Stone, P.: A polynomial-time Nash equilibrium algorithm for repeated games. Decision Support Systems 39(1), 55–66 (2005)

[12] Osborne, M.J., Rubinstein, A.: A Course in Game Theory. MIT Press, Cambridge (1994)

[13] Rubinstein, A.: Equilibrium in supergames with the overtaking criterion. Journal of Economic Theory 21(1), 1–9 (1979)

[14] Selten, R.: Spieltheoretische behandlung eines oligopolmodells mit nachfrageträgheit. Zeitschrift für Gesamte Staatswissenschaft 121, 301–324, 667–689 (1965)

Concise Bid Optimization Strategies with Multiple Budget Constraints

Arash Asadpour[1], Mohammad Hossein Bateni[2],
Kshipra Bhawalkar[2], and Vahab Mirrokni[2]

[1] NYU Stern School of Business
aasadpou@stern.nyu.edu
[2] Google Inc.
{bateni,kshipra,mirrokni}@google.com

Abstract. A major challenge faced by the marketers attempting to optimize their advertising campaigns is to deal with budget constraints. The problem is even harder in the face of multidimensional budget constraints, particularly in the presence of many decision variables involved, and the interplay among the decision variables through these such constraints. Concise bidding strategies help advertisers deal with this challenge by introducing fewer variables to act on.

In this paper, we study the problem of finding optimal concise bidding strategies for advertising campaigns with multiple budget constraints. Given bid landscapes—i.e., predicted value (e.g., number of clicks) and cost per click for any bid—that are typically provided by ad-serving systems, we optimize the value given budget constraints. In particular, we consider bidding strategies that consist of no more than k different bids for all keywords. For constant k, we provide a PTAS to optimize the profit, whereas for arbitrary k we show how constant-factor approximation can be obtained via a combination of solution enumeration and dependent LP-rounding techniques.

Finally, we evaluate the performance of our algorithms on real datasets in two regimes with 1- and 3-dimensional budget constraint. In the former case where uniform bidding has provable performance guarantee, our algorithm beats the state of the art by an increase of 1% to 6% in the expected number of clicks. This is achieved by only two or three clusters—contrast with the single cluster permitted in uniform bidding. With only three dimensions in the budget constraint (one for total consumption, and another two for enforcing minimal diversity), the gap between the performance of our algorithm and an enhanced version of uniform bidding grows to an average of 5% to 6% (sometimes as high as 9%). Although the details of experiments for the multidimensional budget constraint to the full version of the paper are deferred to the full version of the paper, we report some highlights from the results.

1 Introduction

The Internet has become a major advertising medium, with billions of dollars at stake; according to the recent IAB report [18], Internet advertising revenues in the United States totaled $31.7 billion in 2011 with sponsored search accounting for 46.5% of this revenue. Search engines provide simple ways to quickly set up an advertising campaign,

T.-Y. Liu et al. (Eds.): WINE 2014, LNCS 8877, pp. 263–276, 2014.
© Springer International Publishing Switzerland 2014

track expenses, monitor effectiveness of the campaigns, and tinker with campaign parameters, and this has made it relatively easy even for small advertisers to enter online advertising market. Even with all available tools to monitor and optimize ad campaigns, proper allocation of the *marketing budget* is far from trivial. A major challenge faced by the marketers attempting to optimize their campaigns is in the sheer number of variables they can possibly change. The problem is even more challenging in the presence of *multiple budget constraints*; i.e., in setting up a campaign that aims to target various categories of users or queries, or target a diverse set of demographics, the goal of an advertiser may be to allocate at least a fraction of its budget to each category, and therefore it may be facing several budget constraints at the same time. Even within a single advertising channel on a particular search engine, the advertiser can optimize by reallocating the budget across different keywords, choosing a particular bidding strategy to use within a single ad auction, deciding on the daily advertising budget or what demographics of users to target. This is in particular challenging in the presence of many decision variables involved and an interplay among these variables. To deal with the challenge, we propose *concise bidding strategies* to help advertisers by introducing fewer variables to act on. The idea is to consider the set of keywords that an advertiser may be interested in bidding on, and partition them into a small number of clusters such that the advertiser is going to have the same bid on each cluster. Such concise bidding strategies are inspired by *uniform bidding strategies* that have been shown to achieve relatively good results [11]. In this paper, we develop near-optimal concise bidding strategies for allocating advertising budgets across different keywords in a general setting in the presence of multiple budget constraints. In the following, we first motivate the problem and give an overview of our contributions, before elaborating on our model and our results in the following sections.

Setting. Any online advertising market such as sponsored search consists of three main players: *Users, Advertisers, and Publishers (or search engines)*. In sponsored search, users pose queries on a search engine like Bing or Google, declaring their intention and interests. Advertisers seek to place ads and target them to users' intentions as expressed by their queries, and finally publishers (or search engines in the case of sponsored search), provide a suitable mechanism for showing ads to users, through an ad-serving system. A common mechanism for allocating ads to users is based on having advertisers bid on the search query issued by the user, and the search engine run an *auction* at the time the user poses the query to determine the advertisements that will be shown to the user. A lot of research has focused on the algorithmic and game-theoretic problems behind such advertising markets, both from the publisher/search engine's point of view [1, 22, 7, 19, 5, 6, 12], and advertiser's point of view [4, 11, 21, 23, 20, 8, 2]. In this paper, we focus on optimization problems faced by advertisers.

More specifically, when a user submits a search query to a search engine, she receives next to the search results a number of ads. If the user finds any of the ads interesting and relevant, she may click on the ad. Advertisers interested in a search query submit their bids and the auction determines (1) which ads "win" to be displayed to the user, and (2) how much each is charged. Charging can be based on "impressions" (each time the ad being displayed to the user), "clicks" (only if the the user clicks on the ad), or "conversions" (only if the user purchases the product or installs the software).

In sponsored search, advertisers mainly pay if the user clicks on their ad (the "pay-per-click" model), and the amount they pay is determined by the auction mechanism, but will be no larger than their bid.

While the impact of a bidding strategy is a complicated phenomenon based on complex dynamics among other advertisers' bidding strategies and the arrival pattern of user queries, search engines help advertisers optimize their campaigns by providing general statistics about the final predicted cost and value (e.g., number of clicks) of a bidding strategy. In particular, they provide for each advertiser a set of *bid landscapes*[1] [11] for keywords; i.e., for each keyword w, advertisers get bid landscape functions value_w and $\overrightarrow{\text{cost}}_w$ corresponding to different bids on keyword w.

For ease of presentation, here we mostly focus on the most common case of *cost-per-click* (CPC) charging and consider the bid landscapes for cost and number of clicks, however, unlike most previous work [11, 20], our results directly apply to more general pay-per-impression or pay-per-conversion models along with other value functions, and even to settings with nonconcave value or cost functions.

To set up an advertising campaign, advertisers specify a set of user queries (or keywords), determine a bid for each type of query/keyword, and declare an upper bound on their *advertising budget* for the campaign. Next, we discuss these constraints.

Multidimensional Budget Constraints. Budget constraints play a major role in setting up an online advertising campaign, both from the auctioneer point of view and from advertiser's marketing strategy. It gives advertisers a robust knob to hedge against the uncertainty in the cost and benefits of the advertising campaign. In fact, some automated tools provided by search engines ask for a budget as part of the input, e.g., [13, 14]. While setting up an advertising campaign, marketers often aim to target a diverse set of demographics, and therefore need to spread their budget spent on various keywords. One way to enforce a diversified spent is to set an upper bound on the budget spent on a subset of keywords corresponding to a subcategory of users targeted in the campaign or a particular category of keywords.

As an example, consider an advertising campaign by a real-estate agency website to generate customers (or leads) for rentals in three of the boroughs in New York City, namely, Manhattan, Brooklyn, and Queens. Given a $1000 daily budget for the whole campaign, the advertiser might want to diversify the campaign throughout different boroughs, and therefore, spend at most $500 of the budget for the keywords related to Manhattan, at most $400 for those related to Brooklyn, and at most $250 for those related to Queens. Moreover, the advertiser might want to diversify among the different rental types as well, and to spend at most $700 on the keywords relevant to condominiums and/or apartments and at most $600 on those searches relevant to townhouses and/or houses. By this example, we would like to emphasize that even very natural preferences such as the above (and consequently, their relevant budget constraints) could have very complicated structures. In particular, the budget constraints are not limited to the special multidimensional case in which the constraints are only defined over disjoint subsets of keywords. As a result, different budget constraints interact with each other and their corresponding decisions would affect one another. We want our model to be able to

---

[1] Also referred to as "bid simulator" or "traffic estimator" [15, 16].

capture such general multidimensional budget constraints. We describe the details of these budget constraints in Section 2.

Concise Bidding Strategies. Advertisers usually need to submit their bidding strategy to the search engine ahead of time, so that whenever a relevant query enters the system, the auction can run in real time. Advertisers can optimize their campaigns by reallocating their budget across different keywords, choosing a particular bidding strategy to use, or deciding on what demographics of users to target. This optimization is particularly challenging when facing many decision variables or the interplay among them through the multidimensional budget constraints. To deal with this challenge, we propose *concise bidding* strategies by introducing fewer variables to act on. The idea is to represent the bidding strategy by a small number of bids with each bid acting on a cluster of keywords, i.e., partitioning the target set of keywords into a small number of clusters so that the advertiser is going to have the same bid on each cluster.

Such concise bidding strategies are already studied in the context of *uniform bidding strategies*, introduced by the seminal paper of Feldman et al. [11]. In uniform bidding strategies, the advertiser bids uniformly on all keywords. Uniform bidding, although naïve at first glance, has been shown to achieve relatively good results, both in theory and practice [11, 20]. In fact, the simplicity of uniform bidding along with its reasonable performance make it a desirable solution in practice which is robust and less reliant on the uncertain information provided by the advertising tool. Using such strategies, advertisers understand what their campaign is doing and where it is spending the budget. Although effective in simplistic setting, uniform bidding mainly applies to a specific setting with a single budget constraint and concave cost and value functions. Search engines do give advertisers the ability to bid differently on each keyword. Employing more complicated bidding strategies—in particular, using this ability to bid differently on different keywords—may benefit the advertiser, search engine users, and the search engine company. However, finding a different bid value for each keyword will result in information overload for the advertiser. It may make the campaign management overwhelming and impossible. Therefore, we take a middle-ground approach, and instead of declaring only one bid for all keywords, we cluster the keywords into a small number of subsets and apply a uniform bidding strategy on each subset, i.e., we use k distinct bids and let each bid act on an appropriate subset of keywords.

Goal. Given all the above, our goal is to help advertisers find optimal concise bidding strategies respecting multiple budget constraints. Given a number k, a set of keywords relevant to an ad campaign, a value bid landscape and multiple budget landscapes for each keyword, the advertiser's goal is to find k clusters of keywords, and a bid for each cluster so as to maximize the value the advertiser receives from this bidding strategy (e.g., the expected number of clicks) subject to its budget constraints.

Our Results and Techniques. In this paper, we propose concise bidding strategies, and develop an algorithm to find optimal concise bidding strategies for allocating advertising budgets across different keywords in a general setting in the presence of multiple budget constraints. We formalize the concise bid optimization problem with multiple budget constraints as motivated and sketched above, and formally defined in Section 2, and present approximation algorithms for this problem. The problem with super-constant number of budget constraints r does not admit a reasonable approximation algorithm as it is harder than *set packing*. The latter is known not to have any $\omega(r^{1-\epsilon})$ approximation unless $NP \subseteq ZPP$ [17]. In this paper, we focus on the problem with a constant number of budget constraints r.

Our main theoretical contribution in this paper is a constant-factor approximation for arbitrary number of clusters k. This constant-factor approximation algorithm is obtained using a dependent LP-rounding technique (performed in three phases) combined with solution enumeration. The linear-programming (LP) formulation of this problem and the dependent-rounding approach used to obtain an integral solution are of independent interest. The rounding algorithm is very simple to implement and is linear-time, however, its analysis uses a new technique to bound the loss incurred.

For the case of constant number of clusters k, we provide a polynomial-time approximation scheme (PTAS) to optimize the value. This PTAS is based on a careful dynamic program that enumerates various ways to satisfy the budge constraints. If a factor $1 + \epsilon$ violation of budget constraints is permitted, it is relatively easy to extend the standard PTAS for the knapsack problem to solve our problem with multiple budget constraints. However, to eliminate the budget violations completely is pretty involved and requires careful enumeration and modification of the residual instance.

Finally, we evaluate our algorithms on real data sets and compare their performance with the uniform bidding strategy. Even in a simple setting of maximizing the expected number of clicks subject to one budget constraint (for which uniform bidding is provably good), we show that using a small number of clusters can improve the expected number of clicks by 1% to 4%. We see more improvement with increasing number of clusters when the budget constraint is more tight. We also evaluate our algorithm in data sets with more budget constraints, and notice significant improvement (as high as 20%) compared to uniform bidding. Moreover, we observe that we lose less than 1% when we round the solution from fractional LP solution to a feasible integral solution. In the interest of space, some of the proofs will be deferred to the full version of the paper.

1.1   Related Work

As a central issue in online advertising, optimizing under budget constraints have been studied extensively both from publishers' (or search engines') point of view [19, 5, 6, 12], and from advertisers' point of view [4, 11, 21, 23, 20, 8, 2]. One well-studied problem from publisher's perspective is to deal with online allocation of ads in the presence of budget constraints [19, 5, 10, 9], and another line of research is dedicated to designing efficient mechanisms addressing incentive issues, and respecting budget constraints [6, 12]. More relevant to this paper, the bid optimization with budget constraints has also been studied from advertisers' perspective: either in a repeated auction setting [4], or in the context of broad-match ad auctions [8], or the case of long-term carryover effects [2].

This work is most related to the seminal paper of Feldman et al. [11] in which the authors propose uniform bidding as a means for bid optimization in the presence of budget constraints in sponsored-search ad auctions. Our results differ from those of Feldman et al. [11] and Muthukrishnan et al. [20] in several aspects: The uniform bidding result and its guaranteed approximation ratio of $1 - 1/e$ applies to CPC settings where the goal is to maximize the expected number of clicks and the cost and click landscapes follow a specific structure. Besides, those results apply only in the case of one budget constraint and (the proofs) do not easily generalize to settings with multiple budget constraints. Our results however apply to any set of monotone cost and value bid landscape functions (e.g., for the case of maximizing conversions), and more importantly handles multiple budget constraints. In addition, we compare our solution to the best solution with the same number of clusters, however, Feldman et al. compare their solution to the optimum of the knapsack problem with arbitrarily number of clusters and also in a more general query language model. As a result, we can get a PTAS for the case of constant number of clusters, but Feldman et al. can only get a $1 - 1/e$ approximation ratio. In fact, generalizing the results of Feldman et al. to multiple budget constraints is not possible, and we needed a new solution concept and a set of tools and techniques for this problem.

2   Preliminaries

Let $[k]$ for an integer k denote the set $\{1, 2, \dots, k\}$. We denote a vector v by $\boldsymbol{v}$ to emphasize its multidimensionality. The length of the vector is omitted and understood from the context; it is r, unless otherwise specified, since our vectors are mostly used for capturing the multidimensional resource constraints. To denote different components of a vector $\boldsymbol{v}$ of length r, we use the notation $v^{(q)}$ for $q \in [r]$. For any real number z, the vector $\boldsymbol{z}$ is one all whose components are z. The length of these vectors is understood from the context. We say $\boldsymbol{v} \leq \boldsymbol{w}$ if they have the same length and every component of $\boldsymbol{v}$ is at most the corresponding component of $\boldsymbol{w}$. Otherwise, we can write $\boldsymbol{v} \nleq \boldsymbol{w}$.

2.1   Formal Problem Definition

In order to optimize their campaigns, we assume that advertisers get "bid landscapes" [11] as an input: For each keyword w, they get (i) a monotone nonnegative function value$_w$ that maps any bid value to the expected value (e.g., number of clicks), and (ii) a nonnegative function $\overrightarrow{\text{cost}}_w$ mapping any bid value to an r-dimensional cost vector incurred by the advertiser. These functions are left-continuous, but they do not necessarily satisfy Lipschitz smoothness conditions. (See [11] for an example of how these are derived.)

In addition, we have an r-dimensional budget limit vector (or resource usage vector), and a number k indicating the number of clusters we can produce in our suggested bidding strategy. The bid clustering problem is formally the following:

Problem 1. Given are an integer k, a number r of budget constraints (resources), a real vector $\boldsymbol{L} \in \mathbb{R}^r$, a set $\mathcal{K}$ of keywords as well as value and cost landscape functions value$_w$: bids $\mapsto \mathbb{R}$ and $\overrightarrow{\text{cost}}_w$: bids $\mapsto \mathbb{R}^r$ for each keyword $w \in \mathcal{K}$. Find a partition of $\mathcal{K}$ into k clusters $\mathcal{K}_1, \mathcal{K}_2, \dots, \mathcal{K}_k$, and a set of bids b_i for $i \in [k]$ such that the expected resource consumption of the advertiser is no more than his budget vector L, i.e., $\sum_{i \in [k]} \sum_{w \in \mathcal{K}_i} \overrightarrow{\text{cost}}_w(b_i) \leq \boldsymbol{L}$, and the advertiser's value (e.g., expected number of clicks), i.e., $\sum_{i \in [k]} \sum_{w \in \mathcal{K}_i} \text{value}_w(b_i)$ is (approximately) maximized. We can also consider a *weighted* objective where clicks coming from different keywords may be of varying degrees of importance.

For ease of exposition, we use the shorthands $c_{ib}^q = \overrightarrow{\text{cost}}_i^{(q)}(b)$ to refer to each budget constraint limit and $p_{ib} = \text{value}_i(b)$ for values. We also refer to each of the r budget constraints as a resource constraint, i.e., the qth resource (or budget) constraint is the following: $\sum_{i \in [k]} \sum_{w \in \mathcal{K}_i} \overrightarrow{\text{cost}}_i^{(q)}(b) \leq L^q$. Finally, throughout this paper, we use $n = |\mathcal{K}|$ to denote the number of keywords, k for the number of clusters, and r for the number of budget (or resource) constraints.[2]

2.2 Approach

As discussed earlier, we know that if r, the number of different budget constraints (or resource constraints) is not a constant, the bid-clustering problem even with no restriction on the number of clusters is inapproximable. This is due to the fact that this problem is harder than the set packing or the independent set problem which is known to be inapproximable within a factor better than $n^{1-\epsilon}$ unless $NP \subset ZPP$ [17]. As a result, henceforth we assume that r is a small constant. In fact, the running times of our algorithms depend exponentially on this parameter. We note that all the previous work in advertising bid optimization only consider the case of $r = 1$ [11, 20, 8, 2].

Uniform resource limits. First note that we can assume without loss of generality that the resource usage limit vector $L = 1$. To see this, note that we consider each resource separately. Therefore, if a resource limit q in L is positive, we can scale it to 1 while modifying $\text{cost}_w^{(q)}$ appropriately for all $w \in \mathcal{K}$. On the other hand, a limit of zero in L for some resource q implies that we cannot place a bid b on a keyword w if $\text{cost}_w^{(q)}(b) > 0$. Hence, by setting such values of $\text{cost}_w^{(q)}(b)$ to ∞ we can change the limit of q in L to 1.

Small set of potential bids. We next show that, although the cost and value landscapes have a continuous nature (provided to us, perhaps, by oracle access), we can settle with a polynomial-size description thereof while incurring a small loss in the guarantees. In particular, we show that there are only a polynomial number of different bid values that matter. The proof of the following lemma can be found in the full version of the paper.

Lemma 1. *Given any $\delta > 0$, we can find (in polynomial time) a set B of size $\text{poly}(n, \frac{1}{\delta})$ such that there exists a $(1 - \delta)$-approximate solution (to the problem) all whose bids fall in B.*

In what follows, we consider two input regimes and present algorithms for each. For the general case, we present a constant factor approximation algorithm. If k, the number

---

[2] Note that different resource constraints are not for disjoint sets of keywords; had this been the case, the problem would have been decomposed into separate single-resource special cases. We emphasize, however, that in the example provided, different resource constraints correspond to different markets, each drawing from all keywords, albeit with different coefficients. These techniques can be potentially used to obtain lower bounds on each resource consumption, in effect, capturing diversification objectives better.

of permissible clusters, is a constant, the following theorem guarantees the existence of a polynomial-time approximation scheme (PTAS) based on dynamic programming for the problem. The proof is deferred to the full version of the paper.

Theorem 1. *There is a polynomial-time approximation scheme for the bid-clustering problem if k is a constant.*

3   Approximation Algorithm

In the following, we approach to the bid-clustering problem by solving a very simple linear-programming relaxation and then applying a three-stage dependent randomized rounding scheme. Even though the analysis is not straightforward, the algorithm is very simple to implement and use in practice.

3.1   Linear Programming Relaxation

Here we introduce a linear-programming relaxation for the problem. We will argue that we only need to round this LP for the case that each bid has a small contribution to the solution, otherwise, a PTAS from Theorem 1 suffices to find a good solution for keywords with big contributions in the solution.

Consider a variable x_{ib} for each keyword $i \in \mathcal{K}$ and each relevant bid $b \in B$. In the integer linear program, x_{ib} denotes whether the advertiser should place a bid b on keyword i and in the LP relaxation, we relax it to a positive real variable. In addition, there is a variable y_b for each relevant bid b, denoting whether there is a cluster with bid b. To make the LP more concise and readable, we use the shorthands $p_{ib} = \text{value}_i(b)$ and $c_{ib}^q = \overrightarrow{\text{cost}}_i^{(q)}(b)$.

$$\max \ \textstyle\sum_{i,b} p_{ib} x_{ib} \qquad (1)$$
$$\text{s.t.} \ \textstyle\sum_{i,b} c_{ib}^q x_{ib} \le L^{(q)} \ \forall q \in [r]$$
$$\textstyle\sum_b y_b \ \le k \ \ \forall i$$
$$x_{ib} \ \le y_b \ \ \forall i,b$$
$$y_b \ \le 1 \ \ \forall b$$
$$\textstyle\sum_b x_{ib} \ \le 1 \ \ \forall i \qquad (2)$$
$$x_{ib}, y_b \ \ge 0 \ \ \forall i,b. \ (3)$$

For the case when all $c_{ib}^q \le \epsilon L$, this LP has a small integrality gap, and the LP can be rounded to obtain an approximation ratio of $0.54 - \epsilon$. In fact, this can be done if $c_b^q = \frac{\sum_i c_{ib}^q x_{ib}}{y_b} \le \epsilon L^{(q)}$ for all b and q; see Section 3.2.

To solve the problem, we consider two cases. First, if there is a solution of value at least βopt (β to be determined later) for which the above condition holds, we can add $c_b^q \le \epsilon L^{(q)}$ conditions to the LP as follows.

$$\textstyle\sum_i c_{ib}^q x_{ib} \le \epsilon L^{(q)} y_b \qquad \forall b, q. \qquad (4)$$

and then solve and round the LP to get a guarantee of $\beta(0.54 - \epsilon)$.

Second case happens when there is a solution of value at least $(1 - \beta)$opt that uses only large-cost clusters, i.e., each cluster of the solution has cost at least $\epsilon L^{(q)}$ for some q. In this case, there will be at most $r\epsilon^{-1}$ clusters in the solution, therefore, we can use Theorem 1 to get an approximation ratio of $1 - \beta - \epsilon$. Letting $\beta = \frac{1}{1.54}$, and outputting the best solution of the two methods yields an approximation ratio of $1 - \beta \approx 0.3506$ for the general case of the problem.

3.2   Rounding the LP

The above LP is rounded in three stages. In the first stage, we modify the fractional solution so that only k nonzero y_b variables remain. This is done carefully without losing more than $1 - \epsilon$ factor in the objective value. At this point, we have an LP solution that is *almost* feasible—some constraints (2) may be violated. The second stage addresses this issue by modifying x_{ib} variables so that, at the end, all LP constraints are satisfied. The third stage, which we may even skip depending on the type of solution we need, is a standard randomized assignment of each keyword to one bid, and may lose up to a factor $1 - \epsilon$.

Stage 1: Rounding y_b Variables. Variables y_b are considered one by one, and are rounded to either zero or one, and the value of the remaining (i.e., as of now unconsidered) variables y_b are adjusted accordingly. In particular, each variable y_b, when considered, is rounded up to one with probability y_b and is rounded down to zero with probability $1 - y_b$. The remaining y_b variables are scaled such that their sum stays the same. During the process, x_{ib} variables are also scaled such that each x_{ib}/y_b remains a constant throughout. This process is a martingale, hence we have concentration bounds for $\sum_b c_b^q y_b$ (if all individual contributions are small). We scale down all x_{ib} variables by a factor $1 + \epsilon$, so that the cost constraints are satisfied.

Let LP be the objective value of the linear program. Further, denote by $\mathsf{LP}^{(l)}$ the objective values for the LP solutions after stage $l \in [3]$. Notice that, although LP itself is a certain value, each $\mathsf{LP}^{(l)}$ is a random variable. We have $\mathbf{E}\left[\mathsf{LP}^{(1)}\right] \geq \frac{1}{1+\epsilon}\mathsf{LP}$.

Stage 2: Modifying x_{ib} Variables to Get a Feasible Solution. Note that after rounding the y_b variables and scaling the x_{ib} variables appropriately, some constraints (2) may be violated. In particular, for certain keywords i, we may have $\sum_b x_{ib} > 1$. For each such keyword, we scale down all x_{ib} variables at the same rate to obtain $\sum_b x_{ib} = 1$. Clearly, these operations do not violate any new constraints, and fix all the violated ones, hence the result is a feasible solution. It only remains to show the loss in the objective due to these operations is not too much. More specifically, we prove the following.

Lemma 2. *We have* $\mathbf{E}\left[\mathsf{LP}^{(2)}\right] \geq \lambda \mathbf{E}\left[\mathsf{LP}^{(1)}\right]$ *for a positive constant value of* $\lambda = 0.539968$.

Here, we provide a weaker proof of the above lemma for $\lambda = \frac{1}{4}$. At the end of the proof we discuss the ideas to strengthen our analysis to $\lambda = 0.539968$. The complete proof is deferred to the full version of the paper.

Define random variable X_{ib} to be x_{ib}/y_b with probability y_b and zero otherwise. Let random variable X_i denote $\sum_b X_{ib}$. Furthermore, define random variable $P_i = \sum_b p_{ib}X_{ib}$, which is the contribution of keyword i to the objective value after Stage 1. Note that $\mathbf{E}[X_{ib}] = x_{ib}$, $\mathbf{E}[P_i] = \sum_b p_{ib}x_{ib}$, and $\mathbf{E}\left[\mathsf{LP}^{(1)}\right] = \sum_i \mathbf{E}[P_i]$.

Consider the contribution of all keywords i with $X_i > 2$ to the value of $\mathsf{LP}^{(1)}$. Let random variable $\hat{P}_i$ denote this contribution. By the following inequalities, we show that $\mathbf{E}[\hat{P}_i] \leq \mathbf{E}[P_i]/2$, which means that in expectation at least half of the value of $\mathsf{LP}^{(1)}$ comes from keywords i with $X_i \leq 2$.

$$
\mathbf{E}\left[\hat{P}_i\right] = \mathbf{E}\left[P_i \middle| X_i > 2\right] \cdot \mathbf{Pr}\left[X_i > 2\right] = \mathbf{E}\left[\sum_b p_{ib} X_{ib} \middle| X_i > 2\right] \cdot \mathbf{Pr}\left[X_i > 2\right]
$$

$$
= \sum_b \mathbf{E}\left[p_{ib} X_{ib} \middle| X_i > 2\right] \cdot \mathbf{Pr}\left[X_i > 2\right] \tag{5}
$$

$$
= \sum_b \mathbf{E}\left[p_{ib} X_{ib} \middle| X_i > 2 \wedge X_{ib} > 0\right] \cdot \mathbf{Pr}\left[X_{ib} > 0\right] \cdot \mathbf{Pr}\left[X_i > 2 \middle| X_{ib} > 0\right]
$$

$$
= \sum_b \mathbf{E}\left[p_{ib} X_{ib} \middle| X_i > 2 \wedge X_{ib} = \frac{x_{ib}}{y_b}\right] \cdot \mathbf{Pr}\left[X_{ib} = \frac{x_{ib}}{y_b}\right] \cdot \mathbf{Pr}\left[X_i > 2 \middle| X_{ib} = \frac{x_{ib}}{y_b}\right]
$$

$$
= \sum_b p_{ib} \frac{x_{ib}}{y_b} \cdot y_b \cdot \mathbf{Pr}\left[X_i > 2 \middle| X_{ib} = \frac{x_{ib}}{y_b}\right]
$$

$$
= \sum_b p_{ib} x_{ib} \cdot \mathbf{Pr}\left[X_i^{-b} > 2 - \frac{x_{ib}}{y_b} \middle| X_{ib} = \frac{x_{ib}}{y_b}\right] \leq \sum_b p_{ib} x_{ib} \cdot \frac{\mathbf{E}\left[X_i^{-b} \middle| X_{ib} = \frac{x_{ib}}{y_b}\right]}{2 - \frac{x_{ib}}{y_b}}
$$

$$
\leq \sum_b p_{ib} x_{ib} \cdot \frac{1 - \frac{x_{ib}}{y_b}}{2 - \frac{x_{ib}}{y_b}} \leq \sum_b p_{ib} x_{ib} \cdot \frac{1}{2} = \frac{1}{2} \mathbf{E}\left[P_i\right]. \tag{6}
$$

Now, note that in Stage 2, for each keyword i with $X_i > 1$ we scale down all X_{ib} variables by X_i. Hence, for each keyword i with $X_i \leq 2$, we lose at most a factor of 2 in the scaling process of Stage 2. However, Inequality (6) shows that at least half of the value of $\mathbf{E}[\mathsf{LP}^{(1)}]$ is coming from such keywords. Hence, a quarter of $\mathbf{E}[\mathsf{LP}^{(1)}]$ is preserved after Stage 2, or, $\lambda \geq \frac{1}{4}$.

The above analysis is suboptimal for two reasons. First, it ignores the contribution of $p_{ib} x_{ib}$ to the objective if X_i happens to be greater than two. Second, it treats all keywords i for which $X_i \leq 2$ similarly, and divides all of them by two although some may only require a small scaling factor (or none at all). The deferred analysis takes advantage of these observations and some concentration bounds to achieve $\lambda = 0.539968$.

Stage 3: Rounding x_{ib} Variables. We can simply pick one bid b for each keyword i with probability proportional to x_{ib}. This independent rounding enjoys concentration properties (via Chernoff bounds) for total value as well as the cost vector. This follows from the assumption that no c_{ib}^q or p_{ib} is larger than ϵ or ϵopt, respectively, otherwise we would use the PTAS in Theorem 1. Therefore, we argue that, with high probability, both are within a factor $1 \pm \epsilon$ of the semi-integral LP solution. Then, since individual contributions to cost are small, we can remove, and throw away a small portion of the cost with a loss in value that is no more than a $1 - \epsilon$ factor.

The discussions in this section so far can be summarized in the following theorem.

Theorem 2. *The above algorithm provides a 0.54-approximate integral solution to the LP (1)-(3) with additional constraints (4). This, combined with Theorem 1, can be used* *to obtain a 0.35-approximate solution for the general concise bidding problem, i.e., LP (1)-(3).*

In the full version of the paper, we provide an instance of the aforementioned LP with an integrality gap of 0.63.

4 Experimental Study

In order to evaluate the practical performance of our algorithms, we apply our algorithms to real datasets collected from a sponsored search advertising system, and compare our results with a baseline method, i.e., uniform bidding. For a set of (randomly selected, anonymous) advertisers, we consider a set of queries on which they might wish to advertise. We use a traffic estimator tool to estimate the number of clicks the advertiser will get and the cost he will have to pay when he bids a bid b. Such tools are provided for major sponsored search advertising systems [3, 15].

The datasets contain varying number of queries (from tens to tens of thousands). For each query we obtain estimates of clicks and cost for bids in the range [$0.10, $2].

We then run our algorithms, an appropriate version of the uniform bidding algorithm and an algorithm that computes the optimal bid for each query against each of the datasets. We apply these algorithms at different budget values to see the impact of changing the budget in the relative performance of different algorithms.

4.1 A One-Dimensional Budget Constraint

Our initial experiments involve only one budget constraint. Note that this is the setting in which the uniform-bidding algorithm was proposed and analyzed [11].

We first see how the total amount of clicks that can be obtained grows as the number of permitted bids increases.

Figure 1 plots the performance of the bid allocation we find for different number of bids. It shows how the objective value of the fractional LP for each dataset grows with the number of clusters. This interesting point confirms the intuition that additional clusters allow for more refined bidding on various queries, hence better performance. We also note that, conveniently, with a few clusters, we can achieve the almost optimal solution, and there is no need for a complicated strategy.

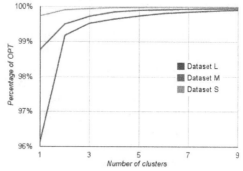

Fig. 1. Comparison of performance by number of clusters for all datasets

Next we consider the deterministic solutions constructed by our algorithm for each of these datasets. The values in the figures are normalized with respect to the optimal solution that chooses an individual bid for each query. We report performance of our algorithm for number of clusters $k = 1, 2, 3, 4$. We also report the performance of our implementation of uniform bidding that chooses an optimal set of two bids, with some

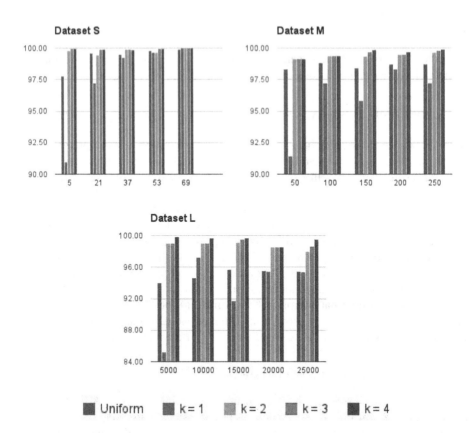

Fig. 2. Plots comparing performance of various algorithms on the three datasets. The x axis has budget in dollars, whereas the y axis shows the percentage of the (unrestricted) optimal solution.

probability chooses the first bid for all queries and otherwise chooses the other bid for all queries. This algorithm was described and analyzed in [11].

Plots in Figure 2 compare the performance of integer solutions produced by LP rounding with the uniform bidding benchmark.

We see that all algorithms perform equally well at high budgets or when the instance is fairly small, where even the optimal fractional solution is almost integral. On the other hand at lower values of budget and specially in the larger instances, we see superiority of our algorithms as the number of clusters grows. In particular, for the large dataset L, we see improvements of 4% to 6% in the expected number of clicks compared to the uniform bidding strategy when we increase the number of clusters to four. For other datasets which are smaller the average improvement in number of clicks is about 1%.

4.2 A Multidimensional Budget Constraint

A virtue of our algorithm is that it is naturally taking care of the setting where multiple budget constraints are present. These additional budget constraints may arise when an advertiser, considering the semantic meaning of different queries, wishes to restrict how much of her budget is spent on specific queries or domains. In the full version of this paper we report detailed results of evaluating our algorithms on experimental data in the presence of multidimensional budget constraint.

5 Conclusion and Future Directions

We formulate the problem of finding the concise bidding strategy for advertisers in order to obtain the maximum number of clicks (or maximize other monotone profit function) subject to a multidimensional budget constraint.

When the budget constraint has constant dimension, we propose a polynomial-time approximation scheme. Otherwise, we present an LP-rounding algorithm that is both fast and simple to implement. While the approximation guarantee for this algorithm is ≈ 0.54, it performs much better in practice. In particular, even for the case of a one-dimensional budget constraint, our algorithm beats the state of the art algorithm (uniform bidding) by 1% to 6%. Conveniently this is achieved by very concise bidding strategies that use only two or three different bids (where uniform bidding uses one). The gap between the performance of our algorithm and the enhanced uniform bidding widens in the case of having a small number (e.g., two) extra dimensions in the budget constraint to guarantee diversity for advertisement targeting. In this case, our algorithms outperforms the state of the art by an average of 5% to 6% (and sometimes up to 9%).

One obvious future direction would be to improve the analysis of our LP rounding. We conjecture that the integrality gap is $1 - \frac{1}{e}$ and that our current rounding approach indeed achieves this approximation factor.

Another possible research direction is to investigate the effect of k (the maximum number of possible bids provided to the advertiser) on the optimum solution of the problem. Currently, we assume that the value of k is given, and based on that we provide a set of—at most—k bids to the advertiser to choose the bid from. However, it is not clear how the value of k itself should be determined. The trade-off here is between simplicity (i.e., lower values k that lead to a more concise set of possible bids) and performance (higher values of k which lead to a broader set of feasible solutions and consequently, improve the optimum solution). One approach to this question would be to examine the value of the optimum solutions for different values of k. A preliminary study of this question for one-dimensional budget constraints (as reported in Figure 1) suggests that the expected marginal gain from allowing one more possible bid (i.e., adding one unit to k) is *diminishing*. In other words, the expected profit is a concave function of k. Also, the reported result suggests that the marginal gains rapidly diminish and most of the gain is captured by going from $k = 1$ to $k = 2$, where we go from "forcing the solution to use the single bid available" to "allowing the solution to optimize over two available bids". Formalizing these observations would be very helpful in providing better insight about the nature of the problem and the challenges we face.

References

[1] Aggarwal, G., Goel, A., Motwani, R.: Truthful auctions for pricing search keywords. In: ACM Conference on Electronic Commerce (EC), pp. 1–7 (2006)

[2] Archak, N., Mirrokni, V., Muthukrishnan, S.: Budget optimization for online campaigns with positive carryover effects. In: Goldberg, P.W. (ed.) WINE 2012. LNCS, vol. 7695, pp. 86–99. Springer, Heidelberg (2012)

[3] Bing Ads. Bing ads intelligence (2013),
http://advertise.bingads.microsoft.com/en-us/
bingads-downloads/bingads-intelligence

[4] Borgs, C., Chayes, J.T., Immorlica, N., Jain, K., Etesami, O., Mahdian, M.: Dynamics of bid optimization in online advertisement auctions. In: World Wide Web, pp. 531–540 (2007)

[5] Devenur, N.R., Hayes, T.P.: The adwords problem: Online keyword matching with budgeted bidders under random permutations. In: ACM Conference on Electronic Commerce (EC), pp. 71–78 (2009)

[6] Dobzinski, S., Lavi, R., Nisan, N.: Multi-unit auctions with budget limits. Games and Economic Behavior 74(2), 486–503 (2012)

[7] Edelman, B., Ostrovsky, M., Schwarz, M.: Internet advertising and the generalized second price auction: Selling billions of dollars worth of keywords. American Economic Review 97(1), 242–259 (2005)

[8] Even-Dar, E., Mirrokni, V.S., Muthukrishnan, S., Mansour, Y., Nadav, U.: Bid optimization for broad match ad auctions. In: World Wide Web, pp. 231–240 (2009)

[9] Feldman, J., Henzinger, M., Korula, N., Mirrokni, V.S., Stein, C.: Online stochastic packing applied to display ad allocation. In: de Berg, M., Meyer, U. (eds.) ESA 2010, Part I. LNCS, vol. 6346, pp. 182–194. Springer, Heidelberg (2010)

[10] Feldman, J., Korula, N., Mirrokni, V., Muthukrishnan, S., Pál, M.: Online ad assignment with free disposal. In: Leonardi, S. (ed.) WINE 2009. LNCS, vol. 5929, pp. 374–385. Springer, Heidelberg (2009)

[11] Feldman, J., Muthukrishnan, S., Pal, M., Stein, C.: Budget optimization in search-based advertising auctions. In: ACM Conference on Electronic Commerce (EC), pp. 40–49 (2007)

[12] Goel, G., Mirrokni, V.S., Paes Leme, R.: Polyhedral clinching auctions and the adwords polytope. In: STOC, pp. 107–122 (2012)

[13] Google Support, Google adwords dynamic search ads (2011),
http://adwords.blogspot.fr/2011/10/
introducing-dynamic-search-ads-beta.html

[14] Google Support. Google adwords automatic bidding tools (2013),
http://support.google.com/adwords/bin/
answer.py?hl=en&answer=2470106

[15] Google Support. Traffic estimator (2013), http://support.google.com/
adwords/bin/answer.py?hl=en&answer=6329

[16] Google Support. Using the bid simulator (2013), http://support.google.com/
adwords/bin/answer.py?hl=en&answer=2470105

[17] Hastad, J.: Clique is hard to approximate within $n^{1-\epsilon}$. Acta Mathematica 182(1) 105–142 (1999)

[18] IAB. Internet advertising bureau 2011 report (2011), http://www.iab.net/media/
file/IAB_Internet_Advertising_Revenue_Report_FY_2011.pdf

[19] Mehta, A., Saberi, A., Vazirani, U.V., Vazirani, V.V.: Adwords and generalized online matching. Journal of ACM 54(5) (2007)

[20] Muthukrishnan, S., Pal, M., Svitkina, Z.: Stochastic models for budget optimization in search-based advertising. Algorithmica 58(4), 1022–1044 (2010)

[21] Rusmevichientong, P., Williamson, D.: An adaptive algorithm for selecting profitable keywords for search-based advertising services. In: ACM Conference on Electronic Commerce (EC), pp. 260–269 (2006)

[22] Varian, H.: Position auctions. Int. J. Industrial Opt. 25(6), 1163–1178 (2007)

[23] Zhou, Y., Chakrabarty, D., Lukose, R.: Budget constrained bidding in keyword auctions and online knapsack problems. In: Papadimitriou, C., Zhang, S. (eds.) WINE 2008. LNCS, vol. 5385, pp. 566–576. Springer, Heidelberg (2008)

Sampling and Representation Complexity of Revenue Maximization

Shaddin Dughmi[1,*], Li Han[1,**], and Noam Nisan[2,***]

[1] University of Southern California
{shaddin,han554}@usc.edu
[2] Hebrew University and Microsoft Research
noam@cs.huji.ac.il

Abstract. We consider (approximate) revenue maximization in mechanisms where the distribution on input valuations is given via "black box" access to samples from the distribution. We analyze the following model: a single agent, m outcomes, and valuations represented as m-dimensional vectors indexed by the outcomes and drawn from an arbitrary distribution presented as a black box. We observe that the number of samples required – the sample complexity – is tightly related to the representation complexity of an approximately revenue-maximizing auction. Our main results are upper bounds and an exponential lower bound on these complexities. We also observe that the computational task of "learning" a good mechanism from a sample is nontrivial, requiring careful use of regularization in order to avoid over-fitting the mechanism to the sample. We establish preliminary positive and negative results pertaining to the computational complexity of learning a good mechanism for the original distribution by operating on a sample from said distribution.

1 Introduction

In the general (quasi-linear, independent-private-value, Bayesian) mechanism design setting, a principal must choose from one from a set A of *outcomes*, and there are n *bidders* each of whom has a *valuation* $v_i : A \to \Re$ mapping outcomes to real values. These valuations are private, and the mechanism designer only knows that each v_i is drawn from a *prior distribution* $\mathcal{D}_i$ on valuations. Based on these distributions, the mechanism designer must design a *mechanism* that determines, for each profile of bidder valuations, an outcome which may be probabilistic – a *lottery* – and a *payment* from each player. The rational behavior of the bidders is captured by two sets of constraints: *Incentive constraints* require that no bidder can improve his expected utility by behaving according to – i.e. "reporting to the mechanism" – another valuation v_i'. *Individual Rationality constraints* require that bidders never lose from participating in the mechanism. Under these two sets of constraints the mechanism designer's goal is to maximize his expected *revenue*.

Myerson's classical work [18] completely solves the problem for the special case of *single parameter* valuations, where each v_i is effectively captured by a scalar. In this

---

* Supported in part by NSF CAREER Award CCF-1350900.
** Supported by NSF grant CCF-1350900.
*** For a full version see "L. Han, S. Dughmi, N. Nisan, Sampling and Representation Complexity of Revenue Maximization, arXiv:1402.4535, 2014".

T.-Y. Liu et al. (Eds.): WINE 2014, LNCS 8877, pp. 277–291, 2014.
© Springer International Publishing Switzerland 2014

case, the optimal mechanism has a very simple form and is deterministic. It turns out that this completely breaks down once we leave the single-parameter settings and it is known that deterministic mechanisms can be significantly inferior to general ones that are allowed to allocate lotteries [4, 11, 16, 17, 19], and that good revenue may require complex mechanisms [14]. Moreover, this is so even in very simple settings such as auctions with a single bidder and two items.

It is well known that even in the general multi-parameter case, the revenue maximizing mechanism is obtained using linear optimization [4]. While this may seem encouraging for both characterization and computation of the optimal mechanism, there is a rub: this LP formulation hides several exponential blowups in the natural parameters in most settings. Two types of such blowups, and how to overcome them, have received considerable attention recently: an exponential blowup in n, the number of bidders, that is a result of the fact that we have variables for each *profile* of valuations (e.g. [1,2,6,8]), and the fact that, in the case of various multi-item auctions, m, the size of the outcome space, is naturally exponential in the number of items (e.g. [7, 10, 12]).

In this paper we study a third type of exponential blowup who's consequences are not yet fully understood: the size of the support of each $\mathcal{D}_i$ – the size of the valuation space – is naturally exponential in the number of outcomes m. Formally, it is often a continuum since a valuation assigns a real value to each alternative, but even once we discretize (as we certainly will have to do for any computational purpose), the valuation space is still exponential in m. Does this exponential blowup necessarily translate to the computational task, or can revenue be maximized in time polynomial in m?

For most bite of our main result, which is negative, we focus on the simplest scenario of this type, one that exhibits only this exponential blowup in the size of the valuation space, and no others. Specifically, we have a *single bidder* bidding for m abstract alternatives in A. For a single bidder, this setting is essentially equivalent[1] to an auction setting studied e.g. in [4, 11] in which A is a set of items for sale, a "unit demand" bidder is interested in acquiring at most a single item and has a potentially different value $v(j)$ for each item $j \in A$. Furthermore, for a single bidder, an auction is just a pricing scheme, giving a *menu* that assigns a price for each possible lottery $(x_1...x_m)$ where $x_j \geq 0$ is the probability of getting item j and $\sum_{j \in A} x_j \leq 1$.

As observed in [4], if $\mathcal{D}$ (the prior distribution over v) happens to have a "small" support then the linear program is small and we are done. However, this is typically not the case: even if we restrict all item values to be 0 or 1 there are 2^m possible valuations and the linear program is exponential. This raises the question of how $\mathcal{D}$ is represented. Sometimes $\mathcal{D}$ admits some special structure — e.g. it may be a product distribution over item values — permitting a succinct representation. In other cases it may come from "nature" and we will, in some sense, have to "learn" $\mathcal{D}$ in order to construct our mechanism. Both of these scenarios can be captured by a black box *sampling* model in which our access to $\mathcal{D}$ is by means of a sequence of samples v, each drawn independently at random from $\mathcal{D}$. Can we design an (approximately) revenue-maximizing auction for $\mathcal{D}$ using a reasonable number of samples?

---

[1] The formal distinction is that in the unit-demand setting, there is special outcome $*$ with fixed value $v(*) = 0$, denoting not allocating any item.

The focus of this paper is the general case in which $\mathcal{D}$ is not necessarily a product distribution. Revenue maximization for product distributions was previously studied by [9, 11] who together achieve a polynomial-time constant-factor approximation, and by [5] who design a quasi-polynomial-time $(1 + \epsilon)$ approximation to the revenue of *deterministic auctions*. It is known, however, that the general case of correlated distributions is harder, e.g. deterministic prices can not provide a constant approximation [4].

The most natural approach for maximizing revenue for a distribution $\mathcal{D}$ given as a black box would be to sample some polynomial number of valuations from it, construct a revenue maximizing auction for this sample, and hope that the constructed auction also has good revenue on the original distribution $\mathcal{D}$. This, however, may fail terribly even for symmetric product distributions as shown in Proposition 3.

The astute reader will recognize this failure as a classic case of over-fitting: the optimal mechanism for the sample is so specifically targeted to the sample that it loses any optimality for the real distribution $\mathcal{D}$. The remedy for such over-fitting is well known: we need to "discourage" such tailoring and encourage "simple" auctions. At this point we need to specify what "simple" auctions are, a question closely related to how auctions are *represented*. The simplest answer is the "menu-complexity" suggested in [14]: we measure the complexity as the number of possible allocations of the auction, i.e. as the number of entries in the menu specifying the auction. More complex representations that may be more succinct for some auctions are also possible. Our lower bounds will apply to any *auction representation language*. Formally, an auction representation language is an arbitrary function that maps binary strings to auctions. The *complexity of an auction* in a given language is just the length of the smallest binary string that is mapped to this auction. Thus for example the menu-size of an auction corresponds to complexity in the representation language where the menu-entries are explicitly represented by listing the probabilities and price for each entry separately.[2]

Our Results

Fixing an auction representation language, we consider the following sample-and-optimize template for revenue maximization that takes into account the complexity of the output auction (in said representation language). The same idea is used in the context of prior-free mechanism design by [3]. In our setting, beyond the dependence on complexity of the auction, the number of samples needs to depend (polynomially) on three other parameters: the number of items m, the required precision ϵ, and the range of the values. Specifically, assume that all valuations in the support of $\mathcal{D}$ lie in the bounded range $1 \le v(j) \le H$ for all j. Since most of the expected value of a valuation may come from events whose probability is $O(1/H)$, it is clear that we will need $\Omega(H)$ samples to even notice these events.[3]

---

[2] Counting bits, we are off from just counting the number of menu entries by a factor of $O(m \log \epsilon)$ where ϵ is the precision in which real numbers are represented. We will focus on exponential versus polynomial complexities, so do not assign much importance to this gap.

[3] This also explains why bounding the range of valuations, as we do, is required for the sampling question to make any sense. Equivalently, we could have instead bounded the variance of $\mathcal{D}$ without significantly changing any of our results.

Sample-and-Optimize Algorithm Template

1. Sample $t = poly(C, m, \epsilon^{-1}, H)$ samples from $\mathcal{D}$.
2. Find an auction of complexity at most C that maximizes (as much as possible) the revenue for the uniform distribution over the sample and output it.

To convert this template to an algorithm, one must specify C and show how to compute an auction of complexity C which achieves high revenue on the sample. (Note that without the complexity bound, even fully maximizing revenue is efficiently done using the basic linear program, but this does not carry-over to complexity-bounded maximization.) Once the complexity is bounded, at least information-theoretically, the "usual" learning-like uniform convergence bounds indeed apply and we have:

Proposition 1. *Fix any auction representation language, and take an algorithm that follows this template and always produces an auction that approximates to within an α factor the optimal revenue from the sample over all auctions of complexity C. Then the produced auction also approximates to within a factor of $(1 - \epsilon)\alpha$ the revenue from the real prior distribution $\mathcal{D}$ over all auctions of complexity C. (see full version)*

Thus we get approximate revenue maximization over all complexity-C auctions. However, if this limited class is inferior to general auctions, this does not yield approximate revenue maximization over all auctions, which is our goal. The following questions thus remain:

1. What is the complexity C required of an auction in order to obtain good revenue? What approximation can we get when we require C to be polynomial in H and m?
2. What is the computational complexity of step 2 of the algorithm template, i.e. of constructively finding a mechanism that maximizes revenue over mechanisms of bounded complexity C?

We provide definitive answers to the first question and preliminary answers to the second. Apriori, it is not even clear that any finite complexity C suffices for getting good revenue (for fixed H and m). Previous work ([12]) implies that arbitrarily good approximations are possible using menu-size complexity that is polynomial in H and exponential in m and for the special case $m = 2$ even poly-logarithmic size in H, [14]. This is done by taking the optimal auction and "rounding" its entries. This is trickier than it may seem since a slight change of probabilities may cause a great change in revenue, so such proofs need to carefully adjust the rounding of probabilities and prices making sure that significant revenue is never lost.[4] We describe a general way to perform this adjustment, allowing us to tighten these results: we get poly-logarithmic dependence in H for general m, stronger bounds for "monotone" valuations, and do it all effectively in a computational sense. Monotone valuations are restricted to have $v(1) \le v(2) \le ... \le v(m)$, and naturally model cases such as values for a sequence of ad-slots or for increasing numbers of items in a multi-unit auction.

---

[4] Technically, there is no countable ϵ-net of auctions in the sense of approximating the revenue for every distribution. Instead, one needs to construct a "one-sided" net.

Theorem 1. *For every distribution $\mathcal{D}$ and every $\epsilon > 0$ there exists an auction with menu-size complexity at most $C = \left(\frac{\log H + \log m + \log \epsilon^{-1}}{\epsilon}\right)^{O(m)}$ whose revenue is at least $(1 - \epsilon)$ fraction of the optimal revenue for $\mathcal{D}$. For the special case of distributions over "monotone" valuations, menu-size complexity of at most $C = m^{O((\log^3 H + \log^2 \epsilon)/\epsilon^2)}$ suffices. Furthermore, in both cases these auctions can be computed in $poly(C, H, \epsilon^{-1}, m)$ time by sampling $poly(C, H, \epsilon^{-1}, m)$ valuations from $\mathcal{D}$.*

So in general a menu of complexity exponential in m suffices. A basic question is whether complexity polynomial in m suffices (in terms of menu-size or perhaps other stronger representation languages). The "usual tricks" suffice to show that an $O(\log H)$-approximation of the revenue is possible with small menus.

Proposition 2. *For every distribution $\mathcal{D}$ there exists an auction with m menu-entries (and with all numbers represented in $O(\log H)$ bits) that extracts $\Omega(1/\log H)$ fraction of the optimal revenue from $\mathcal{D}$. Furthermore, this auction can be computed in polynomial time from $poly(H)$ samples. (see full version)*

Can this be improved? Can we get a constant factor approximation with polynomial-size complexity? Our main result is negative. Previous techniques that separate the revenue of simple auctions from that of general auctions do not suffice for proving an impossibility here for two reasons. First, these bounds only apply to menu-size complexity and not to general auction representations; this is explicit in [14] and implicit in [4].[5] Second, these bounds proceed by giving an upper bound to the revenue that a single menu-entry can extract. Since small menus can extract an $O(1/\log H)$ fraction of the optimum revenue, such techniques can have no implications for sampling complexity since, as mentioned above, $\Omega(H)$ is a trivial lower bound on the sampling complexity. Our main result shows that even for a small range of values H, auctions may need to be exponentially complex in m in order to break the $O\left(\frac{1}{\log H}\right)$ barrier.

Theorem 2. *For every auction representation language and every $1 < H < 2^{m/400}$ there exists a distribution $\mathcal{D}$ on $[1..H]^m$ such that every auction with complexity at most $2^{m/400}$ has revenue that is at most an $O\left(\frac{1}{\log H}\right)$ fraction of the optimal revenue for $\mathcal{D}$.*

Notice that this immediately implies a similar exponential lower bound on the number of samples needed: since we allow any auction description language, simply listing the sample is one such language for which the lower bound holds.

Next, we examine our second question, regarding the computational complexity of "fitting" an auction of low complexity to sampled data. We show that it is NP-hard to compute an approximately optimal auction of a specified menu size.[6]

Theorem 3. *Given as input a sample of valuations and a menu-size C, it is NP-hard to approximate the optimal menu with size C to within any factor better than $1 - \frac{1}{e}\frac{H-1}{H}$.*

---

[5] Since these papers exhibit an explicit distribution providing the separation, the optimal auction can always be specified in some language by just listing the few parameters of said distribution.

[6] Here, we expect stronger auction representation languages to only be harder to deal with.

This hardness result does not preclude a satisfactory answer to our original goal of effectively finding an auction that approximates the revenue also on the original distribution $\mathcal{D}$ since for that it suffices to find a "small" auction with good revenue on the sample, rather than the "smallest" one. Thus a bi-criteria approximation to step 2 suffices, and may be algorithmically easier: find a menu of size $\text{poly}(C, m, H)$ which approximates the revenue of the best menu of size C over a given sample. Whether this bi-criteria problem can be solved in polynomial time is left as our first open problem.

Our second open problem concerns the question of structured distributions, specifically product distributions over item values studied in [5, 9, 11]. Proposition 1 implies that, as these distributions can be succinctly represented, polynomially many samples suffice for finding a nearly optimal auction for product distributions.[7] It is not clear, however, how this can be done algorithmically and whether the simple menu-size auction description language suffices for succinctly representing the (approximately) optimal auction. Constant factor approximation with small menu-size (even deterministic menus) follow from [9, 11], but a $(1 + \epsilon)$-approximation is still open.

2   Preliminaries

2.1   The Model

In the *single-buyer unit-demand mechanism design problem*, or the *pricing problem* for short, we assume that there are m "items" or "outcomes" $[m] = \{1, \ldots, m\}$, and a single risk-neutral buyer equipped with a valuation $v \in \mathbb{R}_+^m$. Additionally, we assume the existence of an additional outcome $*$ for which a buyer has value 0 – e.g. the outcome in which the player receives no item. We assume that v is drawn from a distribution $\mathcal{D}$ supported on some family of valuations $\mathcal{V} \subseteq \mathbb{R}_+^m$.

We adopt the perspective of an auctioneer looking to sell the items in order to maximize his revenue. After soliciting a bid $b \in \mathcal{V}$, the auctioneer chooses an *allocation*, namely a (partial) lottery $x \in \Delta_m = \{x \in \mathbb{R}_+^m : \sum_i x_i \leq 1\}$ over the items, and a *payment* $p \in \mathbb{R}_+$. Formally, the auctioneer's task is to design a *mechanism*, equivalently, an *auction*, (x, p), where $x : \mathcal{V} \to \Delta_m$ maps a player's reported valuation to a lottery on the m items, and $p : \mathcal{V} \to \mathbb{R}_+$ maps the same report to a payment. When each allocation in the range of x is a deterministic choice of an item, we say the mechanism (or auction) is *deterministic*, otherwise it is *randomized*.

To simplify our results, we usually assume that players' valuations lie in a bounded range. Specifically, we require that the support $\mathcal{V}$ of our distribution is contained in $[1, H]^m$, for some finite upper-bound H which may depend on the number of items being sold. Given this assumption, we restrict our attention without loss of generality to mechanisms with payment rules constrained to prices in $[1, H] \cup \{0\}$. Moreover, we assume without loss of generality that $p(v) = 0$ only if $x(p) = \mathbf{0}$.[8]

---

[7] This is directly implied when the item values have finite (polynomial) support; the techniques used in section 4.1 suffice for showing it in general.

[8] An optimal mechanism satisfying these two properties always exists for all the problems we consider.

Whereas our complexity results are independent of the representation of $\mathcal{D}$, our algorithmic results hold in the *black-box model*, in which the auctioneer is given sample access to $\mathcal{D}$, and otherwise knows nothing about $\mathcal{D}$ besides its support $\mathcal{V}$.

2.2 Truthfulness and Menus

We constrain our mechanism (x, p) to be *truthful*: i.e. bidding $b = v$ maximizes the buyer's utility $v \cdot x(b) - p(b)$. The well known characterization below reduces the design of such a mechanism to the design of a *pricing menu*.

Fact 1. *A mechanism (x, p) is truthful if and only if there is a menu $M \subseteq \Delta_m \times \mathbb{R}$ of allocation/price pairs such that $(x(v), p(v)) \in \text{argmax}_{(x,p) \in M}\{v \cdot x - p\}$.*

We adopt the menu perspective through much of this paper, interchangeably referring to a mechanism (aka auction) and its corresponding menu M. When interpreting a menu M as a mechanism, we break ties in $v \cdot x - p$ in favor higher prices. When every allocation in the menu is a deterministic choice of an item, we call M an *item-pricing menu*, otherwise we call it a *lottery-pricing menu*.

We also require our mechanisms to be *individually rational*. To enforce this, we assume that $(0, 0)$ is in every menu. As described in Section 2.1, we usually restrict valuations to $[1, H]^m$ and payments for non-zero lotteries to $[1, H]$. Therefore, we think of a menu as a subset of $\Delta_m \times [1, H]$, and include $(0, 0)$ implicitly.

2.3 Auction Complexity and Benchmarks

Given a mechanism M and valuation v, we use $\text{Rev}(M, v)$ to denote the payment of a buyer with valuation v when participating in the mechanism. Given a distribution $\mathcal{D}$ over valuations, we use $\text{Rev}(M, \mathcal{D}) = \mathbf{E}_{v \sim \mathcal{D}} \text{Rev}(M, v)$ to denote the expected revenue generated by the mechanism when a player is drawn from distribution $\mathcal{D}$. We use $\text{Rev}(\mathcal{D})$ to denote the supremum, over all mechanisms M, of $\text{Rev}(M, \mathcal{D})$. When $\mathcal{M}$ is a family of mechanisms, we use $\text{Rev}(\mathcal{M}, \mathcal{D})$ to denote $\sup_{M \in \mathcal{M}} \text{Rev}(M, \mathcal{D})$.

Recall that a auction description language is just a mapping from binary strings to mechanisms. I.e. it is simply a way of encoding menus in binary strings. The representation complexity of an auction in such a language is simply the length of the shortest string that is mapped to it. For this paper, the only important property of auction description languages is that there are at most 2^C auctions of complexity C. (Of course, in applications we will also worry about its expressive power, its computational difficulty, etc.) The simplest auction description language allows describing an auction by directly listing its menu entries one by one. Each menu entry is composed of $m + 1$ numbers, and if all the numbers can be presented using $O(r)$ bits of precision, then the total complexity of a k-entry auction in this format is $O(kmr)$. In this paper we never need more than $r = O(\log m + \log H + \log \epsilon^{-1})$ bits of precision, so the gap between menu-size (the number of menu entries) and complexity using this language (the total number of bits used in such a description) is not significant.

We use $\text{Rev}_k(\mathcal{D})$ to denote the maximum revenue of a mechanism with complexity at most k. When using menu-size complexity, we say M is a k-menu if $|M| \leq k$, and use $\mathcal{M}_k$ to denote the set of all k-menus, and $\mathcal{M}_\infty$ to denote the set of all menus.

3   Sampling vs. Auction Complexity

3.1   Over Fitting with Complex Auctions

In this subsection we will consider the basic sampling algorithm that makes a small number of samples and optimizes the auction for this sample.

Naive Sample-and-Optimize Algorithm

1. Sample $t = poly(m)$ samples from $\mathcal{D}$.
2. Find an auction that maximizes revenue for the uniform distribution over samples.

We will show that this does not work even for symmetric product distributions. Let $\delta > 0$ be some small constant and let $\mathcal{D}$ be the distribution on valuations where item values are chosen identically and independently at random as follows: with probability δ: $v(j) = 1$; with probability δ/m: $v(j) = 2$; and otherwise: $v(j) = 0$. We will show that optimizing for a sample may give very low revenue on $\mathcal{D}$ itself:

Proposition 3. *Take a polynomial-size sample, with high probability, there is an auction that is optimal for the sample and yet its revenue from $\mathcal{D}$ is $O(\delta)$. (see full version)*

3.2   Uniform Convergence over Simple Auctions

When we limit the "complexity" of the auction that our algorithm is allowed to produce to be significantly smaller than the sample size, we can guarantee that the produced auction approximately maximizes revenue for the original distribution $\mathcal{D}$. Since there can not be too many auctions of low complexity, this follows by a standard application of tail bounds and the union bound as in [3].

Sample-and-Optimize Algorithm Template

1. Sample $t = poly(C, m, \epsilon^{-1}, H)$ samples from $\mathcal{D}$.
2. Output an auction of complexity at most C that approximately maximizes the revenue for the uniform distribution over the sample.

Proposition 1. *Fix any auction representation language, and take an algorithm that follows this template and always produces an auction that approximates to within an α factor the optimal revenue from the sample over all auctions of complexity C. Then the produced auction also approximates to within a factor of $(1 - \epsilon)\alpha$ the revenue from the real prior distribution $\mathcal{D}$ over all auctions of complexity C. (see full version)*

4   Constructions of Simple Approximating Auctions

4.1   From Rounding Lotteries to "Rounding" Auctions

When trying to approximate a given auction, it is natural to simply round all entries in the menu and hope that this does not hurt the revenue significantly. As mentioned in the introduction, this is not trivial since tiny decreases in probabilities or tiny increases in price may be the "last straw" chasing away bidders that made knife's-edge choice of the entry. This subsection shows that, never the less, this may be done with a little further tweaking: once we have a good way to round lotteries we can "round" entire menus, losing an approximation factor that is polynomially related to the rounding error.

Several previous works (e.g. [3, 15]) have considered discretization of pricing mechanisms, most of which operate on item prices and therefore admit simpler "covers" of the space of mecanisms. Recently, [8] applied some of these ideas to lottery pricing, though their lemma is not at the level of generality required for our purposes. In particular, if we use their lemma directly, the additive loss in revenue due to discretization could be ϵH, which cannot guarantee any multiplicative approximation ratio.

Definition 1. *Let V be a set of valuations, and L be a set of lotteries. We say that L ϵ-covers V if for every lottery $x \in \Delta_m$ there exists a lottery $\widetilde{x} \in L$ such that for every $v \in V$ we have that $x \cdot v \geq \widetilde{x} \cdot v \geq (1 - \epsilon)x \cdot v - \epsilon$.*

Lemma 1. *Let L be a set of lotteries that ϵ-covers a set of valuations V, for every menu M there exists a menu $\widetilde{M}$ all of whose entries have lotteries in L and have prices represented in $O(\log \epsilon^{-1} + \log H + \log m)$ bits such that for every $v \in V$ $Rev(\widetilde{M}, v) \geq (1 - \epsilon')Rev(M, v) - \epsilon'$, where $\epsilon' = O(\log H \sqrt{\epsilon})$. Moreover, if the calculation of $\widetilde{x}$ from x is efficient then so is the calculation of $\widetilde{M}$ from M. (see full version)*

4.2 Approximations for General Valuations

So at this point we know that we just need to worry about rounding lotteries. Once we round all values to a small number of discrete values, we will get a small number of lotteries. Unfortunately, we need to use both an additive and multiplicative approximation error: the multiplicative approximation error allows a large additive error when values are close to H; and the additive error saves us from having to approximate multiplicatively very small probabilities. Combining these two notions of error allows us to make do with $O(\log H/\epsilon)$ discrete levels of approximation.

Proposition 4. *Let R_ϵ be the set of real numbers containing zero and all integer powers of $(1 - \epsilon)$ in the range $[\epsilon/(Hm), 1]$, and let L_ϵ be the set of lotteries all of whose entries are in R_ϵ. Then L_ϵ ϵ-covers the set of all valuations $v \in [1, H]^m$. Moreover, calculating $\widetilde{x}$ from x can be done efficiently. (see full version).*

Corollary 1. *There exists an ϵ-cover of the set of all valuations $v : \{1...m\} \to [1, H]$ whose size is $((\log m + \log H + \log \epsilon^{-1})/\epsilon)^m$.*

Corollary 2. *(Part I of theorem 1 from the introduction) For every distribution $\mathcal{D}$ on $[1, H]^m$ and every $\epsilon > 0$ there exists an auction with menu-size complexity at most $C = \left(\frac{\log H + \log m + \log \epsilon^{-1}}{\epsilon}\right)^{O(m)}$ whose revenue is at least $(1 - \epsilon)$ fraction of the optimal revenue for $\mathcal{D}$. Furthermore, this auction can be computed effectively (in polynomial time in its size) from a sample of size $\text{poly}(C, m, H, \epsilon^{-1})$.*

Proof. Combining corollary 1 using $O((\epsilon/\log H)^2)$ in place of ϵ with lemma 1 we get the existence of mechanism with menu-size complexity of $((\log m + \log H)/\epsilon)^{O(m)}$

whose approximation error (both additive and multiplicative) is ϵ. The additive approximation error of the whole mechanism is subsumed by the multiplicative one since optimal revenue is at least 1. We now plug this family of low complexity mechanisms into proposition 1, and obtain the required result, in the information-theoretic sense.

To compute the actual menu, we solve the linear program on the sample (that is of size polynomial in C, thus exponential in m), obtain the optimal mechanism M for the sample, and then round it to a mechanism $\widetilde{M}$ that provides the required approximation for the sample and – since it is of the right complexity – also for the distribution.

4.3   Approximations for Monotone Valuations

In this section, we consider a limited class of valuations and show that for distributions over this class a much smaller complexity is needed. The class we consider fixes an order on items, without loss of generality, the order $1, \ldots, m$. A valuation $v \in [1, H]^m$ is *monotone* if $v_i \leq v_{i+1}$ for $i \in \{1, \ldots, m - 1\}$. Monotone valuations are natural in contexts such as *multi-unit auctions*, where m identical goods are being sold, and an outcome corresponds to the number of goods allocated to the buyer. In this setting, v_i is the player's value for i goods. Monotone valuations then correspond to a free disposal assumption in multi-unit auctions.

Next we show that for monotone valuations, we can find a small ϵ-cover of all lotteries, which implies, using our "Rounding Lotteries to Rounding Auctions" paradigm, small complexity auctions that approximate revenue well for all monotone valuations. This family of auctions has menu-size complexity polynomial in m when ϵ and H are constant, and quasi-polynomial when H is polynomial in m (and ϵ poly-logarithmic).

Theorem 4. *(Part II of theorem 1 from the introduction) If $\mathcal{D}$ is supported on monotone valuations then for every $\epsilon > 0$ there exists a menu M with $C = m^{O(\frac{\log^3 H + \log^2 \epsilon^{-1}}{\epsilon^2})}$ entries (and with all numbers with $O(\log m + \log H + \log \epsilon^{-1})$ bits of precision) such that $Rev(M, \mathcal{D}) \geq (1 - \epsilon)Rev(\mathcal{D})$. Furthermore, this auction can be computed in $poly(C, H, \epsilon^{-1}, m)$ time by sampling $poly(C, H, \epsilon^{-1}, m)$ valuations from $\mathcal{D}$.*

As in the proof of corollary 2, using lemma 1 and proposition 1, this theorem follows from the following lemma (proof in full version):

Lemma 2. *For every ϵ, there is a set of lotteries L whose size is $m^{O((\log H + \log \epsilon^{-1})/\epsilon)}$, that ϵ-covers the set of all monotone valuations with $v : \{1...m\} \to [1, H]$. Moreover, calculating $\widetilde{x}$ from x can be done efficiently.*

5   Lower Bound for Auction Complexity

Before we embark on our lower bound, we note the matching upper bound.

Proposition 2. *For every distribution $\mathcal{D}$ there exists an auction with m menu-entries (and with all numbers represented in $O(\log H)$ bits) that extracts $\Omega(1/\log H)$ fraction of the optimal revenue from $\mathcal{D}$. Furthermore, this auction can be computed in polynomial time from $poly(H)$ samples. (see full version)*

Theorem 2. *For every auction representation language and every* $1 < H < 2^{m/400}$ *there exists a distribution* $\mathcal{D}$ *on* $[1..H]^m$ *such that every auction with complexity at most* $2^{m/400}$ *has revenue that is at most an* $O\left(\frac{1}{\log H}\right)$ *fraction of the optimal revenue for* $\mathcal{D}$.

Proof. We will construct the distribution $\mathcal{D}$ probabilistically. Our starting point will be a fixed baseline distribution $\mathcal{B}$ that takes an "equal revenue" one-dimensional distribution and spreads it symmetrically over a random subset of the items. Each valuation in the support of $\mathcal{B}$ is specified by a set $S \subset \{1..m\}$ of size exactly $k = m/3$ and an integer scale value $1 \leq z \leq \log H$. The valuation will give value 2^z for every item in S and value 1 for every other item. The probability distribution over these is induced by choosing S uniformly at random among sets of size k and choosing z as to obtain an "equal revenue distribution" $Pr[z = x] = 2^{-x}$. We can view this distribution over the v's as choosing uniformly at random from a multi-set V of exactly $\binom{m}{k}(H-1)$ valuations (for every set S of size k we have $H/2$ copies of a valuation with value 2, $H/4$ copies of a valuation with value 4 ... and a single copy of a valuation with value H). The point is that due to symmetry, it can be shown that, just like in the corresponding single dimensional case, $\text{Rev}(\mathcal{B})$ is constant (despite the expected value being $O(\log H)$). This is proven formally in lemma 3 below.

Taking the point of view of $\mathcal{B}$ being a random choice of a valuation from the multi-set V, we will now construct our distribution $\mathcal{D}$ as being a uniform choice over a random subset V' of V, where V' is of size $|V'| = K = 2^{m/100}$. We will now be able to provide two estimates. On one hand, since V' is a random sample from V, we expect that every fixed mechanism will extract approximately the same revenue from $\mathcal{D}$ as from $\mathcal{B}$. This can be shown to hold, w.h.p., simultaneously for *all* mechanisms in a small enough family and thus all mechanisms with sub-exponential complexity can only extract constant revenue. On the other hand, as V' is sparse, w.h.p. it does not contain two valuations whose subsets have a large intersection. This will suffice for extracting at east half of the expected value as revenue, an expected value that is $O(\log H)$. Lemma 4 below proves the former fact and lemma 6 below proves the latter.

Lemma 3. *Let* $\mathcal{B}$ *denote the distribution above then* $\text{Rev}(\mathcal{B}) \leq 2$.

Proof. We will prove this by reduction the the single dimensional case where Myerson's theorem can be used. Let us define the single dimensional distribution $\mathcal{G}$ that gives value 2^x with probability 2^{-x} for $x \in \{1...\log H\}$. The claim is that $Rev(\mathcal{B}) \leq \text{Rev}(\mathcal{G}) \leq 2$. Since $\mathcal{G}$ is single dimensional, the second inequality follows from Myerson's result stating that a single price mechanism maximizes revenue, as it is easy to verify that every possible single price gives revenue of at most 2.

To prove the first claim we build a single-parameter mechanism for $\mathcal{G}$ with the same revenue as a given multidimensional one for $\mathcal{B}$. Given a value 2^x distributed as in $\mathcal{G}$, our mechanism chooses a random subset S of size k and constructs a valuation v by combining the given single-parameter value with this set, so now v is distributed according to $\mathcal{B}$. We run the mechanism that was given to us for $\mathcal{B}$ and when it returns an lottery $a = a(v)$, we sell the item in the single parameter auction with probability $\sum_{j \in S} a_j$, asking for the same payment as asked for the lottery a in the $\mathcal{B}$-auction. Now notice that the same outcome that maximizes utility for v also maximizes utility for the single parameter buyer.

Lemma 4. *Let M be the set of mechanisms with complexity at most $2^{m/400}$ and choose the distribution $\mathcal{D}$ as described above then, w.h.p., $\mathrm{Rev}(\mathcal{M}, \mathcal{D}) \leq 3$.*

Proof. As $|M| \leq 2^{2^{m/400}}$, it follows from the following lemma and union bound.

Lemma 5. *Fix some mechanism M and choose the distribution $\mathcal{D}$ as described above then $Pr[\mathrm{Rev}(M, \mathcal{D}) > 3] \leq exp(-K/H^2) \leq 2^{-2^{m/300}}$.*

Proof. Let $r_M(v)$ be the revenue that M extracts on valuation v. By definition $Rev(M, \mathcal{B}) = E_{v \in V} r_M(v)$ while $Rev(M, \mathcal{D}) = E_{v \in V'} r_M(v)$ (where the distribution is uniform over the multi-sets V and V' respectively). Lemma 3 bounded the former: $Rev(M, \mathcal{B}) \leq 2$. Since we are choosing V' to be a random multi-set of size K and since for all v we have $0 \leq r_M(v) \leq H$ then we can use Chernoff bounds to bound the probability that the expectation of $r_M(v)$ over the sample V' is larger than its expectation over the population V to be $Pr[|E_{v \in V'} r_M(v) - E_{v \in V} r_M(v)| > 1] \leq exp(-K/H^2)$.

Lemma 6. *Choose the distribution $\mathcal{D}$ as described above then, w.h.p, $\mathrm{Rev}(\mathcal{D}) \geq \log H/2$.*

Proof. We will use the following property that holds, w.h.p., for V': for every two different valuations in V' the sets of items S and T associated with them satisfy $|S \cap T| < m/6$. The reason that this property holds is that for any fixed T, since S is a random set of size $m/3$ the probability that $|S \cap T|/|T| \geq 1/2$ is $exp(-|T|) \leq 2^{-m/40}$. Now we can take a union bound over all $K^2 = 2^{m/50}$ possible pairs of S and T.

Using this property of $\mathcal{D}$ here is a mechanism that extracts as revenue at least half of the expected value of v, i.e. at least $(\log H)/2$ revenue: we have a menu entry for each element $v \in V'$. For v that gives value 2^z to the set S, this entry will offer every item in S with probability $1/|S| = 3/m$, and will ask for payment of 2^{z-1} for this lottery. Clearly if v chooses this entry it gets net utility of exactly 2^{z-1}, we need to show that the net utility from any other menu entry is less than this. Observe that v's value from a menu entry that corresponds to a set T is exactly $2^z \cdot |S \cap T|/|T|$ which due to our property is bounded from above by 2^{z-1}.

6   Computational Complexity

In this section, we examine the computational complexity of the algorithmic task associated with Proposition 1 when valuations lie in $[1, H]^m$. We restrict our attention to the menu-complexity model. The computational bottleneck is Step 2 of the algorithm, which computes a C-menu maximizing revenue for the uniform distribution over samples. Specifically, it requires the solution of the following optimization problem $MAXREV$. An instance of $MAXREV$ is given by an integer C and a sample $X = \{v_1, \ldots, v_n\} \subseteq [1, H]^m$. Feasible solutions of $MAXREV$ are menus with at most C entries, and the objective is to maximize revenue for a buyer drawn uniformly from X. We leave essentially open the exact computational complexity of approximating $MAXREV$, yet make some progress by showing the problem APX-hard.

Theorem 3. *Given as input a sample of valuations and a menu-size C, it is NP-hard to approximate the optimal menu with size C to within any factor better than $1 - \frac{1}{e}\frac{H-1}{H}$.*

Proof. We reduce from a promise problem of the NP-hard optimization problem *max cover*. For convenience, we use the equivalent *hitting set* formulation of max cover. The input is a family $\mathcal{S} = \{S_1, \ldots, S_n\}$ of subsets of $[m]$, and an integer k, and the output is a "hitting set" $T \subseteq [m]$ of size at most k maximizing the number of sets $S \in \mathcal{S}$ with which T has a non-empty intersection — we say those sets S are "hit" by T. We use the fact that it is NP-hard to distinguish between instances of hitting set in which the optimal solution hits all sets in $\mathcal{S}$, and instances in which the optimal solution hits less than a $1 - \frac{1}{e} + \epsilon$ fraction of the sets in $\mathcal{S}$, for any constant $\epsilon > 0$ (see Feige [13]).

Given an instance $(\mathcal{S}, k)$ of hitting set, we produce an instance (X, C) of $MAXREV$ as follows. We let $C = k$, and for each $S_i \in \mathcal{S}$ we include a valuation $v_i \in X$ such that $v_i(j) = H$ for $j \in S_i$, and $v_i(j) = 1$ otherwise. If there is a hitting set T of size k which hits every $S_i \in \mathcal{S}$, then the item-pricing C-menu $\{(e_j, H) : j \in T\}$, which prices every item $j \in T$ at H, generates a revenue of H from every valuation $v_i \in X$. On the other hand, we show that if there is a C-menu with average revenue at least $R = H - (\frac{1}{e} - \epsilon)(H - 1)$ over X, then there is a hitting set of size k hitting at least a $\frac{R-1}{H-1} = 1 - \frac{1}{e} + \epsilon$ fraction of the sets in $\mathcal{S}$. Consider such a C-menu $M = \{(x_1, p_1), \ldots, (x_C, p_C)\}$, and draw an item j_t from each lottery x_t in M.[9] Let $T = \{j_1, \ldots, j_C\}$ be the resulting random hitting set of size $\leq C = k$. It suffices to show that T hits at least an $\frac{R-1}{H-1}$ fraction of the sets in $\mathcal{S}$ in expectation.

$$
\begin{aligned}
R = \operatorname*{avg}_{i=1}^{n} \operatorname{Rev}(M, v_i) &\leq \operatorname*{avg}_{i=1}^{n} \max_{t=1}^{C} v_i \cdot x_t && (\text{ by individual rationality }) \\
&= \operatorname*{avg}_{i=1}^{n} \max_{t=1}^{C} [H \cdot x_t(S_i) + 1 \cdot x_t([m] \setminus S_i)] && (\ x_t(S) \text{ denotes } \textstyle\sum_{j \in S} x_t(j)\ ) \\
&\leq \operatorname*{avg}_{i=1}^{n} \max_{t=1}^{C} [H \cdot x_t(S_i) + 1 - x_t(S_i)] && (\text{ because } \textstyle\sum_j x_t(j) \leq 1\ ) \\
&= 1 + (H-1) \operatorname*{avg}_{i=1}^{n} \max_{t=1}^{C} x_t(S_i) \\
&= 1 + (H-1) \operatorname*{avg}_{i=1}^{n} \max_{t=1}^{C} \mathbf{Pr}[j_t \in S_i] && (\text{ because } j_t \sim x_t\ ) \\
&\leq 1 + (H-1) \operatorname*{avg}_{i=1}^{n} \mathbf{Pr}[T \cap S_i \neq \emptyset]
\end{aligned}
$$

The reader might have noticed that step 2 of the 'Sample-and-Optimize' algorithm template, requiring the solution of an instance of $MAXREV$, is too restrictive as stated. An auctioneer may constrain the complexity of his sought mechanism either because it is believed that such a mechanism is approximately optimal[10], or because computational and/or practical considerations limit the auctioneer to only "simple" mechanisms. In both cases, it is perhaps more natural to seek a *bicriteria guarantee*: a mechanism of complexity polynomial in C, m, and $\log H$ which nevertheless approximates the revenue of the best mechanism of complexity C.

To illustrate this idea, consider the following variant of the 'Sample-and-Optimize' algorithm with step 2 replaced by its *bicriteria* version:

1. Sample $t = poly_1(C, m, \epsilon^{-1}, H)$ samples from $\mathcal{D}$;

---

[9] Since our lotteries are partial (i.e. $\sum_j x_t(j) \leq 1$) some of the items j_t may be the "null" item.
[10] For product distributions, such belief can be formally proved.

2. Find an auction of complexity at most $poly_2(C, m, \epsilon^{-1}, \log H)$ that approximates the optimal auction of complexity C on the t samples;

Using the same idea in the proof of Prop 1, we can see that, in order to avoid overfitting for auctions of complexity at most $poly_2(C, m, \epsilon^{-1}, \log H)$, a sample size of $poly_1(C, m, \epsilon^{-1}, H)$ suffices, as long as $poly_1$ is a larger polynomial than $poly_2$. An α-approximation for the bicriteria $MAXREV$ problem implies one in the *black-box* model. We leave the approximability of the bicriteria $MAXREV$ as an open question.

References

1. Alaei, S.: Bayesian combinatorial auctions: Expanding single buyer mechanisms to many buyers. In: Proceedings of the Symposium on Foundations of Computer Science, pp. 512–521 (2011)
2. Alaei, S., Fu, H., Haghpanah, N., Hartline, J., Malekian, A.: Bayesian optimal auctions via multi-to single-agent reduction. In: ACM Conference on Electronic Commerce, p. 17 (2012)
3. Balcan, M.-.F., Blum, A., Hartline, J.D., Mansour, Y.: Mechanism design via machine learning. In: Foundations of Computer Science, pp. 605–614 (2005)
4. Briest, P., Chawla, S., Kleinberg, R., Matthew Weinberg, S.: Pricing randomized allocations. In: Proceedings of the Twenty-First Annual ACM-SIAM Symposium on Discrete Algorithms, pp. 585–597 (2010)
5. Cai, Y., Daskalakis, C.: Extreme-value theorems for optimal multidimensional pricing. In: Proceedings of the Symposium on Foundations of Computer Science, pp. 522–531 (2011)
6. Cai, Y., Daskalakis, C., Matthew Weinberg, S.: An algorithmic characterization of multidimensional mechanisms. In: Proceedings of the ACM Symposium on Theory of Computing, pp. 459–478 (2012)
7. Cai, Y., Daskalakis, C., Matthew Weinberg, S.: Optimal multi-dimensional mechanism design: Reducing revenue to welfare maximization. In: Proceedings of the Symposium on Foundations of Computer Science, pp. 130–139 (2012)
8. Cai, Y., Huang, Z.: Simple and nearly optimal multi-item auctions. In: SODA, pp. 564–577 (2013)
9. Chawla, S., Hartline, J.D., Kleinberg, R.D.: Algorithmic pricing via virtual valuations. In: ACM Conference on Electronic Commerce, pp. 243–251 (2007)
10. Chawla, S., Hartline, J.D., Malec, D.L., Sivan, B.: Multi-parameter mechanism design and sequential posted pricing. In: Proceedings of the 42nd ACM Symposium on Theory of Computing, pp. 311–320 (2010)
11. Chawla, S., Malec, D.L., Sivan, B.: The power of randomness in bayesian optimal mechanism design. In: Proceedings of the 11th ACM Conference on Electronic Commerce (2010)
12. Daskalakis, C., Matthew Weinberg, S.: Symmetries and optimal multi-dimensional mechanism design. In: ACM Conference on Electronic Commerce, pp. 370–387 (2012)
13. Feige, U.: A threshold of ln n for approximating set cover. J. ACM 45(4), 634–652 (1998)
14. Hart, S., Nisan, N.: The menu-size complexity of auctions. In: ACM Conference on Electronic Commerce, p. 565 (2013)
15. Hartline, J.D., Koltun, V.: Near-optimal pricing in near-linear time. In: Dehne, F., López-Ortiz, A., Sack, J.-R. (eds.) WADS 2005. LNCS, vol. 3608, pp. 422–431. Springer, Heidelberg (2005)
16. Manelli, A.M., Vincent, D.R.: Bundling as an optimal selling mechanism for a multiple-good monopolist. Journal of Economic Theory 127(1), 1–35 (2006)

17. Preston McAfee, R., McMillan, J.: Multidimensional incentive compatibility and mechanism design. Journal of Economic Theory 46(2), 335–354 (1988)
18. Myerson, R.: Optimal auction design. Mathematics of Operations Research 6(1), 58–73 (1981)
19. Thanassoulis, J.: Haggling over substitutes. Journal of Economic Theory 117(2), 217–245 (2004)

Bounds on the Profitability of a Durable Good Monopolist

Gerardo Berbeglia[1], Peter Sloan[2], and Adrian Vetta[3]

[1] Melbourne Business School, The University of Melbourne
g.berbeglia@mbs.edu
[2] Department of Mathematics and Statistics, McGill University
ptrsln@gmail.com
[3] Department of Mathematics and Statistics and School of Computer Science,
McGill University
vetta@math.mcgill.ca

Abstract. A durable good is a long-lasting good that can be consumed repeatedly over time, and a duropolist is a monopolist in the market of a durable good. Theoretically, less is known about durable goods than their more well-studied counterparts, consumable and perishable goods. It was quite startling, therefore, when Ronald Coase (1972) conjectured that a duropolist has no monopoly power at all! Specifically, a duropolist who lacks commitment power cannot sell the good above the competitive price if the time between periods approaches zero. The Coase conjecture was first proved by Gul et al. (1986) under an infinite time horizon model with non-atomic consumers. Remarkably, the situation changes dramatically for atomic consumers and an infinite time horizon. Bagnoli et al. (1989) showed the existence of a subgame perfect Nash equilibrium where the duropolist extracts all the consumer surplus, provided the discount factor is large enough. Thus, for atomic consumers, the duropolist may have perfect price discriminatory power! Observe that, in these cases, duropoly profits are either arbitrarily smaller or arbitrarily larger than the corresponding static monopoly profits – the profit a monopolist for an equivalent consumable good could generate. Neither situation accords in practice with the profitability of durable good producers. Indeed we show that the results of Gul et al. (1986) and Bagnoli et al. (1989) are driven by the infinite time horizons. For finite time horizons, duropoly profits for any equilibrium satisfying the standard skimming property closely relate to static monopoly profits. In particular, for atomic agents, we prove that duropoly profits are always at least as large as static monopoly profits, but never exceed double the static monopoly profits.

1 Our Results

Bagnoli et al. (1989) studied very small examples of the durable good monopoly problem with finite time horizon and atomic consumers. They showed that in such games with two or three consumers, it is possible to obtain subgame perfect equilibria where the duropolist extracts more revenue than the static price strategy. Several questions arise immediately from their work. Does this phenomenon

T.-Y. Liu et al. (Eds.): WINE 2014, LNCS 8877, pp. 292–293, 2014.
© Springer International Publishing Switzerland 2014

arise for more natural games where the number of consumers and the number of time periods is much larger than three? If so, how would a duropolist actually compute a profit maximizing strategy? Finally, from an optimization perspective, can we quantify *exactly* how much more profit a duropolist can obtain at equilibria in comparison to a static monopolist?

Our main contributions is to answer those three questions. To achieve this, we first characterize the class of subgame perfect equilibria that satisfy the standard skimming property: high-value consumers buy before lower-valued consumers. Our main result is then that, at equilibria, duropoly profits are *at least* static monopoly profits but *at most twice* static monopoly profits, regardless of the number of consumers, their values, and the number of time periods. We also prove that this factor two bound is tight. To conclude the paper, we examine subgame perfect equilibria in the absence of the skimming property. We provide the first example of a subgame perfect equilibrium in which the skimming-property does not hold. Furthermore, we conjecture that amongst all equilibria that maximize duropoly profits at least one satisfies the skimming property. We prove this conjecture is true for the case of two time periods.

We believe that our results shed light into this classical problem in at least three ways. First, this is the first theoretical result that concurs with the practical experience that duropolists and static monopolists have comparable profitability. Second, our result shows that a duropolist can obtain at least half the optimum profit by mimicking a static monopolist via a price commitment strategy. From a practical perspective this is important because a price commitment strategy can generally be implemented by the duropolist very easily. Finally, the standard view in the literature is that the surprising and well-known result of Bagnoli et al. (1989), namely that the duropolist can extract all consumer surplus, is due to the assumption of atomic consumers. Our results showed that their result is, in fact, driven by the infinite time horizon. For finite time horizons, the power of a duropolist is limited.

A full version of this paper is available at http://arxiv.org/abs/1409.7979

Acknowledgements. This work was partially supported by an NSERC posdoctoral fellowship award. This support is gratefully acknowledged. We are very grateful to Juan Ortner and Sven Feldmann for their helpful comments and suggestions. The authors are also very grateful to an anonymous conference referee for suggestions that greatly simplified the proof of Theorem 4.4.

References

Bagnoli, M., Salant, S.W., Swierzbinski, J.E.: Durable-goods monopoly with discrete demand. The Journal of Political Economy 97, 1459–1478 (1989)

Coase, R.H.: Durability and monopoly. Journal of Law and Economics 15, 143–149 (1972)

Gul, F., Sonnenschein, H., Wilson, R.: Foundations of dynamic monopoly and the coase conjecture. Journal of Economic Theory 39, 155–190 (1986)

To Save Or Not To Save: The Fisher Game

Ruta Mehta[1], Nithum Thain[2], László A. Végh[3], and Adrian Vetta[4]

[1] College of Computing, Georgia Institute of Technology
rmehta@cc.gatech.edu
[2] Department of Mathematics and Statistics, McGill University
nithum@gmail.com
[3] London School of Economics
L.Vegh@lse.ac.uk
[4] Department. of Mathematics and Statistics, and School of Computer Science,
McGill University
vetta@math.mcgill.ca

Abstract. We examine the Fisher market model when buyers, as well as sellers, have an intrinsic value for money. We show that when the buyers have oligopsonistic power they are highly incentivized to act strategically with their monetary reports, as their potential gains are unbounded. This is in contrast to the bounded gains that have been shown when agents strategically report utilities [5]. Our main focus is upon the consequences for social welfare when the buyers act strategically. To this end, we define the *Price of Imperfect Competition (PoIC)* as the worst case ratio of the welfare at a Nash equilibrium in the induced game compared to the welfare at a Walrasian equilibrium. We prove that the PoIC is at least $\frac{1}{2}$ in markets with CES utilities with parameter $0 \leq \rho \leq 1$ – this includes the classes of Cobb-Douglas and linear utility functions. Furthermore, for linear utility functions, we prove that the PoIC increases as the level of competition in the market increases. Additionally, we prove that a Nash equilibrium exists in the case of Cobb-Douglas utilities. In contrast, we show that Nash equilibria need not exist for linear utilities. However, in that case, good welfare guarantees are still obtained for the best response dynamics of the game.

1 Introduction

General equilibrium is a fundamental concept in economics, tracing back to 1872 with the seminal work of Walras [20]. Traditionally, the focus has been upon *perfect competition*, where the number of buyers and sellers in the market are so huge that the contribution of any individual is infinitesimal. In particular, the participants are *price-takers*.

In practice, however, this assumption is unrealistic. This observation has motivated researchers to study markets where the players have an incentive to act strategically. A prominent example is the seminal work of Shapely and Shubik [17]. They defined *trading post games* for exchange markets and examined whether Nash equilibria there could implement competitive equilibrium prices

T.-Y. Liu et al. (Eds.): WINE 2014, LNCS 8877, pp. 294–307, 2014.
© Springer International Publishing Switzerland 2014

and allocations. Another example, and a prime motivator of our research, is the Cournot-Walras market model introduced by Codognato and Gabszewicz [6] and Gabszewicz and Michel [10], which extends oligopolistic competition into the Arrow-Debreu setting. The importance of this model was demonstrated by Bonniseau and Florig [2] via a connection, in the limit, to traditional general equilibria models under the standard economic technique of agent *replication*. More recently, in the computer science community, Babaioff et al [3] extended Hurwicz's framework [12] to study the welfare of Walrasian markets acting through an auction mechanism.

Our interest is in analyzing the robustness of the pricing mechanism against strategic manipulation. Specifically, our primary goal is to quantify the loss in social welfare due price-making rather than price-taking behaviour. To do this, we define the *Price of Imperfect Competition (PoIC)* as the ratio of the social welfare at the worst Nash equilibrium to the social welfare at the perfectly-competitive Walrasian equilibrium.

Two remarks are pertinent here. First, we are interested in changes in the welfare produced by the market mechanism under the two settings of price-takers and price-makers. We are not interested in comparisons with the optimum social welfare, which requires the mechanism to possess the unrealistic power to perform total welfare redistribution. In particular, we are not concerned here with the *Price of Anarchy* or *Price of Stability*. Interestingly, though, the groundbreaking Price of Anarchy results of Johari and Tzitsiklis [15] on the proportional allocation mechanism for allocating one good (bandwidth) can be seen as the first Price of Imperfect Competition results. This is because in their setting the proportional allocation mechanism will produce optimal allocations in non-stategic settings; in contrast, for our markets, Walrasian equilibrium can be arbitrarily poor in comparison to optimal allocations.

Second, in some markets the Price of Imperfect Competition may actually be larger than one. Thus, strategic manipulations by the agents can lead to improvements in social welfare! Indeed, we will discuss examples where the social welfare increases by an arbitrarily large factor when the agents act strategically.

In this paper, we analyze the Price of Imperfect Competition in Fisher markets with strategic buyers, a special case of the Cournot-Walras model. This scenario models the case of an oligopsonistic market, where the price-making power lies with the buyers rather than the sellers (as in an oligopoly).[1] Adsul et al. [1] study Fisher markets where buyers can lie about their preferences. They gave a complete characterization of its symmetric Nash equilibria (SNE) and showed that market equilibrium prices can be implemented at one of the SNE. Later Chen et. al. [5] studied *incentive ratios* in such markets to show that a buyer can gain no more than twice by strategizing in markets with linear, Leontief and Cobb-Douglas utility functions. In upcoming work, Branzei et al [4] study the Price of Anarchy in the game of Adsul et al. and prove polynomial lower and

---

[1] The importance of oligopsonies was recently highlighted by the price-fixing behaviour of massive technology companies in San Francisco.

upper bounds for it. Furthermore, they show Nash equilibria exist for linear, Leontieff, and Cobb-Douglas utilities.

In the above games (and the Fisher model itself), only the sellers have an intrinsic utility for money. In contrast, we postulate that buyers (and not just sellers) have utility for money. Thus, buyers may also benefit by saving money for later use. This incentivizes buyers to withhold money from the market. This defines our *Fisher Market Game*, where agents strategize on the amount of money they wish to spend, and obtain utility one from each unit of saved money. Contrary to the bound of two on gains when strategizing on utility functions [5], we observe that strategizing on money may facilitate unbounded gains (see the full paper). These incentives can induce large variations between the allocations produced at a Market equilibrium and at a Nash equilibrium. Despite this, we prove the Price of Imperfect Competition is at least $\frac{1}{2}$ for Fisher markets when the buyers' utility functions belong to the utililty class of Constant Elasticity of Substitution (CES) with the weak gross substitutability property – this class includes linear and Cobb-Douglas functions.

1.1 Overview of Paper

In Section 2, we define the Fisher Game, give an overview of CES utility functions, and present our welfare metrics. In Section 3, we prove that Price of Imperfect Competition is at least $\frac{1}{2}$, for CES utilities which satisfy the weak gross substitutability property. In Section 4, we apply the economic technique of replication to demonstrate that, for linear utilities, the PoIC bound improves as the level of competition in the market increases. In Section 5, we turn our attention to the question of existence of Nash equilibria. We establish that Nash equilibria exist for the subclass of Cobb-Douglas utilities. However, they need not exist for all CES utilities. In particular, Nash equilibria need not exist for linear utilities. To address this possibility of non-existence, in Section 6, we examine the dynamics of the linear Fisher Game and provide logarithmic welfare guarantees.

2 Preliminaries

We now define the Fisher market model and the corresponding game where agents strategize on how much money to spend. We require the following notation. Vectors are shown in bold-face letters, and are considered as column vectors. To denote a row vector we use $\boldsymbol{x}^T$. The ith coordinate of $\boldsymbol{x}$ is denoted by x_i, and $\boldsymbol{x}_{-i}$ denotes the vector $\boldsymbol{x}$ with the ith coordinate removed.

2.1 The Fisher Market

A Fisher market $\mathcal{M}$, introduced by Irving Fisher in his 1891 PhD thesis, consists of a set $\mathcal{B}$ of buyers and and a set $\mathcal{G}$ of divisible goods (owned by sellers). Let $n = |\mathcal{B}|$ and $g = |\mathcal{G}|$. Buyer i brings m_i units of money to the market and wants to buy a bundle of goods that maximizes her utility. Here, a non-decreasing, concave function $U_i : \mathbb{R}_+^g \to \mathbb{R}_+$ measures the utility she obtains from a bundle of goods. Without loss of generality, the aggregate quantity of each good is one.

Given prices $\boldsymbol{p} = (p_1, \ldots, p_g)$, where p_j is price of good j, each buyer demands a utility maximizing (an optimal) bundle that she can afford. The prices $\boldsymbol{p}$ are said to be a *market equilibrium* (ME) if agents can be assigned an optimal bundle such that demand equals supply, *i.e.* the market clears. Formally, let x_{ij} be the amount of good j assigned to buyer i. So $\boldsymbol{x}_i = (x_{i1}, \ldots, x_{ig})$ is her bundle. Then,

1. Supply = Demand: $\forall j \in \mathcal{G}$, $\sum_i x_{ij} = 1$ whenever $p_j > 0$.
2. Utility Maximization: $\boldsymbol{x}_i$ is a solution of $\max U_i(\boldsymbol{z})$ s.t $\sum_j p_j z_{ij} \leq m_i$.

We denote by y_{ij} the amount of money player i invests in item j after prices are set. Thus $y_{ij} = p_j x_{ij}$. Equivalently y_{ij} can be thought of as player i's demand for item j in monetary terms.

Utility Functions
An important sub-class of Fisher markets occurs when we restrict utility functions to what are known as *Constant Elasticity of Substitution (CES)* utilities [18]. These functions have the form:

$$U_i(\boldsymbol{x}_i) = \left(\sum_j u_{ij} x_{ij}^\rho\right)^{\frac{1}{\rho}}$$

for some fixed $\rho \leq 1$ and some coefficients $u_{ij} \geq 0$. The elasticity of substitution for these markets are $\frac{1}{1-\rho}$. Hence, for $\rho = 1$, *i.e.* linear utilities, the goods are perfect substitutes; for $\rho \to -\infty$, the goods are perfect complements. As $\rho \to 0$, we obtain the well-known Cobb-Douglas utility function:

$$U_i(\boldsymbol{x}_i) = \prod_j x_{ij}^{u_{ij}}$$

where each $u_{ij} \geq 0$ and $\sum_j u_{ij} = 1$. In this paper, we will focus on the cases of $0 < \rho \leq 1$ and the case $\rho \to 0$. These particular markets satisfy the property of *weak gross substitutability*, meaning that increasing the price of one good cannot decrease demand for other goods. It is also known that for these particular markets, one can determine the market prices and allocations by solving the Eisenberg-Gale convex program (see [8], [9], [14]):

$$\max \left(\sum_i m_i \log U_i(\boldsymbol{x}_i) : \sum_i x_{ij} \leq 1, \forall j; \ x_{ij} \geq 0, \forall i, j.\right) \tag{1}$$

2.2   The Fisher Game

An implicit assumption within the Fisher market model is that money has an intrinsic value *to the sellers*, stemming from its potential use outside of the market or at a later date. Thus, money is not just a numéraire. We assume this intrinsic value applies to all market participants including the buyers. This assumption induces a strategic game in which the buyers may have an incentive to save some of their money.

This *Fisher Game* is a special case of the general Cournot-Walras game introduced by Codognato, Gabszewicz, and Michel ([6], [10]). Here the buyers can choose some strategic amount of money $s_i < m_i$ to bring to the market, which will affect their budget constraint. They gain utility both from the resulting market equilibria (with s_i substituted for m_i) and from the money they withhold from the market. Observe, in the Fisher market model, the sellers have no value for the goods in the market. Thus, in the corresponding game, they will place all their goods on sale as their only interest is in money. (Equivalently, we may assume the sellers are non-strategic.)

Thus, we are in an oligopsonistic situation where buyers have indirect price-making power. The set of strategies available to buyer i is $M_i = \{s \geq 0 \mid s \leq m_i\}$. When each buyer decides to spend $s_i \in M_i$, then $\boldsymbol{p}(\boldsymbol{s})$ and $\boldsymbol{x}(\boldsymbol{s})$ are the prices and allocations, respectively, produced by the Fisher market mechanism. These can be determined from the Eisenberg-Gale program (1) by substituting s_i for m_i. Thus, total payoff to buyer i is

$$T_i(\boldsymbol{s}) = U_i(\boldsymbol{x}_i(\boldsymbol{s})) + (m_i - s_i) \tag{2}$$

Our primary tool to analyze the Fisher Game is via the standard solution concept of a Nash equilibrium. A strategy profile $\boldsymbol{s}$ is said to be a *Nash equilibrium* if no player gains by deviating unilaterally. Formally, $\forall i \in \mathcal{B}$, $T_i(\boldsymbol{s}) \geq T_i(s', \boldsymbol{s}_{-i})$, $\forall s' \in M_i$. For the market game defined on market $\mathcal{M}$, let $NE(\mathcal{M})$ denote its set of NE strategy profiles.

The incentives in the Fisher Game can be high. In particular, in the full paper, we show that for any $L \geq 0$, there is a market with linear utility functions where an agent improve his payoff by a multiplicative factor of L by acting strategically.

The Price of Imperfect Competition

The social welfare of a strategy is the aggregate payoff of both buyers and sellers. At a state $\boldsymbol{s}$, with prices $\boldsymbol{p} = \boldsymbol{p}(\boldsymbol{s})$ and allocations $\boldsymbol{x} = \boldsymbol{x}(\boldsymbol{s})$, the social welfare is:

$$\mathcal{W}(\boldsymbol{s}) = \sum_{i \in \mathcal{B}} (U_i(\mathbf{x_i}) + m_i - s_i) + \sum_{j \in \mathcal{G}} p_j = \sum_{i \in \mathcal{B}} U_i(\mathbf{x_i}) + \sum_{i \in \mathcal{B}} m_i \tag{3}$$

Note, here, that the cumulative payoff of sellers is $\sum_{j \in \mathcal{G}} p_j = \sum_{i \in \mathcal{B}} s_i$.

The focus of this paper is how strategic manipulations of the market mechanism affect the overall social welfare. Thus, we must compare the social welfare of the strategic Nash equilibrium to that of the unstrategic market equilibrium where all buyers simply put all of their money onto the market. This latter equilibrium is the *Walrasian equilibrium (WE)*. This comparison gives rise to a welfare ratio, which we term the *Price of Imperfect Competition (PoIC)*, the ratio of the minimum welfare amongst strategic Nash equilibria in the market game to the welfare of the unstrategic Walrasian equilibrium. Formally, for a given market $\mathcal{M}$,

$$\text{PoIC}(\mathcal{M}) = \min_{s \in NE(\mathcal{M})} \frac{\mathcal{W}(s)}{\mathcal{W}(m)}$$

Thus the Price of Imperfect Competition is a measure of how robust, with respect to social welfare, the market mechanism is against oligopsonist behaviour. Observe that the Price of Imperfect Competition could be either greater or less than 1. Indeed, in the full paper, we show that a Nash Equilibrium may produce arbitrarily higher welfare than a Walrasian Equilibrium. Of course, one may expect that welfare falls when the mechanism is gamed and we do present an example in the full paper where the welfare at a Nash Equilibrium is slightly lower than at the Walrasian Equilibrium. This leads to the question of whether the welfare at a Nash can be much worse than at a market equilibrium. We will show that the answer is no; a Nash always produces at least a constant factor of the welfare of a market equilibrium.

3   Bounds on the Price of Imperfect Competition

In this section we establish bounds on the PoIC for the Fisher Game for CES utilities with $0 < \rho \leq 1$ and for Cobb-Douglas utilities. The example discussed above shows that there is no upper bound on PoIC for the Fisher Game. Thus, counterintuitively, even for linear utilities, it may be extremely beneficial to society if the players are strategic.

In the rest of this section, we demonstrate a lower bound of $\frac{1}{2}$ on the PoIC.

Consider a market with Cobb-Douglas or CES utility functions (where $0 < \rho \leq 1$). The key to proving the factor $\frac{1}{2}$ lower bound on the PoIC is the following lemma showing the monotonicity of prices.

Lemma 1. *Given two strategic allocations of money* $\boldsymbol{s}^* \leq \boldsymbol{s}$, *then the corresponding equilibrium prices satisfy* $\boldsymbol{p}^* \leq \boldsymbol{p}$, *where* $\boldsymbol{p}^* = \boldsymbol{p}(\boldsymbol{s}^*)$ *and* $\boldsymbol{p} = \boldsymbol{p}(\boldsymbol{s})$.

Proof. We break the proof up into three classes of utility function.
(i) **Cobb-Douglas Utilities**
The case of Cobb-Douglas utility functions is simple. To see this, recall a result of Eaves [7]. He showed that, when buyer i spends s_i, the prices and allocations for the Fisher market are given by

$$p_j = \sum_i u_{ij} s_i \qquad x_{ij} = \frac{u_{ij} s_i}{\sum_k u_{kj} s_k} \tag{4}$$

It follows that if strategic allocations of money increase, then so must prices.

(ii) **CES Utilities with** $0 < \rho < 1$
Recall that market equilibria for CES Utilities can be calculated via the Eisenberg-Gale convex program (1). From the KKT conditions of this program, where p_j is the dual variable of the budget constraint, we observe that:

$$\forall j, \qquad p_j > 0 \Rightarrow \sum_i x_{ij} = 1$$
$$\forall (i,j), \qquad \frac{s_i u_{ij}}{U_i(x)^\rho x_{ij}^{1-\rho}} \leq p_j \quad \text{and} \quad x_{ij} > 0 \Rightarrow \frac{s_i u_{ij}}{U_i(x)^\rho x_{ij}^{1-\rho}} = p_j \tag{5}$$

Claim. If players have CES utilities with $0 < \rho < 1$ and $s \geq 0$, then $x_{ij} > 0$, $\forall(i, j)$ with $u_{ij} > 0$.

Proof. Consider the derivative of U_i with respect to x_{ij} as $x_{ij} \to 0$:

$$\lim_{x_{ij} \to 0} \frac{\partial U_i(\boldsymbol{x}_i)}{\partial x_{ij}} = \lim_{x_{ij} \to 0} \frac{u_{ij} U_i(\boldsymbol{x}_i)^{1-\rho}}{x_{ij}^{1-\rho}} = +\infty \qquad (6)$$

The claim follows since $p_j \leq \sum_i s_i$ and is, thus, finite. □

We may now proceed by contradiction. Suppose $\exists k$ s.t. $p_k < p_k^*$. Choose a good j such that $\frac{p_j}{p_j^*}$ is minimal and therefore less than 1, by assumption. Take any player i such that $u_{ij} > 0$. By the above claim, we have $x_{ij}, x_{ij}^* > 0$. Consequently, by the KKT conditions (5), we have:

$$\frac{u_{ij}}{p_j x_{ij}^{1-\rho}} = \frac{U_i(\boldsymbol{x}_i)^\rho}{s_i} \quad \text{and} \quad \frac{u_{ij}}{p_j^* x_{ij}^{*1-\rho}} = \frac{U_i(\boldsymbol{x}_i^*)^\rho}{s_i^*} \qquad (7)$$

Taking a ratio gives:

$$\frac{p_j x_{ij}^{1-\rho}}{p_j^* x_{ij}^{*1-\rho}} = \frac{U_i(\boldsymbol{x}_i^*)^\rho s_i}{U_i(\boldsymbol{x}_i)^\rho s_i^*} \qquad (8)$$

Indeed, this equation also holds for every good $t \in \mathcal{G}$ with $u_{it} > 0$. Next consider the following two cases:

Case 1: $x_{ij} \leq x_{ij}^*$ for some player i.
From (8) we must then have that $U_i(\boldsymbol{x}_i) > U_i(\boldsymbol{x}_i^*)$. However, by the minimality of $\frac{p_j}{p_j^*}$, and since (8) holds for every $t \in \mathcal{G}$ with $u_{it} > 0$, we obtain $x_{it} \leq x_{it}^*$ for all such t. This implies $U_i(\boldsymbol{x}_i) \leq U_i(\boldsymbol{x}_i^*)$, a contradiction.

Case 2: $x_{ij} > x_{ij}^*$ for every player i.
Since $p_j^* > p_j$, we must have $p_j^* > 0$. By (5) it follows that $\sum_i x_{ij}^* = 1$. But now we obtain the contradiction that demand must exceed supply as $\sum_i x_{ij} > \sum_i x_{ij}^* = 1$.

(iii) Linear Utilities
We begin with some notation. Let $S_i = \{j \in \mathcal{G} : x_{ij} > 0\}$ be the set of goods purchased by buyer i at strategy s. Let $\beta_{ij} = \frac{u_{ij}}{p_j}$ be the *rate-of-return* of good j for buyer i at prices $\mathbf{p}$. Let $\beta_i = \max_{j \in \mathcal{G}} \beta_{ij}$ be the *bang-for-buck* buyer i can obtain at prices $\mathbf{p}$. It can be seen from the KKT conditions of the Eisenberg-Gale program (1) that at $\{\mathbf{p}, \mathbf{x}\}$, every good $j \in S_i$ will have a rate-of-return equal to the bang-for-buck (see, for example, [19]). Similarly, let S_i^*, β_i^* be correspondingly defined for strategy s^*.

Note that, assuming for each good j, $\exists i$, $u_{ij} > 0$, we have that $\mathbf{p}, \mathbf{p}^* > 0$. Thus, we can partition the goods into groups based on the *price ratios* $\frac{p_j^*}{p_j}$. Suppose there are k distinct price ratios over all the goods (thus $k \leq g$), then partition the goods into k groups, say $\mathcal{G}_1, \ldots, \mathcal{G}_k$ such that all the goods in a group have the same ratio. Let the ratio in group j be λ_j and let $\lambda_1 < \lambda_2 < \cdots < \lambda_k$. Thus $\mathcal{G}_1$ are the goods whose prices have fallen the most (risen the least) and $\mathcal{G}_k$ are the goods whose prices have fallen the least (risen the most).

Let $\mathcal{I}_k = \{i : \exists j \in \mathcal{G}_k, x_{ij} > 0\}$ and $\mathcal{I}_k^* = \{i : \exists j \in \mathcal{G}_k, x_{ij}^* > 0\}$. Thus $\mathcal{I}_k$ and $\mathcal{I}_k^*$ are the collections of buyers that purchase goods in $\mathcal{G}_k$ in each of the allocations. Take any buyer $i \in \mathcal{I}_k^*$; so there is some good $j \in S_i^* \cap \mathcal{G}_k$.

If $S_i \cap \bigcup_{\ell=1}^{k-1} \mathcal{G}_\ell \neq \emptyset$ then buyer i would not desire good j at prices p_j^*. To see this, take a good $j' \in S_i \cap \bigcup_{\ell=1}^{k-1} \mathcal{G}_\ell$. Then $\beta_{ij'} = \beta_i \geq \beta_{ij}$. Therefore

$$
\begin{aligned}
\beta_i^* \geq \frac{u_{ij'}}{p_{j'}^*} &\geq \frac{u_{ij'}}{\lambda_{k-1} \cdot p_{j'}} > \frac{u_{ij'}}{\lambda_k \cdot p_{j'}} \\
&= \frac{1}{\lambda_k} \cdot \frac{u_{ij'}}{p_{j'}} \geq \frac{1}{\lambda_k} \cdot \frac{u_{ij}}{p_j} \\
&= \frac{u_{ij}}{p_j^*} = \beta_i^*
\end{aligned}
$$

This contradiction tells us that $S_i \subseteq \mathcal{G}_k$ and $\mathcal{I}_k^* \subseteq \mathcal{I}_k$. It follows that $\cup_{i \in \mathcal{I}_k^*} S_i \subseteq \mathcal{G}_k$. Putting this together, we obtain that

$$
\sum_{i \in \mathcal{I}_k^*} s_i \leq \sum_{i \in \mathcal{I}_k} s_i \leq \sum_{j \in \mathcal{G}_k} p_j \tag{9}
$$

Now recall that all goods must be sold by the market mechanism (as $\boldsymbol{p}, \boldsymbol{p}^* > 0$). Thus the buyers $\mathcal{I}_k^*$ must be able to afford all of the goods in $\mathcal{G}_k$. Thus

$$
\sum_{i \in \mathcal{I}_k^*} s_i^* \geq \sum_{j \in \mathcal{G}_k} p_j^* = \lambda_k \cdot \sum_{j \in \mathcal{G}_k} p_j \tag{10}
$$

But $s_i^* \leq s_i$ for all i. Consequently, Inequalities (9) and (10) imply that $\lambda_k \leq 1$. Thus no price in $\boldsymbol{p}^*$ can be higher than in $\boldsymbol{p}$. $\qquad \square$

First we use Lemma 1 to provide lower bounds on the individual payoffs.

Lemma 2. *Let s_i be a best response for agent i against the strategies s_{-i}. Then $T_i(s) \geq \max(\hat{U}_i, m_i)$, where $\hat{U}_i$ is her utility at the Walrasian equilibrium.*

Proof. Clearly $T_i(s) \geq m_i$, otherwise player i could save all her money and achieve a payoff of m_i. For $T_i(s) \geq \hat{U}_i$, let $\boldsymbol{p} = \boldsymbol{p}(\boldsymbol{m})$ and $\boldsymbol{x} = \boldsymbol{x}(\boldsymbol{m})$ be the prices and allocation at Walrasian equilibrium. If buyer i decides to spend all his money when the others play s_{-i}, the resulting equilibrium prices will be less than $\boldsymbol{p}$, by Lemma 1. Therefore, she can afford to buy bundle $\boldsymbol{x}_i$. Thus, her best response payoff must be at least $\hat{U}_i$. $\qquad \square$

It is now easy to show the lower bound on the Price of Imperfect Competition.

Theorem 1. *In the Fisher Game with Cobb-Douglas or CES utilities with $0 < \rho \leq 1$, we have PoIC $\geq \frac{1}{2}$. That is, $\mathcal{W}(\boldsymbol{s}^*) \geq \frac{1}{2}\mathcal{W}(\boldsymbol{m})$, for any Nash equilibrium $\boldsymbol{s}^*$.*

Proof. Let $p^* = p(s^*)$ and $x^* = x(s^*)$. Let p and x be the Walrasian equilibrium prices and allocations, respectively. At the Nash equilibrium s^* we have $T_i(s^*) \geq \max(m_i, U_i(x_i))$ for each player i, by Lemma 2. Thus, we obtain:

$$2 \sum_i T_i(s^*) \geq \sum_i U_i(x_i) + \sum_i m_i \tag{11}$$

Therefore $\mathcal{W}(s^*) \geq \frac{1}{2}\mathcal{W}(m)$, as desired.   □

4   Social Welfare and the Degree of Competition

In this section, we examine how the welfare guarantee improves with the degree of competition in the market. To model the degree of competition, we apply a common technique in the economics literature, namely *replication* [17]. In a replica economy, we take each buyer type in the market and make N duplicates (the budgets of each duplicate is a factor N smaller than that of the original buyer). The *degree of competition* in the resultant market is N. We now consider the Fisher Game with linear utility functions and show how the lower bound on Price of Imperfect Competition improves with N.

Theorem 2. *Let s^* be a NE in a market with degree of competition N. Then*

$$\mathcal{W}(s^*) \geq (1 - \frac{1}{N+1}) \cdot \mathcal{W}(m)$$

In order to prove Theorem 2, we need a better understanding of how prices adjust to changes in strategy under different degrees of competition. Towards this goal, we need the following two lemmas.

Lemma 3. *Given an arbitrary strategic money allocation s. If player i increases (resp. decreases) her spending from s_i to $(1 + \delta)s_i$ then the price of any good increases (resp. decreases) by at most a factor of $(1 + \delta)$.*

Proof. We focus on the case of increase; the argument for the decrease case is analogous. Suppose all players increase their strategic allocation by a factor of $(1 + \delta)$. Then the allocations to all players would remain the same by the market mechanism and all prices would be scaled up by a factor of $(1+\delta)$. Then suppose each player $k \neq i$ subsequently lowers its money allocation back down to the original amount s_k. By Lemma 1, no price can now increase. The result follows.   □

Lemma 4. *Given an arbitrary strategic money allocation s in a market with degree of competition N. Let buyer i be the duplicate player of her type with the smallest money allocation s_i. If she increases her spending to $(1 + N \cdot \delta)s_i$ then the price of any good increases by at most a factor $(1 + \delta)$.*

Proof. We utilize the symmetry between the N identical players. Let players $i_1 = i, i_2, ..., i_N$ be the replicas identical to player i. If each of these players increased their spending by a factor of $(1 + \delta)$ then, by Lemma 3, prices would go up by at most a factor $(1 + \delta)$. From the market mechanism's perspective, this is equivalent to player i increasing her strategic allocation to $s_i + \delta \cdot \sum_k s_{i_k}$. But this is greater than $(1 + N \cdot \delta)s_i$. Thus, by Lemma 1, the new prices are larger by a factor of at most $(1 + \delta)$. $\qquad\square$

Now let $x = x(m)$ and $x^* = x(s^*)$. Since we have rational inputs, $\mathbf{x}$ and $\mathbf{x}^*$ must be rational [14]. Therefore, by appropriately duplicating the goods and scaling the utility coefficients, we may assume that there is exactly one unit of each good and that both $\mathbf{x}$ and $\mathbf{x}^*$ are $\{0, 1\}$-allocations. Recall from the proof of Lemma 1 our definition of S_i, S_i^* and β_i, β_i^*. Under this assumption, $S_i = \{j \in \mathcal{G} : x_{ij} = 1\}$ and similarly for S_i^*. We are now ready to prove the following welfare lemma.

Lemma 5. *For any Nash equilibrium $\{s^*, p^*, x^*\}$ and any Walrasian equilibrium $\{s = m, p, x\}$, we have*

$$\sum_{i \in \mathcal{B}} \sum_{j \in S_i^*} u_{ij} \geq \left(1 - \frac{1}{N}\right) \cdot \sum_{i \in \mathcal{B}} \sum_{j \in S_i} u_{ij} \tag{12}$$

Proof. To prove the lemma we show that total utility produced by goods at NE, after scaling by a factor $\frac{N}{N-1}$, is at least as much as the utility they produce at the Walrasian equilibrium. We do this by partitioning goods into the sets S_i. We then notice that for each good, the player who receives it at NE must receive utility from it in excess of the price he paid for it. In many cases, this price is more than the utility of the player who receives it in Walrasian equilibrium and we are done. Otherwise we will set up a transfer system where players in NE who receive more utility for the good than the price paid for it transfer some of this excess utility to players who need it. This will ultimately allow us to reach the desired inequality.

For the rest of this proof wlog we will restrict our attention to Nash equilibria where each identical copy of a certain type of player has the same strategy. We are able to do this as the market could treat the sum of these copies as a single player and thus we are able to manipulate the allocations between these players without changing market prices or the total utility derived from market allocations. Thus if our argument holds for Nash equilibria where identical players have the same strategy, it will also hold for heterogeneous Nash equilibria. Now take any player i. There are two cases:

Case 1: $s_i^* = m_i$.
By Lemma 1, we know that

$$\sum_{j \in S_i^* \cap S_i} p_j^* \leq \sum_{j \in S_i^* \cap S_i} p_j \tag{13}$$

Therefore, by the assumption that $s_i^* = m_i$, we have

$$\sum_{j \in S_i \setminus S_i^*} p_j = m_i - \sum_{j \in S_i^* \cap S_i} p_j = s_i^* - \sum_{j \in S_i^* \cap S_i} p_j \leq s_i^* - \sum_{j \in S_i^* \cap S_i} p_j^* = \sum_{j \in S_i^* \setminus S_i} p_j^* \tag{14}$$

Thus buyer i spends more on $S_i^* \setminus S_i$ than she did on $S_i \setminus S_i^*$. But, by Lemma 1, she also receives a better bang-for-buck on $S_i^* \setminus S_i$ than on $S_i \setminus S_i^*$, as $\beta_i^* \geq \beta_i$ (Lemma 1). Let $\beta_i^* = 1 + \epsilon_i^*$. Thus, at the Nash equilibrium, her total utility on $S_i^* \setminus S_i$ is

$$\sum_{j \in S_i^* \setminus S_i} u_{ij} = \sum_{j \in S_i^* \setminus S_i} \beta_i^* \cdot p_j^* = (1 + \epsilon_i^*) \cdot \sum_{j \in S_i^* \setminus S_i} p_j^*$$

Of this utility, buyer i will allocate p_j^* units of utility to each item $j \in S_i^* \setminus S_i$. The remaining $\epsilon_i^* \cdot p_j^*$ units of utility derived from good j is reallocated to goods in $S_i \setminus S_i^*$.

Consider the goods in S_i. Clearly goods in $S_i \cap S_i^*$ contribute the same utility to both the Walrasian equilibrium and the Nash equilibrium. So take the items in $S_i \setminus S_i^*$. The buyers of these items at NE have obtained at least $\sum_{j \in S_i \setminus S_i^*} p_j^*$ units of utility from them (as $\beta_d^* \geq 1$, $\forall d$). In addition, buyer i has reallocated $\epsilon_i^* \cdot \sum_{j \in S_i^* \setminus S_i} p_j^*$ to goods in $S_i \setminus S_i^*$. So the total utility allocated to goods in $S_i \setminus S_i^*$ is

$$\sum_{j \in S_i \setminus S_i^*} p_j^* + \epsilon_i^* \cdot \sum_{j \in S_i^* \setminus S_i} p_j^* \geq \sum_{j \in S_i \setminus S_i^*} p_j^* + \epsilon_i^* \cdot \sum_{j \in S_i \setminus S_i^*} p_j^* = (1 + \epsilon_i^*) \cdot \sum_{j \in S_i \setminus S_i^*} p_j^*$$

$$= \beta_i^* \cdot \sum_{j \in S_i \setminus S_i^*} p_j^* \geq \sum_{j \in S_i \setminus S_i^*} u_{ij}$$

Here the first inequality follows by (14) and the final inequality follows as $\beta_i^* \geq \frac{u_{ij}}{p_j^*}$, for any good $j \notin S_i^*$. Thus the reallocated utility on S_i at NE is greater than the utility it provides in the Walrasian equilibrium (even without scaling by $\frac{N}{N-1}$).

Case 2: $s_i^* < m_i$.

Suppose buyer i increases her spending from s_i^* to $(1 + N \cdot \delta) \cdot s_i^*$. Then the prices of the goods she buys increase by at most a factor $(1 + \delta)$ by Lemma 4. Thus her utility changes by

$$(m_i - (1 + \delta \cdot N) \cdot s_i^*) + s_i^* \cdot \beta_i^* \cdot \frac{1 + N \cdot \delta}{1 + \delta} - (m_i - s_i^*) - s_i^* \cdot \beta_i^* \leq 0$$

where the inequality follows as s^* is a Nash equilibrium. This simplifies to

$$s_i^* \cdot \left(-\delta \cdot N + \beta_i^* \cdot \left(\frac{1 + N \cdot \delta}{1 + \delta} - 1 \right) \right) \leq 0$$

Now suppose (i) $s_i^* = 0$. In this case we must have $u_{ij}/p_j^* \leq 1$ for every good j. To see this, we argue by contradiction. Suppose $u_{ij}/p_j^* = 1 + \epsilon$ for some good

j. Notice that if player i changes s_i^* to γ the price of good j can go up by at most γ as we know each price increases by Lemma 1 and the sum of all prices is at most γ higher (by the market conditions). Thus, if player i puts $\gamma < \epsilon$ money onto the market then good j will still have bang-for-buck greater than 1 and so player i will gain more utility than the loss of savings. Thus, s_i^* cannot be an equilibrium, a contradiction.

Thus $u_{ij} \leq p_j^* \leq u_{i^*j}$ where i^* is the player who receives good j at NE. Therefore this player obtains more utility from good j than player i did in the Walrasian equilibrium, even without scaling or a utility transfer.

On the other hand, suppose (ii) $s_i^* > 0$. This can only occur if we have both $\beta_i^* \geq 1$ and

$$\beta_i^* \cdot \frac{(N-1)\cdot\delta}{1+\delta} \leq \delta\cdot N \tag{15}$$

Therefore $1 \leq \beta_i^* \leq (1+\delta)\cdot(1+\frac{1}{N-1})$. Since this holds for all δ, as we take $\delta \to 0$ we must have $\beta_i^* \leq \frac{N}{N-1}$. Thus $\frac{u_{ij}}{p_j^*} \leq \frac{N}{N-1}$ for every good j. Thus if we multiply the utility of the player receiving good j in the Nash equilibrium by $\frac{N}{N-1}$ he will be getting more utility from it than player i did in the Walrasian equilibrium. $\qquad\square$

Proof of Theorem 2. Given the other buyers strategies $\boldsymbol{s}_{-i}^*$ suppose buyer i sets $s_i = m_i$. Then, by Lemma 1, prices cannot be higher for $(m_i, \boldsymbol{s}_{-i}^*)$ than at the Walrasian equilibrium $\boldsymbol{p}(\boldsymbol{m})$. Therefore, by selecting $s_i = m_i$, buyer i could afford to buy the entire bundle S_i at the resultant prices. Consequently, her best response strategy $\boldsymbol{s}_i^*$ must offer at least that much utility. This is true for each buyer, so we have

$$\sum_{i\in B}\left((m_i - s_i^*) + \sum_{j\in G} u_{ij}\cdot x_{ij}^*\right) \geq \sum_{i\in B}\sum_{j\in G} u_{ij}\cdot x_{ij} \tag{16}$$

Thus

$$\mathcal{W}(\boldsymbol{s}^*) = \sum_{i\in B}\sum_{j\in G} u_{ij}\cdot x_{ij}^* + \sum_{i\in B} m_i = \sum_{i\in B}\left((m_i - s_i^*) + \sum_{j\in G} u_{ij}\cdot x_{ij}^*\right) + \sum_{i\in B} s_i^*$$

$$\geq \sum_{i\in B}\sum_{j\in G} u_{ij}\cdot x_{ij} + \sum_{i\in B} s_i^* \tag{17}$$

On the other hand, Lemma 5 implies that

$$\mathcal{W}(\boldsymbol{s}^*) = \sum_{i\in B}\sum_{j\in G} u_{ij}\cdot x_{ij}^* + \sum_{i\in B} m_i \geq \left(1 - \frac{1}{N}\right)\cdot\sum_{i\in B}\sum_{j\in G} u_{ij}\cdot x_{ij} + \sum_{i\in B} m_i \tag{18}$$

Taking a convex combination of Inequalities (17) and (18) gives

$$\mathcal{W}(\boldsymbol{s}^*) \geq \left(\alpha\cdot(1 - \frac{1}{N}) + (1-\alpha)\right)\cdot\sum_{i\in B}\sum_{j\in G} u_{ij}\cdot x_{ij} + \alpha\cdot\sum_{i\in B} m_i + (1-\alpha)\cdot\sum_{i\in B} s_i^*$$

$$\geq \left(\alpha \cdot (1 - \frac{1}{N}) + (1 - \alpha)\right) \cdot \sum_{i \in \mathcal{B}} \sum_{j \in \mathcal{G}} u_{ij} \cdot x_{ij} + \alpha \cdot \sum_{i \in \mathcal{B}} m_i$$

$$= \left(1 - \frac{\alpha}{N}\right) \cdot \sum_{i \in \mathcal{B}} \sum_{j \in \mathcal{G}} u_{ij} \cdot x_{ij} + \alpha \cdot \sum_{i \in \mathcal{B}} m_i \tag{19}$$

Thus plugging $\alpha = \frac{N}{N+1}$ in (19) gives

$$\mathcal{W}(s^*) \geq \left(1 - \frac{1}{N+1}\right) \cdot \left(\sum_{i \in \mathcal{B}} \sum_{j \in \mathcal{G}} u_{ij} \cdot x_{ij} + \sum_{i \in \mathcal{B}} m_i\right) = \left(1 - \frac{1}{N+1}\right) \cdot \mathcal{W}(\boldsymbol{m})$$
$$\tag{20}$$

This completes the proof.   □

5   Existence of Nash Equilibria

We have demonstrated bounds for the Price of Imperfect Competition in the Fisher Game under both CES and Cobb-Douglas utilities. However, these welfare results only apply to strategies that are Nash equilibria. In the full paper, we prove that Nash equilibria exist for the Cobb-Douglas case, but need not exist for linear utilities. For games without Nash equilibria, we may still recover some welfare guarantees; we discuss this in Section 6, by examining the dynamics of the Fisher Game with linear utilities.

6   Social Welfare under Best Response Dynamics

Whilst Nash equilibria need not exist in the Fisher Game with linear utilities, we can still obtain a good welfare guarantee in the dynamic setting. Specifically, in the dynamic setting we assume that in every round (time period), each player simultaneously plays a best response to what they observed in the previous round. Dynamics are a natural way to view how a game is played and a well-studied question is whether or not the game dynamics converge to an equilibrium. Regardless of the answer, it is possible to quantify the average social welfare over time of the dynamic process. This method was introduced by Goemans et al in [11] and we show how it can be applied here to bound the *Dynamic Price of Imperfect Competition* - the worst case ratio of the average welfare of states in the dynamic process to the welfare of the Walrasian equilibrium.

For best responses to be well defined in the dynamic Fisher Game, we need the concept of a minimum monetary allocation s_i. Thus we discretize the game by allowing players to submit strategies which are rational numbers of precision up to Φ. This has the added benefit of making the game finite. In the full paper, we prove the following bound on the Dynamic Price of Imperfect Competition.

Theorem 3. *In the dynamic Fisher Game with linear utilities, the Dynamic Price of Imperfect Competition is lower bounded by $\Omega(1/\log(\frac{M}{\phi}))$ where $M = \max_i m_i$.*

References

1. Adsul, B., Babu, C.S., Garg, J., Mehta, R., Sohoni, M.: Nash equilibria in Fisher market. In: Kontogiannis, S., Koutsoupias, E., Spirakis, P.G. (eds.) SAGT 2010. LNCS, vol. 6386, pp. 30–41. Springer, Heidelberg (2010)
2. Bonnisseau, J., Florig, M.: Existence and optimality of oligopoly equilibria in linear exchange economies. Economic Theory 22(4), 727–741 (2002)
3. Babaioff, M., Lucier, B., Nisan, N., Paes Leme, R.: On the efficiency of the Walrasian mechanism. In: EC 2014, pp. 783–800 (2014)
4. Branzei, S., Chen, Y., Deng, X., Filos-Ratsikas, A., Frederiksen, S., Zhang, J.: The Fisher market game: Equilibrium and welfare. To appear in AAAI (2014)
5. Chen, N., Deng, X., Zhang, H., Zhang, J.: Incentive ratios of Fisher markets. In: Czumaj, A., Mehlhorn, K., Pitts, A., Wattenhofer, R. (eds.) ICALP 2012, Part II. LNCS, vol. 7392, pp. 464–475. Springer, Heidelberg (2012)
6. Codognato, G., Gabszewicz, J.: Equilibre de Cournot-Walras dans une économie d'échange. Revue Économique 42(6), 1013–1026 (1991)
7. Eaves, B.: Finite solution of pure trade markets with Cobb-Douglas utilities. In: Economic Equilibrium: Model Formulation and Solution, pp. 226–239 (1985)
8. Eisenberg, E., Gale, D.: Consensus of subjective probabilities: The pari-mutuel method. The Annals of Mathematical Statistics 30(1), 165–168 (1959)
9. Eisenberg, E.: Aggregation of utility functions. Management Sciences 7(4), 337–350 (1961)
10. Gabszewicz, J., Michel, P.: Oligopoly equilibria in exchange economies. In: Trade, Technology and Economics. Essays in Honour of Richard G. Lipsey, pp. 217–240 (1997)
11. Goemans, M., Mirrokni, V., Vetta, A.: Sink equilibria and convergence. In: Foundations of Computer Science (2005)
12. Hurwicz, L.: On informationally decentralized systems. In: Decision and Organization: A Volume in Honor of Jacob Marschak. Studies in Mathematical and Managerial Economics, vol. 12, pp. 297–336 (1972)
13. Jain, K.: A polynomial time algorithm for computing an Arrow-Debreu equilibrium for linear utilities. SIAM Journal on Computing 37(1), 291–300 (2007)
14. Jain, K., Vazirani, V.: Eisenberg–Gale markets: Algorithms and game-theoretic properties. Games and Economic Behavior 70(1), 84–106 (2010)
15. Johari, R., Tsitsiklis, J.: Efficiency loss in network resource allocation game. Mathematics of Operations Research 57(4), 823–839 (2004)
16. Rosen, J.B.: Existence and Uniqueness of Equilibrium Points for Concave N-person Games. Econometrica 33(3), 520–534 (1965)
17. Shapley, L., Shubik, M.: Trade using one commodity as a means of payment. The Journal of Political Economy, 937–968 (1977)
18. Solov, R.: A contribution to the theory of economic growth. Quarterly Journal of Economics 70, 65–94 (1956)
19. Vazirani, V.: Combinatorial Algorithms for Market Equilibria. In: Algorithmic Game Theory, pp. 103–133 (2007)
20. Walras, L.: Principe d'une théorie mathématique de l'échange (1874)

Coalitional Games on Sparse Social Networks

Edith Elkind

University of Oxford, UK

Abstract. We consider coalitional games played on social networks (graphs), where feasible coalitions are associated with connected subsets of agents. We characterize families of graphs that have polynomially many feasible coalitions, and show that the complexity of computing common solution concepts and parameters of coalitional games on social networks is polynomial in the number of feasible coalitions. Also, we establish a connection between coalitional games on social networks and the *synergy coalition group* representation [5], and provide new complexity results for this representation. In particular, we identify a variant of this representation where computing the cost of stability [2] is easy, but computing the value of the least core [12] is hard.

1 Introduction

Coalitional game theory models many aspects of collaboration among self-interested agents. In the most basic model of a coalitional game, an arbitrary subset of players can form a coalition in order to make a profit or share costs; the benefits from forming the coalition are then split among the players. However, in practice not all subsets of players can collaborate in a productive manner; e.g., it may be infeasible to form a coalition where some of the agents do not get along with each other or lack communication channels. For instance, in a parliamentary democracy we are unlikely to see a governing coalition that includes an extreme right-wing party (R) and an extreme left-wing party (L), but no centrist parties, even if R and L together have a majority of seats.

Such settings can often be described succinctly by explicitly specifying the social network that governs the interaction among the agents: the agents are viewed as vertices of a graph, an edge between two vertices indicates that the respective agents know each other, and feasible coalitions are associated with connected subgraphs of this graph. This graph is usually called the *interaction graph*. This model was proposed by Myerson [14], and has received a lot of attention since then. It has been shown that the structure of the interaction graph provides useful information about the game: for instance, if this graph is a tree, the game is guaranteed to admit stable outcomes (i.e., has non-empty core) [6], and, more generally, if it is close to being a tree (as measured by its treewidth of pathwidth), it is inexpensive to stabilize by external subsidies [13].

One can also expect that the complexity of computing various solution concepts for a given game (such as the core or the Shapley value) can be bounded in terms of natural parameters of the interaction graph. Variants of the latter question were explored by a number of authors in recent years, for various algorithmic problems, such as optimal coalition structure generation [21] and computation of stable or fair outcomes [8,4,19]. While some of these papers deal with designing practical algorithms for reasonably

T.-Y. Liu et al. (Eds.): WINE 2014, LNCS 8877, pp. 308–321, 2014.

large games, others focus on formulating conditions on the interaction graph that guarantee polynomial-time solvability of the problems they consider. In particular, Malizia et al. [8] show that many natural core-related questions are Δ_2^P-hard (Δ_2^P is a complexity class that subsumes NP and coNP) even if the treewidth of the interaction graph is 2. In contrast, Chalkiadakis et al. [4] observe that these questions become easy if the interaction graph is a line or a cycle. They use a simple, but important observation that in such games the number of feasible coalitions is polynomial (in fact, quadratic) in the number of players, and combine it with the fact that many stability-related questions can be captured by a linear program with one constraint for each feasible coalition (and a small number of additional constraints).

Motivated by the observation of Chalkiadakis et al. [4], in this paper we explore the following questions: (1) under which conditions on the interaction graph is the number of feasible coalitions at most polynomial in the number of players? (2) which coalitional game theory concepts for games on social networks can be computed in time polynomial in the number of feasible coalitions?

For the first question, we identify a number of simple checks that allow us to answer it (either in the positive or in the negative) for many classes of graphs. For cases that are not captured by these checks, we describe a procedure that is based on enumerating polynomially many subsets of vertices and, for each subset, comparing two easy-to-compute quantities. We believe that this analysis provides useful intuition about the families of graphs with few connected coalitions.

For the second question, we consider both the setting where the value of each disconnected coalition is assumed to be 0 (we refer to such games as *Demange games*, as they are considered in the seminal work of Demange [6]), and the setting where the value of each disconnected coalition is computed as the sum of the values of its connected components (we call such games *Myerson games*, as they are based on the same intuition as the Myerson value [14]). For both settings, we consider a number of standard computational tasks (finding an optimal coalition structure, checking if an outcome is in the core, determining whether the core is non-empty, computing the value of the least core, the cost of stability, the nucleolus, or players' Shapley values), and show that they admit algorithms whose running time is polynomial in the number of connected coalitions. While some of these algorithms have been suggested in prior work, others are new, and for known algorithms we are sometimes able to provide simplified proofs of correctness and/or better bounds on the running time.

Some of the results presented in this paper do not use the graph structure at all, i.e., they hold for any family of coalitional games that can be described by a small number of "base" coalitions (in the sense that the values of all other coalitions are 0, as in Demange games, or are set to the value of their best partition into base coalitions, as in Myerson games). We classify our algorithmic results according to this criterion, and, for those that rely on the graph structure, show that this reliance is necessary. To this end, we prove hardness results for the respective computational problems under the representation where the "base" coalitions are listed explicitly. The variant of this model where the value of each coalition is computed as the value of its best partition into base coalitions (i.e., the analogue of Myerson games) is exactly the well-known *synergy coalition group* representation of Conitzer and Sandholm [5], and we obtain new computational complexity results for this representation. In particular, we identify a variant of the synergy coalition group representation for which computing the cost of stability is in P, whereas computing the value of the least core is NP-hard, thus obtaining the first complexity-theoretic separation result between these two notions.

2   Preliminaries and Notation

We start by reviewing basic definitions of graph theory and coalitional game theory that will be used in this paper.

Graph Theory. A *graph* is a pair $\Gamma = (N, E)$, where $N = \{1, \ldots, n\}$ is a finite set of *vertices* and $E = \{e_1, \ldots, e_m\}$ is a list of *edges*. Each edge is labeled with an element of $N \times N$; if e is labeled with (a, b), then a and b are said to be the *endpoints* of e. An edge e is a *loop* if it is labeled with (a, a) for some $a \in N$. The *degree* of a vertex $a \in N$ is the number of non-loop edges in E that have a as one of their endpoints plus twice the number of loop edges in E that are labeled with (a, a). Two edges $e_1, e_2 \in E$ are said to be *parallel* if they are labeled with the same pair $(a, b) \in N \times N$. A graph is said to be *simple* if it has no loops and no parallel edges; in a simple graph, we associate each edge with its label, i.e., we write $e = (a, b)$. A *path* in a graph is a sequence of edges $e_1, \ldots, e_k$ with the following property: there exists a set of vertices $\{a_0, a_1, \ldots, a_k\}$ such that for each $i = 1, \ldots, k$ the edge e_i is labeled with (a_{i-1}, a_i); the *length* of a path is the number of edges in it. A subset of vertices $S \subseteq N$ is said to be *connected* if for every pair of vertices $a, b \in S$ the graph G contains a path between a and b. Given a set of vertices $S \subseteq N$ of a simple graph (N, E), we let $\mathcal{N}(S) = \{a \in N \mid a \in S \text{ or } (a, b) \in E \text{ for some } b \in S\}$; we refer to the set $\mathcal{N}(S)$ as the *neighborhood* of S.

Coalitional Game Theory. A *coalitional game* is a pair $G = (N, v)$, where $N = \{1, \ldots, n\}$ is a finite set of *players*, and $v : 2^N \to \mathbb{R}$ is a *characteristic function*, which associates every subset, or a *coalition*, of players $S \subseteq N$ with its *worth*, or *value*, $v(S)$. The set N is called the *grand coalition*. In what follows, we assume that $v(S) \geq 0$ for all $S \subseteq N$, and $v(\emptyset) = 0$. A *coalition structure* for G is a partition of players into disjoint coalitions, i.e., a collection of subsets $\pi = \{S_1, \ldots, S_k\}$ such that $S_i \cap S_j = \emptyset$ for all $1 \leq i, j \leq k, i \neq j$, and $\cup_{i=1}^k S_i = N$. We denote the set of all coalition structures over N by $\Pi(N)$, and extend this notation to subsets of N. The *value* of a coalition structure $\pi = \{S_1, \ldots, S_k\}$ is the sum of values of the coalitions in π: $v(\pi) = \sum_{i=1}^k v(S_i)$.

A game $G = (N, v)$ is said to be *superadditive* if $v(S \cup T) \geq v(S) + v(T)$ for every pair of disjoint coalitions $S, T \subseteq N$; it is said to be *cohesive* if $v(N) \geq v(\pi)$ for every $\pi \in \Pi(N)$. A superadditive game is necessarily cohesive, but the converse is not true. A related notion is that of an essential coalition: a coalition S is said to be *essential* if $v(S) > v(\pi)$ for all $\pi \in \Pi(S)$. In a cohesive game, it is reasonable to assume that the grand coalition forms. A *payoff vector* for a cohesive game $G = (N, v)$ with $N = \{1, \ldots, n\}$ is a vector $\mathbf{p} = (p_1, \ldots, p_n) \in \mathbb{R}^n$ such that $p_1 + \cdots + p_n = v(N)$; a payoff vector $\mathbf{p}$ is an *imputation* if $p_i \geq v(\{i\})$ for each $i \in N$. We denote the set of all payoff vectors for a game G by $I(G)$. We associate outcomes of cohesive games with payoff vectors, i.e., we assume that players form the grand coalition and share its payoff according to a payoff vector. In what follows, given a vector $\mathbf{x} = (x_1, \ldots, x_n) \in \mathbb{R}^n$ and a set $S \subseteq N$, we write $x(S)$ to denote $\sum_{i \in S} x_i$.

Given a cohesive game G, the set $I(G)$ describes all possible outcomes of G. There are several approaches to defining the most desirable among these outcomes; these are known as *solution concepts*. In this paper, we consider several solution concepts for (cohesive) coalitional games, including the *core*, the *least core*, the *nucleolus*, the *Shapley value*, and a related notion of the *cost of stability*.

The *core* is the set of all payoff vectors that are *stable*, in the sense that no coalition has a profitable deviation: formally, a payoff vector $\mathbf{p} \in I(G)$ is in the core of G if $p(S) \geq v(S)$ for all $S \subseteq N$. The core of a game G is captured by the following linear feasibility program with variables $p_1, \ldots, p_n$.

$$\sum_{i \in N} p_i = v(N), \qquad p_i \geq 0 \text{ for all } i \in N$$
$$\sum_{i \in S} p_i \geq v(S) \text{ for all } S \subseteq N \tag{1}$$

As the core of a game may be empty, it is often useful to consider relaxations of this concept. In particular, for each $\varepsilon \in \mathbb{R}$ we define the *ε-core of G* as the set of all vectors in $\mathbb{R}^n$ that satisfy a modification of the LP (1) where for each $S \subseteq N$ the constraint $\sum_{i \in S} p_i \geq v(S)$ is relaxed to $\sum_{i \in S} p_i \geq v(S) - \varepsilon$. The smallest value of ε for which the ε-core is non-empty is known as the *value of the least core* [12], and is denoted by $\varepsilon(G)$. It equals to the value of the following LP with variables $p_1, \ldots, p_n, \varepsilon$.

$$\min \varepsilon$$
$$\sum_{i \in N} p_i = v(N), \qquad p_i \geq 0 \text{ for all } i \in N$$
$$\sum_{i \in S} p_i \geq v(S) - \varepsilon \text{ for all } S \subseteq N \tag{2}$$

The set of all vectors $\mathbf{p} \in \mathbb{R}^n$ such that $(p_1, \ldots, p_n, \varepsilon(G))$ is a feasible solution of LP (2) is known as the *least core* of G. Intuitively, this is the set of all payoff divisions that are stable when a coalitional deviation carries a cost of $\varepsilon(G)$.

The notion of the least core is based on the idea of punishing the agents for deviating; alternatively, we can offer them an incentive to stay together, by providing a subsidy to the grand coalition. This is captured by the notion of the *cost of stability* [2], which can be defined as the value of the following linear program with variables $p_1, \ldots, p_n, \Delta$:

$$\min \Delta$$
$$\sum_{i \in N} p_i = v(N) + \Delta, \qquad p_i \geq 0 \text{ for all } i \in N$$
$$\sum_{i \in S} p_i \geq v(S) \text{ for all } S \subseteq N \tag{3}$$

We denote the cost of stability of a game G by $\Delta(G)$.

The *nucleolus* [16] is a single-point solution concept that refines the least core. It is based on lexicographic minimization of coalitional *deficits*, i.e., the differences between the value of a coalition and the payoff it receives. Instead of providing a formal definition, we describe a procedure for computing the nucleolus that was proposed by

Kopelowitz [11] (see also [12]). Given a game $G = (N, v)$, we construct a sequence of linear programs $\text{LPN}_0, \ldots, \text{LPN}_k$, a sequence of values $\varepsilon_0, \ldots, \varepsilon_k$, and a sequence of sets of coalitions $\mathcal{Q}_0, \ldots, \mathcal{Q}_k$ for some $k \geq 1$ so that LPN_k has a unique feasible solution $(\mathbf{p}, \varepsilon)$; the resulting vector $\mathbf{p}$ (which is a payoff vector for G) is called the *nucleolus* of G.

We define LPN_0 to coincide with LP (2), and set $\mathcal{Q}_0 = \emptyset$, $\varepsilon_0 = -\infty$. For $j \geq 1$, LPN_j is constructed from LPN_{j-1} by replacing each constraint of the form $p(S) \geq v(S) - \varepsilon$, $S \in \mathcal{Q}_{j-1}$, with $p(S) \geq v(S) = \varepsilon_{j-1}$; note that $\text{LPN}_1 = \text{LPN}_0$. Further, ε_j is defined to be the value of LPN_j. It remains to describe how to construct $\mathcal{Q}_j$. Given an optimal solution $(\mathbf{p}, \varepsilon_j)$ to LPN_j, let $\mathcal{Q}(\mathbf{p})$ be the set of coalitions such that the respective constraint of LPN_j is tight, i.e., $p(S) = v(S) - \varepsilon_j$. Let $\mathbf{p}_j$ be an *interior optimizer* for LPN_j, i.e., $\mathcal{Q}(\mathbf{p}_j) \subseteq \mathcal{Q}(\mathbf{p})$ for every $\mathbf{p}$ such that $(\mathbf{p}, \varepsilon_j)$ is an optimal solution to LPN_j, and set $\mathcal{Q}_j = \mathcal{Q}(\mathbf{p}_j)$. It can be shown that $\mathcal{Q}_j$ is well-defined (see, e.g., [7]). Moreover, finding an interior optimizer for a given LP is as easy as finding an arbitrary optimal solution to it; in particular, this can be done in polynomial time if this LP admits a polynomial-time separation oracle [17].

We continue this procedure until each inequality of the form $p(S) \geq v(S) - \varepsilon$ is replaced with an equality; clearly, this happens after at most 2^n steps. It can be shown that the last LP has a unique solution $(\mathbf{p}, \varepsilon)$; the payoff vector $\mathbf{p}$ is the nucleolus.[1] In what follows, it will be convenient to modify LPN_j, $j > 0$, by adding the constraint $\varepsilon \geq \varepsilon_{j-1}$; this constraint may change the set of feasible solutions to LPN_j, but does not affect the set of optimal solutions. The advantage of adding this constraint is that for the modified sequence of LPs it holds that the set of feasible solutions to LPN_j is exactly the set of optimal solutions to LPN_{j-1}.

Besides stability, another important consideration in the analysis of coalitional games is *fairness*, usually captured by the notion of the *Shapley value* [18]. Formally, the *Shapley value* of a player i in a coalitional game $G = (N, v)$ is given by

$$\phi_i(G) = \sum_{S \subseteq N: i \in S} \frac{|S - 1|!(|N| - |S|)!}{|N|!} (v(S) - v(S \setminus \{i\})). \tag{4}$$

The Shapley value of a player i can be interpreted as his average marginal contribution, where the average is taken over all permutations of players in N; we refer the reader to [3] for a discussion.

If a game is not cohesive, it may be suboptimal for the players to form the grand coalition, as they can work more productively in smaller teams. For such games, a fundamental task is *coalition structure generation*, i.e., partitioning players into teams so as to maximize the social welfare. Formally, the *optimal coalition structure generation problem* asks for a coalition structure $\pi \in \arg\max_{\pi \in \Pi(N)} v(\pi)$. Various stability-related solution concepts can be extended to non-cohesive games by allowing the players to form coalition structures [1]; however, we do not consider the associated computational problems in this work due to space constraints.

---

[1] More precisely, this procedure computes the *pre-nucleolus* of the game. However, the two notions often coincide, so in what follows we refer to the output of our sequence of LPs as the nucleolus.

When investigating the complexity of algorithmic problems associated with a coalitional game $G = (N, v)$, we assume that v takes values in the set of non-negative rational numbers, and its values are represented in binary; also, we set $V = \max_{S \subseteq N} v(S)$.

3   The Model

We will now formally define the two types of coalitional games on social networks that will be studied in this paper. While both of them can be traced back to the seminal work of Myerson [14], we refer to games of the first type as *Demange games*, to acknowledge the fact that Demange [6] proved important results about the core of such games, and to games of the second type as *Myerson games*, since they are based on the same intuition as the classic Myerson value [14]. In both types of games, we are given a (simple, connected) graph Γ that has the set of players N as its vertex set; the edges of Γ are interpreted as communication links between the players. Also, for both types of games, the characteristic function $v : 2^N \to \mathbb{R}^+ \cup \{0\}$ is fully described by its values on coalitions that are connected in Γ. However, Demange games and Myerson games differ in their treatment of coalitions that are not connected: the former assign a value of 0 to every such coalition, whereas the latter compute the value of such coalition as the sum of the values of its connected components.

Formally, given a simple, connected graph $\Gamma = (N, E)$, let $\mathcal{K}(\Gamma)$ be the collection of all subsets of N that are connected in Γ, and let $K(\Gamma) = |\mathcal{K}(\Gamma)|$; we omit Γ from the notation when it is clear from the context. A *base game* on Γ is a triple $G = (N, v, \Gamma)$, where $v : \mathcal{K}(\Gamma) \to \mathbb{R}^+ \cup \{0\}$ is a *partial characteristic function*. The *Demange game* associated with a base game $G = (N, v, \Gamma)$ is the triple $G^0 = (N, v^0, \Gamma)$, where $v^0 : 2^N \to \mathbb{R}^+ \cup \{0\}$ is a characteristic function given by $v^0(S) = v(S)$ if $S \in \mathcal{K}(\Gamma)$ and $v^0(S) = 0$ otherwise. The *Myerson game* associated with a base game $G = (N, v, \Gamma)$ is the triple $G^+ = (N, v^+, \Gamma)$, where $v^+ : 2^N \to \mathbb{R}^+ \cup \{0\}$ is a characteristic function given by $v^+(S) = \sum_{i=1}^{k} v(S_i)$, where $S_1, \ldots, S_k$ is the list of the connected components of S (in particular, $v^+(S) = v(S)$ for all $S \in \mathcal{K}(\Gamma)$). We refer to both Demange games and Myerson games as *graph-restricted games*. The graph Γ is called the *interaction graph* for G, G^0, and G^+.

Both Demange games and Myerson games aim to capture the intuition that, to collaborate, agents should be able to communicate. However, in Demange games we make the rather strong assumption that a disconnected coalition can earn no profit whatsoever, whereas in Myerson games we allow the players in each connected component to work on their own. The graph-restricted games studied by Greco et al. [8], Chalkiadakis et al. [4] and Voice et al. [21] are Demange games (though, as we will see, for the optimal coalition structure generation problem the two types of games are equivalent), whereas Skibski et al. [19] consider both types of games.

Note that a Demange game is typically not superadditive, but it may still be cohesive. When analyzing the complexity of computing solution concepts for graph-restricted games, we assume that the input games are cohesive; however, we do not make this assumption when we consider the optimal coalition structure generation problem, as this problem is trivially solvable for cohesive games.

4 Interaction Graphs with a Few Connected Subgraphs

In this section we present a characterization of graph-restricted games that have at most polynomially many connected coalitions. This question is essentially graph-theoretic in nature, as it does not refer to the properties of the characteristic function. As we are interested in asymptotic results, we will consider families of simple connected graphs $(\Gamma_n)_{n>0}$, where Γ_n has n vertices, and try to identify sufficient and necessary conditions on such families for $K(\Gamma_n)$ to be at most polynomial in n.

Chalkiadakis et al. [4] observe that, if the degree of each vertex in Γ_n is at most 2, then $K(\Gamma_n)$ is polynomial in n. This suggests that vertices of degree 2 do not contribute much to $K(\Gamma_n)$, and motivates the following definition.

Definition 1. *Given a simple graph $\Gamma = (N, E)$, its* condensed graph $\Gamma^* = (N^*, E^*)$ *is a weighted graph (N^*, E^*, ν) that is defined as follows. Let $N(2) = \{a \in N \mid \deg(a) = 2\}$. We set $N^* = N \setminus N(2)$. Further, for each pair of vertices $a, b \in N^*$ (where a and b may be equal) and each path in Γ of the form $(a, c_1, \ldots, c_k, b)$, where $k \geq 0$, $a, b \in N^*$ and $c_1, \ldots, c_k \in N(2)$, we include in E^* an edge e between a and b with weight $\nu(e) = \log(k + 1)$. We denote the set of positive-weight edges of Γ^* by E^+; note that $E^+ = E^* \setminus E$. Given an edge $e \in E^+$ that corresponds to a path $\pi = (a, c_1, \ldots, c_k, b)$ in Γ, we set $P(e) = \{c_1, \ldots, c_k\}$, and let $\pi(e) = \pi$.*

Our first observation is that, if the number of vertices in Γ_n^* is superlogarithmic, then $K(\Gamma_n)$ is superpolynomial.

Theorem 1. *For every family of graphs $(\Gamma_n)_{n>0}$ where the respective family of condensed graphs $(\Gamma_n^*)_{n>0}$, $\Gamma_n^* = (N_n^*, E_n^*, \nu_n)$, satisfies $|N_n^*| = \omega(\log n)$, it holds that $K(\Gamma_n)$ is superpolynomial in n.*

Proof. Karpov [10] shows that every simple connected graph with s vertices of degree 1 and 3 and t vertices of degree 4 or more has a spanning tree with at least $s/4 + t/3 + 3/2$ leaves. This implies that for every $n > 0$ the graph Γ_n has a spanning tree with at least $|N_n^*|/4$ leaves. Deleting any subset of these leaves results in a connected subgraph of Γ_n; as the number of such subsets is at least $2^{|N_n^*|/4} = 2^{\omega(\log n)}$, our claim follows. □

Theorem 1 is tight, as illustrated by the following example.

Example 1. Consider the family of graphs $(\Gamma_n^{\text{kite}})_{n>0}$ (Figure 1). The n-th graph in this family consists of a clique of size $\log n$ with a "tail" of length $n - \log n$ attached to one of the vertices of the clique. A connected subgraph of Γ_n^{kite} consists of a (possibly empty) subset of the clique and a contiguous segment of the tail, and therefore its size is at most $2^{\log n} \cdot n^2 = \text{poly}(n)$.

Fig. 1. Γ_n^{kite} for $n = 64$

It is natural to conjecture that the converse of Theorem 1 is also true, i.e., if $|N_n^*| = O(\log n)$, then $K(\Gamma_n)$ is polynomial in n. However, this is not the case: in fact, we can construct a family of graphs $(\Gamma_n)_{n>0}$ with $|N_n^*| = 1$ such that $K(\Gamma_n)$ grows superpolynomially.

Example 2. Consider the family of graphs $(\Gamma_n^{\text{flower}})_{n>0}$ (Figure 2). The n-th graph in this family has a central node a, and, for each $i = 1, \ldots, k$ (where the value of k will be specified later), there is a path P_i consisting of $\ell_i \in \{\lfloor \frac{n}{k} \rfloor, \lceil \frac{n}{k} \rceil\}$ vertices of degree 2 such that the first and the last vertex on this path are connected to a; the values $\ell_1, \ldots, \ell_k$ are chosen so that the total number of vertices is n.

Observe that Γ_n^* has a single vertex and k loop edges that start and end at this vertex. Further, each list of numbers $(s_1, \ldots, s_k)$ with $0 \le s_i \le \ell_i$ for $i = 1, \ldots, k$ defines a distinct subgraph of Γ, namely, the graph that contains a, and, for each $i = 1, \ldots, k$, the path of length s_i that starts at a and goes along P_i. For $k <$ $\log n$ there are at least $(\frac{n}{\log n})^k \ge n^{k/2}$ such sequences. If k is not bounded by a constant, this quantity is superpolynomial.

Fig. 2. Γ_n^{flower} for $n = 49, k = 8$

Thus, if $|N_n^*| = \omega(\log n)$, then $K(\Gamma_n)$ is superpolynomial, but for smaller values of $|N_n^*|$ no conclusion can be derived. Therefore, for $|N_n^*| = O(\log n)$, we have to look at other parameters of Γ_n (or Γ_n^*). A natural next step is to consider the total weight of edges in Γ_n^*, i.e., $\nu(\Gamma_n^*) = \sum_{e \in E_n^*} \nu(e)$. We will now show that $\nu(\Gamma_n^*)$ is indeed a very useful measure: if $|N^*| = O(\log n)$, then $\nu(\Gamma_n^*) = O(\log n)$ implies that $K(\Gamma_n)$ grows at most polynomially, whereas $\nu(\Gamma_n^*) = \omega(\log^2 n)$ implies that $K(\Gamma_n)$ grows superpolynomially.

We first prove the upper bound.

Proposition 1. *For every family of graphs $(\Gamma_n)_{n>0}$ with $|N_n^*| = O(\log n)$, $\nu(\Gamma_n^*) = O(\log n)$ it holds that $K(\Gamma_n)$ is at most polynomial in n.*

Proof. Note first that, since the weight of each positive-weight edge is at least 1, Γ_n^* contains at most $O(\log n)$ positive-weight edges.

Now, consider a connected subgraph Γ' of Γ_n and an edge e with $\nu(e) > 0$ in Γ_n^*; let u and v be the endpoints of this edge. It could the the case that Γ' is contained in $\pi(e)$; there are $O(2^{2\nu(e)})$ such subgraphs. Now, suppose that this is not the case. If $u, v \in \Gamma'$, then either $\Gamma' \cap \pi(e) = \pi(e)$ or $\Gamma' \cap \pi(e)$ consists of two contiguous segments of $\pi(e)$: one containing u and one containing v. If only one of u, v appears in Γ', then $\Gamma' \cap \pi(e)$ consists of a single contiguous segment of $\pi(e)$, and if none of them appears in Γ', then $\Gamma' \cap \pi(e)$ is empty.

This argument shows that the number of connected subgraphs that are fully contained in some path corresponding to a positive-weight edge of Γ_n can be bounded by $\sum_{e \in E_n} O(2^{2\nu(e)}) = O(\log n) \cdot O(2^{2\nu(\Gamma_n^*)}) = \text{poly}(n)$. On the other hand, each connected subgraph Γ' of Γ_n such that $\Gamma' \not\subseteq \pi(e)$ for every $e \in E_n^*$ can be uniquely identified by specifying (a) the vertices of N_n^* that appear in Γ', and (b) for each edge e of Γ_n^* that has weight $\nu(e) > 0$ and endpoints u, v, the lengths of the segments (u, u') and (v', v) formed by the intersection of Γ' and $\pi(e)$, i.e., two numbers between 0 and $2^{\nu(e)}$. Therefore, the total number of such subgraphs is at most

$$2^{|N_n^*|} \cdot \prod_{e \in E_n^*} (2^{\nu(e)} + 1)^2 = \text{poly}(n) \cdot O(2^{2\nu(\Gamma^*)}) = \text{poly}(n). \qquad \square$$

To prove the lower bound, we first consider graphs with many "heavy" edges.

Proposition 2. *For every family of graphs* $(\Gamma_n)_{n>0}$ *with* $|N_n^*| = O(\log n)$, $|E_n^+| = \omega(\log n)$ *it holds that* $K(\Gamma_n)$ *is superpolynomial in* n.

Proof. Construct a spanning tree for Γ_n^*. It has $|N_n^*| - 1 = O(\log n)$ vertices, and hence $O(\log n)$ edges. Therefore, there are $\omega(\log n)$ positive-weight edges not used by the spanning tree. For every such edge e, pick a vertex on $\pi(e)$ that is adjacent to one of the endpoints of e. Denote the set of all such vertices by M_n. Now, we can obtain a connected subgraph of Γ_n by taking all vertices in N_n^* and an arbitrary subset of M_n; as $|M_n| = \omega(\log n)$, the number of distinct connected subgraphs that can be obtained in this way is superpolynomial in n. □

Corollary 1. *For every family of graphs* $(\Gamma_n)_{n>0}$ *with* $|N_n^*| = O(\log n)$, $\nu(\Gamma_n^*) = \omega(\log^2 n)$ *it holds that* $K(\Gamma_n)$ *is superpolynomial in* n.

Proof. The proof follows immediately from Proposition 2 by observing that the weight of each edge is at most $\log n$ and therefore $\nu(\Gamma_n^*) = \omega(\log^2 n)$ implies that Γ_n^* has $\omega(\log n)$ edges with positive weight. □

The proof of Corollary 1 uses a fairly crude argument. Nevertheless, the following example shows that the bound of $\omega(\log^2 n)$ is tight.

(a) The graph $\Gamma_n^{\text{cat-1}}$ (b) The graph $\Gamma_n^{\text{cat-2}}$

Fig. 3. Two families of caterpillars

Example 3. A *caterpillar* of length $k > 0$ is a graph with the set of vertices $A \cup B$, where $A = \{a_1, \ldots, a_k\}$, $B = \{b_1, \ldots, b_k\}$, and the set of edges $\{(a_i, b_i)\}_{i=1}^{k} \cup \{(a_i, a_{i+1})\}_{i=1}^{k-1}$. The edges of the form (a_i, b_i) are the *legs* of the caterpillar, and edges of the form (a_i, a_{i+1}) form its *spine*. Consider two families of graphs, $(\Gamma_n^{\text{cat-1}})_{n>0}$ and $(\Gamma_n^{\text{cat-2}})_{n>0}$, illustrated in Figure 3. The n-th graph in the first family is obtained by taking a caterpillar of length $k = \lfloor \log n \rfloor$ and subdividing its i-th leg into a path of length $\ell_i \in \{\lfloor \frac{n-2k}{k} \rfloor, \lceil \frac{n-2k}{k} \rceil\}$, whereas the n-th graph in the second family is obtained by applying the same procedure to the edges in the caterpillar's spine; $\ell_1, \ldots, \ell_k$ are chosen so that the total number of vertices is n. It is easy to see that $K(\Gamma_n^{\text{cat-1}})$ is superpolynomial, but $K(\Gamma_n^{\text{cat-2}})$ is polynomial in n.

Example 3 illustrates that simply considering the topology of the condensed graph or its total weight is not sufficient: the two families of graphs in this example are indistinguishable according to these criteria. However, Example 3, together with the proof of Proposition 2, indicates that it may be useful to look at spanning trees of vertex subsets. To pursue this approach, we need the following additional notation.

Given a graph Γ and its respective condensed graph $\Gamma^* = (N^*, E^*, \nu)$, for every connected subset $S \subseteq N^*$ we let $\nu^+(S)$ be the total weight of edges in E^* with at least one endpoint in S and we let $\nu^-(S)$ be the weight of a minimum-weight spanning tree of S. The following theorem only considers graphs with $|N^*| = O(\log n)$, $|E^+| = O(\log n)$, as we have argued that in all other cases the number of connected subgraphs grows superpolynomially (Theorem 1 and Proposition 2). The proof (omitted) combines ideas from the proofs of Propositions 1 and 2.

Theorem 2. *Consider a family of graphs* $(\Gamma_n)_{n>0}$ *with* $|N_n^*| = O(\log n)$, $|E_n^+| = O(\log n)$. *It holds that* $K(\Gamma_n)$ *is polynomial in* n *if and only if there exists an* $\alpha > 0$ *such that for every subset* $S \subseteq N_n^*$ *it holds that* $\nu^+(S) - \nu^-(S) \le \alpha \log n$.

5 Demange Games

In this section, we show that, given a Demange game $G^0 = (N, v^0, \Gamma)$ with $|N| = n$, $K(\Gamma) = K$, we can solve computational problems associated with the notions defined in Section 2 in time polynomial in K, n, and $\log V$, assuming that we can compute the value of every coalition in $\mathcal{K}(\Gamma)$ in unit time. We remark that it is possible to list all connected subgraphs of a given graph $\Gamma = (N, E)$ in time $O(K \cdot |E|)$ (see, e.g., [19]), so we will assume that we are explicitly given the list of all coalitions in $\mathcal{K}$, together with their values.

Shapley Value. When computing the Shapley value of player i in a Demange game $G^0 = (N, v^0, \Gamma)$ via formula (4), we can ignore all terms in the summation such that neither S nor $S \setminus \{i\}$ are connected. Thus, we need to consider at most $2K$ terms, and, for each term, perform $\mathrm{poly}(n, \log V)$ computational steps. This implies the following simple (folklore) result (see also [19] for a more practical algorithm).

Proposition 3. *Given a Demange game* $G^0 = (N, v^0, \Gamma)$, *we can compute the Shapley value of an arbitrary player in time* $K \cdot \mathrm{poly}(n, \log V)$.

Optimal Coalition Structure Generation. Voice et al. [21] show how to adapt the standard dynamic programming algorithm for computing the value of an optimal coalition structure to Demange games. The following result is implicit in their work.

Proposition 4. *Given a Demange game* $G^0 = (N, v^0, \Gamma)$, *we can find an optimal coalition structure for* G^0 *in time* $K^2 \cdot \mathrm{poly}(n, \log V)$.

Core, Least Core, and Cost of Stability. We have seen that checking non-emptiness of the core, finding an imputation in the core, and computing the value of the least core or the cost of stability reduces to solving LPs (1), (2), and (3), respectively. For a Demange game (N, v^0, Γ), we can simplify these LPs by removing constraints associated with disconnected coalitions. Indeed, if $S \notin \mathcal{K}$ (and hence $v^0(S) = 0$), then in LP (1) and LP (3) the constraint $p(S) \ge v^0(S)$ is implied by the constraints $p_i \ge 0$, $i \in S$, and in LP (2) the constraint $p(S) \ge v^0(S) - \varepsilon$ is implied by the constraints $p_i \ge 0$, $i \in S$, when $\varepsilon \ge 0$ and by the constraints $p_i \ge v^0(\{i\}) - \varepsilon$, $i \in S$, when $\varepsilon < 0$. Thus, we can assume that our LPs have at most $K + n + 1$ constraints and n variables, and are therefore polynomial-time solvable (see, e.g., [17]). Moreover, as the coefficients in the right-hand side of each constraint are in $\{0, 1\}$, these LPs admit a strongly polynomial-time algorithm [20]. A similar argument shows that, to check if a given payoff vector

p is in the core, it suffices to verify that $p_i \geq 0$ for all $i \in N$ and $p(S) \geq v(S)$ for all $S \in \mathcal{K}$; the constraints associated with coalitions in $2^N \setminus \mathcal{K}$ are implied by the non-negativity constraints. These (folklore) observations imply the following proposition.

Proposition 5. *Given a Demange game $G^0 = (N, v^0, \Gamma)$, we can check non-emptiness of the core, find an imputation in the core (if one exists), check if a given imputation is in the core, and compute the value of the least core and the cost of stability in time* $\mathrm{poly}(K, n, \log V)$.

Nucleolus. We can try to compute the nucleolus of a Demange game (N, v^0, Γ) using the same approach as for the least core, i.e., ignore the constraints associated with coalitions in $2^N \setminus \mathcal{K}(\Gamma)$. That is, all such constraints are dropped from LPN$_0$ and are not taken into account when computing interior optimizers for each LP. As we start with K inequality constraints for coalitions, we have to solve at most K LPs. Each of these LPs has at most $K + n + 2$ constraints, so the running time of this procedure is polynomial in K, n and $\log V$. It remains to argue that the last LP is this sequence has a unique solution, and that this solution coincides with the nucleolus.

This approach was first proposed by Huberman [9], who showed that, when the core is non-empty, removing constraints associated with non-essential coalitions from LPN$_0$ does not affect the final outcome. Disconnected coalitions in Demange games are non-essential, so his result applies in our case, too. However, in our setting we can prove a stronger claim: our sequence of reduced LPs computes the nucleolus correctly even when the core is empty. The proof of the following theorem (omitted) is similar to the one given by Huberman.

Theorem 3. *Given a Demange game $G^0 = (N, v^0, \Gamma)$, we can compute its nucleolus in time* $\mathrm{poly}(K, n, \log V)$.

6 Myerson Games

Recall that in Myerson games the value of each disconnected coalition is defined as the sum of the values of its connected components. Thus, even if $K(\Gamma)$ is small, there can be many coalitions with non-zero value. We will now argue that, nevertheless, most of the algorithms described in Section 5 extend to Myerson games.

Shapley Value. The Shapley value of a player in a Myerson game $G^+ = (N, v^+, \Gamma)$ is exactly her Myerson value in the associated base game $G = (N, v, \Gamma)$, and Skibski et al. [19] provide an algorithm for computing the Myerson value of each player in G, which runs in time polynomial in $K(\Gamma)$ and $\log V$. We complement their results by giving a closed-form expression for the Shapley value of player i in G^+.

Proposition 6. *Given a Myerson game $G^+ = (N, v^+, \Gamma)$ with $|N| = n$, let $S_1, \ldots, S_K$ be the list of connected coalitions in G, and for each $j = 1, \ldots, K$ let $s_j = |S_j|$, $n_j = n - |\mathcal{N}(S_j)|$, where $\mathcal{N}(S)$ in the neighborhood of the coalition S in Γ. Then the Shapley value of player i in G^+ is given by*

$$\phi_i(G^+) = \sum_{j:i \in S_j} \sum_{\ell=0}^{n_j} \binom{n}{\ell} \frac{(\ell + s_j - 1)!(n - \ell - s_j)!}{n!} \left(v^+(S_j) - v^+(S_j \setminus \{i\}) \right),$$

and therefore can be computed in time $K \cdot \text{poly}(n, \log V)$.

Optimal Coalition Structure Generation. Consider a Myerson game $G^+ = (N, v^+, \Gamma)$ and the Demange game $G^0 = (N, v^0, \Gamma)$ with the same base game (N, v, Γ). It is easy to see that G^+ admits an optimal coalition structure in which all coalitions are connected, as any disconnected coalition can be replaced with its connected components without changing the value of the coalition structure. Therefore, a coalition structure that is optimal for G^0 is also optimal for G^+, and we can use the optimal coalition structure generation algorithm from Section 5 without any changes.

Core, Least Core, Cost of Stability, and Nucleolus. It is not hard to give a direct proof that Myerson games admit efficient algorithms for computational problems related to the core. However, for expositional purposes we make use of the *synergy coalition group (SCG)* representation for superadditive games that was introduced by Conitzer and Sandholm [5]. Under this representation, a coalitional game is described by its set of players N, a set of coalitions $\mathcal{C} = \{C_1, \ldots, C_s\}$, which contains all singleton coalitions, and a partial characteristic function $v : \mathcal{C} \to \mathbb{Q}^+ \cup \{0\}$, which is described by explicitly listing its values on the coalitions from $\mathcal{C}$. The function v is extended to 2^N by setting $v(S) = \max_{\pi \in \Pi(S)} v(\pi)$ for all $S \in 2^N \setminus \mathcal{C}$. That is, if the value of a coalition is not listed explicitly, it is computed as the value of its best partition. While this representation is intended for superadditive games, it can be used for non-superadditive games as long as all coalitions that "violate" superadditivity (i.e., all S such that $v(S) < v(\pi)$ for some $\pi \in \Pi(S)$) are included in $\mathcal{C}$ [15].

Now, if $G^+ = (N, v^+, \Gamma)$ is a Myerson game, we can obtain its SCG representation by simply listing the values of all coalitions in $\mathcal{K}$. Note that the resulting representation $(N, \mathcal{C}, v)$ satisfies $N \in \mathcal{C}$. This is important since, in general, core-related problems are computationally hard for coalitional games in SCG representation, but they become polynomial-time solvable if $N \in \mathcal{C}$ [5]. This easiness result is based on the observation that constraints corresponding to coalitions in $2^N \setminus \mathcal{C}$ can be removed from LP (1). Indeed, if $S \notin \mathcal{C}$, then $v(S) = \sum_{i=1}^{k} v(S_i)$ for some $S_1, \ldots, S_k \in \mathcal{C}$, so if a payoff vector $\mathbf{p}$ satisfies $p(S_i) \geq v(S_i)$ for $i = 1, \ldots, k$, we also have $p(S) = \sum_{j=1}^{k} p(S_j) \geq \sum_{j=1}^{k} v(S_j) = v(S)$. In fact, this argument also applies to LP (3). We summarize these observations as follows.

Proposition 7. *Given a Myerson game* $G^+ = (N, v^+, \Gamma)$, *we can check non-emptiness of the core, find an imputation in the core (if one exists), check if a given imputation is in the core, and compute the cost of stability in time* $\text{poly}(K, n, \log V)$.

We can also develop an efficient algorithm for the value of the least core, by reducing this problem to that of optimal coalition structure generation. The algorithm described in the proof of Proposition 8 (omitted) works for superadditive games, but it can be extended to arbitrary cohesive games.

Proposition 8. *Given a superadditive Myerson game* $G^+ = (N, v^+, \Gamma)$, *we can compute the value of the least core in time* $\text{poly}(K, n, \log V)$.

It is not clear if the algorithm for computing the nucleolus of Demange games (Section 5) extends to Myerson games. However, we can use the fact that disconnected coalitions in a Myerson game are not essential, and apply the result of Huberman [9]. We obtain the following proposition.

Proposition 9. *Given a Myerson game $G^+ = (N, v^+, \Gamma)$, with a non-empty core, we can compute its nucleolus in time* $\mathrm{poly}(K, n, \log V)$.

7   The Role of the Interaction Graph

The reader may have observed that some of our results do not rely on the graph structure at all, and only use the fact that the number of coalitions with non-zero value (in Demange games) or the number of essential coalitions (in Myerson games) is bounded by K. In particular, this applies to all algorithms in Section 5 except for the one for optimal coalition structure generation, and to algorithms related to the core and the cost of stability in Section 6. However, the rest of our algorithms make active use of the fact that the coalitions in $\mathcal{K}$ correspond to connected subsets of vertices of a given graph. We will now argue that this is necessary, by showing that the associated problems become computationally hard if the set of "base" coalitions has no special structure.

Optimal Coalition Structure Generation. It is immediate that the optimal coalition structure generation problem is NP-hard for coalitional games represented by the list of coalitions with non-zero values, even if the size of this list is polynomial in the number of players and the value of each coalition is 0 or 1; this can be shown by a straightfoward reduction from EXACT COVER BY 3-SETS. Similarly, while this problem is easy for Myerson games, it is NP-hard for the SCG representation (see [15]).

Shapley Value under SCG Representation. To compute the Shapley value in Myerson games, we use the graph-theoretic notion of a neighborhood. There is no obvious analogue of this notion for the SCG representation, and, indeed, computing the Shapley value under this representation turns out to be NP-hard. Interestingly, despite a considerable number of papers on the SCG representation, this result appears to be new.

Theorem 4. *Let $(N, \mathcal{C}, v)$ be an SCG representation of a coalitional game G, and let i be an agent in N. Then deciding whether $\phi_i(G) = 0$ is* NP-*hard even if G is superadditive, $N \in \mathcal{C}$, and for each $C \in \mathcal{C}$ the value $v(C)$ is either* 1 *or* 0.

Least Core under SCG Representation. To compute the value of the least core in a Myerson game, we use the algorithm for optimal coalition structure generation as a subroutine, so it is natural to expect that our approach does not extend to arbitrary coalitional games under SCG representation. Indeed, we can show that computing the value of the least core under SCG representation is NP-hard, even if $N \in \mathcal{C}$. Observe that, in contrast, as argued in Section 6, when given an SCG representation $(N, \mathcal{C}, v)$ with $N \in \mathcal{C}$, we can compute the cost of stability in polynomial time. To the best of our knowledge, this is the first example of a formalism for coalitional games under which the computational complexity of the cost of stability differs from that of the least core, and, as such, may be of independent interest.

Theorem 5. *Let $(N, \mathcal{C}, v)$ be an SCG representation of a coalitional game G, and let ε be a positive rational number. Then deciding whether $\varepsilon(G) \leq \varepsilon$ is* coNP-*hard, even if G is superadditive, $N \in \mathcal{C}$, and $v(C)$ is an integer between* 0 *and* $3|N|$ *for each $C \in \mathcal{C}$.*

Acknowledgements. The author would like to thank Leslie Ann Goldberg, Tomasz Michalak, and Dima Pasechnik for useful discussions.

References

1. Aumann, R.J., Dréze, J.: Cooperative games with coalition structures. International Journal of Game Theory 3(4), 217–237 (1974)
2. Bachrach, Y., Elkind, E., Meir, R., Pasechnik, D., Zuckerman, M., Rothe, J., Rosenschein, J.S.: The cost of stability in coalitional games. In: Mavronicolas, M., Papadopoulou, V.G. (eds.) SAGT 2009. LNCS, vol. 5814, pp. 122–134. Springer, Heidelberg (2009)
3. Brânzei, R., Dimitrov, D., Tijs, S.: Models in cooperative game theory. Springer (2005)
4. Chalkiadakis, G., Markakis, E., Jennings, N.R.: Coalitional stability in structured environments. In: AAMAS 2012, pp. 779–786 (2012)
5. Conitzer, V., Sandholm, T.: Complexity of constructing solutions in the core based on synergies among coalitions. Artificial Intelligence 170, 607–619 (2006)
6. Demange, G.: On group stability in hierarchies and networks. Journal of Political Economy 112(4), 754–778 (2004)
7. Elkind, E., Pasechnik, D.: Computing the nucleolus of weighted voting games. In: SODA 2009, pp. 327–335 (2009)
8. Greco, G., Malizia, E., Palopoli, L., Scarcello, F.: On the complexity of the core over coalition structures. In: IJCAI 2011, pp. 216–221 (2011)
9. Huberman, G.: The nucleolus and essential coalitions. In: Bensoussan, A., Lions, J.L. (eds.) Analysis and Optimization of Systems. LNCIS, vol. 28, pp. 416–422. Springer, Heidelberg (1980)
10. Karpov, D.V.: Spanning trees with many leaves: Lower bounds in terms of the number of vertices of degree 1, 3, and at least 4. Journal of Mathematical Sciences 196(6), 768–783 (2014)
11. Kopelowitz, A.: Computation of the kernels of simple games and the nucleolus of n-person games. Technical report, Hebrew University (1967)
12. Maschler, M., Peleg, B., Shapley, L.S.: Geometric properties of the kernel, nucleolus, and related solution concepts. Mathematics of Operations Research 4, 303–338 (1979)
13. Meir, R., Zick, Y., Elkind, E., Rosenschein, J.: Bounding the cost of stability in games over interaction networks. In: AAAI 2013, pp. 690–696 (2013)
14. Myerson, R.: Graphs and cooperation in games. Mathematics of Operations Research 2(3), 225–229 (1977)
15. Ohta, N., Conitzer, V., Ichimura, R., Sakurai, Y., Iwasaki, A., Yokoo, M.: Coalition structure generation utilizing compact characteristic function representations. In: Gent, I.P. (ed.) CP 2009. LNCS, vol. 5732, pp. 623–638. Springer, Heidelberg (2009)
16. Schmeidler, D.: The nucleolus of a characteristic function game. SIAM Journal on Applied Mathematics 17, 1163–1170 (1969)
17. Schrijver, A.: Combinatorial Optimization: Polyhedra and Efficiency. Springer (2003)
18. Shapley, L.S.: A value for n-person games. In: Contributions to the Theory of Games, vol. II, pp. 307–317. Princeton University Press (1953)
19. Skibski, O., Michalak, T., Rahwan, T., Wooldridge, M.: Algorithms for the Shapley and Myerson values in graph-restricted games. In: AAMAS 2014, pp. 197–204 (2014)
20. Tardos, É.: A strongly polynomial algorithm to solve combinatorial linear programs. Operations Research 34(2), 250–256 (1986)
21. Voice, T., Ramchurn, S.D., Jennings, N.R.: On coalition formation with sparse synergies. In: AAMAS 2012, pp. 223–230 (2012)

The Value of Temporally Richer Data
for Learning of Influence Networks

Munther A. Dahleh, John N. Tsitsiklis, and Spyros I. Zoumpoulis

Laboratory for Information and Decision Systems,
MIT Massachusetts Institute of Technology
77 Massachusetts Avenue, Cambridge MA 02139
{dahleh,jnt,szoumpou}@mit.edu

Consumers adopting a new product; an epidemic spreading across a population; a sovereign debt crisis hitting several countries; a cellular process during which the expression of a gene affects the expression of other genes; an article trending in the blogosphere, a topic trending on an online social network, computer malware spreading across a network; all of these are temporal processes governed by local interactions of networked entities, which influence one another. Due to the increasing capability of data acquisition technologies, rich data on the outcomes of such processes are oftentimes available (possibly with time stamps), yet the underlying network of local interactions is hidden. In this work, we infer who influences whom in a network of interacting entities based on data of their actions/decisions, and quantify the gain of learning based on sequences of actions versus sets of actions. We answer the following question: how much faster can we learn influences with access to increasingly informative temporal data (sets versus sequences)?

Clearly, having access to richer temporal information allows, in general, for faster and more accurate learning. Nevertheless, in some contexts, the temporally poor data mode of sets could provide almost all the information needed for learning, or at least suffice to learn key network relations. In addition, collecting, organizing, storing, and processing temporally richer data may require more effort and more cost. In some contexts, data on times of actions, or even sequences of actions, is noisy and unreliable; for example, the time marking of epilepsy seizure events is done by physicians on an empirical basis and is not exact. In some other contexts, having access to time stamps or sequences of actions is almost impossible. For example, in the context of retailing, data exist on sets of purchased items per customer (and are easily obtained by scanning the barcodes at checkout); however, no data exist on the order in which the items a customer checked out were picked up from the shelf (and obtaining such data would be practically hard). In this light, the question of quantifying the gain of learning with increasingly informative temporal data, and understanding in what scenarios learning with temporally poor data modes is good enough, is highly relevant in various contexts.

The overarching theme of our work is to quantify the gain in speed of learning of parametric models of influence, due to having access to richer temporal information. We seek to compare the speed of learning under three different cases of available data: (i) the data provides merely the set of agents/entities who took

T.-Y. Liu et al. (Eds.): WINE 2014, LNCS 8877, pp. 322–323, 2014.
© Springer International Publishing Switzerland 2014

an action; (ii) the data provides the (ordered) sequence of agents/entities who took an action, but not the times; and (iii) the data provides the times of the actions. It is clear that learning is no slower with times than it is with sequences, and no slower with sequences than with sets; yet, what can we say about *how much* faster learning is with times than with sequences, and with sequences than with sets? This is, to the best of our knowledge, a comparison that has not been studied systematically before. In this paper, we focus on the comparison between learning with sets and learning with sequences.

We propose a parametric model of influence which captures directed pairwise interactions and provide theoretical guarantees on the sample complexity for correct learning with sets and sequences. Our results characterize the sufficient and necessary scaling of the number of i.i.d. samples required for correct learning. The asymptotic gain of having access to richer temporal data à propos of the speed of learning is thus quantified in terms of the gap between the derived asymptotic requirements under different data modes. We first assume prior knowledge of a "super graph" that includes all the candidate edges, and we infer which edges of the super graph truly exist; restricting to each edge having either very large or no influence, we provide sufficient and necessary conditions on the graph topology for learnability, and we come up with upper and lower bounds for the minimum number of i.i.d. samples required to learn the correct hypothesis for the star topology, for different variations of the learning problem: learning one edge or learning all the edges, under different prior knowledge over the hypotheses, under different scaling of the horizon rate, and learning with sets or with sequences. We then study more general networks and relax the assumption that each edge carries an influence rate that is either very large or zero; we provide a learning algorithm and theoretical guarantees on the sample complexity for correct learning in the hard problem of telling between the complete graph and the complete graph that is missing one edge.

We also evaluate learning with sets and sequences *experimentally*. Given real data on outcomes, we learn the parametric influence model by maximum likelihood estimation. The value of learning with data of richer temporal detail is quantified, and our methodology is shown to recover the underlying network structure well. The real data come from observations of mobile app installations of users, along with data on their communications and social relations.

Link to full paper: http://web.mit.edu/ szoumpou/Public/learning_WINE2014_working_paper.pdf

Randomized Revenue Monotone Mechanisms for Online Advertising

Gagan Goel[1], MohammadTaghi Hajiaghayi[2,*], and Mohammad Reza Khani[2,*]

[1] Google Inc., New York, NY
gagangoel@google.com
[2] University of Maryland, College Park, MD
{hajiagha,khani}@cs.umd.edu

Abstract. Online advertising is the main source of revenue for many Internet firms; thus designing effective mechanisms for selecting and pricing ads become an important research question. In this paper, we seek to design truthful mechanisms for online advertising that satisfy Revenue Monotonicity (RM) - a natural property which states that the revenue of a mechanism should not decrease if the number of participants increase or if a participant increases her bid. In a recent work Goel and Khani [5], it was argued that RM is a desired goal for proper functioning of an online advertising business. Since popular mechanisms like VCG are not revenue-monotone, they introduced the notion of Price of Revenue Monotonicity (PoRM) to capture the loss in social welfare of a revenue-monotone mechanism. Goel and Khani [5] then studied the price of revenue-monotonicity of *Combinatorial Auction with Identical Items*(CAII). In CAII, there are k identical items to be sold to a group of bidders, where bidder i wants either exactly $d_i \in \{1, \dots, k\}$ number of items or nothing. CAII generalizes important online advertising scenarios such as *image-text* and *video-pod* auctions. In an image-text auction we want to fill an advertising slot with either k text-ads or a single image-ad. In video-pod auction we want to fill a video advertising break of k seconds with video-ads of possibly different durations. Goel and Khani [5] showed that no deterministic RM mechanism can attain PoRM of less than $\ln(k)$ for CAII, *i.e.*, no deterministic mechanism can attain more than $\frac{1}{\ln(k)}$ fraction of the maximum social welfare. Goel and Khani [5] also design a mechanism with PoRM of $O(\ln^2(k))$ for CAII.

In this paper, first we overcome the impossibility result of Goel and Khani [5] for deterministic mechanisms by using the power of randomization. We show that by using randomization, one can attain a constant PoRM; in particular, we design a randomized RM mechanism with PoRM of 3 for CAII. Then, we study a more general Multi-group Combinatorial Auction with Identical Items (MCAII). In MCAII, the bidders are partitioned into multiple groups, and the set of winners are constrainted to be from a single group. The motivation for MCAII is from scenarios where the set of selected ads may be required to have the same

* Supported in part by NSF CAREER award 1053605, ONR YIP award N000141110662, DARPA/AFRL award FA8650-11-1-7162, and a Google faculty research award.

T.-Y. Liu et al. (Eds.): WINE 2014, LNCS 8877, pp. 324–337, 2014.

format. We give a randomized mechanism which satisfies RM and IC and has PoRM of $O(\ln k)$. This is in contrast to $\log^2(k)$ deterministic mechanism that follows from [5].

1 Introduction

Many Internet firms including search engines, social networks, and online publishers rely on online advertising revenue for their business; thus, making online advertising an essential part of the Internet. Online advertising consists of showing a few ads to a user when she accesses a web-page from a publisher's domain. The advertising can happen in different formats such as text-ads, image-ads, video-ads, or a hybrid of them.

A key component in online advertising is a mechanism which selects and prices the set of winning ads. In this paper we study the design of mechanisms for Combinatorial Auction with Identical Items (CAII). In CAII we want to sell k identical items to a group of bidders; each demand a number of items from $\{1, \ldots, k\}$ and has a single-parameter valuation for obtaining them. Although CAII is a well-motivated model on its own, we note that a few important advertising scenarios such as image-text and video-pod auctions can be modeled by CAII. In image-text auction we want to fill an advertising box on a publisher's web-page with either one image-ad or k text-ads. We note that a large portion of Google AdSense's revenue is from this auction. Image-text auction is a special case of CAII where participants either demand only one item (text-ads) or all k items (image-ads). In video-pod auction there is an advertising break of k seconds which should be filled with video-ads each with certain duration and valuation.

When designing a mechanism, typically one focusses on attaining incentive-compatibility, and maximizing social welfare and/or revenue. In a recent work, Goel and Khani [5] argue that the mechanisms for online advertising should satisfy an additional property of revenue-monotonicity. Revenue-monotonicity is a natural property which states that the revenue of a mechanism should not decrease as the number of bidders increase or if the bidders increase their bids. The motivation is that any online firm typically has a large sales team to attract more bidders on their inventory or they invest in new technologies to make bids more attractive. The typical reasoning is that more bidders (or higher bids) lead to more competition which should lead to higher prices. However, lack of revenue-monotonicity of a mechanism is conflicting with this intuitive and natural reasoning process, and can create significant confusion from a strategic decision-making point of view.

Even though Revenue Monotonicity (RM) seems very natural, we note that majority of the well-known mechanisms do not satisfy this property [11, 12, 5]. For example the famous Vickrey-Clarke-Groves (VCG) mechanism fails to satisfy RM as adding one more bidder might decreases the revenue to zero. To see this, consider two identical items to be sold to two bidders. One wants one item with a bid 2, and the other one wants both items with a bid 2. In this case the revenue of VCG mechanism is 2 (for a proof, see for instance [10, Chapter 9]). Now suppose we add one more bidder who wants one item with a bid of 2. In this case the revenue of VCG goes down to 0!

It is known that if we require mechanisms to satisfy both RM and IC, not only the mechanism cannot get the maximum social welfare but it can also not achieve Pareto-optimality in social welfare [12]. In light of this, [5] introduced the notion of *Price of Revenue Monotonicity* (PoRM) to capture the loss in social welfare for RM mechanisms. Here a mechanism has PoRM of α if its social welfare is at least $\frac{1}{\alpha}$ fraction of the maximum social welfare in any type profile of participants. It is shown that, under a mild condition, the PoRM of any deterministic mechanism for the CAII problem is at least $\ln(k)$, *i.e.*, no deterministic mechanism can obtain more than $\frac{1}{\ln(k)}$ fraction of the maximum social welfare [5]. In fact this impossibility result holds even for the case when participants demand either all the items or only one item. On the positive side, [5] give a deterministic mechanism with PoRM of $O(\ln^2(k))$ for CAII. We note that satisfying RM is hard especially since it is an *across instance* constraint.

This work is motivated by the desire to design better mechanisms for CAII. However, the above impossibility result of [5] is a bottleneck towards this goal. To overcome this, in this paper, we resort to randomized mechanisms. We say a randomized mechanism satisfies RM if it satisfies RM in expectation[1]. Similarly, a randomized mechanism has PoRM of α if its expected social welfare is not less than $\frac{1}{\alpha}$ fraction of the maximum social welfare. We significantly improve the performance by designing a randomized mechanism with a constant PoRM. In particular, our randomized mechanism achieves a PoRM of 3.

Finally, we study Multi-group Combinatorial Auction with Identical Items (MCAII) that generalizes CAII. In MCAII bidders are partitioned into multiple groups and the set of winners has to be only from one group. The motivation is that the publisher sometimes require the ads to be of same format or size for a given ad slot. We design a randomized mechanism for MCAII that satisfies IC and RM with PoRM $O(\log k)$. An easy corollary of [5] gives a deterministic mechanism with a PoRM $O(\log^2 k)$. We give evidence that this factor for randomized mechanisms cannot be improved. The study of MCAII appears in the full version of the paper.

2   Related Works

Goel and Khani [5] show that RM is a desirable property for web-centeric companies and consider designing mechanisms which satisfy both RM and IC. They introduced the notion of PoRM and study CAII and a special case of it - namely, image-text auction. They [5] give a deterministic mechanism with PoRM of $\ln(k)$ and prove that no mechanism which satisfies RM and IC can obtain PoRM of better than $\ln(k)$ under the following two mild conditions. The first condition is anonymity which states that the outcome shouldn't depend on the identities

---

[1] Since in a typical online advertising setting, there is a large number of auctions being run everyday, we get sharp concentration bounds.

of the bidders but their type profile. The second condition is independence of irrelevant alternatives which states that decreasing the bid of any losing participant should not hurt a winning participant. Goel and Khani [5] also give a deterministic mechanism for CAII with PoRM of $O(\ln^2(k))$ that satisfies IC and RM.

Rastegari et al. [12] show that for combinatorial auctions, no deterministic mechanism that satisfies RM and IC can get weak maximality. A mechanism is Weakly Maximal (WM) if it chooses an allocation which cannot be augmented to make a losing participant a winner without hurting a winning participant. Rastegari et al. [11] study randomized mechanisms for combinatorial auctions which satisfy RM and IC. Note that a simple mechanism which chooses a maximal allocation uniformly at random ignoring the valuations of bidders satisfies RM, IC, and WM. Rastegari et al. [11] add another constraint that a mechanism has to also satisfy Consumer Sovereignty (CS) which means that if a bidder increases her bid high enough, she can win her desired items. Now a new issue is that there is no randomized mechanism which satisfies RM, IC, WM, and CS [11]. In order to avoid this issue they relax CS constraint as follows. For each participant i there has to be λ different valuations $v_1 > v_2 > \ldots > v_\lambda$ such that for $j \in \{1, \ldots, \lambda\}$, we have $w_i(v_j) > w_i(v_{j+1}) + \sigma$ where w_i is the probability of winning for participant i and $\sigma > 0$. Roughly speaking relaxed CS constraint means that if participant i increases her bid from zero to infinity she sees at least λ jumps of length σ in her winning probability. The idea of their mechanism is that for each participant i they find λ constant values $c_{i,1} > c_{i,2} > \ldots > c_{i,\lambda}$ such that regardless of valuations of the other bidders; if the bid of bidder i is between $c_{i,j}$ and $c_{i,j+1}$ then her winning probability is at least $j * \sigma$. In order to find the constants for each participant they solve a LP whose constraints force RM, IC, Relaxed CS, and WM. As you may notice although this mechanism achieves WM, RM and relaxed CM, but can do very poorly in terms of PoRM. For example suppose you have n participants and each of them wants all items. The valuation of each participant i is bigger than its highest constant $c_{i,1}$. In this case all the participants can win with probability at most $1/n$. Now suppose that the valuation of one of the participants is infinity. She still wins with probability $1/n$ which shows that the PoRM of their mechanism is at least n.

Dughmi et al. [4] show that VCG is revenue monotone if and only if the feasible subsets of winners form a matroid. Ausubel and Milgrom [1] show that if valuations of bidders satisfy *bidder-submodularity* then VCG satisfies RM. Here valuations satisfy bidders submodularity if and only if for any bidder i and any two sets of bidders S, S' with $S \subseteq S'$ we have $\text{WELFARE}(S \cup \{i\}) - \text{WELFARE}(S) \geq \text{WELFARE}(S' \cup \{i\}) - \text{WELFARE}(S')$, where $\text{WELFARE}(S)$ is the maximum social welfare achievable using only bidders in S. Note that we can restrict the set of possible allocations in a way such that bidder-submodularity holds. Then we can use VCG on this restricted set of allocations and hence achieve RM. However we can show that it is not possible to get a mechanism with PoRM better than $\Omega(k)$ by restricting the set of allocations in order to get bidder-submodularity.

Ausubel and Milgrom [1] design a mechanism which is in the core of the exchange economy for combinatorial auctions. A mechanism is in the core if there is no subset of participants including the seller which can collude and trade among each other such that all of them benefit more than the result of the mechanism. Day and Milgrom [3] show that a core-selecting mechanism which selects an allocation that minimizes the seller's revenue satisfies RM given bidders follow so called *best-response truncation strategy*. Therefore, the mechanism of [1] satisfies RM if it selects an allocation that minimizes the seller's revenue and the participants follow best-response strategy, however, this mechanism does not satisfy IC.

Another line of related works is around characterizing incentive compatible mechanisms. The classic result of Roberts [13] tells that affine maximizers are the only social choice functions which can be implemented using mechanisms that satisfy IC when bidders have unrestricted quasi-linear valuations. Subsequent works study some restricted cases, see *e.g.* [14, 8, 2, 15].

There is also a large body of research around designing mechanisms with good bounds on the revenue. In the single parameter Bayesian setting Myerson [9] designs a mechanism which achieves the optimal expected revenue. [6, 7] consider optimizing revenue in prior-free settings (see *e.g.* [10] for a survey on this).

3   Our Results and Overview of Techniques

To give intuition about our approach, we first start with ideas that will not work but are potentially good candidates. To keep the explanation easier let us focus on deterministic mechanisms. Note that the payment of each participant in a deterministic mechanism which satisfies IC is her critical value, *i.e.*, the minimum valuation for which she still remains a winner. Assume that all participants demand only one item. In this case we can simply give all the items to the highest k bidders, which sets the critical value (the payment) of each winner to the valuation of the $(k + 1)$th highest bidder. If we add one more participant the valuation of the $(k + 1)$th highest bidder increases, therefore, the payment of each winner increases and hence the mechanism satisfies RM.

Now assume we have two types of bidders: A bidder of type A who demand all k items, and a bidder of type B who demands a single item. This scenario is equivalent to the image-text auction for which there is a lower-bound of $\ln(k)$ for the PoRM of deterministic mechanisms [5]. However using randomization we can simply get a PoRM of 2. Flip a coin and with probability half give all items to the highest type A bidder and with probability half give k items to the k highest bidders of type B. Here, the expected social welfare is at least half of the maximum social welfare. Note that when the coin flip selects bidders of type A the auction simply transforms to the second price auction of selling one package of items which has RM. When it selects bidders of type B the auction transforms to the case when all bidders demand one item which we explained earlier and has RM. Therefore, the expected revenue is monotone and hence the mechanism satisfies RM. Expanding the above idea we can partition the bidders into $\log(k)$ groups such that the bidders of each group $i \in \log(k)$ has demand in $[2^i, 2^{i+1})$. Then, we randomly select one group and choose the winners from the selected group. However, this partitioning approach does not lead to a PoRM better than $\log(k)$.

As a second approach instead of partitioning the bidders and sort them by their valuation, we can sort them according to their Price Per Item (PPI) which is the valuation of a participant divided by the number of items she demands. Now consider a simple greedy algorithm as follows. Start from the top of the sorted list of bidders and at each step do the following. If the number of remaining items is enough to serve the current bidder give the items to the bidder and proceed; otherwise stop. Let us call the bidder at which the greedy algorithm stops the *runner-up bidder*. Note that the runner-up bidder has the largest PPI among the loser bidders and let p be her PPI. If each of the winner participant had PPI less than p then she could not win. Therefore, the critical value of each winner participant is her demand multiplied by p. Although value p increases if we add more bidders, the number of items sold might decrease. For example consider the case when the bidder with the highest PPI demands all k items. In this scenario she wins all items and pays k multiplied by the PPI of the runner-up bidder. Now if we add one more bidder whose PPI is more than the highest bidder but demands only one item; the new bidder wins and we sell only one item. This potentially decreases the revenue of the greedy mechanism.

For our mechanism we use a combination of the above ideas and an extra interesting technique. We partition the bidders into two groups: high-demand bidders who demand more than $k/2$ items, and low-demand bidders who demand less than or equal to $k/2$ items. With probability $1/3$ the winner is a high-demand bidder with the largest valuation. Similar to the partitioning approach the critical value of the winner is the second largest valuation of the high-demand bidders which can only increase if we add more bidders. With probability $2/3$ we do the following with the low-demand bidders. First we run the greedy algorithm over the low-demand bidders and find the runner-up bidder. The important observation here is that because there is no high-demand bidder, the sum of winners' demands (A) is larger than $k/2$. Therefore we are sure that we sell at least $k/2$ items where the price of each item is the PPI of the runner-up bidder. Now we select each winner of the greedy algorithm with probability $\frac{k/2}{A}$ as the true winner of our mechanism. This random selection makes sure that the expected number of sold items is exactly $k/2$. The exact number $k/2$ is important since the expected revenue of the mechanism is $k/2$ multiplied by the PPI of the runner-up bidder. Therefore as the PPI of the runner-up bidder increases if we add more bidders the expected revenue is monotone.

Now we explain ideas used to design our mechanism for MCAII. We first note that as a corollary of the result of [5], we get a deterministic mechanism with a PoRM of $\log^2(n)$. In our mechanism, we assign a value to each group and use it as the criterion in order to select the winner group. Note that a simple value that can be assigned to each group is the maximum social welfare obtainable by the group. However, this way we cannot guarantee RM. Because suppose participant $i^{(g)}$ of group $G^{(g)}$ increases her bid high enough which guarantees that $G^{(g)}$ wins against all other groups no matter what are the valuations of the other participants of $G^{(g)}$. Therefore, the critical values of the other members of $G^{(g)}$ decreases as $i^{(g)}$ increases her bid and hence can decrease the revenue of the mechanism.

We refer to our assigned value to each group as the Maximum Possible Revenue of the Group (MPRG). As name MPRG suggests, it shows the maximum revenue we can obtain from each group without the fear of violating RM. For each $j \in \{1, \ldots, k\}$ and group $G^{(g)}$, let $u_j^{(g)}$ be the maximum price can be set for a single item so that we can sell at least j items to low-demand bidders of group $G^{(g)}$. More formally, $u_j^{(g)}$ is the maximum value where the sum of demands of low-demand bidders whose PPI is larger than $u_j^{(g)}$ in group $G^{(g)}$ is at least j. The MPRG of group $G^{(g)}$ is $\max(V^{(g)}, \max_{j \in \{1, \ldots, k/2\}} j \cdot u_j^{(g)})$ where $V^{(g)}$ is the highest valuation of high-demand bidders. Intuitively, MPRG either sells items to high-demand bidders and obtains revenue of at most $V^{(g)}$ or sells items to low-demand bidders in which we can sell a number of items between 1 and $k/2$. We select a group with the highest MPRG and choose the winners from this group. We are able to show that we can obtain a revenue of at least the second highest MPRG. We prove that our mechanism satisfies RM by showing that the second highest MPRG increases if we add more bidders.

We show that the MPRG of each group is at least $1/\ln(k)$ fraction of the maximum social welfare obtainable by the group. Therefore, as we select the winning group using the MPRGs of groups, the PoRM of our mechanism is $O(\ln(k))$. We provide evidence that indeed the MPRG of each group is the closest value to its social welfare that can be safely used for selecting the winning group without violating RM. Moreover, any randomization over the groups for selecting the winning one according to MPRG cannot improve the PoRM factor.

4   Preliminary

Let assume we have a set of n bidders $\{1, \ldots, n\}$ and a set of k identical items. Let type profile θ be a vector containing the type of each bidder i which we show by θ_i. Here θ_i is pair $(d_i, v_i) \in [k] \times \mathbb{R}^+$ where d_i is the number of items she demands and v_i shows her valuation for getting d_i items. Here we assume the demands are publicly known because in our scenario they represent the length of video-ads stored in database while the valuations are private to bidders.

Note that having higher valuation does not necessarily mean that the bidder is more desirable to the seller as she might have a large demand. We define Price Per Item (PPI) of bidder i to be $\frac{v_i}{d_i}$ which we use in our mechanism to compare bidders.

We show a randomized mechanism $(\mathcal{M})$ by pair (w, p) where $w_i(\theta)$ shows the winning probability of bidder i in type profile θ and $p_i(\theta)$ is her expected payment.

We use the following Theorem in this paper frequently which is a well-known characteristic of the truthful randomized mechanisms in the single parameter model (see $e.g.$ [10]).

Theorem 1. *Randomized mechanism $\mathcal{M} = (w, p)$ is truthful if and only if for any type profile θ and any bidder i with type (d_i, v_i) the followings hold.*

1. *Function $w_i ((d_i, v_i), \theta_{-i})$ is weakly monotone in v_i.*
2. $p_i(\theta) = v_i \cdot w_i(\theta) - \int_0^{v_i} w_i ((d_i, t), \theta_{-i}) \, dt$

5 Combinatorial Auction with Identical Items

We build a randomized mechanism $(\mathcal{M} = (w, p))$ satisfying revenue monotonicity and incentive compatibility such that $\mathrm{PoRM}(\mathcal{M})$ is equal to 3.

We call a bidder *high-demand* bidder if her demand is greater than $\lfloor k/2 \rfloor$ otherwise we refer it as *low-demand* bidder. Mechanism $\mathcal{M}$ partitions the bidders into two groups of low-demand and high-demand bidders and with probability $1/3$ selects the winning set from the high-demand bidders and with probability $2/3$ from the low-demand bidders.

We will see that mechanism $\mathcal{M}$ favors high-demand bidders with larger valuations and favors low-demand-bidders with larger PPIs while breaking the ties by the index number of the bidders.

Definition 1. *We say low-demand bidder l_1 is* more valuable *than low-demand bidder l_2 and show it by $(l_1 \succ l_2)$ if $\mathrm{PPI}_{l_1} > \mathrm{PPI}_{l_2} \vee (\mathrm{PPI}_{l_1} = \mathrm{PPI}_{l_2} \wedge l_1 < l_2)$. Similarly we call high-demand bidder h_1 is* more valuable *than high-demand bidder h_2 and show it by $(h_1 \succ h_2)$ if $v_{h_1} > v_{h_2} \vee (v_{h_1} = v_{h_2} \wedge h_1 < h_2)$.*

Let's assume that there are ℓ low-demand bidders and h high-demand bidders. By adding some dummy bidders with demand 1 and valuation zero we assume that the sum of demands of low-demand bidders is always greater than k. Without loss of generality we assume that the first ℓ bidders are low-demand bidders and $i \succ i + 1$ for any $i \in [\ell - 1]$ (the PPIs of the low-demand bidders decreases by their index) and the remaining h bidders are high-demand-bidders while $i \succ i + 1$ for any $i \in \{\ell + 1, \ldots n - 1\}$ (the valuations of the high-demand bidders decreases by their index).

Definition 2. *We call low-demand bidder r the* runner-up bidder *if r is the smallest value in set $[\ell]$ for which $\sum_{i=1}^{r} d_i \geq k$.*

Later we will see that the runner-up bidder is the bidder with the largest PPI and smallest index number who has zero probability of winning. We simply refer to the runner-up bidder as r.

We define A to be $\sum_{i=1}^{r-1} d_i$ which is the sum of demands of low-demand bidders that have PPIs greater than or equal to that of r and have positive probability of winning (see Fig 1).

Observation 1 *We have $\lceil k/2 \rceil \leq A < k$.*

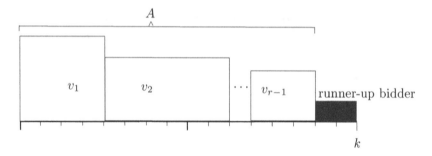

Fig. 1. Each rectangle corresponds to a bidder where the height, width, and area represent PPI, demand, and valuation of the bidder respectively. The dark rectangle corresponds to the runner-up bidder whose demand crosses the value k.

Proof. Inequality $A < k$ is the direct result of the way we select runner-up bidder r. Inequality $\lceil \frac{k}{2} \rceil \leq A$ follows from the fact that $\sum_i^r d_i \geq k$ and the demand of the runner-up bidder is less than or equal to $\lfloor \frac{k}{2} \rfloor$ by definition of low-demand bidders. $\qquad \square$

Now we are ready to precisely define how $\mathcal{M}$ selects and charges the set of winners. With probability $1/3$ $\mathcal{M}$ selects the most valuable high-demand bidder (which is the high-demand bidder with largest valuation breaking the ties by index). Therefore, the winning bidder in this case is $\ell + 1$ and she pays $v_{\ell+2}$ which is the second highest valuation among high-demand bidders. Therefore her expected payment is $p_{\ell+1}^{\mathcal{M}}(\theta) = \frac{v_{\ell+2}}{3}$.

If we did not select the largest high-demand bidder then mechanism $\mathcal{M}$ uniformly at random selects the winner set from the first $r - 1$ low-demand bidders where the probability of selecting each bidder $i \in [r - 1]$ is $\frac{\lceil k/2 \rceil}{A}$. In this case if bidder i gets selected she has to pay $d_i \cdot \text{PPI}_r$. Therefore, her expected payment is $p_i^{\mathcal{M}}(\theta) = \frac{2\lceil k/2 \rceil}{3A} \cdot d_i \cdot \text{PPI}_r$ since with probability $2/3$ we select low-demand-bidders and with probability $\frac{\lceil k/2 \rceil}{A}$ bidder i gets selected. The probability $\frac{\lceil k/2 \rceil}{A}$ is selected in a way such that if the low-demand bidders win, the expected number of allocated items is $\lceil k/2 \rceil$ since the sum of demands of the first $r-1$ low-demand bidders is A and each of them gets selected with probability $\frac{\lceil k/2 \rceil}{A}$.

In summary the expected payments of the bidders in mechanism $\mathcal{M}$ is the following.

$$
p_i^{\mathcal{M}}(\theta) = \begin{cases} 0 & \ell + 1 < i \\ \frac{v_{\ell+2}}{3} & i = \ell + 1 \\ 0 & r \leq i \leq \ell \\ \frac{2\lceil k/2 \rceil}{3A} \cdot d_i \cdot \text{PPI}_r & 1 \leq i < r \end{cases} \tag{1}
$$

In the following first we prove that the allocation function of $\mathcal{M}$ is monotone and then we show that the unique expected payments of the winners calculated using Theorem 1 is equal to the expected payment of mechanism $\mathcal{M}$ which proves that $\mathcal{M}$ truthful.

Observation 2 $w_i\left((d_i, v_i), \theta_{-i}\right)$ is monotone in v_i.

Proof. If bidder i is a high-demand bidder then clearly increasing her bid just increases her chance to be the high-demand bidder with the largest valuation and hence win with probability $1/3$. If bidder i is a low-demand bidder then increasing her bid just increases her PPI and hence can help her to go over the PPI of the runner-up bidder and win with probability $\frac{2\lceil\frac{k}{2}\rceil}{3\cdot A}$. $\qquad\square$

The following lemma shows the expected payment of each winner.

Lemma 1. *The truthful expected payment of bidder i $(p_i(\theta))$ calculated by Condition 2 of Theorem 1 is the following.*

$$
p_i(\theta) = \begin{cases}
0 & \ell + 1 < i \\
\frac{v_{\ell+2}}{3} & i = \ell + 1 \\
0 & r \le i \le \ell \\
\frac{2\lceil k/2\rceil}{3A} \cdot d_i \cdot \text{PPI}_r & 1 \le i < r
\end{cases}
\tag{2}
$$

Proof. Remember that the first ℓ bidders are low-demand bidders which have non-decreasing PPIs, r is the low-demand runner-up bidder, and finally among high-demand bidders, bidder $\ell + 1$ has the largest valuation and bidder $\ell + 2$ has the second largest valuation.

The probability of winning for bidder i when $\ell + 1 < i$ is zero since she is a high-demand bidder who either does not have the highest valuation or has the highest valuation but has larger index number (see Definition 1). Because function w_i is monotone we conclude that $w_i\left((d_i, t), \theta_{-i}\right)$ is equal to zero for any $t \le v_i$. Hence by calculating the formula in Condition 2 of Theorem 1 we get $p_i(\theta) = 0$.

We calculate the truthful expected payment of bidder $\ell + 1$ by using the formula in Condition 2 of Theorem 1.

$$
\begin{aligned}
p_{\ell+1}(\theta) &= v_{\ell+1} \cdot w_{\ell+1}(\theta) - \int_0^{v_{\ell+1}} w_{\ell+1}\left((d_{\ell+1}, t), \theta_{-\ell+1}\right) dt \\
&= \frac{1}{3} v_{\ell+1} - \int_0^{v_{\ell+1}} w_{\ell+1}\left((d_{\ell+1}, t), \theta_{-\ell+1}\right) dt \\
&= \frac{1}{3} v_{\ell+1} - \int_0^{v_{\ell+2}} w_{\ell+1}\left((d_{\ell+1}, t), \theta_{-\ell+1}\right) dt - \int_{v_{\ell+2}}^{v_{\ell+1}} w_{\ell+1}\left((d_{\ell+1}, t), \theta_{-\ell+1}\right) dt \\
&= \frac{1}{3} v_{\ell+1} - \int_{v_{\ell+2}}^{v_{\ell+1}} w_{\ell+1}\left((d_{\ell+1}, t), \theta_{-\ell+1}\right) dt \\
&= \frac{1}{3} v_{\ell+1} - \frac{1}{3}(v_{\ell+1} - v_{\ell+2}) \\
&= \frac{v_{\ell+2}}{3}
\end{aligned}
$$

The first equality is Condition 2 of Theorem 1, the second equality follows from the fact that probability of winning for bidder $\ell+1$ $(w_{\ell+1}(\theta))$ is $1/3$, the third one is breaking the domain of integration, the forth and fifth equalities are followed by noting that probability of winning for bidder $\ell + 1$ is zero if his valuation is less than $v_{\ell+2}$ and is $1/3$ if his valuation is greater than or equal to $v_{\ell+2}$.

The probability of winning for bidder i when $r \leq i \leq \ell$ is zero since she is a low-demand bidder which has PPI less than or equal to PPI_r. Because function w_i is monotone we conclude that $w_i\left((d_i, t), \theta_{-i}\right)$ is equal to zero for any $t \leq v_i$. Hence by calculating the formula in Condition 2 of Theorem 1 we get $p_i(\theta) = 0$.

The only part remaining is to show that $p_i(\theta) = \frac{2\lceil k/2 \rceil}{3A} \cdot d_i \cdot \text{PPI}_r$ for $1 \leq i < r$ using Condition 2 of Theorem 1. In order to calculate $\int_0^{v_i} w_i\left((d_i, t), \theta_{-i}\right) dt$ we consider the curve of allocation function $w_i\left((d_i, t), \theta_{-i}\right)$ when t increases from zero to v_i (see Fig 2).

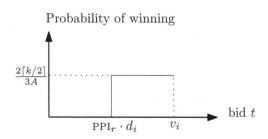

Fig. 2. The horizontal axis represents the bid of bidder i and the vertical axis shows the probability of bidder i winning. As bidder i increases her bid; at the point when her PPI is equal to the PPI of the runner-up bidder she gets allocated with probability $\frac{2\lceil k/2 \rceil}{3A}$.

Observation 3 *For any bidder $1 \leq i < r$ allocation function $w_i\left((d_i, t), \theta_{-i}\right)$ is equal to zero when $t < d_i \cdot \text{PPI}_r$ and is equal to $\frac{2\lceil k/2 \rceil}{3A}$ when $t \geq d_i \cdot \text{PPI}_r$.*

Proof. Remember the runner-up bidder r has the smallest index for which $\sum_{j=1}^r d_j \geq k$. Mechanism $\mathcal{M}$ allocates all the low-demand bidders which have index less than r (have PPIs greater than or equal to the runner-up bidder) with probability $\frac{2\lceil k/2 \rceil}{3A}$. Therefore as far as $t \geq d_i \cdot \text{PPI}_r$ bidder i is more valuable than the runner-up bidder (see Definition 1) and wins with probability $\frac{2\lceil k/2 \rceil}{3A}$ in type profile $\left((d_i, t), \theta_{-i}\right)$.

Now assume that $t < d_i \cdot \text{PPI}_r$ and $\theta' = \left((d_i, t), \theta_{-i}\right)$. Our objective is to show that the probability of bidder i winning is zero for type profile θ' and hence finish the proof of the observation. Note that $\sum_{j=1}^r d_j \geq k$ and in the new type profile θ' bidder i has PPI less than the PPIs of all bidders $j \in [r]$ where $j \neq i$ since $t < d_i \cdot \text{PPI}_r$. In other words, bidder i is the least valuable bidder in $[r]$ (see Definition 1) while $\sum_{j=1}^r d_j \geq k$. Therefore, bidder i is either the runner-up bidder in θ' or has PPI less than the runner-up bidder (see Definition 2). Hence has zero probability of winning. ☐

The following equalities shows the expected payment of bidder i for $1 \le i < r$.

$$
\begin{aligned}
p_i(\theta) &= v_i \cdot w_i(\theta) - \int_0^{v_i} w_i\left((d_i, t), \theta_{-i}\right) dt \\
&= \frac{2\lceil k/2 \rceil}{3A} v_i - \int_0^{v_i} w_i\left((d_i, t), \theta_{-i}\right) dt \\
&= \frac{2\lceil k/2 \rceil}{3A} v_i - \int_0^{d_i \cdot \mathrm{PPI}_r} w_i\left((d_i, t), \theta_{-i}\right) dt - \int_{d_i \cdot \mathrm{PPI}_r}^{v_i} w_i\left((d_i, t), \theta_{-i}\right) dt \\
&= \frac{2\lceil k/2 \rceil}{3A} v_i - \int_{d_i \cdot \mathrm{PPI}_r}^{v_i} w_i\left((d_i, t), \theta_{-i}\right) dt \\
&= \frac{2\lceil k/2 \rceil}{3A} v_i - \frac{2\lceil k/2 \rceil}{3A}\left(v_i - d_i \cdot \mathrm{PPI}_r\right) \\
&= \frac{2\lceil k/2 \rceil}{3A}\left(d_i \cdot \mathrm{PPI}_r\right)
\end{aligned}
$$

The first equality is Condition 2 of Theorem 1, the second equality follows from the fact that probability of winning for bidder i ($w_i(\theta)$) is $\frac{2\lceil k/2 \rceil}{3A}$, the third one is breaking the domain of integration, the forth and fifth equalities are followed from Observation 3. □

Let REVENUE$(\mathcal{M}, \theta)$ denotes the expected revenue of mechanism $\mathcal{M}$ in type profile θ. We prove the following.

$$
\begin{aligned}
\text{REVENUE}(\mathcal{M}, \theta) &= \sum_{i=1}^{n} p_i(\theta) && \text{definiton of REVENUE} \\
&= \sum_{i=1}^{r-1} p_i(\theta) + \sum_{i=r}^{\ell} p_i(\theta) + p_{\ell+1}(\theta) + \sum_{i=\ell+2}^{n} p_i(\theta) \\
&= \sum_{i=1}^{r-1} \frac{2\lceil k/2 \rceil}{3A}\left(d_i \cdot \mathrm{PPI}_r\right) + \frac{v_{\ell+2}}{3} && \text{Lemma 1} \\
&= \frac{2\lceil k/2 \rceil}{3A} \cdot \mathrm{PPI}_r \cdot \sum_{i=1}^{r-1} d_i + \frac{v_{\ell+2}}{3} \\
&= \frac{2\lceil k/2 \rceil}{3} \cdot \mathrm{PPI}_r + \frac{v_{\ell+2}}{3} && \text{as } A = \sum_{i=1}^{r-1} d_i
\end{aligned}
$$

$$(3)$$

The following lemma proves that $\mathcal{M}$ is revenue monotone.

Lemma 2. *The expected revenue of mechanism $\mathcal{M}$ does not decrease if we add one more bidder or a bidder increases her bid.*

Proof. The expected revenue of mechanism $\mathcal{M}$ is $\frac{2\lceil k/2 \rceil}{3} \cdot \mathrm{PPI}_r + \frac{v_{\ell+2}}{3}$ by Equation (3). Remember that $v_{\ell+2}$ is the high-demand bidder with the second highest valuation, therefore, if we add one more bidder or a bidder increases her bid this value does not decrease. On the other hand PPI_r is the PPI of the runner-up bidder (see Definition 2) which is the PPI of the first low-demand bidder that crosses value k (see Fig 1) where the bidders are sorted according to their PPIs. The proof of the lemma follows by the fact that PPI_r also does not decrease as we add one more bidder or a bidder increases her bid. □

Finally, the following lemma (included in the full version of the paper) shows that Price of Revenue Monotoncity (PoRM) of $\mathcal{M}$ is 3 and finishes this section.

Lemma 3. PoRM($\mathcal{M}$) = 3.

6   Discussion and Future Works

Note that our mechanism satisfies the desired IC property and gets a good portion of the maximum social welfare. However, one may worry that by enforcing revenue monotonicity we may lose in total revenue since it is an additional constraint. To address this issue, firstly, we emphasize that lack of revenue-monotonicity can lead to loss of revenue and efficiency from second-order effects that could be much higher than leaving some revenue to attain this property. Most teams in a technology firm treat auction as a black box without knowledge of its internal procedures. For example, assume a team designs a new innovative ad format that increases the click-through-rate of certain ads. Without revenue-monotonicity, such changes can actually lower the revenue. The problem now is that this can result in this innovative change not getting into production system as it might be seen as a *bad* change. This can be a real problem in practice, and as auction designers, we need to address this problem. Secondly, our ultimate goal is indeed to design auctions that satisfy good properties in different dimensions including total revenue. However, one must realize that almost nothing is known theoretically about this important property of *revenue-monotonicity*. Therefore, to fully understand it formally, in our model, we isolate and just focus on RM property while maximizing social welfare. This work can be a starting point for the community to build more results around RM property, and hopefully a general framework to design RM mechanisms emerges. Once we have the state of the art understanding of RM, the next goal is to understand more objectives simultaneously.

References

[1] Ausubel, L.M., Milgrom, P.: Ascending auctions with package bidding. Frontiers of Theoretical Economics 1(1), 1–42 (2002)
[2] Bikhchandani, S., Chatterji, S., Lavi, R., Mu'alem, A., Nisan, N., Sen, A.: Weak monotonicity characterizes deterministic dominant-strategy implementation. Econometrica 74(4), 1109–1132 (2006)

[3] Day, R., Milgrom, P.: Core-selecting package auctions. International Journal of Game Theory 36(3-4), 393–407 (2008)

[4] Dughmi, S., Roughgarden, T., Sundararajan, M.: Revenue submodularity. In: Proceedings of the 10th ACM Conference on Electronic Commerce, pp. 243–252. ACM (2009)

[5] Goel, G., Khani, M.R.: Revenue monotone mechanisms for online advertising. In: International World Wide Web Conference, WWW (2014), https://www.cs.umd.edu/~khani/papers/rm.pdf

[6] Goldberg, A.V., Hartline, J.D., Wright, A.: Competitive auctions and digital goods. In: Symposium on Discrete Algorithms, pp. 735–744 (2001)

[7] Goldberg, A.V., Hartline, J.D., Karlin, A.R., Saks, M., Wright, A.: Competitive auctions. Games and Economic Behavior 55(2), 242–269 (2006)

[8] Lavi, R., Mu'Alem, A., Nisan, N.: Towards a characterization of truthful combinatorial auctions. In: Foundations of Computer Science, pp. 574–583 (2003)

[9] Myerson, R.B.: Optimal auction design. Mathematics of Operations Research 6(1), 58–73 (1981)

[10] Nisan, N., Roughgarden, T., Tardos, E., Vazirani, V.V.: Algorithmic game theory. Cambridge University Press (2007)

[11] Rastegari, B., Condon, A., Leyton-Brown, K.: Stepwise randomized combinatorial auctions achieve revenue monotonicity. In: Symposium on Discrete Algorithms, pp. 738–747 (2009)

[12] Rastegari, B., Condon, A., Leyton-Brown, K.: Revenue monotonicity in deterministic, dominant-strategy combinatorial auctions. Artificial Intelligence 175(2), 441–456 (2011)

[13] Roberts, K.: The characterization of implementable choice rules. Aggregation and Revelation of Preferences 12(2), 321–348 (1979)

[14] Rochet, J.-C.: A necessary and sufficient condition for rationalizability in a quasilinear context. Journal of Mathematical Economics 16(2), 191–200 (1987)

[15] Saks, M., Yu, L.: Weak monotonicity suffices for truthfulness on convex domains. In: Electronic Commerce, pp. 286–293 (2005)

Learning Economic Parameters
from Revealed Preferences

Maria-Florina Balcan[1], Amit Daniely[2],
Ruta Mehta[3], Ruth Urner[1], and Vijay V. Vazirani[3]

[1] Department of Machine Learning, Carnegie Mellon University
{ninamf,rurner}@cs.cmu.edu
[2] Department of Mathematics, The Hebrew University
amit.daniely@mail.huji.ac.il
[3] School of Computer Science, Georgia Institute of Technology
{rmehta,vazirani}@cc.gatech.edu

Abstract. A recent line of work, starting with Beigman and Vohra [4] and Zadimoghaddam and Roth [30], has addressed the problem of *learning* a utility function from revealed preference data. The goal here is to make use of past data describing the purchases of a utility maximizing agent when faced with certain prices and budget constraints in order to produce a hypothesis function that can accurately forecast the *future* behavior of the agent.

In this work we advance this line of work by providing sample complexity guarantees and efficient algorithms for a number of important classes. By drawing a connection to recent advances in multi-class learning, we provide a computationally efficient algorithm with tight sample complexity guarantees ($\tilde{\Theta}(d/\epsilon)$ for the case of d goods) for learning linear utility functions under a linear price model. This solves an open question in Zadimoghaddam and Roth [30]. Our technique yields numerous generalizations including the ability to learn other well-studied classes of utility functions, to deal with a misspecified model, and with non-linear prices.

Keywords: revealed preference, statistical learning, query learning, efficient algorithms, Linear, SPLC and Leontief utility functions.

1 Introduction

A common assumption in Economics is that agents are utility maximizers, meaning that the agent, facing prices, will choose to buy the bundle of goods that she most prefers among all bundles that she can afford, according to some concave, non-decreasing utility function [21]. In the classical "revealed preference" analysis [29], the goal is to produce a model of the agent's utility function that can explain her behavior based on past data. Work on this topic has a long history in economics [26,19,20,14,23,1,28,10,15,11], beginning with the seminal work by Samuelson (1948) [24]. Traditionally, this work has focused on the "rationalization" or "fitting the sample" problem, in which explanatory utility functions are

T.-Y. Liu et al. (Eds.): WINE 2014, LNCS 8877, pp. 338–353, 2014.

constructively generated from finitely many agent price/purchase observations. For example, the seminal work of Afriat [1] showed (via an algorithmic construction) that any finite sequence of observations is rationalizable if and only if it is rationalizable by a piecewise linear, monotone, concave utility function. Note, however, that just because a function agrees with a set of data does not imply that it will necessarily predict future purchases well.

A recent exciting line of work, starting with Beigman and Vohra [4], introduced a statistical learning analysis of the problem of learning the utility function from past data with the explicit formal goal of having predictive or forecasting properties. The goal here is to make use of the observed data describing the behavior of the agent (i.e., the bundles the agent bought when faced with certain prices and budget constraints) in order to produce a hypothesis function that can accurately predict or forecast the *future* purchases of a utility maximizing agent. [4] show that without any other assumptions on the utility besides monotonicity and concavity, the sample complexity of learning (in a statistical or probably approximately correct sense [27]) a demand and hence utility function is infinite. This shows the importance of focusing on important sub-classes since fitting just any monotone, concave function to the data will not be predictive for future events.

Motivated by this, Zadimoghaddam and Roth [30] considered specific classes of utility functions including the commonly used class of linear utilities. In this work, we advance this line of work by providing sample complexity guarantees and efficient algorithms for a number of important classical classes (including linear, separable piecewise-linear concave (SPLC), and Leontief [21]), significantly expanding the cases where we have strong learnability results. At a technical level, our work establishes connections between learning from revealed preferences and problems of multi-class learning, combining recent advances on intrinsic sample complexity of multi-class learning based on compression schemes [9] with a new algorithmic analysis yielding time- and sample-efficient procedures. We believe that this technique may apply to a variety of learning problems in economic and game theoretic contexts.

1.1 Our Results

For the case of linear utility functions, we establish a connection to the so-called structured prediction problem of D-*dimensional linear classes* in theoretical machine learning (see e.g., [6,7,16]). By using and improving very recent results of [9], we provide a computationally efficient algorithm with *tight* sample complexity guarantees for learning linear utility functions under a linear price model (i.e., additive over goods) for the statistical revealed preference setting. This improves over the bound in Zadimoghaddam and Roth [30] by a factor of d and resolves their open question concerning the right sample complexity of this problem. In addition to noting that we can actually fit the types of problems stemming from revealed preference in the structured prediction framework of Daniely and Shalev-Shwartz [9], we also provide a much more efficient and practical algorithm for this learning problem. We specifically show that we can reduce their compression based technique to a classic SVM problem which can be solved via convex programming [1]. This latter result could be of independent interest to Learning Theory.

The connection to the structured prediction problem with D-dimensional linear classes is quite powerful and it yields numerous generalizations. It immediately implies strong sample complexity guarantees (though not necessarily efficient algorithms) for other important revealed preference settings. For linear utility functions we can deal with non-linear prices (studied for example in [17]), as well as with a misspecified model — in learning theoretic terms this means the agnostic setting where the target function is consistent with a linear utility function on a $1 - \eta$ fraction of bundles; furthermore, we can also accommodate non-divisible goods. Other classes of utility functions including SPLC can be readily analyzed in this framework as well.

We additionally study *exact* learning via revealed preference queries: here the goal of the learner is to determine the underlying utility function exactly, but it has more power since it can choose instances (i.e., prices and budgets) of its own choice and obtain the labels (i.e., the bundles the buyer buys). We carefully exploit the structure of the optimal solution (which can be determined based on the KKT conditions) in order to design query efficient algorithms. This could be relevant for scenarios where sellers/manufacturers with many different products have the ability to explicitly set desired prices for exploratory purposes (e.g., with the goal to be able to predict how demands change with change in prices of different goods, so that they can price their goods optimally).

As a point of comparison, for both statistical and the query setting, we also analyze learning classes of utility functions directly (from utility values instead of from revealed preferences). Table 1 summarizes our sample complexity bounds for learning from revealed preferences (RP) and from utility values (Value) as well as our corresponding bounds on the query complexity (in the table we omit log-factors). Previously known results are indicated with a $*$.

Table 1. Markets with d goods, and parameters of (bit-length) size n

	RP, Statistical	RP, Query	Value, Statistical	Value, Query
Linear	$\Theta(d/\epsilon)$	$O(nd)$	$O(d/\epsilon)^*$	$O(d)^*$
SPLC (at most κ segments per good)	$O(\kappa d/\epsilon)$ (known segment lengths)	$O(n\kappa d)$	$O(\kappa d/\epsilon)$ (known segment lengths)	$O(n\kappa d)$
Leontief	$O(1)$	$O(1)$	$O(d/\epsilon)$	$O(d)$

2   Preliminaries

Following the framework of [30], we consider a market that consists of a set of agents (buyers), and a set $\mathcal{G}$ of d goods of unit amount each. The prices of the

---

[1] Such an algorithm has been used in the context of revealed preferences in a more applied work of [17]; but we prove correctness and tight sample complexity.

goods are indicated by a price vector $\boldsymbol{p} = (p_1, \ldots, p_d)$. A buyer comes with a budget of money, say B, and intrinsic preferences over bundles of goods. For most of the paper we focus on divisible goods. A bundle of goods is represented by a vector $\boldsymbol{x} = (x_1, \ldots, x_d) \in [0, 1]^d$, where the i-th component x_i denotes the amount of the i-th good in the bundle. The price of a bundle is computed as the inner product $\langle \boldsymbol{p}, \boldsymbol{x} \rangle$. Then the preference over bundles of an agent is defined by a non-decreasing, non-negative and concave utility function $U : [0, 1]^d \to \mathbb{R}_+$. The buyer uses her budget to buy a bundle of goods that maximizes her utility.

In the revealed preference model, when the buyer is provided with $(\boldsymbol{p}, B)$, we observe the optimal bundle that she buys. Let this optimal bundle be denoted by $\mathcal{B}_U(\boldsymbol{p}, B)$, which is an optimal solution of the following optimization problem:

$$\begin{aligned} \arg\max{}_{\boldsymbol{x} \in [0,\ 1]^d} &: U(\boldsymbol{x}) \\ s.t. \quad &\quad \langle \boldsymbol{p}, \boldsymbol{x} \rangle \le B \end{aligned} \tag{1}$$

We assume that if there are multiple optimal bundles, then the buyer will choose a cheapest one, i.e., let $S = \arg\max_{\boldsymbol{x} \in [0,\ 1]^d} U(\boldsymbol{x})$ at $(\boldsymbol{p}, B)$, then $\mathcal{B}_U(\boldsymbol{p}, B) \in \arg\min_{\boldsymbol{x} \in S} \langle \boldsymbol{x}, \boldsymbol{p} \rangle$. Furthermore, if there are multiple optimal bundles of the same price, ties are broken according to some rule (e.g. , the buyer prefers lexicographically earlier bundles).

Demand functions While a utility function U, by definition, maps bundles to values, it also defines a mapping from pairs $(\boldsymbol{p}, B)$ of price vectors and budgets to optimal bundles under U. We denote this function by $\widehat{U}$ and call it the *demand function* corresponding to the utility function U. That is, we have $\widehat{U} : \mathbb{R}_+^d \times \mathbb{R}_+ \to [0, 1]^d$, and $\widehat{U}(\boldsymbol{p}, B) = \mathcal{B}_U(\boldsymbol{p}, B)$. For a class of utility function $\mathcal{H}$ we denote the corresponding class of demand functions by $\widehat{\mathcal{H}}$.

2.1 Classes of Utility Functions

Next we discuss three different types of utility functions that we analyze in this paper, namely linear, SPLC and Leontief [21], and define their corresponding classes formally. Note that at given prices $\boldsymbol{p}$ and budget B, $\mathcal{B}_U(\boldsymbol{p}, B) = \mathcal{B}_{\alpha U}(\boldsymbol{p}, B)$, for all $\alpha > 0$, i.e., positive scaling of a utility function does not affect optimal bundles. Since we are interested in learning U by asking queries to $\mathcal{B}_U$ we will make some normalizing assumptions in the following definitions. We start with linear utilities, the simplest and the most studied class of functions.

Definition 1 (Linear $\mathcal{H}_{lin}$). *A utility function U is called linear if the utility from a bundle $\boldsymbol{x}$ is linear in each good. Formally, for some $\boldsymbol{a} \in \mathbb{R}_+^d$, we have $U(\boldsymbol{x}) = U_{\boldsymbol{a}}(x) = \sum_{j \in \mathcal{G}} a_j x_j$. It is wlog to assume that $\sum_j a_j = 1$. We let $\mathcal{H}_{lin}$ denote the class of linear utility functions.*

Next, is a generalization of linear functions that captures decreasing marginal utility, called separable piecewise-linear concave.

Definition 2. *[Separable Piecewise-Linear Concave (SPLC) $\mathcal{H}_{splc}$] A utility function function U is called SPLC if, $U(\boldsymbol{x}) = \sum_{j \in \mathcal{G}} U_j(x_j)$ where each U_j : $\mathbb{R}_+ \to \mathbb{R}_+$ is non-decreasing piecewise-linear concave function. The number of (pieces) segments in U_j is denoted by $|U_j|$ and the kth segment of U_j denoted by (j, k). The slope of a segment specifies the rate at which the agent derives utility per unit of additional good received. Suppose segment (j, k) has domain $[a, b] \subseteq \mathbb{R}_+$, and slope c. Then, we define $a_{jk} = c$ and $l_{jk} = b - a$; $l_{j|U_j|} = \infty$. Since U_j is concave, we have $a_{j(k-1)} > a_{jk}$, $\forall k \geq 2$. We can view an SPLC function, with $|U_j| \leq \kappa$ for all j, as defined by to matrices $\boldsymbol{A}, \boldsymbol{L} \in \mathbb{R}_+^{d \times \kappa}$ and we denote it by $U_{\boldsymbol{AL}}$. We let $\mathcal{H}_{splc}$ denote the class of all SPLC functions.*

Linear and SPLC functions are applicable when goods are substitutes, i.e., one good can be replaced by another to maintain a utility value. The other extreme is when goods are complementary, i.e., all goods are needed in some proportions to obtain non-zero utility. Next, we describe a class of functions, used extensively in economic literature, that captures complementarity.

Definition 3 (Leontief $\mathcal{H}_{leon}$). *A utility function U is called a Leontief function if $U(\boldsymbol{x}) = \min_{j \in \mathcal{G}} x_j/a_j$, where $\boldsymbol{a} \geq 0$ and (wlog) $\sum_j a_j = 1$. Let $\mathcal{H}_{leon}$ be the set of all Leontief functions on d goods.*

In order to work with finite precision, in all the above definitions we assume that the parameters are rational numbers of size (bit-length) at most n.

2.2   Learning Models: Statistical and Query

We now introduce the formal models under which we analyze the learnability of utility functions. We start by reviewing the general model from statistical learning theory for multi-class classification. We then explain the more specific model for learning from revealed preferences as introduced in [30]. Finally, we also consider a non-statistical model of exact learning from queries, which is explained last in this section.

General Model for Statistical Multi-class Learning. Let $\mathcal{X}$ denote a *domain* set and let $\mathcal{Y}$ denote a *label* set. A *hypothesis* (or *label predictor* or *classifier*), is a function $h : \mathcal{X} \to \mathcal{Y}$, and a *hypothesis class* $\mathcal{H}$ is a set of hypotheses. We assume that data is generated by some (unknown) probability distribution P over $\mathcal{X}$. This data is labeled by some (unknown) *labeling function* $l : \mathcal{X} \to \mathcal{Y}$. The quality of a hypothesis h is measured by its *error* with respect to P and l: $\mathrm{err}_P^l(h) = \Pr_{x \sim P}[l(x) \neq h(x)]$. A *learning algorithm* (or *learner*) gets as input a sequence $S = ((x_1, y_1), \dots, (x_m, y_m))$ and outputs a hypothesis.

Definition 4 (Multi-class learnability (realizable case)). *We say that an algorithm $\mathcal{A}$ learns some hypothesis class $\mathcal{H} \subseteq \mathcal{Y}^{\mathcal{X}}$, if there exists a function $m : (0, 1) \times (0, 1) \to \mathbb{N}$ such that, for all distributions P over $\mathcal{X}$, and for all $\epsilon > 0$ and $\delta > 0$, when given a sample $S = ((x_1, y_1), \dots, (x_m, y_m))$ of size at least*

$m = m(\epsilon, \delta)$ *with the* x_i *generated i.i.d. from* P *and* $y_i = h(x)$ *for some* $h \in \mathcal{H}$, *then, with probability at least* $1 - \delta$ *over the sample,* $\mathcal{A}$ *outputs a hypothesis* $\mathcal{A}(S) : \mathcal{X} \to \mathcal{Y}$ *with* $\mathrm{err}_P^h(\mathcal{A}(S)) \leq \epsilon$.

The complexity of a learning task is measured by its *sample complexity*, that is, informally, the amount of data with which an optimal learner can achieve low error. We call the (point-wise) smallest function $m : (0,1) \times (0,1) \to \mathbb{N}$ that satisfies the condition of Definition 4 the *sample complexity of the algorithm* $\mathcal{A}$ *for learning* $\mathcal{H}$. We denote this function by $m[\mathcal{A}, \mathcal{H}]$. We call the smallest function $m : (0,1) \times (0,1) \to \mathbb{N}$ such that there exists a learning algorithm $\mathcal{A}$ with $m[\mathcal{A}, \mathcal{H}] \leq m$ the *sample complexity of learning* H and denote it by $m[\mathcal{H}]$.

Statistical Learning from Revealed Preferences. As in [30], we consider a statistical learning setup where data is generated by a distribution P over pairs of price vectors and budgets (that is, P is a distribution over $\mathbb{R}_+^d \times \mathbb{R}_+$). In this model, a learning algorithm $\mathcal{A}$ gets as input a sample $S = (((\boldsymbol{p}_1, B_1), \mathcal{B}_U(\boldsymbol{p}_1, B_1)), \ldots, ((\boldsymbol{p}_m, B_m), \mathcal{B}_U(\boldsymbol{p}_m, B_m)))$, where the $(\boldsymbol{p}_i, B_i)$ are generated *i.i.d.* from the distribution P and are labeled by the optimal bundles under some utility function U. It outputs some function $\mathcal{A}(S) : \mathbb{R}_+^d \times \mathbb{R}_+ \to [0,1]^d$ that maps pairs of price vectors and budgets to bundles. A learner is considered successful if it learns to predict a bundle of value that is the optimal bundles' value.

Definition 5 (Learning from revealed preferences [30]). *An algorithm* $\mathcal{A}$ *is said to* learn *a class of utility functions* $\mathcal{H}$ *from revealed preferences, if for all* $\epsilon, \delta > 0$, *there exists a sample size* $m = m(\epsilon, \delta) \in \mathbb{N}$, *such that, for any distribution* P *over* $\mathbb{R}_+^d \times \mathbb{R}_+$ *(pairs of price vectors and budgets) and any target utility function* $U \in \mathcal{H}$, *if* $S = (((\boldsymbol{p}_1, B_1), \mathcal{B}_U(\boldsymbol{p}_1, B_1)), \ldots, ((\boldsymbol{p}_m, B_m), \mathcal{B}_U(\boldsymbol{p}_m, B_m)))$ *is a sequence of i.i.d. samples generated by* P *with* U, *then, with probability at least* $1 - \delta$ *over the sample* S, *the output utility function* $\mathcal{A}(S)$ *satisfies*

$$\Pr_{(\boldsymbol{p}, B) \sim P} \left[U(\mathcal{B}_U(\boldsymbol{p}, B)) \neq U(\mathcal{B}_{\mathcal{A}(S)}(\boldsymbol{p}, B)) \right] \leq \epsilon.$$

Note that the above learning requirement is satisfied if the learner "learns to output the correct optimal bundles". That is, to learn a class $\mathcal{H}$ of utility functions from revealed preferences, in the sense of Definition 5, it suffices to learn the corresponding class of demand functions $\widehat{\mathcal{H}}$ in the standard sense of Definition 4 (with $\mathcal{X} = \mathbb{R}_+^d \times \mathbb{R}_+$ and $\mathcal{Y} = [0,1]^d$). This is what the algorithm in [30] and our learning algorithms for this setting actually do. The notion of sample complexity in this setting can be defined analogously to the above.

Model for Exact Learning from Queries. In the query learning model, the goal of the learner is to determine the underlying utility function exactly. The learner can choose instances and obtain the labels of these instances from some oracle. A *revealed preference query learning algorithm* has access to an oracle that, upon given the input (query) of a price vector and a budget $(\boldsymbol{p}, B)$, outputs the corresponding optimal bundle $\mathcal{B}_U(\boldsymbol{p}, B)$ under some utility function U. Slightly abusing notation, we also denote this oracle by $\mathcal{B}_U$.

Definition 6 (Learning from revealed preference queries). *A learning algorithm learns a class $\mathcal{H}$ from m revealed preference queries, if for any function $U \in \mathcal{H}$, if the learning algorithm is given responses from oracle $\mathcal{B}_U$, then after at most m queries the algorithm outputs the function U.*

Both in the statistical and the query setting, we analyze a revealed preference learning model as well as a model of learning classes of utility function "directly" from utility values. Due to limited space, for these latter definition and results refer to the full-version at [2].

3   Efficiently Learning Linear Multi-class Hypothesis Classes

We start by showing that certain classes of multi-class predictors, so-called D-*dimensional linear classes* (see Definition 7 below), can be learnt efficiently both in terms of their sample complexity and in terms of computation. For this, we make use of a very recent upper bound on their sample complexity by Daniely and Shalev-Shwartz [9]. At a high level, their result obtains strong bounds on the sample complexity of D-dimensional linear classes (roughly D/ϵ) by using an algorithm and sample complexity analysis based on a compression scheme — which roughly means that the hypothesis produced can be uniquely described by a small subset of D of the training examples. We show that their algorithm is actually equivalent to a multi class SVM formulation, and thereby obtain a computationally efficient algorithm with optimal sample complexity. In the next sections we then show how learning classes of utility functions from revealed preferences can be cast in this framework.

Definition 7. *A hypothesis class $\mathcal{H} \subseteq \mathcal{Y}^{\mathcal{X}}$ is a D-dimensional linear class, if there exists a function $\Psi : \mathcal{X} \times \mathcal{Y} \to \mathbb{R}^D$ such that for every $h \in \mathcal{H}$, there exists a vector $\boldsymbol{w} \in \mathbb{R}^D$ such that $h(x) \in \arg\max_{y \in \mathcal{Y}} \langle \boldsymbol{w}, \Psi(x, y) \rangle$ for all $x \in \mathcal{X}$. We then also denote the class by $\mathcal{H}_\Psi$ and its members by $h_{\boldsymbol{w}}$.*

For now, we assume that (the data generating distribution is so that) the set $\arg\max_{y \in \mathcal{Y}} \langle \boldsymbol{w}, \Psi(x, y) \rangle$ contains only one element, that is, there are no ties[2]. The following version of the multi-class support vector machine (SVM) has been introduced by Crammer and Singer [8].

Algorithm 1. Multi-class (hard) SVM [8]

Input: Sample $(\boldsymbol{x}_1, y_1), \ldots, (\boldsymbol{x}_m, y_m) \in \mathcal{X} \times \mathcal{Y}$
Solve: $\boldsymbol{w} = \arg\min_{\boldsymbol{w} \in \mathbb{R}^d} \|\boldsymbol{w}\|$
such that $\langle \boldsymbol{w}, \Psi(\boldsymbol{x}_i, y_i) - \Psi(\boldsymbol{x}_i, y) \rangle \geq 1 \quad \forall i \in [m], y \neq y_i$
Return: vector $\boldsymbol{w}$

---

[2] The work of [9] handled ties using a "don't know" label; to remove technicalities, we make this distributional assumption in this version of our work.

Remark 1. Suppose that given $w \in \mathbb{R}^d$ and $x \in \mathcal{X}$, it is possible to efficiently compute some $y' \in \text{argmax}_{y \notin \text{argmax}_{y''}\langle w, \Psi(x,y'')\rangle}\langle w, \Psi(x,y)\rangle$. That is, it is possible to compute a label y in the set of "second best" labels. In that case, it is not hard to see that SVM can be solved efficiently, since this gives a separation oracle. SVM minimizes a convex objective subject to, possibly exponentially many, linear constraints. For a given w, a violated constraint can be efficiently detected (by one scan over the input sample) by observing that $\langle w, \Psi(x_i, y_i) - \Psi(x_i, y')\rangle < 1$.

The following theorem on the sample complexity of the above SVM formulation, is based on the new analysis of linear classes by [9]. We show that the two algorithms (the SVM and the one in [9]) are actually the same.

Theorem 1. *For a D-dimensional linear class $\mathcal{H}_\Psi$, with Ψ having finite range, the sample complexity of SVM is $m[SVM, \mathcal{H}_\Psi](\epsilon, \delta) = O\left(\frac{D \log(1/\epsilon) + \log(1/\delta)}{\epsilon}\right).$*

Proof. Let $S = (x_1, y_1), \ldots, (x_m, y_m)$ be a sample that is realized by $\mathcal{H}_\Psi$. That is, there exists a vector $w \in \mathbb{R}^d$ with $\langle w, \Psi(x_i, y_i)\rangle > \langle w, \Psi(x_i, y)\rangle$ for all $y \neq y_i$. Consider the set $Z = \{\Psi(x_i, y_i) - \Psi(x_i, y) \mid i \in [m], y \neq y_i\}$. The learning algorithm for $\mathcal{H}_\Psi$ of [9] outputs the minimal norm vector $w' \in \text{conv}(Z)$. According to Theorem 5 in [9] this algorithm successfully learns $\mathcal{H}_\Psi$ and has sample complexity $O\left(\frac{D \log(1/\epsilon) + \log(1/\delta)}{\epsilon}\right)$. We will show that the hypothesis returned by that algorithm is the same hypothesis as the one returned by SVM. Indeed, let w be the vector that solves the SVM program and let w' be the vector found by the algorithm of [9]. We will show that $w = \frac{\|w\|}{\|w'\|} \cdot w'$. This is enough since in that case $h_w = h_{w'}$.

We note that w is the same vector that solves the *binary* SVM problem defined by the sample $\{(z, 1)\}_{z \in Z}$. It is well known (see, e.g. , [25], Lemma 15.2) that the hyperplane defined by w has maximal margin. That is, the unit vector $e = \frac{w}{\|w\|}$ maximizes the quantity $\text{mar}(e'') := \min\{\langle e'', z\rangle \mid z \in Z\}$ over all unit vectors e''. The proof of the theorem now follows from the following claim:

Claim. Over all unit vectors, $e' = \frac{w'}{\|w'\|}$ maximizes the margin.

Proof. Let $e'' \neq e'$ be a unit vector. We must show that $\text{margin}(e'') < \text{margin}(e')$. Note that $\text{margin}(e') > 0$, since w' is shown in [9] to realize the sample S (that is $\langle w', z\rangle > 0$ for all $z \in Z$ and thus also for all $z \in \text{conv} Z$). Therefore, we can assume w.l.o.g. that $\text{margin}(e'') > 0$. In particular, since $\text{margin}(-e') = -\text{margin}(e') < 0$, we have that $e'' \neq -e'$.

Since, $\text{margin}(e'') > 0$, we have that $\text{margin}(e'')$ is the distance between the hyperplane $H'' = \{x \mid \langle e'', x\rangle = 0\}$ and $\text{conv}(Z)$. Since $e'' \notin \{e', -e'\}$, there is a vector in $v \in H''$ with $\langle e', v\rangle \neq 0$. Now, consider the function

$$t \mapsto \|t \cdot v - w'\|^2 = t^2 \cdot \|v\|^2 + \|w'\|^2 - 2t\langle v, w'\rangle.$$

Since the derivative of this function at 0 is not 0, for some value of t we have $\text{dist}(t \cdot v, w') < \text{dist}(0, w')$. Therefore, $\text{margin}(e'') = \text{dist}(H'', Z) \leq \text{dist}(t \cdot v, w') < \text{dist}(0, w') = \text{margin}(e')$.

4 Statistical Learning from Revealed Preferences

In the next section, we show that learning utility functions from revealed preferences can in many cases be cast as learning a D-dimensional linear class $\mathcal{H}_\Psi$ for a suitable encoding function Ψ and D. Throughout this section, we assume that the data generating distribution is so that there are no ties for the optimal bundle with respect to the agents' utility function (with probability 1). This is, for example, the case if the data-generating distribution has a density function.

4.1 Linear

Learnability of $\mathcal{H}_{lin}$ from revealed preferences is analyzed in [30]. They obtain a bound of (roughly) d^2/ϵ on the sample complexity. We show that the quadratic dependence on the number of goods is not needed. The sample complexity of this problem is (roughly) d/ϵ. We will show that the corresponding class of demand functions $\widehat{\mathcal{H}_{lin}}$ is actually a d-dimensional linear class. Since learnability of a class of utility functions in the revealed preference model (Definition 5) is implied by learnability of the corresponding class of demand functions (in the sense of Definition 4), Theorem 1 then implies the upper bound in the following result:

Theorem 2. *The class $\mathcal{H}_{lin}$ of linear utility functions is efficiently learnable in the revealed preference model with sample complexity $O\left(\frac{d\log(1/\epsilon)+\log(1/\delta)}{\epsilon}\right)$.*

Moreover, the sample complexity is lower bounded by $\Omega\left(\frac{d+\log(1/\delta)}{\epsilon}\right)$.

Proof. Let $U_{\boldsymbol{a}}$ be a linear utility function. By definition, the optimal bundle given a price vector $\boldsymbol{p}$ and a budget B is $\arg\max_{\boldsymbol{x}\in[0,1]^n,\langle\boldsymbol{p},\boldsymbol{x}\rangle\leq B}\langle\boldsymbol{a},\boldsymbol{x}\rangle$. Note that, for a linear utility function, there is always an optimal bundle $\boldsymbol{x}$ where all (except at most one) of the x_i are in $\{0,1\}$ (this was also observed in [30]; see also Section 5.1). Essentially, given a price vector $\boldsymbol{p}$, in an optimal bundle, the goods are bought greedily in decreasing order of a_i/p_i (value per price).

Thus, given a pair of price vector and budget $(\boldsymbol{p}, B)$, we call a bundle $\boldsymbol{x}$ *admissible*, if $|\{i\,:\,x_i\notin\{0,1\}\}|\leq 1$ and $\langle\boldsymbol{p},\boldsymbol{x}\rangle = B$. In case $\langle\boldsymbol{p},\boldsymbol{1}_d\rangle=\sum_{i\in\mathcal{G}}p_i\leq B$, we also call the all 1-bundle $\boldsymbol{1}_d$ admissible (and in this case, it is the only admissible bundle). We now define the function Ψ as follows:

$$\Psi((\boldsymbol{p},B),\boldsymbol{x}) = \begin{cases} \boldsymbol{x} & \text{if } \boldsymbol{x} \text{ admissible} \\ \boldsymbol{0}_d & \text{otherwise} \end{cases}$$

where $\boldsymbol{0}_d$ denotes the all-0 vector in $\mathbb{R}^d$. With this, we have $\mathcal{H}_\Psi = \widehat{\mathcal{H}_{lin}}$.

We defer the proof of the lower bound to the full version [2]. To outline the argument, we prove that the Natarajan dimension of $\widehat{\mathcal{H}_{lin}}$ is at least $d-1$. This implies a lower bound for learning $\widehat{\mathcal{H}_{lin}}$. It is not hard to see that the construction also implies a lower bound for learning $\mathcal{H}_{lin}$ in the revealed preference model.

To prove computational efficiency, according to Remark 1, we need to show that for a linear utility function $U_{\boldsymbol{a}}$, we can efficiently compute some

$$y' \in \arg\max_{y\notin\arg\max_{y''}\langle\boldsymbol{a},\Psi(x,y'')\rangle}\langle\boldsymbol{a},\Psi(x,y)\rangle;$$

that is a second best bundle with respect to the mapping Ψ. This will be shown in Theorem 3 of the next subsection.

Efficiently Computing the Second Best Bundle under Linear Utilities.
In this section show how to compute a second best *admissible bundle* (with respect to the mapping Ψ) efficiently. Recall that *admissible bundles* at prices $\boldsymbol{p}$ and budget B are defined (in the proof of the above theorem) to be the bundles that cost exactly B with at most one partially allocated good (or the all-1 bundle $\mathbf{1}_d$, in case it is affordable). Note that, in case $\langle \boldsymbol{p}, \mathbf{1}_d \rangle \leq B$, *any* other bundle is second best with respect to Ψ, since all other bundles are mapped to $\mathbf{0}_d$. For the rest of this section, we assume that $\langle \boldsymbol{p}, \mathbf{1}_d \rangle > B$. At any given $(\boldsymbol{p}, B)$ the optimal bundle is always admissible. We now design an $O(d)$-time algorithm to compute the second best admissible bundle, i.e., $\boldsymbol{y} \in \arg\max_{\boldsymbol{x} \text{ admissible} ,\boldsymbol{x} \neq \boldsymbol{x}^*} \langle \boldsymbol{a}, \boldsymbol{x} \rangle$, where $\boldsymbol{x}^*$ is the optimal bundle. At prices $\boldsymbol{p}$, let $\frac{a_1}{p_1} \geq \frac{a_2}{p_2} \geq \cdots \geq \frac{a_d}{p_d}$, and let the first k goods be bought at the optimal bundle, i.e., $k = \max_{j:\ x_j^* > 0} j$. Then, clearly $\forall j < k$, $x_j^* = 1$ and $\forall j > k$, $x_j^* = 0$ as $\boldsymbol{x}^*$ is admissible.

Note that, to obtain the second best admissible bundle $\boldsymbol{y}$ from $\boldsymbol{x}^*$, amounts of only the first k goods can be lowered and amounts of only the last k to d goods can be increased. Next we show that the number of goods whose amounts are lowered and increased at exactly one each. In all the proofs we crucially use the fact that if $\frac{a_j}{p_j} > \frac{a_k}{p_k}$, then transferring money from good k to good j gives a better bundle, i.e., $a_j \frac{m}{p_j} - a_k \frac{m}{p_k} > 0$.

Lemma 1. *There exists exactly one $j \geq k$, such that $y_j > x_j^*$.*

Proof. To the contrary suppose there are more than one goods with $y_j > x_j^*$. Consider the last such good, let it be l. Clearly $l > k$, because the first good that can be increased is k. If $y_l < 1$ then there exists $j < l$ with $y_j = 0$, else if $y_l = 1$ then there exists $j < l$ with $y_j < 1$. In either case transfer money from good l to good j such that the resulting bundle is admissible. Since, $\frac{a_j}{p_j} > \frac{a_l}{p_l}$ it is a better bundle different from $\boldsymbol{x}^*$. The latter holds since there is another good whose amount still remains increased. A contradiction to $\boldsymbol{y}$ being second best.

Lemma 2. *There exists exactly one $j \leq k$, such that $y_j < x_j^*$.*

Proof. To the contrary suppose there are more than one goods with $y_j < x_j^*$. Let l be the good with $y_l > x_l^*$; there is exactly one such good due to Lemma 1. Let i be the first good with $y_i < x_i^*$ and let p be the good that is partially allocated in $\boldsymbol{y}$. If p is undefined or $p \in \{i, l\}$, then transfer money from l to i to get a better bundle. Otherwise, $p < l$ so transfer money from l to p. In either case we can do the transfer so that the resulting bundle is admissible and is better than $\boldsymbol{y}$ but different from $\boldsymbol{x}^*$. A contradiction.

Lemmas 1 and 2 gives an $O(d^2)$ algorithm to compute the second best admissible bundle, where we can check all possible ways of transferring money from a good in $\{1, \ldots, k\}$ to a good in $\{k, \ldots, d\}$. The next lemma leads to time $O(d)$.

Lemma 3. *If $x_k^* < 1$, and for $j > k$ we have $y_j > x_j^*$, then $y_k < x_k^*$. Further, if $x_k^* = 1$ and $y_j > x_j^*$ then $j = k + 1$.*

Proof. To the contrary suppose, $y_k = x_k^* < 1$ and for a unique $i < k$, $y_i < x_i^*$ (Lemma 2). Clearly, $y_i = 0$ and $y_j = 1$ because $0 < y_k < 1$. Thus, transferring money from j to k until either $y_j = 0$ or $y_k = 1$ gives a better bundle different from $\boldsymbol{x}^*$, a contradiction. For the second part, note that there are no partially bought good in $\boldsymbol{x}^*$ and $y_{k+1} = 0$. To the contrary suppose $j > k + 1$, then transferring money from good j to good $k + 1$ until either $y_j = 0$ or $y_{k+1} = 1$ gives a better bundle other than $\boldsymbol{x}^*$, a contradiction.

The algorithm to compute second best bundle has two cases. First is when $x_k^* < 1$, then from Lemma 3 it is clear that if an amount of a good in $\{k+1, \ldots, d\}$ is increased then the money has to come from good k. This leaves exactly $d - 1$ bundles to be checked, namely when money is transferred from good k to one of $\{k + 1, \ldots, d\}$, and when it is transferred from one of $\{1, \ldots, k - 1\}$ good k. The second case is when $x_k^* = 1$, then we only need to check k bundles namely, when money is transferred from one of $\{1, \ldots, k\}$ to good $k + 1$. Thus we get:

Theorem 3. *Given prices $\boldsymbol{p}$ and budget B, the second best bundle with respect to the mapping Ψ for $U \in \mathcal{H}_{lin}$ at $(\boldsymbol{p}, B)$ can be computed in $O(d)$ time.*

4.2   Other Classes of Utility Functions

By designing appropriate mappings Ψ as above, we also obtain bounds on the sample complexity of learning other classes of utility functions from revealed preferences. In particular, we can employ the same technique for the class of SPLC functions with known segment lengths. See Table 1 for an overview on the results and the full version [2] for for the technical details.

4.3   Extensions

Modeling learning tasks as learning a D-dimensional linear class is quite a general technique. We now discuss how it allows for a variety of interesting extensions.

Agnostic setting In this work, we mostly assume that the data was generated by an agent that has a utility function that is a member of some specific class (for example, the class of linear utilities). However, this may not always be a realistic assumption. For example, an agent may sometimes behave irrationally and deviate from his actual preferences. In learning theory, such situations are modeled in the *agnostic learning* model. Here, we do not make any assumption about membership of the agents' utility function in some fixed class. The goal then is, to output a function from some class, say the class of linear utility functions, that predicts the agents' behavior with error that is at most ϵ worse than the best linear function would.

Formally, the requirement on the output classifier $\mathcal{AS}$ in Definition 4 then becomes $\mathrm{err}_P^l(\mathcal{AS}) \leq \eta + \epsilon$ (instead of $\mathrm{err}_P^l(\mathcal{AS}) \leq \epsilon$), where η is the error of the best classifier in the class. Since our sample complexity bounds are based on a compression scheme, and compression schemes also imply learnability in the agnostic learning model (also see the full version [2]) we get that the classes of utility functions with D-dimensional linear classes as demand functions that we have analyzed are also learnable in the agnostic model. That is, we can replace the assumption that the data was generated exactly according to a linear (or SPLC) function with an assumption that the agent behaves according to such a function at least a $1 - \eta$ fraction of the time.

Non-linear prices, indivisible goods, quasi-linear utilities So far, we looked at a market where pricing is always linear and goods are divisible (see Section 2). We note that the sample complexity results for $\mathcal{H}_{lin}$ and $\mathcal{H}_{splc}$ that we presented here actually apply in a broader context. Prices per unit could vary with the amount of a good in a bundle (e.g. [17]). For example, there may be discounts for larger volumes and prices could be SPLC . Also, goods may not be arbitrarily divisible (e.g. [12]). Instead of one unit amount of each good in the market, there may then be a number of non-divisible items of each good on offer. Note that we can still define the functions Ψ to obtain a D-dimensional linear demand function class and the classes of utility functions discussed above are learnable with the same sample complexity.

In another common model the agent chooses a bundle to maximize $U(\boldsymbol{x}) - \langle \boldsymbol{p}, \boldsymbol{x} \rangle$ (with or without a budget constraint). Note that for linear utility functions, the optimal bundles under this model are also well structured. Without a budget constraint, the agent buys a good only if $a_i - p_i > 0$. With a budget constraint, goods are bought greedily in decreasing order of $(a_i - p_i)/p_i$. This gives us a means to define admissible bundles for these scenarios and we can employ the mapping Ψ (written for the case without budget) $\Psi(\boldsymbol{p}, \boldsymbol{x}) = (\boldsymbol{x}, \langle \boldsymbol{p}, \boldsymbol{x} \rangle)$, if $\boldsymbol{x}$ is admissible and $\mathbf{0}_{d+1}$ otherwise. This shows that learning to predict a buyers behavior in this model can be cast as learning a $(d+1)$-dimensional linear class.

Learning preference orderings Consider the situation where we would like to not only learn the preferred choice (over a number d of options) of an agent, but the complete ordering of preferences given some prices over the options.

We can model this seemingly more complex task as a learning problem as follows: Let $\mathcal{X} = \mathbb{R}^d_+$ be our instance space of price vectors. Denote by $\mathcal{Y} = S_d$ the group of permutations on d elements. Let a vector $\boldsymbol{w} \in \mathbb{R}^d$ represent the unknown valuation of the agent, that is w_i indicates how much the agent values option i. Consider the functions $h_{\boldsymbol{w}} : \mathbb{R}^d_+ \to S_d$ such that $h_{\boldsymbol{w}}(\boldsymbol{p})$ is the permutation corresponding to the ordering over the values w_i/p_i (i.e. $\pi(1)$ is the index with the largest value per money w_i/p_i and so on).

Finally, consider the hypothesis class $\mathcal{H}_\pi = \{h_{\boldsymbol{w}} : \boldsymbol{w} \in \mathbb{R}^d_+\}$. We show below that $\mathcal{H}_\pi$ is a d-dimensional linear class. Therefore, this class can also be learned with sample complexity $O\left(\frac{d \log(1/\epsilon) + \log(1/\delta)}{\epsilon}\right)$. With the same construction as for linear demand functions (see the full version [2] for details), we can also show that the Natarajan dimension of $\mathcal{H}_\pi$ is lower bounded by $d - 1$, which implies that this bound on the sample complexity is essentially optimal.

To see that $\mathcal{H}_\pi$ is d-dimensional linear class, consider the map $\Psi : \mathcal{X} \times S_d \to \mathbb{R}^d$ defined by $\Psi(\boldsymbol{p}, \pi) = \sum_{1 \leq i < j \leq d} \pi_{ij} \cdot ((1/p_j)e_j - (1/p_i)e_i)$, where, π_{ij} is 1 if $\pi(i) < \pi(j)$ and else -1; $e_1, \ldots, e_d$ is the standard basis of $\mathbb{R}^d$

5   Learning via Revealed Preference Queries

In this section we design algorithms to learn classes $\mathcal{H}_{lin}$, $\mathcal{H}_{splc}$, or $\mathcal{H}_{leon}$ using $\text{poly}(n, d)$ revealed preference queries.[3] Recall that we have assumed all defining parameters of a function to be rationals of size (bit length) at most n. In what follows we discuss the case of linear functions ($\mathcal{H}_{lin}$), for SPLC ($\mathcal{H}_{splc}$) and Leontief ($\mathcal{H}_{leon}$) refer to the full-version [2].

5.1   Characterization of Optimal Bundles

In this section we characterize optimal bundles for linear utility functions. In other words, given $(\boldsymbol{p}, B)$ we characterize $\mathcal{B}_U(\boldsymbol{p}, B)$ when U is in $\mathcal{H}_{lin}$. Since function U is concave, formulation (1) is a convex formulation, and therefore the Karush-Kuhn-Tucker (KKT) conditions characterize its optimal solution [5,3]. For a general formulation $\min\{f(\boldsymbol{x}) \mid g_i(\boldsymbol{x}) \leq 0, \ \forall i \leq n\}$, the KKT conditions are as follows, where μ_i is the dual variable for constraint $g_i(\boldsymbol{x}) \leq 0$.

$$L(\boldsymbol{x}, \boldsymbol{\mu}) = f(\boldsymbol{x}) + \sum_{i \leq n} \mu_i g_i(\boldsymbol{x}); \quad \frac{dL}{dx_i} = 0, \ \forall i \leq n$$
$$\forall i \leq n : \ \mu_i g_i(\boldsymbol{x}) = 0, \quad g_i(\boldsymbol{x}) \leq 0, \quad \mu_i \geq 0$$

In (1), let μ, μ_j and μ_j' be dual variables for constraints $\langle \boldsymbol{p}, \boldsymbol{x} \rangle \leq B$, $x_j \leq 1$ and $-x_j \leq 0$ respectively. Then its optimal solution $\boldsymbol{x}^* = \mathcal{B}_U(\boldsymbol{p}, B)$ satisfies the KKT conditions: $dL/dx_j|_{\boldsymbol{x}^*} = -dU/dx_j|_{\boldsymbol{x}^*} + \mu p_j + \mu_j - \mu_j' = 0$, $\mu_j' x_j^* = 0$, and $\mu_j(x_j^* - 1) = 0$. Simplifying these gives us:

$$
\begin{array}{llll}
\forall j \neq k, & x_j^* > 0, \ x_k^* = 0 & \Rightarrow & \frac{dU/dx_j|_{x^*}}{p_j} \geq \frac{dU/dx_k|_{x^*}}{p_k} \\
\forall j \neq k, & x_j^* = 1, \ 0 \leq x_k^* < 1 \Rightarrow & & \frac{dU/dx_j|_{x^*}}{p_j} \geq \frac{dU/dx_k|_{x^*}}{p_k} \\
\forall j \neq k, & 0 < x_j^*, x_k^* < 1 & \Rightarrow & \frac{dU/dx_j|_{x^*}}{p_j} = \frac{dU/dx_k|_{x^*}}{p_k}
\end{array}
\tag{2}
$$

Linear functions: Given prices $\boldsymbol{p}$, an agent derives a_j/p_j utility per unit money spent on good j (bang-per-buck). Thus, she prefers the goods where this ratio is maximum. The characterization of optimal bundle exactly reflects this,

$$
\begin{array}{llll}
\forall j \neq k, & x_j^* > 0, \ x_k^* = 0 & \Rightarrow & \frac{a_j}{p_j} \geq \frac{a_k}{p_k} \\
\forall j \neq k, & x_j^* = 1, \ 0 \leq x_k^* < 1 \Rightarrow & & \frac{a_j}{p_j} \geq \frac{a_k}{p_k} \\
\forall j \neq k, & 0 < x_j^*, x_k^* < 1 & \Rightarrow & \frac{a_j}{p_j} = \frac{a_k}{p_k}
\end{array}
\tag{3}
$$

The next theorem follows using the KKT conditions (2).

---

[3] Learning budget, when it is private to the buyer, requires only one extra query: For prices $p_j = 2^{2n}, \forall j$, the amount of money spent by the buyer is her budget. This is because $B \leq 2^n$ if $size(B) \leq n$. Further, the algorithms designed in this section can be easily modified to handle this fixed-budget case.

Theorem 4. *Given prices p and budget B, conditions of (3) together with the feasibility constraints of (1) exactly characterizes $x^* = \mathcal{B}_U(p, B)$ for $U \in \mathcal{H}_{lin}$.*

5.2   An Algorithm for Linear Functions

Recall that, if $U \in \mathcal{H}_{lin}$ then $U(x) = \sum_j a_j x_j$, where $\sum a_j = 1$. First we need to figure out which a_js are non-zero.

Lemma 4. *For $p_j = 1$, $\forall j$ and $B = n$, if $x = \mathcal{B}_U(p, B)$, then $x_j = 0 \Rightarrow a_j = 0$.*

Proof. Since $B = \sum_j p_j$, the agent has enough money to buy all the good completely, and the lemma follows as the agent buys cheapest optimal bundle.

Lemma 4 implies that one query is enough to find the set $\{j \mid a_j > 0\}$. Therefore, wlog we now assume that $\forall j \in \mathcal{G}$, $a_j > 0$.

Note that, it suffices to learn the ratios $\frac{a_j}{a_1}$, $\forall j \neq 1$ exactly in order to learn U, as $\sum_j a_j = 1$. Since the bit length of the numerator and the denominator of each a_j is at most n, we have that $1/2^{2n} \leq a_j/a_1 \leq 2^{2n}$. Using this fact, next we show how to calculate each of these ratios using $O(n)$ revealed preference queries, and in turn the entire function using $O(dn)$ queries.

Recall the optimality conditions (3) for linear functions. Algorithm 2 determines a_j/a_1 when called with $H = 2^{2n}$, $q = 1$ and $x_j^e = 0$.[4] The basic idea is to always set budget B so low that the agent can buy only the most preferred good, and then do binary search by varying p_j appropriately. Correctness of the algorithm follows using (3) and the fact that bit length of a_j/a_1 is at most $2n$.

Algorithm 2. Learning Linear Functions: Compute a_j/a_1

Input: Good j, upper bound H, quantity q of goods, extra amount x_j^e.
Initialize: $L \leftarrow 0$; $p_1 \leftarrow 1$; $p_k \leftarrow 2^{10n}$, $\forall k \in \mathcal{G} \setminus \{j, 1\}$; $i \leftarrow 0$; flag $\leftarrow$ nil
while $i <= 4n$ **do**
   $i \leftarrow i + 1$; $p_j \leftarrow \frac{H+L}{2}$; $B \leftarrow x_j^e * p_j + \frac{\min\{p_1, p_j\}}{q}$; $x \leftarrow \mathcal{B}_U(p, B)$
   if $x_j > 0$ & $x_1 > 0$ **then   Return** p_j;
   if $x_j > 0$ **then** $L \leftarrow p_j$; flag $\leftarrow 1$; **else** $H \leftarrow p_j$; flag $\leftarrow 0$;
  if flag $= 1$ **then** Round up p_j to nearest rational with denominator at most 2^n
  else Round down p_j to nearest rational with denominator at most 2^n
Return p_j.

Theorem 5. *The class $\mathcal{H}_{lin}$ is learnable from $O(nd)$ revealed preference queries.*

Acknowledgments. This work was supported in part by AFOSR grant FA9550-09-1-0538, ONR grant N00014-09-1-0751, NSF grants CCF-0953192 and CCF-1101283, a Microsoft Faculty Fellowship, and a Google Research Award.

---

[4] Last two inputs are irrelevant for learning linear functions, however they are used to learn SPLC functions in full-version [2].

References

1. Afriat, S.N.: The construction of utility functions from expenditure data. International Economic Review (1967)
2. Balcan, M.F., Daniely, A., Mehta, R., Urner, R., Vazirani, V.V.: Learning economic parameters from revealed preferences (2014), http://arxiv.org/abs/1407.7937
3. Bazarra, M.S., Sherali, H.D., Shetty, C.M.: Nonlinear Programming: Theory and Algorithms. John Wiley & Sons (2006)
4. Beigman, E., Vohra, R.: Learning from revealed preference. In: EC, pp. 36–42 (2006)
5. Boyd, S., Vandenberghe, L.: Convex Optimization. Cambridge University Press (2009)
6. Collins, M.: Discriminative reranking for natural language parsing. In: ICML, pp. 175–182 (2000)
7. Collins, M.: Discriminative training methods for hidden markov models: Theory and experiments with perceptron algorithms. In: Proceedings of the ACL 2002 Conference on Empirical Methods in Natural Language Processing, EMNLP 2002, vol. 10, pp. 1–8. Association for Computational Linguistics, Stroudsburg (2002)
8. Crammer, K., Singer, Y.: On the algorithmic implementation of multiclass kernel-based vector machines. Journal of Machine Learning Research 2, 265–292 (2001)
9. Daniely, A., Shalev-Shwartz, S.: Optimal learners for multiclass problems. In: COLT, pp. 287–316 (2014)
10. Diewert, E.: Afriat and revealed preference theory. Review of Economic Studies 40, 419–426 (1973)
11. Dobell, A.R.: A comment on A. Y. C. Koo's an empirical test of revealed preference theory. Econometrica 33(2), 451–455 (1965)
12. Echenique, F., Golovin, D., Wierman, A.: A revealed preference approach to computational complexity in economics. In: EC, pp. 101–110 (2011)
13. Haussler, D., Welzl, E.: Epsilon-nets and simplex range queries. In: Symposium on Computational Geometry, pp. 61–71 (1986)
14. Houthakker, H.S.: Revealed preference and the utility function. Economica 17, 159–174 (1950)
15. Koo, A.Y.C.: An empirical test of revealed preference theory. Econometrica 31(4), 646–664 (1963)
16. Lafferty, J.D., McCallum, A., Pereira, F.C.N.: Conditional random fields: Probabilistic models for segmenting and labeling sequence data. In: ICML, pp. 282–289 (2001)
17. Lahaie, S.: Kernel methods for revealed preference analysis. In: European Conference on Artificial Intelligence, pp. 439–444 (2010)
18. Littlestone, N., Warmuth, M.K.: Relating data compression and learnability. Unpulished manuscript (1986)
19. Mas-Colell, A.: The recoverability of consumers' preferences from market demand. Econometrica 45(6), 1409–1430 (1977)
20. Mas-Colell, A.: On revealed preference analysis. The Review of Economic Studies 45(1), 121–131 (1978)
21. Mas-Colell, A., Whinston, M.D., Green, J.R.: Microeconomic Theory. Oxford University Press, New York (1995)
22. Natarajan, B.: On learning sets and functions. Machine Learning 4(1), 67–97 (1989)
23. Richter, M.: Revealed preference theory. Econometrica 34(3), 635–645 (1966)

24. Samuelson, P.: Consumption theory in terms of revealed preference. Econometrica 15 (1948)
25. Shalev-Shwartz, S., Ben-David, S.: Understanding Machine Learning. Cambridge University Press (2014)
26. Uzawa, H.: Preference and rational choice in the theory of consumption. In: Arrow, K.J., Karlin, S., Suppes, P. (eds.) Mathematical Models in Social Science (1960)
27. Valiant, L.G.: A theory of the learnable. Commun. ACM 27(11), 1134–1142 (1984)
28. Varian, H.R.: The non-parametric approach to demand analysis. Econometrica 50, 945–974 (1982)
29. Varian, H.R.: Revealed preference. In: Szenberg, M., Ramrattand, L., Gottesman, A.A. (eds.) Samuelsonian Economics and the 21st Century, pp. 99–115 (2005)
30. Zadimoghaddam, M., Roth, A.: Efficiently learning from revealed preference. In: Goldberg, P.W. (ed.) WINE 2012. LNCS, vol. 7695, pp. 114–127. Springer, Heidelberg (2012)

General Truthfulness Characterizations
via Convex Analysis

Rafael Frongillo and Ian Kash

Microsoft Research

Abstract. We present a model of truthful elicitation which generalizes and extends mechanisms, scoring rules, and a number of related settings that do not quite qualify as one or the other. Our main result is a characterization theorem, yielding characterizations for all of these settings, including a new characterization of scoring rules for non-convex sets of distributions. We generalize this model to eliciting some property of the agent's private information, and provide the first general characterization for this setting. We also show how this yields a new proof of a result in mechanism design due to Saks and Yu.

1   Introduction

We examine a general model of information elicitation where a single agent is endowed with some type t that is private information and is asked to reveal it. After doing so, he receives a score $A(t', t)$ that depends on both his report t' and his true type t. We allow A to be quite general, with the main requirement being that $A(t', \cdot)$ is an affine[1] function of the true type t, and seek to understand when it is optimal for the agent to truthfully report his type. Given this truthfulness condition, it is immediately clear why convexity plays a central role—when an agent's type is t, the score for telling the truth is $A(t, t) = \sup_{t'} A(t', t)$, which is a convex function of t as the pointwise supremum of affine functions.

One special case of our model is mechanism design with a single agent[2], where the designer wishes to select an outcome based on the agent's type. In this setting, $A(t', \cdot)$ can be thought of as the allocation and payment given a report of t', which combine to determine the utility of the agent as a function of his type. In this context, $A(t, t)$ is the consumer surplus function (or indirect utility function), and Myerson's well-known characterization [50] states that, in single-parameter settings, a mechanism is truthful if and only if the consumer surplus function is convex and its derivative (or subgradient at points of non-differentiability) is the allocation rule. More generally, this remains true in higher dimensions (see [4]).[3]

---

[1] A mapping between two vector spaces is affine if it consists of a linear transformation followed by a translation.

[2] This is not a real restriction because notions of truthfulness are phrased in terms of holding the behavior of other agents constant. See [4, 23] for additional discussion.

[3] Note that here the restriction that $A(t', \cdot)$ be affine is without loss of generality, because we view types as functions and function application is a linear operation. (See Section 2.2 for more details.)

T.-Y. Liu et al. (Eds.): WINE 2014, LNCS 8877, pp. 354–370, 2014.

Another special case is a scoring rule, also called a *proper loss* in the machine learning literature, where an agent is asked to predict the distribution of a random variable and given a score based on the observed realization of that variable. In this setting, types are distributions over outcomes, and $A(t', t)$ is the agent's subjective expected score for a report that the distribution is t' when he believes the distribution is t. As an expectation, this score is linear in the agent's type. Gneiting and Raftery [33] unified and generalized existing results in the scoring rules literature by characterizing proper scoring rules in terms of convex functions and their subgradients.

Further, the generality of our model allows it to include settings that do not quite fit into the standard formulations of mechanisms or scoring rules. These include counterfactual scoring rules for decision-making [20,21,56], proper losses for machine learning with partial labels [24], mechanism design with partial allocations [17], and responsive lotteries [27].

In many settings, it is difficult, or even impossible, to have agents report an entire type $t \in \mathcal{T}$. For example, when allocating a divisible good (e.g. water), a mechanism that needs to know how much an agent would value each possible allocation requires him to submit an infinite-dimensional type. Even type spaces which are exponential in size, such as those that arise in combinatorial auctions, can be problematic from an algorithmic perspective. Moreover, in many situations, the principal is *uninterested* in all but some small aspect of an agent's private type. For example, the information is often to be used to eventually make a specific decision, and hence only the information directly pertaining to the decision is actually needed—why ask for the agent's entire probability distribution of rainfall tomorrow if a principal wanting to choose between {umbrella, no umbrella} would be content with its expected value, or even just whether she should carry an umbrella or not?

It is therefore natural to consider an indirect elicitation model where agents provide some sort of summary information about their type. Such a model has been studied in the scoring rules literature, where one wishes to elicit some statistic, or *property*, of a distribution, such as the mean or quantile [32,47,54,61]. We follow this line of research, and extend the affine score framework to accept reports from a different (intuitively, much smaller) space than $\mathcal{T}$.

1.1   Our Contribution

Our main theorem (Section 2) is a general characterization theorem that generalizes and extends known characterization theorems for proper scoring rules (substantially) and truthful mechanisms (slightly, by removing a technical assumption). For scoring rules, this provides the first characterization of proper scoring rules with non-convex sets of distributions, an idea that has proved useful as a way of separating informed and uninformed experts [9,26], but for which no characterization was known. We also survey applications to related settings and show our theorem can be used to provide characterizations for them as well, including new results about mechanism design with partial allocation and responsive lotteries. Thus, our theorem eliminates the need to independently derive characterizations for such settings.

This unified characterization of mechanisms and scoring rules also clarifies their relationship: both are derived from convex functions in the exact same manner, with mechanisms merely facing additional constraints on the choice of convex function so that it yields a valid allocation rule. This aids in understanding when results or techniques from one setting can be applied in the other. Indeed, the proof of our characterization begins with Gneiting and Raftery's scoring rule construction [33] and adapts it with a variant of a technique from Archer and Kleinberg [4] for handling mechanisms with non-convex type spaces (see their Theorem 6.1). As an example of the new insights this can provide, results from mechanism design show that a scoring rule is proper if and only if it is locally proper (see Section C.2 and Corollary 3). More broadly, we show how results from mechanism design about implementability and revenue equivalence generalize to our framework.

We then move on to two general results for eliciting a particular property of the agent's private information. The first is essentially a direct generalization of Theorem 1, which keeps the same general structure but adds the constraint that the convex function must be flat on sets of types which share an optimal report. This is the first general result for arbitrary properties; in addition to serving as our main tool to derive the remainder of our results, this theorem provides several ways to show that a property is not elicitable (by showing that no such convex function can exist). The second result is a transformation of this theorem using *duality*, which shows that there is a strong sense in which properties *are* subgradients of convex functions. We use this result to introduce notions of dual properties and scores, which gives a new construction to convert between scoring rules and randomized mechanisms (see Corollary 9).

We conclude by examining properties that take on a finite number of values, which Lambert and Shoham [48] showed correspond to *power diagrams*. We extend their result to settings where the private information need not be a probability distribution, and give a tight characterization for a particular restricted "simple" case. We also give an explicit construction for generating power diagrams from other measures of distances via a connection to *Bregman Voronoi diagrams* [15]. Finally, we show how these results imply a new proof of an implementability theorem from mechanism design due to Saks and Yu [60].

1.2   Relation to Prior Work

The similarities between mechanisms and scoring rules were noted by (among others) Fiat et al. [29], who gave a construction to convert mechanisms into scoring rules and vice versa, and Feige and Tennenholtz [27], who gave techniques to convert both to "responsive lotteries." Further, techniques from convex analysis have a long history in the analysis of both models (see [33,65]). However, we believe that our results use the "right" representation and techniques, which leads to more elegant characterizations and arguments. For example, the construction used by Fiat et al. has the somewhat awkward property that the scoring rule corresponding to a mechanism has one more outcome than the mechanism did, a complication absent from our results. Similarly, the constructions used by Feige and Tennenholtz only handle special cases and they claim "there is no immediate equivalence between lottery rules and scoring rules," while we can give such an equivalence. So while prior work has understood that there is a connection, the nature of that connection has been far from clear.

A large literature in mechanism design has explored characterizations of when allocation rules can be truthfully implemented; see e.g. [4, 5, 14, 19, 40–42, 49, 51, 60]. Similarly, work on revenue equivalence can be cast in our framework as well [18, 37, 44, 50]. For scoring rules, our work connects to a literature that has used non-convex sets of probability distributions to separate (usefully) informed exports from uninformed experts [9, 26].

Indirect elicitation has a long history in the scoring rules literature, starting with Savage [61]. While the bulk of the literature focuses on specific statistics, such as means and quantiles [32, 33, 35, 54], Osband [55] and Lambert, Pennock, and Shoham [47] first considered the problem of eliciting a more general property Γ. Several authors have made significant contributions toward the general problem for the case where Γ is real-valued [32, 34, 46, 47, 62] and vector-valued [30, 47, 55], but our results are the first for arbitrary multivalued maps. Mechanisms that elicit a ranking over outcomes rather than a utility for each outcome (common in, e.g., matching contexts) are a form of property elicitation, and our results are related to characterizations due to Carroll [19].

Notation. We define $\overline{\mathbb{R}} = \mathbb{R} \cup \{-\infty, \infty\}$ to be the extended real numbers. Given a set of measures M on X, a function $f : X \to \overline{\mathbb{R}}$ is M-quasi-integrable if $\int_X f(x)d\mu(x) \in \overline{\mathbb{R}}$ for all $\mu \in M$. Let $\Delta(X)$ be the set of all probability measures on X. We denote by $\mathsf{Aff}(X \to Y)$ and $\mathsf{Lin}(X \to Y)$ the set of functions from X to Y which are affine and linear, respectively. We write $\mathsf{Conv}(X)$ to denote the convex hull of a set of vectors X, the set of all (finite) convex combinations of elements of X. Some useful facts from convex analysis are collected in § A of the full version [31].

2 Affine Scores

We consider a very general model with an agent who has a given type $t \in \mathcal{T}$ and reports some possibly distinct type $t' \in \mathcal{T}$, at which point the agent is rewarded according to some score $\mathsf{A}(t', t)$ which is affine in the true type t. This reward we call an affine score. We wish to characterize all *truthful* affine scores, those which incentivize the agent to report her true type t.

Definition 1. *Any function* $\mathsf{A} : \mathcal{T} \times \mathcal{T} \to \overline{\mathbb{R}}$, *where* $\mathcal{T} \subseteq \mathcal{V}$ *for some vector space* $\mathcal{V}$ *over* $\mathbb{R}$ *and* $\mathcal{A} \doteq \{\mathsf{A}(t, \cdot) \mid t \in \mathcal{T}\} \subseteq \mathsf{Aff}(\mathcal{T} \to \overline{\mathbb{R}})$, *is a affine score with score set* $\mathcal{A}$. *We say* A *is truthful if for all* $t, t' \in \mathcal{T}$,

$$\mathsf{A}(t', t) \leq \mathsf{A}(t, t). \tag{1}$$

If this inequality is strict for all $t \neq t'$, *then* A *is* strictly truthful.

Our characterization uses convex analysis, a central concept of which is the subgradient of a function, which is a generalization of the gradient yielding a linear approximation that is always below the function.

Definition 2. *Given some function* $G : \mathcal{T} \to \mathbb{R}$, *a function* $d \in \mathsf{Lin}(\mathcal{V} \to \overline{\mathbb{R}})$ *is a subgradient to* G *at* t *if for all* $t' \in \mathcal{T}$,

$$G(t') \geq G(t) + d(t' - t). \tag{2}$$

We denote by $\partial G : \mathcal{T} \rightrightarrows \mathsf{Lin}(\mathcal{V} \to \overline{\mathbb{R}})$ *the multivalued map such that* $\partial G(t)$ *is the set of subgradients to* G *at* t. *We say a parameterized family of linear functions* $\{d_t \in \mathsf{Lin}(\mathcal{V} \to \overline{\mathbb{R}})\}_{t \in \mathcal{T}'}$ *for* $\mathcal{T}' \subseteq \mathcal{T}$ *is a selection of subgradients if* $d_t \in \partial G(t)$ *for all* $t \in \mathcal{T}'$; *we denote this succinctly by* $\{d_t\}_{t \in \mathcal{T}'} \in \partial G$.

For mechanism design, it is typical to assume that utilities are always real-valued. However, the log scoring rule (one of the most popular scoring rules) has the property that if an agent reports that an event has probability 0, and then that event does occur, the agent receives a score of $-\infty$. Essentially solely to accommodate this, we allow affine scores and subgradients to take on values from the extended reals. In the next paragraph we provide the relevant definitions, but for most purposes it suffices to ignore these and simply assume that all affine scores are real-valued.

It is standard (cf. [33]) to restrict consideration to the "regular" case, where intuitively only things like the log score are permitted to be infinite. In particular, an affine score A is *regular* if $\mathsf{A}(t, t) \in \mathbb{R}$ for all $t \in \mathcal{T}$, and $\mathsf{A}(t', t) \in \mathbb{R} \cup \{-\infty\}$ for $t' \neq t$. Similarly, a parameterized family of linear functions (e.g. subgradients) $\{d_t \in \mathsf{Lin}(\mathcal{V} \to \overline{\mathbb{R}})\}_{t \in \mathcal{T}}$ is $\mathcal{T}$-*regular* if $d_t(t) \in \mathbb{R}$ for all $t \in \mathcal{T}$, and $d_{t'}(t) \in \mathbb{R} \cup \{-\infty\}$ for $t' \neq t$.[4] Likewise, $\mathcal{T}$-regular affine functions have $\mathcal{T}$-regular linear parts with finite constants (i.e. we exclude the constant functions $\pm\infty$). For the remainder of the paper we assume all affine scores and parameterized families of linear or affine functions are $\mathcal{T}$-regular, where $\mathcal{T}$ will be clear from context.

We now state our characterization theorem. The proof takes Gneiting and Raftery's [33] proof for the case of scoring rules on convex domains and extends it to the non-convex case using a variant of a technique Archer and Kleinberg [4] introduced for mechanisms with non-convex type spaces. This technique is essentially that used in prior work on extensions of convex functions [57, 66].

Theorem 1. *Let an affine score* $\mathsf{A} : \mathcal{T} \times \mathcal{T} \to \overline{\mathbb{R}}$ *with score set* $\mathcal{A}$ *be given.* A *is truthful if and only if there exists some convex* $G : \mathsf{Conv}(\mathcal{T}) \to \overline{\mathbb{R}}$ *with* $G(\mathcal{T}) \subseteq \mathbb{R}$, *and some selection of subgradients* $\{d_t\}_{t \in \mathcal{T}} \in \partial G$, *such that*

$$\mathsf{A}(t', t) = G(t') + d_{t'}(t - t'). \tag{3}$$

In the remainder of this section, we show how scoring rules, mechanisms, and other related models fit comfortably within our framework.

---

[4] To define linear functions to $\overline{\mathbb{R}}$, we adopt the convention $0 \cdot \infty = 0 \cdot (-\infty) = 0$. Thus, any $\ell \in \mathsf{Lin}(\mathcal{V} \to \overline{\mathbb{R}})$ can be written as $\ell_1 + \infty \cdot \ell_2$ for some $\ell_1, \ell_2 \in \mathsf{Lin}(\mathcal{V} \to \mathbb{R})$.

2.1   Scoring Rules for Non-convex $\mathcal{P}$

In this section, we show that the Gneiting and Raftery characterization is a simple special case of Theorem 1, and moreover that we *generalize* their result to the case where the set of distributions $\mathcal{P}$ may be non-convex. We also give a result about local properness derived using tools from mechanism design in the full version [31, § C.2]. To begin, we formally introduce scoring rules and show that they fit into our framework. The goal of a scoring rule is to incentivize an expert who knows a probability distribution to reveal it to a principal who can only observe a single sample from that distribution.

Definition 3. *Given outcome space $\mathcal{O}$ and set of probability measures $\mathcal{P} \subseteq \Delta(\mathcal{O})$, a scoring rule is a function* S $: \mathcal{P} \times \mathcal{O} \to \overline{\mathbb{R}}$. *We say* S *is proper if for all $p, q \in \mathcal{P}$,*

$$\mathbb{E}_{o \sim p}[\mathsf{S}(q, o)] \le \mathbb{E}_{o \sim p}[\mathsf{S}(p, o)]. \tag{4}$$

If the inequality in (4) is strict for all $q \ne p$, then S *is strictly proper.*

To incorporate this into our framework, take the type space $\mathcal{T} = \mathcal{P}$. Thus, we need only construct the correct score set $\mathcal{A}$ of affine functions available to the scoring rule as payoff functions. Intuitively, these are the functions that describe what payment the expert receives given each outcome, but we have a technical requirement that the expert's expected utility be well defined. Thus, following Gneiting and Raftery, we take $\mathcal{F}$ to be the set of $\mathcal{P}$-quasi-integrable[5] functions $f : \mathcal{O} \to \overline{\mathbb{R}}$, and the score set $\mathcal{A} = \{p \mapsto \int_{\mathcal{O}} f(o) \, dp(o) \mid f \in \mathcal{F}\}$.

We now apply Theorem 1 for our choice of $\mathcal{T}$ and $\mathcal{A}$, which yields the following generalization of Gneiting and Raftery [33].

Corollary 1. *For an arbitrary set $\mathcal{P} \subseteq \Delta(\mathcal{O})$ of probability measures, a regular[6] scoring rule* S $: \mathcal{P} \times \mathcal{O} \to \overline{\mathbb{R}}$ *is proper if and only if there exists a convex function $G : \mathsf{Conv}(\mathcal{P}) \to \mathbb{R}$ with functions $G_p \in \mathcal{F}$ such that*

$$\mathsf{S}(p, o) = G(p) + G_p(o) - \int_{\mathcal{O}} G_p(o) \, dp(o), \tag{5}$$

where $G_p : q \mapsto \int_{\mathcal{O}} G_p(o) \, dq(o)$ is a subgradient of G for all $p \in \mathcal{P}$.

Importantly, Corollary 1 immediately generalizes [33] to the case where $\mathcal{P}$ is not convex, which is new to the scoring rules literature. One direction of this extension is obvious (if S is truthful on the convex hull of a set then it is truthful on that set). The other is not, however, and is an important negative result, ruling out the possibility of new scoring rules arising by restricting the set of distributions (provided the restriction does not alter the convex hull).

In the absence of a characterization, several authors have worked in the non-convex $\mathcal{P}$ case. For example, Babaioff et al. [9] examine when proper scoring

---

[5] We say that $f : \mathcal{O} \to \overline{\mathbb{R}}$ is $\mathcal{P}$-quasi-integrable if $\int_{\mathcal{O}} f(o) dp(o) \in \overline{\mathbb{R}}$ for all $p \in \mathcal{P}$.
[6] This is the same concept as with affine scores: scores cannot be ∞ and only incorrect reports can yield $-\infty$.

rules can have the additional property that uninformed experts do not wish to make a report (have a negative expected utility), while informed experts do wish to make one. They show that this is possible in some settings where the space of reports is not convex. Our characterization shows that, despite not needing to ensure properness on reports outside $\mathcal{P}$, essentially the only possible scoring rules are still those that are proper on all of $\Delta(\mathcal{O})$. We state the simplest version of such a characterization, for perfectly informed experts, here.

Corollary 2. *Let a non-convex set $\mathcal{P} \subseteq \Delta(\mathcal{O})$ and $\bar{p} \in \Delta(\mathcal{O}) - \mathcal{P}$ be given. A scoring rule S is proper and guarantees that experts with a belief in $\mathcal{P}$ receive a score of at least δ_A while experts with a belief of $\bar{p}$ receive a score of at most δ_R if and only if S is of the form (5) with $G(p) \geq \delta_A \forall p \in \mathcal{P}$ and $G(\bar{p}) \leq \delta_R$.*

With a similar goal to Babaioff et al., Fang et al. [26] find conditions on $\mathcal{P}$ for which every continuous "value function" $G : p \mapsto S(p,p)$ on $\mathcal{P}$ can be attained by some S with the motivation of eliciting the expert's information when it is known to come from some family of distributions (which in general will not be a convex set). As such, they provide sufficient conditions on particular non-convex sets, as opposed to our result which provides necessary and sufficient conditions for all non-convex sets. Beyond these specific applications, our characterization is useful for answering practical questions about scoring rules. For example, suppose we assume that people have beliefs about probabilities in increments of 0.01. Does that change the set of possible scoring rules? No. What happens if they have finer-grained beliefs but we restrict them to such reports? They will end up picking a "nearby" report (see the discussion of convexity in Section 3.2).

In the full version [31, § C.2], we show how local truthfulness conditions from mechanism design, where one verifies that an affine score is truthful by checking that it is truthful in a small neighborhood around every point, generalize to our framework. In particular, Corollary 11 shows that local properness (i.e. properness for distributions in a neighborhood) is equivalent to global properness for scoring rules on convex $\mathcal{P}$, an observation that is also new to the scoring rules literature. See [31, § C.2] for the precise meaning of (weak) local properness.

Corollary 3. *For a convex set $\mathcal{P} \subseteq \Delta(\mathcal{O})$ of probability measures, a scoring rule $S : \mathcal{P} \times \mathcal{O} \to \overline{\mathbb{R}}$ is proper if and only if it is (weakly) locally proper.*

2.2 Mechanism Design

We now show how to view a mechanism as an affine score. First, we formally introduce mechanisms in the single agent case (see below for remarks about multiple agents). Then we show how known characterizations of truthful mechanisms follow easily from our main theorem. This allows us to relax a minor technical assumption from the most general such theorem.

Definition 4. *Given outcome space $\mathcal{O}$ and a type space $\mathcal{T} \subseteq (\mathcal{O} \to \mathbb{R})$, consisting of functions mapping outcomes to reals, a (direct) mechanism is a pair (f,p) where $f : \mathcal{T} \to \mathcal{O}$ is an allocation rule and $p : \mathcal{T} \to \mathbb{R}$ is a payment. The utility of* the agent with type t and report t' to the mechanism is $U(t', t) = t(f(t')) - p(t')$; we say the mechanism (f, p) is truthful if $U(t', t) \leq U(t, t)$ for all $t, t' \in \mathcal{T}$.

Here we suppose that the mechanism can choose an allocation from some set $\mathcal{O}$ of outcomes, and there is a single agent whose type $t \in \mathcal{T}$ is itself the valuation function. That is, the agent's net utility upon allocation o and payment p is $t(o) - p$. Thus, following Archer and Kleinberg [4], we view the type space $\mathcal{T}$ as lying in the vector space $\mathcal{V} = \mathbb{R}^{\mathcal{O}}$. The advantage of this representation is that while agent valuations in mechanism design can generally be complicated functions, viewed this way they are all linear: for any $v_1, v_2 \in \mathcal{V}$, we have $(v_1 + \alpha v_2)(o) = v_1(o) + \alpha v_2(o)$. Thus, we have an affine score $\mathsf{A}(t', t) \doteq U(t', t)$, with score set $\mathcal{A} = \{t \mapsto t(o) + c \mid o \in \mathcal{O}, c \in \mathbb{R}\}$, so that every combination of outcome and payment a mechanism could choose is an element of $\mathcal{A}$.

As an illustration of our theorem, consider the following characterization, due to Myerson [50], for a single parameter setting (i.e. when the agent's type can be described by a single real number). The result states that an allocation rule is implementable, meaning there is some payment rule making it truthful, if and only if it is *monotone* in the agent's type.

Corollary 4 (Myerson [50]). *Let $\mathcal{T} = \mathbb{R}_+$, $\mathcal{O} \subseteq \mathbb{R}$, so that the agent's valuation is $t \cdot o$. Then a mechanism f, p is truthful if and only if: (i) f is monotone non-decreasing in t, and (ii) $p(t) = tf(t) - \int_0^t f(t')dt' + p_0$.*

More generally, applying our theorem gives the following characterization. It is essentially equivalent to that of Archer and Kleinberg [4] (their Theorem 6.1), although our approach allows the relaxation of a technical assumption their version requires when the set of types is non-convex.

Corollary 5. *A mechanism f, p is truthful if and only if there exists a convex function $G : \mathsf{Conv}(\mathcal{T}) \to \mathbb{R}$ and some selection of subgradients $\{dG_t\}_{t \in \mathcal{T}}$, such that for all $t \in \mathcal{T}$, $f(t) = dG_t$ and $G(t) = t(f(t)) - p(t)$*

Of course, mechanism design asks many questions beyond whether a particular mechanism is truthful, and some of these can be reframed as questions in convex analysis. The study of *implementability* focuses on the question of when there exist payments that make a given allocation rule truthful, whereas *revenue equivalence* asks when all mechanisms with a given allocation rule charge the same prices (up to a constant). By focusing on the subgradient, we recover and extend previous results for both, which we detail in the full version [31, § C, § D].

2.3   Other Applications

There are a number of other application domains that are not quite mechanisms or scoring rules, yet for which our main theorem yields characterization theorems. In the full version [31], we survey four such domains where our theorem could have directly provided the characterization ultimately used rather than requiring effort to conceptualize and prove it. We summarize two of the four below; the others are decision rules [20,21,56] and machine learning with partial labels [24]).

Mechanism design with partial allocation. Cai, Mahdian, Mehta, and Waggoner [17], consider a setting where the mechanism designer wants to elicit two pieces of information: the agent's (expected) value for an item in an auction and the probability distribution of a random variable conditional on that agent winning, with the goal of understanding how the organizer of a daily deal site can take into account the value that will be created for users (as opposed to just the advertiser) when a particular deal is chosen to be advertised (e.g. the site operator may prefer deals that sell to many users over equally profitable deals that sell only to a few because this keeps users interested for future days). Our approach allows us to provide a characterization (given in [31, § E.3]), of a more general setting where a mechanism designer wishes to elicit two pieces of information, but the second need not be restricted to probability distributions. For example the mechanism designer could have two distinct sets of goods to allocate and want to design a truthful mechanism that is consistent with a partial allocation rule that determines how the primary goods should be allocated given the agent's preferences over both types of goods.

Responsive lotteries. Feige and Tennenholtz [27] study the problem of how an agent can be incentivized to indirectly reveal his utility function over outcomes by being given a choice of lotteries over those outcomes, an approach with applications to experimental psychology, market research, and multiagent mechanism design. They give a geometric description of how such lotteries can be created with a finite set of outcomes. Our approach allows us to give a complete characterization, which highlights the relationship between natural desiderata and underlying geometric properties of the set of possible lotteries: strict truthfulness and continuity of the lottery rule jointly correspond to strict convexity of the lottery set, and uniqueness of the utility given the optimal lottery corresponds to smoothness of the boundary.

3 Property Elicitation

We wish to generalize the notion of truthful elicitation from eliciting private information from some set $\mathcal{T}$ to accept reports from a space $\mathcal{R}$ which is different from $\mathcal{T}$. To even discuss truthfulness in this setting, we need a notion of a truthful report r for a given type t. We encapsulate this notion by a general multivalued map which specifies all (and only) the correct values for t.

3.1 Affine Scores for Properties

Definition 5. *Let $\mathcal{T}$ be a give type space, where $\mathcal{T} \subseteq \mathcal{V}$ for some vector space $\mathcal{V}$ over $\mathbb{R}$, and $\mathcal{R}$ be some given report space. A property is a multivalued map $\Gamma : \mathcal{T} \rightrightarrows \mathcal{R}$ which associates a nonempty set of correct report values to each type. We let $\Gamma_r \doteq \{t \in \mathcal{T} \mid r \in \Gamma(t)\}$ denote the set of types t corresponding to report value r.*

One can think of Γ_r as the "level set" of Γ corresponding to value r. This concept will be especially useful when we consider finite-valued properties in Section 5. A natural bookkeeping constraint to impose on these level sets is *non-redundancy*, meaning no property value r has a level set entirely contained in another.

We extend the notion of an affine score to this setting, where the report space is $\mathcal{R}$ instead of $\mathcal{T}$ itself. Note that the score set $\mathcal{A} = \{A(r, \cdot) \mid r \in \mathcal{R}\}$ is still a subset of $\mathsf{Aff}(\mathcal{V} \to \overline{\mathbb{R}})$.

Definition 6. *An affine score* $A : \mathcal{R} \times \mathcal{T} \to \overline{\mathbb{R}}$ *elicits a property* $\Gamma : \mathcal{T} \rightrightarrows \mathcal{R}$ *if for all* t,

$$\Gamma(t) = \operatorname*{argsup}_{r \in \mathcal{R}} A(r, t). \qquad (6)$$

If we merely have $\Gamma(t) \subseteq \operatorname{argsup}_{r \in \mathcal{R}} A(r, t)$, *we say* A *weakly elicits* Γ. *Property* $\Gamma : \mathcal{T} \rightrightarrows \mathcal{R}$ *is elicitable if some affine score* $A : \mathcal{R} \times \mathcal{T} \to \overline{\mathbb{R}}$ *elicits* Γ.

Note that it is certainly possible to write down A such the argsup in (6) is not well defined. This corresponds to some types not having an optimal report, which we view as violating a minimal requirement for a sensible affine score. Thus, in order for A to be an affine score, we require (6) to be well defined for all $t \in \mathcal{T}$.

We now state our property characterization theorem, proved in the full version [31, §E], which in essence says that eliciting a property Γ is equivalent to eliciting subgradients of a convex function G. Intuitively, by truthfulness the linear part of $A(r, \cdot)$ must be a subgradient of G at all $t \in \Gamma_r$. We show that this is equivalent to G being flat along Γ_r, meaning we can calculate G on Γ_r by picking any $t_r \in \Gamma_r$ and following the subgradient. Since all choices of t_r lead to the same value, we could just as easily ask for this subgradient $\varphi(r)$ to be reported directly. As subgradients are functions (in this case from $\mathcal{T}$ to $\overline{\mathbb{R}}$), we use the curried notation $\varphi(r)(t)$ for the application of this function.

Theorem 2. *Let non-redundant property* $\Gamma : \mathcal{T} \rightrightarrows \mathcal{R}$ *and* Γ-*regular[7] affine score* $A : \mathcal{R} \times \mathcal{T} \to \overline{\mathbb{R}}$ *be given. Then* A *elicits* Γ *if and only if there exists some convex* $G : \mathsf{Conv}(\mathcal{T}) \to \overline{\mathbb{R}}$ *with* $G(\mathcal{T}) \subseteq \mathbb{R}$, *some* $\mathcal{D} \subseteq \partial G$, *and some bijection* $\varphi : \mathcal{R} \to \mathcal{D}$ *with* $\Gamma(t) = \varphi^{-1}(\mathcal{D} \cap \partial G_t)$, *such that for all* $r \in \mathcal{R}$ *and* $t \in \mathcal{T}$,

$$A(r, t) = G(t_r) + \varphi(r)(t - t_r), \qquad (7)$$

where $\{t_r\}_{r \in \mathcal{R}} \subseteq \mathcal{T}$ *satisfies* $r' \in \Gamma(t_{r'})$ *for all* r'.

3.2   What Properties Are Not Elicitable?

In the remainder of this section, we examine three features that subgradient mappings of convex functions possess and thus that the level sets of elicitable properties must possess.

---

[7] This is defined similarly to regularity; see [31, §E].

Convexity. A well-known property of subgradient mappings is that their level sets are convex (for completeness, we provide a proof in the full version [31, § A]). In light of our characterizations, this fact about convex functions immediately applies to elicitable properties:

Corollary 6. *If* $\Gamma : \mathcal{T} \rightrightarrows \mathcal{R}$ *is elicitable, then* Γ_r *is convex for all* r.

To see this, just note that $\varphi(r) \in \partial G_t \cap \partial G_{t'}$ implies that $\varphi(r) \in \partial G_{\hat{t}}$ for all $\hat{t} = \alpha t + (1 - \alpha)t'$. Corollary 6 was previously known for special cases [47, 48], where it was used to show variance, skewness, and kurtosis are not elicitable, and was also known in mechanism design (i.e. the set of types for which a given (allocation, payment) pair is optimal is convex).

Cardinality. Combining Theorem 2 with the fact that finite-dimensional convex functions are differentiable almost everywhere (cf. [3, Thm 7.26]) yields the following corollary, which shows that elicitable properties have unique values almost everywhere.

Corollary 7. *Let* $\Gamma : \mathcal{T} \rightrightarrows \mathcal{R}$ *be an elicitable property with* $\mathcal{T} \subseteq \mathcal{V} = \mathbb{R}^n$. *If* $\mathcal{T}$ *is of positive measure in* $\mathsf{Conv}(\mathcal{T})$, *and* Γ *is non-redundant, then* $|\Gamma(t)| = 1$ *almost everywhere.*

Using an appropriate notion of "almost everywhere", in some cases this holds in infinite-dimensional vector spaces as well (see e.g. [16, p. 195] and [3, p. 274]). One can use this fact to show that $\Gamma(p) = \{(a, b) : \int_a^b p(x)dx = 0.9\}$, the set of 90% confidence intervals for a distribution p, is not an elicitable property. This was previously only known for the case where p has finite support [47].

Topology. Combining Theorem 2 with a closure property of convex functions [59, Thm 24.4] yields the following.

Corollary 8. *Let* $\Gamma : \mathcal{T} \rightrightarrows \mathcal{R}$ *be an elicitable property with* $\mathcal{T} \subseteq \mathcal{V} = \mathbb{R}^n$ *convex that can be elicited by a closed, convex* G. *Then* Γ_r *is closed for all* r.

Requiring G to be closed is a technical issue regarding the boundary of of $\mathcal{T}$, and is irrelevant for level sets in the relative interior. While [48] showed this for finite report spaces $\mathcal{R}$, this more general statement shows, for example, that if $\mathcal{T} = \mathbb{R}$ the property $\Gamma(t) = \mathrm{floor}(t) = \max\{z \in \mathbb{Z} \mid z \leq t\}$ is not elicitable. More generally, this often provides a tool for showing that we cannot get around issues of cardinality by finding a tie-breaking rule to make the value unique.

Closure appears is a more delicate property to work with in infinite dimensions, but intuitive violations of it can still be used to show that properties are not elicitable. As an illustration, we provide a direct proof that a property is not elicitable. We already saw that confidence intervals are not elicitable due to their cardinality, but a natural practical request would be for this "smallest" such interval. Can we elicit this, or even just the length of this interval? The following sketch shows we cannot. For probability distribution F represented by a CDF, let $\Gamma(F) = \inf\{b - a \mid F(b) - F(a) = 1\}$ be the property that is the length of the smallest interval of probability 1^8. Consider the family of distributions defined by their pdfs as $f_c(x) = 1 - c$ for $0 \leq x \leq 1$ and $f_c(x) = c$ for $1 < x \leq 2$ with corresponding CDFs F_c. Note that for $0 < c < 1$, $\Gamma(F_c) = \{2\}$ but $\Gamma(F_0) = \{1\}$. Suppose we could elicit this with a scoring rule S. Let $X(F) = \mathsf{S}(2, F) - \mathsf{S}(1, F)$. By elicitability $X(F_c) > 0$ for $0 < c < 1$ but $X(F_0) < 0$, which violates the continuity of X.

4   Duality in Property Elicitation

In the full version [31, § G], we inspect Theorem 2 further and apply convex duality to reveal two notions of duality between affine scores: *report* duality, which asks the agent to report his desired allocation instead of his type, and *type* duality, which swaps the roles of the type and the allocation. Table 1 gives a particular instantiation of our duality notions, with $\mathcal{T} = \Delta(\mathcal{O})$ and $\mathcal{T}^* = (\mathcal{O} \to \mathbb{R})$; that is, we construct our affine scores and their duals upon the classic duality between integrable functions and probability measures. Note that G^* is the convex conjugate of G; see Definition 17.

Table 1. The duality quadrangle for the duality between distributions and functionals

| | | Type | |
		Primal	Dual
	Primal	$\mathsf{A}(p', p)$ Scoring rule	$\mathsf{A}^*(p', q)$ Menu auction
Report	Dual	$\mathsf{A}(q', p)$ Prediction market	$\mathsf{A}^*(q', q)$ Randomized mechanism
		$\sup \mathsf{A}(\cdot, p) = G(p)$	$\sup \mathsf{A}^*(\cdot, q) = G^*(q)$

As discussed in Section G.2, the columns of Table 1 are well-understood already; the first gives prediction market duality, the well-known fact that market scoring rules are dual to prediction markets, and the second gives the taxation principle, which says that without loss of generality one could think of a mechanism as assigning prices to probability distributions over outcomes o.

The rows of this table, however, are new: in essence, scoring rules are dual mechanisms. In the scoring rule or prediction market setting, an agent has a private distribution (their belief) and the principal gives the agent a utility vector (the score or the bundle of securities), which assigns the agent a real-valued payoff for each possible state of the world. Dually, in a mechanisms, the agent possesses a private type encoding their utility for each state of the world, and the principal assigns a distribution over these states. This observation allows us to give a very simple and natural construction to convert between scoring rules

---

[8] Essentially the same construction can be applied for an $\alpha < 1$ confidence interval.

and mechanisms. Unlike previous constructions (e.g., [29]) we do not require any normalization, or even that the set of outcomes be finite.

Corollary 9. *Let* $\mathsf{S}(p, o) = G(p) + G_p(o) - \int_{\mathcal{O}} G_p(o) \, dp(o)$ *be a proper scoring rule. Then* $f(t) = dG^*(t)$ *and* $p(t) = G^*(t) - t(dG^*(t))$ *is a truthful randomized mechanism. Conversely, let* (f, p) *be a truthful randomized mechanism and* $G(t) = t(f(t)) - p(t)$. *Then* $\mathsf{S}(p, o) = G^*(p) + G_p^*(o) - \int_{\mathcal{O}} G_p^*(o) \, dp(o)$ *is a proper scoring rule.*

The connections go much deeper than swapping types, however. To illustrate this with a somewhat whimsical example, suppose a gambler in a casino examines the rules of a dice-based game of chance and forms belief p about the probabilities of possible outcomes, assuming the dice are fair. The gambler then participates in a prediction market A to predict the outcome of the game, and purchases a bundle q. Before the game is played however, the casino informs the gambler that the dice used need not be fair, and offers the gambler the opportunity to select from among different choices of dice using a truthful mechanism where the gambler's private information is q. If the mechanism used is A*, then the outcome of the mechanism will be using fair dice. The power of duality is that this holds regardless of our choice of A.

5 Finite-Valued Properties

We now examine the special case where $\mathcal{R}$ is a finite set of reports, using the additional structure to provide stronger characterizations. In the scoring rules literature, Lambert and Shoham [48] view this as eliciting answers to multiple-choice questions. There are also applications to mechanism design, discussed in Section 5.1. Assume throughout that $\mathcal{R}$ is finite and that $\mathcal{T}$ is a convex subset of a vector space $\mathcal{V}$ endowed with an inner product, so that we may write $\langle t, t' \rangle$ and in particular $\|t\|^2 = \langle t, t \rangle$. In this setting, we will use the concept of a power diagram from computational geometry.

Definition 7. *Given a set of points* $P = \{p_i\}_{i=1}^m \subset \mathcal{V}$, *called* sites, *and weights* $w \in \mathbb{R}^m$, *a power diagram* $D(P, w)$ *is a collection of cells* cell$(p_i) \subseteq \mathcal{T}$ *defined by*

$$\text{cell}_{P,w}(p_i) = \left\{ t \in \mathcal{T} \mid i \in \text{argmin}_j \left\{ \|p_j - t\|^2 - w_j \right\} \right\}. \tag{8}$$

The following result is a straightforward generalization of Theorem 4.1 of Lambert and Shoham [48], and is essentially a restatement of results due to Aurenhammer [6,8]. See the full version [31, § H] for a discussion about Bregman Voronoi digrams and the role of $\| \cdot \|^2$ in Theorem 3.

Theorem 3. *A property* $\Gamma : \mathcal{T} \rightrightarrows \mathcal{R}$ *for finite* $\mathcal{R}$ *is elicitable if and only if the level sets* $\{\Gamma_r\}_{r \in \mathcal{R}}$ *form a power diagram* $D(P, w)$.

We have now seen what kinds of finite-valued properties are elicitable, but how can we elicit them? More precisely, as the proof above gives sufficient conditions, what are all ways of eliciting a given power-diagram? In general, it is difficult to provide a "closed form" answer, so we restrict to the *simple* case, where essentially the cells of a power diagram are as constrained as possible.

Definition 8 ([7]). *A j-polyhedron is the intersection of dimension j of a finite number of closed halfspaces of $\mathcal{V}$, where $0 \leq j \leq \dim(\mathcal{V}) < \infty$. A cell complex C in $\mathcal{V}$ is a covering of $\mathcal{V}$ by finitely many j-polyhedra, called j-faces of C, whose (relative) interiors are disjoint and whose non-empty intersections are faces of C. C is called simple if each of its j-faces is in the closure of exactly $(d - j + 1)$ d-faces (cells).*

Theorem 4. *Let finite-valued, elicitable, simple property $\Gamma : \mathcal{T} \rightrightarrows \mathcal{R}$ be given. Then there exist points $\{p_r\}_\mathcal{R} \subseteq \mathcal{V}$ such that an affine score $A : \mathcal{R} \times \mathcal{T} \to \overline{\mathbb{R}}$ elicits Γ if and only if there exist $\alpha > 0$, and $p_0 \in \mathcal{V}$ such that*

$$A(r, t) = 2 \langle \alpha p_r + p_0, t \rangle - \|\alpha p_r + p_0\|^2 + w_r, \tag{9}$$

where the choice $w \in \mathbb{R}^\mathcal{R}$ is determined by α and p_0.

5.1 Finite Properties in Mechanism Design

Mechanisms with a finite set of allocations are common. Carroll [19] examines them and observes they give rise to polyhedral typespaces. Theorem 3 strengthens this characterization to power diagrams, which rules out polyhedral examples such as the one shown in Figure 2. Suppose we have are in a such a mechanism design setting with a finite set of allocations $\mathcal{X}$ and we have picked an allocation rule a. Under what circumstances is a implementable (i.e. having a payment rule that makes the resulting mechanism truthful)? If the set of types is convex, Saks and Yu [60] showed that the following condition is necessary and sufficient.

Definition 9. *Allocation rule a satisfies* weak monotonicity *(WMON) if $a(t) \cdot (t' - t) \leq a(t') \cdot (t' - t)$ for all $t, t' \in \mathcal{T}$.*

From Theorem 1, we know that a being implementable means that there exists a G such that a is a selection of its subgradients. But this is equivalent to saying that the property $\Gamma(t) = \mathcal{X} \cap dG_t$ is directly elicitable! Leveraging results from computational geometry, this gives us a new proof of this theorem by showing that WMON characterizes power diagrams.

Theorem 5. *A cell complex C is a power diagram with sites $\{p_1, \ldots, p_n\}$ iff for all $t \in Z_i$ and $t' \in Z_j$ we have $p_i \cdot (t' - t) \leq p_j \cdot (t' - t)$ (i.e. C satisfies WMON)*

Corollary 10 (Saks and Yu). *If $\mathcal{X}$ is finite, $\mathcal{T}$ is convex, and a satisfies WMON, then a is implementable.*

Acknowledgements We would like to thank Aaron Archer, Gabriel Carroll, Yiling Chen, Philip Dawid, Felix Fischer, Hu Fu, Philippe Jehiel, Nicolas Lambert, Peter Key, David Parkes, Colin Rowat, Greg Stoddard, Matus Telgarsky, and Rakesh Vohra for helpful discussions and anonymous reviewers for helpful feedback.

References

1. Abernethy, J., Frongillo, R.: A characterization of scoring rules for linear properties. In: Proceedings of the 25th Conference on Learning Theory (2012)
2. Abernethy, J., Chen, Y., Vaughan, J.W.: Efficient market making via convex optimization, and a connection to online learning. ACM Transactions on Economics and Computation 1(2), 12 (2013)
3. Aliprantis, C.D., Border, K.C.: Infinite Dimensional Analysis: A Hitchhiker's Guide. Springer (2007)
4. Archer, A., Kleinberg, R.: Truthful germs are contagious: a local to global characterization of truthfulness. In: Proceedings of the 9th ACM Conference on Electronic Commerce, pp. 21–30 (2008)
5. Ashlagi, I., Braverman, M., Hassidim, A., Monderer, D.: Monotonicity and implementability. Econometrica 78(5), 1749–1772 (2010)
6. Aurenhammer, F.: Power diagrams: properties, algorithms and applications. SIAM Journal on Computing 16(1), 78–96 (1987)
7. Aurenhammer, F.: Recognising polytopical cell complexes and constructing projection polyhedra. Journal of Symbolic Computation 3(3), 249–255 (1987)
8. Aurenhammer, F.: A criterion for the affine equivalence of cell complexes in r d and convex polyhedra in r d+1. Discrete & Computational Geometry 2(1), 49–64 (1987)
9. Babaioff, M., Blumrosen, L., Lambert, N.S., Reingold, O.: Only valuable experts can be valued. In: Proceedings of the 12th ACM Conference on Electronic Commerce, pp. 221–222 (2011)
10. Babaioff, M., Sharma, Y., Slivkins, A.: Characterizing truthful multi-armed bandit mechanisms. In: Proceedings of the 10th ACM Conference on Electronic Commerce, pp. 79–88 (2009)
11. Baldwin, E., Klemperer, P.: Tropical geometry to analyse demand. Tech. rep., Working paper, Oxford University (2012)
12. Berger, A., Müller, R., Naeemi, S.H.: Characterizing incentive compatibility for convex valuations. In: Mavronicolas, M., Papadopoulou, V.G. (eds.) SAGT 2009. LNCS, vol. 5814, pp. 24–35. Springer, Heidelberg (2009)
13. Berger, A., Müller, R., Hossein, N.S.: Path-monotonicity and incentive compatibility. Tech. rep., Maastricht: METEOR, Maastricht Research School of Economics of Technology and Organization (2010)
14. Bikhchandani, S., Chatterji, S., Lavi, R., Mu'alem, A., Nisan, N., Sen, A.: Weak monotonicity characterizes deterministic dominant-strategy implementation. Econometrica 74(4), 1109–1132 (2006)
15. Boissonnat, J.D., Nielsen, F., Nock, R.: Bregman voronoi diagrams: Properties, algorithms and applications. CoRR abs/0709.2196 (2007)
16. Borwein, J.M., Vanderwerff, J.D.: Convex Functions: Constructions, Characterizations and Counterexamples. Cambridge University Press (January 2010)
17. Cai, Y., Mahdian, M., Mehta, A., Waggoner, B.: Designing markets for daily deals. Preprint (2013)
18. Carbajal, J.C., Ely, J.C.: Mechanism design without revenue equivalence. Journal of Economic Theory (2012)
19. Carroll, G.: When are local incentive constraints sufficient? Econometrica 80(2), 661–686 (2012)
20. Chen, Y., Kash, I., Ruberry, M., Shnayder, V.: Decision markets with good incentives. In: Chen, N., Elkind, E., Koutsoupias, E. (eds.) WINE 2011. LNCS, vol. 7090, pp. 72–83. Springer, Heidelberg (2011)

21. Chen, Y., Kash, I.A.: Information elicitation for decision making. In: AAMAS (2011)
22. Chen, Y., Ruberry, M., Wortman Vaughan, J.: Cost function market makers for measurable spaces. In: Proceedings of the Fourteenth ACM Conference on Electronic Commerce, pp. 785–802 (2013)
23. Chung, K.S., Ely, J.C.: Ex-post incentive compatible mechanism design. Working Paper (2002),
    http://www.kellogg.northwestern.edu/research/math/dps/1339.pdf
24. Cid-Sueiro, J.: Proper losses for learning from partial labels. In: Advances in Neural Information Processing Systems 25, pp. 1574–1582 (2012)
25. Diakonikolas, I., Papadimitriou, C., Pierrakos, G., Singer, Y.: Efficiency-revenue trade-offs in auctions. In: Czumaj, A., Mehlhorn, K., Pitts, A., Wattenhofer, R. (eds.) ICALP 2012, Part II. LNCS, vol. 7392, pp. 488–499. Springer, Heidelberg (2012)
26. Fang, F., Stinchcombe, M.B., Whinston, A.B.: Proper scoring rules with arbitrary value functions. Journal of Mathematical Economics 46(6), 1200–1210 (2010)
27. Feige, U., Tennenholtz, M.: Responsive lotteries. In: Kontogiannis, S., Koutsoupias, E., Spirakis, P.G. (eds.) SAGT 2010. LNCS, vol. 6386, pp. 150–161. Springer, Heidelberg (2010)
28. Feldman, J., Muthukrishnan, S.: Algorithmic methods for sponsored search advertising. In: Liu, Z., Xia, C.H. (eds.) Performance Modeling and Engineering, pp. 91–122. Springer US (January 2008)
29. Fiat, A., Karlin, A., Koutsoupias, E., Vidali, A.: Approaching utopia: strong truthfulness and externality-resistant mechanisms. In: Proceedings of the 4th Conference on Innovations in Theoretical Computer Science, pp. 221–230 (2013)
30. Frongillo, R.M., Kash, I.A.: Vector-valued property elicitation. Preprint (2014)
31. Frongillo, R.M., Kash, I.A.: General truthfulness characterizations via convex analysis. arXiv:1211.3043 [cs] (November 2012)
32. Gneiting, T.: Making and evaluating point forecasts. Journal of the American Statistical Association 106(494), 746–762 (2011)
33. Gneiting, T., Raftery, A.: Strictly proper scoring rules, prediction, and estimation. Journal of the American Statistical Association 102(477), 359–378 (2007)
34. Gneiting, T., Katzfuss, M.: Probabilistic forecasting. Annual Review of Statistics and Its Application 1, 125–151 (2014)
35. Grant, K., Gneiting, T.: Consistent scoring functions for quantiles. In: From Probability to Statistics and Back: High-Dimensional Models and Processes – A Festschrift in Honor of Jon A. Wellner, pp. 163–173. Institute of Mathematical Statistics (2013)
36. Halpern, J.: Reasoning about uncertainty. MIT Press (2003)
37. Heydenreich, B., Müller, R., Uetz, M., Vohra, R.V.: Characterization of revenue equivalence. Econometrica 77(1), 307–316 (2009)
38. Ioffe, A.D., Tikhomirov, V.M.: Theory of extremal problems. North-Holland Pub. Co.; sole distributors for the U.S.A. and Canada, Elsevier, North-Holland, Amsterdam, New York (1979)
39. Iyer, R., Bilmes, J.: The lovász-bregman divergence and connections to rank aggregation, clustering, and web ranking: Extended version. In: Uncertainity in Artificial Intelligence (2013)
40. Jehiel, P., Moldovanu, B.: Efficient design with interdependent valuations. Econometrica 69(5), 1237–1259 (2001)
41. Jehiel, P., Moldovanu, B., Stacchetti, E.: How (not) to sell nuclear weapons. The American Economic Review 86(4), 814–829 (1996)

42. Jehiel, P., Moldovanu, B., Stacchetti, E.: Multidimensional mechanism design for auctions with externalities. Journal of Economic Theory 85(2), 258–293 (1999)
43. Kos, N., Messner, M.: Extremal incentive compatible transfers. Journal of Economic Theory (2012)
44. Krishna, V., Maenner, E.: Convex potentials with an application to mechanism design. Econometrica 69(4), 1113–1119 (2001)
45. Lai, H.C., Lin, L.J.: The fenchel-moreau theorem for set functions. Proceedings of the American Mathematical Society, 85–90 (1988)
46. Lambert, N.: Elicitation and evaluation of statistical forecasts. Preprint (2011)
47. Lambert, N., Pennock, D., Shoham, Y.: Eliciting properties of probability distributions. In: Proceedings of the 9th ACM Conference on Electronic Commerce, pp. 129–138 (2008)
48. Lambert, N., Shoham, Y.: Eliciting truthful answers to multiple-choice questions. In: Proceedings of the 10th ACM Conference on Electronic Commerce, pp. 109–118 (2009)
49. McAfee, R., McMillan, J.: Multidimensional incentive compatibility and mechanism design. Journal of Economic Theory 46(2), 335–354 (1988)
50. Myerson, R.B.: Optimal auction design. Mathematics of Operations Research, 58–73 (1981)
51. Müller, R., Perea, A., Wolf, S.: Weak monotonicity and bayes-nash incentive compatibility. Games and Economic Behavior 61(2), 344–358 (2007)
52. Negahban, S.N., Ravikumar, P., Wainwright, M.J., Yu, B.: A unified framework for high-dimensional analysis of m-estimators with decomposable regularizers. arXiv preprint arXiv:1010.2731 (2010)
53. Ok, E.A.: Real analysis with economic applications, vol. 10. Princeton University Press (2007)
54. Osband, K., Reichelstein, S.: Information-eliciting compensation schemes. Journal of Public Economics 27(1), 107–115 (1985)
55. Osband, K.H.: Providing Incentives for Better Cost Forecasting. University of California, Berkeley (1985)
56. Othman, A., Sandholm, T.: Decision rules and decision markets. In: Proceedings of the 9th International Conference on Autonomous Agents and Multiagent Systems, vol. 1, pp. 625–632 (2010)
57. Peters, H.J.M., Wakker, P.P.: Convex functions on non-convex domains. Economics Letters 22(2-3), 251–255 (1987)
58. Rochet, J.C.: A necessary and sufficient condition for rationalizability in a quasi-linear context. Journal of Mathematical Economics 16(2), 191–200 (1987)
59. Rockafellar, R.: Convex analysis, Princeton Mathematics Series, vol. 28. Princeton University Press (1997)
60. Saks, M., Yu, L.: Weak monotonicity suffices for truthfulness on convex domains. In: Proceedings of the 6th ACM Conference on Electronic Commerce, pp. 286–293 (2005)
61. Savage, L.: Elicitation of personal probabilities and expectations. Journal of the American Statistical Association, 783–801 (1971)
62. Steinwart, I., Pasin, C., Williamson, R., Zhang, S.: Elicitation and identification of properties. Technical Report Stuttgart University (2014)
63. Urruty, J.B.H., Lemaréchal, C.: Fundamentals of Convex Analysis. Springer (2001)
64. Van Manen, M., Siersma, D.: Power diagrams and their applications. arXiv preprint math/0508037 (2005)
65. Vohra, R.V.: Mechanism design: a linear programming approach. Cambridge University Press, Cambridge (2011)
66. Yan, M.: Extension of convex functions. arXiv preprint arXiv:1207.0944 (2012)

Privacy Games

Yiling Chen*, Or Sheffet**, and Salil Vadhan***

Center for Research on Computation and Society
School of Engineering and Applied Sciences
Harvard University
{yiling,osheffet,salil}@seas.harvard.edu

Abstract. The problem of analyzing the effect of privacy concerns on the behavior of selfish utility-maximizing agents has received much attention lately. Privacy concerns are often modeled by altering the utility functions of agents to consider also their privacy loss [24,13,19,4]. Such privacy aware agents prefer to take a randomized strategy even in very simple games in which non-privacy aware agents play pure strategies. In some cases, the behavior of privacy aware agents follows the framework of Randomized Response, a well-known mechanism that preserves differential privacy.

Our work is aimed at better understanding the behavior of agents in settings where their privacy concerns are explicitly given. We consider a toy setting where agent A, in an attempt to discover the secret type of agent B, offers B a gift that one type of B agent likes and the other type dislikes. As opposed to previous works, B's incentive to keep her type a secret isn't the result of "hardwiring" B's utility function to consider privacy, but rather takes the form of a payment between B and A. We investigate three different types of payment functions and analyze B's behavior in each of the resulting games. As we show, under some payments, B's behavior is very different than the behavior of agents with hardwired privacy concerns and might even be deterministic. Under a different payment we show that B's BNE strategy does fall into the framework of Randomized Response.

1 Introduction

In recent years, as the subject of privacy becomes an increasing concern, many works have discussed the potential privacy concerns of economic utility-maximizing agents. Obviously, utility-maximizing agents are worried about the effect of revealing personal information in the current game on future transactions, and wish to minimize potential future losses. In addition, some agents may simply care about what some outside observer, who takes no part in the current game, believes about them. Such agents would like to optimize the effect of their behavior in the current game on the beliefs of that outside observer. Yet

* Supported in part by NSF grant CCF-1301976.
** Supported in part by NSF grant CNS-1237235.
*** Supported by NSF grant CNS-1237235, a gift from Google, Inc., and a Simons Investigator grant.

T.-Y. Liu et al. (Eds.): WINE 2014, LNCS 8877, pp. 371–385, 2014.
© Springer International Publishing Switzerland 2014

specifying the exact way in which information might affect the agents' future payment or an outside observer's beliefs is a complicated and intricate task.

Differential privacy (DP), a mathematical model for privacy, developed for statistical data analysis [9,8], avoids the need for such intricate modeling by providing a worst-case bound on an agents' exposure to privacy-loss. Specifically, by using a ϵ-differentially private mechanism, agents can guarantee that the belief of *any* observer about them changes by no more than a multiplicative factor of $e^\epsilon \approx 1 + \epsilon$ once this observer sees the outcome of the mechanism [7] . Furthermore, as pointed out in [13,19], using a ϵ-differentially private mechanism the agents guarantee that, in expectation, *any* future loss increases by no more than a factor of $e^\epsilon - 1 \approx \epsilon$. A recent line of work [24,13,19,4] has used ideas from differential privacy to model and analyze the behavior of privacy-awareness in game-theoretic settings. The aforementioned features of DP allow these works to bypass the need to model future transactions. Instead, they model privacy aware agents as selfish agents with utility functions that are "hardwired" to trade off between two components: a (positive) reward from the outcome of the mechanism vs a (negative) loss from their non-private exposure. This loss can be upper-bounded using DP, and hence in some cases can be shown to be dominated by the reward (of carefully designed mechanisms), showing that privacy concerns don't affect an agent's behavior.

However, in other cases, the behavior of privacy-aware agents may differ drastically from the behavior of classical, non-privacy aware agents. For example, consider a toy-game in which B tells A which of the two free gifts that A offers (or *coupons* as we call it, for reasons to be explained later) B would like to receive. We characterize B using one of two types, 0 or 1; where type 0 prefers the first gift and type 1 prefers the second one. (This is a rephrasing of the "Rye or Wholewheat" game discussed in [19].) Therefore it is simple to see that a non-privacy-aware agent always (deterministically) asks for the gift that matches her type. In contrast, if we model the privacy loss of a privacy-aware agent using DP as in the work of Ghosh and Roth [13] (and the value of the coupon is large enough), a privacy-aware agent takes a randomized strategy. (See Section 2.2.) Specifically, the agent plays *Randomized Response*, a standard differentially private mechanism that outputs a random choice slightly biased towards the agent's favorable action.

However, it was argued [19,4] that it is not realistic to use the worst-case model of DP to quantify the agent's privacy loss and predict her behavior. Differential privacy should only serve as an *upper bound* on the privacy loss, whereas the agent's expected privacy loss can (and should in fact) be much smaller — depending on the agent's predictions regarding future events, adversary's prior belief about her, the types and strategies of other agents, and the random choices of the mechanism and of other agents. As discussed above, these can be hard to model, so it is tempting to use a worst-case model like differential privacy.

But what happens if we can formulate the agent's future transactions? What if we know that the agent is concerned with the belief of a specific adversary, and we can quantify the effects of changes to that belief? Is the behavior of a classical selfish agent in that case well-modeled by such a "DP-hardwired" privacy-aware agent? Will she even randomize her strategy? In other words, we ask:

What is the behavior of a selfish utility-maximizing agent in a setting with clear privacy costs?

More specifically, we ask whether we can take the above-mentioned toy-game and alter it by introducing payments between A and B such that the behavior of a privacy-aware agent in the toy-game matches the behavior of classical (non-privacy aware) agent in the altered game. In particular, in case B takes a randomized strategy — does her behavior preserve ϵ-differential privacy, and for what value of ϵ? The study of these questions may also provide insights relevant for traditional, non-game-theoretic uses of differential privacy — helping us understand how tightly differential privacy addresses the concerns of data subjects, and thus providing guidance in the setting of the privacy parameter ϵ or the use of alternative, non-worst-case variants of differential privacy (such as [1]).

Our model. In this work we consider multiple games that model an interaction between an agent which has a secret type and an adversary whose goal is to discover this type. Though the games vary in the resulting behavior of the agents, they all follow a common outline which is similar to the toy game mentioned above. Agent A offers B a free coupon, that comes in one of two types $\{0,1\}$. Agent B has a secret type $t \in \{0,1\}$ chosen from a known prior (D_0, D_1), such that a type-t agent has positive utility ρ_t for type-t coupon and zero utility for a type-$(1-t)$ coupon. And so the game starts with B sending A a signal $\hat{t}$ indicating the requested type of coupon. (Formally, B's utility for the coupon is $\rho_t \mathbb{1}_{[\hat{t}=t]}$ for some parameters ρ_0, ρ_1.) Following this interaction, agent C, who viewed the signal $\hat{t}$ that B sent, challenges B into a game — with C taking action $\tilde{t}$ and incurring a payment from B of $P(\tilde{t}, t)$. To avoid the need to introduce a third party into the game, we identify C with A.[1] Figure 1 gives a schematic representation of the game's outline.

We make a few observations of the above interaction. We aim to model a scenario where B has the most incentive to hide her true type whereas A has the most incentive to discover B's type. Therefore, all of the payments we consider have the property that if B's type is t^* then $t^* = \arg\max_{\tilde{t}} P(\tilde{t}, t^*)$. Furthermore, the game is modeled so that the payments are transferred from B to A, which makes A's and B's goals as opposite as possible. (In fact, past the stage where B sends a signal $\hat{t}$, we have that A and B plays a zero-sum game.) We also note that A and B play a Bayesian game (in extensive form) as A doesn't know the private type of B, only its prior distribution. We characterize Bayesian Nash Equilibria (BNE) in this paper and will show that in each game, the BNE is unique except when parameters of the game satisfy certain equality constraints. It is not difficult to show that the strategies at every BNE of our games are part

---

[1] Hence the reason for the name "The Coupon Game". We think of A as G – an "evil" car-insurance company that offers its client a coupon either for an eyewear store or for a car race; thereby increasing the client's insurance premium based on either the client's bad eyesight or the client's fondness for speedy and reckless driving.

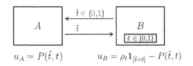

Fig. 1. A schematic view of the privacy game we model

of a Perfect Bayesian Equilibrium (PBE), i.e. a subgame-perfect refinement of the BNE. However, we focus on BNE in this paper as the equilibrium refinement doesn't bring any additional insight to our problem.

Our results and paper organization. First, in Section 2, following preliminaries we discuss the DP-hardwired privacy-aware agent as defined by Ghosh and Roth [13] and analyze her behavior in our toy game. Our analysis shows that given sufficiently large coupon valuations ρ_t, both types of B agent indeed play Randomized Response. We also discuss conditions under which other models of DP-hardwired privacy-aware agents play a randomized strategy.

Following preliminaries, we consider three different games. These games follow the general coupon-game outline, yet they vary in their payment function. The discussion for each of the games follows a similar outline. We introduce the game, then analyze the two agents' BNE strategies and see if the strategy of the B agent is indeed randomized or pure (and in case it is randomized — whether or not it follows Randomized Response for some value of ϵ). We also compare the coupon game to a "benchmark game" where B takes no action and A guesses B's type without any signal from B. Investigating whether it is even worth while for A to offer such a coupon, we compare A's profit between the two games.[2] The payment functions we consider are the following.

1. In Section 3 we consider the case where the payment function is given by a *proper scoring rule*. Proper scoring rules allows us to quantify the B's cost to any change in A's belief about her type. We show that in the case of symmetric scoring rules (scoring rules that are invariant to relabeling of event outcomes) both types of B agent follow a randomized strategy that causes A's posterior belief on the types to resemble Randomized Response. That is, initially A's belief on B being of type-0 (resp. type-1) is D_0 (resp. D_1); but B plays in a way such that after viewing the $\hat{t} = 0$ signal, A's belief that B is of type-0 (resp. type-1) is $\frac{1+\epsilon}{2}$ (resp. $\frac{1-\epsilon}{2}$) for some value of ϵ (and vice-versa in the case of the $\hat{t} = 1$ signal with the same ϵ).
2. In Section 4 we consider the case where the payments between A and B are the result of A guessing correctly B's type. A views the signal $\hat{t}$ and then guesses a type $\tilde{t} \in \{0, 1\}$ and receives a payment of $\mathbb{1}_{[\tilde{t}=t]}$ from B. This payment models the following viewpoint of B's future losses: there is a constant gap (of one "unit of utility") between interacting with an agent that

---

[2] The benchmark game is not to be confused with the toy-game we discussed earlier in this introduction. In the toy game, A takes no action and B decides on a signal. In the benchmark game, B takes no action and A decides which action to take based on the specific payment function we consider in each game.

knows B's type to an agent that does not know her type. We show that in this case, if the coupon valuations are fixed as ρ_0 and ρ_1, then at least one type of B agent plays deterministically. However, if B's valuation for the coupon is sampled from a continuous distribution, then A's strategy effectively dictates a threshold with the following property: any B agent whose valuation for the coupon is below the threshold lies and signals $\hat{t} = 1 - t$, and any agent whose valuation is above the threshold signals truthfully $\hat{t} = t$. Hence, an A agent who does not know B's valuation thinks of B as following a randomized strategy.

3. In Section 5 we consider a variation of the previous game where A also has the option to opt out and not challenge B into a payment game — to report $\bot$ and in return get no payment (i.e., $P(\bot, t) = 0$). We show that in such a game, under a very specific setting of parameters, the only BNE is such where both types of B agent take a randomized strategy. Under alternative settings of the game's parameters, the strategy of B is such that at least one of the two types plays deterministically.

Future directions are deferred to the full version of the paper, due to space limitation. We find it surprising to see how minor changes to the privacy payments lead to diametrically different behaviors. In particular, we see the existence of a threshold phenomena. Under certain parameter settings in the game we consider in item 3 above, we have that if the value of the coupon is above a certain threshold then at least one of the two types of B agent plays deterministically; and if the value of the coupon is below this threshold, B randomizes her behavior s.t. $\hat{t} = t$ w.p. close to $\frac{1}{2}$.

1.1   Related Work

The study of the intersection between mechanism design and differential privacy began with the seminal work of McSherry and Talwar [18], who showed that an ϵ-differentially private mechanism is also ϵ-truthful. The first attempt at defining a privacy-aware agent was of Ghosh and Roth [13] who quantified the privacy loss using a linear approximation $v_i \cdot \epsilon$ where v_i is an individual parameter and ϵ is the level of differential privacy that a mechanism preserves. Other applications of differentially privacy mechanisms in game theoretic settings were studied by Nissim et al [20]. The work of Xiao [24] initiated the study of mechanisms that are truthful even when you incorporate the privacy loss into the agents' utility functions. Xiao's original privacy loss measure was the mutual information between the mechanism's output and the agent's type. Nissim et al [19] (who effectively proposed a preliminary version of our coupon game called "Rye or Wholewheat") generalized the models of privacy loss to only assume that it is *upper bounded* by $v_i \cdot \epsilon$. Chen et al [4] proposed a refinement where the privacy loss is measured with respect to the given input and output. Fleischer and Lyu [11] considered the original model of agents as in Ghosh and Roth [13] but under the assumption that v_i, the value of the privacy parameter of each agent, is sampled from a known distribution.

Several papers in economics look at the potential loss of agents from having their personal data revealed. In fact, one folklore objection to the Vickrey auction is that in a repeated setting, by providing the sellers with the bidders' true valuations for the item, the bidders subject themselves to future loss should the seller prefer to run a reserved-price mechanism in the future. In the context of repeated interaction between an agent and a company, there have been works [6,2] studying the effect of price differentiation based on an agent allowing the company to remember whether she purchased the same item in the past. Interestingly, strategic agents realize this effect and so they might "haggle" — reject a price below their valuation for the item in round 1 so that they'd be able to get even lower price in round 2. In that sense, the fact that the agents publish their past interaction with the company actually helps the agents. Other work [3] discusses a setting where a buyer sequentially interacts with two different sellers, and characterizes the conditions under which the first seller prefers not to give the buyer's information to the second seller. Concurrently with our work, Gradwohl and Smorodinsky [15], whose motivation is to analyze the effect of privacy concerns, introduce a framework of games in which an agent's utility is affected by both her actions and how her actions are perceived by a third party.

The privacy games that we propose and analyze in this paper fall into the class of signaling games [17], where a sender (B in our game) with a private type sends a message (i.e. a signal) to a receiver (A in our game) who then takes an action. The payoffs of both players depend on the sender's message, the receiver's action, and the sender's type. Signaling games have been widely used in modeling behavior in economics and biology. The focus is typically on understanding when signaling is informative, i.e. when the message of the sender allows the receiver to infer the sender's private type with certainty, especially in settings when signaling is costly (e.g. Spence's job market signaling game [21]). In our setting, however, informative signaling violates privacy. We are interested in characterizing when the sender plays in a way such that the receiver cannot infer her type deterministically.

2   Preliminaries

2.1   Equilibrium Concept

We model the games between A and B as Bayesian extensive-form games. However, instead of using the standard Perfect Bayesian Equilibrium (PBE), which is a refinement of Bayesian Nash Equilibrium (BNE) for extensive-form games, as our solution concept, we analyze BNE for our games. It can be shown that all of the BNEs considered in our paper can be "extended" to PBEs (by appropriately defining the beliefs of agent A about agent B at all points in the game). We thus avoid defining the more subtle concept of PBE as the refinement doesn't provide additional insights for our problem. Below we define BNE.

A *Bayesian* game between two agents A and B is specified by their type spaces (Γ_A, Γ_B), a prior distribution Π over the type spaces (according to which nature draws the private types of the agents), sets of available actions (C_A, C_B), and utility functions, $u_i : \Gamma_A \times \Gamma_B \times C_A \times C_B \to \mathbb{R}$, $i \in \{A, B\}$. A *mixed* or *randomized* strategy of agent i maps a type of agent i to a distribution over her available actions, i.e. $\sigma_i : \Gamma_i \to \Delta(C_i)$, where $\Delta(C_i)$ is the probability simplex over C_i.

Definition 1. *A strategy profile (σ_A, σ_B) is a Bayesian Nash Equilibrium if*

$$\mathbf{E}[u_i(T_i, T_{-i}, \sigma_i(T_i), \sigma_{-i}(T_{-i}))|T_i = t_i] \geq \mathbf{E}[u_i(T_i, T_{-i}, \sigma_i'(T_i), \sigma_{-i}(T_{-i}))|T_i = t_i]$$

for all $i \in \{A, B\}$, all types $t_i \in \Gamma_i$ occurring with positive probability, and all strategies σ_i', where σ_{-i} and T_{-i} denote the strategy and type of the other agent respectively and the expectation is taken over the randomness of agent type T_{-i} and the randomness of the strategies, σ_i, σ_{-i} and σ_i'.

2.2 Differential Privacy

In order to define differential privacy, we first need to define the notion of neighboring inputs. Inputs are elements in $\mathcal{X}^n$ for some set $\mathcal{X}$, and two inputs $\mathcal{I}, \mathcal{I}' \in \mathcal{X}^n$ are called neighbors if the two are identical on the details of all individuals (all coordinates) except for at most one.

Definition 2 ([9]). *An algorithm ALG which maps inputs into some range $\mathcal{R}$ satisfies ϵ-differential privacy if for all pairs of neighboring inputs $\mathcal{I}, \mathcal{I}'$ and for all subsets $\mathcal{S} \subset \mathcal{R}$ it holds that $\mathbf{Pr}[\text{ALG}(\mathcal{I}) \in \mathcal{S}] \leq e^\epsilon \mathbf{Pr}[\text{ALG}(\mathcal{I}') \in \mathcal{S}]$.*

One of the simplest algorithms that achieve ϵ-differential privacy is called *Randomized Response* [16,10], which dates back to the 60s [22]. This algorithm is best illustrated over a binary input, where each individual is represented by a single binary bit (therefore a neighboring instance is a neighbor in which one individual is represented by a different bit), Randomized Response works by perturbing the input. For each individual i represented by the bit b_i, the algorithm randomly and independently picks a bit $\hat{b}_i$ s.t. $\mathbf{Pr}[\hat{b}_i = b_i] = \frac{1+\epsilon}{2}$ for some $\epsilon \in [0, 1)$. It follows from the definition of the algorithm that it satisfies $\ln(\frac{1+\epsilon}{1-\epsilon}) \approx 2\epsilon$-differential privacy. Randomized Response is sometimes presented as a distributed algorithm, where each individual randomly picks $\hat{b}_i$ locally, and reports $\hat{b}_i$ publicly. Therefore, it is possible to view this work as an investigation of the type of games in which selfish utility-maximizing agents truthfully follow Randomized Response, rather than sending some arbitrary bit as $\hat{b}_i$.

In this work, we define certain games and analyze the behavior of the two types of B agent in the BNE of these games. And so, denoting B's strategy as σ_B, we consider the implicit algorithm $\sigma_B(t)$ that tells a type-t agent what probability mass to put on the 0-signal and on the 1-signal. Knowing B's strategy σ_B, we say that B satisfies $\ln(X_{\text{game}})$-differential privacy where[3]

$$X_{\text{game}} \stackrel{\text{def}}{=} X_{\text{game}}(\sigma_B) = \max_{t, \hat{t} \in \{0,1\}} \left(\frac{\mathbf{Pr}[\sigma_B(t) = \hat{t}]}{\mathbf{Pr}[\sigma_B(1 - t) = \hat{t}]} \right)$$

---

[3] We use the convention $\frac{0}{0} = 1$.

We are interested in finding settings where $X_{\text{game}}(\sigma_B^*)$ is finite, where σ_B^* denotes B's BNE strategy. We say B *plays a Randomized Response strategy* in a game whenever her BNE strategy σ_B^* satisfies $\mathbf{Pr}[\sigma_B^*(0) = 0] = \mathbf{Pr}[\sigma_B^*(1) = 1] = p$ for some $p \in [1/2, 1)$.

Privacy-Aware Agents. The notion of privacy-aware agents has been developed through a series of works [24,13,19,4]. The utility function of our privacy-aware agent B is of the form $u_B = u_B^{out} - u_B^{priv}$. The first term, u_B^{out} is the utility of agent B from the mechanism. The second term, u_B^{priv}, represents the agent's privacy loss. The exact definition of u_B^{priv} (and even the variables u_B^{priv} depends on) varies between the different works mentioned above, but all works bound the privacy-loss of an agent that interacts with a mechanism that satisfies ϵ-differential privacy by $u_B^{priv} \leq v \cdot \epsilon$ for some $v > 0$. Here we argue about the behavior of a privacy-aware agent with the maximal privacy loss function, which is the type of agent considered by Ghosh and Roth [13] (i.e., the agent's privacy loss when interacting with a mechanism that satisfies ϵ-differential privacy is exactly $v \cdot \epsilon$ for some $v > 0$).

Recall our toy game: B sends a signal $\hat{t}$ and gets a coupon of type $\hat{t}$. Therefore, the outcome of this simple game is $\hat{t}$, precisely the action that B takes. B's type is picked randomly to be 0 w.p. D_0 and 1 w.p. D_1, and a B agent of type t has valuation of ρ_t for a coupon of type t. Therefore, in this game $u_B^{out} = \rho_t \mathbb{1}_{[\hat{t}=t]}$. The mechanism we consider is σ_B^*, B's utility-maximizing strategy, which we think of as the implicit algorithm that tells a type-t agents what probability mass to put on sending the $\hat{t} = 0$ signal and what mass to put on the $\hat{t} = 1$ signal. As noted above, this strategy satisfies $\ln(X_{\text{game}})$-differential privacy, and so $u_B^{priv}(\sigma_B^*) = v \cdot \ln(X_{\text{game}})$ for some parameter $v > 0$. Assuming $D_0\rho_0 \neq D_1\rho_1$, our proof shows that this privacy-aware agent chooses essentially between two alternatives in our toy game: either both types take the same deterministic strategy and send the same signal ($\mathbf{Pr}[\sigma_B^*(0) = b] = \mathbf{Pr}[\sigma_B^*(1) = b] = 1$ for some $b \in \{0, 1\}$); or the agent randomizes her behavior and plays using Randomized Response: $\mathbf{Pr}[\sigma_B^*(0) = 0] = \mathbf{Pr}[\sigma_B^*(1) = 1] \in [\frac{1}{2}, 1)$. We show that for sufficiently large values of the coupon the latter alternative is better than the first.

Theorem 3. *Let B be a privacy-aware agent, whose privacy loss is given by $v \ln(X_{\text{game}})$ for some $v > 0$. Assume that there exists an $\alpha > 0$ s.t. for sufficiently large values of ρ_0, ρ_1 it holds that $\min\{\rho_0, \rho_1\} \geq \alpha \cdot (\rho_0 + \rho_1)$. Then, the unique strategy σ_B^* that maximizes B's utility is randomized and satisfies: $\mathbf{Pr}[\sigma_B^*(0) = 0] = \mathbf{Pr}[\sigma_B^*(1) = 1] = p^*$ for some $p^* \in [\frac{1}{2}, 1)$.*

The proof is deferred to the full version of the paper. The proof of Theorem 3 also applies to some alternative models of a privacy-aware agent. In addition to Theorem 3, we also analyze, for completeness, an alternative scenario where type 0 and type 1 are two competing agents. Observe that this is no longer a Bayesian game with a single player but rather a standard complete-information game with two players. We show that this game also has NEs where both types play randomized strategies that follow Randomized Response (i.e., $\mathbf{Pr}[\sigma_B^*(0) = 0] = \mathbf{Pr}[\sigma_B^*(1) = 1]) > \frac{1}{2}$).

3 The Coupon Game with Scoring Rules Payments

In this section, we model the payments between A and B using a proper scoring rule (see below). This model is a good "first-attempt" model for the following two reasons. (i) Proper scoring rules assign profit to A based on the accuracy of her belief, so A has incentives to improve her prior belief on B's type. (ii) As we show, in this model it is possible to quantify the B's trade-off between an ϵ-change in the belief and the cost that B pays A. In that aspect, this model gives a clear quantifiable trade-off that explains what each additional unit of ϵ-differential privacy buys B. Interestingly, proper scoring rules were recently applied in the context of differential privacy [12] (yet in a very different capacity).

Proper scoring rules (see surveys [23,14]) were devised as a method to elicit experts to report their true prediction about some random variable. For a $\{0, 1\}$-valued random variable X, an expert is asked to report a prediction $x \in [0, 1]$ about the probability that $X = 1$. We pay her $f_1(x)$ if indeed $X = 1$ and $f_0(x)$ otherwise. A *proper scoring rule* is a pair of functions (f_0, f_1) such that $\arg\max_x \mathbf{E}_{t \leftarrow X}[f_t(x)] = \mathbf{Pr}[X = 1]$. Hence a risk-neutral agent's best strategy is to report $x = \mathbf{Pr}[X = 1]$. Most frequently used proper scoring rules are *symmetric* (or label-invariant) rules, where $\forall x, f_1(x) = f_0(1 - x)$ (also referred to as neutral scoring rules in [5]). With symmetric proper scoring rules, the payment to an expert reporting x as the probability of a random variable X to be 1, is identical to the payment of an expert reporting $(1 - x)$ as the probability of the random variable $(1 - X)$ to be 1. Additional background regarding proper scoring rules is deferred to the full version of this paper.

3.1 The Game with Scoring Rule Payments

We now describe the game, and analyze its BNE. In this game A interacts with a random B from a population that has D_0 fraction of type 0 agents and D_1 fraction of type 1 agents. Wlog we assume throughout Sections 3, 4 and 5 that $D_0 \geq D_1$. A aims to discover B's secret type. She has utility that is directly linked to her posterior belief on B's type and A reports her belief that B is of type 1. A's payments are given by a proper scoring rule, composed of two functions (f_0, f_1), so that after reporting a belief of x, a B agent of type t pays $f_t(x)$ to A.

A benchmark game. First consider the following straight forward (and more boring) game where B does nothing, A merely reports x – her belief that B is of type 1. In this game A gets paid according to a proper scoring rule — i.e., A gets a payment of $F_{D_1}(x) \stackrel{\text{def}}{=} D_0 f_0(x) + D_1 f_1(x)$ in expectation. Since (f_0, f_1) is a proper scoring rule, A maximizes her expected payment by reporting $x = D_1$. So, in this game A gets paid $g(D_1) \stackrel{\text{def}}{=} f_{D_1}(D_1)$ in expectation, whereas B's expected cost is $g(D_1)$. (Alternatively, a B agent of type 0 pays $f_0(D_1)$ and a B agent of type 1 pays $f_1(D_1)$.)

The full game. We now turn our attention to a more involved game. Here A, aiming to have a more accurate posterior belief on B's type, offers B a coupon. Agents of type t prefer a coupon of type t. And so, B chooses what type to report A, who then gives B the coupon and afterwards makes a prediction about B's probability of being of type 1. The formal stages of the game are as follows.

0. B's type, t, is drawn randomly with $\mathbf{Pr}[t = 0] = D_0$ and $\mathbf{Pr}[t = 1] = D_1$.
1. B reports to A a type $\hat{t} = \sigma_B(t)$ and receives utility of ρ_t if indeed $\hat{t} = t$. We assume throughout this section that $\rho_0 = \rho_1 = \rho$.
2. A reports a prediction x, representing $\mathbf{Pr}[t = 1 \mid \sigma_B(t) = \hat{t}]$, and receives a payment from B of $f_t(x)$.

Theorem 4. *Consider the coupon game with payments in the form of a symmetric proper scoring rule and with the following added assumption about the value of the coupon: $f_1(D_0) - f_1(D_1) < \rho < f_1(1) - f_1(0) = f_0(0) - f_0(1)$. The unique BNE strategy of B in this game, denoted σ_B^*, satisfies that $\mathbf{Pr}[t = 0 \mid \sigma_B^*(t) = 0] = \mathbf{Pr}[t = 1 \mid \sigma_B^*(t) = 1]$.*

Note that a Randomized Response strategy σ_B for B would instead have $\mathbf{Pr}[\sigma_B(0) = 0] = \mathbf{Pr}[\sigma_B(1) = 1]$. This condition is different from the condition in Theorem 4 when $\mathbf{Pr}[t = 0] \neq \mathbf{Pr}[t = 1]$ (i.e., $D_0 \neq D_1$). The proof of Theorem 4 is in the full version of this paper, where we also compare A's profit in the benchmark game to her profit from her BNE strategy in the full game.

4   The Coupon Game with the Identity Payments

In this section, we examine a different variation of our initial game. As always, we assume that B has a type sampled randomly from $\{0, 1\}$ w.p. D_0 and D_1 respectively, and wlog $D_0 \geq D_1$. Yet this time, the payments between A and B are given in the form of a 2×2 matrix we denote as M. This payment matrix specifies the payment from B to A in case A "accuses" B of being of type $\hat{t} \in \{0, 1\}$ and B is of type t. In general we assume that A strictly gains from finding out B's true type and potentially loses otherwise (or conversely, that a B agent of type t strictly loses utility if A accuses B of being of type $\hat{t} = t$ and potentially gains money if A accuses B of being of type $\hat{t} = 1 - t$). In this section specifically, we consider one simple matrix M – the identity matrix $I_{2\times 2}$. Thus, A gets utility of 1 from correctly guessing B's type (the same utility regardless of B's type being 0 or 1) and 0 utility if she errs.

4.1   The Game and Its Analysis

The benchmark game. The benchmark for this work is therefore a very simple "game" where B does nothing, A guesses a type and B pays A according to M. It is clear that A maximizes utility by guessing $\hat{t} = 0$ (since $D_0 \geq D_1$) and so

A gains in expectation D_0; where an agent B of type $t = 0$ pays 1 to A, and an agent B of type $t = 1$ pays 0 to A.

The full game. Aiming to get a better guess for the actual type of B, we now assume A first offers B a coupon. As before, B gets a utility of ρ_t from a coupon of the right type and 0 utility from a coupon of the wrong type. And so, the game takes the following form now.

0. B's type, denoted t, is chosen randomly, with $\mathbf{Pr}[t = 0] = D_0$ and $\mathbf{Pr}[t = 1] = D_1$.
1. B reports a type $\hat{t} = \sigma_B(t)$ to A. A in return gives B a coupon of type $\hat{t}$.
2. A accuses B of being of type $\tilde{t} = \sigma_A(\hat{t})$ and B pays 1 to A if indeed $\tilde{t} = t$.

And so, the utility of agent A is $u_A = \mathbb{1}_{[\tilde{t}=t]}$. The utility of agent B is a summation of two factors – reporting the true type to get the right coupon and the loss of paying A for finding B's true type. So $u_B = \rho_t \mathbb{1}_{[\hat{t}=t]} - \mathbb{1}_{[\tilde{t}=t]}$.

Theorem 5. *In the coupon game with payments given by the identity matrix with $\rho_0 \neq \rho_1$, any BNE strategy of B is pure for at least one of the two types of B agent. Formally, for any BNE strategy of B, denoted σ_B^*, there exist $t, \hat{t} \in \{0, 1\}$ s.t. $\mathbf{Pr}[\sigma_B^*(t) = \hat{t}] = 1$.*

In the case where $\rho_0 = \rho_1$ then B has infinitely many randomized BNE strategies, including a BNE strategy σ_B^* s.t. $\frac{1}{2} \leq \mathbf{Pr}[\sigma_B^*(0) = 0] = \mathbf{Pr}[\sigma_B^*(1) = 1] < 1$ (Randomized response).

4.2 Continuous Coupon Valuations

We now consider the same game with the same payments, but under a different setting. Whereas before we assumed the valuations that the two types of B agents have for the coupon are fixed (and known in advance), we now assume they are not fixed. In this section we assume the existence of a continuous prior over ρ, where each type $t \in \{0, 1\}$ has its own prior, so $\mathsf{CDF}_0(x) \stackrel{\text{def}}{=} \mathbf{Pr}[\rho < x \mid t = 0]$ with an analogous definition of $\mathsf{CDF}_1(x)$. We use CDF_B to denote the cumulative distribution function of the prior over ρ (i.e., $\mathsf{CDF}_B(x) = \mathbf{Pr}[\rho < x] = D_0 \mathsf{CDF}_0(x) + D_1 \mathsf{CDF}_1(x)$). We assume the CDF is continuous and so $\mathbf{Pr}[\rho = y] = 0$ for any y. Given any $z \geq 0$ we denote $\mathsf{CDF}_B^{-1}(z)$ the set $\{y : \mathsf{CDF}_B(y) = z\}$.

Theorem 6. *In every BNE (σ_A^*, σ_B^*) of the coupon game with identity payments, where $D_0 \neq D_1$ and the valuations of the B agents for the coupon are taken from a continuous distribution over $[0, \infty)$, the BNE-strategies are as follows.*

- *Agent A always plays $\tilde{t} = 0$ after viewing the $\hat{t} = 0$ signal (i.e., $\mathbf{Pr}[\sigma_A^*(0) = 0] = 1$); and plays $\tilde{t} = 1$ after viewing the $\hat{t} = 1$ signal with probability y^* (i.e., $\mathbf{Pr}[\sigma_A^*(1) = 1] = y^*$), where y^* is any value in $\mathsf{CDF}_B^{-1}(D_1)$ when $\mathbf{Pr}[\rho < 1] \geq D_1$ and $y^* = 1$ when $\mathbf{Pr}[\rho < 1] < D_1$.*

– Agent B reports truthfully (sends the signal $\hat{t} = t$) whenever her valuation for the coupon is greater than y^*, and lies (sends the signal $\hat{t} = 1 - t$) otherwise. That is, for every $t \in \{0, 1\}$ and $\rho \in [0, \infty)$, we have that if $\rho > y^*$ then $\mathbf{Pr}[\sigma_B^*(t) = t] = 1$ and if $\rho < y^*$ then $\mathbf{Pr}[\sigma_B^*(t) = t] = 0$.

Due to space constraints, this analysis is deferred to the full version of the paper.

5   The Coupon Game with an Opt Out Strategy

In this section, we consider a version of the game considered in Section 4. The revised version of the game we consider here is very similar to the original game, except for A's ability to "opt out" and not guess B's type.

In this section, we consider the most general form of matrix payments. We replace the identity-matrix payments with general payment matrix M of the form $M = \begin{bmatrix} M_{0,0} & -M_{0,1} \\ -M_{1,0} & M_{1,1} \end{bmatrix}$ with the (i, j) entry in M means A guessed $\tilde{t} = i$ and B's true type is $t = j$, and so B pays A the amount detailed in the (i,j)-entry. We assume $M_{0,0}, M_{0,1}, M_{1,0}, M_{1,1}$ are all non-negative.

Indeed, when previously considering the identity matrix payments, we assumed the for A, realizing that B has type $t = 0$ is worth just as much as finding B has type $t = 1$. But it might be the case that finding a person of $t = 1$ should be more worthwhile for A. For example, type $t = 1$ (the minority, since we always assume $D_0 \geq D_1$) may represent having some embarrassing medical condition while type $t = 0$ representing not having it. Therefore, $M_{1,1}$ can be much larger than $M_{0,0}$, but similarly $M_{1,0}$ is probably larger than $M_{0,1}$. (Falsely accusing B of being of the embarrassing type is costlier than falsely accusing a B of type 1 of belonging to the non-embarrassing majority.) Our new payment matrix still motivates A to find out B's true type — A gains utility by correctly guessing B's type, and loses utility by accusing B of being of the wrong type.

The "strawman" game. First, consider a simple game where B makes no move (A offers no coupon) and A tries to guess B's type without getting any signal from B. Then A has three possible pure strategies: (i) guess that B is of type 0; (ii) guess that B is of type 1; and (iii) guess nothing. In expectation, the outcome of option (i) is $D_0 M_{0,0} - D_1 M_{0,1}$ and the outcome of option (ii) is $D_1 M_{1,1} - D_0 M_{1,0}$. If the parameters of M are set such that both options are negative then A's preferred strategy is to opt out and gain 0. We assume throughout this section that indeed the above holds. (Intuitively, this assumption reflects the fact that we don't make assumptions about people's type without first getting any information about them.) So we have

$$\frac{M_{0,0}}{M_{0,1}} < \frac{D_1}{D_0}, \qquad \text{and} \qquad \frac{M_{1,1}}{M_{1,0}} < \frac{D_0}{D_1} \qquad (1)$$

A direct (and repeatedly used) corollary of Equation (1) is that $\frac{M_{0,0}}{M_{0,1}} < \frac{M_{1,0}}{M_{1,1}}$.

The full game. We now give the formal description of the game.

0. B's type, denoted t, is chosen randomly, with $\mathbf{Pr}[t = 0] = D_0$ and $\mathbf{Pr}[t = 1] = D_1$.
1. B reports a type $\hat{t}$ to A. A in return gives B a coupon of type $\hat{t}$.
2. A chooses whether to accuse B of being of a certain type, or opting out.
   - If A opts out (denoted as $\tilde{t} = \perp$), then B pays A nothing.
   - If A accuses B of being of type $\tilde{t}$ then: if $\tilde{t} = t$ then B pays $M_{t,t}$ to A, and if $\tilde{t} = 1 - t$ then B pays $-M_{1-t,t}$ to A (or A pays $M_{1-t,t}$ to B).

Introducing the option to opt out indeed changes significantly the BNE strategies of A and B.

Theorem 7. *If we have that $D_0^2 M_{0,0} M_{1,0} = D_1^2 M_{0,1} M_{1,1}$ and the parameters of the game satisfy the following condition:*

$$0 < \rho_1 M_{1,0} - \rho_0 M_{1,1} < M_{0,1} M_{1,0} - M_{0,0} M_{1,1}$$
$$0 < \rho_0 M_{0,0} - \rho_1 M_{0,0} < M_{0,1} M_{1,0} - M_{0,0} M_{1,1} \qquad (2)$$

then the unique BNE strategy of B, denote σ_B^*, is such that B plays Randomized Response: $\frac{1}{2} \leq \mathbf{Pr}[\sigma_B^*(0) = 0] = \mathbf{Pr}[\sigma_B^*(1) = 1] < 1$.

Proving Theorem 7 is the goal of this section. The proof itself is deferred to the full version of this paper, where we also give a complete summary of the various BNEs of this game. We detail 6 different cases that cover all possible settings of the game. Each of these 6 cases is defined by a different *feasibility* condition. These conditions guarantee that A is able to find a strategy that cause at least one of the two types of B agent to be indifferent as to the signal she sends.

The feasibility condition detailed in Equation (2) can be realized starting with any matrix M satisfying $M_{0,0} M_{1,1} < M_{0,1} M_{1,0}$ (which is a necessary condition derived from Equation (1)), which intuitively can be interpreted as having a wrong "accusation" being costlier than the gain from a correct "accusation" (on average and in absolute terms). Given such M, one can set D_0 and D_1 s.t. $\frac{D_0}{D_1} = \sqrt{\frac{M_{0,1}}{M_{0,0}} \cdot \frac{M_{1,1}}{M_{1,0}}}$ as to satisfy Equation (1). This can be interpreted as balancing the "significance" of type 0 (i.e. $M_{0,0} M_{0,1}$) with the "significance" of type 1 (i.e. $M_{1,0} M_{1,1}$), setting the more significant type as the less probable (i.e. if type 1 is more significant than type 0, than $D_1 < D_0$). We then pick ρ_0, ρ_1 that satisfy $\frac{M_{1,1}}{M_{1,0}} < \frac{\rho_1}{\rho_0} < \frac{M_{0,1}}{M_{0,0}}$ and scale both by the sufficiently small multiplicative factor so we satisfy the other inequality in Equation (2). (In particular, setting $\frac{\rho_1}{\rho_0} = \frac{D_0}{D_1}$ is a feasible solution.) Here, ρ_0 and ρ_1 are set such that the ratio $\frac{\rho_1}{\rho_0}$ balances the significance ratio w.r.t type 1 accusation (i.e. $\frac{\rho_1}{\rho_0} > \frac{M_{1,1}}{M_{0,0}}$) and the ratio $\frac{\rho_0}{\rho_1}$ balances the significance ratio w.r.t to type 0 accusation (i.e. $\frac{\rho_0}{\rho_1} > \frac{M_{0,0}}{M_{1,0}}$). More concretely, for any matrix $M = \begin{pmatrix} 1 & c \\ c & d \end{pmatrix}$ with parameters c, d satisfying $d < c^2$, we can set $\frac{D_0}{D_1} = \sqrt{d}$ and any sufficiently small ρ_0, ρ_1 satisfying $\frac{\rho_1}{\rho_0} \in (\frac{d}{c}, c)$ and satisfy the requirements of Theorem 7.

Recall, in addition to the conditions specifically stated in Equation (2), we also require that $D_0^2 M_{0,0} M_{1,0} = D_1^2 M_{0,1} M_{1,1}$ in order for the two types of agent

B to play Randomized Response. In other words, the feasibility condition in Equation (2) implies that B's BNE strategy, denoted by $p^* = \mathbf{Pr}[\sigma_B^*(0) = 0]$ and $q^* = \mathbf{Pr}[\sigma_B^*(1) = 1]$, is given by

$$(p^*, q^*) = \left(\frac{D_0 D_1 M_{0,1} M_{1,0} - D_1^2 M_{0,1} M_{1,1}}{D_0 D_1 M_{0,1} M_{1,0} - D_0 D_1 M_{0,0} M_{1,1}}, \frac{D_0 D_1 M_{0,1} M_{1,0} - D_0^2 M_{0,0} M_{1,0}}{D_0 D_1 M_{0,1} M_{1,0} - D_0 D_1 M_{0,0} M_{1,1}} \right)$$

The additional condition of $D_0^2 M_{0,0} M_{1,0} = D_1^2 M_{0,1} M_{1,1}$ implies therefore that $p^* = q^*$. And so, in this case the B agent plays a Randomized Response strategy that preserves ϵ-differential privacy for $\epsilon = \ln(\frac{p^*}{1-q^*}) = \ln\left(\frac{D_1 M_{0,1}}{D_0 M_{0,0}}\right)$. Observe that this value of ϵ is *independent* from the value of the coupon (i.e., from ρ_0 and ρ_1). This is due to the nature of BNE in which an agent plays her Nash-strategy in order to make her opponent indifferent between various strategies rather than maximizing her own utility. Therefore, the coordinates (p^*, q^*) are such that they make agent A indifferent between several pure strategies. And since the utility function of A is independent of ρ_0, ρ_1, we have that perturbing the values of ρ_0, ρ_1 does not affect the coordinates (p^*, q^*). (Yet, perturbing the values of ρ_0, ρ_1 does affect the various relations between the parameters of the game, and so it may determine which of the 6 feasibility conditions does in fact hold.)

Acknowledgments. We would like to thank Kobbi Nissim for many helpful discussions and helping us in initiating this line of work.

References

1. Bassily, R., Groce, A., Katz, J., Smith, A.: Coupled-worlds privacy: Exploiting adversarial uncertainty in statistical data privacy. In: FOCS (2013)
2. Bergemann, D., Brooks, B., Morris, S.: The Limits of Price Discrimination. Cowles Foundation Discussion Papers 1896, Cowles Foundation for Research in Economics, Yale University (May 2013), http://ideas.repec.org/p/cwl/cwldpp/1896.html
3. Calzolari, G., Pavan, A.: On the optimality of privacy in sequential contracting. Journal of Economic Theory 130(1) (2006)
4. Chen, Y., Chong, S., Kash, I.A., Moran, T., Vadhan, S.P.: Truthful mechanisms for agents that value privacy. In: EC (2013)
5. Chen, Y., Devanur, N.R., Pennock, D.M., Vaughan, J.W.: Removing arbitrage from wagering mechanisms. In: EC (2014)
6. Conitzer, V., Taylor, C.R., Wagman, L.: Hide and seek: Costly consumer privacy in a market with repeat purchases. Marketing Science 31(2) (2012)
7. Dwork, C.: Differential privacy. In: Bugliesi, M., Preneel, B., Sassone, V., Wegener, I. (eds.) ICALP 2006, Part II. LNCS, vol. 4052, pp. 1–12. Springer, Heidelberg (2006)
8. Dwork, C., Kenthapadi, K., McSherry, F., Mironov, I., Naor, M.: Our data, ourselves: Privacy via distributed noise generation. In: Vaudenay, S. (ed.) EUROCRYPT 2006. LNCS, vol. 4004, pp. 486–503. Springer, Heidelberg (2006)
9. Dwork, C., McSherry, F., Nissim, K., Smith, A.: Calibrating noise to sensitivity in private data analysis. In: Halevi, S., Rabin, T. (eds.) TCC 2006. LNCS, vol. 3876, pp. 265–284. Springer, Heidelberg (2006)

10. Dwork, C., Smith, A.: Differential privacy for statistics: What we know and what we want to learn. Journal of Privacy and Confidentiality 1(2), 2 (2010)
11. Fleischer, L., Lyu, Y.H.: Approximately optimal auctions for selling privacy when costs are correlated with data. In: EC (2012)
12. Ghosh, A., Ligett, K., Roth, A., Schoenebeck, G.: Buying private data without verification. In: EC (2014)
13. Ghosh, A., Roth, A.: Selling privacy at auction. In: EC (2011)
14. Gneiting, T., Raftery, A.E.: Strictly proper scoring rules, prediction, and estimation. Journal of the American Statistical Association 102(477), 359–378 (2007)
15. Gradwohl, R., Smorodinsky, R.: Subjective perception games and privacy. CoRR abs/1409.1487 (2014), http://arxiv.org/abs/1409.1487
16. Kasiviswanathan, S.P., Lee, H.K., Nissim, K., Raskhodnikova, S., Smith, A.: What can we learn privately? In: FOCS (2008)
17. Mas-Colell, A., Whinston, M.D., Green, J.R.: Microeconomic Theory. Oxford University Press (June 1995)
18. McSherry, F., Talwar, K.: Mechanism design via differential privacy. In: FOCS, pp. 94–103 (2007)
19. Nissim, K., Orlandi, C., Smorodinsky, R.: Privacy-aware mechanism design. In: EC (2012)
20. Nissim, K., Smorodinsky, R., Tennenholtz, M.: Approximately optimal mechanism design via differential privacy. In: ITCS (2012)
21. Spence, M.: Job market signalling. Quarterly Journal of Economics 87(3), 355–374 (1973)
22. Warner, S.L.: Randomized Response: A Survey Technique for Eliminating Evasive Answer Bias. Journal of the American Statistical Association 60(309) (March 1965)
23. Winkler, R.: Scoring rules and the evaluation of probabilities. Test 5(1), 1–60 (1996)
24. Xiao, D.: Is privacy compatible with truthfulness? In: ITCS (2013)

Simple and Near-Optimal Mechanisms
for Market Intermediation

Rad Niazadeh, Yang Yuan, and Robert Kleinberg*

Cornell University, Department of Computer Science, Ithaca, NY, 14850, USA

Abstract. A prevalent market structure in the Internet economy consists of buyers and sellers connected by a platform (such as Amazon or eBay) that acts as an intermediary and keeps a share of the revenue of each transaction. While the optimal mechanism that maximizes the intermediary's profit in such a setting may be quite complicated, the mechanisms observed in reality are generally much simpler, e.g., applying an affine function to the price of the transaction as the intermediary's fee. Loertscher and Niedermayer [7, 8] initiated the study of such fee-setting mechanisms in two-sided markets, and we continue this investigation by addressing the question of when an affine fee schedule is approximately optimal for worst-case seller distribution. On one hand our work supplies non-trivial sufficient conditions on the buyer side (i.e. linearity of marginal revenue function, or MHR property of value and value minus cost distributions) under which an affine fee schedule can obtain a constant fraction of the intermediary's optimal profit for all seller distributions. On the other hand we complement our result by showing that proper affine fee-setting mechanisms (e.g. those used in eBay and Amazon selling plans) are *unable* to extract a constant fraction of optimal profit in the worst-case seller distribution. As subsidiary results we also show there exists a constant gap between maximum surplus and maximum revenue under the aforementioned conditions. Most of the mechanisms that we propose are also prior-independent with respect to the seller, which signifies the practical implications of our result.

1 Introduction

A prevalent market structure in the Internet economy consists of buyers and sellers connected by a platform (such as Amazon or eBay) that acts as an intermediary and keeps a share of the revenue each time a buyer makes a purchase from a seller. What mechanism should the intermediary use to maximize its profit? In cases the optimal mechanism is unacceptably complicated, can simpler mechanisms closely approximate the profit of the optimal mechanism? We approach these questions using the framework of Bayesian mechanism design and worst-case approximation guarantees.

* All three authors were supported by NSF grant AF-0910940. Robert Kleinberg was also supported by a Microsoft Research New Faculty Fellowship and a Google Research Grant. Parts of this work were completed while the third author was a Visiting Researcher at Microsoft Research New England.

T.-Y. Liu et al. (Eds.): WINE 2014, LNCS 8877, pp. 386–399, 2014.

To motivate our investigation it is instructive to consider the transaction fees that are commonly used by intermediaries in reality. For example, when an item is sold on eBay using a fixed price listing (as opposed to an auction), the seller is charged a fee of $0.3 + 0.1P$, where P is the total amount of the sale in dollars[1]. Amazon uses a similar pricing rule for individual sellers, which is $0.99 + \alpha P$, where α is a real number determined by the category of the product, typically ranging from 8% to 15% [2]. Generalizing these examples, we say that a *fee-setting mechanism* is one in which the intermediary names a function $w(\cdot)$, the seller names a price P, and the buyer chooses whether or not to take the item at price P. If the transaction takes place, then the intermediary keeps $w(P)$ and pays $P - w(P)$ to the seller. Otherwise, no money changes hands. We refer to w as the *fee schedule* of the mechanism. We say that w is *affine* if it can be represented in the form $w = (1 - \alpha)P + \beta$ for some constants α, β, and we say that an affine schedule $w(P) = (1 - \alpha)P + \beta$ is *proper* if $\alpha \in [0, 1], \beta \geq 0$. Note that the fee schedule used by eBay and Amazon (and many other intermediaries, for example real estate brokers) are affine and proper.

Loertscher and Niedermayer [7, 8] initiated the study of fee-setting mechanisms in two-sided markets. They showed that if it is possible for the intermediary to choose a mechanism that implements a given allocation rule in Bayes-Nash equilibrium, then there is a fee-setting mechanism that does so. They also provided necessary and sufficient conditions for the intermediary's optimal mechanism to be implemented by an affine fee-setting mechanism. The necessary and sufficient condition discovered by Loertscher and Niedermayer [7, 8] requires the seller's cost to be drawn from a generalized Pareto distribution (see Definition 1 below). Using results from extreme value theory, they show that in the limit as only the sellers with lowest cost and the buyers with highest value enter the market, the conditional distribution of the seller's cost (conditional on entering the market) approaches a generalized Pareto distribution, thus providing a partial justification for the prevalence of affine fee-setting mechanisms in two-sided markets.

Our work draws inspiration from the aforementioned work of Loertscher and Niedermayer [7, 8] and seeks a different type of justification for affine fee-setting mechanisms by asking the question, "When are affine fee-setting mechanisms approximately optimal?" Our results pertain to the case when the buyer's virtual valuation function is affine, which is the characterization of generalized Pareto distributions, in ex-post IR setting. We first show that a specific choice of seller prior-independent affine fee schedule $w(P) = P - \phi_{\mathcal{B}}(P)$ is ex-post IR for every possible seller's distribution, where prior-independent means the fee schedule only depends on the buyer's value distribution but not on the seller's cost distribution. Moreover, this affine fee schedule also achieves a constant-approximation to the maximum surplus — and hence, also, a constant-approximation to the optimal revenue. The approximation factor depends on the exponent of the buyer's generalized power distribution but it is no more than 4 comparing to optimal

---

[1] See http://pages.ebay.com/help/sell/fees.html
[2] See http://services.amazon.com/selling/pricing.htm

intermediary's profit when the buyer's PDF is monotone. Our results complement the results of Loertscher and Niedermayer [7, 8] in the sense that combined with their results, we show that if either of the buyer side or the seller side has affine virtual valuation function, and the other side follows regular distributions, then the best affine fee schedule guarantees either optimal or near optimal revenue, which provides explanation for the phenomenon that affine fee schedule is widely used in the daily life.

Our second main result explores the setting that the difference between the values of the seller and the buyer follows MHR distribution, which indicates that the surplus and revenue are constant approximation to each other. Under this assumption, we may further extend the buyer's distribution to MHR distributions, and still get constant approximation ratio with constant (and hence affine) fee schedule.

Intriguingly, without proper MHR assumptions the ex-post IR affine fee schedule in the aforementioned approximation result is *not* proper; in contrast to intermediaries in typical two-sided markets in practice, the intermediary in our approximation result may charge a transaction fee which is a decreasing function of the seller's price. Our third main result shows that this reliance on improper affine fee schedules is unavoidable: even when the buyer's value is assumed to be uniformly distributed on $[0, 1]$, there exist seller cost distributions for which no proper affine fee-setting mechanism can achieve a constant-approximation to the optimal revenue.

In the special case that the buyer's distribution is uniform $[0, 1]$, we propose an improved mechanism, which gives 3-approximation fee-setting mechanism to the optimal revenue. We also prove that if one needs a prior independent affine fee schedule when the buyer's distribution is uniform $[0, 1]$, then $\alpha - \beta = 1$ is necessary. Moreover, among all the prior independent affine fee schedule, $w(P) = 1 - P$ gets the best approximation ratio 8 comparing to maximum surplus. From this perspective, our proposed affine fee schedule is optimal. Finally, our proof techniques reveal the fact that there exists a constant gap between optimal revenue and maximum surplus when buyer's distribution is generalized Pareto distribution as a side dish.

The primary source of difficulty in proving these results is that fee-setting mechanisms are not Bayes-Nash incentive compatible (BNIC). Thus, deriving a revenue guarantee for the intermediary requires first solving for the Bayes-Nash equilibrium of the mechanism. Our paper adopts the approach introduced by Loertscher and Niedermayer [7, 8] for deriving the Bayes-Nash equilibrium. The technical heart of our paper lies in some surprising connections between the affine fee schedule, Bayes-Nash equilibrium payment function, and the cumulative hazard rate function. These connections are non-trivial, which make the proof succinct while the results are still general. Starting from that, we got expressions of the three quantities of interest — the maximum surplus, the optimal revenue, and the affine fee-setting mechanism's revenue — in a closely related form. Then, leveraging our assumption that the buyer's virtual value function is affine, we are able to choose an affine fee schedule to approximate the optimal revenue.

1.1   Related Work

Myerson and Satterthwaite [10] showed that for one seller one buyer setting, if there is no intermediary between them, then no incentive-compatible individually rational mechanism can produce post efficient outcome, where post efficient outcome means the trade should take place whenever the buyer's value is larger than the seller's cost. Based on this impossibility result, they also considered the case that intermediary is allowed, and both the seller and the buyer can trade with the intermediary only.

Deng et al. [3] studied the double auction, in which the intermediary designs mechanism for the buyers and the sellers to extract maximum revenue. In the paper, they provided optimal or near-optimal mechanisms for both single dimensional and multi-dimensional environments with continuous or discrete distributions. Jain and Wilkens [6] studied the same problem with single unit-demand buyer and multiple sellers, and gave a characterization for the optimal solution in this setting. Since the optimal mechanism is generally hard to implement, they also proposed several approximation mechanisms, including picking the best item and sell, or using anonymous virtual reserve price combined with greedy algorithm.

Contract problem has a similar setting as the intermediary problem: the principle (intermediary) proposed a contract ($w(\cdot)$ function) to the agent (the seller), and the agent will choose his action and get a output (P payment), and then give the principle $w(P)$, keep $P - c$ as its utility. Previously, researchers have found evidence showing that linear contract is powerful in this setting. Pal et al. [11] studied linear contract problem, and found that linear contracts are common in practice not only because the simplicity, but also due to the fact that the optimal linear contract guarantees at least 90% of the fully optimal contract in the canonical moral hazard setting. Carroll [2] proved that under mild assumptions, the optimal contract is actually linear.

Simple mechanisms and their approximation ratios to the corresponding optimal mechanisms have been an important research topic in the literature. For example, Bulow and Klemperer [1] showed that in the i.i.d., regular, single dimensional setting, second price auction with $n+1$ bidder will give more revenue than the optimal auction with n bidders. Hartline and Roughgarden [5] investigated the single dimensional setting where bidders have independent valuations, and showed that VCG with anonymous reserve price can achieve 4-approximation to the optimal revenue. Dhangwatnotai et al. [4] considered the auctions that are prior-independent, in the sense that the auction will achieve good approximation to the optimal revenue while the specific value distributions of the bidders are not used in the auction.

2   Preliminaries

In this paper we consider the problem of single-item trade, in which a profit-maximizing broker mediates the exchange between a buyer and a seller. In particular, we follow the Bayesian mechanism design approach wherein a Bayesian designer looks to find the trade mechanism with the maximum possible revenue in expectation over the distributions from which the preferences of the buyer and seller are drawn. We assume the preferences of buyer and seller are private values drawn from product distributions, which are common knowledge.

2.1   Setting, Notations, Solution Concepts, and Basics

We assume the reader is familiar with the general model of single dimensional mechanism design for risk neutral agents, including the definitions of incentive compatibility and individual rationality, basics of Bayesian mechanism design, and adapting these concepts to the exchange setting (see Appendix in the online full-version of our paper). Still, it is worth identifying a few aspects of our notations and terminology.

Suppose the seller $\mathcal{S}$ has a private cost c and the buyer $\mathcal{B}$ has a private value v for the item. We use F (and f) to denote the CDF(and PDF) of v, and G (and g) to denote the CDF (and PDF) of c. Unless stated otherwise, we assume the support of f is $[0, \overline{v}]$ and the support of g is $[0, \overline{c}]$. We define the marginal revenue functions (a.k.a. *virtual preferences*) of seller and buyer as follows. Let $\phi_{\mathcal{S}}(c) \triangleq c + \frac{G(c)}{g(c)}$ be defined as the virtual cost of the seller and $\phi_{\mathcal{B}}(v) \triangleq v - \frac{1-F(v)}{f(v)}$ be defined as the virtual value of the buyer. We also define buyer's *hazard rate*, $h_{\mathcal{B}}(v) \triangleq \frac{f(v)}{1-F(v)}$, and *cumulative hazard rate*, $H_{\mathcal{B}}(v) \triangleq \int_0^v h_{\mathcal{B}}(z)dz$. It can be easily shown that $1 - F(v) = e^{-H_{\mathcal{B}}(v)}$, which is a famous property of cumulative hazard rate.

We say a buyer (or a seller) is *buyer-regular* (or *seller-regular*) if $\phi_{\mathcal{B}}(v)$ (or $\phi_{\mathcal{S}}(c)$) is monotone non-decreasing. A buyer's distribution is said to be *MHR (monotone hazard rate)* if $h_{\mathcal{B}}(v)$ is monotone non-decreasing (or equivalently $H_{\mathcal{B}}(v)$ is convex). For a regular buyer v, *monopoly price* is defined to be $\eta_v = \phi_{\mathcal{B}}^{-1}(0)$ (i.e. if $v \geq \eta_v$ virtual value is non-negative). Moreover, *monopoly revenue* $R_\eta^v \triangleq \eta_v(1 - F(\eta_v))$ is the expected revenue one gets by posting η_v to a buyer with value v.

2.2   Characterization of Distributions with Affine Virtual Value/Cost

A critical constraint throughout this paper, which is appearing in different forms in many of our results and background results on this subject, is when the buyer or seller has an affine virtual preference, i.e. when $\phi_{\mathcal{S}}(c) = xc + y$ or when $\phi_{\mathcal{B}}(v) = xv - y$ for $x, y \in \mathbb{R}$. We now characterize the buyer distributions and seller distributions with the above property as follows.

Definition 1. *A generalized Pareto distribution F with parameters μ, λ, and ξ, where $\mu, \lambda, \xi \in \mathbb{R}$, $\lambda > 0$ and $\xi \geq 0$, is defined by the following cumulative density function.*

$$F(x) = \begin{cases} 1 - (1 - \xi\lambda(x-\mu))^{\frac{1}{\xi}} & \text{if } \xi > 0 \\ 1 - e^{\lambda(x-\mu)} & \text{if } \xi = 0 \end{cases}$$

and the support is bounded and equal to $[\mu, \mu + \frac{1}{\xi\lambda}]$ if $\xi > 0$, and is unbounded and equal to $[\mu, +\infty)$ if $\xi = 0$. When $\xi > 0$ we refer to the distribution as generalized power distribution *and when $\xi = 0$ we refer to it as* generalized exponential distribution.

It is worth mentioning that the family of Pareto distributions are skewed, heavy-tailed distributions that are sometimes used to model the distributions of incomes and other financial variables. For the cost of the seller, we define a similar distribution as follows.

Definition 2. *The seller with cost c has a reverse-generalized Pareto distribution with parameters μ, λ, and ξ if $-c$ is a random variable drawn from a generalized Pareto distribution with parameters μ, λ and ξ.*

For generalized Pareto distribution family, one can easily prove the following corollary by definition.

Corollary 1. *If v is drawn from a generalized Pareto distribution with parameters μ, λ, and ξ, then $\phi_B(v) = (1 + \xi)v - (\frac{1}{\lambda} - \xi\mu)$. If c is drawn from a reverse-generalized Pareto distribution with parameters μ, λ, and ξ, then $\phi_S(c) = (1 + \xi)c + (\frac{1}{\lambda} + \xi\mu)$.*

We can also prove that the inverse is true, i.e. affine virtual preferences implies the generalized Pareto distribution (To prove this, solve the corresponding differential equations coming from the definitions, which we omit here)

Lemma 1. *A buyer (or seller) has affine virtual value (or cost) only if its value (or cost) is drawn from a generalized Pareto distribution (or reverse-generalized Pareto distribution).*

3   Background Results

In this section, we investigate a class of mechanisms known as *fee-setting*, introduced first by Loertscher and Niedermayer [7]. In these mechanisms, the intermediary asks the seller to bid her preferred price. If a buyer is willing to buy the item with this price, the intermediary takes a share of the trade money and gives the rest to the seller. Fee-setting mechanisms are simple, intuitive, easy to implement and more robust compared with Myerson's optimal mechanism.

3.1   Fee-Setting Exchange Mechanisms

We first define a *fee-setting mechanism* as follows.

Definition 3. *A a fee-setting mechanism with common knowledge fee schedule $w(.) : \mathbb{R} \to \mathbb{R}$ is an indirect mechanism for single buyer single seller exchange that runs the following steps subsequently:*

- *Trader asks the seller to bid its desired price P,*
- *Trader then posts the price P for the buyer,*

- *If $v < P$ then the trade doesn't happen and all the payments will be zero.*
- *If $v \geq P$ then the item will be traded, trader charges the buyer P, keeps its share of the trade $w(P)$, and pays $P - w(P)$ to the seller.*

We now define *affine fee setting exchange mechanisms* formally below.

Definition 4. *An* affine fee setting exchange mechanism *with parameters α and β is a fee-setting mechanism with affine fee schedule $w(P) \triangleq (1 - \alpha)P + \beta$, $\alpha, \beta \in \mathbb{R}$.*

In this paper, we refer to an affine exchange fee mechanism with parameters α and β as $\text{APX}(\alpha, \beta)$. We also define $\text{Rev-APX}(\alpha, \beta)$ to be the revenue of $\text{APX}(\alpha, \beta)$ when strategy profile of agents is a BNE (As we will discuss below, for affine exchange mechanisms there is a unique BNE under the regularity assumption). Moreover, OPT-Rev is defined to be the revenue of optimal Myerson mechanism, and OPT-Surplus to be the surplus of VCG mechanism.

3.2 Characterization of BNE Strategy of the Seller

By a standard argument similar to those used in the Bayes-Nash equilibrium characterization of single dimension mechanism [9] one can characterize the BNE of the fee-setting mechanism. More formally, we have the following theorem, proved in [7], that characterizes the BNE of the fee-setting mechanisms.

Theorem 1. *[7] Consider a fee-setting mechanism with differentiable fee-setting $w(.)$, then $P : [0, \bar{c}] \to \mathbb{R}^+$ is a BNE strategy of the seller if and only if:*

- *$P(c)$ is monotone non-decreasing with respect to c.*
- *$P(c)$ satisfies $\phi_{\mathcal{B}}(P(c)) = P(c) - \frac{P(c) - w(P(c)) - c}{1 - \frac{\partial w}{\partial p}(P(c))}$.*

Although the characterization in Theorem 1 is indirect, it has many nice implications in the special case of fee-settings mechanisms with affine fee schedule.

Corollary 2. *Suppose in an exchange setting seller is regular. Then for an affine fee-setting mechanism with fee schedule $w(P) = (1 - \alpha)P + \beta$, $P(c) = \phi_{\mathcal{B}}^{-1}(\frac{c+\beta}{\alpha})$ is the unique BNE strategy of seller.*

Proof. From Theorem 1 we know in any BNE, we have

$$\phi_{\mathcal{B}}(P(c)) = P(c) - \frac{P(c) - w(P(c)) - c}{1 - \frac{\partial w}{\partial p}(P(c))} = P(c) - \frac{\alpha P(c) + \beta + c}{1 - (1 - \alpha)} = \frac{c + \beta}{\alpha}$$

and as buyer is regular, $\phi_{\mathcal{B}}$ is invertible, so in any BNE $P(c) = \phi_{\mathcal{B}}^{-1}(\frac{c+\beta}{\alpha})$.

3.3 Optimality of Affine and Non-affine Fee-Setting Mechanisms

Considering the class of fee-setting mechanisms, one important question is how well these mechanisms can perform comparing to Myerson's optimal mechanism. Loertscher and Niedermayer [7, 8] showed that with a proper choice of function $w(P)$ (not necessarily affine) one can design a fee-setting mechanism that extracts the same revenue in expectation as in Myerson's optimal mechanism. While this result is surprising by itself, they also could show that optimal fee-setting mechanism will be affine when seller's cost is drawn form a reverse-generalized Pareto distribution as in Definition 2 (in other words, when the seller's virtual cost is affine). For more details on this result and a simple proof using revenue equivalence theorem [9], see the online full-version of our paper.

4   Main Results

As can be seen from the discussion in the last section, Loertscher and Niedermayer [7] initiated the study of affine fee-setting mechanisms in two-sided markets and identified necessary and sufficient conditions for the intermediary's optimal fee schedule to be affine for worst-case buyer distribution. In this section, we continue this investigation by addressing the question of when an affine fee schedule is optimal or approximately optimal for worst-case seller distribution. By simulation, one can show that there exists a pair of seller and buyer distributions for which the best affine mechanism is not optimal (for example see [7]). However, in those cases, we may still be able to get constant approximations to maximum intermediary profit with affine fee-settings. We have three main results following this line of thought.

As our first result, intuitively when at least one side of the bilateral market has some linear behaviors it might be possible for the mechanism designer to extract optimal or approximately optimal revenue from the buyer and seller using affine fee-settings. Under this condition, we propose improper fee-setting mechanisms that can extract constant approximations to optimal revenue. More formally:

Main Result 1. *If the buyer has affine virtual value, under some mild assumptions, the affine fee-setting mechanism $w(P) = P - \phi_B(P)$ extracts a constant approximation of optimal intermediary's revenue in expectation for any seller-regular distributions. Moreover, optimal intermediary's revenue and maximum surplus are in constant approximation of each other in expectation.*

As the second result, when surplus and revenue are in constant approximation of each other (for example when the distributions involved in the trade are not heavy-tailed) posting a proper price for the buyer can always extract constant approximations to optimal surplus, and hence optimal revenue, and seller's cost will not be an important issue. More formally:

Main Result 2. *If the random variables v (buyer's value) and $v - c$ (difference of buyer's value and seller's cost) are MHR, the constant fee-setting mechanism $w(P) = \eta_{v-c}$ extracts constant approximations to optimal intermediary's revenue in expectation for any seller distributions, in which η_{v-c} is the monopoly price for the random variable $v - c$ ($\eta_{v-c} = \phi_{v-c}^{-1}(0)$). Moreover, optimal intermediary's revenue and maximum surplus are in constant approximation of each other in expectation.*

As the final result, we show that a mechanism designer who tries to get constant approximation to optimal revenue for all seller's distribution (especially for heavy-tailed distributions), cannot avoid using the improper fee-setting mechanisms. Formally:

Main Result 3. *Even when the buyer's value is drawn from $unif [0, 1]$, there exists seller cost distributions for which no proper affine fee-setting mechanism can achieve a constant-approximation to the optimal intermediary's revenue.*

In the next Section, we first provide a proof sketch for our first main result, and then for the special case when buyer's value is uniform we propose an improved fee-setting mechanism accompanied by a refined analysis, which gives us a better approximation ratio. Then in Section 4.3 we sketch the proof of second main result. Finally in Section 5 we elaborate on our third result.

4.1   Approximations for Affine Buyer's Virtual Value

Suppose buyer's virtual value is affine, i.e. $\phi_{\mathcal{B}}(v) = \alpha v - \beta,$[3] and now look at the affine fee-setting mechanism $w(P) = P - \phi_{\mathcal{B}} = (1-\alpha)P + \beta$. We start by proving some properties of this mechanism, which also show the mechanism is ex-post IR for seller, buyer and trader (hence no party regrets attending the trade).

Lemma 2. *If $\phi_{\mathcal{B}}(v) = \alpha v - \beta$ and $P(c)$ is the BNE strategy of seller, then affine fee-setting mechanism $w(P) = P - \phi_{\mathcal{B}}(P) = (1 - \alpha)P + \beta$ has the following properties:*

(a) $\forall c : w(\phi_{\mathcal{B}}(P)) = \alpha w(P)$ and $\phi_{\mathcal{B}}(\phi_{\mathcal{B}}(P)) = c$.
(b) Ex-post utilities of seller and trader are always non-negative.
(c) $\forall v : e^{-H_{\mathcal{B}}(v)} = (\frac{w(v)}{\beta})^{\frac{1}{\alpha-1}}$, when $\alpha \neq 1$.

Proof. To prove (a) we have $w(\phi_{\mathcal{B}}(P)) = (1-\alpha)(\alpha P - \beta) + \beta = \alpha((1-\alpha)P + \beta) = \alpha w(P)$. Moreover, due to Corollary 2, $\phi_{\mathcal{B}}(P) = \frac{c+\beta}{\alpha}$ and hence $c = \alpha \phi_{\mathcal{B}}(P) - \beta = \phi_{\mathcal{B}}(\phi_{\mathcal{B}}(P))$. To prove (b), note that utility of trader is equal to $w(P) = P - \phi_{\mathcal{B}}(P) \geq 0$, due to properties of virtual value. Also, seller's ex-post utility when trade happens is equal to $P - w(P) - c = \phi_{\mathcal{B}}(P) - c \geq \phi_{\mathcal{B}}(\phi_{\mathcal{B}}(P)) - c = 0$, due to property (a). To prove (c) we have $h_{\mathcal{B}}(v) = (v - \phi_{\mathcal{B}}(v))^{-1} = (w(v))^{-1}$. Now, the following calculation finds cumulative hazard rate $H_{\mathcal{B}}(v)$ which completes the proof of (c).

$$H_{\mathcal{B}}(v) = \int_0^v h_{\mathcal{B}}(z)dz = \frac{\ln(w(v))}{1-\alpha} - \frac{\ln(w(0))}{1-\alpha} = \frac{\ln(\frac{w(v)}{\beta})}{1-\alpha} \qquad \square$$

Now, using the above properties we prove one can extract a constant portion of optimal revenue and optimal surplus by the above mechanism. The intuition

---

[3] Note that due to Corollary 1 and Lemma 1, v is drawn from a generalized Pareto distribution, and hence α should be in $[1, \infty)$.

behind the proof is as follows. Look at the special case when the buyer's distribution is uniform on $[0, 1]$. Then the fee schedule that we propose is $w(P) = 1 - P$. At the first glance this appears counterintuitive: as a seller, if you ask for a higher price then the broker gets less money from you. But the seller needs to take a trade-off when setting the price: if the seller picks $P = 1$, which minimizes the broker's fee as $w(1) = 0$, then the chance of finding a buyer with this price will be zero, which produces zero utility to the seller. So the seller needs to find a balanced price, at which the chance of finding a buyer is large, and the fee paid to the broker is reasonable as well. In other words, the seller is buying "chance of trade" from the broker by paying $1 - P$ to it. We formalize this argument by the following theorem. (Figure 1 presents a geometric proof sketch.)

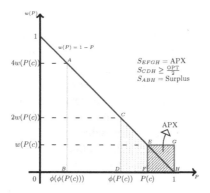

Fig. 1. In this figure, buyer value is unif $[0, 1]$ and $w(P) = 1 - P$. This fee-setting mechanism (APX) extracts $\frac{1}{4}$ fraction of optimal revenue (OPT) and $\frac{1}{8}$ fraction of optimal surplus (Surplus) in expectation, which can be seen by comparing the area of corresponding regions.

Theorem 2. *Suppose buyer's virtual value is affine: $\phi_B(v) = \alpha v - \beta$ for some $\alpha \geq 1$. Then the revenue of affine fee-setting mechanism $w(P) = P - \phi_B(P)$ is $\alpha^{\frac{1}{\alpha-1}}-approximation$ to optimal revenue and $\alpha^{\frac{\alpha+1}{\alpha-1}}-approximation$ to optimal surplus in expectation.*

Due to space constraint, we put the proof in the online version of this paper.

We are now ready to obtain approximation ratios for different cases of generalized Pareto distributions, namely general power distributions and exponential distributions. This is exactly the same class of distributions that Loertscher and Niedermayer [7, 8] investigated.

Corollary 3 (Exponential distribution). *Suppose $F(v) = 1 - e^{-\lambda v}$ over $[0, \infty)$ for $\lambda > 0$. Then revenue of $APX(1, \frac{1}{\lambda})$ (i.e. fee-setting with $w(P) = \frac{1}{\lambda}$) is e^2-approximation to maximum surplus, and e-approximation to the optimal revenue in expectation.*

Proof. This is the special case of Theorem 2 when $\phi_B(v) = v - \frac{1-F(v)}{f(v)} = v - \frac{1}{\lambda}$. That gives us $\alpha = 1, \beta = \frac{1}{\lambda}$. Following the fact that $\lim_{\alpha \to 1} \alpha^{\frac{1}{\alpha-1}} = e$ and $\lim_{\alpha \to 1} \alpha^{\frac{\alpha+1}{\alpha-1}} = e^2$, we prove the desired approximation factors.   □

Corollary 4 (Power distributions). *Suppose $F(v) = 1 - (1 - \frac{v}{\bar{v}})^a$ over the support $[0, \bar{v}]$ for some $a \geq 1$. Then the revenue of $APX(\frac{a+1}{a}, \frac{\bar{v}}{a})$ (i.e. fee-setting with $w(P) = \frac{-1}{a}P + \frac{\bar{v}}{a}$) is $8-$approximation to the maximum surplus, and $4-$approximation to the maximum revenue.*

Proof. This is the special case of Theorem 2 when $\phi_B(v) = v - \frac{1-F(v)}{f(v)} = \frac{a+1}{a}v - \frac{\bar{v}}{a}$. So $\alpha = \frac{a+1}{a}, \beta = \frac{\bar{v}}{a}$. Note that as $a \geq 1$, we have $\alpha \leq 2$. Following the fact that for $\alpha \leq 2$, we have $\alpha^{\frac{1}{\alpha-1}} \leq 4$ and $\alpha^{\frac{\alpha+1}{\alpha-1}} \leq 8$, which completes the proof.   □

4.2   Approximations for the Uniform Distribution

Uniform distribution on $[0, 1]$ is a special case of power distributions, so based on the results of the last section we can get approximation factors 4 and 8 with respect to optimal revenue and surplus respectively. However, we propose a different fee-setting mechanism that is $3-$approximation with respect to optimal revenue in expectation. Our technique is based on the "best of two" technique for designing approximation algorithms, which picks the best of two mechanisms each performs well on some class of input seller's distribution. For the proof, see the online full-version of our paper.

Theorem 3. *Suppose $F = unif[0, 1]$. Let $y \triangleq \min\{\phi_S^{-1}(1), \bar{c}\}$[4]. Then the mechanism which is best of $APX(2, 1)$ and $APX(1, \frac{1-y}{2})$ in terms of revenue is 3-approximation to optimal revenue in expectation.*

Corollary 5. *The best affine fee-setting mechanism is at least a 3-approximation to optimal revenue expectation when $F = unif[0, 1]$.*

Proof. The best affine fee-setting mechanism has expected revenue at least as large as both $APX(2, 1)$ and $APX(1, \frac{1-y}{2})$, and hence is a $3-$approximation to the maximum intermediary's revenue.

4.3   Approximations for MHR Distributions

In this section, we investigate the question of approximating surplus and revenue when neither buyer's virtual value nor seller's virtual cost is affine, but instead we have some proper distributional assumptions on the buyer and seller distributions. We look at the setting that the difference between the values of the seller and the buyer follows MHR distribution, which indicates that the surplus and revenue of an imaginary bidder with value $v - c$ are in constant approximation to each other. Moreover, we assume v is coming from a MHR distribution and hence surplus approximation and revenue approximation are equivalent for

---

[4]   We set $\phi_S^{-1}(1) = +\infty$ when $\phi_S(1) = 1$ doesn't have a solution.

this bidder. It is important to mention that many distributions in real economic exchange settings satisfy the following properties under independence assumption of seller and buyer (like uniform, normal, exponential, and etc.). Now, under these assumptions we get constant approximation ratio to both surplus and revenue in expectation with a constant fee schedule. Formally we have this theorem (for the proof, see the online full-version of our paper).

Theorem 4. *Suppose buyer's value v is MHR, and random variable $v - c$ is also MHR. Then a constant fee-schedule mechanism $w(P) = \eta_{v-c}$ is $e^2 - approximation$ to optimal surplus, and hence $e^2 - approximation$ to optimal revenue in expectation, where η_{v-c} is monopoly price of random variable $v - c$.*

5   Inapproximability Results

In this section, we give two inapproximability results. The first one shows that the proper fee schedules eBay and Amazon are currently using are not revenue-efficient, in the sense that for unif$[0, 1]$ buyer distribution no *proper* fee schedule can get constant approximation to the optimal revenue for the worst case seller distribution. Meanwhile, as we showed before, there is an improper fee-setting mechanism that always gets 4-approximation to the optimal revenue. The second result shows that for unif$[0, 1]$ buyer distribution, $APX(\alpha, \beta)$ gives seller prior independent constant approximation to the maximum surplus for worst-case seller distribution *if and only if* $\alpha - \beta = 1$ and $\alpha \neq 1$.

5.1   Inapproximability Result for Proper Fee Schedule

First we investigate the question of how good proper fee schedule works. We define a proper fee schedule as the following.

Definition 5. *A proper fee schedule is an affine fee schedule with parameters α and β such that $0 \leq \alpha \leq 1$ and $\beta \geq 0$.*

Then we give definitions on the approximability of proper fee schedule.

Definition 6. *Proper fee schedule revenue gap $RG_{F,G}$ under buyer distribution F, and seller distribution G is the ratio of the optimal revenue to the approximation revenue using the best proper fee schedule.*

Definition 7. *Proper fee schedule surplus gap $SG_{F,G}$ under buyer distribution F, and seller distribution G is the ratio of the maximum surplus to the approximation revenue using the best proper fee schedule.*

As a direct consequence of Corollary 4, we can say optimal revenue is $8-$ approximation to optimal surplus in expectation. Hence, for the special case of unif$[0,1]$ we have,

Corollary 6. *If F is uniform distribution on $[0, 1]$, then for any seller distribution G, $RG_{F,G} \geq \frac{1}{8}SG_{F,G}$.*

We now show the following theorem (for the proof, see the online full-version of our paper), which shows that $RG_{F,G}$ could be arbitrarily large even if the buyer distribution is as simple as the uniform $[0,1]$ distribution. At the same time, APX(2, 1) is 4-approximation to the optimal revenue, which means proper fee schedule can be arbitrarily worse than APX(2, 1).

Theorem 5. *When F is uniform distribution on $[0, 1]$, for every constant d, there exists a regular seller distribution G with $RG_{F,G} \geq d$.*

Proof Sketch. Based on Corollary 6, it suffices to show that for every constant d, there exists a regular seller distribution G with $SG_{F,G} \geq d$. Assume F is uniform distribution on $[0, 1]$. Consider the following family of distributions with parameter δ, defined on the interval $\left[0, 1 - \sqrt{\delta}\right]$,

$$g_\delta(x) = \frac{2\delta}{(1-\delta)(1-x)^3}, \quad G_\delta(x) = \frac{\delta}{1-\delta}\left(\frac{1}{(1-x)^2} - 1\right), \quad x \in \left[0, 1 - \sqrt{\delta}\right].$$

the rest of the proof shows that for any $d > 0$, $\exists \delta$ such that $RG_{F,G} \geq d$ □

5.2   Inapproximability Result for Prior-Independent Approximation

For the setting of seller prior-independent, one might still expect the existence of other constant approximations. However, we show our mechanism is the unique fee-setting mechanism that can get constant seller prior-independent approximations to surplus. More formally, we show that in the seller prior-independent setting when buyer's value is drawn from uniform $[0, 1]$ distribution, $w(P) = (1 - \alpha)P + \beta$ gives constant approximation to the surplus if and only if $\alpha - \beta = 1$. The proof is provided in the online full-version of our paper.

Theorem 6. *If the buyer's distribution is uniform $[0, 1]$, $w(x) = (1 - \alpha)x + \beta$, where α and β are parameters independent form the seller distribution, then the revenue obtained using w is a constant approximation to the surplus for every possible seller's distribution if and only if $\alpha - \beta = 1$ and $\alpha \neq 1$. Moreover, when $\alpha = 2, \beta = 1$, it achieves the best approximation ratio 8.*

6   Extension to Multi-buyers Case

Some of our results can extend to multi-buyers case, when the buyers are regular and i.i.d. In fact, if there are n buyers with regular i.i.d. values $v_1, v_2, \ldots, v_n$ drawn from distribution F, one can replace the pool of buyers with one *effective* buyer $v = \max_i v_i$ and still get the same revenue in expectation for any fee-setting mechanisms and optimal Myerson mechanism (because all buyers have the same non-decreasing virtual value function), and also the same surplus in expectation for VCG mechanism. Now, using the following lemma and the above reduction we can extend Theorem 4 to multi-buyers case, whose proof is found in the online full-version of our paper.

Lemma 3. *Suppose $v_1, v_2, \ldots, v_n$ are i.i.d. random variables drawn from MHR distribution F. Then $v = \max_i v_i$ is also MHR.*

By combining Lemma 3 and Theorem 4 we have the following direct corollary.

Corollary 7 (Multi-buyers setting). *Suppose F is a MHR distribution and there are n i.i.d. buyers whose values are drawn from F. Seller's cost c is drawn from G and is independent from all buyers. Moreover, assume the random variable $\max_i v_i - c$ is MHR. Then the revenue of constant fee-setting mechanism $w(P) = \eta_{\max_i v_i - c}$, where $\eta_{\max_i v_i - c}$ is the monopoly price for the distribution of $\max_i v_i - c$, is e^2-approximation to optimal surplus and revenue in expectation.*

Acknowledgment. The authors would like to express their very great appreciations to Prof. Jason Hartline for his valuable and constructive suggestions during this research work, especially in developing Theorem 4. His willingness to give his time so generously has been very much appreciated.

References

[1] Bulow, J., Klemperer, P.: Auctions vs. negotiations. Working Paper 4608, National Bureau of Economic Research (January 1994)

[2] Carroll, G.: Robustness and linear contracts. Working paper, Stanford University (2013)

[3] Deng, X., Goldberg, P., Tang, B., Zhang, J.: Revenue maximization in a bayesian double auction market. In: Chao, K.-M., Hsu, T.-S., Lee, D.-T. (eds.) ISAAC 2012. LNCS, vol. 7676, pp. 690–699. Springer, Heidelberg (2012)

[4] Dhangwatnotai, P., Roughgarden, T., Yan, Q.: Revenue maximization with a single sample. In: Proceedings of the 11th ACM Conference on Electronic Commerce, EC 2010, pp. 129–138 (2010)

[5] Hartline, J.D., Roughgarden, T.: Simple versus optimal mechanisms. In: Proceedings of the 10th ACM Conference on Electronic Commerce, EC 2009, pp. 225–234. ACM, New York (2009)

[6] Jain, K., Wilkens, C.A.: ebay's market intermediation problem. CoRR, abs/1209.5348 (2012)

[7] Loertscher, S., Niedermayer, A.: When is seller price setting with linear fees optimal for intermediaries? Working paper (2007),
http://www.vwl.unibe.ch/papers/dp/dp0706.pdf

[8] Loertscher, S., Niedermayer, A.: Fee-setting mechanisms: On optimal pricing by intermediaries and indirect taxation, Working paper (2013),
http://andras.niedermayer.ch/uploads/File/LN2013-10-10.pdf

[9] Myerson, R.B.: Optimal auction design. Discussion Papers 362, Northwestern University, Center for Mathematical Studies in Economics and Management Science (December 1978)

[10] Myerson, R.B., Satterthwaite, M.A.: Efficient mechanisms for bilateral trading. Journal of Economic Theory 29(2), 265–281 (1983)

[11] Pal, D., Bose, A., Sappington, D.: On the performance of linear contracts. University of Cincinnati, economics working papers series, Department of Economics (2007)

GSP with General Independent Click-through-Rates

Ruggiero Cavallo[1] and Christopher A. Wilkens[2]

[1] Yahoo Labs, New York, NY, USA
cavallo@yahoo-inc.com
[2] Yahoo Labs, Sunnyvale, CA, USA
cwilkens@yahoo-inc.com

Abstract. The popular generalized second price (GSP) auction for sponsored search is built upon a *separable* model of click-through-rates that decomposes the likelihood of a click into the product of a "slot effect" and an "advertiser effect"—if the first slot is twice as good as the second for some bidder, then it is twice as good for everyone. Though appealing in its simplicity, this model is quite suspect in practice. A wide variety of factors including externalities and budgets have been studied that can and do cause it to be violated. In this paper we adopt a view of GSP as an iterated second price auction (see, e.g., Milgrom [2010]) and study how the most basic violation of separability—position dependent, arbitrary public click-through-rates that do not decompose—affects results from the foundational analysis of GSP [Varian, 2007; Edelman *et al.*, 2007]. For the two-slot setting we prove that for arbitrary click-through-rates, for arbitrary bidder values, an efficient pure-strategy equilibrium always exists; however, without separability there always exist values such that the VCG outcome and payments *cannot* be realized by any bids, in equilibrium or otherwise. The separability assumption is therefore necessary in the two-slot case to match the payments of VCG but not for efficiency. We moreover show that without separability, generic existence of efficient equilibria is sensitive to the choice of tie-breaking rule, and when there are more than two slots, no (bid-independent) tie-breaking rule yields the positive result. In light of this we suggest alternative mechanisms that trade the simplicity of GSP for better equilibrium properties when there are three or more slots.

1 Introduction

The generalized second price (GSP) auction is the predominant auction for sponsored search advertising today. The auction takes per-click bids and proceeds as follows: a score is computed *independently* for each advertiser, reflecting its bid and propensity to be clicked; ads are ranked according to these scores, matched to slots accordingly, and finally charged the minimum bid required to maintain their allocated slot (i.e., to stay above the winner of the slot below). Fundamental to this procedure is the fact that the optimal assignment can be computed based on a ranking of independently-computed scores, which requires that: (a)

T.-Y. Liu et al. (Eds.): WINE 2014, LNCS 8877, pp. 400–416, 2014.

the differences between slots affect all ads equally, and (b) an ad's propensity to be clicked is unaffected by the other ads shown around it. Formally, this amounts to *separability* of click-through-rates: any given ad i's probability of being clicked when shown in slot j decomposes into two factors, μ_j (a "slot-effect") and β_i (an "advertiser effect"). The GSP auction, as well as the theory underlying it (Varian [2007]; Edelman *et al.* [2007]), all critically rely on this model.

Unfortunately, separability generally does not hold in practice (one recent work challenging the model is Jeziorski and Segal [forthcoming]). Moreover, the inadequacy of the model is becoming more acute as online advertising evolves to incorporate more heterogeneous bidders and slots. Instead of a uniform column of vanilla text ads, it is now common for different ad formats (images, text with sitelinks, etc.) to appear together on the same search results page. New ad marketplaces with richer formats, such as Yahoo's "native" stream, have emerged. For advertisers that are seeking clicks, *click-through-rate* is the relevant metric, but for brand advertisers the "view rate" of a slot is more relevant (see, e.g., Hummel and McAfee [2014]).

In this paper we examine what happens if we move beyond the separable model: besides assuming—as in the standard model—that click-through-rates can be determined independent of context (i.e., surrounding ads), we make virtually no structural assumptions and determine to what extent the most important classical findings hold up.

Our main results in the two-slot setting show that efficiency is achievable but revenue may suffer. For arbitrary click-through-rates and values, there exist efficient equilibria. However, for arbitrary click-through-rates, there exist values such that the VCG outcome and payments are *not* achievable (in equilibrium or otherwise). Put another way: *all* click-through-rate profiles ensure existence of efficient equilibria, but *no* non-separable click-through-rate profiles ensure the feasibility of VCG payments. We also show that the price of anarchy in a two-slot setting without the separability assumption is 2 (Caragiannis *et al.* [2014] showed that it is at most 1.282 with separability).

When there are three or more slots, we show that efficient equilibria do not always exist if the tie-breaking rule cannot be chosen dynamically in response to bids. We present an alternate mechanism that restores efficient equilibria by expanding the bid space so that agents can specify a bid for every slot, with items left unallocated if there is not sufficient competition. Several proofs are sketched or wholly omitted due to space constraints; the interested reader can find the complete proofs in a longer version of the paper available online.

1.1 Related Work

Besides providing one of the earliest models of the sponsored search setting, Edelman *et al.* [2007] proved that—in the complete-information model with separable click-through-rates—GSP has an equilibrium that realizes the VCG result, i.e., an efficient allocation with each winner paying a price equal to the negative externality his presence exerts on the other advertisers. In another important early paper, Lahaie [2006] provides equilibrium analysis for GSP (including for the version where advertiser effects are ignored) and first-price variants, in both the complete and incomplete information settings. A good early survey is Lahaie *et al.* [2007].

In a recent paper, Caragiannis *et al.* [2014] examine the space of equilibria that may exist under GSP with separable click-through-rates, and bound the efficiency loss that can result in any of the sub-optimal equilibria. Part of this work involves a straightforward price of anarchy analysis for the complete information setting, to which we provide a counterpoint without separability in Section 3.4.

The prior literature contains some empirical evidence against the separability assumption. For instance, Craswell *et al.* [2008] demonstrate clear violations of separability for *organic* search results. Gomes *et al.* [2009] take three prominent keywords and show that the separable model is a poorer fit to observed clicks than an alternate "ordered search" model of click-through-rates. Most of the work that steps outside of the classic separable model is motivated by externalities between advertisements [Kempe and Mahdian, 2008; Ghosh and Mahdian, 2008; Giotis and Karlin, 2008; Athey and Ellison, 2011; Aggarwal *et al.*, 2008; Gomes *et al.*, 2009; Ghosh and Sayedi, 2010]. The context in which an ad is shown may matter: for instance, an ad may yield more clicks if shown below poor ads than it would if shown below very compelling competitors. Our model in the current paper removes the separability assumption but does not capture externalities, as it assumes click-through-rates are context-independent.

Aggarwal *et al.* [2006] show that in the absence of the separability assumption, there are cases where truthful bidding under GSP will not lead to an efficient allocation. The authors go on to design a truthful mechanism that implements the allocation that would result under GSP (which is not truthful) with truthful bidding. Gonen and Vassilvitskii [2008] extend this analysis in a setting with reserve prices.

Finally, without separability a set of agents could have arbitrary "expected values" for each slot—no common structure is assumed. Though types in our model are single-dimensional since click-through-rates are not private knowledge, there is a connection to work that shows existence of efficient equilibria when agents have a private value for each slot [Leonard, 1983; Abrams *et al.*, 2007].

2   Preliminaries

The basic sponsored search model can be described as follows: a set of m slots are to be allocated among $n \geq m$ advertisers. When ad i is shown in slot j, regardless of what is shown in other slots, a user clicks on ad i with probability ("click-through-rate") $\alpha_{i,j}$, generating value v_i for the advertiser. We let I denote the set of advertisers, and assume throughout that lower slots yield weakly lower click-through-rates, i.e., $\forall i \in I$, $\forall k \in \{1, \ldots, m-1\}$, $\alpha_{i,k} \geq \alpha_{i,k+1}$, and that $\forall i \in I$, $\forall k \in \{1, \ldots, m\}$, $\alpha_{i,k} > 0$. Our model places no further assumptions on click-through-rates.

In the *separable* refinement of this model, click-through-rates $\alpha_{i,j}$ can be decomposed multiplicatively into $\alpha_{i,j} = \mu_j \beta_i$, where μ_j is the *slot effect* that depends only on the position and β_i is the *ad effect* that depends only on the bidder. Slots are ordered so that $\mu_1 \geq \mu_2 \geq \cdots \geq \mu_m$. In that setting, the GSP auction can be defined like such:

Definition 1 (GSP auction). *The* generalized second price (GSP) *auction proceeds as follows:*

1. *Each bidder $i \in I$ submits a per-click bid b_i.*
2. *Bidders are ranked by $\beta_i b_i$ and matched to slots according to their rank.*
3. *The bidder in position j pays "the ad-effect-adjusted bid of the bidder in position $j + 1$" when her ad is clicked; specifically, she pays the minimum amount required to be ranked in position j:*

$$p_j = \frac{\beta_{j+1} b_{j+1}}{\beta_j}$$

To move beyond separable click-through-rates, we must generalize the GSP mechanism. We will work from a common observation (see, e.g., Milgrom [2010]) that the GSP auction can be viewed as a special sequence of second-price auctions—each slot is sold in order as if it were the only slot for sale. This view allows us to naturally handle general click-through-rates.

Definition 2 (Iterated second price auction). *An* iterated second price auction *for sponsored search proceeds as follows:*

1. *Each bidder $i \in I$ submits a per-click bid b_i.*
2. *An order-of-sale σ is selected for the slots.*
3. *For j from 1 to m, with slots indexed according to σ:*
   (a) *A second-price auction is used to sell slot j as follows: let i^* be the remaining bidder with the highest $\alpha_{i,j} b_i$ and let i^+ be the bidder with the second-highest $\alpha_{i,j} b_i$. i^* wins the auction and pays $\frac{\alpha_{i^+,j} b_{i^+}}{\alpha_{i^*,j}}$ per click or $\alpha_{i^+,j} b_{i^+}$ per impression.*
   (b) *Bidder i^* is removed from the auction and cannot win future slots.*

This auction, with "best to worst" as the order of sale adopted in step 2, is the implicit context for all results in this paper except where explicitly stated otherwise.

Another important auction mechanism is the Vickrey-Clarke-Groves (VCG) mechanism, which yields truthful bidding and an efficient allocation in dominant strategies.

Definition 3 (VCG mechanism). *In sponsored search, the* Vickrey-Clarke-Groves (VCG) mechanism *proceeds as follows:*

1. *Each bidder $i \in I$ submits a per-click bid b_i to the auction.*
2. *Bids are interpreted as values per-click, and a matching of bidders to slots $i(j)$ is chosen that maximizes welfare, i.e that maximizes $\sum_{j \in I} \alpha_{i(j),j} b_{i(j)}$.*

3. *Each bidder $i \in I$ is charged an amount equal to the welfare other bidders would gain, according to their reported bids, if i were removed from the auction.*

In this paper we will compare the outcome of our GSP generalization (Definition 2) to that of VCG:

Definition 4 (VCG result). *The VCG result refers to the allocation and payments realized by the VCG mechanism.*

Given a set of advertiser bids, if we say that an auction has "realized the VCG result" we are saying that its allocation and payments match those of the VCG mechanism.

3   Two Slots

We focus much of our analysis on the two-slot case, for a few reasons. First, this is the simplest case in which GSP deviates from a straightforward Vickrey auction (which it reduces to in the case of a single slot); second, with two slots "separability" is cleanly and simply defined, holding whenever the ratio of click-through-rate for the first slot to the click-through-rate for the second (henceforth, the *click-ratio*) is the same across all agents (i.e., $\forall i, j \in I$, $\frac{\alpha_{i,1}}{\alpha_{i,2}} = \frac{\alpha_{j,1}}{\alpha_{j,2}}$); and finally, we will be able to show important positive results for the two-slot case that do not extend to larger numbers of slots.

3.1   Efficient Equilibria

Among the first questions one might ask about an auction mechanism is: does it yield *efficient* equilibria? The foundational work of Edelman *et al.* [2007] and Varian [2007] demonstrated that efficient equilibria do exist under GSP in the separable model, and we now ask whether the assumption of separability is necessary. We resolve this in the negative.

To build intuition, we will start by considering an especially "problematic" example for the non-separable setting that reveals some of the challenges that can arise.

Table 1. A two-slot, three-bidder example in which two bidders are indifferent between the two slots. There is no pure strategy equilibrium unless ties are broken in favor of bidder 3.

bidder	value	$\alpha_{i,1}$	$\alpha_{i,2}$
1	1	1	1
2	1	1	1
3	2	0.4	0.2

The first thing to notice about the example in Table 1 is that in any pure strategy equilibrium bidders 1 and 2 win the slots and bidder 3 gets nothing.[1] So now assume without loss of generality that bidder 1 wins slot 1 and bidder 2 wins slot 2. Bidder 2 has the better deal, since he'll have to pay at most half of what bidder 1 pays (since the bid of bidder 3 will set the price for slot 2 and lower-bound the price for slot 1), and slot 2 is as good as slot 1 (in the eyes of bidders 1 and 2). Thus, in order for bidder 1 to be best-responding, it must be impossible for him to bid so as to win slot 2 (which would sell at a lower price) instead of slot 1. In other words, if he were to underbid bidder 2, he must end up with nothing. This can only be the case if $0.4b_3 = b_2$ *and* a hypothetical tie between bidders 2 and 3 for slot 1 is broken in favor of bidder 3.

Therefore, interestingly, in the above example there exists a pure strategy equilibrium—efficient or otherwise—*only* if ties are broken in a specific way. This would seem to bode very poorly for the prospects of a general result establishing existence of efficient equilibria. However, we will see in this section that, at least in the two-slot case, efficient equilibria do in fact always exist (given the right tie-breaking rule).

Theorem 1 (Efficient equilibria exist). *In a two-slot setting with any number of bidders, for arbitrary values and click-through-rates, if there is a unique efficient allocation and ties are broken in favor of an agent with highest click-ratio, then there is an efficient equilibrium without overbidding.*

Proof sketch. Consider arbitrary click-through-rates α and values v. Let 1 and 2 denote the respective winners of slots 1 and 2 in the efficient allocation, and let 3 denote $\arg\max_{j \in I \setminus \{1,2\}} \alpha_{j,2} v_j$. We dichotomize the set of possible click-through-rate profiles into those in which $\frac{\alpha_{2,1}}{\alpha_{2,2}} \geq \frac{\alpha_{3,1}}{\alpha_{3,2}}$ and those in which $\frac{\alpha_{2,1}}{\alpha_{2,2}} < \frac{\alpha_{3,1}}{\alpha_{3,2}}$. In the former case, the following bid profile is an efficient equilibrium: $b_1 = v_1$, $b_2 = \frac{\alpha_{3,2} v_3 + (\alpha_{2,1} - \alpha_{2,2}) v_2}{\alpha_{2,1}}$, $b_3 = v_3$, and $b_i = 0$, $\forall i \in I \setminus \{1,2,3\}$. In the latter, the following is: $b_1 = v_1$, $b_2 = \frac{\alpha_{3,2}}{\alpha_{2,2}} v_3$, $b_3 = \frac{\alpha_{2,1}}{\alpha_{2,2}} \frac{\alpha_{3,2}}{\alpha_{3,1}} v_3$, and $b_i = 0$, $\forall i \in I \setminus \{1,2,3\}$. The proof verifies that an exhaustive set of sufficient equilibrium conditions holds in each case. □

It is interesting to see what the above tells us about the problematic example of Table 1. To derive bids yielding an efficient equilibrium, we can note the following about the example: an efficient allocation gives slots 1 and 2 to bidders 1 and 2, and thus the agents are labeled in a way consistent with the convention of Theorem 1. Now, since $\frac{\alpha_{2,1}}{\alpha_{2,2}} < \frac{\alpha_{3,1}}{\alpha_{3,2}}$, the above proof indicates that the following bids—combined with a tie-breaking rule that favors bidder 3 over bidder 2— yields an efficient equilibrium: $b_1 = v_1 = 1$, $b_2 = \frac{\alpha_{3,2}}{\alpha_{2,2}} v_3 = 0.4$, $b_3 = \frac{\alpha_{2,1}}{\alpha_{2,2}} \frac{\alpha_{3,2}}{\alpha_{3,1}} v_3 = 1$.

---

[1] Assume otherwise. If bidder 3 were winning the first slot in equilibrium, he must be paying less than his value in expectation (0.8), but in that case the loser amongst bidders 1 and 2 could benefit by bidding between 0.8 and 1, winning a slot for at most 0.8. Likewise, if bidder 3 were winning the second slot in equilibrium, he must be paying less than his value in expectation (0.4), but in that case the loser amongst bidders 1 and 2 could benefit by bidding between 0.4 and 1.

3.2   Globally Envy-Free Equilibria

In the previous subsection we demonstrated that efficient equilibria always exist. We proved this constructively, giving bid functions that yield efficiency for all valuations. However, these bids do not generally lead to global envy-freeness:

Definition 5 (Globally envy-free outcome). *Consider an arbitrary alloca- tion and prices. Let* k *denote the winner of slot* k *and* p_k *denote the price paid by* k*, for* $k \in \{1, \ldots, n\}$*; let* $n+1$ *denote the agent that receives nothing; and let* $p_{n+1} = 0$*. The allocation and prices constitute a globally envy-free outcome if and only if, for all* $i, j \in \{1, \ldots, n+1\}$*,*

$$\alpha_{i,i} v_i - p_i \geq \alpha_{i,j} v_i - p_j$$

Envy-freeness is a major focus of the classic work on GSP [Edelman *et al.*, 2007; Varian, 2007], because of its relationship to VCG results, the salience it arguably confers on equilibria, and perhaps most importantly, the fact that envy-freeness implies that an equilibrium generates at least as much revenue as VCG. Unfortunately, we will now see that this guarantee does not extend to our setting, and an envy-free equilibrium is not guaranteed to exist.

We will give a necessary condition for global envy-freeness (Proposition 1), which will not always be satisfied. We will then show that whenever the condition is satisfied, global envy-freeness *can* be achieved, and moreover done so in the context of an efficient equilibrium (Theorem 2).

Proposition 1. *In a two-slot, three-bidder setting, for arbitrary values* v *and click-through-rates* α*, there exist no bids yielding a globally envy-free outcome unless, letting 1 and 2 denote the respective winners of slots 1 and 2 in the efficient allocation:*

$$(\alpha_{3,1} - \alpha_{3,2}) v_3 \leq (\alpha_{1,1} - \alpha_{1,2}) v_1$$

Proof. Take arbitrary values v, click-through-rates α, and bids b. First assume $b_2 \geq \frac{\alpha_{3,1}}{\alpha_{2,1}} b_3$ (i.e., 2 sets the price for 1). For 1 to not be envious of 2, it must be the case that $b_2 \leq \frac{\alpha_{3,2} b_3 + (\alpha_{1,1} - \alpha_{1,2}) v_1}{\alpha_{2,1}}$. The combination of these two constraints yields $(\alpha_{3,1} - \alpha_{3,2}) b_3 \leq (\alpha_{1,1} - \alpha_{1,2}) v_1$. Now instead assume $b_2 \leq \frac{\alpha_{3,1}}{\alpha_{2,1}} b_3$ (i.e, 3 sets the price for 1). 1 is not envious of 2 if and only if $\alpha_{1,1} v_1 - \alpha_{3,1} b_3 \geq \alpha_{1,2} v_1 - \alpha_{3,2} b_3$, i.e., $(\alpha_{3,1} - \alpha_{3,2}) b_3 \leq (\alpha_{1,1} - \alpha_{1,2}) v_1$, again. Finally, noting that envy-freeness for 3 requires that $b_3 \geq v_3$ (otherwise 3 would envy 2), global envy-freeness requires:

$$(\alpha_{3,1} - \alpha_{3,2}) v_3 \leq (\alpha_{3,1} - \alpha_{3,2}) b_3 \leq (\alpha_{1,1} - \alpha_{1,2}) v_1$$

If $(\alpha_{3,1} - \alpha_{3,2}) v_3 > (\alpha_{1,1} - \alpha_{1,2}) v_1$, this cannot be satisfied.   □

Theorem 2 (GEF and efficient equilibria condition). *In a two-slot, three- bidder setting, for arbitrary click-through-rates* α *and values* v*, there exist bids* *yielding a globally envy-free and efficient equilibrium if and only if, letting 1 and 2 denote the respective winners of slots 1 and 2 in the efficient allocation:*

$$(\alpha_{3,1} - \alpha_{3,2})v_3 \leq (\alpha_{1,1} - \alpha_{1,2})v_1$$

If a globally envy-free and efficient equilibrium exists, one exists that yields the VCG result and does not require overbidding.

Proof sketch. The full proof follows similar lines to that of Theorem 1, and considers three cases: (i) $(\alpha_{3,1} - \alpha_{3,2})v_3 \leq (\alpha_{2,1} - \alpha_{2,2})v_2$; (ii) $(\alpha_{3,1} - \alpha_{3,2})v_3 > (\alpha_{2,1} - \alpha_{2,2})v_2$ and $\frac{\alpha_{3,1}}{\alpha_{2,1}}v_3 \leq v_2$; and (iii) $(\alpha_{3,1} - \alpha_{3,2})v_3 > (\alpha_{2,1} - \alpha_{2,2})v_2$ and $\frac{\alpha_{3,1}}{\alpha_{2,1}}v_3 > v_2$. In each case it is assumed that $(\alpha_{3,1} - \alpha_{3,2})v_3 \leq (\alpha_{1,1} - \alpha_{1,2})v_1$. We specify bids yielding efficient and globally envy-free equilibria: in case (i) $b_1 = v_1$, $b_2 = \frac{\alpha_{3,2}v_3 + (\alpha_{2,1} - \alpha_{2,2})v_2}{\alpha_{2,1}}$, and $b_3 = v_3$; in case (ii), $b_1 = v_1$, $b_2 = \frac{\alpha_{3,1}}{\alpha_{2,1}}v_3$, and $b_3 = v_3$; and in case (iii), $b_1 = v_1$, $b_2 = v_2$, and $b_3 = v_3$. $\square$

For instance, consider a 3-agent example with $v_1 = v_2 = v_3 = 1$, $\alpha_{1,1} = 0.9$, $\alpha_{1,2} = 0.5$, $\alpha_{2,1} = 0.5$, $\alpha_{2,2} = 0.4$, $\alpha_{3,1} = 0.6$, and $\alpha_{3,2} = 0.1$. The unique efficient allocation gives slots 1 and 2 to bidders 1 and 2, respectively. But we have: $0.5 = (\alpha_{3,1} - \alpha_{3,2})v_3 > (\alpha_{1,1} - \alpha_{1,2})v_1 = 0.4$. Thus Theorem 2 implies that there can be no globally envy-free and efficient equilibrium.

A characterization for more than three bidders is harder to state in a concise form, but the following theorem gives sufficient conditions for efficiency and global envy-freeness.

Theorem 3. *For arbitrary click-through-rates and values, letting 1 and 2 denote the respective winners of slots 1 and 2 in the efficient allocation, if $\frac{\alpha_{2,1}}{\alpha_{2,2}} \geq \frac{\alpha_{i,1}}{\alpha_{i,2}}$, $\forall i \in I \setminus \{1,2\}$, there exists an efficient and globally envy-free equilibrium without overbidding.*

3.3   VCG Results Cannot Always Be Achieved

In the results of Edelman *et al.* [2007], existence of an efficient equilibrium in the separable setting is demonstrated via proof that an equilibrium realizing the VCG result always exists. In some sense the VCG result is the most salient kind of efficient equilibrium, and it would be surprising if efficient equilibria exist generically but VCG equilibria do not. But that is exactly what we now demonstrate. Whenever a set of click-through-rates violates separability,[2] one can never be assured that a VCG result is feasible, in equilibrium or otherwise. That is, there always exist values that make it impossible for the agents to bid in a way that yields an efficient allocation and VCG prices.

---

[2] Interestingly, there is one very minor exception to this "whenever": if there is exactly one agent whose click-ratio is not equal to the maximum across all bidders—i.e., click-through-rates are separable except in the case of one bidder, and his click-ratio is *lower*—then the VCG result will be supported.

Theorem 4 (Always a bad value profile). *Assume strictly decreasing click-through-rates. In a two-slot setting with three bidders, one of whom has a strictly higher click-ratio than the other two, there always exist values such that the VCG result is not supported.*

Proof. Consider three agents with strictly decreasing click-through-rates α such that one agent's click-ratio is strictly higher than that of the other two. Label the three bidders in a non-decreasing order of $\alpha_{i,1}/\alpha_{i,2}$. Strictly decreasing click-through-rates entails that $\alpha_{1,1}/\alpha_{1,2} > 1$, and $\alpha_{1,1}/\alpha_{1,2} \leq \alpha_{2,1}/\alpha_{2,2} < \alpha_{3,1}/\alpha_{3,2}$ by assumption. In other words, for some $\epsilon \geq 0$ and $\delta > 0$,

$$1 < \frac{\alpha_{1,1}}{\alpha_{1,2}} = \frac{\alpha_{2,1}}{\alpha_{2,2}} - \epsilon = \frac{\alpha_{3,1}}{\alpha_{3,2}} - \epsilon - \delta \tag{1}$$

Fix arbitrary $v_3 > 0$. Let $\lambda_1 = \left(\frac{\alpha_{3,1} - \alpha_{3,2}}{\alpha_{1,1} - \alpha_{1,2}} - \frac{\alpha_{3,1}}{\alpha_{1,1}}\right) v_3$. Note that:

$$\frac{\alpha_{3,1} - \alpha_{3,2}}{\alpha_{1,1} - \alpha_{1,2}} > \frac{\alpha_{3,1}}{\alpha_{1,1}} \Leftrightarrow 1 - \frac{\alpha_{3,2}}{\alpha_{3,1}} > 1 - \frac{\alpha_{1,2}}{\alpha_{1,1}}$$

$$\Leftrightarrow \frac{\alpha_{1,1}}{\alpha_{1,2}} < \frac{\alpha_{3,1}}{\alpha_{3,2}}$$

This holds by (1), and thus $\lambda_1 > 0$. Now let $\lambda_2 = \left(\frac{\alpha_{3,1} - \alpha_{3,2}}{\alpha_{2,1} - \alpha_{2,2}} - \frac{\alpha_{3,2}}{\alpha_{2,2}}\right) v_3$. Note that:

$$\frac{\alpha_{3,1} - \alpha_{3,2}}{\alpha_{2,1} - \alpha_{2,2}} > \frac{\alpha_{3,2}}{\alpha_{2,2}} \Leftrightarrow \frac{\alpha_{3,1}}{\alpha_{3,2}} - 1 > \frac{\alpha_{2,1}}{\alpha_{2,2}} - 1$$

$$\Leftrightarrow \frac{\alpha_{2,1}}{\alpha_{2,2}} < \frac{\alpha_{3,1}}{\alpha_{3,2}}$$

This also holds by (1), and thus $\lambda_2 > 0$. Now let $v_1 = \frac{\alpha_{3,1} - \alpha_{3,2}}{\alpha_{1,1} - \alpha_{1,2}} v_3 - \gamma_1$, for some $\gamma_1 \in (0, \lambda_1)$. We have:

$$\frac{\alpha_{3,1}}{\alpha_{1,1}} < \frac{v_1}{v_3} < \frac{\alpha_{3,1} - \alpha_{3,2}}{\alpha_{1,1} - \alpha_{1,2}} \tag{2}$$

And let $v_2 = \frac{\alpha_{3,2}}{\alpha_{2,2}} v_3 + \gamma_2$, for some $\gamma_2 \in (0, \lambda_2)$. We have:

$$\frac{\alpha_{3,2}}{\alpha_{2,2}} < \frac{v_2}{v_3} < \frac{\alpha_{3,1} - \alpha_{3,2}}{\alpha_{2,1} - \alpha_{2,2}} \tag{3}$$

We refine our specification of γ_1 and γ_2 such that:

$$\frac{1}{\alpha_{3,2} v_3} \left[(\alpha_{1,1} - \alpha_{1,2})\gamma_1 + (\alpha_{2,1} - \alpha_{2,2})\gamma_2 \right] < \delta,$$

$$\gamma_2 > \frac{\alpha_{1,1} - \alpha_{1,2}}{\alpha_{2,2}} \gamma_1, \text{ and}$$

$$\frac{\alpha_{1,1} - \alpha_{1,2}}{\alpha_{1,1} v_3} \left(\frac{\alpha_{1,1}}{\alpha_{3,2}} \gamma_1 + \frac{\alpha_{2,1} - \alpha_{2,2}}{\alpha_{3,2}} \gamma_2 \right) < \delta + \frac{\alpha_{1,2}}{\alpha_{1,1}} \epsilon$$

Note that such values can be chosen consistent with everything specified above, for arbitrary $\delta > 0$.

Letting (i, j) denote the allocation in which agent i receives slot 1 and agent j receives slot 2, if we can establish that (1,2) is an efficient allocation, then the bidder labels here correspond to those used in Proposition 1. Letting $w(i, j)$ denote $\alpha_{i,1}v_i + \alpha_{j,2}v_j$, i.e., the social value of allocation (i, j), this can be established by demonstrating that: $w(1, 2) > w(2, 1)$, $w(1, 2) > w(1, 3)$, $w(1, 2) > w(2, 3)$, $w(1, 2) > w(3, 2)$, and $w(1, 2) > w(3, 1)$. Due to space constraints, we omit demonstration of these inequalities, which are relatively straightforward.

Now, since a VCG result is always globally envy-free (see, e.g., Leonard [1983]), in light of Proposition 1, to complete the proof it is sufficient to show that $(\alpha_{3,1} - \alpha_{3,2})v_3 > (\alpha_{1,1} - \alpha_{1,2})v_1$. We have:

$$(\alpha_{3,1} - \alpha_{3,2})v_3 - (\alpha_{1,1} - \alpha_{1,2})v_1$$

$$= (\alpha_{3,1} - \alpha_{3,2})v_3 - (\alpha_{1,1} - \alpha_{1,2})\left(\frac{\alpha_{3,1} - \alpha_{3,2}}{\alpha_{1,1} - \alpha_{1,2}}v_3 - \gamma_1\right)$$

$$= (\alpha_{1,1} - \alpha_{1,2})\gamma_1$$

$$> 0$$

$\square$

The result extends almost immediately to the n-bidder case if we forbid overbidding (note that overbidding is weakly dominated in GSP). We can fix the values of all but three agents to 0; then the problem is equivalent to one in which the 0-valued agents do not exist, since they can't bid anything other than 0.

Corollary 1. *Assume strictly decreasing click-through-rates. In a two-slot setting with any number of bidders greater than two, if there exists a bidder with click-ratio strictly greater than that of two other agents, there always exist values such that the VCG result is not supported without overbidding.*

In light of this negative result, one might ask whether the VCG result can be recovered if we are willing to experiment with different orders of sale. It turns out this can never help in the two-slot case.

Proposition 2. *In settings with at most three bidders, if the VCG result is not supported when selling slots in-order, it is not supported when selling slots in reverse order.*

Proof. Let 1 and 2 denote the bidders that receive items 1 and 2, respectively, in a VCG result, and let p_1 and p_2 denote the respective (per-impression) VCG prices. Suppose first that we sell the items in order to achieve the VCG result. Since bidder 3 will be the only competition for bidder 2, it must be that $\alpha_{3,2}b_2 = p_2$. Moreover, we can suppose that $\alpha_{2,1}b_2 = p_1$ (lowering b_2 cannot help, bidding higher will interfere with the auction for item 1 either by winning the item or by raising the price). Thus, suppose bidders bid as follows:

$$b_1 = v_1 , \quad b_2 = \frac{p_1}{\alpha_{2,1}} , \quad \text{and} \quad b_3 = \frac{p_2}{\alpha_{3,2}} .$$

By construction, these bids will achieve the VCG result as long as two other conditions are met: $\alpha_{2,2}b_2 \geq p_2$ so bidder 2 still wins item 2, and $\alpha_{3,1}b_3 \leq p_1$ so bidder 3 does not interfere in the sale of item 1. The first condition is always true — envy-freeness of VCG prices implies $\alpha_{2,1}v_2 - p_1 \leq \alpha_{2,2}v_2 - p_2$ and so

$$\alpha_{2,2}(v_2 - b_2) \leq \alpha_{2,1}(v_2 - b_2) = \alpha_{2,1}v_2 - p_1 \leq \alpha_{2,2}v_2 - p_2$$

$$\alpha_{2,1}b_2 \geq p_2$$

as desired. The second condition may indeed be violated.

It remains to show that whenever $\alpha_{3,1}b_3 > p_1$, then selling items in reverse order cannot achieve the VCG result. Suppose we find bids that support the VCG result selling out of order. Then bidder 1 must choose a bid b_1 that wins item 1 without interfering in the auction for item 2, i.e., a bid b_1 such that $\alpha_{1,2}b_1 \leq p_2$ and $\alpha_{1,1}b_1 \geq p_1$. We thus get

$$\alpha_{1,1}v_1 - p_1 \geq \alpha_{1,1}(v_1 - b_1) > \alpha_{1,2}(v_1 - b_1) \geq \alpha_{1,2}v_1 - p_2$$

$$\alpha_{1,1}v_1 - p_1 > \alpha_{1,2}v_1 - p_2$$

Now, since VCG prices are the minimal envy-free prices (see Leonard [1983]), some bidder's envy constraint must be tight for item 2 (otherwise we could lower the price of item 2 while preserving envy-freeness). It cannot be bidder 3 because, when $\alpha_{3,1}b_3 > p_1$, bidder 3 strictly prefers item 1 at VCG prices:

$$\alpha_{3,2}v_3 - p_2 = \alpha_{3,2}(v_3 - b_3) \leq \alpha_{3,1}(v_3 - b_3) < \alpha_{3,1}v_3 - p_1 \ .$$

The only remaining bidder who can be indifferent is 1, so we can conclude that $\alpha_{1,1}v_1 - p_1 = \alpha_{1,2}v_1 - p_2$, which contradicts the prior statement that $\alpha_{1,1}v_1 - p_1 > \alpha_{1,2}v_1 - p_2$. Thus, when $\alpha_{3,1}b_3 > p_1$, selling items in reverse order cannot support the VCG result either. $\square$

3.4   Price of Anarchy

We established in Section 3.1 that our generalization of GSP will always have an efficient equilibrium, but there may be many inefficient equilibria as well. In this section we consider how much efficiency may be lost if one of those other equilibria occurs. We will make the natural assumption that agents don't bid more than their value; this is standard in the literature—overbidding is a weakly dominated strategy, and with overbidding very strange equilibria can be constructed.

We find that the efficient equilibrium is never more than twice as good as the worst equilibrium, and this bound is tight. This result stands in contrast to the results of Caragiannis et al. [2014], who showed that in the separable setting with two slots, the efficient equilibrium is never more than 28.2 percent better than (i.e., yields no more than 1.282 times the social welfare of) the worst. One could thus say there is a significant added "efficiency risk" in a setting without separability.

Definition 6 (Price of anarchy). *Given click-through-rates α and values v, the price of anarchy is the ratio of the social welfare in the efficient (best) equilibrium to that in the worst equilibrium; i.e., letting 1 and 2 denote the respective winners of slots 1 and 2 in the efficient allocation, letting A denote the set of equilibrium allocations, and letting a_1 and a_2 denote the respective winners of slots 1 and 2 in allocation $a \in A$,*

$$\frac{\alpha_{1,1}v_1 + \alpha_{2,2}v_2}{\min_{a \in A}\left[\alpha_{a_1,1}v_{a_1} + \alpha_{a_2,2}v_{a_2}\right]}$$

The following lemma, and especially its corollary, will be critical for the proof bounding price of anarchy in our setting.

Lemma 1. *Let (i, j) denote an allocation in which i receives slot 1 and j receives slot 2. For arbitrary click-through-rates α and values v, letting 1 and 2 denote the respective winners of slots 1 and 2 in the efficient allocation, the only possible inefficient equilibria are: $(\arg\max_{i \in I \setminus \{1\}} \alpha_{i,1}v_i, 1)$ and $(2, \arg\max_{i \in I \setminus \{2\}} \alpha_{i,2}v_i)$.*

Corollary 2. *Given click-through-rates α and values v, letting 1 and 2 denote the respective winners of slots 1 and 2 in the efficient allocation, letting j denote $\arg\max_{i \in I \setminus \{1\}} \alpha_{i,1}v_i$ and k denote $\arg\max_{i \in I \setminus \{2\}} \alpha_{i,2}v_i$, the price of anarchy is:*

$$\max\left\{e(1,2) \cdot 1, \ e(j,1) \cdot \frac{\alpha_{1,1}v_1 + \alpha_{2,2}v_2}{\alpha_{j,1}v_j + \alpha_{1,2}v_1}, \ e(2,k) \cdot \frac{\alpha_{1,1}v_1 + \alpha_{2,2}v_2}{\alpha_{2,1}v_2 + \alpha_{k,2}v_k}\right\},$$

where $e(i, j) = 1$ if allocation (i, j) is attainable in equilibrium[3] and 0 otherwise.

Proposition 3. *For the two-slot, n-bidder setting, for any $n \geq 2$, for arbitrary click-through-rates and values, the price of anarchy is at most 2.*

We now show that this bound is tight by way of an example.

Proposition 4. *For the two-slot, n-bidder setting, for any $n \geq 2$, for arbitrary $\epsilon > 0$, there exist click-through-rates and values such that the price of anarchy is at least $2 - \epsilon$.*

Proof. Consider a setting with n bidders, for arbitrary $n \geq 2$. Consider the case where two bidders, which we'll call 1 and 2, have value 1 and all other bidders (if there are any) have value 0. Take $\alpha_{1,1} = 1 - \delta$, $\alpha_{1,2} = \delta$, $\alpha_{2,1} = 1$, and $\alpha_{2,2} = 1 - \delta$, for arbitrary $\delta \in (0, \frac{1}{3})$. The efficient allocation is $(1, 2)$, and this is supported, e.g., by equilibrium bids $b_1 = 1$ and $b_2 = \delta$. But allocation $(2, 1)$ is also supported as an equilibrium, e.g., by bids $b_1 = 0$ and $b_2 = 1$. The price of anarchy is thus:

$$\frac{\alpha_{1,1}v_1 + \alpha_{2,2}v_2}{\alpha_{2,1}v_2 + \alpha_{1,2}v_1} = \frac{(1 - \delta) + (1 - \delta)}{1 + \delta} = \frac{2 - 2\delta}{1 + \delta}$$

For any $\epsilon > 0$, if $\delta < \frac{\epsilon}{4 - \epsilon}$ then $\frac{2 - 2\delta}{1 + \delta} > 2 - \epsilon$. Therefore, for any $\epsilon > 0$, we can choose $\delta \in (0, \min\{\frac{1}{3}, \frac{\epsilon}{4 - \epsilon}\})$, in which case the price of anarchy will exceed $2 - \epsilon$. $\square$

---

[3] Note that Theorem 1 entails that $e(1, 2) = 1$ in all cases.

This also shows that equilibrium revenue, as a fraction of the VCG revenue, may be arbitrarily bad. In the example above, the $b_1 = 0$, $b_2 = 1$ equilibrium yields 0 revenue, while the $b_1 = 1$, $b_2 = \delta$ equilibrium yields the VCG outcome, with revenue δ.

4   Three or More Slots

So far, we have seen that many of the important properties of the GSP auction break in a two-slot setting. In this section, we will explore additional complexities that arise with more than two slots. Notably, we will see that the order in which slots are sold becomes critical — it will no-longer be sufficient to sell slots from "best to worst" as in a standard GSP auction.

4.1   Absence of Equilibrium

First, we show that even the existence of equilibrium is in doubt. The following example with 4 bidders and 3 slots illustrates that no bid-independent tie-breaking rule can guarantee the existence of an equilibrium for every set of valuations:

Table 2. An example in which no pure-strategy equilibrium exists for all v with a fixed, bid-independent tie-breaking rule

bidder	value	$\alpha_{i,1}$	$\alpha_{i,2}$	$\alpha_{i,3}$
1	v_1	1	1	0
2	v_2	1	1	0
3	v_3	1	0.5	0.5
4	v_4	1	0.5	0.5

The example in Table 2 uses similar techniques to the simpler one in Section 3.1, so we will only sketch the reasoning here. It is straightforward to argue that any equilibrium must achieve the efficient allocation, otherwise some bidder could deviate and benefit. In Section 3, we saw that it was important to break ties in favor of the bidder who had a greater incremental value for slot 1 over slot 2. In this example, if the efficient allocation chooses bidders 1 and 2 (as well as either bidder 3 or 4), then we see the same structure replicated here — it will be important to break ties in favor of bidder 3 and/or 4. On the other hand, if the efficient allocation chooses bidders 3 and 4, with one of bidder 1 or 2, then the same structure arises across slots 1 and 3. However, bidders 1 and 2 have a greater incremental value for slot 1 over slot 3 and therefore it is important to break ties in their favor. Thus, any tie-breaking rule that does not depend on bids will necessarily fail for at least one of these scenarios.

4.2   The Importance of the Order of Sale

We just saw that selling slots in a different order can be beneficial, but is it ever necessary? In fact, we show that it is.

Observation 1. *With four bidders and three slots, there exist values and click-through-rates such that the VCG result can be achieved, but not by selling slots in order.*

Table 3. A four-bidder, three-slot example demonstrating that selling items out of order may facilitate VCG results

bidder	value	$\alpha_{i,1}$	$\alpha_{i,2}$	$\alpha_{i,3}$
1	10	1	0.4	0.4
2	8	1	0.75	$\frac{1}{7}$
3	8	1	0.5	0.5
4	5	1	1	0

Proof. Consider the four-bidder, three-slot example depicted in Table 3. One can check that the optimal assignment is (1,2,3) and VCG prices for the slots are $p = [7, 5, 1]$. If slots are sold in order, then bidder 4 must set p_3. Thus, bidder 4 must be bidding such that $\alpha_{4,3}b_4 = p_3$, which implies $0 \times b_4 = 1$. Clearly, this is not possible, and there will be similar problems even if we require that $\alpha_{4,3}$ is strictly positive.

However, VCG prices can be achieved by selling slots in the order 1,3,2. One can check that the bids $b = [10, 7, 7, 5]$ achieve VCG prices. $\square$

4.3   An Auction with Expressive Bidding

Finally, we show how we can build an auction that always yields the VCG result as an equilibrium by selling slots in a different order. For this mechanism, we will need bidders to place a distinct bid $b_{i,j}$ for each slot (WLOG we ignore α values here). First, we need to argue that an appropriate ordering exists, then we will construct a mechanism that exploits this ordering.

Price Support Orderings and Forests We first establish that the VCG result is a feasible outcome of an iterated auction with expressive bidding. If i is paying price p_i, then some other bidder who has not already been allocated is bidding p_i for the slot i wins. It is not a priori clear that this is possible without requiring some bidder to overbid her true value. We call an ordering that achieves this a *price support ordering* (PSO).

Our first lemma shows that a price support ordering always exists for VCG prices More specifically, we show that a *price support forest* (PSF) exists — a price support forest is a directed forest that captures the ability of bidders to support prices:

Definition 7. *A price support forest (PSF) for prices p_j with n slots and bidders is a graph F on n nodes with the following properties:*

- F is a directed forest with edges pointing away from the roots.
- Root nodes (nodes with no incoming edges) have price $p_j = 0$.
- Edge (i,j) in F implies that bidder i can set the price for slot j without overbidding.

We will formalize "i can set the price for slot j" below.

Assume that the VCG mechanism assigns bidder i to slot i, and let p_j denote the minimum Walrasian equilibrium price for slot j (the VCG price of bidder j). The following lemma says that VCG prices always admit a PSF in which edges capture indifferences. A precisely equivalent lemma appears in Mehta and Vazirani [2013], so we omit the proof.

Lemma 2 (VCG Price Support Lemma). *There exists a directed forest F with the following property: for any slot j, either $p_j = 0$, or there is an edge (i,j) corresponding to a bidder who is indifferent between getting slot i at price p_i and getting slot j at price p_j, ergo i is happy to bid $b_{i,j} = p_j$ for slot j and thereby set its price. Thus, F is a price support forest.*

Corollary 3. *There exists an ordering σ of slots with the following property: for any slot j, either $p_j = 0$, or there is some bidder with $i > j$ who is indifferent between getting slot i at price p_i and getting slot j at price p_j, ergo i is happy to bid $b_{i,j} = p_j$ for slot j and thereby set its price.*

Proof. By Lemma 2, we know that a price support forest F exists. Compute an ordering σ such that any parent in F comes after all its children (e.g.) by a breadth-first traversal of F. $\qquad\square$

Auctions Leveraging Price Support. Finally, we show how the existence of a PSF can be used to construct an auction that supports the VCG result as an equilibrium:

Definition 8 (Auction with a Price Support Order). *An iterated second-price auction can be implemented leveraging a price support order as follows:*

1. *Choose an order of sale σ and tie-breaking rules that maximize seller revenue given bids. If a slot has only one nonzero bid, it does not get sold.*
2. *Run an iterated second-price auction according to the order σ and rules selected in (1).*

Theorem 5 (Equilibrium). *The iterated second-price auction with unit-demand bidders and expressive bids has an efficient equilibrium in which bidders pay VCG prices.*

Proof. Choose an arbitrary PSF and define bids as follows:

$$b_{i,j} = \begin{cases} v_{i,j} & i = j \\ p_j & i \text{ supports the price of } j \text{ in the PSF, or} \\ 0 & \text{otherwise.} \end{cases}$$

Consider deviations by a particular bidder k. Notice that no slot j can have a bid less than p_j unless it was placed by bidder k. We can thus conclude that if k wins any slot for less than the VCG price through this defection (which is necessary for it to be profitable), then k must have won the slot for free. However, our auction rules stipulate that slots will not be sold if they only have one nonzero bid, so this is impossible. □

5 Conclusion

The primary theoretical justification for GSP builds on the analyses of Varian [2007] and Edelman *et al.* [2007] to argue that GSP will perform at least as well as VCG. Unfortunately, our results demonstrate that this is a very fragile phenomenon—when GSP is naturally generalized as an iterated second price auction, these performance guarantees fall apart even with small deviations from GSP's separable model. Our work suggests a few techniques for recovering desirable performance guarantees, such as varying the order of sale and allowing expressive bidding, but perhaps even more importantly it points to significant open questions that might suggest new mechanisms and principles for implementing auctions:

- Is there a better way to generalize GSP that would preserve the performance guarantees of Varian [2007] and Edelman *et al.* [2007]?
- What are the key principles that define GSP in theory?
- What are the properties that capture GSP's practical popularity?

That said, our results also include a surprising positive result: *all* click-through-rate profiles ensure existence of efficient equilibria in the two-slot setting, given a specific bid-independent tie-breaking rule. We proved that this result does not generalize to the case with more slots, but whether bid-*dependent* tie-breaking rules could yield generic existence of efficient equilibria remains an open question. And even if no meaningful extension beyond the two-slot setting is possible, the positive result we have may turn out to be specifically relevant for a world of mobile devices where only a small number of slots can be shown per page.

References

Abrams, Z., Ghosh, A., Vee, E.: Cost of conciseness in sponsored search auctions. In: Deng, X., Graham, F.C. (eds.) WINE 2007. LNCS, vol. 4858, pp. 326–334. Springer, Heidelberg (2007)

Aggarwal, G., Goel, A., Motwani, R.: Truthful auctions for pricing search keywords. In: Proceedings of the 7th ACM Conference on Electronic Commerce, pp. 1–7 (2006)

Aggarwal, G., Feldman, J., Muthukrishnan, S., Pál, M.: Sponsored search auctions with markovian users. In: Papadimitriou, C., Zhang, S. (eds.) WINE 2008. LNCS, vol. 5385, pp. 621–628. Springer, Heidelberg (2008)

Athey, S., Ellison, G.: Position auctions with consumer search. The Quarterly Journal of Economics 126(3), 1213–1270 (2011)

Caragiannis, I., Kaklamanis, C., Kanellopoulos, P., Kyropoulou, M., Lucier, B., Leme, R.P., Tardos, E.: Bounding the inefficiency of outcomes in generalized second price auctions. Journal of Economic Theory (2014)

Craswell, N., Zoeter, O., Taylor, M., Ramsey, B.: An experimental comparison of click position-bias models. In: Proceedings of the 2008 International Conference on Web Search and Data Mining, pp. 87–94 (2008)

Edelman, B., Ostrovsky, M., Schwarz, M.: Internet advertising and the generalized second-price auction: Selling billions of dollars worth of keywords. American Economic Review 97(1), 242–259 (2007)

Ghosh, A., Mahdian, M.: Externalities in online advertising. In: Proceedings of the 17th International World Wide Web Conference, pp. 161–168 (2008)

Ghosh, A., Sayedi, A.: Expressive auctions for externalities in online advertising. In: Proceedings of the 19th International Conference on World Wide Web, pp. 371–380 (2010)

Giotis, I., Karlin, A.R.: On the equilibria and efficiency of the GSP mechanism in keyword auctions with externalities. In: Papadimitriou, C., Zhang, S. (eds.) WINE 2008. LNCS, vol. 5385, pp. 629–638. Springer, Heidelberg (2008)

Gomes, R., Immorlica, N., Markakis, E.: Externalities in keyword auctions: An empirical and theoretical assessment. In: Leonardi, S. (ed.) WINE 2009. LNCS, vol. 5929, pp. 172–183. Springer, Heidelberg (2009)

Gonen, R., Vassilvitskii, S.: Sponsored search auctions with reserve prices: Going beyond separability. In: Papadimitriou, C., Zhang, S. (eds.) WINE 2008. LNCS, vol. 5385, pp. 597–608. Springer, Heidelberg (2008)

Hummel, P., McAfee, R.P.: Position auctions with externalities. In: Liu, T.-Y., Qi, Q., Ye, Y. (eds.) WINE 2014. LNCS, vol. 8877, pp. 410–415. Springer, Heidelberg (2014)

Jeziorski, P., Segal, I.: What makes them click: Empirical analysis of consumer demand for search advertising. American Economic Journal: Microeconomics (forthcoming)

Kempe, D., Mahdian, M.: A cascade model for externalities in sponsored search. In: Papadimitriou, C., Zhang, S. (eds.) WINE 2008. LNCS, vol. 5385, pp. 585–596. Springer, Heidelberg (2008)

Lahaie, S., Pennock, D., Saberi, A., Vohra, R.: Sponsored search auctions. In: Nisan, N., Roughgarden, T., Tardos, E., Vazirani, V. (eds.) Algorithmic Game Theory. Cambridge University Press (2007)

Lahaie, S.: An analysis of alternative slot auction designs for sponsored search. In: Proceedings of the 7th ACM Conference on Electronic Commerce, pp. 218–227 (2006)

Leonard, H.B.: Elicitation of honest preferences for the assignment of individuals to positions. The Journal of Political Economy 91(3), 461–479 (1983)

Mehta, R., Vazirani, V.V.: An incentive compatible, efficient market for air traffic flow management. CoRR, abs/1305.3241 (2013)

Milgrom, P.: Simplified mechanisms with an application to sponsored-search auctions. Games and Economic Behavior 70(1), 62–70 (2010)

Varian, H.R.: Position auctions. International Journal of Industrial Organization 25, 1163–1178 (2007)

Position Auctions with Externalities

Patrick Hummel[1] and R. Preston McAfee[2]

[1] Google Inc.
phummel@google.com
[2] Microsoft Corp.
preston@mcafee.cc

Abstract. This paper presents models for predicted click-through rates in position auctions that take into account the externalities ads shown in other positions may impose on the probability that an ad in a particular position receives a click. We present a general axiomatic methodology for how click probabilities are affected by the qualities of the ads in the other positions, and illustrate that using these axioms will increase revenue as long as higher quality ads tend to be ranked ahead of lower quality ads. We also present appropriate algorithms for selecting the optimal allocation of ads when predicted click-through rates are governed by a natural special case of this axiomatic model of externalities.

1 Introduction

In sponsored search auctions, advertisements appear alongside search results in a variety of positions on the page, some of which are more prominent and thus more likely to be clicked than others. In both academic work and practice, it is standard to model each position as having some quality score that reflects the relative probability that an ad will receive a click in that position and then ranking the ads by a product of their bid, the maximum amount the advertisers will pay per click, and a quality score, which reflects the probability an ad will receive a click if the advertiser is shown in the top position.

Although it is almost universal to assume that an ad's click probability is a product of the ad's quality score and a quality score of a position, this formulation may be suboptimal. The formulation implicitly assumes that the probability an ad receives a click in a given position is independent of the identities of the other ads on the page. However, this assumption is unlikely to hold in practice. [3] notes empirically that many consumers are likely to search for what they are looking for by beginning their search at the top and ceasing to search after they have found what they are looking for, and [11] presents evidence that ads impose large negative externalities on other ads by virtue of the fact that the ads can be substitutes for one another. Consequently, placing higher quality ads at the top of the page decreases the probability that a user clicks on other ads.

How then, might one incorporate this possibility into sponsored search auctions to choose a more efficient allocation of ads? This paper presents methods for achieving this goal. We begin by presenting a general axiomatic model of

T.-Y. Liu et al. (Eds.): WINE 2014, LNCS 8877, pp. 417–422, 2014.
© Springer International Publishing Switzerland 2014

predicted click-through rates when the probability an ad receives a click may depend not only on the quality score of the ad and the position in question, but also on the quality scores of the other ads that are shown in the other positions. We analyze the properties of this axiomatic formulation, and illustrate that as long as higher quality ads are typically ranked ahead of lower ads, then moving towards this new axiomatic model will increase revenue in expectation.

A drawback of the most general possible formulation is that computing the optimal allocation of ads is unlikely to be computationally feasible because one would likely need to try each possible configuration of ads in order to choose the optimal configuration, and this is likely to be too slow to be useful in practice. For this reason, we also develop a second formulation that is a special case of our most general methodology that has the advantage of admitting a rapidly converging algorithm for computing the optimal allocation of ads.

While a few papers have presented theoretical analyses of circumstances where the click-through rates are not equal to a product of the quality score of an ad and the quality score of a position, these papers differ significantly from our paper. [1] and [12] consider models in which users search from the top to the bottom that lead to non-separable click probabilities and tractable algorithms for choosing the allocation of ads, but do not consider more general models, as we do in this paper. [7] and [8] further analyze the equilibrium and efficiency properties of such a model, but [11] finds empirical evidence that models in which users search from the top of the page to the bottom do not fully match the data. Other papers that consider different models of externalities (e.g. [2], [5], [6], and [10]) also do not present algorithms for choosing the allocation of ads.

2   Model of Externalities

There is an auction for s advertising positions on a page. Each advertising position k has a quality score n_k, where we assume without loss of generality that n_k is non-increasing in k. There are also m advertisers. Each advertiser i has a quality score q_i reflecting the relative clickability of the ad and makes a bid b_i reflecting the maximum amount that this advertiser will pay per click.

In this setting, a standard model of position auctions such as [4] or [13] would assume that the probability advertiser i receives a click in position k is $n_k q_i$. We instead allow the probability an advertiser receives a click to depend on these quality scores in a more nuanced way. Let $p_{(j)} = f_j(q_{(1)}, \ldots, q_{(s)}; n_1, \ldots, n_s)$ denote the probability that the advertiser in the jth position receives a click as a function of the quality scores of the ads in the first s positions as well as quality scores of the s positions. In addition to requiring this probability to be increasing in the underlying quality scores of the ad and the position, $q_{(j)}$ and n_j, we stipulate that this probability should satisfy these axioms:

(A) $f_j(q_{(1)}, \ldots, q_{(s)}; n_1, \ldots, n_s)$ is non-increasing in $q_{(k)}$ for all $k \neq j$.

(B) Increasing the quality score of an ad in a higher quality position decreases the click-through rates of ads in other positions by more than increasing the quality score of an ad in a lower quality position. Formally, let $q \equiv (q_{(1)}, \ldots, q_{(s)})$

denote a vector of qualities for which $q_{(i)} = q_{(k)} = q^*$ for some particular i and k satisfying $n_i > n_k$. Also let $\boldsymbol{q}_{(i)}$ denote the vector of qualities that would result from replacing $q_{(i)} = q^*$ with $q_{(i)} = \hat{q}$ for some $\hat{q} \neq q^*$, and let $\boldsymbol{q}_{(k)}$ denote the vector of qualities that would result from replacing $q_{(k)} = q^*$ with $q_{(k)} = \hat{q}$ for the same $\hat{q}$. Then $|f_j(\boldsymbol{q}_{(i)}; n_1, \ldots, n_s) - f_j(\boldsymbol{q}; n_1, \ldots, n_s)| \geq |f_j(\boldsymbol{q}_{(k)}; n_1, \ldots, n_s) - f_j(\boldsymbol{q}; n_1, \ldots, n_s)|$ for all $j \notin \{i, k\}$.

Axiom (A) simply reflects the possibility that when a higher quality ad assumes a particular position, the ad is likely to decrease the probability that ads in other positions receive a click. This axiom is plausible because if the quality of an ad in a particular position increases, users are relatively more likely to click on this ad, which in turn draws their attention from the other ads.

Similarly, axiom (B) reflects the fact that increasing the quality of an ad in a higher quality position does more to increase the probability that users will click on that ad, so increasing the quality of an ad in a higher quality position also draws more user attention from other ads than increasing the quality of an ad in a lower quality position. Thus both axioms (A) and (B) reflect sensible properties on how changing the qualities of ads in other positions is likely to affect the probabilities that other ads receive a click.

Throughout our analysis, we focus on mechanisms in which the auctioneer seeks to maximize total expected welfare with respect to the bids of the advertisers. That is, the auctioneer maximizes $\sum_{j=1}^{s} b_{(j)} p_{(j)}$, where $b_{(j)}$ denotes the cost per click bid of the advertiser in the jth position and $p_{(j)}$ denotes the probability that the advertiser in the jth position receives a click. We also focus on a generalization of the generalized second price auction in which the advertiser in the jth position is charged a cost per click $c_{(j)}$ that represents the smallest bid that this advertiser could make while still maintaining the jth position when the allocation of ads is chosen using the above algorithm.

3   General Results

We first derive some general results on how using an alternative model of predicted click-through rates meeting the axioms given in the previous section would affect revenue from online auctions. To do this, we compare two otherwise identical methods for predicting the click-through rates of ads in position auctions. The first method is one in which the predicted click-through rates of the ads in slots $j \notin \{k, k + 1\}$ are independent of the quality scores of the ads in positions k and $k + 1$, as in a standard model. The other method we consider is one in which the predicted click-through rates of the ads in positions $j \notin \{k, k + 1\}$ may depend on the quality scores of the ads in positions k and $k+1$ in a manner that satisfies the axioms (A) and (B) presented in the previous section.

There are two different ways that incorporating the possibility that the quality scores of ads may affect the click-through rates of ads in other positions could affect revenue. First there is the possibility that this could affect the allocation of ads that is shown in the auction. In this case, if the revised model of predicted click-through rates is more accurate, then one would choose a more efficient allocation of ads, and thereby typically achieve higher revenue.

However, in a substantial percentage of auctions, allowing for the possibility that an ad's predicted click-through rate may depend on the quality scores of the other ads will not change the allocation of ads but will affect the pricing. It is thus important to assess how the prices that the advertisers pay would be affected by the changed model of predicted click-through rates even if this does not affect the allocation of ads. This is addressed in the following theorem:

Theorem 1. *Consider two different models of predicted click-through rates for position auctions that are identical except for the following:*

(1) For the first model, the predicted click-through rates of ads in slots $j \notin \{k, k+1\}$ are independent of the quality scores of the ads in slots k and $k+1$.

(2) For the second model, the predicted click-through rates of ads in slots $j \notin \{k, k+1\}$ depend on the quality scores of the ads in slots k and $k+1$ in a manner that satisfies axioms (A) and (B).

Then if the allocation of ads that is selected by the two models of predicted click-through rates is identical, the advertiser in position k pays more per click under the second model if and only if $q_{(k)} > q_{(k+1)}$.

All proofs are in the appendix of the full paper [9]. Theorem 1 indicates that if we take into account the externalities that the ads in positions k and $k+1$ impose on the other ads, then the advertiser in position k will pay more per click if and only if this advertiser has a higher quality ad. Since Theorem 1 applies to all slots k, repeatedly applying Theorem 1 to every slot suggests that if a model with externalities has no effect on the allocation of ads, then this model will typically increase the cost per click paid by an advertiser if and only if this advertiser's quality score exceeds that of the advertiser just below him.

The results of this section suggest that if one can more accurately describe click probabilities by using a model of the form in Section 2, then one should be able to increase revenue. Typically higher quality ads will be ranked higher than lower quality ads, so the result in Theorem 1 suggests that even if this model does not change the allocation of ads, revenue should still increase. And if one is able to choose a more efficient allocation, then one would also expect revenue to increase. Thus revenue is likely to increase from using predicted click-through rates of the form in Section 2 as long as such a model is more accurate.

4   Practical Formulation

For general models of the form in Section 2, it may be difficult to select the efficiency-maximizing configuration because there are an exponentially large number of feasible configurations and it is not obvious how one can rule out different configurations as dominated by others. Thus it is important to use a model where one can select the efficiency-maximizing configuration in a computationally tractable way. In this section we present a specific formulation of the model in Section 2 that permits such a practical implementation.

In particular, in this section we consider a model in which the predicted click-through rates for the ads in position i are of the form

$$p_i = \frac{\nu n_i q_i}{1 + \lambda \sum_{j=1}^{s} n_j q_j}$$

where λ and ν are positive constants, n_i denotes the quality score of the ith position, and q_i denotes the quality score of the ad in the ith position. This formulation is sensible because one would expect the percentage decrease in an ad's click-through rate due to the negative externalities imposed by the other ads to be proportional to the total click-through rates of these ads, meaning an ad's click-through rate is likely to be decreased by a factor proportional to $1 + \lambda \sum_{j=1}^{s} n_j q_j$. Also note that in this formulation, setting $\lambda = 0$ and $\nu = 1$ would recover the standard formulation of predicted click-through rates, so optimally choosing these parameters can never result in less accurate predicted click-through rates than the standard formulation. Further note that changing the value of ν would never change the optimal allocation of ads. Here ν is a term that only serves to make the predicted click-through rates unbiased on average.

Now define S to be the expected social welfare from a given ranking of ads when $\nu = 1$. We first begin our analysis of this formulation by noting when using a non-zero value of λ would result in changing the allocation of ads:

Theorem 2. *Welfare is enhanced by switching the order of the ads in positions k and m where $k < m$ if and only if $b_m q_m - \lambda q_m S > b_k q_k - \lambda q_k S$.*

Theorem 2 suggests that if one can obtain a good estimate of the social welfare S that will result in the efficiency-maximizing configuration, then it may be feasible to rank the ads on the basis of scores of the form $b_m q_m - \lambda q_m S$ to achieve the efficiency maximizing allocation. We now exploit this insight to derive a computationally efficient way of selecting the optimal ordering of ads.

The algorithm proceeds by selecting a value S_L that is lower than the social welfare S that will result in the efficiency-maximizing configuration and another value S_H that is higher than this social welfare S. The algorithm then repeatedly replaces either S_L or S_H with $\hat{S} \equiv \frac{1}{2}(S_L + S_H)$ until it finds some such value of $\hat{S}$ that is guaranteed to result in the efficiency-maximizing allocation when ranking ads by the scores $b_m q_m - \lambda q_m S$ when $S = \hat{S}$. Such an algorithm will typically require very few steps in practice because after n passes, $\hat{S}$ will be within a factor of 2^{-n} of the true social welfare S corresponding to the efficiency-maximizing configuration. The detailed steps for the algorithm are as follows:

(1) Define S_L to be the expected social welfare that would result if the ads were ranked by the scores $b_m q_m$.
(2) Define $S_H \equiv \sum_{m=1}^{s} n_m b_m q_m$ when the ads are ranked by the scores $b_m q_m$.
(3) Calculate the rankings of the ads when the ads are ranked by the scores $b_m q_m - \lambda q_m S$ for $S = S_L$ and $S = S_H$.
(4) If the rankings of the ads in step (3) are the same for both $S = S_L$ and $S = S_H$, then choose this ranking of the ads.
(5) If these rankings are different, let $\hat{S} \equiv \frac{1}{2}(S_L + S_H)$ and calculate the ranking of the ads when the ads are ranked by the scores $b_m q_m - \lambda q_m \hat{S}$.

(6) Let $\phi(\hat{S}) \equiv \sum_{m=1}^{s} n_m(b_m q_m - \lambda q_m \hat{S})$ when the ads are ranked by the scores $b_m q_m - \lambda q_m \hat{S}$. If $\phi(\hat{S}) < \hat{S}$, then let $S_H = \hat{S}$. Otherwise let $S_L = \hat{S}$.

(7) Repeat steps (3)-(6) until the rankings in step (4) are the same for both $S = S_L$ and $S = S_H$, and choose the resulting ranking of ads.

This algorithm indeed results in the efficiency-maximizing allocation:

Theorem 3. *The ranking of ads that results from the algorithm considered above is the efficiency-maximization allocation.*

This completes our results for the model of position auctions with externalities. In the full version of the paper [9], we also present an additional model of position auctions that takes into account the fact that ads from well-known brands are less adversely affected by being shown in a lower position than ads from better-known brands [10]. In this model of brand effects, we again present appropriate algorithms for selecting the optimal allocation of ads and show that a purely greedy approach of ranking the ads will potentially cost as much as half of the total possible social welfare. We refer the reader to [9] for more details.

References

[1] Aggarwal, G., Feldman, J., Muthukrishnan, S., Pál, M.: Sponsored search auctions with Markovian users. In: Papadimitriou, C., Zhang, S. (eds.) WINE 2008. LNCS, vol. 5385, pp. 621–628. Springer, Heidelberg (2008)

[2] Athey, S., Ellison, G.: Position auctions with consumer search. Quarterly Journal of Economics 126(3), 1213–1270 (2011)

[3] Craswell, N., Zoeter, O., Taylor, M., Ramsey, B.: An experimental comparison of click position-bias models. In: WSDM 2008, pp. 87–94 (2008)

[4] Edelman, B., Ostrovsky, M., Schwarz, M.: Internet advertising and the generalized second price auction: Selling billions of dollars of keywords. American Economic Review 97(1), 242–259 (2007)

[5] Fotakis, D., Krysta, P., Telelis, O.: Externalities among advertisers in sponsored search. In: Persiano, G. (ed.) SAGT 2011. LNCS, vol. 6982, pp. 105–116. Springer, Heidelberg (2011)

[6] Ghosh, A., Mahdian, M.: Externalities in online advertising. In: WWW 2008, pp. 161–168 (2008)

[7] Giotis, I., Karlin, A.R.: On the equilibria and efficiency of the GSP mechanism in keyword auctions with externalities. In: Papadimitriou, C., Zhang, S. (eds.) WINE 2008. LNCS, vol. 5385, pp. 629–638. Springer, Heidelberg (2008)

[8] Gomes, R., Immorlica, N., Markakis, E.: Externalities in keyword auctions: An empirical and theoretical assessment. In: Leonardi, S. (ed.) WINE 2009. LNCS, vol. 5929, pp. 172–183. Springer, Heidelberg (2009)

[9] Hummel, P., McAfee, R.P.: Position auctions with externalities and brand effects. arXiv:1409.4687 [cs.GT] (2014)

[10] Jerath, K., Ma, L., Park, Y.-H., Srinivasan, K.: A "position paradox" in sponsored search auctions. Marketing Science 30(4), 612–627 (2011)

[11] Jeziorski, P., Segal, I.: What makes them click: Empirical analysis of consumer demand for search advertising. Typescript, University of California Berkeley, Berkeley, CA (2014)

[12] Kempe, D., Mahdian, M.: A cascade model for externalities in sponsored search. In: Papadimitriou, C., Zhang, S. (eds.) WINE 2008. LNCS, vol. 5385, pp. 585–596. Springer, Heidelberg (2008)

[13] Varian, H.: Position auctions. International Journal of Industrial Organization 25(6), 1163–1178 (2007)

Quality of Service in Network Creation Games[*]

Andreas Cord-Landwehr, Alexander Mäcker,
and Friedhelm Meyer auf der Heide

Heinz Nixdorf Institute & Department of Computer Science
University of Paderborn, Germany

Abstract Network creation games model the creation and usage costs of networks formed by n selfish nodes. Each node v can buy a set of edges, each for a fixed price $\alpha > 0$. Its goal is to minimize its private costs, i.e., the sum (SUM-game, Fabrikant et al., PODC 2003) or maximum (MAX-game, Demaine et al., PODC 2007) of distances from v to all other nodes plus the prices of the bought edges. The above papers show the existence of Nash equilibria as well as upper and lower bounds for the prices of anarchy and stability. In several subsequent papers, these bounds were improved for a wide range of prices α. In this paper, we extend these models by incorporating quality-of-service aspects: Each edge cannot only be bought at a fixed quality (edge length one) for a fixed price α. Instead, we assume that quality levels (i.e., edge lengths) are varying in a fixed interval $[\check{\beta}, \hat{\beta}]$, $0 < \check{\beta} \le \hat{\beta}$. A node now cannot only choose which edge to buy, but can also choose its quality x, for the price $p(x)$, for a given price function p. For both games and all price functions, we show that Nash equilibria exist and that the price of stability is either constant or depends only on the interval size of available edge lengths. Our main results are bounds for the price of anarchy. In case of the SUM-game, we show that they are tight if price functions decrease sufficiently fast.

1 Introduction

Network creation games (NCG) aim to model the evolution and outcome of networks created by selfish nodes. In these games, nodes can decide individually which edges they want to buy in order to minimize their private costs, i.e., the costs of the bought edges plus costs for communicating with other nodes. Each node v can buy a set of edges, each for a price $\alpha > 0$. Its goal is to minimize its private costs, i.e., the sum (SUM-game) or maximum (MAX-game) of the distances from v to all other nodes in the network plus the costs of the bought edges. Since all decisions are taken individually and only with respect to optimize their private costs, analyzing the resulting network by comparing it to an overall good structure constitutes the central aspect in the study of NCGs. This task

[*] This work was partially supported by the German Research Foundation (DFG) within the Collaborative Research Centre "On-The-Fly Computing" (SFB 901) and by the EU within FET project MULTIPLEX under contract no. 317532.

T.-Y. Liu et al. (Eds.): WINE 2014, LNCS 8877, pp. 423–428, 2014.

was formalized as analyzing the *price of anarchy* and was first discussed by [8] for the SUM-game and by [7] for the MAX-game. These papers inspired a series of subsequent works.

In this paper, we incorporate a kind of quality-of-service into the classical network creation games model: An edge can be bought for different prices, with different latencies. This is a well-established method, e.g., for internet service providers who offer different bandwidths of connection for different prices. We formalize this game on individual connection qualities and prove the existence of equilibria and present bounds for the prices of stability and anarchy.

For the omitted proofs please refer to the full version of this paper [6].

1.1   Model and Notations

An instance of our NCG is given by a set V of n nodes and a price function $p : [\check{\beta}, \hat{\beta}] \to \mathbb{R}^+$ on an interval of possible edge weights $[\check{\beta}, \hat{\beta}] \subseteq \mathbb{R}^+$. A price function is assumed to be monotonically decreasing and the interval to fulfill $0 < \check{\beta} \leq \hat{\beta}$. Each $v \in V$ aims to minimize its private costs by selfishly selecting a *strategy* $s_v \subset V \times [\check{\beta}, \hat{\beta}]$ such that each $(u, x) \in s_v$ represents an undirected weighted edge $(\{v, u\}, x)$ from v to u of weight x, which is created by v and has price $p(x)$. For a strategy profile $S = (s_1, \ldots, s_n)$, the resulting weighted graph $G[S]$ consists of vertices V and the weighted edges $\bigcup_{v \in V} \{(\{v, u\}, x) | (u, x) \in s_v\}$.

The costs of a node in the SUM-game are given by $c_v(S) = \sum_{(u,x) \in s_v} p(x) + \sum_{u \in V} d_{G[S]}(v, u)$. Here, $d_{G[S]}(v, u)$ denotes the shortest weighted path distance from v to u in the weighted graph $G[S]$. For the MAX-game, the private cost function is given by $c_v(S) = \sum_{(u,x) \in s_v} p(x) + \max_{u \in V} d_{G[S]}(v, u)$.

The social costs in both games are $c(S) = \sum_{v \in V} c_v(S)$. We refer to the edge cost term of the cost function as *edge costs* and to the distance term as *distance costs*. A strategy profile $S = (s_1, \ldots, s_n)$ is called a *Nash equilibrium* (NE) if for every node i and every strategy s_i' it holds: Let $s_i' \neq s_i$ be a strategy change, then $S' := (s_1, \ldots, s_{i-1}, s_i', s_{i+1}, \ldots, s_n)$ does not have lower costs for i, i.e, $c_i(S) \leq c_i(S')$. Depending on the game, we call such an equilibrium a SUM-NE or a MAX-NE. If a strategy profile is not a NE, then there exists at least one node that can perform an *improving response* (IR), i.e., it can decrease its costs by changing its strategy. An improving response is called a *best response* (BR) if this strategy change is optimal regarding the maximum private costs decrease.

A main objective of the research on NCGs is the analysis of the *price of anarchy* (PoA), introduced in [10]. The PoA is defined as the ratio of a largest social cost of any Nash equilibrium and the optimal social cost. The minimal loss by selfish behavior is given by the *price of stability*, see for example [3, 4], and it is defined as the ratio of the smallest social cost of any Nash equilibrium and the optimal social cost.

1.2   Related Work

In the original SUM- and MAX-games by [8] and [7], nodes can only buy edges of fixed length one for a fixed price $\alpha > 0$. In [8], the authors introduced the

SUM-game and proved (among other things) an upper bound of $\mathcal{O}(\sqrt{\alpha})$ on the price of anarchy (PoA) in the case of $\alpha < n^2$, and a constant PoA otherwise. Later, [1] proved a constant PoA for $\alpha = \mathcal{O}(\sqrt{n})$ and the first sublinear worst case bound of $\mathcal{O}(n^{1/3})$ for general α. [7] proved an $\mathcal{O}(n^\varepsilon)$ bound for α in the range of $\Omega(n)$ and $o(n \lg n)$. Recently, by [13] and improved by [12], it was shown that for $\alpha \geq 65n$ all equilibria are trees (and thus the PoA is constant).

For the MAX-game, [7] showed that the PoA is at most 2 for $\alpha \geq n$, $\mathcal{O}\left(\min\{4^{\sqrt{\lg n}}, (n/\alpha)^{1/3}\}\right)$ for $2\sqrt{\lg n} \leq \alpha \leq n$, and $\mathcal{O}\left(n^{2/\alpha}\right)$ for $\alpha < 2\sqrt{\lg n}$. For $\alpha > 129$, [13] showed, like in the SUM version, that all equilibria are trees and the PoA is constant.

In [2], a simpler model, the *basic network creation game* (BNCG), was introduced. Here, the operation of a node consists of swapping some of its incident edges, i.e., redirecting them to other nodes. There are no costs associated with such operations. Restricting the initial network to trees, the only equilibrium in the SUM-game is a star graph. Without restrictions, all (swap) equilibria are proven to have a diameter of $2^{\mathcal{O}(\sqrt{\log n})}$, which is also the PoA. For the MAX-version, the authors provide an equilibrium network with diameter $\Theta(\sqrt{n})$. In [11], it is shown for the SUM-game that this model is fundamentally different to the original network creation game in the following sense: There are equilibria for the BNCG that are not equilibria for NCG for any α, and vice versa.

An interesting extension of the SUM-game was introduced and investigated by [1]. They weight each pair (u, v) of nodes, indicating the importance of the connection to v for u. The special case of 0-1-weights, defining a friendship graph between the nodes, was examined by [9] and [5].

1.3   Our Results

We show that equilibria exist for both games, for every monotonically decreasing price function $p : [\check{\beta}, \hat{\beta}] \to \mathbb{R}^+$. For the SUM-game with n nodes, the price of stability is at most $\mathcal{O}(1 + \hat{\beta}/\check{\beta})$. For the MAX-game, it is always constant.

For the price of anarchy for the SUM-game, we provide an upper bound of $\mathcal{O}\left(\min\{n, (p(x^*) + x^*)/\check{\beta}\}\right)$, with $x^* \in [\check{\beta}, \hat{\beta}]$ being the edge quality that minimizes $p(x) + x$. This value can be understood to be the edge weight with optimal price-weight trade-off for an edge, if used for exactly one shortest path. For example, for $p : [\check{\beta}, \hat{\beta}] \to \mathbb{R}^+$ with $p(x) = \alpha/x$ and $\alpha > 0$, the price of anarchy is $\mathcal{O}(\sqrt{\alpha}/\check{\beta})$.

If $x^* = \hat{\beta}$, $p(\hat{\beta}) \leq \check{\beta}$, and $p(\check{\beta}) \leq \hat{\beta}$ hold, then this upper bound is tight up to constant factors. Examples for such price functions are linear functions $p : [1, \alpha - 2\varepsilon] \to \mathbb{R}^+$ with $p(x) = \alpha - (1 + \varepsilon)x$, for $\alpha > 0$ and $0 < \varepsilon < 1/2$. For these functions the price of anarchy is $\Theta(\alpha - \varepsilon)$.

For the MAX-game we provide a price of anarchy upper bound of $\mathcal{O}(1 + \sqrt[3]{n})$.

2 The Sum-Game

Lemma 1. *Let S be a strategy profile such that $G[S]$ is connected and no edge can be removed without increasing the social cost. Denote by $\check{x}$ the minimal weight of any edge in $G[S]$ and by m the number of all edges. Then, for $x^* \in [\check{\beta}, \hat{\beta}]$ being the value minimizing $p(x) + x$, it holds $c(S) \geq 2\check{x}n(n-1) + m(p(x^*) + x^* - 4\check{x})$.*

Lemma 2. *Let $p : [\check{\beta}, \hat{\beta}] \to \mathbb{R}^+$ be a price function. Define $\chi^* \in [\check{\beta}, \hat{\beta}]$ to be the value minimizing $p(x) + 2x$ and $\bar{\chi} \in [\check{\beta}, \hat{\beta}]$ the value minimizing $p(x) + 2(n-1)x$. Then, the optimal social cost is given by a star with all edges having weight $\bar{\chi}$ or by a complete graph with all edges having weight χ^*.*

Theorem 1. *For every price function $p : [\check{\beta}, \hat{\beta}] \to \mathbb{R}^+$ a SUM-NE exists. Let $x^* \in [\check{\beta}, \hat{\beta}]$ be the value minimizing $p(x) + x$ and $\bar{x} \in [\check{\beta}, \hat{\beta}]$ the value minimizing $p(x) + (n-1)x$, then either a star with all edges having weight $\bar{x}$ or a complete graph with all edges having weight x^* forms a SUM-NE graph.*

Corollary 1. *Let $x^* \in [\check{\beta}, \hat{\beta}]$ be the value minimizing $p(x) + x$ and $\bar{x} \in [\check{\beta}, \hat{\beta}]$ the value minimizing $p(x) + (n-1)x$. Then, the price of stability in the SUM-game is constant if $p(x^*) > \bar{x}$ or $x^* > p(\bar{x})$ and otherwise $\mathcal{O}(1 + x^*/\bar{x})$.*

Similar to [1], we start our analysis for the price of anarchy by bounding the social cost of a SUM-NE graph essentially by the diameter of the graph. Using arguments about the maximum weights and prices in SUM-NE graphs, we can further bound this diameter and get a PoA upper bound only depending on the price function and its domain.

Lemma 3. *Let $p : [\check{\beta}, \hat{\beta}] \to \mathbb{R}^+$ be a price function and S a SUM-NE strategy profile. Then $c(S) \leq n\delta_G(v) + x^*(n-1)^2 + 2(p(x^*) + x^*)n(n-1)$ with $G := G[S], \delta_G(v) := \sum_{u \in V} d_G(v, u)$ being the distance costs of an arbitrary node in the equilibrium graph, and $x^* \in [\check{\beta}, \hat{\beta}]$ chosen such that it minimizes $p(x) + x$.*

Lemma 4. *Let $p : [\check{\beta}, \hat{\beta}] \to \mathbb{R}^+$ be a price function and S a strategy profile forming a SUM-NE graph G. Then, the diameter of G is at most $\mathcal{O}(p(x^*) + x^*)$, with $x^* \in [\check{\beta}, \hat{\beta}]$ minimizing $p(x) + x$.*

Theorem 2. *Let $p : [\check{\beta}, \hat{\beta}] \to \mathbb{R}^+$ be a price function and $x^* \in [\check{\beta}, \hat{\beta}]$ the value minimizing $p(x) + x$, then in the SUM-game $\mathrm{PoA} = \mathcal{O}\left(\min\{n, (p(x^*) + x^*)/\check{\beta}\}\right)$.*

Applying the price and weight value ranges, we can deduce a price of anarchy upper bound that is independent of the price function.

Corollary 2. *For every price function $p : [\check{\beta}, \hat{\beta}] \to \mathbb{R}^+$, in the SUM-game it holds $\mathrm{PoA} = \mathcal{O}\left(\min\{1 + p(\check{\beta})/\check{\beta}, (p(\hat{\beta}) + \hat{\beta})/\check{\beta}, n\}\right)$.*

The price of anarchy upper bound is even tight for a broad class of price functions. In particular, for all price functions $x \mapsto p(x)$ that decrease faster than the linear function $x \mapsto -x$ and where both $p(\hat{\beta}) \leq \check{\beta}$ and $p(\check{\beta}) \leq \hat{\beta}$ hold, it is PoA $= \Omega(\min\{1 + p(\check{\beta})/\check{\beta}, (p(\hat{\beta}) + \hat{\beta})/\check{\beta}, n\})$. Yet, the bound cannot be tight for every function as can be seen when considering $p : [1, 1] \to [\alpha, \alpha]$, which constitutes the original game by [8], for which it is known that for most ranges of α the price of anarchy is constant (cf. related work).

Theorem 3. *Let $p : [\check{\beta}, \hat{\beta}] \to \mathbb{R}^+$ be a price function with $p(\hat{\beta}) \leq \check{\beta}$, $p(\check{\beta}) \leq \hat{\beta}$, and $\bar{\beta} = \arg\min_{x \in [\check{\beta}, \hat{\beta}]} p(x) + x$, then PoA $= \Omega\left(\min\{n, (p(x^*) + x^*)/\check{\beta}\}\right)$.*

Concluding the analysis, we apply our results to explicit price functions.

Corollary 3. *For the price function $p : [\check{\beta}, \hat{\beta}] \to \mathbb{R}^+, x \mapsto \alpha/x$ with $\alpha > 0$ the bounds PoS $= \mathcal{O}(1)$ and PoA $= \mathcal{O}\left(\sqrt{\alpha}/\check{\beta}\right)$ hold.*

Corollary 4. *For the price function $p : [1, \alpha - 2\varepsilon] \to \mathbb{R}^+, x \mapsto \alpha - (1 + \varepsilon)x$ with $\alpha > 0, \varepsilon \in (0, 1/n-1)$ the bounds PoS $= \mathcal{O}(1)$ and PoA $= \Theta(\alpha - \varepsilon)$ hold. The optimal solution is given by a star with all edges having weight of 1.*

3   The Max-Game

Lemma 5. *Let $p : [\check{\beta}, \hat{\beta}] \to \mathbb{R}^+$ be a price function, $x^* \in [\check{\beta}, \hat{\beta}]$ the value minimizing $x + p(x)/2$, and S a strategy profile. Then, $c(S) \geq (x^* + p(x^*)/2)n$.*

Theorem 4. *For any price function $p : [\check{\beta}, \hat{\beta}] \to \mathbb{R}^+$, equilibrium graphs exist and the price of stability is constant.*

Lemma 6. *Let $p : [\check{\beta}, \hat{\beta}] \to \mathbb{R}^+$ be a price function with $x^* \in [\check{\beta}, \hat{\beta}]$ minimizing $x + p(x)/2$ and S a MAX-NE strategy profile. Then, $c(S) \leq n\delta_{G[S]}(v) + x^*(n - 1) + 2(p(x^*) + x^*)(n - 1)$, with $\delta_{G[S]}(v)$ the distance costs of an arbitrary $v \in V$.*

Using a similar approach like [7], we derive a bound for the diameter and hence for the social cost of every MAX-NE graph.

Lemma 7. *Let $p : [\check{\beta}, \hat{\beta}] \to \mathbb{R}^+$ be a price function and S a strategy profile forming a MAX-NE. Then, the diameter of $G[S]$ is at most $\mathcal{O}(\sqrt[3]{p(x)^2 xn} + x)$, for $x \in [\check{\beta}, \hat{\beta}]$ arbitrary.*

Theorem 5. *Let $p : [\check{\beta}, \hat{\beta}] \to \mathbb{R}^+$ be a price function. Then, the price of anarchy in the MAX-game is bounded by $\mathcal{O}(1 + \sqrt[3]{n})$.*

4   Conclusion

Our model extension captures the effects of quality of service agreements in autonomous distributed networks and provides theoretical results regarding the stable states of these networks. Interestingly, despite of the considerably increased freedom in the strategic decisions of the nodes (e.g., for a continuous price function the strategy set is unbounded), equilibria always exist. In the SUM-game for a given price function p, we discovered the value that minimizes the term $p(x) + x$ to characterize the worst case loss by selfish behavior. This value can be understood as the optimal trade-off for using one edge for exactly one shortest path and effectively bounds the maximal investment into any edge.

References

[1] Albers, S., Eilts, S., Even-Dar, E., Mansour, Y., Roditty, L.: On nash equilibria for a network creation game. In: Proceedings of the 17th Annual ACM-SIAM Symposium on Discrete Algorithm (SODA). ACM (2006)

[2] Alon, N., Demaine, E.D., Hajiaghayi, M., Leighton, T.: Basic network creation games. In: Proceedings of the 22nd ACM Symposium on Parallelism in Algorithms and Architectures (SPAA). ACM (2010)

[3] Anshelevich, E., Dasgupta, A., Tardos, É., Wexler, T.: Near-optimal network design with selfish agents. In: Proceedings of the 35th Annual ACM Symposium on Theory of Computing (STOC). ACM (2003)

[4] Anshelevich, E., Dasgupta, A., Kleinberg, J., Tardos, É., Wexler, T., Roughgarden, T.: The Price of Stability for Network Design with Fair Cost Allocation. In: Proceedings of the 45th Annual IEEE Symposium on Foundations of Computer Science (FOCS). IEEE (2004)

[5] Cord-Landwehr, A., Hüllmann, M., Kling, P., Setzer, A.: Basic network creation games with communication interests. In: Serna, M. (ed.) SAGT 2012. LNCS, vol. 7615, pp. 72–83. Springer, Heidelberg (2012)

[6] Cord-Landwehr, A., Mäcker, A., Meyer auf der Heide, F.: Quality of Service in Network Creation Games. CoRR (2014), arxiv.org/abs/1409.5366

[7] Demaine, E.D., Hajiaghayi, M., Mahini, H., Zadimoghaddam, M.: The price of anarchy in network creation games. In: Proceedings of the 26th Symposium on Principles of Distributed Computing (PODC). ACM (2007)

[8] Fabrikant, A., Luthra, A., Maneva, E., Papadimitriou, C.H., Shenker, S.: On a network creation game. In: Proceedings of the 22nd Annual Symposium on Principles of Distributed Computing (PODC). ACM (2003)

[9] Halevi, Y., Mansour, Y.: A Network Creation Game with Nonuniform Interests. In: Deng, X., Graham, F.C. (eds.) WINE 2007. LNCS, vol. 4858, pp. 287–292. Springer, Heidelberg (2007)

[10] Koutsoupias, E., Papadimitriou, C.: Worst-case equilibria. In: Meinel, C., Tison, S. (eds.) STACS 1999. LNCS, vol. 1563, pp. 404–413. Springer, Heidelberg (1999)

[11] Lenzner, P.: Greedy selfish network creation. In: Goldberg, P.W. (ed.) WINE 2012. LNCS, vol. 7695, pp. 142–155. Springer, Heidelberg (2012)

[12] Mamageishvili, A., Mihalák, M., Müller, D.: Tree Nash Equilibria in the Network Creation Game. In: Bonato, A., Mitzenmacher, M., Prałat, P. (eds.) WAW 2013. LNCS, vol. 8305, pp. 118–129. Springer, Heidelberg (2013)

[13] Mihalák, M., Schlegel, J.C.: The Price of Anarchy in Network Creation Games is (Mostly) Constant. In: Kontogiannis, S., Koutsoupias, E., Spirakis, P.G. (eds.) SAGT 2010. LNCS, vol. 6386, pp. 276–287. Springer, Heidelberg (2010)

The Sequential Price of Anarchy for Atomic Congestion Games[*]

Jasper de Jong and Marc Uetz

University of Twente, P.O. Box 217, 7500 AE Enschede, The Netherlands
{j.dejong-3,m.uetz}@utwente.nl

Abstract. In situations without central coordination, the price of anarchy relates the quality of any Nash equilibrium to the quality of a global optimum. Instead of assuming that all players choose their actions simultaneously, we consider games where players choose their actions sequentially. The sequential price of anarchy, recently introduced by Paes Leme, Syrgkanis, and Tardos [13], relates the quality of any subgame perfect equilibrium to the quality of a global optimum. The effect of sequential decision making on the quality of equilibria, depends on the specific game under consideration. We analyze the sequential price of anarchy for atomic congestion games with affine cost functions. We derive several lower and upper bounds, showing that sequential decisions mitigate the worst case outcomes known for the classical price of anarchy [2,5]. Next to tight bounds on the sequential price of anarchy, a methodological contribution of our work is, among other things, a "factor revealing" linear programming approach we use to solve the case of three players.

1 Model and Notation

We consider atomic congestion games with affine cost functions. The input of an instance $I \in \mathcal{I}$ consists of a finite set of resources R, a finite set of players $N = \{1, \ldots, n\}$, and for each player $i \in N$ a collection $\mathcal{A}_i$ of possible actions $A_i \subseteq R$. We say a resource $r \in R$ is chosen by player i if $r \in A_i$, where A_i is the action chosen by player i. By $A = (A_i)_{i \in N}$ we denote a possible outcome, that is, a complete profile of actions chosen by all players $i \in N$.

Each resource $r \in R$ has a constant activation cost $d_r \geq 0$ and a variable cost or weight $w_r \geq 0$ that expresses the fact that the resource gets more congested the more players choose it. The total cost of resource $r \in R$, for outcome A, is then $f_r(A) = d_r + w_r \cdot n_r(A)$, where $n_r(A)$ denotes the number of players choosing resource r in A. Given outcome A, the total cost of all resources chosen by player i is $\mathrm{cost}_i(A) = \sum_{r \in A_i} f_r(A)$. Players aim to minimize their costs. The total cost over all players of an outcome A is denoted by $\mathrm{cost}(A) = \sum_{i \in N} \mathrm{cost}_i(A)$.

Note that this class of problems includes as a special case the celebrated network routing games as studied e.g. in [2,15]. Another special case is singleton

---

[*] Research supported by CTIT (www.ctit.nl) and 3TU.AMI (www.3tu.nl), project "Mechanisms for Decentralized Service Systems".

T.-Y. Liu et al. (Eds.): WINE 2014, LNCS 8877, pp. 429–434, 2014.

congestion games, where actions A_i are all singletons, $|A_i| = 1$. This model, and variants thereof, are also known as load balancing games and, with respect to the quality of equilibria, have a vast literature, e.g. [4,11].

Pure Nash equilibria are outcomes $(A_i)_{i \in N}$ in which no player can decrease his costs by unilaterally deviating from choosing A_i. The price of anarchy PoA [9], measures the quality of any Nash equilibrium relative to the quality of a globally optimal allocation, OPT. Here OPT is an outcome minimizing the total costs over all players[1]. Our goal is to compare the quality of Nash equilibria to the quality of subgame perfect equilibria of an extensive form game as introduced in [10,16]. We assume that the players choose their actions in an arbitrary, predefined order $1, 2, \ldots, n$, so that the i-th player must choose his action A_i, observing the actions of players preceding i, but not knowing the actions of the players succeeding him. A strategy S_i then specifies for player i the actions he chooses, one for each potential profile of actions chosen by his predecessors $1, \ldots, i-1$. We denote by S a strategy profile $(S_i)_{i \in N}$. The outcome $A(S) = (A(S)_i)_{i \in N}$ of a game is then the set of actions chosen by each player resulting from a given strategy profile S. We denote by $\text{cost}(S)$ the cost in the outcome $A(S)$.

Extensive form games can be represented in a game tree, with the nodes on one level representing the possible situations that a single player can encounter, and the edges emanating from any node representing the possible actions of that player in the given situation. The nodes of the game tree are also called information sets[2]. Subgame perfect equilibria are defined by Selten [16] as strategy profiles that induce Nash equilibria in any subgame of the game tree. The sequential price of anarchy of an instance I is defined by

$$SPoA(I) = \max_{S \in SPE(I)} \frac{\text{cost}(S)}{\text{cost}(OPT(I))}, \tag{1}$$

where $SPE(I)$ denotes the set of subgame perfect equilibria of instance I in extensive game form, and $OPT(\text{I})$ denotes a social optimum outcome of I. The sequential price of anarchy of a class of instances $\mathcal{I}$ is defined as in [13] by $SPoA(\mathcal{I}) = \sup_{I \in \mathcal{I}} SPoA(I)$. Throughout the paper, when the class of instances is clear from the context, we write PoA and $SPoA$. Also, we use OPT and SPE to denote optimal and subgame perfect equilibrium outcomes respectively.

2   Related Work and Contribution

Recently, the sequential price of anarchy was introduced by Paes Leme et al. [13] as an alternative way to measure the costs of decentralization. Compared to the classical price of anarchy of Papadimitriou and Koutsoupias [9], it avoids

---

[1] Note that we consider a utilitarian global objective, that is, the global objective is to minimize the sum of the costs of all players. This is one of the standard models, yet different than the egalitarian makespan objective as studied, e.g., in [9].

[2] We deal with a game with perfect information, so all information sets are trivial, and subgame perfect equilibria can be computed by backward induction.

the "curse of simultaneity" inherent in certain games [13]. More specifically, for machine cost sharing games, generic unrelated machine scheduling games and generic consensus games, the *SPoA* is smaller than the *PoA* [13]. However, for the latter two games, the 'generic' condition is indeed necessary [3]. Also, Bilò et al. [3] show that for many games myopic behaviour leads to better equilibria than the farsighted behaviour of subgame perfect equilibria. For throughput scheduling games, or more generally, set packing games, the *SPoA* is lower than the *PoA* [6]. For isolation games, however, the *PoA* is not worse than the *SPoA* in general [1]. These results leave a mixed impression, and lead to the natural question which classes of games possess an *SPoA* which is lower than the *PoA*. We address this question for atomic congestion games with affine cost functions. Congestion games were introduced by Rosenthal [14]. A special case is linear atomic congestion games, for which the price of anarchy is known to equal 2 in the case of two players, and 2.5 in the case of three or more players [2,5].

Our contributions are both lower and upper bounds on the sequential price of anarchy for atomic congestion games with affine cost functions. For two and three players, we prove tight bounds of 1.5. and $2\frac{63}{488} \approx 2.13$, respectively. For $n = 4$ players, we derive a lower bound ≈ 2.46, yet we have not been able to derive a nontrivial constant upper bound (yet). In that respect note that, trivially, $SPoA \leq n$. We also consider the special case of singleton congestion games for which the *PoA* is 2.5 [4]. Here we give a parametric family of instances that yields a lower bound of $2 + 1/e \approx 2.37$, and we give an upper bound of $n - 1$. We substantially improve on these results for symmetric singleton congestion games, where we show that the *SPoA* equals 4/3, which matches the bound known for the *PoA* [8]. For each of the theorems in this paper we only give an outline of the proof. For full proofs and lower bound examples, we refer to our full paper[7].

3   General Linear Atomic Congestion Games

Theorem 1. *SPoA* $= 1.5$ *for atomic congestion games with two players and affine cost functions.*

We prove the theorem by considering only the relevant part of the game tree. For player 1, we only need to consider two actions; the action he chooses in a social optimum, and the action he chooses in a subgame perfect equilibrium. For player 2 we only need to consider 3 actions; the action he chooses in a social optimum, and his subgame perfect responses to both of player 1's actions. Therefore we only need to consider 6 outcomes. The general situation is shown in Figure 1. We lower bound the total cost in the subgame perfect equilibrium in terms of the total cost in the social optimum. The tight lower bound example uses only 2 actions per player and 3 resources in total.

Considering the simplicity of the lower bound example for 2 players, one might wonder whether it is possible to prove upper bounds in a more elegant fashion, for instance using smoothness or potential arguments. But, contrary to what one might expect, not every outcome of a subgame perfect equilibrium

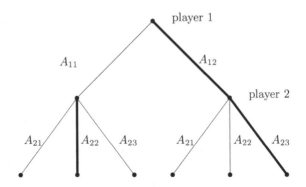

Fig. 1. All relevant actions in the game tree for 2 players. Fat lines correspond to subgame perfect actions.

is a Nash equilibrium of the corresponding strategic form game.[3] In fact, we have constructed examples where it is subgame perfect for a player to choose an action that is strictly dominated in the corresponding strategic game. Therefore it is not easy to derive useful properties of *SPE* outcomes. Instead, for 3 players we use a linear programming (LP) approach.

Theorem 2. *SPoA* $= 2\frac{63}{488} \approx 2.13$ *for atomic congestion games with three players and affine cost functions.*

We first use simple combinatorial arguments to argue that a worst case instance is moderate in size. Specifically, we show that for any instance I, we can construct an instance I' with the same *SPoA* using only 2,3 and 7 actions for players 1,2 and 3 respectively. Moreover, I' has at most 4096 resources, one for every subset of all actions. Intuitively, the LP works as follows: It maximizes the *SPoA* over all instances with the properties described above. The only decision variables are the weights and constant costs of each of the 4096 resources. This completely determines the costs in all outcomes. We prespecify all subgame perfect actions in the game tree and normalize the costs in the social optimum to 1. Our only set of constraints enforces that in each node of the game tree, each subgame perfect action has a lower cost than any other action. Our objective is simply to maximize the total cost in the *SPE* outcome.

We have implemented this using the AIMMS modeling framework, and using CPLEX 12.5 we obtain an optimal solution with value $2\frac{63}{488}$. Given the techniques used so far, problems with $n > 3$ players become increasingly difficult. Extending the LP straightforwardly to the case with 4 players is problematic; using the same reasoning as in the thee player case, we would need to consider 43 actions for

---

[3] Note that both games have different strategy spaces: In the strategic form game both players have as strategy space their feasible actions, $\mathcal{A}_i$. In the extensive form game, however, the strategy space for the second player is more complex, as it specifies an action $A_2 \in \mathcal{A}_2$ for all information sets (= possible actions of player 1).

congestion game	# players	PoA	SPoA
general	$n = 2$	2[5,2]	1.5
general	$n = 3$	2.5[5,2]	$2\frac{63}{488}$
general	$n = 4$	2.5[5,2]	> 2.46
singleton	$n \geq 3$	2.5[4]	$\leq n - 1$
singleton	$n \to \infty$	2.5[4]	$\geq 2\frac{1}{e}$
singleton & symmetric	$n \geq 2$	4/3 [8]	4/3

Fig. 2. Results for the *SPoA* in comparison to the *PoA*

player 4, and 2^{55} resources. However, using ILP techniques, we have been able to construct lower bound examples for more than 3 players.

Theorem 3. *SPoA* ≥ 2.46 *for atomic congestion games with four players and affine cost functions.*

4 Singleton Linear Atomic Congestion Games

Next, we present results for the special case of singleton congestion games.

Theorem 4. *Asymptotically for* $n \to \infty$, *SPoA* $\geq 2 + \frac{1}{e} \approx 2.37$ *for singleton atomic congestion games with linear cost functions.*

The proof is by a parametric set of lower bound instances.

Theorem 5. *For singleton atomic congestion games with affine cost functions,* *SPoA* $\leq n - 1$.

The proof is by contradiction. Suppose the theorem does not hold, then for some instance I, *SPoA*$(I) > n - 1$. Therefore there exists at least one player i for whom $\text{cost}_i(SPE) \geq (n - 1)\,\text{cost}_i(OPT)$. With this, we can construct a contradiction. However, note that this bound is close to the trivial upper bound n that holds for general congestion games.

Theorem 6. *For symmetric singleton atomic congestion games with affine cost functions,* *SPoA* $= 4/3$.

To prove the theorem, we first prove that any *SPE* outcome of a sequential game is also an *NE* outcome of the corresponding strategic game. Note that this is not trivial or even true in a more general setting as mentioned in Section 2. Also note that the theorem is not implied by results in [12]; for the non-generic case, Milchtaich proves only the existence of an *SPE* outcome that is an *NE* outcome. Intuitively our proof is as follows: we show that for any player i for whom there exists a resource r' in an *SPE* outcome that is less costly than the resource r he chose, we can find a successor j for whom there exists a less costly resource in the *SPE* outcome in the subgame where player i chooses r'. With this, we construct a contradiction. The theorem follows from the fact that $PoA = 4/3$, as shown in [8], and a matching lower bound example. Figure 2 gives an overview.

Acknowledgements. Thanks to Sebastian Stiller and Christoph Hansknecht for helpful discussions. Special thanks to our summer intern Yuzixuan Zhu from USTC for careful proofreading, and for carrying out the experiments that lead to the 2.46 lower bound for the case of four players.

References

1. Angelucci, A., Bilò, V., Flammini, M., Moscardelli, L.: On the Sequential Price of Anarchy of Isolation Games. In: Du, D.-Z., Zhang, G. (eds.) COCOON 2013. LNCS, vol. 7936, pp. 17–28. Springer, Heidelberg (2013)
2. Awerbuch, B., Azar, Y., Epstein, A.: The Price of Routing Unsplittable Flow. In: Proceedings 37th STOC, pp. 57–66 (2005)
3. Bilò, V., Flammini, M., Monaco, G., Moscardelli, L.: Some Anomalies of Farsighted Strategic Behavior. In: Erlebach, T., Persiano, G. (eds.) WAOA 2012. LNCS, vol. 7846, pp. 229–241. Springer, Heidelberg (2013)
4. Caragiannis, I., Flammini, M., Kaklamanis, C., Kanellopoulos, P., Moscardelli, L.: Tight Bounds for Selfish and Greedy Load Balancing. In: Bugliesi, M., Preneel, B., Sassone, V., Wegener, I. (eds.) ICALP 2006, Part I. LNCS, vol. 4051, pp. 311–322. Springer, Heidelberg (2006)
5. Christodoulou, G., Koutsoupias, E.: The Price of Anarchy of Finite Congestion Games. In: Proceedings 37th STOC, pp. 67–73 (2005)
6. de Jong, J., Uetz, M., Wombacher, A.: Decentralized Throughput Scheduling. In: Spirakis, P.G., Serna, M. (eds.) CIAC 2013. LNCS, vol. 7878, pp. 134–145. Springer, Heidelberg (2013)
7. de Jong, J., Uetz, M.: The sequential price of anarchy for atomic congestion games, TR-CTIT-14-09, CTIT, University of Twente (2014)
8. Fotakis, D.: Stackelberg Strategies for Atomic Congestion Games. Theory of Computing Systems 47, 218–249 (2010)
9. Koutsoupias, E., Papadimitriou, C.: Worst-case equilibria. In: Meinel, C., Tison, S. (eds.) STACS 1999. LNCS, vol. 1563, pp. 404–413. Springer, Heidelberg (1999)
10. Kuhn, H.W.: Extensive Games and the Problem of Information, Contribution to the Theory of Games. Annals of Math. Studies, vol. II, 28, pp. 193–216 (1953)
11. Lücking, T., Mavronicolas, M., Monien, B., Rode, M.: A New Model for Selfish Routing. In: Diekert, V., Habib, M. (eds.) STACS 2004. LNCS, vol. 2996, pp. 547–558. Springer, Heidelberg (2004)
12. Milchtaich, I.: Crowding games are sequentially solvable. International Journal of Game Theory 27, 501–509 (1998)
13. Paes Leme, R., Syrgkanis, V., Tardos, É.: The Curse of Simultaneity. In: Proceedings 3rd ITCS, pp. 60–67. ACM (2012)
14. Rosenthal, R.W.: A class of games possessing pure-strategy Nash equilibria. International Journal of Game Theory 2, 65–67 (1973)
15. Roughgarden, T.: Selfish routing with atomic players. In: Proceedings 16th SODA, pp. 1184–1185 (2005)
16. Selten, R.: A simple model of imperfect competition, where 4 are few and 6 are many. International Journal of Game Theory 2, 141–201 (1973)

Multilevel Network Games*

Sebastian Abshoff, Andreas Cord-Landwehr,
Daniel Jung, and Alexander Skopalik

Heinz Nixdorf Institute & Computer Science Department
University of Paderborn, Germany
Fürstenallee 11, 33102 Paderborn

Abstract We consider a multilevel network game, where nodes can improve their communication costs by connecting to a high-speed network. The n nodes are connected by a static network and each node can decide individually to become a gateway to the high-speed network. The goal of a node v is to minimize its private costs, i.e., the sum (SUM-game) or maximum (MAX-game) of communication distances from v to all other nodes plus a fixed price $\alpha > 0$ if it decides to be a gateway. Between gateways the communication distance is 0, and gateways also improve other nodes' distances by behaving as shortcuts. For the SUM-game, we show that for $\alpha \leq n - 1$, the price of anarchy is $\Theta\left(n/\sqrt{\alpha}\right)$ and in this range equilibria always exist. In range $\alpha \in (n-1, n(n-1))$ the price of anarchy is $\Theta\left(\sqrt{\alpha}\right)$, and for $\alpha \geq n(n-1)$ it is constant. For the MAX-game, we show that the price of anarchy is either $\Theta\left(1 + n/\sqrt{\alpha}\right)$, for $\alpha \geq 1$, or else 1. Given a graph with girth of at least 4α, equilibria always exist. Concerning the dynamics, both games are not potential games. For the SUM-game, we even show that it is not weakly acyclic.

1 Introduction

Today's networks, like the Internet, do not consist of one but a mixture of several interconnected networks. Every network has individual qualities and hence the total performance of the network becomes a mixture of these individual properties. Typically, one can categorize those different networks into high-speed backbone networks and low-speed general purpose networks. Given the fact that nodes in Internet-like networks establish their connections in an uncoordinated and selfish way, it becomes a challenging question to understand the evolution and outcome of those networks.

We model and analyze the interaction of two networks: a low speed general purpose network and a high-speed backbone network. Every node can decide individually if it wants to connect to the high-speed network for a fixed price α in order to minimize its private costs, i.e., the costs of connecting to the

---

* This work was partially supported by the German Research Foundation (DFG) within the Collaborative Research Center "On-The-Fly Computing" (SFB 901), by the EU within FET project MULTIPLEX under contract no. 317532, and the International Graduate School "Dynamic Intelligent Systems".

T.-Y. Liu et al. (Eds.): WINE 2014, LNCS 8877, pp. 435–440, 2014.

high-speed network plus the costs for communicating with other nodes. The communication costs of a node are given by the sum or maximum distance to all other nodes in the network, possibly improved by shortcuts through the high-speed network. Having two nodes that are both connected to the high-speed network, they provide a shortcut of a fixed (very small) edge length. In our model, we assume the shortcut edge length to be less than 1 divided by the number of nodes and normalize it to be 0.

For the omitted proofs please refer to the full version of this paper [1].

Model and Notations. We consider a set V of n nodes forming an undirected connected graph $G := (V, E)$. Each node of this graph can connect to a high-speed network by paying a fixed price $\alpha > 0$. A node connected to the high-speed network is called a *gateway* and we assume communication distances between each pair of gateway nodes to be 0. The shortest path distance between two nodes u, v in G is given by $d(u, v)$, whereas we consider $d(u, v)$ to be the hop distance. Having a set of gateways S, we define the communication distance $\delta(u, v) := \min\{d(u, v), d(u, S) + d(S, v)\}$. Each node $v \in V$ aims to minimize its private costs by selfishly deciding whether to connect to the high-speed network. We identify the set of gateways S with the current strategy profile, i.e., nodes in S are gateways and nodes in $V \setminus S$ are non-gateways.

The private costs of a node in the *SUM-game* are $c_v(S) := |S \cap \{v\}|\alpha + \sum_{u \in V} \delta(v, u)$. For the *MAX-game*, the private cost function is $c_v(S) := |S \cap \{v\}|\alpha + \max_{u \in V} \delta(v, u)$. For both games, the social costs are $c(S) := \sum_{v \in V} c_v(S)$.

If a node improves its private costs by changing its strategy from non-gateway to gateway or vice versa, we call this an *improving response* (IR). For an IR where a node v changes its strategy to be a gateway, we say that v *opens*. Analogously, we say v *closes* if it changes its strategy from gateway to non-gateway. We call a strategy profile S a (pure) Nash equilibrium (NE) if no node can perform an IR. We require that there is always at least one gateway in the graph, i.e., the last gateway is not allowed to close even if that strategy change is an IR.

Our Questions. A main objective of the research on network games is the analysis of the *price of anarchy*. The price of anarchy (PoA), introduced in [7], measures the quality of equilibria by computing the ratio of the biggest social costs of any Nash equilibrium and the optimal social costs. We further question if our games provide the *finite improvement property* or (lesser) whether they are *weakly acyclic*. A game with the finite improvement property (FIPG) guarantees that, when starting from any initial state, *every* sequence of IRs eventually converges to a NE state, i.e., every sequence of IRs is finite. Monderer and Shapley [11] showed that a game is a FIPG if and only if there exists a generalized ordinal potential function $\Phi : V \to \mathbb{R}$ that maps strategy profiles to real numbers such that if a node performs an IR the potential value decreases. A game is called *weakly acyclic* (WAG) [12] if, starting from any initial strategy profile, there exists *some* finite sequence of IRs that eventually converges to a NE state.

Related Work. Network creation games (NCG) are an established model to study the evolution and quality of networks established by selfishly acting nodes.

In these games, nodes can decide individually which edges they want to buy (each for a fixed price $\alpha > 0$) in order to minimize their private costs. For a node, the private costs are either the sum (SUM-game, Fabrikant et al. [5]) or maximum (MAX-game, Demaine et al. [4]) of the distances to all other nodes in the network plus the costs of the bought edges.

The task of describing the maximal possible loss by selfish behavior was formalized as the *price of anarchy* and first discussed by Fabrikant et al. [5] for the SUM-game. The authors proved an upper bound of $\mathcal{O}(\sqrt{\alpha})$ on the price of anarchy (PoA) in the case of $\alpha < n^2$, and a constant PoA otherwise. Later, Albers et al. [2] proved a constant PoA for $\alpha = \mathcal{O}(\sqrt{n})$ and the first sublinear worst case bound of $\mathcal{O}(n^{1/3})$ for general α. Demaine et al. [4] were the first to prove an $\mathcal{O}(n^\varepsilon)$ bound for α in the range of $\Omega(n)$ and $o(n \lg n)$. Recently, by Mihalák and Schlegel [10] and improved by [9], it was shown that for $\alpha \geq 65n$ all equilibria are trees (and thus the PoA is constant).

For the MAX-game, Demaine et al. [4] showed that the PoA is at most 2 for $\alpha \geq n$, $\mathcal{O}\left(\min\{4^{\sqrt{\lg n}}, (n/\alpha)^{1/3}\}\right)$ for $2\sqrt{\lg n} \leq \alpha \leq n$, and $\mathcal{O}(n^{2/\alpha})$ for $\alpha < 2\sqrt{\lg n}$. For $\alpha > 129$, Mihalák and Schlegel [10] showed, like in the average distance version, that all equilibria are trees and the PoA is constant.

In several subsequent papers, different approaches were done to simplify the games and also to enable nodes to compute their best responses in polynomial time (which is not possible in the original games). Alon et al. [3] introduced the *basic network creation game*, where the operation of a node only consists of swapping some of its incident edges, i.e., redirecting them to other nodes. Restricting the initial network to trees, the only equilibrium in the SUM-game is a star graph. Without restrictions, all (swap) equilibria are proven to have a diameter of $2^{\mathcal{O}(\sqrt{\log n})}$, which is also the PoA. For the MAX-version, the authors provide an equilibrium network with diameter $\Theta(\sqrt{n})$.

In [8], Lenzner introduced a different approach by taking the original NCGs from [5], but restricting the operation of a node to single edge changes. This model allows for polynomial time computable best responses, but at the same time its equilibria give a 3-approximation to the equilibria of the original game.

For a variety of these games, Kawald and Lenzner [6] studied the convergence. For all researched games, with the only exception of basic network creation games on initial tree networks, they provided negative convergence results.

Our Results. We introduce a new network game that focuses on dynamics in multilevel networks. In particular, we study how nodes of a general purpose network interact with a high-speed network when deciding selfishly whether to connect to the high-speed network. For both the SUM- and the MAX-game it is NP-hard to find an optimal placement of gateways (Theorem 1 and 5).

For the SUM-game, we show that for $\alpha \leq n - 1$ and $\alpha > n(n - 1)$ equilibria always exist and that the PoA is $\Theta(1 + n/\sqrt{\alpha})$ (Theorem 4). For the range $\alpha \in (n - 1, n(n - 1))$ we upper bound the PoA by $\mathcal{O}(\sqrt{\alpha})$. Concerning the dynamics, the SUM-game is no FIPG for wide ranges of parameter values α (Theorem 2). And we further show that it is not even a WAG (3).

For the MAX-game, equilibria always exist if the girth is at least 4α (which is always true for trees). Like in the SUM-game, the PoA is $\Theta\left(1 + n/\sqrt{\alpha}\right)$ for $\alpha \geq 1$ (Theorem 7), and otherwise 1. The MAX-game is also not a FIPG (Theorem 6).

2   The SUM-Game

Theorem 1. *Given a graph $G = (V, E)$ it is NP-hard to compute an optimal set of gateways $S \subseteq V$ that minimizes the social costs in the SUM-game.*

Sketch. For $n, m > 4$, let $X := \{x_1, \ldots, x_m\}$ be elements and $S_1, \ldots, S_n \subseteq X$ sets that form an instance of the NP-complete Set-Cover problem. Given the Set-Cover instance, we construct an instance of the SUM-game as follows: First, we create a clique C of k nodes and mark one of its nodes as c. For every set S_i, we create a corresponding node S_i and connect each set node to c. For every element $x_i \in X$, we create w-many nodes $x_i^1, \ldots, x_i^w$ and connect all $x_i^j, i = 1, \ldots, m, j = 1, \ldots, w$ to the set nodes S_l with $x_i \in S_l$. The parameters are $w := n$, $k := m - 1$, and $\alpha := 4n(m - 1)$.

We can now show the NP-hardness by proving that the socially optimal SUM-game solution is given by a gateway node c and a minimal number of set node gateways such that all element nodes are covered.

Proposition 1. *Given a network $G = (V, E)$ and $\alpha \leq n - 1$ or $\alpha > n \cdot \mathrm{diam}(G)$, then a Nash equilibrium always exists.*

Lemma 1. *Given a network $G = (V, E)$, $n := |V|$, and $\alpha \leq n - 1$, then $S = V$ minimizes the social costs in the SUM-game.*

2.1   Convergence Properties

Proposition 2. *Let $G = (V, E)$ be a graph and $S \subseteq V$ an initial set of gateways, then for $\alpha < 1$ or $\alpha > n \cdot \mathrm{diam}(G)$ the SUM-game is a FIPG.*

Proposition 3. *Let $G = (V, E)$ be a graph and S an initial set of gateways with $|S| = 1$. If $\mathrm{diam}(G) > 2\alpha + 1$ and $4 \leq \alpha \leq n - 1$, then in the SUM-game there exists a sequence of IRs such that the game converges to a NE.*

Theorem 2. *Given $n \in \mathbb{N}$ with either $n > 16$ and $\alpha \in (\frac{3}{32}n^2 + n, \frac{5}{32}n^2)$, or $n > 7$ and $\alpha \in (4, n - 1)$, the SUM-game is not a FIPG.*

Theorem 3. *The SUM-game is not a weakly acyclic game in general.*

Proof. We consider $\alpha := 7$ and a graph that consists of three nodes u, v, and w, which are connected as a line, a clique X of $\lceil \alpha/2 \rceil$ nodes, a clique Y of $\lfloor \alpha/2 \rfloor$ nodes, and a center node c. All nodes of X are connected to c and to u, all nodes of Y are connected to c and to w, and, additionally, c is connected to v. Now, for the initial strategy profile $S = \{w\}$, there exists a unique sequence of improving responses, such that u and v change their strategy in turn. $\square$

Theorem 4. *In the SUM-game, for $0 < \alpha < 1$, and $n(n - 1) \leq \alpha$, the PoA is 1, for $\alpha \in [1, n - 1]$, it is $\Theta\left(n/\sqrt{\alpha}\right)$, and for $\alpha \in (n - 1, n(n - 1))$ it is $\mathcal{O}\left(\sqrt{\alpha}\right)$.*

3 The MAX-Game

Theorem 5. *Given a graph $G = (V, E)$, it is NP-hard to compute an optimal set of gateways $S \subseteq V$ that minimizes the social costs for the MAX-game.*

For $\alpha < 1$, the MAX-game is a FIPG with the only equilibrium of all nodes being gateways. Similar for $\alpha > \mathrm{diam}(G)$, for a gateway, it is always an IR to close and a non-gateway will never open. Hence, in both cases equilibria exist.

Lemma 2. *For each graph $G = (V, E)$ with $\mathrm{girth}(G) \geq 4\alpha$, for $\alpha \in [1, \mathrm{diam}(G))$ a MAX-game NE exists.*

Proof. Let x_1, x_2 be two maximal distant nodes in G. If $d(x_1, x_2) < 2\alpha$, we get with $\mathrm{girth}(G) \geq 4\alpha$ that G is a tree and there exists a node v that has maximal distance of less than α to every node. In this case, opening v gives a NE.

Otherwise, define $R := \lfloor \min\{\alpha - 1, (d(x_1, x_2) - \alpha)/2\} \rfloor$. Since x_1 and x_2 are at maximal distance, none of them can be connected to a leaf node. For both of these nodes, we do the following: We consider the breadth-first-search trees T up to level R, rooted in x_1 and x_2, respectively. From the nodes at level R, we open a maximal set such that no two gateways are at distance less than R.

We now claim that for every node x in such a tree, there exists a gateway in distance of at most R. For this, consider a shortest path to a node u at level R. If u is not a gateway, there must be another node u' also at level R that is a gateway. Since the girth is at least 4α and $R < \alpha < \mathrm{diam}(G)$, the shortest path from u to u' can only consist of nodes of the tree and hence $d(x, u') < R$.

Next, iteratively open a maximal set of further nodes such that each new node has minimal distance of exactly $\lceil \alpha \rceil$ to a gateway. By construction, since every non-gateway has maximal distance of $\lfloor \alpha \rfloor$ to a gateway, a non-gateway can improve its maximal distance by at most $\lfloor \alpha \rfloor$ and hence cannot perform any IR. For every gateway v, it holds that its private costs are $c(v) = \alpha + R$ (with both x_1 and x_2 at maximal distance, since otherwise we get a contradiction to the maximal distance of x_1 and x_2.) Considering the private cost change of closing v, its maximal distance increases by exactly $\lceil \alpha \rceil$ and hence is not an IR.   □

Theorem 6. *For $\alpha > 1$, in general the MAX-game is not a FIPG.*

Theorem 7. *In the MAX-game for $\alpha \geq 1$, the PoA is $\Theta(1 + n/\sqrt{\alpha})$.*

4 Conclusion and Future Work

The PoA results emphasize that for very small or big α (i.e., when tending to the number of nodes), equilibria are nearly optimal solutions despite of the selfish behavior of the nodes. In comparison to NCGs, the existence of equilibria is much harder to show. Here, the challenge is to combine the drastically reduced strategy space with the global influences of single strategy changes. For the SUM-game, with $\alpha \in (n - 1, n(n - 1))$, and the MAX-game, with graphs of girth less than 4α, computing NEs seems to be an interesting problem.

Regarding the convergence, both games do not provide the finite improvement property and remarkably, the SUM-game is not even weakly acyclic. For the MAX-game, due to the symmetry of the maximum, the equilibria and convergence properties seem to be more stable than for the sum.

References

[1] Abshoff, S., Cord-Landwehr, A., Jung, D., Skopalik, A.: Multilevel Network Games. CoRR (2014), arxiv.org/abs/1409.5383
[2] Albers, S., Eilts, S., Even-Dar, E., Mansour, Y., Roditty, L.: On nash equilibria for a network creation game. In: Proceedings of the 17th Annual ACM-SIAM Symposium on Discrete Algorithms (SODA). ACM (2006)
[3] Alon, N., Demaine, E.D., Hajiaghayi, M., Leighton, T.: Basic network creation games. In: Proceedings of the 22nd ACM Symposium on Parallelism in Algorithms and Architectures (SPAA). ACM (2010)
[4] Demaine, E.D., Hajiaghayi, M., Mahini, H., Zadimoghaddam, M.: The price of anarchy in network creation games. In: Proceedings of the 26th Annual ACM Symposium on Principles of Distributed Computing (PODC). ACM (2007)
[5] Fabrikant, A., Luthra, A., Maneva, E., Papadimitriou, C.H., Shenker, S.: On a network creation game. In: Proceedings of the 22nd Annual Symposium on Principles of Distributed Computing (PODC). ACM (2003)
[6] Kawald, B., Lenzner, P.: On Dynamics in Selfish Network Creation. In: Proceedings of the 25th Annual ACM Symposium on Parallelism in Algorithms and Architectures (SPAA). ACM (2013)
[7] Koutsoupias, E., Papadimitriou, C.: Worst-case equilibria. In: Meinel, C., Tison, S. (eds.) STACS 1999. LNCS, vol. 1563, pp. 404–413. Springer, Heidelberg (1999)
[8] Lenzner, P.: Greedy Selfish Network Creation. In: Goldberg, P.W. (ed.) WINE 2012. LNCS, vol. 7695, pp. 142–155. Springer, Heidelberg (2012)
[9] Mamageishvili, A., Mihalák, M., Müller, D.: Tree Nash Equilibria in the Network Creation Game. In: Bonato, A., Mitzenmacher, M., Prałat, P. (eds.) WAW 2013. LNCS, vol. 8305, pp. 118–129. Springer, Heidelberg (2013)
[10] Mihalák, M., Schlegel, J.C.: The Price of Anarchy in Network Creation Games is (Mostly) Constant. In: Kontogiannis, S., Koutsoupias, E., Spirakis, P.G. (eds.) SAGT 2010. LNCS, vol. 6386, pp. 276–287. Springer, Heidelberg (2010)
[11] Monderer, D., Shapley, L.S.: Potential Games. Games and Economic Behavior 14(1) (1996)
[12] Young, H.P.: The evolution of conventions. Econometrica: Journal of the Econometric Society (1993)

Coordination Games on Graphs
(Extended Abstract)

Krzysztof R. Apt[1,2], Mona Rahn[1], Guido Schäfer[1,3], and Sunil Simon[4]

[1] Centre for Mathematics and Computer Science (CWI),
Amsterdam, The Netherlands
[2] ILLC, University of Amsterdam, The Netherlands
[3] VU University Amsterdam, The Netherlands
[4] IIT Kanpur, Kanpur, India

Abstract. We introduce natural strategic games on graphs, which capture the idea of coordination in a local setting. We show that these games have an exact potential and have strong equilibria when the graph is a pseudoforest. We also exhibit some other classes of graphs for which a strong equilibrium exists. However, in general strong equilibria do not need to exist. Further, we study the (strong) price of stability and anarchy. Finally, we consider the problems of computing strong equilibria and of determining whether a joint strategy is a strong equilibrium.

1 Introduction

Motivation. In game theory coordination games are used to model situations in which players are rewarded for agreeing on a common strategy, e.g., by deciding on a common technological or societal standard. In this paper we propose and study a very simple and natural class of coordination games, which we call *coordination games on graphs*: We are given an undirected graph the nodes of which correspond to the players of the game. Each player chooses a colour from a set of colours available to her. The payoff of a player is the number of neighbours who choose the same colour.

This model captures situations in which players have to choose between multiple competing providers offering the same service (or product), such as peer-to-peer networks, social networks, photo sharing platforms, mobile phone providers, etc. In these applications the benefit of a player subscribing to a specific provider increases as certain other players (e.g., friends, relatives, etc.) opt for the same provider. As a consequence, players have an interest to coordinate their choices in order to maximize their benefit.

Our Contributions. The focus of our investigations is on coalitional equilibria in coordination games on graphs. Recall that in a *strong equilibrium* (*k-equilibrium*) no coalition of players (of size at most k) can deviate so that every player of the coalition strictly improves her payoff. Our main contributions are as follows:

1. *Existence.* We show that k-equilibria for $k \geq 5$ do not exist in general. Further, we identify several graph structural properties that guarantee the

T.-Y. Liu et al. (Eds.): WINE 2014, LNCS 8877, pp. 441–446, 2014.

existence of strong equilibria and also ensure that every sequence of profitable joint deviations terminates. Further, we show that 2-equilibria (and hence Nash equilibria) always exist.

2. *Inefficiency.* We derive almost matching lower and upper bounds of $2\frac{n-1}{k-1} - 1$ and $2\frac{n-1}{k-1}$, respectively, on the k-price of anarchy. Further, the strong price of anarchy is exactly 2. We also provide conditions on the graph guaranteeing that the strong price of stability is 1.

3. *Computability.* We prove that the problem of deciding whether a given joint strategy is a k-equilibrium is co-NP-complete. On the positive side, for certain graph classes the decision problem is in P and we can efficiently compute a strong equilibrium.

Related Work. Given their simplicity, it is not surprising that coordination games on graphs are related to various well-studied types of games. Due to lack of space, we only mention the most relevant references below.

First, they are similar to *additively separable hedonic games* [6,4]. Here players are nodes on a weighted graph and form coalitions. The payoff of a node is the total weight of all incident edges to neighbours in the same coalition. These games were originally introduced in a cooperative setting but have more recently also been investigated in a strategic setting, with a particular focus on computational issues (e.g., [8]); for a survey see [7]. Aziz and Brandl [3] study the existence of strong equilibria in these games. Despite the similarity between these games and our coordination games, in the former every player can choose to enter every possible coalition and hence they do not generalize the games we study here.

Next, coordination games on graphs are *polymatrix games* (see [10]). Recall that this is a finite strategic game in which the payoff for each player is the sum of the payoffs obtained from the individual 2-player games she plays with each other player separately. Hoefer [9] studied clustering games that are also polymatrix games based on graphs. However, in his setup each player has the same set of strategies, so the resulting games are not comparable to ours.

When the graph is complete, coordination games on graphs are special cases of congestion games with monotone increasing utility functions. Rozenfeld and Tennenholtz [12] give a characterization of the existence of strong equilibria for these games. Bilò et al. [5] study congestion games in which the players form a (possibly directed) influence graph, focusing on the existence of Nash equilibria. However, because the latency functions are assumed to be increasing in the number of players, these games do not cover the games we study here.

As for the solution concepts, strong equilibria were introduced in [2]; the strong price of anarchy was defined in [1]; and finally, exact potentials were introduced in [11].

2   Coordination Games on Graphs

We next introduce some standard notion and define our coordination games on graphs.

A *strategic game* $\mathcal{G} := (N, (S_i)_{i \in N}, (p_i)_{i \in N})$ consists of a set $N := \{1, \ldots, n\}$ of $n > 1$ players and a non-empty set S_i of *strategies* and a *payoff function* $p_i : S_1 \times \cdots \times S_n \to \mathbb{R}$ for each player $i \in N$. We denote $S_1 \times \cdots \times S_n$ by S and call each element $s \in S$ a *joint strategy*.

We call a non-empty subset $K := \{k_1, \ldots, k_m\}$ of N a *coalition*. Given a joint strategy s we abbreviate the sequence $(s_{k_1}, \ldots, s_{k_m})$ of strategies to s_K; we also write (s_K, s_{-K}) instead of s. Given two joint strategies s and s' and a coalition K, we say that the players in K can profitably deviate from s to s' if $s' = (s'_K, s_{-K})$ and $p_i(s') > p_i(s)$ for every player $i \in K$. A joint strategy s a *k-equilibrium* ($1 \le k \le n$) if no coalition of at most k players that can profitably deviate from s. Using this definition, a *Nash equilibrium* is a 1-equilibrium and a *strong equilibrium* is an n-equilibrium.

Given a joint strategy s, its *social welfare* is defined as $SW(s) = \sum_{i \in N} p_i(s)$. When the social welfare of s is maximal we call s a *social optimum*. Given a finite game that has a k-equilibrium its *k-price of anarchy (resp. stability)* is the ratio $SW(s)/SW(s')$, where s is a social optimum and s' is a k-equilibrium with the lowest (resp. highest) social welfare. In the case of division by zero, we interpret the outcomes as ∞. The *(strong) price of anarchy* refers to the k-price of anarchy with $k = 1$ (resp. $k = n$). The *(strong) price of stability* is defined analogously.

A *coalitional improvement path*, in short a *c-improvement path*, is a maximal sequence $(s^1, s^2, \ldots)$ of joint strategies such that for every $k > 1$ there is a coalition K such that s^k is a profitable deviation of the players in K from s^{k-1}. Clearly, if a c-improvement path is finite, its last element is a strong equilibrium. We say that $\mathcal{G}$ has the *finite c-improvement property* (*c-FIP*) if every c-improvement path is finite.

Our *coordination games on graphs* are defined as follows: We are given a finite set of *colours* M, an undirected graph $G = (V, E)$ without self-loops, and a *colour assignment* A. The latter is a function that assigns to each node $i \in V$ a non-empty set of colours $A_i \subseteq M$. Let N_i denote the set of all *neighbours* of node i, i.e., $N_i = \{j \in V \mid \{i, j\} \in E\}$. We define a strategic game $\mathcal{G}(G, A)$ as follows:

- the players are identified with the nodes, i.e., $N = V$,
- the set of strategies of player i is the set of colours $A_i \subseteq M$,
- the payoff function of player i is $p_i(s) = |\{j \in N_i \mid s_i = s_j\}|$.

So each node simultaneously chooses a colour and the payoff to the node is the number of neighbours who chose the same colour. Subsequently, we refer to these games simply as *coordination games*.

3   Existence

We identify several graph structural properties that guarantee the existence of strong equilibria in coordinate games. Most of our existence results are based on the following key lemma.

Given a set of nodes K, we denote by $G[K]$ the subgraph of G induced by K and by $E[K]$ the set of edges in E that have both endpoints in K. Recall that an edge set $F \subseteq E[K]$ is a **feedback edge set** of $G[K]$ if the graph $(K, E[K] \setminus F)$ is acyclic. Given a joint strategy s we denote by E_s^+ the set of edges $\{i, j\} \in E$ such that $s_i = s_j$.

Lemma 1 (Key lemma). *Suppose a coalition K can profitably deviate from s to s'. Let F be a feedback edge set of $G[K]$. Then*

$$SW(s') - SW(s) > 2|F \cap E_s^+| - 2|F \cap E_{s'}^+|.$$

Using this key lemma, we can derive several existence results.

Theorem 1. *Every c-improvement path in which deviations of coalitions of size at most 2 are allowed is finite. In particular, 2-equilibria (and thus Nash equilibria) always exist.*

Theorem 2. *Every coordination game with at most 2 colours has the c-FIP.*

For a colour $x \in M$ let $V_x = \{i \in V \mid x \in A_i\}$ be the set of nodes that can choose x. We call G a **colour forest** (with respect to A) if $G[V_x]$ is a forest for all $x \in M$.

Theorem 3. *Every coordination game on a colour forest has the c-FIP.*

Recall that a **pseudoforest** is a graph in which every connected component contains at most one cycle.

Theorem 4. *Every coordination game on a pseudoforest has the c-FIP.*

Theorem 5. *Let G be such that cycles are pairwise edge-disjoint. Let k be the minimum length of a cycle in G. Then every coalitional improvement path of coalitions of size at most k is finite. Hence a k-equilibrium exists.*

We also establish the c-FIP property for some additional classes of coordination games. We call a coordination game on a graph G **uniform** if for every joint strategy s and for every edge $\{i, j\} \in E$ it holds: if $s_i = s_j$ then $p_i(s) = p_j(s)$.

Theorem 6. *Every uniform coordination game has the c-FIP.*

A class of coordination games that we can capture by Theorem 6 is as follows. We say that G is **colour complete** (with respect to A) if each component of $G[V_x]$ is complete for every $x \in M$. In particular, every complete graph is colour complete.

Corollary 1. *Every coordination game on a colour complete graph has the c-FIP.*

Above we identified sufficient properties of graphs that ensure the existence of strong equilibria. In general, coordination games may not admit strong equilibria. To see this, consider the coordination game depicted in Figure 1. It is not hard to verify that for every joint strategy there is an improving move by a coalition of size at most 5. Thus, 5-equilibria (and hence strong equilibria) do not need to exist.

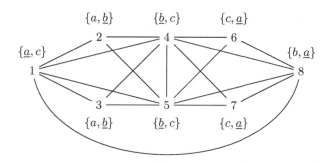

Fig. 1. A coordination game with three colours that does not admit a 5-equilibrium

4   Inefficiency

The next two theorems summarize our results on the inefficiency of k-equilibria.

Theorem 7. *The price of anarchy of coordination games is ∞; the strong price of anarchy is 2. Further, for all $k \in \{2, \ldots, n-1\}$, the k-price of anarchy for coordination games is between $2\frac{n-1}{k-1} - 1$ and $2\frac{n-1}{k-1}$.*

Theorem 8. *The strong price of stability is 1 in each of the following cases: G is a pseudoforest; G is a colour forest; there are only two colours.*

5   Computation

In general it is hard to decide whether a given joint strategy is a k-equilibrium.

Theorem 9. *Given a joint strategy s of a coordination game and $k \in \{1, \ldots, n\}$, it is co-NP-complete to decide whether s is a k-equilibrium.*

However, we can derive positive results for colour forests and pseudoforests.

Theorem 10. *Let G be a colour forest. Then there exists an algorithm that determines in polynomial time whether a given joint strategy is a k-equilibrium. Further, a strong equilibrium can be computed in polynomial time.*

Theorem 11. *Let G be a pseudoforest. Then a strong equilibrium can be computed in polynomial time.*

6   Extensions and Future Work

A natural generalization of our games are coordination games on *weighted* graphs. For these games, Theorem 7 continues to hold, while Theorem 1 does not. An interesting direction which we leave for future work is to derive a characterization of graph classes that guarantee the existence of strong equilibria. Yet another generalization is to allow players to choose multiple colours. Our results on the existence and inefficiency of equilibria then continue to hold; details are deferred to the full version of the paper.

An intriguing open question is whether k-equilibria exist for $k = 3, 4$. Recall that they are guaranteed to exist for $k \leq 2$ and may not exist for $k \geq 5$. Also it would be interesting to derive existence results for other graph classes.

Acknowledgements. Dariusz Leniowski first observed the fact that for the case of a ring the coordination game has the c-FIP. We thank José Correa for allowing us to use his lower bound in Theorem 7. It improves on our original one by a factor of 2.

References

1. Andelman, N., Feldman, M., Mansour, Y.: Strong price of anarchy. Games and Economic Behavior 65(2), 289–317 (2009)
2. Aumann, R.J.: Acceptable points in general cooperative n-person games. In: Luce, R.D., Tucker, A.W. (eds.) Contribution to the Theory of Game IV. Annals of Mathematical Study, vol. 40, pp. 287–324. University Press (1959)
3. Aziz, H., Brandl, F.: Existence of stability in hedonic coalition formation games. In: Proc. 11th International Conference on Autonomous Agents and Multiagent Systems, pp. 763–770 (2012)
4. Banerjee, S., Konishi: Core in a simple coalition formation game. Social Choice and Welfare 18(1), 135–153 (2001)
5. Bilò, V., Fanelli, A., Flammini, M., Moscardelli, L.: Graphical congestion games. Algorithmica 61(2), 274–297 (2011)
6. Bogomolnaia, A., Jackson, M.O.: The stability of hedonic coalition structures. Games and Economic Behavior 38(2), 201–230 (2002)
7. Cechlárová: Stable partition problem. In: Encyclopedia of Algorithms, pp. 885–888 (2008)
8. Gairing, M., Savani, R.: Computing stable outcomes in hedonic games. In: Kontogiannis, S., Koutsoupias, E., Spirakis, P.G. (eds.) SAGT 2010. LNCS, vol. 6386, pp. 174–185. Springer, Heidelberg (2010)
9. Hoefer, M.: Cost sharing and clustering under distributed competition, Ph.D. Thesis, University of Konstanz (2007)
10. Janovskaya, E.: Equilibrium points in polymatrix games. Litovskii Matematicheskii Sbornik 8, 381–384 (1968)
11. Monderer, D., Shapley, L.S.: Potential games. Games and Economic Behaviour 14, 124–143 (1996)
12. Rozenfeld, O., Tennenholtz, M.: Strong and correlated strong equilibria in monotone congestion games. In: Spirakis, P., Mavronicolas, M., Kontogiannis, S. (eds.) WINE 2006. LNCS, vol. 4286, pp. 74–86. Springer, Heidelberg (2006)

On the Existence of Low-Rank Explanations for Mixed Strategy Behavior

Siddharth Barman, Umang Bhaskar, Federico Echenique, and Adam Wierman

California Institute of Technology, Pasadena, CA, USA
{barman,umang,fede,adamw}@caltech.edu

Abstract. Nash equilibrium is used as a model to explain the observed behavior of players in strategic settings. For example, in many empirical applications we observe player behavior, and the problem is to determine if there exist payoffs for the players for which the equilibrium corresponds to observed player behavior. Computational complexity of Nash equilibria is important in this framework. If the payoffs that explain observed player behavior requires players to have solved a computationally hard problem, then the explanation provided is questionable. In this paper we provide conditions under which observed behavior of players can be explained by games in which Nash equilibria are easy to compute. We identify three structural conditions and show that if the data set of observed behavior satisfies any of these conditions, then it can be explained by payoff matrices for which Nash equilibria are efficiently computable.

Keywords: equilibrium computation, revealed preference, matrix rank.

1 Introduction

The computational complexity of equilibria in economic models is at the core of recent research in algorithmic game theory. In general, the basic message of this research is negative: Computing Nash equilibria is PPAD-complete even for 2-player games [7], and computing Walrasian equilibria is PPAD-hard [6, 20]. The fact that the standard notions of equilibrium used by economists are hard to compute raises a concern that they are flawed models for economic behavior, because they lack a plausible rationale for how one would arrive at equilibrium.

These hardness results have motivated the study of instances in which equilibrium can be computed efficiently, e.g., [1, 8, 9]. These results — both positive and negative — assume a fixed and literal interpretation of economic models. For example, in two-player games the assumption is that payoff matrices are explicitly specified, and agents seek to maximize their payoffs given the strategy of the other player.

However, models are frequently used as explanations of behavior, rather than literal descriptions. In empirical applications of game theory, for example, one rarely observes payoffs of the players. Rather, what we observe is the behavior of the players, and a first-order task is to determine if the model explains observed behavior or not ([4, 5] are classical examples of this exercise). In particular, a

T.-Y. Liu et al. (Eds.): WINE 2014, LNCS 8877, pp. 447–452, 2014.
© Springer International Publishing Switzerland 2014

good model instance (i.e., payoffs specification) is one where the observed behavior of the players is as if they were playing equilibrium. This is certainly how
economists use game theory: as a modeling tool to explain observed behavior.
This perspective however cannot ignore computational complexity. Even if a
model explains observed behavior, it is unreasonable if it requires players to solve
computationally hard problems. Thus, an important question that arises from
the perspective of models as explanations of observed behavior and the computational complexity of equilibrium is: *when is an economic model a reasonable
explanation for observed behavior?* We address this question in the context of
Nash equilibrium as a model for two-player games, and computational complexity as a measure of reasonableness.

This framework of starting with observed behavior is consistent with much of
economics, and is formalized in *revealed preference theory*, which was pioneered
by Samuelson in 1938 [15] and has a long tradition in economics (e.g., [2, 16–
19]). Classical revealed preference theory asks, "Does there exist an instance
of the model that is consistent with the observed behavior?" If there is such
a model instance, then the observed behavior is said to be consistent with the
theory, and thus *rationalizable*. Our work augments the fundamental question
of rationalizability in revealed preference theory with complexity considerations.
The question we address is then, "Does there exist an instance of the model that
is consistent with the observed behavior *and* for which the observations could
have been computed efficiently?"

We focus on addressing this question in the context of bimatrix games. We
consider a setting where mixed strategy behavior (i.e., probability distributions
over the actions of the players) is observed. In particular, with multiple instances
of mixed strategy behavior as input, we want to know if there is some tractable
instance of the game such that the given observations correspond to Nash equilibria. We focus on low *player rank* — the minimum of the ranks of the payoff
matrices of the players — as our notion of tractability given recent algorithmic
results, e.g., [8].

Summary of results. Our results show that large and structurally complex data
sets of observations — including data sets with overlapping observed strategies,
each of which may be an arbitrary distribution — can be rationalized by games
that admit efficient computation of the observed Nash equilibria. Specifically,
we identify three measures of structural complexity in data sets, and show that
if a data set has a low value on any one of these measures for either player, or
can be partitioned in a manner such that each partition has a low value on any
one of these measures, then it has a rationalization with low player rank. The
three measures we study are (i) the *dimensionality* of the observed strategies
(Theorem 2), (ii) the *support size* of the observed strategies (Theorem 3), and
(iii) the *chromatic number* of the data set (Theorem 4). These are natural and
complementary measures to evaluate the structural complexity of a data set, and
our contribution is to show that each of these measures individually translates
to the existence of rationalizing games with low player rank.

Proofs of the mentioned results appear in the full version of the paper; see [3]. Also, in the full version [3] we show that the bounds we obtain on the player rank for these measures are nearly tight. In addition, the extended version presents a unifying result that combines the above mentioned results to provide a more robust low-rank construction.

2 Preliminaries

Bimatrix Games. Bimatrix games are two player games in normal form. Such games are specified by a pair of matrices (A, B) of size $n \times n$, which are termed the payoff matrices for the players. The first player, also called the row player, has payoff matrix A, and the second player, or the column player, has payoff matrix B. The strategy set for each player is $[n] = \{1, 2, \ldots, n\}$, and, if the row player plays strategy i and column player plays strategy j, then the payoffs of the two players are A_{ij} and B_{ij} respectively. The player rank of game (A, B) is defined to be $\min\{\text{rank}(A), \text{rank}(B)\}$. Our focus on player rank stems from a number of important properties. In particular, if a game has player rank $k \in \{1, 2, \ldots, n\}$, then an equilibrium can be computed in time $O(n^{O(k)})$ [8, 10].

Let Δ^n be the set of probability distributions over the set of pure strategies $[n]$. For $x \in \Delta^n$, we define $\text{Supp}(x) := \{i : x_i > 0\}$. Further, $e_i \in \mathbb{R}^n$ is the vector with 1 in the ith coordinate and 0's elsewhere, and $u_k \in \Delta^n$ is the uniform distribution over the set $\{1, 2, \ldots, k\}$. The players can randomize over their strategies by selecting any probability distribution in Δ^n, called a mixed strategy. When the row and column players play mixed strategies x and y respectively, the expected payoff of the row player is $x^T A y$ and the expected payoff of the column player is $x^T B y$.

Given a mixed strategy $y \in \Delta^n$ for the column player, the best-response set of the row player, β_r, is defined as $\beta_r(y) := \{i \in [n] \mid e_i^T A y \geq e_k^T A y \ \forall k \in [n]\}$. Similarly, the best-response set, β_c, of the column player (against mixed strategy $x \in \Delta^n$ of the row player) is defined as $\beta_c(x) := \{j \in [n] \mid x^T B e_j \geq x^T B e_k \ \forall k \in [n]\}$. The best response sets β_r and β_c are defined with respect to the payoff matrices A and B. When we want to emphasize this fact we use superscripts: β_r^A and β_c^B.

Definition 1 (Nash Equilibrium). *A pair of mixed strategies (x, y), $x, y \in \Delta^n$, is a Nash equilibrium if and only if:*

$$x^T A y \geq e_i^T A y \ \forall i \in [n], \ \text{and} \ x^T B y \geq x^T B e_j \quad \forall j \in [n].$$

The Nash equilibrium is strict *if additionally the support and the best-response sets are equal, i.e., $\text{Supp}(x) = \beta_r(y)$ and $\text{Supp}(y) = \beta_c(x)$.*

Observed behavior. We consider settings in which the payoff matrices A and B are not explicitly specified. Instead, we are given a collection of observed mixed strategy pairs. Our framework of observing mixed strategies is entirely analogous to the theory of individual stochastic choice: see for example

[11–14]. The idea is that repeated observation of pure play allows one to infer a probability distribution over pure strategies.

A data set $\mathcal{D}$ (of size m) is a collection of mixed-strategy pairs, $\mathcal{D} = \{(x_k, y_k) \in \Delta^n \times \Delta^n \mid k \in [m]\}$. We refer to mixed-strategy pairs (x_k, y_k) as observations.

We denote the set of observed mixed strategies of the row and column player in a data set $\mathcal{D}$ by $\mathcal{O}_r(\mathcal{D})$ and $\mathcal{O}_c(\mathcal{D})$ respectively: $\mathcal{O}_r(\mathcal{D}) := \{x \in \Delta^n \mid \exists y \in \Delta^n \text{ such that } (x, y) \in \mathcal{D}\}$ and $\mathcal{O}_c(\mathcal{D}) := \{y \in \Delta^n \mid \exists x \in \Delta^n \text{ such that } (x, y) \in \mathcal{D}\}$. When there is a single data set under consideration, for ease of notation, we simply refer to these sets as $\mathcal{O}_r$ and $\mathcal{O}_c$.

Given observed behavior (data), the first-order goal of classical revealed preference theory is to understand whether the data is rationalizable.

Definition 2 (Rationalizable Data). *A data set $\mathcal{D} = \{(x_k, y_k)\}_k$ is rationalizable if there exist payoff matrices A and B such that for all k, (x_k, y_k) is a strict Nash equilibrium in the game (A, B).*

Strictness is required in the above definition in order to avoid rationalization by trivial games.

Proposition 1. *The rationalizability of a given data set $\mathcal{D} = \{(x_k, y_k) \in \Delta^n \times \Delta^n \mid 1 \le k \le m\}$ can be determined in polynomial time by solving a linear program.*

3   Rationalizations with Low Player Rank

This section identifies structural properties of data sets that guarantee the existence of rationalizations for which the observed Nash equilibria can be computed efficiently. For efficient computation, we construct rationalizations with low player rank and make use of the following result from [8].

Theorem 1 ([8]). *If the player rank of a bimatrix game is k then all extreme Nash equilibria can be computed in time $O(n^{O(k)})$.*

The algorithm implicit in this theorem computes all extreme equilibria, and so it can be used to compute the observations in the data set rather than simply some arbitrary equilibria. This fact is crucial to the exercise, and provides strong motivation for a focus on player rank, since the goal is to explain the specific observations in the data set.

Observations from a low-dimensional subspace Given a finite set $S \subset \mathbb{R}^n$ of m vectors $s_1, \dots, s_m$, write $dim(S)$ to denote the maximum number of linearly independent vectors in S. Observed strategies that form a low dimensional subspace are natural candidates for low player rank rationalizations and, the following theorem shows that — independent of the size of the data set — if the observations form a low dimensional subspace then they can be rationalized by a game of low player rank.

Theorem 2. *If a data set $\mathcal{D}$ is rationalizable then it can be rationalized by a game of player rank at most $\min\{dim(\mathcal{O}_r), dim(\mathcal{O}_c)\}$.*

Small support size. The second structural property of the data set we consider is the support size of the observations. In spirit, the following theorem complements the result of Lipton et al. [10] wherein they establish that if the rank of both the payoff matrices is low then the game contains a small-support equilibrium. The following result highlights that there is a connection in the other direction as well.

Theorem 3. *Let $\mathcal{D} = \{(x_k, y_k) \in \Delta^n \times \Delta^n \mid 1 \leq k \leq m\}$ be a data set in which $|Supp(x_k)| \leq s$ for all $k \in [m]$ or $|Supp(y_k)| \leq s$ for all $k \in [m]$. If the observed strategies $\mathcal{O}_r(\mathcal{D})$ and $\mathcal{O}_c(\mathcal{D})$ are generic then $\mathcal{D}$ can be rationalized by a game with player rank $\leq 2s + 1$.*

Low chromatic number. Intuitively, the chromatic number quantifies the degree of intersection between the observed mixed strategies, and hence it is a relevant measure of the structural complexity of data. For a data set $\mathcal{D}$, we define the row chromatic number $\kappa_r(\mathcal{D})$ and the column chromatic number $\kappa_c(\mathcal{D})$ as the chromatic numbers of graphs G_r and G_c, defined as follows. For the row chromatic number, $\kappa_r(\mathcal{D})$, construct graph G_r with a vertex corresponding to each observation in $\mathcal{O}_r$. For distinct observations (x, y) and (x', y') in $\mathcal{D}$, if $\text{Supp}(x) \cap \text{Supp}(x') \neq \emptyset$ then the graph G_r has an edge between the corresponding vertices. Then set $\kappa_r(\mathcal{D}) = \chi(G_r)$, i.e., the chromatic number of graph G_r. The column chromatic number is defined similarly using intersections $\text{Supp}(y) \cap \text{Supp}(y')$. The chromatic number of the data set, $\kappa(\mathcal{D})$, is defined to be the minimum of $\kappa_r(\mathcal{D})$ and $\kappa_c(\mathcal{D})$.

Theorem 4. *Let $\mathcal{D}$ be a data set with chromatic number equal to $\kappa(\mathcal{D})$. If the observed mixed-strategy sets $\mathcal{O}_r(\mathcal{D})$ and $\mathcal{O}_c(\mathcal{D})$ are generic then $\mathcal{D}$ can be rationalized by a game of player rank at most $2\kappa(\mathcal{D})$.*

Of course, in general the chromatic number of a graph is hard to compute. However, an easy upper bound is the maximum degree of any vertex in G_r and G_c plus one, which then can be interpreted as follows: $\kappa_r(\mathcal{D}) \leq \max_{(x,y)\in\mathcal{D}} |\{(x', y') \in \mathcal{D} : \text{Supp}(x) \cap \text{Supp}(x') \neq \phi\}|$ and $\kappa_c(\mathcal{D}) \leq \max_{(x,y)\in\mathcal{D}} |\{(x', y') \in \mathcal{D} : \text{Supp}(y) \cap \text{Supp}(y') \neq \phi\}|$. Though these bounds provide intuition, it is obvious the chromatic numbers can be much less than these upper bounds, e.g., if the graph G_r is a star.

Acknowledgments. This research was supported by NSF grants CNS-0846025, EPAS-1307794, and CCF-1101470, along with a Linde/SISL postdoctoral fellowship.

References

1. Adsul, B., Garg, J., Mehta, R., Sohoni, M.: Rank-1 bimatrix games: a homeomorphism and a polynomial time algorithm. In: Proceedings of the 43rd Annual ACM Symposium on Theory of Computing, STOC 2011, pp. 195–204. ACM (2011)

2. Afriat, S.N.: The construction of utility functions from expenditure data. International Economic Review 8(1), 67–77 (1967)
3. Barman, S., Bhaskar, U., Echenique, F., Wierman, A.: On the existence of low-rank explanations for mixed strategy behavior. arXiv preprint arXiv:1311.2655 (2014)
4. Berry, S., Levinsohn, J., Pakes, A.: Automobile prices in market equilibrium. Econometrica: Journal of the Econometric Society, 841–890 (1995)
5. Bresnahan, T.F.: Empirical studies of industries with market power. In: Handbook of Industrial Organization, vol. 2, pp. 1011–1057 (1989)
6. Chen, X., Dai, D., Du, Y., Teng, S.H.: Settling the complexity of arrow-debreu equilibria in markets with additively separable utilities. In: FOCS (2009)
7. Chen, X., Deng, X., Teng, S.H.: Settling the complexity of computing two-player nash equilibria. J. ACM 56(3) (2009)
8. Garg, J., Jiang, A.X., Mehta, R.: Bilinear games: Polynomial time algorithms for rank based subclasses. In: Chen, N., Elkind, E., Koutsoupias, E. (eds.) WINE 2011. LNCS, vol. 7090, pp. 399–407. Springer, Heidelberg (2011)
9. Jain, K.: A polynomial time algorithm for computing an arrow-debreu market equilibrium for linear utilities. SIAM Journal on Computing 37(1), 303–318 (2007)
10. Lipton, R.J., Markakis, E., Mehta, A.: Playing large games using simple strategies. In: Proceedings of the 4th ACM Conference on Electronic Commerce, pp. 36–41. ACM (2003)
11. Luce, R.D.: Individual Choice Behavior a Theoretical Analysis. John Wiley and Sons (1959)
12. McFadden, D.: Conditional logit analysis of qualitative choice behavior. In: Zarembka, P. (ed.) Frontiers in Econometrics, p. 105. Academic Press, New York (1974)
13. McFadden, D., Richter, M.: Stochastic rationality and revealed stochastic preference. In: Preferences, Uncertainty, and Optimality, Essays in Honor of Leo Hurwicz, pp. 161–186. Westview Press, Boulder (1990)
14. McFadden, D.: Revealed stochastic preference: a synthesis. Economic Theory 26(2), 245–264 (2005)
15. Samuelson, P.A.: A note on the pure theory of consumer's behaviour. Economica 5(17), 61–71 (1938)
16. Varian, H.R.: The nonparametric approach to demand analysis. Econometrica 50(4), 945–974 (1982)
17. Varian, H.R.: Non-parametric tests of consumer behaviour. Review of Economic Studies 50(1), 99–110 (1983)
18. Varian, H.R.: The nonparametric approach to production analysis. Econometrica 52(3), 579–598 (1984)
19. Varian, H.R.: Revealed preference. In: Samuelsonian Economics and the Twenty-first Century, pp. 99–115 (2006)
20. Vazirani, V.V., Yannakakis, M.: Market equilibrium under separable, piecewise-linear, concave utilities. J. ACM 58(3) (2011)

Congestion Games
with Higher Demand Dimensions

Max Klimm* and Andreas Schütz

Institut für Mathematik, Technische Universität Berlin, Berlin, Germany
{klimm,schuetz}@math.tu-berlin.de

Abstract. We introduce a generalization of weighted congestion games in which players are associated with k-dimensional demand vectors and resource costs are k-dimensional functions $c : \mathbb{R}_{\geq 0}^k \to \mathbb{R}$ of the aggregated demand vector of the players using the resource. Such a cost structure is natural when the cost of a resource depends on different properties of the players' demands, e.g., total weight, total volume, and total number of items. A complete characterization of the existence of pure Nash equilibria in terms of the resource cost functions for all $k \in \mathbb{N}$ is given.

1 Introduction

The study of selfish resource allocation problems is one of the core topics of the algorithmic game theory and operations research literature and has proven to be an important source for innovations in the field. E.g., central notions like the price of anarchy or the price of stability have been defined and studied first for such games, see Koutsoupias and Papadimitriou [11] and Anshelevich et al. [3].

In a congestion game, as introduced by Rosenthal [15], we are given a set of resources and players choose subsets of this set. Each player strives to minimize her private cost which is defined as the sum of the costs of the chosen resources, where the cost of each resource is a function of the number of players using it. Congestion games model a wide range of applications including road traffic, animal behavior, and telecommunication networks. In most cases, the resources correspond to the edges of a graph and each player aims to establish a path connecting her source and target vertex. In practical applications it is desirable that the system converges to a stable point because unstable behavior often leads to inefficiency. This can be observed, e.g., in telecommunication networks with distance vector routing protocols where route flapping is a major issue.

The most important stability concept is that of a pure Nash equilibrium, a deterministic state from which no user of the system can improve. Rosenthal showed that unweighted congestion games, in which each user controls one unit of demand, always admit a pure Nash equilibrium. A natural extension of congestion games are *weighted congestion games*, in which an unsplittable demand $d_i > 0$ is assigned to each player i and the cost function $c_r : \mathbb{R}_{\geq 0} \to \mathbb{R}$ of a

---

* The research of the first author was carried out in the framework of MATHEON supported by the Einstein Foundation Berlin.

T.-Y. Liu et al. (Eds.): WINE 2014, LNCS 8877, pp. 453–459, 2014.

resource r depends on the cumulated demands of all players sharing r rather than the number of players. In contrast to the original unweighted model studied by Rosenthal, weighted congestion games do not always possess a pure Nash equilibrium [6–8, 13]. Consequently, one line of research focused on finding (maximal) subclasses of weighted congestion games for which the existence of a pure Nash equilibrium can be guaranteed.

In a *singleton* game, each strategy of each player consists of a single resource only. Fabrikant et al. [5] remarked that every singleton weighted congestion game with non-decreasing costs admits a pure Nash equilibrium. This existence result can be strengthened towards the existence of a strong equilibrium – a strengthening of the Nash equilibrium concept due to Aumann [4] – see Kukushkin [12] and Andelman et al. [2], Harks et al. [10], and Rozenfeld and Tennenholz [16] for subsequent work in this direction. Ackermann et al. [1] showed that weighted congestion games with non-decreasing costs always admit a pure Nash equilibrium if all strategy spaces are equal to the set of bases of a matroid, and that this is the maximal property defined on the strategy spaces ensuring the existence of a pure Nash equilibrium for arbitrary non-decreasing cost functions. For *arbitrary* strategy spaces, Fotakis et al. [6] showed that every weighted congestion game with affine cost functions always admits a pure Nash equilibrium. Panagopoulou and Spirakis [14] proved the same result for exponential resource costs $c_r(x) = e^x$. Harks et al. [9] additionally confirmed the existence of pure Nash equilibria in weighted congestion games with exponential cost functions of type $a_c e^{\phi x} + b_c$, where $a_c, b_c \in \mathbb{R}$ may depend on c and $\phi \in \mathbb{R}$ is independent of c. There are no further sets of cost functions that guarantee the existence of a pure Nash equilibrium in weighted congestion games [8].

All these games are single-dimensional in the sense that the cost of a resource depends only on a single parameter – the aggregated demand of all players using it. In many situations, however, the cost of a resource depends on different parameters. E.g., in a transportation network, it is reasonable to assume that the cost to ship the player's aggregated goods depends both on the total volume and the total weight of the goods; in a telecommunication network the delay of an arc may depend both on the amount of data and the total number of files handled through the corresponding arc, respectively. To capture such situations more precisely, in this paper, we study *congestion games with k-dimensional demands*, where for $k \in \mathbb{N}_{\geq 1}$ the demand of each player i is represented as a k-dimensional vector $\mathbf{d}_i \in \mathbb{R}_{>0}^k$ and the cost of each resource r is given by a k-dimensional function $c_r : \mathbb{R}_{\geq 0}^k \to \mathbb{R}$. For $k = 1$, we obtain weighted congestion games for which the existence of pure Nash equilibria is reasonably well understood. To formally capture the dependence of the existence of pure Nash equilibria on the underlying cost structure, Harks and Klimm [8] call a set $\mathcal{C}$ of cost functions *consistent*, if all weighted congestion games with cost functions in $\mathcal{C}$ have a pure Nash equilibrium. They also give a complete characterization of the set of consistent cost functions. We extend this terminology to k-dimensional cost functions. For $k \geq 1$, we call a set $\mathcal{C}$ of cost functions $c : \mathbb{R}_{\geq 0}^k \to \mathbb{R}$ k-consistent if each congestion game with k-dimensional demand and cost functions in $\mathcal{C}$ has a pure Nash equilibrium. The main question of this paper is: How large are the sets of k-consistent cost functions?

Our Results. We first give a complete characterization of 2-consistent sets of cost functions. For a set $\mathcal{C}$ of continuous cost functions $c : \mathbb{R}^2_{\geq 0} \to \mathbb{R}$, we show that $\mathcal{C}$ is 2-consistent if and only if there are $\phi_1, \phi_2 \geq 0$ or $\phi_1, \phi_2 \leq 0$ such that $\mathcal{C}$ only contains functions of type $c(x_1, x_2) = a_c(\phi_1 x_1 + \phi_2 x_2) + b_c$ or $\mathcal{C}$ only contains functions of type $c(x_1, x_2) = a_c e^{\phi_1 x_1 + \phi_2 x_2} + b_c$, where $a_c, b_c \in \mathbb{R}$ may depend on c.

We then extend this characterization to congestion games with k-dimensional demands for any $k \in \mathbb{N}_{\geq 3}$. A set $\mathcal{C}$ of continuous cost functions $c : \mathbb{R}^k_{\geq 0} \to \mathbb{R}$ is k-consistent if and only if there is a vector $\boldsymbol{\Phi} \in \mathbb{R}^k_{\geq 0}$ or $\boldsymbol{\Phi} \in \mathbb{R}^k_{\leq 0}$ such that $\mathcal{C}$ only contains functions of type $c(\mathbf{x}) = a_c \boldsymbol{\Phi}^\top \mathbf{x} + b_c$ or $\mathcal{C}$ only contains functions of type $c(\mathbf{x}) = a_c e^{\boldsymbol{\Phi}^\top \mathbf{x}} + b_c$, where $a_c, b_c \in \mathbb{R}$ may depend on c. A set $\mathcal{C}$ that contains only functions of one of these types is called *degenerate*. Provided that $\mathcal{C}$ is degenerate, our results imply that every congestion game with k-dimensional demands and cost functions in $\mathcal{C}$ is isomorphic to a congestion game with 1-dimensional demands and the same sets of players, resources, strategies and private costs. Our contributions to k-consistency for $k \in \mathbb{N}_{\geq 1}$ generalize the complete characterization of 1-consistent sets for weighted congestion games due to Harks and Klimm [8].

All proofs missing in this extended abstract are deferred to the full version of this paper.

2   Preliminaries

We consider strategic minimization games $G = (N, S, \pi)$, where $N = \{1, \ldots, n\}$ is the finite set of players, S_i is the finite set of strategies available to player i, $S = S_1 \times \cdots \times S_n$ is the nonempty strategy space and $\pi : S \to \mathbb{R}^n$ is the combined private cost functions assigning a private cost vector $\pi(s) = (\pi_i(s))_{i \in N}$ to each strategy profile $s \in S$. For $i \in N$, we write $S_{-i} = S_1 \times \ldots S_{i-1} \times S_{i+1} \times \cdots \times S_n$ for the joint strategy set of all players except i. For $s \in S$, we write $s = (s_i, s_{-i})$ meaning that $s_i \in S_i$ and $s_{-i} \in S_{-i}$. A strategy profile is a *pure Nash equilibrium*, if $\pi_i(s) \leq \pi_i(t_i, s_{-i})$ for all $i \in N$ and $t_i \in S_i$.

Let $k \in \mathbb{N}$ with $k \geq 1$ be a demand dimension. We write $[k]$ shorthand for $\{1, \ldots, k\}$ and write vectors $\mathbf{x} \in \mathbb{R}^k$ with bold face. We denote the subset of k-dimensional non-negative vectors as $\mathbb{R}^k_{\geq 0}$, i.e., $\mathbb{R}^k_{\geq 0} = \{\mathbf{x} = (x_1, \ldots, x_k) \in \mathbb{R}^k : x_i \geq 0 \ \forall i \in [k]\}$. When k is clear from the context, we use $\mathbf{0}$ to denote the k-dimensional zero vector and we write $\mathbb{R}^k_{>0}$ for $\mathbb{R}^k_{\geq 0} \setminus \{\mathbf{0}\}$.

Let R be a finite set of resources, each endowed with a k-dimensional cost function $c_r : \mathbb{R}^k_{\geq 0} \to \mathbb{R}$. A k-*dimensional congestion game* is given by a set N of players, where for each player i, her set of strategies $S_i \subseteq 2^R \setminus \{\emptyset\}$ is a set of non-empty subsets of R, and her demand vector $\mathbf{d}_i \in \mathbb{R}^k_{>0}$ is a non-negative k-dimensional vector. In the corresponding k-dimensional congestion game the private cost of player i is defined as $\pi_i(s) = \sum_{r \in s_i} c_r(\mathbf{x}_r(s))$, where $\mathbf{x}_r(s) = \sum_{j \in N : r \in s_j} \mathbf{d}_j$ is the k-dimensional aggregated demand of resource r under strategy profile s. For two vectors $\mathbf{x}, \mathbf{y} \in \mathbb{R}^k$ with $\mathbf{x} = (x_1, \ldots, x_k)$ and $\mathbf{y} = (y_1, \ldots, y_k)$, we write $\mathbf{x} \leq \mathbf{y}$ if and only if $x_i \leq y_i$ for all $i \in [k]$. We call a function $c : \mathbb{R}^k_{\geq 0} \to \mathbb{R}$ non-decreasing if $c_r(\mathbf{x}) \leq c_r(\mathbf{y})$ for all $\mathbf{x}, \mathbf{y} \in \mathbb{R}^k_{\geq 0}$ with $\mathbf{x} \leq \mathbf{y}$. Non-increasing functions are defined analogously. Functions that are both non-decreasing and non-increasing are called *constant*, functions that are either non-decreasing or non-increasing are called *monotonic*. For a set $\mathcal{C}$ of cost functions $c : \mathbb{R}^k_{\geq 0} \to \mathbb{R}$, we say that $\mathcal{C}$ is k-*consistent* if all k-dimensional congestion games with cost functions contained in $\mathcal{C}$ have a pure Nash equilibrium. For $k = 1$, we obtain the well known class of weighted congestion games for which in previous work Harks and Klimm [8] obtained the following characterization of 1-consistency.

Theorem 1 (Harks and Klimm [8]). *A set C of continuous cost functions $c : \mathbb{R}_{\geq 0} \to \mathbb{R}$ is 1-consistent if and only if $\mathcal{C}$ only contains affine functions or $\mathcal{C}$ only contains functions of type $c(x) = a_c e^{\phi x} + b_c$ where $a_c, b_c \in \mathbb{R}$ may depend on c while $\phi \in \mathbb{R}$ is independent of c.*

3 Sufficient Conditions on k-Consistency

To obtain a full characterization of the sets of k-consistent cost functions, we first give sufficient conditions for the consistency of k-dimensional cost functions. We introduce the notion of *degeneracy* of sets of cost functions. In a sense, this notion of degeneracy forecloses the characterization we are going to prove in the remainder of this paper.

Definition 2 (Degeneracy). *A set $\mathcal{C}$ of cost functions $c : \mathbb{R}^k_{\geq 0} \to \mathbb{R}$ is $\boldsymbol{\Phi}$-degenerate, or simply degenerate, if there is a vector $\boldsymbol{\Phi} \in \mathbb{R}^k_{\geq 0}$ or $\boldsymbol{\Phi} \in \mathbb{R}^k_{\leq 0}$ with one of the following properties:*
1. *For every $c \in C$ there is a function $f_c : \mathbb{R} \to \mathbb{R}$ of type $f(x) = a_c x + b_c$ such that $c(\mathbf{x}) = f(\boldsymbol{\Phi}^\top \mathbf{x})$ for some $a_c, b_c \in \mathbb{R}$ and all $\mathbf{x} \in \mathbb{R}^k_{\geq 0}$.*
2. *For every $c \in C$ there is a function $f_c : \mathbb{R} \to \mathbb{R}$ of type $\overline{f}(x) = a_c e^x + b_c$ such that $c(\mathbf{x}) = f(\boldsymbol{\Phi}^\top \mathbf{x})$ for some $a_c, b_c \in \mathbb{R}$ and all $\mathbf{x} \in \mathbb{R}^k_{\geq 0}$.*

In case (1) holds, we call C and every $c \in C$ affinely $\boldsymbol{\Phi}$-degenerate, in case (2) holds, we call C and every $c \in C$ exponentially $\boldsymbol{\Phi}$-degenerate.

As our first result, we show that degeneracy is sufficient for k-consistency. Specifically, we show that any congestion games with k-dimensional demands G for which all cost functions are taken from a degenerate set $\mathcal{C}$ is isomorphic to a congestion game with 1-dimensional demands G' that admits a pure Nash equilibrium.

Theorem 3. *Let $k \in \mathbb{N}_{\geq 1}$ and let $\mathcal{C}$ be a set of cost functions $c : \mathbb{R}^k_{\geq 0} \to \mathbb{R}$. If $\mathcal{C}$ is degenerate, then $\mathcal{C}$ is k-consistent.*

4   Necessary Conditions on Consistency

In order to show that degeneracy is necessary for the consistency of a set $\mathcal{C}$ of continuous functions, we first derive three necessary conditions that are captured in the Extended Monotonicity Lemma, the Hyperplane Restriction Lemma, and the Line Restriction Lemma. In Sections 5 and 6, we then use these three key lemmas to derive necessary conditions on 2-consistency and k-consistency for $k \geq 3$, respectively.

The Extended Monotonicity Lemma states that any integer linear combination of functions contained in a k-consistent set of cost functions $\mathcal{C}$ is monotonic. A similar lemma has been given by Harks and Klimm [8] for the case $k = 1$. However, the proof of the Extended Monotonicity Lemma turns out to be more intricate as the $\leq$-relation does not give a complete order on $\mathbb{R}^k_{\geq 0}$ which makes the monotonicity of functions defined on $\mathbb{R}^k_{\geq 0}$ somewhat harder to characterize.

Lemma 4 (Extended Monotonicity Lemma). *Let $\mathcal{C}$ be a k-consistent set of continuous cost functions $c : \mathbb{R}^k_{\geq 0} \to \mathbb{R}$ and let*

$$\mathcal{L}_k(\mathcal{C}) = \{c : \mathbb{R}^k_{\geq 0} \to \mathbb{R} : c(x) = \lambda_1 c_1(x) + \lambda_2 c_2(x), c_1, c_2 \in \mathcal{C}, \lambda_1, \lambda_2 \in \mathbb{Z}\}.$$

Then, every $c \in \mathcal{L}_k(\mathcal{C})$ is monotonic.

In order to state the Hyperplane Restriction Lemma, we need some additional notation. For an index $i \in [k]$ and a scalar $\hat{x}_i \geq 0$, the *insertion function* $\tau^i_{\hat{x}_i} : \mathbb{R}^{k-1}_{\geq 0} \to \mathbb{R}^k_{\geq 0}$ maps a $(k-1)$-dimensional vector $\mathbf{x}_{-i} \in \mathbb{R}^{k-1}_{\geq 0}$ to the k-dimensional vector $(x_1, \ldots, x_{i-1}, \hat{x}_i, x_{i+1}, \ldots, x_k)^\top \in \mathbb{R}^k_{\geq 0}$ by inserting $\hat{x}_i$ at position i. For a function $c : \mathbb{R}^k_{\geq 0} \to \mathbb{R}$ the function composition $c \circ \tau^i_{\hat{x}_i} : \mathbb{R}^{k-1}_{\geq 0} \to \mathbb{R}$, which can be interpreted as the *restriction of c to the hyperplane $H^i_{\hat{x}_i} = \{\mathbf{x} \in \mathbb{R}^k_{\geq 0} : x_i = \hat{x}_i\}$* for which the ith component of every vector $\mathbf{x}$ is fixed.

For $k \geq 2$, the following Hyperplane Restriction Lemma establishes a link between k-consistent cost functions and $(k-1)$-consistent cost functions.

Lemma 5 (Hyperplane Restriction Lemma). *Let $\mathcal{C}$ be a k-consistent set of cost functions $c : \mathbb{R}^k_{\geq 0} \to \mathbb{R}$, $k \geq 2$. Then, $\mathcal{C}^i = \{c \circ \tau^i_{\hat{x}_i} : c \in \mathcal{C}, \hat{x}_i \geq 0\}$ is $(k-1)$-consistent for every $i \in [k]$.*

The next lemma establishes a similar connection between k-consistency and 1-consistency. Specifically, we show that given a k-consistent set $\mathcal{C}$ of cost functions $c : \mathbb{R}^k_{\geq 0} \to \mathbb{R}$ and a vector $\mathbf{v} \in \mathbb{R}^k_{\geq 0}$, the restrictions of functions $c \in \mathcal{C}$ to the line $L_\mathbf{v} = \{\mathbf{z} \in \mathbb{R}^k_{\geq 0} : \mathbf{z} = x\mathbf{v}, x \geq 0\}$ constitutes a 1-consistent set of cost functions. The proof uses similar ideas as the proof of the Hyperplane Restriction Lemma.

Lemma 6 (Line Restriction Lemma). *Let $\mathcal{C}$ be a k-consistent set of cost functions $c : \mathbb{R}^k_{\geq 0} \to \mathbb{R}$, $k \geq 1$. Then, $\mathcal{C}^\mathbf{v} = \{c^\mathbf{v} : \mathbb{R}_{\geq 0} \to \mathbb{R}, x \mapsto c(x\mathbf{v}) : c \in \mathcal{C}\}$ is 1-consistent for every $\mathbf{v} \in \mathbb{R}^k_{> 0}$.*

5 A Characterization of 2-Consistency

Combining the the Extended Monotonicity Lemma (Lemma 4), the Hyperplane Restriction Lemma (Lemma 5), the Line Restriction Lemma (Lemma 6) and Theorem 1, we establish the following complete characterization of 2-consistent sets of continuous cost functions.

Theorem 7. *Let C be a set of continuous cost functions $c : \mathbb{R}^2_{\geq 0} \to \mathbb{R}$. Then, C is 2-consistent if and only if C is degenerate, i.e., there are $\phi_1, \phi_2 \in \mathbb{R}_{\geq 0}$ or $\phi_1, \phi_2 \in \mathbb{R}_{\leq 0}$ such that one of the following two cases holds:*
  1. *C only contains functions of type $c(x_1, x_2) = a_c(\phi_1 x_1 + \phi_2 x_2) + b_c$ with $a_c, b_c \in \mathbb{R}$,*
  2. *C only contains functions of type $c(x_1, x_2) = a_c e^{\phi_1 x_1 + \phi_2 x_2} + b_c$ with $a_c, b_c \in \mathbb{R}$.*

6 A Characterization of k-Consistency

In this section, we generalize the characterization of 2-consistency discussed in the previous section to arbitrary dimensions $k \in \mathbb{N}_{\geq 3}$. Specifically, we show that a set C of continuous cost functions is k-consistent if and only if C is degenerate.

For the proof, we use that for $k \geq 3$, the intersection of two $(k-1)$-dimensional hyperplanes contains a line. This allows us to consider partial derivatives of the cost functions along this intersection which enables us to establish a connection between $c \circ \tau^i_{\hat{x}_i}$ and $c \circ \tau^j_{\hat{x}_j}$. The following straightforward lemma takes a first step in that direction.

Lemma 8. *Let $k \in \mathbb{N}_{\geq 3}$ and $c : \mathbb{R}^k_{\geq 0} \to \mathbb{R}$ and let $\mathbf{x} \in H^i_{\hat{x}_i} \cap H^j_{\hat{x}_j}$ for $i, j \in [k]$ with $i \neq j$ and some $\hat{x}_i, \hat{x}_j \geq 0$. If for $z \in [k] \setminus \{i, j\}$ the partial derivatives $\partial(c \circ \tau^i_{\hat{x}_i})/\partial x_z(\mathbf{x}_{-i})$ and $\partial(c \circ \tau^j_{\hat{x}_j})/\partial x_z(\mathbf{x}_{-j})$ exist, then $\partial c/\partial x_z(\mathbf{x})$ exists and satisfies $\partial c/\partial x_z(\mathbf{x}) = \partial(c \circ \tau^i_{\hat{x}_i})/\partial x_z(\mathbf{x}_{-i}) = \partial(c \circ \tau^j_{\hat{x}_j})/\partial x_z(\mathbf{x}_{-j})$.*

Using Lemma 8, we can derive the following complete characterization of k-consistency.

Theorem 9. *Let C be a set of continuous cost functions $c : \mathbb{R}^k_{\geq 0} \to \mathbb{R}$, $k \geq 1$. Then, C is k-consistent if and only if C is degenerate, i.e., there is a vector $\Phi \in \mathbb{R}^k_{\geq 0}$ or $\Phi \in \mathbb{R}^k_{\leq 0}$ such that one of the following statements holds:*
  1. *C only contains functions of type $c(\mathbf{x}) = a_c \Phi^\top \mathbf{x} + b_c$ for some $a_c, b_c \in \mathbb{R}$.*
  2. *C only contains functions of type $c(\mathbf{x}) = a_c e^{\Phi^\top \mathbf{x}} + b_c$ for some $a_c, b_c \in \mathbb{R}$.*

References

1. Ackermann, H., Röglin, H., Vöcking, B.: Pure Nash equilibria in player-specific and weighted congestion games. Theoret. Comput. Sci. 410(17), 1552–1563 (2009)
2. Andelman, N., Feldman, M., Mansour, Y.: Strong price of anarchy. Games Econom. Behav. 65(2), 289–317 (2009)
3. Anshelevich, E., Dasgupta, A., Kleinberg, J., Tardos, É., Wexler, T., Roughgarden, T.: The price of stability for network design with fair cost allocation. SIAM J. Comput. 38(4), 1602–1623 (2008)

4. Aumann, R.: Acceptable points in general cooperative n-person games. In: Luce, R., Tucker, A. (eds.) Contributions to the Theory of Games IV, pp. 287–324. Princeton University Press, Princeton (1959)
5. Fabrikant, A., Papadimitriou, C.H., Talwar, K.: The complexity of pure Nash equilibria. In: Proc. 36th Annual ACM Sympos. Theory Comput., pp. 604–612 (2004)
6. Fotakis, D., Kontogiannis, S., Spirakis, P.G.: Selfish unsplittable flows. Theoret. Comput. Sci. 348(2-3), 226–239 (2005)
7. Goemans, M.X., Mirrokni, V.S., Vetta, A.: Sink equilibria and convergence. In: Proc. 46th Annual IEEE Sympos. Foundations Comput. Sci., pp. 142–154 (2005)
8. Harks, T., Klimm, M.: On the existence of pure Nash equilibria in weighted congestion games. Math. Oper. Res. 37(3), 419–436 (2012)
9. Harks, T., Klimm, M., Möhring, R.H.: Characterizing the existence of potential functions in weighted congestion games. Theory Comput. Syst. 49(1), 46–70 (2011)
10. Harks, T., Klimm, M., Möhring, R.H.: Strong equilibria in games with the lexicographical improvement property. Internat. J. Game Theory 42(2), 461–482 (2012)
11. Koutsoupias, E., Papadimitriou, C.: Worst-case equilibria. In: Meinel, C., Tison, S. (eds.) STACS 1999. LNCS, vol. 1563, pp. 404–413. Springer, Heidelberg (1999)
12. Kukushkin, N.S.: Acyclicity in games with common intermediate objectives, Russian Academy of Sciences, Dorodnicyn Computing Center, Moscow (2004)
13. Libman, L., Orda, A.: Atomic resource sharing in noncooperative networks. Telecommun. Syst. 17(4), 385–409 (2001)
14. Panagopoulou, P.N., Spirakis, P.G.: Algorithms for pure Nash equilibria in weighted congestion games. ACM J. Exp. Algorithmics 11, 1–19 (2006)
15. Rosenthal, R.W.: A class of games possessing pure-strategy Nash equilibria. Internat. J. Game Theory 2(1), 65–67 (1973)
16. Rozenfeld, O., Tennenholtz, M.: Strong and correlated strong equilibria in monotone congestion games. In: Spirakis, P., Mavronicolas, M., Kontogiannis, S. (eds.) WINE 2006. LNCS, vol. 4286, pp. 74–86. Springer, Heidelberg (2006)

Time-Decaying Bandits for Non-stationary Systems

Junpei Komiyama[1,*] and Tao Qin[2]

[1] The University of Tokyo, 7-3-1 Hongo, Bunkyo-ku, Tokyo, Japan
junpei@komiyama.info
[2] Microsoft Research, No. 5 Danling Street, Haidian District, Beijing, 100080, P.R. China
taoqin@microsoft.com

Abstract. Contents displayed on web portals (e.g., news articles at Yahoo.com) are usually adaptively selected from a dynamic set of candidate items, and the attractiveness of each item decays over time. The goal of those websites is to maximize the engagement of users (usually measured by their clicks) on the selected items. We formulate this kind of applications as a new variant of bandit problems where new arms are dynamically added into the candidate set and the expected reward of each arm decays as the round proceeds. For this new problem, a direct application of the algorithms designed for stochastic MAB (e.g., UCB) will lead to over-estimation of the rewards of old arms, and thus cause a misidentification of the optimal arm. To tackle this challenge, we propose a new algorithm that can adaptively estimate the temporal dynamics in the rewards of the arms, and effectively identify the best arm at a given time point on this basis. When the temporal dynamics are represented by a set of features, the proposed algorithm is able to enjoy a sub-linear regret. Our experiments verify the effectiveness of the proposed algorithm.

1 Introduction

The multi-armed bandit (MAB) problem is a typical example of sequential decision-making problems under uncertain environments and can model many real-world applications such as an adaptive routing, clinical trials, and a variety of recommendation problems. Among those applications, the recommendation problems, such as news recommendation [10] and social bookmarks [12], are attracting more and more attention from both the academia and the industry. Using the language of MABs, a recommendation problem can be described as follows. Given a set of K arms (candidate items) to select (display), in each round (user visit) the system selects one arm from the set and show it to the user. The system then receives a reward (whether the user clicks on the item or not) for the arm. The goal of MAB is to design an algorithm that optimizes the cumulative reward (the total number of user clicks given a number of user visits), which is achieved by accurately identifying the arm with the best expected reward (click-through rate (CTR)).

A well studied MAB problem is the so-called stochastic MAB, in which it is assumed that the rewards of each arm is i.i.d. drawn from a fixed but unknown distribution. The upper confidence bound (UCB) algorithm [6] is the standard algorithm in this problem.

---

* This work was done while the author was visiting Microsoft Research Asia.

T.-Y. Liu et al. (Eds.): WINE 2014, LNCS 8877, pp. 460–466, 2014.

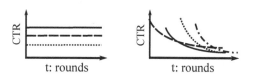

Fig. 1. Comparison between stochastic bandits and time-decaying bandits. The left figure shows a stochastic bandit where CTRs of the arms do not change over time. The right one shows a time-decaying bandit, where CTRs decay over rounds.

While the stochastic MAB successfully models many problems, it does not match well with the recommendation problems under our investigation, because it ignores an important factor of recommender systems: the attractiveness of an item to users decays over time. For example, it has been reported that new items (e.g., news articles in a web portals, and tweets in social networks) usually have larger CTRs than old ones [12], and a specific content will lose its attractiveness after being repeatedly displayed to the users [3]. In this situation, a simple application of the algorithms designed for stochastic MAB (e.g., UCB) will lead to over-estimation of the rewards of old arms, and thus cause a misidentification of the optimal arm.

Actually, the recommendation problems correspond to a new type of MAB problems, which we call the "time-decaying MAB", where the expected reward of each arm decays with respect to time (see Fig. 1). Before investigating such problems, the very first step is to characterize the decay factor. A simple way is to adopt a constant decay factor and integrate it into the stochastic MAB algorithms. However, in many real applications, such a characterization is inaccurate. This is because the decay factor (including magnitude and decreasing speed) varies largely among arms. Take news articles as examples. A breaking news usually quickly attracts a lot of attention, but the attention may drop significantly in just several hours. In contrast, news articles such as an enforcement of some national law usually warm up relatively slowly, but may attract a long-term attention like a week or so. In this case, it would be more appropriate to assume that the decaying factors for individual arms differ from each other and to learn them in an online manner. For this purpose, the learning algorithm needs to make exploration to simultaneously understand both the stochastic properties and the decaying factors of the rewards.

In this work, to solve the time-decaying MAB problems, we generalize the UCB algorithm by incorporating the information about the temporal dynamics into the computation of the upper confidence bounds of the arms. In particular, we represent the temporal dynamics by a set of basic time-dependent functions which consists of both fast and slow decays. The weights of individual functions are optimized by an application of the linear bandit technology. As a result, our algorithm is able to estimate the decay factor of each arm, which leads to an accurate estimation of the expected reward. Also, by choosing the arm of the largest index like the UCB algorithm, our algorithm balances exploration (give more chances to less selected arms for best arm identification) and exploitation (choosing the arm with the largest observed reward).

To summarize, the major contributions of our work lie in two aspects: (1) According to our knowledge, this is the first work that embeds temporal decay of the rewards into MAB problems. (2) We design an algorithm to solve the time-decaying MAB problems, the effectiveness of which is verified both theoretically and empirically.

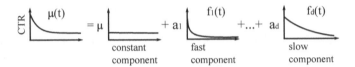

Fig. 2. CTR of an arm

2 Problem Setup

Time-decaying MAB extends stochastic MAB from two aspects: (1) new arms are continuously added to the candidate set, and (2) the expected reward of each arm decays in rounds. Let n be the total number of rounds, and $\mathcal{K}_t$ be the set of available arms in round $t \in [n]$. Let $r_{i,t}$ be the reward of arm i if it is selected at round t. In this work we take news recommendation as an example and exclusively consider the case of click-through feedback. Thus, in this case, $r_{i,t}$ is either 0 or 1, and the CTR of a news article corresponds to the expected reward of an arm. Henceforth, we use "news article" and "arm" interchangeably.

A time-decaying MAB goes as follows. At each round $t = 1, 2, ..., n$, a system selects one arm I_t from the candidate set $\mathcal{K}_t$ and receives a random reward $r_{I_t,t}$. Note that the reward information of the other arms are not available. The reward of arm i is drawn from a Bernoulli distribution parameterized by $\mu_{i,t}$, which assumes to be represented as the sum of a constant part μ_i and several basic decaying functions (see Fig. 2). Let $f_1(t - t_i), ..., f_d(t - t_i)$ be the set of basic decaying functions and $t - t_i$ be the number of rounds since arm i appears for the first time. The expected reward of arm i at round t can be modeled as $\mu_{i,t} = \mu_i + \sum_{k=1}^{d} a_{i,k} f_k(t-t_i)$, where $a_{i,k}$ is the weight associated with the k-th decaying function for arm i. Equivalently, by defining $\boldsymbol{x}_{i,t} = (1, f_1(t - t_i), \cdots, f_d(t - t_i)) \in R^{d+1}$ and $\boldsymbol{\theta}_i = (\mu_i, a_{i,1}, a_{i,2}, \cdots, a_{i,d}) \in R^{d+1}$, we can write $\mu_{i,t} = \boldsymbol{x}_{i,t}^\top \boldsymbol{\theta}_i$. That is, $\mu_{i,t}$ can be represented as a linear combination of a $(d + 1)$-dimensional "context" $\boldsymbol{x}_{i,t}$ which consists of the constant 1 and the values of functions $f_1(t - t_i), ..., f_d(t - t_i)$. We assume that the contexts and the weights are bounded as $||\boldsymbol{x}_{i,t}|| \leq L$ ($||\boldsymbol{x}|| = \sqrt{\boldsymbol{x}^\top \boldsymbol{x}}$) and $||\boldsymbol{\theta}_i|| \leq S$, respectively.

We define the optimal arm $i^*(t)$ as the arm with the largest expected reward at round t: $i^*(t) = \arg \max_{i \in \mathcal{K}_t} \mu_{i,t}$. Unlike the stochastic MAB, the optimal arm in our problem may vary in rounds, which is the essential difficulty in this problem. The performance of an algorithm is measured by the (pseudo) regret $R(n)$, which is defined as the difference between the cumulative expected reward of the optimal pulling policy (which knows the expected rewards of all arms at each round) and that of the arms selected by the algorithm: $R(n) = \sum_{t=1}^{n} \mu_{i^*(t),t} - \sum_{t=1}^{n} \mu_{I_t,t}$.

3 Algorithm

The key to solve the time-decaying MAB problem, where the reward of an arm can be represented as a linear combination of decaying functions, is to effectively estimate $\boldsymbol{\theta}_i$, the weights of individual decaying functions, for each arm. This falls into the framework

Algorithm 1. Time-decaying UCB

1: Inputs: $a(t), f_1(t - t_i), ..., f_d(t - t_i)$.
2: **for** $t = 1, 2, 3, ..., n$ **do**
3:     **for** $i \in \mathcal{K}_t$ **do**
4:         **if** arm i is new **then**
5:             $t_i = t$, $\mathbf{A}_{i,t} \leftarrow \mathbf{I}_{d+1}$ and $\boldsymbol{b}_{i,t} \leftarrow \mathbf{0}_{(d+1) \times 1}$
6:         **end if**
7:         $\boldsymbol{x}_{i,t} \leftarrow (1, f_1(t - t_i), ..., f_d(t - t_i))^T$
8:         $c_{i,t} \leftarrow a(t - t_i + 1)\|\boldsymbol{x}_{i,t}\|_{\mathbf{A}_{i,t}^{-1}}$, and $\hat{\mu}_{i,t} \leftarrow \boldsymbol{x}_{i,t}^\top \mathbf{A}_{i,t}^{-1} \boldsymbol{b}_{i,t}$
9:         $g_{i,t} \leftarrow \hat{\mu}_{i,t} + c_{i,t}$
10:     **end for**
11:     Choose arm $I_t = \arg\max\limits_{i \in \mathcal{K}_t} g_{i,t}$, and receive reward $r_{I_t,t} \in \{0, 1\}$
12:     $\mathbf{A}_{I_t,t+1} \leftarrow \mathbf{A}_{I_t,t} + \boldsymbol{x}_{I_t,t} \boldsymbol{x}_{I_t,t}^\top$ and $\boldsymbol{b}_{I_t,t+1} \leftarrow \boldsymbol{b}_{I_t,t} + r_{I_t,t} \boldsymbol{x}_{I_t,t}$
13:     **for** $i \neq I_t \in \mathcal{K}_t$ **do**
14:         $\mathbf{A}_{i,t+1} \leftarrow \mathbf{A}_{i,t}$ and $\boldsymbol{b}_{i,t+1} \leftarrow \boldsymbol{b}_{i,t}$
15:     **end for**
16: **end for**

---

of linear bandits [2,5,9,1], which perform an online estimation of linear weights with bandit feedback. The difference is that our problem contains multiple linear bandits: each arm can be considered as an instance of a linear bandit problem, whose context consists of a constant term and a series of temporal functions, while there is only one linear bandit in classical linear bandit problems[1]. In this sense, our problem is a hybrid of multi-armed bandits and linear bandits plus temporal decays.

Our proposed Algorithm 1 is shown as above, which we call time-decaying UCB. As can be seen, at each round of the algorithm, for each arm it constructs a matrix $\mathbf{A}_{i,t}$ and a vector $\boldsymbol{b}_{i,t}$, which are the sum of the covariance and the reward-weighted sum of features, respectively. $\hat{\mu}_{i,t}$, the least square estimation of the reward at round t, is given as $\boldsymbol{x}_{i,t}^\top \mathbf{A}_{i,t}^{-1} \boldsymbol{b}_{i,t}$. To guarantee the sufficient amount of exploration, we additionally introduce a confidence bound term $c_{i,t} = a(t)\|\boldsymbol{x}_{i,t}\|_{\mathbf{A}_{i,t}^{-1}}$, where $\|\boldsymbol{x}\|_\mathbf{A}$ is the matrix-induced vector norm $\sqrt{\boldsymbol{x}^\top \mathbf{A} \boldsymbol{x}}$. For the choice of $a(t)$, we show in the next section that a $O(\sqrt{\log t})$ function is appropriate to give a reliable confidence bound. Time-decaying UCB chooses the arm with the maximum UCB index $g_{i,t} = \hat{\mu}_{i,t} + c_{i,t}$.

4 Regret Bound

The following theorem shows that the proposed algorithm possesses a sublinear regret bound. The proof of the theorem, which combines the multi-armed bandit and the linear bandit techniques, is in the full version of this paper.

---

[1] There are several papers that analyze the regret of a linear bandit problem with multiple regressors (e.g., Cesa-Bianchi et al. [11], and Agrawal and Goyal [4]). However, The analysis in these papers are limited to the case where the set of arms does not change over time.

Theorem 1. *Let* $C(t, \delta') = \frac{1}{2}\sqrt{(d+1)\log\left(\frac{1+tL^2}{\delta'}\right)} + S$. *By setting* $\alpha(t) = C(t,$
$\delta/|\mathcal{K}_t|)$, *the regret of the proposed algorithm is upper-bounded as follows with probability at least* $1 - \delta^2$

$$R(n) \leq 2C(n, \delta/|\mathcal{K}_{all}|)\sqrt{|\mathcal{K}_{all}|n(d+1)(L^2+1)\log\left(1 + \frac{nL^2}{d+1}\right)} = \tilde{O}(\sqrt{|\mathcal{K}_{all}|n}),$$

$$(1)$$

where $\tilde{O}$ *hides a polylog factor, and* $\mathcal{K}_{all}$ *is the set of all the arms through the run.*

5   Experiments

In this section, we report the results of our simulation. The goal here is to compare the empirical performance of the proposed algorithm with that of existing ones.

We simulate a news recommender system, where the decay pattern of CTR of each news article is different from the others and new articles are continuously added into the system.

Rounds and Articles: We try different values: $n = \{10^5, 10^{5\frac{1}{3}}, 10^{5\frac{2}{3}}, ..., 10^7\}$. For each n, all the algorithms are run for 20 times and the results are averaged over the runs. At the beginning of each run, there are 20 articles in the candidate set. Then new articles are continuously added into the set. At the end of each run, 100 articles are involved.

CTRs and Decay Factor: We set the CTR of the i-th article as $\mu_{i,t} = m_i y(\Delta_i(t)/t_{h,i})$, where m_i is its initial CTR when it is added into the system and $y(\Delta_i(t)/t_{h,i})$ is the decay function. The initial CTRs of all the news articles are independently drawn from a uniform distribution in $[0, 0.15]$. We adopt the square root decay function $y(x) = 1/\sqrt{x+1}$, which is reported and used in a contest of news article recommendation for Yahoo! Homepage [8]. $t_{h,i}$ defines how fast CTR decays, and is independently drawn from an exponential distribution $P(t_{h,i}) = -\lambda \exp(-t/\lambda)$ with $\lambda = 0.02n$. $\Delta_i(t) = t - t_i$ was the number of the rounds after the article is added into the system. In this setting, CTR of the optimal article averaged over time is around 0.1, which is similar to the case of the Yahoo! news article dataset [13]. Note that the above parameters (including the number of rounds, decay function, etc.) are notified to none of the algorithms. Fig. 3 displays a part of time series of CTRs of the articles in a run.

Compared Algorithms: We take RANDOM, Exp3.S [7] and UCB [6] as baselines for comparison: RANDOM is the algorithm that uniformly samples an article from all available ones; Exp3.S is a variant of the Exp3 algorithm for switching environment; and UCB is a stochastic bandit algorithm that ignores temporal dynamics. For our time-decaying UCB, we implement three variants with different sets of the temporal feature: (1) Decaying-UCB-3 has three temporal components $\{f_1(\Delta_i(t)), f_2(\Delta_i(t)),$
$f_3(\Delta_i(t))\} = \{y(\Delta_i(t)/\lambda), y(2^4\Delta_i(t)/\lambda), y(2^8\Delta_i(t)/\lambda)\}$, (2) Decaying-UCB-5 has five temporal components $\{f_1(\Delta_i(t)), f_2(\Delta_i(t)), ..., f_5(\Delta_i(t))\} = \{y(\Delta_i(t)/\lambda), y(2^2\Delta_i(t)/\lambda), ..., y(2^8\Delta_i(t)/\lambda)\}$, and (3) Decaying-UCB-9 has nine

---

^{2} We can set $\delta = O(1/n)$.

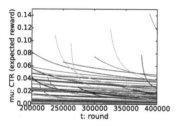

Fig. 3. CTRs (= expected rewards) of articles in a single run with $n = 10^6$. Each curve represents a CTR of an article. Most articles have low CTR, and the optimal article switches frequently.

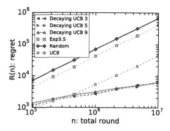

Fig. 4. The log-log plot of the regret of the algorithms. The horizontal axis is the number of total rounds (depend on the scale factor s) and the vertical line is the regret.

temporal components $\{f_1(\Delta_i(t)), f_2(\Delta_i(t)), ..., f_9(\Delta_i(t))\} = \{y(\Delta_i(t)/\lambda), y(2\Delta_i(t)/\lambda), ..., y(2^8\Delta_i(t)/\lambda)\}$. The hyper-parameters of the algorithms are set as follows: K in Exp3.S is set to 100, and S (switching number) is chosen best among $\{1, 2, 5, 10, 20, 50, 100\}$. $a(t)$ in UCB and in our time-decaying UCB, which determine the magnitude of the exploration, are chosen to be the best among $\{0.01, 0.02, 0.05, 0.1, 0.2, 0.5, 1.0\} \times \sqrt{\log t}$.

Regret Comparison: Fig. 4 shows the regrets of all the algorithms. RANDOM and Exp3.S are clearly worse than UCB and time-decaying UCB. The performances of the three variants of time-decaying UCB are very close: our algorithm is not very sensitive to the selection of the basic decaying functions. Further, UCB and time-decaying UCB perform similarly when n is small, and the latter performs much better when $n \geq 10^6$. Considering that the number of daily visitors of a web portal spans from millions to hundreds of millions, it is rather easy to obtain a large n, and therefore our algorithm is expected to perform better than other algorithms in real-world recommender systems.

6   Conclusion

In this paper, we have proposed a new type of bandit problems in which new arms are dynamically added into the candidate set and the expected reward of each arm decays as the round proceeds. The performance of the proposed algorithm is verified both theoretically and empirically. For future works, we will (1) design new algorithms with better regret bounds and (2) consider more complicated dynamics in real-world applications that go beyond simple time decay.

References

1. Abbasi-Yadkori, Y., Pál, D., Szepesvári, C.: Improved algorithms for linear stochastic bandits. In: NIPS, pp. 2312–2320 (2011)
2. Abe, N., Long, P.M.: Associative reinforcement learning using linear probabilistic concepts. In: ICML, pp. 3–11 (1999)

3. Agarwal, D., Chen, B.C., Elango, P.: Spatio-temporal models for estimating click-through rate. In: WWW, pp. 21–30 (2009)
4. Agrawal, S., Goyal, N.: Thompson sampling for contextual bandits with linear payoffs. In: ICML (3). JMLR Proceedings, vol. 28, pp. 127–135. JMLR.org (2013)
5. Auer, P.: Using confidence bounds for exploitation-exploration trade-offs. Journal of Machine Learning Research 3, 397–422 (2002)
6. Auer, P., Cesa-bianchi, N., Fischer, P.: Finite-time Analysis of the Multiarmed Bandit Problem. Machine Learning 47, 235–256 (2002)
7. Auer, P., Freund, Y., Schapire, R.E.: The non-stochastic multi-armed bandit problem. Siam Journal on Computing (2002)
8. Chou, K.C., Lin, H.T.: Balancing between estimated reward and uncertainty during news article recommendation for ICML 2012 exploration and exploitation challenge. ICML 2012 Workshop: Exploration and Exploitation 3 (2012)
9. Dani, V., Hayes, T.P., Kakade, S.M.: Stochastic linear optimization under bandit feedback. In: COLT, pp. 355–366 (2008)
10. Li, L., Chu, W., Langford, J., Schapire, R.E.: A contextual-bandit approach to personalized news article recommendation. In: WWW, pp. 661–670 (2010)
11. Cesa-Bianchi, N., Gentile, C., Zappella, G.: A Gang of Bandits. In: NIPS (2013)
12. Wu, F., Huberman, B.A.: Novelty and collective attention. Tech. rep., Proceedings of National Academy of Sciences (2007)
13. Yahoo!: Yahoo! Webscope dataset R6A/R6B. ydata-frontpage-todaymodule-clicks (2011), http://webscope.sandbox.yahoo.com/

Market Equilibrium under Piecewise Leontief Concave Utilities

[Extended Abstract]

Jugal Garg[*]

Max-Planck-Institut für Informatik, Germany
jugal.garg@gmail.com

Abstract. Leontief function is one of the most widely used function in economic modeling, for both production and preferences. However it lacks the desirable property of diminishing returns. In this paper, we consider piecewise Leontief concave (p-Leontief) utility function which consists of a set of Leontief-type segments with decreasing returns and upper limits on the utility. Leontief is a special case when there is exactly one segment with no upper limit.

We show that computing an equilibrium in a Fisher market with p-Leontief utilities, even with two segments, is PPAD-hard via a reduction from Arrow-Debreu market with Leontief utilities. However, under a special case when coefficients on segments are uniformly scaled versions of each other, we show that all equilibria can be computed in polynomial time. This also gives a non-trivial class of Arrow-Debreu Leontief markets solvable in polynomial time.

Further, we extend the results of [13,2] for Leontief to p-Leontief utilities. We show that equilibria in case of pairing economy with p-Leontief utilities are rational and we give an algorithm to find one using the Lemke-Howson scheme.

1 Introduction

Market equilibrium is a fundamental concept in mathematical economics and has been studied extensively since the work of Walras [11]. The notion of equilibrium is inherently algorithmic, with many applications in policy analysis and recently in e-commerce [4,7,9]. The Arrow-Debreu (exchange) market model consists of a set of agents and a set of goods, where each agent has an initial endowment of goods and a utility (preference) function over bundle of goods. At equilibrium, each agent buys a utility maximizing bundle from the money obtained by selling its initial endowment and the market clears.

It is customary in economics to assume utility functions to be concave and satisfying the law of diminishing returns. Leontief utility function is a well-studied concave function, where goods are complementary and they are needed in a fixed

---

[*] Work done while at Georgia Tech, Atlanta, USA.

T.-Y. Liu et al. (Eds.): WINE 2014, LNCS 8877, pp. 467–473, 2014.

proportion for deriving a positive utility, for e.g., bread and butter. It is a homogeneous function of degree one, where the utility is multiplied by α when the amount of each good is multiplied by α, for any $\alpha > 0$; hence it does not, as such, model diminishing returns. Consider the following example.

Example. Suppose Alice wants to consume sandwiches and for making a sandwich, she needs two slices of bread and one slice of cheese. It seems her utility function for bread and cheese can be modeled as a Leontief function, but it is not appropriate because her utility for the second sandwich is less than the first one due to satiation, and so on.

In this paper, we define piecewise Leontief concave (p-Leontief) utility function, which not only generalizes Leontief but also captures diminishing returns to scale and seems to be more relevant in economics. Further, we derive algorithmic and hardness results for both Fisher[1] and exchange market models under these functions. A p-Leontief utility function consists of a set of segments, where utility obtained on each segment is as per a Leontief function with a limit on the utility. The extra bundle needed, to obtain another unit of utility on segment k, is strictly more than that on segment k-1[2]. This puts a natural ordering on the segments, so that function remains concave and captures diminishing returns (see Section 2 for the precise definition). Observe that a Leontief function is simply a p-Leontief function with exactly one segment and no upper limit.

Recall the above example. Alice's utility for bread and cheese can be modeled as a p-Leontief function as follows: On the first segment, a unit of utility can be derived by consuming 2 slices of bread and 1 slice of cheese, and the upper limit is 1, *i.e.*, at most 1 unit of utility can be derived on this segment. On the second segment, a unit of utility can be derived by consuming 4 slices of bread and 2 slices of cheese, and the upper limit is 2, and so on.

Since Leontief function is a special case of p-Leontief function, all hardness results for Leontief utilities [2] simply carry over to p-Leontief utilities and we get the following theorem.

Theorem 1 (Hardness of Exchange p-Leontief). *Computing an equilibrium in an exchange market with p-Leontief utilities is PPAD-hard, and all equilibria can be irrational even if all input parameters are rational numbers.*

There is a qualitative difference between the complexity of computing an equilibrium in Fisher and Arrow-Debreu markets under Leontief utilities; while polynomial time in the former case through Eisenberg's convex program [6], it is PPAD-hard in the latter case [2]. In contrast, we show that Fisher is no easier than Arrow-Debreu under p-Leontief utilities and obtain the following theorem.

Theorem 2 (Hardness of Fisher p-Leontief). *Computing an equilibrium in Fisher market with p-Leontief utilities, even with two segments, is PPAD-hard.*

---

[1] A special case of exchange market model, defined in Section 2.

[2] By *strictly more than*, we mean at least one good is needed in greater amount.

For the above theorem, we essentially give a reduction from exchange p-Leontief with k segments to Fisher p-Leontief with $k + 1$ segments. Further we show that when coefficients on segments are uniformly scaled versions of each other, then Fisher market equilibria can be computed in polynomial time. This special case arises in many practical situations, like in the above example of Alice's utility function for bread and cheese. The proportion of bread and cheese on each segment remains 2:1, however her utility per unit of sandwich decreases.

This also gives us a non-trivial class of tractable exchange Leontief markets, where the sum of endowment matrix (W) and Leontief utility coefficient matrix (U) is a constant times all one matrix. We note that Fisher is a special case of exchange market model for which W is very special, however an exchange market satisfying our condition does not require W to be special and hence it does not arise from a Fisher market. To the best of our knowledge, apart from the Fisher markets, we are not aware of any other non-trivial tractable classes of exchange Leontief markets.

Pairing economy is a special case of exchange markets, where each agent brings a different good to the market (see Section 2 for precise definition). In case of a pairing economy with Leontief utilities, [2] showed that equilibria are rational and they are in one-to-one correspondence with the symmetric Nash equilibria in a symmetric bimatrix game. We extend the results of [2,13] for Leontief to p-Leontief and obtain the following (informal) theorem.

Theorem 3 (Pairing Economy: Rationality and Algorithm). *In a pairing economy with p-Leontief utilities, equilibrium prices are rational if all input parameters are rational. Further computing an equilibrium is PPAD-complete and there is a finite time algorithm to find one using the Lemke-Howson scheme.*

For this, we first characterize equilibrium conditions for exchange market with p-Leontief utilities using the *right* set of variables: a variable to capture price for each good and a variable to capture utility on each segment. In case of pairing economy, these conditions can be divided into two parts. The first part captures the utility on each segment, at equilibrium, as a linear complementarity problem (LCP) formulation, where we use the power of complementarity to ensure that segments are allocated in the correct order. The second part is a linear system of equations of type $Ap = p$ in prices given the utilities on each segment. Next we show that the LCP of first part can be solved using the Lemke-Howson scheme [8] and then we obtain the equilibrium prices by solving $Ap = p$. For this to work, we need a positive solution of $Ap = p$, which is guaranteed by the Perron-Frobenius theorem as A turns out to be a positive stochastic matrix.

Related Work. Since Leontief is a homogeneous function of degree one, equilibria in a Fisher market with Leontief utilities are captured by Eisenberg's convex program [6] and hence it is computable in polynomial time. Mas-Colell (in [5] by Eaves) gave an example of Leontief economy (both Fisher and exchange), where all equilibria are irrational, even if the input parameters are rational numbers; this discards the possibility of LCP based approach for Leontief economy.

Pairing economy model is used by [2] to show that computing an equilibrium in a Leontief exchange market is PPAD-hard and it has also been studied in many other settings, for e.g., [13,12,3,14]. There are generalizations of Leontief studied by [13,1]. [13] considered a class of piecewise linear concave (PLC) utility functions and showed that equilibrium in pairing economy is equivalent to solving an LCP. [1] studied market equilibrium under hybrid linear-Leontief utility function. Leontief is a special case in both of them, however these classes are still homogeneous of degree one and do not model the diminishing returns to scale. Hence they are quite different and not comparable with p-Leontief.

In this version of the paper, we only give an outline of the reduction from exchange to Fisher market, and refer the reader to the full version for details.

2   Preliminaries

Exchange Market. An exchange market consists of a set of agents $\mathcal{A}$ and a set of goods $\mathcal{G}$. Let $m \overset{\text{def}}{=} |\mathcal{A}|$ and $n \overset{\text{def}}{=} |\mathcal{G}|$. Each agent comes to the market with an initial endowment of goods, where W_{ij} is the amount of good j with agent i, and a utility function $u_i : \mathbb{R}_+^n \to \mathbb{R}_+$ over bundle of goods. Given prices of goods $\boldsymbol{p} = (p_1, \ldots, p_n)$, where p_j is the price of good j, each agent i earns $\sum_{j \in \mathcal{G}} W_{ij} p_j$ by selling its initial endowment and buys a (optimal) bundle which maximizes its utility function from the earned money. At *equilibrium* prices, market clears, i.e., demand of each good matches with its supply.

Fisher Market. A Fisher market consists of a set of agents $\mathcal{A}$ and a set of goods $\mathcal{G}$. Each agent i has money E_i, and a utility function $u_i : \mathbb{R}_+^n \to \mathbb{R}_+$ over bundle of goods. Let Q_j denotes the quantity of good j in the market. Given prices of goods, each agent i buys an optimal bundle subject to its budget constraints. At *equilibrium* prices, market also clears.

Leontief Utility Function. The Leontief utility function of agent i from a bundle $\boldsymbol{x}_i = (x_{i1}, \ldots, x_{in})$ of goods is defined as $u_i(\boldsymbol{x}_i) = \min_j \{ \frac{x_{ij}}{U_{ij}} \}$.

A way to represent Leontief utility function is by choosing x-axis to denote the amount of a good whose coefficient is positive. The amount of the remaining goods are just a fixed proportion of this amount. Fig. 1 depicts a simple example of Leontief utility function on two goods. The goods are required in 2:1 ratio, i.e., one unit of utility is obtained from consuming 2 units of good 1 and 1 unit of good 2.

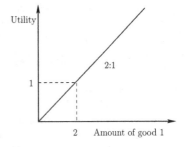

Fig. 1. Leontief utility function

Here agent i derives one unit of utility when it gets U_{ij} amount of each good j. If the utility function of each agent is Leontief, then it can be represented as a matrix $U = [U_{ij}]_{i \in \mathcal{A}, j \in \mathcal{G}}$, whose i^{th} row $U_i = [U_{ij}]_{j \in \mathcal{G}}$ contains all the coefficients of agent i.

p-Leontief Utility Function. A piecewise Leontief concave (p-Leontief) utility function consists of a set of segments (pieces), where the utility derived on each segment is a Leontief function with an upper limit. Further, the coefficient of segments are such that the function remains concave. Formally, let $u_i : \mathbb{R}^n_+ \to \mathbb{R}_+$ be the p-Leontief utility function of agent i with l segments. Since each segment k represents a Leontief function with a limit, it can be represented as $(U^k_i = [U^k_{ij}]_{j \in \mathcal{G}}, L^k_i)$, where U^k_i stores the coefficients of Leontief function and L^k_i stores the limit. The utility u_i from a bundle $\boldsymbol{x}_i = (x_{i1}, \ldots, x_{in})$ is defined as

$$u_i(\boldsymbol{x}_i) = \min_j \left\{ \frac{x_{ij}}{U^1_{ij}}, L^1_i \right\} + \max \left\{ \min_j \left\{ \frac{x_{ij} - L^1_i U^1_{ij}}{U^2_{ij}}, L^2_i \right\}, 0 \right\} + \cdots$$

$$\cdots + \max \left\{ \min_j \left\{ \frac{x_{ij} - \sum_{k=1}^{l-1} L^k_i U^k_{ij}}{U^l_{ij}}, L^l_i \right\}, 0 \right\}.$$

A way to represent p-Leontief utility function is by choosing x-axis to denote the amount of a good whose coefficient is positive. The amount of the remaining goods can be easily obtained from this amount. Fig. 2 depicts a simple example of p-Leontief utility function from two goods. It has three segments; on the first segment, one unit of utility is obtained from 2 units of good 1 and 1 unit of good 2, and the maximum utility that can be derived at this rate is L^1. After that the rate decreases to one unit of utility from 4 units of good 1 and 2 units of good 2 on the second segment, and the maximum utility at this rate is L^2, and so on.

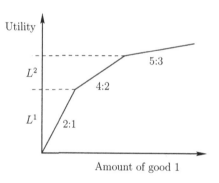

Fig. 2. p-Leontief utility function

Note that $L^k_i U^k_{ij}$ is the amount of good j needed to utilize segment k completely; essentially segments are utilized in order from 1 to l. Further, there is no upper limit on the last segment, i.e., $L^l_i = \infty$. To ensure diminishing returns and concavity, we enforce $U^{k+1}_i \geq U^k_i, \forall k \geq 1$.

3   Fisher Market with p-Leontief Utility Functions

In this section, we give a reduction from Leontief exchange market, where $U > 0$, to Fisher market with p-Leontief utility function which has two segments.

Theorem 4. *A Leontief exchange market $\mathcal{M}$, where $U > 0$, can be reduced to a Fisher market $\mathcal{M}'$ with p-Leontief utility function such that equilibria of $\mathcal{M}$ are in one-to-one correspondence with equilibria of $\mathcal{M}'$ (up to scaling).*

Proof. Let $\mathcal{M}$ is defined by (W, U) (see Section 2 for details), where W is initial endowment matrix and U is Leontief utility function matrix, such that $U_{ij} > 0, \forall(i, j)$. Without loss of generality, we assume that the total quantity of each good is unit, i.e., $\sum_i W_{ij} = 1, \forall j$. We will construct a Fisher market $\mathcal{M}'$ defined by $(E, Q, \widetilde{U}^1, \widetilde{U}^2, L^1)$, where E is initial money vector, Q is the quantity vector, $\widetilde{U}^k$ is Leontief utility function matrix for segment k for $k = 1, 2$, and $L^1 = [L_i^1]_{i \in \mathcal{A}}$ is the bound on maximum utility that can be obtained on the first segment for each agent i. Note that there is no bound on the maximum utility on the last segment.

The idea is to define the first segment, i.e., $\widetilde{U}^1$, such that at any prices p, each agent i buys it completely and the remaining money after that is equal to $\sum_j W_{ij} p_j$. Further, we also make sure that exactly unit amount of each good remains after consuming the first segment of each agent entirely. In that case, it is clear that if we define $\widetilde{U}^2 = U$, then on the second segment, Fisher becomes exactly same as exchange, and any equilibrium of $\mathcal{M}'$ will give an equilibrium of $\mathcal{M}$ and vice versa.

Let $m \stackrel{\text{def}}{=} |\mathcal{A}|$, $U_{max} \stackrel{\text{def}}{=} \max_{i,j} U_{ij}$, and $\Delta \stackrel{\text{def}}{=} m U_{max}$. We set

$$E_i = 1, \qquad \forall i \in \mathcal{A}$$
$$Q_j = m + 1, \qquad \forall j \in \mathcal{G}$$
$$\widetilde{U}_{ij}^1 = \frac{1}{\Delta}(\frac{m+1}{m} - W_{ij}), \forall(i, j) \in (\mathcal{A}, \mathcal{G})$$
$$L_i^1 = \Delta, \qquad \forall i \in \mathcal{A}$$
$$\widetilde{U}^2 = U.$$

Note that $\widetilde{U}_{ij}^1 > 0, \forall(i, j)$ as $W_{ij} \leq 1, \forall(i, j)$, and $\widetilde{U}_{ij}^1 \leq \widetilde{U}_{ij}^2, \forall(i, j)$ due to the choice of Δ. Market clearing condition implies that $(m+1)\sum_j p_j = \sum_i E_i = m$, we have $\sum_j p_j = \frac{m}{m+1}$. The money spent on the first segment by agent i is $\Delta \sum_j \frac{1}{\Delta}(\frac{m+1}{m} - W_{ij}) p_j = 1 - \sum_j W_{ij} p_j$. The remaining money left with agent i is $\sum_j W_{ij} p_j$ to spend on the second segment, which is exactly equal to the money with agent i in $\mathcal{M}$. Further, the total amount of good j needed to completely buy the first segment of each agent is $\sum_i(\frac{m+1}{m} - W_{ij}) = m$, hence the remaining amount is $1, \forall j$. Since the utility on the second segment $\widetilde{U}^2$ is same as U, hence each market equilibrium of $\mathcal{M}'$ will give a market equilibrium of $\mathcal{M}$ (up to scaling) and vice versa. □

Remark 5. The idea of designing the first segment so that it consumes extra money was also used in [10] for proving that Fisher market with separable piecewise-linear and concave utilities is PPAD-hard. However our reduction is more general and does not require the instance of exchange market to be special satisfying *price regulation* property as in [10].

References

1. Chen, X., Huang, L.S., Teng, S.H.: Market equilibria with hybrid linear-Leontief utilities. Theor. Comput. Sci. 410(17), 1573–1580 (2009)
2. Codenotti, B., Saberi, A., Varadarajan, K., Ye, Y.: Leontief economies encode two-player zero-sum games. In: SODA (2006)
3. Dang, C., Ye, Y., Zhu, Z.: An interior-point path-following algorithm for computing a Leontief economy equilibrium. Comp. Opt. and Appl. 50(2), 223–236 (2011)
4. Dixon, P.B., Jorgenson, D.W.: Handbook of Computable General Equilibrium Modeling SET, vols. 1A, 1B. Elsevier (Editors) (2013)
5. Eaves, B.C.: A finite algorithm for the linear exchange model. Journal of Mathematical Economics 3, 197–203 (1976)
6. Eisenberg, E.: Aggregation of utility functions. Management Sciences 7, 337–350 (1961)
7. Ellickson, B.: Competitive equilibrium: Theory and applications. Cambridge University Press (1994)
8. Lemke, C.E., Howson Jr., J.T.: Equilibrium points of bimatrix games. SIAM J. on Applied Mathematics 12(2), 413–423 (1964)
9. Shoven, J.B., Whalley, J.: Applying General Equilibrium. Cambridge University Press (1992)
10. Vazirani, V.V., Yannakakis, M.: Market equilibrium under separable, piecewise-linear, concave utilities. Journal of ACM 58(3), 10:1–10:25 (2011)
11. Walras, L.: Éléments d'économie politique pure ou théorie de la richesse sociale (Elements of Pure Economics, or the theory of social wealth). Lausanne, Paris (1874) (1899, 4th edn.; 1926, rev edn., 1954, Engl. transl.)
12. Wilkens, C.A.: The complexity of models of international trade. In: Leonardi, S. (ed.) WINE 2009. LNCS, vol. 5929, pp. 328–339. Springer, Heidelberg (2009)
13. Ye, Y.: Exchange market equilibria with Leontief's utility: Freedom of pricing leads to rationality. Theor. Comput. Sci. 378(2), 134–142 (2007)
14. Zhu, Z., Dang, C., Ye, Y.: A FPTAS for computing a symmetric Leontief competitive economy equilibrium. Math. Program. 131(1-2), 113–129 (2012)

Computing the Least-Core and Nucleolus for Threshold Cardinality Matching Games[*]

Qizhi Fang[1], Bo Li[1], Xiaoming Sun[2], Jia Zhang[2], and Jialin Zhang[2]

[1] School of Mathematical Sciences, Ocean University of China, Qingdao, China
qfang@ouc.edu.cn, boli198907@gmail.com
[2] Institute of Computing Technology, Chinese Academy of Sciences, Beijing, China
{sunxiaoming,zhangjia,zhangjialin}@ict.ac.cn

Abstract. In this paper, we study the algorithmic issues on the least-core and nucleolus of threshold cardinality matching games (TCMG). We first show that for a TCMG, the problems of computing least-core value, finding and verifying least-core payoff are all polynomial time solvable. We also provide a general characterization of the least core for a large class of TCMG. Next, based on Gallai-Edmonds Decomposition in matching theory, we give a concise formulation of the nucleolus for a typical case of TCMG which the threshold T equals 1. When the threshold T is relevant to the input size, we prove that the nucleolus can be obtained in polynomial time in bipartite graphs and graphs with a perfect matching.

1 Introduction

One of the important problems in cooperative games is how to distribute the total profit generated by a group of agents to individual participants. The prerequisite here is to make all the agents work together, *i.e.*, form a grand coalition. To achieve this goal, the collective profit should be distributed properly so as to minimize the incentive of subgroups of agents to deviate and form coalitions of their own. This intuition is formally captured by several solution concepts, such as the *core*, the *least-core*, and the *nucleolus*, which will be the focus of this paper.

The algorithmic issues in cooperative games are especially interesting since the definitions of many solution concepts would involve in an exponential number of constraints [11]. Megiddo [9] suggested that finding a solution should be done by an efficient algorithm, *i.e.*, within time polynomial in the number of agents. Deng and Papadimitriou [5] suggested the computational complexity be taken into consideration as another measure of fairness for evaluating and comparing different solution concepts. Subsequently, various interesting complexity and algorithmic results have been investigated [4, 6, 7].

---

[*] The work is partially supported by National Natural Science Foundation of China (NSFC) (NO. 61170062, 61222202, 61433014, 61173009, 11271341). Full version can be seen at: http://arxiv.org/abs/1409.5987.

T.-Y. Liu et al. (Eds.): WINE 2014, LNCS 8877, pp. 474–479, 2014.
© Springer International Publishing Switzerland 2014

Matching game is one of the most important combinatorial cooperative games which has attracted much attention [2,3,7]. Kern and Paulusma [7] presented an efficient algorithm for computing the nucleolus for cardinality matching games. Then Biró, Kern, and Paulusma [2] developed an efficient algorithm for computing the nucleolus for matching games on weighted graphs when the core is nonempty. Chen, Lu and Zhang [3] further discussed the fractional matching games. We follow the stream and study the least-core and nucleolus of a natural variation of matching games, called threshold matching games [1].

In this paper, we aim at computing the least-core and the nucleolus for the threshold matching games on unweighted graph, especially when the core is empty. Firstly, we show that for an arbitrary threshold value, the least-core can be obtained in polynomial time through separation oracle technique. By linear program duality, we further provide a general characterization of the least core for a large class of threshold cardinality matching games, which can be used to simplify the sequence of linear programs of the nucleolus. Secondly, we discuss the algorithms for the nucleolus. Especially, when the threshold being one (which is called *edge coalitional games*), we know that finding the least-core and the nucleolus can be done efficiently based on a clear description of the least-core. When the threshold value is relevant to the input size, we prove that the least-core and the nucleolus can also be computed in polynomial time for the games on two typical graphs, the graphs with a perfect matching or bipartite graphs. To our surprise, in all the cases considered, the least-core and the nucleolus do not depend on the value of the threshold. We conjecture our method can be generalized into dealing with general graphs.

2 Preliminaries and Definitions

A cooperative game $\Gamma = (N, v)$ consists of a player set $N = \{1, 2, \cdots, n\}$ and a value function $v : 2^N \to R$ with $v(\emptyset) = 0$. $\forall S \subseteq N$, $v(S)$ represents the profit obtained by S without the help of others. We use $x = (x_1, x_2, \cdots, x_n)$ to represent the payoff vector while x_i is the payoff for player i. For convenience, let $x(S) \triangleq \sum_{i \in S} x_i$. The *core* of Γ is defined as: $\mathcal{C}(\Gamma) := \{x \in R^n : x(N) = v(N) \text{ and } x(S) \geq v(S), \forall S \subseteq N\}$.

A payoff vector in $\mathcal{C}(\Gamma)$ guarantees that any coalition S cannot get more profit if it breaks away from the grand coalition. When $\mathcal{C}(\Gamma) = \emptyset$, there is a nature relaxation of the core: the *least-core*. Given $\varepsilon \leq 0$, an imputation x is in the ε-*core* of Γ, if it satisfies $x(S) \geq v(S) + \varepsilon$ for all $S \subset N$. Let $\varepsilon^* := \sup\{\varepsilon | \varepsilon\text{-core of } \Gamma \text{ is nonempty}\}$. The ε^*-core is called the least-core of Γ, denoted by $\mathcal{LC}(\Gamma)$, and the value ε^* is called the $\mathcal{LC}(\Gamma)$ value. Obviously, the optimal solution of the following linear program LP_1 is exactly the value and the imputations in $\mathcal{LC}(\Gamma)$:

$$LP_1 : \quad \begin{array}{c} \max \quad \varepsilon \\ \text{s.t.} \end{array} \begin{cases} x(S) \geq v(S) + \varepsilon, & \forall S \subset N \\ x_i \geq v(\{i\}), & \forall i \in N \\ x(N) = v(N). \end{cases}$$

Now we turn to the concept of the *nucleolus*. Given any payoff x, the excess of a coalition S under x is defined as $e(x, S) = x(S) - v(S)$, which can be viewed as the satisfaction degree of the coalition S under the given x. The *excess vector* is the vector $\theta(x) = (e(x, S_1), e(x, S_2), \cdots, e(x, S_{2^n-2}))$, where $S_1, \cdots, S_{2^n-2}$ is a list of all nontrivial subsets of N that satisfies $e(x, S_1) \leq e(x, S_2) \leq \cdots \leq e(x, S_{2^n-2})$. The nucleolus of the game Γ, denoted by $\eta(\Gamma)$, is the payoff x that lexicographically maximizes the excess vector $\theta(x)$.

Kopelowitz [8] proposed that $\eta(\Gamma)$ can be computed by recursively solving the following sequential linear programs $SLP(\eta(\Gamma))$ ($k = 1, 2, \cdots$):

$$LP_k : \quad \begin{array}{l} \max \quad \varepsilon \\ \text{s.t.} \quad \begin{cases} x(S) = v(S) + \varepsilon_r, & \forall S \in \mathcal{J}_r \quad r = 0, 1, \cdots, k-1 \\ x(S) \geq v(S) + \varepsilon, & \forall S \in 2^N \setminus \cup_{r=0}^{k-1} \mathcal{J}_r \\ x_i \geq v(\{i\}), & \forall i \in N \\ x(N) = v(N). \end{cases} \end{array}$$

Initially, we set $\mathcal{J}_0 = \{\emptyset, N\}$ and $\varepsilon_0 = 0$. The number ε_r is the optimal value of the r-th program LP_r, and $\mathcal{J}_r = \{S \subseteq N : x(S) = v(S) + \varepsilon_r, \forall x \in X_r\}$, where $X_r = \{x \in R^n : (x, \varepsilon_r) \text{ is an optimal solution of } LP_r\}$. We call a coalition in $\mathcal{J}_r$ *fixed* since its allocation is fixed to a number. Kopelowitz [8] showed that this procedure converges in at most n steps.

We now introduce the definitions of threshold matching games. For a weighted graph $G = (V, E; w)$ and a threshold $T \in R^+$, the corresponding *threshold matching game* (TMG) is a cooperative game defined as $\Gamma = (V, w; T)$. We have the player set V and $\forall S \subseteq V$,

$$v(S) \triangleq \begin{cases} 1, & \text{if } w(M) \geq T, \text{ where } M \text{ is the maximum weight matching of } G[S] \\ 0, & \text{otherwise} \end{cases}$$

where $G[S]$ is the induced subgraph by S on G, $w(M) = \sum_{e \in M} w(e)$. By Theorem 1 in [6], when $\mathcal{C}(\Gamma) \neq 0$, the core and the nucleolus can be given directly. However, when $\mathcal{C}(\Gamma) = 0$, the least-core and the nucleolus is hard to compute [1].

In the following we restrict ourselves to *threshold cardinality matching game* (TCMG) $\Gamma = (V; T)$ based on unweighted graph $G = (V, E)$. That is, $\forall S \subseteq N$, $v(S) = 1$ if the size of a maximum matching in $G[S]$ is no less than T, and $v(S) = 0$ otherwise.

Let $G = (V, E)$ be a graph. Given $A \subseteq V$, we use $\mathcal{B}$ and $\mathcal{D}$ denote the set of even components and odd components in $G \setminus A$, respectively. A set $A \subseteq V$ is called a *Tutte set* if each maximum matching M^* of G can be decomposed as $M^* = M_{\mathcal{B}} \cup M_{A,\mathcal{D}} \cup M_{\mathcal{D}}$, where $M_{\mathcal{B}}$ ($M_{\mathcal{D}}$) induces a perfect (nearly perfect) matching in any component $B \in \mathcal{B}$ ($D \in \mathcal{D}$), and $M_{A,\mathcal{D}}$ is a matching which matches every vertex in A to some vertex in an odd component in $\mathcal{D}$.

Lemma 1 (Gallai-Edmonds Decomposition) [10] *Given $G = (V, E)$, one can construct a Tutte set $A \subseteq V$ in polynomial time such that*

1. *all odd components $D \in \mathcal{D}$ are factor-critical;*
2. *$\forall D \in \mathcal{D}$ there is a maximum matching M^* of G which does not completely cover D (we say M^* leaves D uncovered).*

3   Least-Core of TCMG

Throughout this section, let $\Gamma = (V; T)$ be the TCMG defined on an unweighted graph $G = (V, E)$ with threshold $T : 1 \leq T \leq v^*$. Since both testing the core nonemptiness and finding a core member can be done efficiently, we focus on the case where $\mathcal{C}(\Gamma) = \emptyset$.

From a subtle analysis, we can conclude that the least-core $\mathcal{LC}(\Gamma)$ of TCMG can be characterized as the optimal solution of the following linear program LP_1^T:

$$\max \varepsilon$$

$$LP_1^T : \quad \text{s.t.} \quad \begin{cases} x(M_T) \geq 1 + \varepsilon, & \forall M_T \in \mathcal{M}_T \\ x(V) = 1 \\ x_i \geq 0, & i = 1, 2, \cdots, n. \end{cases}$$

We can show that least-core can be solved efficiently by ellipsoid method with a polynomial time separation oracle.

Theorem 1. *If $\Gamma = (V; T)$ is a TCMG with empty core, then the problems of computing the $\mathcal{LC}(\Gamma)$ value, finding a $\mathcal{LC}(\Gamma)$ member and checking if an imputation is in $\mathcal{LC}(\Gamma)$ are all polynomial time solvable.*

In the following, we further provide a characterization of the least core of TCMG under some conditions. Denote $\mathcal{M}_T = \{M_1, M_2, \cdots, M_m\}$ be the set of all matchings whose sizes are exact T, and let $a_1, a_2, \cdots, a_m$ be the the indicator vectors of the set of vertices that are covered by the matchings in $\mathcal{M}_T$. We have the following result which is quite useful in the algorithm design for the nucleolus in next sections.

Theorem 2. *Let $\Gamma = (V; T)$ be a TCMG with empty core. If $(\frac{2T}{n}, \cdots, \frac{2T}{n})_n$ is a convex combination of $a_1, a_2 \cdots, a_m$, then the value of $\mathcal{LC}(\Gamma)$ is $\varepsilon = \frac{2T}{n} - 1$ and $(\frac{1}{n}, \cdots, \frac{1}{n})_n \in \mathcal{LC}(\Gamma)$.*

4   Nucleolus of TCMG

We firstly consider the *edge coalitional game* (ECG) $\Gamma^1 = (V; 1)$ defined on an unweighted graph $G = (V, E)$, *i.e.*, the TCMG with threshold $T = 1$. When $\mathcal{C}(\Gamma^1) = \emptyset$, the linear program for $\mathcal{LC}(\Gamma^1)$ is as follows:

$$\max \quad \varepsilon$$

$$LP_1^1 : \quad \text{s.t.} \quad \begin{cases} x_i + x_j \geq 1 + \varepsilon, & \forall e = (i, j) \in E \\ x(V) = 1 \\ x_i \geq 0, & i = 1, 2, \cdots, n. \end{cases}$$

According to Gallai-Edmonds Decomposition, every graph can be decomposed into $\mathcal{A}$, $\mathcal{B}$, $\mathcal{D}$. Let $\mathcal{D}_0$ be the set of singletons in $\mathcal{D}$ ($\mathcal{D}_0$ may be empty). Let G_0 be a bipartite graph with vertex set $A \cup \mathcal{D}_0$ and edge set consisting of edges with two endpoints in A and $\mathcal{D}_0$ separately. Find a maximum matching M_0 in G_0. Denote the matched vertices in A and $\mathcal{D}_0$ by A_1 and $\mathcal{D}_{01}$ with respect to M_0. Let $A_2 = A \setminus A_1$ and $\mathcal{D}_{02} = \mathcal{D} \setminus \mathcal{D}_{01}$.

If $\mathcal{D}_{02} = \emptyset$, by making use of Theorem 2, the least-core value and an imputation in the least-core can be obtained directly:

Proposition 1 *Given an ECG $\Gamma^1 = (V; 1)$, if $\mathcal{D}_{02} = \emptyset$, then the value of $\mathcal{LC}(\Gamma^1)$ is $\varepsilon = \frac{2}{n} - 1$ and $(\frac{1}{n}, \cdots, \frac{1}{n})_n \in \mathcal{LC}(\Gamma)$.*

When $\mathcal{D}_{02} \neq \emptyset$, we cannot find such a convex combination. But if we delete $\mathcal{D}_{02}$ from G, we can find a convex combination in $G' = G[V \setminus \mathcal{D}_{02}]$ by using the similar argument Proposition 1. Denote Γ' to be the corresponding ECG defined on G' and the value of $\mathcal{LC}(\Gamma')$ is $\frac{2}{n'} - 1$ where $n' = n - |\mathcal{D}_{02}|$. Consider the following imputation $\widetilde{x}$:

$i \in V$	$i \in V(\mathcal{B})$	$i \in V(A)$ and $\mathcal{D}_{02} \to i$	$i \in V(A)$ and $\mathcal{D}_{02} \nrightarrow i$	$i \in V(\mathcal{D}_{01})$ and $\mathcal{D}_{02} \to i$	$i \in V(\mathcal{D}_{01})$ and $\mathcal{D}_{02} \nrightarrow i$	$i \in V(\mathcal{D}_{02})$
$\widetilde{x}_i$	$\frac{1}{n'}$	$\frac{2}{n'}$	$\frac{1}{n'}$	0	$\frac{1}{n'}$	0

Here, $\mathcal{D}_{02} \to i$ (or $\mathcal{D}_{02} \nrightarrow i$) represents i is reachable (or unreachable) from $\mathcal{D}_{02}$ by M_0-alternating path in G_0. We can easily check that the imputation $\widetilde{x}$ with $\varepsilon = \frac{2}{n'} - 1$ is feasible, *i.e.*, the value of $\mathcal{LC}(\Gamma^1)$ is also $\frac{2}{n'} - 1$.

We then focus on the computation of nucleolus. Since we have seen $\varepsilon_1 = \frac{2}{n'} - 1$, we can prove LP_k^1 in $SLP(\eta(\Gamma^1))$ can be rewritten as:

$$LP_k^1 : \quad \max \quad \varepsilon$$
$$\text{s.t.} \quad \begin{cases} x(e) = \frac{2}{n'} - \varepsilon_1 + \varepsilon_r, & e \in E_r, r = 1, \cdots, k-1 \\ x_i = -\varepsilon_1 + \varepsilon_r, & i \in V_r, r = 1, \cdots, k-1 \\ x(e) \geq \frac{2}{n'} - \varepsilon_1 + \varepsilon, & e \in E \setminus \bigcup_{r=1}^{k-1} E_r \\ x_i \geq -\varepsilon_1 + \varepsilon, & i \in V \setminus \bigcup_{r=1}^{k-1} V_r \\ x(V) = 1, \ x_i \geq 0, & i \in V. \end{cases}$$

Initially set $E_0 = V_0 = \emptyset$ and $\varepsilon_0 = 0$. The number ε_r is the optimal value of the r-th program LP_r^1, and $E_r = \{e \in E : x(e) = 1 + \varepsilon_r, \forall x \in X_r\}$, $V_r = \{i \in N : x_i = 1 - \frac{2}{n'} + \varepsilon_r, \forall x \in X_r\}$, where $X_r = \{x \in R^n : (x, \varepsilon_r)$ is an optimal solution of $LP_r^1\}$. Therefore, the size of the linear programs in LP_1^1 and $SLP(\eta(\Gamma^1))$ are all polynomial. It follows that the least-core and the nucleolus of ECG can be computed efficiently.

Theorem 3. *Given an ECG $\Gamma^1 = (V; 1)$, the nucleolus $\eta(\Gamma^1)$ can be obtained in polynomial time.*

Now we consider the general case $\Gamma^T = (V; T)$ with arbitrary threshold $1 \leq T \leq v^*$. In the following theorem, we firstly show that for the graphs with a perfect matching, the least-core of Γ^T is independent of T. Then we use this characterization to prove that the nucleolus of Γ^T can be obtained in polynomial time and $\eta(\Gamma^T)$ is also independent of T.

Theorem 4. *Suppose $G = (V, E)$ is a simple graph which has a perfect matching and $\Gamma^T = (V; T)$ is a TCMG defined on G. Let $\Gamma^1 = (V; 1)$ be the corresponding ECG defined also on G. Then the value of $\mathcal{LC}(\Gamma^T)$ is $\varepsilon_1^T = \frac{2T}{n} - 1$ and $\mathcal{LC}(\Gamma^T) = \mathcal{LC}(\Gamma^1)$. Furthermore, $\eta(\Gamma^T) = \eta(\Gamma^1)$.*

Let $G = (L, R; E)$ be a bipartite graph with vertex set $L \cup R$ and edge set E. Find a maximum matching M^* in G. Denote the matched vertices in L and R as L_1 and R_1 with respect to M^* respectively. Let $L_2 = L \setminus L_1$ and $R_2 = R \setminus R_1$. If both L_2 and R_2 are empty, it is reduced to the situation in Theorem 4. So we assume at least one of L_2 and R_2 is not empty. If we delete L_2 and R_2 from G, we can find the least-core value and an imputation in least-core by Theorem 4. Denote Γ' to be the corresponding TCMG defined on G' where G' is the induced subgraph by $(L \cup R) \setminus (L_2 \cup R_2)$ in G. Then the value of $\mathcal{LC}(\Gamma')$ is $\frac{2T}{n'} - 1$ where $n' = n - |L_2| - |R_2|$. It is obvious that $\frac{2T}{n'} - 1$ is an upper bound of the value of $\mathcal{LC}(\Gamma^T)$. Actually, we can show that this is actually the value of the least-core in the bipartite graphs.

Theorem 5. *Suppose $G = (L, R; E)$ is a bipartite graph and $\Gamma^T = (V; T)$ is a TCMG defined on G. Let $\Gamma^1 = (V; 1)$ be the corresponding ECG defined also on G. Then the value of $\mathcal{LC}(\Gamma^T)$ is $\varepsilon_1^T = \frac{2T}{n'} - 1$ and $\mathcal{LC}(\Gamma^T) = \mathcal{LC}(\Gamma^1)$, here $n' = n - |L_2| - |R_2|$. Furthermore, $\eta(\Gamma^T) = \eta(\Gamma^1)$.*

References

1. Aziz, H., Brandt, F., Harrenstein, P.: Monotone cooperative games and their threshold versions. In: Proceedings of the 9th International Conference on Autonomous Agents and Multiagent Systems, vol. 1, pp. 1107–1114 (2010)
2. Biró, P., Kern, W., Paulusma, D.: Computing solutions for matching games. International Journal of Game Theory 41(1), 75–90 (2012)
3. Chen, N., Lu, P., Zhang, H.: Computing the nucleolus of matching, cover and clique games. In: Proceedings of the 26th AAAI Conference on Artificial Intelligence (2012)
4. Deng, X., Fang, Q., Sun, X.: Finding nucleolus of flow game. Journal of Combinatorial Optimization 18(1), 64–86 (2009)
5. Deng, X., Papadimitriou, C.H.: On the complexity of cooperative solution concepts. Mathematics of Operations Research 19(2), 257–266 (1994)
6. Elkind, E., Goldberg, L.A., Goldberg, P.W., Wooldridge, M.: Computational complexity of weighted threshold games. In: Proceedings of the National Conference on Artificial Intelligence, vol. 22, p. 718 (2007)
7. Kern, W., Paulusma, D.: Matching games: the least-core and the nucleolus. Mathematics of Operations Research 28(2), 294–308 (2003)
8. Kopelowitz, A.: Computation of the kernels of simple games and the nucleolus of n-person games. Technical report, DTIC Document (1967)
9. Megiddo, N.: Computational complexity of the game theory approach to cost allocation for a tree. Mathematics of Operations Research 3(3), 189–196 (1978)
10. Plummer, M.D., Lovász, L.: Matching theory. Access Online via Elsevier (1986)
11. Schmeidler, D.: The nucleolus of a characteristic function game. SIAM Journal on Applied Mathematics 17(6), 1163–1170 (1969)

Approximate Pure Nash Equilibria in Social Context Congestion Games

Martin Gairing[1], Grammateia Kotsialou[1], and Alexander Skopalik[2]

[1] University of Liverpool, U.K.
{gairing,gkotsia}@liverpool.ac.uk
[2] University of Paderborn, Germany
skopalik@mail.upb.de

Abstract. We study the existence of approximate pure Nash equilibria in social context congestion games. For any given set of allowed cost functions $\mathcal{F}$, we provide a threshold value $\mu(\mathcal{F})$, and show that for the class of social context congestion games with cost functions from $\mathcal{F}$, α-Nash dynamics are guaranteed to converge to α-approximate pure Nash equilibrium if and only if $\alpha > \mu(\mathcal{F})$.

Interestingly, $\mu(\mathcal{F})$ is related and always upper bounded by Roughgarden's anarchy value [19].

1 Introduction

In recent years, *social context games* [1] have been used to model other-regarding preferences in multiple scenarios.

In this paper, we continue the study of altruistic social context in congestion games. Congestion games always admit a *pure* Nash equilibrium, where players pick a single strategy and do not randomise. Rosenthal [18] showed this by introducing an (exact) potential function. Such a function has the property that if a single player deviates to an alternative strategy, then the potential changes by the same amount as the cost of the deviating player.

The existence of pure Nash equilibria is a desirable property of games. Unfortunately, in congestion games this property is very fragile. Several generalisations of congestion games do not possess such states in general. Examples include *weighted* congestion games [8, 10, 15], *player specific* congestion games [16], and *social context* congestion games [1]. A natural question to ask is how much we have to relax the equilibrium condition in order to guarantee the existence of pure equilibria. More precisely, we are interested in the existence of an α-approximate pure Nash equilibrium, a pure strategy profile in which no player can improve by a factor $\alpha > 1$. For weighted congestion games, this question has recently been addressed by Hansknecht et al. [11], who showed that α-approximate pure Nash equilibria exist for reasonable small values of α.

Our contribution. In this paper, we study the existence of approximate pure Nash equilibria in *social context congestion games*.

T.-Y. Liu et al. (Eds.): WINE 2014, LNCS 8877, pp. 480–485, 2014.

As our main result, we show that for the class of social context congestion games with asymmetric social context and with cost functions from some given set $\mathcal{F}$ of allowed cost functions, there is a threshold value $\mu(\mathcal{F})$, such that:

- For any $\alpha > \mu(\mathcal{F})$, α-Nash dynamics converge to an α-approximate Nash equilibrium (Theorem 1). In other words, such games are α-potential games.
- For $\alpha = \mu(\mathcal{F})$, there exits a social context congestion game with cost functions in $\mathcal{F}$, where α-Nash dynamics cycle. We construct even a game with binary social context where each player can choose between one of two resources with identical cost function (Theorem 2).

The threshold value $\mu(\mathcal{F})$ is defined as follows:

Definition 1. *For a set of allowed cost functions $\mathcal{F}$, define*

$$\mu(\mathcal{F}) = \sup_{d \in \mathcal{F}} \sup_{x \in \mathbb{N}} \left\{ \frac{x \cdot d(x)}{(x-1) \cdot d(x-1) + d(x)} \right\}.$$

Note that $\mu(\mathcal{F})$ is related to the *anarchy value* $\beta(\mathcal{F})$ introduced by Roughgarden [19]. He showed that the *price of anarchy* of non-atomic congestion games with cost functions in $\mathcal{F}$ is upper bounded by

$$\beta(\mathcal{F}) = \sup_{d \in \mathcal{F}} \sup_{x, y \geq 0} \left\{ \frac{x \cdot d(x)}{y \cdot d(y) + (x-y) \cdot d(x)} \right\}.$$

Obviously, $\mu(\mathcal{F}) \leq \beta(\mathcal{F})$ for all sets of cost functions $\mathcal{F}$, since $\mu(\mathcal{F})$ is more restrictive, i.e., it requires $y = x - 1$ and $x \in \mathbb{N}$. For some $\mathcal{F}$, e.g., polynomials of maximum degree Δ with non-negative coefficients, $\mu(\mathcal{F}) \approx \beta(\mathcal{F})$. However, $\mu(\mathcal{F})$ can also be significantly better, e.g. for exponential cost functions.

For general cost functions, $\mu(\mathcal{F})$ can also be unbounded. Consider, for example, a convex function where $d(x - 1) = 0$ and $d(x) = 1$. For such functions, one can easily adapt our analysis to show that α-improvements cycle for some $\alpha = \Theta(n)$. In Section 3, we show that if we restrict to *symmetric* social context, there can be a cycle of $\Theta(\sqrt{n})$-improvements even for singleton games with binary context on two resources with convex cost functions. We also show that in this case $\Theta(\sqrt{n})$ is worst possible.

Related work. In recent years, the impact of altruism and spite in games has been widely studied (see e.g.[13, 14] and references therein). Hoefer and Skopalik [13] studied the existence of pure Nash equilibria in social context games. They showed that such games admit an exact potential function if and only if they are isomorphic to a social context congestion game with linear cost functions. They also showed that singleton congestion games with binary social context might not admit a pure Nash equilibrium for concave cost functions.[1]For convex cost functions they left the existence of a pure Nash equilibrium as an open problem.

---

[1] Our analysis contrasts this by showing that they admit 4/3-approximate pure Nash equilibria.

Congestion games without social context always admit a pure Nash equilibrium [18] and computing such an equilibrium is PLS-complete [7]. Skopalik and Vöcking [20] and Caragiannis et al. [2, 3] study the complexity of α-approximate pure Nash equilibria in different scenarios.

Harks et al. [12] characterise weighted congestion games admitting a potential function. Gairing and Klimm [9] provide such a characterisation for player-specific congestion games.

Chien and Sinclair [5] studied the convergence to α-approximate Nash equilibria in symmetric congestion games. Chen and Roughgarden [4] used approximate potential functions to show the existence of approximate pure Nash equilibria in network design games. Christodoulou et al. [6] used approximate potential functions to provide tight bound on the efficiency of approximate pure Nash equilibria.

Model. Let $N = \{1, \cdots, n\}$ be a non-empty finite set of n players and let $R = \{1, \cdots, m\}$ be a non-empty finite set of m resources. A *congestion game* is a tuple $(N, R, (S_i)_{i \in N}, (d_r)_{r \in R})$, where each player chooses as his pure strategy a set $s_i \subseteq R$ from a given set of available strategies $S_i \subseteq 2^R$. A *state* or *strategy profile* $\mathsf{s} = (s_1, \ldots, s_n)$ specifies a strategy for every player. Each resource $r \in R$ is associated with a *cost* or *delay* function $d_r : \mathbb{N} \to \mathbb{R}^+$. The *load* $n_r(\mathsf{s})$ of resource r in a state s is the number of players using resource r, i.e., $n_r(\mathsf{s}) = |\{i \in N : r \in s_i\}|$. The *personal cost* of a player i is given by $c_i(\mathsf{s}) = \sum_{r \in s_i} d_r(n_r(\mathsf{s}))$.

We extend the definition of congestion games by embedding in it a social context. A *social context* is defined by an $n \times n$ matrix $F = (f_{ij})_{i,j \in N}$ where f_{ij} expresses player i's interest towards player j. A social context is *symmetric*, if $f_{ij} = f_{ji}$ for all $i, j \in N$. Otherwise, the context *assymetric*. Throughout, we assume that $f_{ii} \geq f_{ij}$ for all $i, j \in N$ and that the *self-interest* value for every player i is scaled to $f_{ii} = 1$. This implies that $f_{ij} \leq 1$.

The *perceived cost* of a player $i \in N$ is given by a linear combination of his personal cost and a weighted sum of personal costs of the remaining players,

$$c_i(\mathsf{s}, F) = c_i(\mathsf{s}) + \sum_{j \in N, j \neq i} f_{ij} \cdot c_j(\mathsf{s}) = \sum_{j \in N} f_{ij} \cdot c_j(\mathsf{s}).$$

The social context extension of congestion games is classified as a cost minimisation game where every player wishes to minimise his perceived cost.

In a social context congestion game, for $\alpha \geq 1$, a unilateral deviation is called an α-*improvement move* for player i if

$$c_i(s_i, \mathsf{s}_{-i}, F) > \alpha \cdot c_i(s_i', \mathsf{s}_{-i}, F).$$

A sequence of α-improvement moves is called α-*Nash dynamics*. An α-*approximate pure Nash equilibrium* in a game with social context is a state $\mathsf{s} \in S$ where

$$c_i(s_i, \mathsf{s}_{-i}, F) \leq \alpha \cdot c_i(s_i', \mathsf{s}_{-i}, F), \qquad \forall i, \forall s_i' \in S_i.$$

For $\alpha = 1$, such a state s is a pure Nash equilibrium.

For $\alpha \geq 1$, a function Φ is called an α-*potential function* if $c_i(s_i, \mathbf{s}_{-i}, F) > \alpha \cdot c_i(s_i', \mathbf{s}_{-i}, F)$ implies $\Phi(\mathbf{s}) > \Phi(s_i', \mathbf{s}_i)$. For $\alpha = 1$, this definition coincides with the definition of *generalised potential functions* in [17]. Such a function is called an *exact potential function* if $c_i(\mathbf{s}) - c_i(s_i', \mathbf{s}_{-i}) = \Phi(\mathbf{s}) - \Phi(s_i', \mathbf{s}_{-i})$ for every state $\mathbf{s}$, player $i \in N$ and strategy $s_i' \in S_i$.

2 General Social Context

In this section, we allow for general asymmetric social context. We show that for the class of social context congestion games with cost functions from any given set of functions $\mathcal{F}$, α-Nash dynamics are guaranteed to converge to α-approximate pure Nash equilibrium if and only if $\alpha > \mu(\mathcal{F})$. We start by showing convergence for any $\alpha > \mu(\mathcal{F})$.

Theorem 1. *In congestion games under social context with cost functions in* $\mathcal{F}$, α-*Nash dynamics converge to an* α-*approximate Nash equilibrium for any* $\alpha > \mu(\mathcal{F})$.

Proof. Denote $\phi_i^r(\mathbf{s}) = \sum_{j \in [n]: s_j = r} f_{ij}$. Assume by way of contradiction that there exists a cycle of α-improving steps. On this cycle fix a step $s \to s'$, where $s' = (s_{-i}, s_i')$ of some player i, such that

$$c_i(\mathbf{s}) = \sum_{r \in s_i} d_r(n_r(\mathbf{s})) \leq c_i(\mathbf{s}') = \sum_{r \in s_i'} d_r(n_r(\mathbf{s}')). \tag{1}$$

Such a step must exist, since otherwise each step in the cycle improves Rosenthal's potential function [18]. In this step, player i improves by a factor

$$\frac{\sum_{r \in R} \phi_i^r(\mathbf{s}) \cdot d_r(n_r(\mathbf{s}))}{\sum_{r \in R} \phi_i^r(\mathbf{s}') \cdot d_r(n_r(\mathbf{s}'))}$$

$$\leq \frac{\sum_{r \in s_i \setminus s_i'} \phi_i^r(\mathbf{s}) \cdot d_r(n_r(\mathbf{s})) + \sum_{r \in s_i' \setminus s_i} \phi_i^r(\mathbf{s}) \cdot d_r(n_r(\mathbf{s}))}{\sum_{r \in s_i \setminus s_i'} \phi_i^r(\mathbf{s}') \cdot d_r(n_r(\mathbf{s}')) + \sum_{r \in s_i' \setminus s_i} \phi_i^r(\mathbf{s}') \cdot d_r(n_r(\mathbf{s}'))}$$

Now for all $r \in s_i' \setminus s_i$, we have $d_r(n_r(\mathbf{s}')) \geq d_r(n_r(\mathbf{s}))$ and $\phi_i^r(\mathbf{s}') = \phi_i^r(\mathbf{s}) + 1$, and for $r \in s_i \setminus s_i'$, we have $d_r(n_r(\mathbf{s}')) = d_r(n_r(\mathbf{s}) - 1)$ and $\phi_i^r(\mathbf{s}') = \phi_i^r(\mathbf{s}) - 1$. Moreover, (1) implies $\sum_{r \in s_i \setminus s_i'} d_r(n_r(\mathbf{s})) \leq \sum_{r \in s_i' \setminus s_i} d_r(n_r(\mathbf{s}'))$. Using these, we can upper bound our factor by

$$\frac{\sum_{r \in s_i \setminus s_i'} \phi_i^r(\mathbf{s}) \cdot d_r(n_r(\mathbf{s})) + \sum_{r \in s_i' \setminus s_i} \phi_i^r(\mathbf{s}) \cdot d_r(n_r(\mathbf{s}))}{\sum_{r \in s_i \setminus s_i'} \phi_i^r(\mathbf{s}') \cdot d_r(n_r(\mathbf{s}')) + \sum_{r \in s_i' \setminus s_i} (\phi_i^r(\mathbf{s}) + 1) \cdot d_r(n_r(\mathbf{s}'))}$$

$$\leq \frac{\sum_{r \in s_i \setminus s_i'} \phi_i^r(\mathbf{s}) \cdot d_r(n_r(\mathbf{s}))}{\sum_{r \in s_i \setminus s_i'} \phi_i^r(\mathbf{s}') \cdot d_r(n_r(\mathbf{s}')) + \sum_{r \in s_i' \setminus s_i} d_r(n_r(\mathbf{s}'))}$$

$$\leq \frac{\sum_{r \in s_i \setminus s_i'} \phi_i^r(\mathbf{s}) \cdot d_r(n_r(\mathbf{s}))}{\sum_{r \in s_i \setminus s_i'} (\phi_i^r(\mathbf{s}) - 1) \cdot d_r(n_r(\mathbf{s}) - 1) + \sum_{r \in s_i \setminus s_i'} d_r(n_r(\mathbf{s}))}$$

$$\leq \max_{r \in s_i \setminus s_i'} \frac{\phi_i^r(\mathbf{s}) \cdot d_r(n_r(\mathbf{s}))}{(\phi_i^r(\mathbf{s}) - 1) \cdot d_r(n_r(\mathbf{s}) - 1) + d_r(n_r(\mathbf{s}))}.$$

where we used (1) in the second to last step. Observe, that this expression is increasing in $\phi_i^r(\mathsf{s})$ and for each $r \in s_i$, we have $\phi_i^r(\mathsf{s}) = \sum_{j \in [n]:s_j = r} f_{ij} \leq \sum_{j \in [n]:s_j = r} 1 = n_r(\mathsf{s})$. Thus

$$\max_{r \in s_i \backslash s_i'} \frac{\phi_i^r(\mathsf{s}) \cdot d_r(n_r(\mathsf{s}))}{(\phi_i^r(\mathsf{s}) - 1) \cdot d_r(n_r(\mathsf{s}) - 1) + d_r(n_r(\mathsf{s}))}$$

$$\leq \max_{r \in s_i \backslash s_i'} \frac{n_r(\mathsf{s}) \cdot d_r(n_r(\mathsf{s}))}{(n_r(\mathsf{s}) - 1) \cdot d_r(n_r(\mathsf{s}) - 1) + d_r(n_r(\mathsf{s}))} \leq \mu(\mathcal{F}),$$

which is a contradiction to $\alpha > \mu(\mathcal{F})$. $\qquad\square$

We proceed by providing a matching lower bound.

Theorem 2. *Given a set of cost functions $\mathcal{F}$, there exists a singleton congestion game with asymmetric binary social context with cost functions from $\mathcal{F}$, where $\mu(\mathcal{F})$-Nash dynamics cycle, even for $|R| = 2$ resources with identical latency functions.*

Proof. Given $\mathcal{F}$ we construct a congestion game with asymmetric binary social context as follows. Let $d \in \mathcal{F}$ be the cost function and $x \in \mathbb{N}$ the integer that achieve $\mu(\mathcal{F})$ in Definition 1. Construct a game with two resources with identical cost function d and a cyclic ordered set $N = \{0, \ldots, 2x - 2\}$ of $n = 2x - 1$ players. The asymmetric binary social context F is defined as follows: Each player $i \in N$ considers the next $x - 1$ in N as friend, i.e., $f_{ij} = 1$ if $j \in [i, i + x - 1]$ and $f_{ij} = 0$, otherwise. Here intervals are considered modulo $2x - 1$.

Define the initial state s where the x players in $\{0, \ldots, x - 1\}$ are assigned to one resource and the remaining $x - 1$ players $\{x, \ldots, 2x - 2\}$ to the other resource. In this profile, the perceived cost of player 0 is $c_0(\mathsf{s}) = x \cdot d(x)$. By deviating to the other resource, player 0 can achieve a perceived cost of $d(x) + (x - 1) \cdot d(x - 1)$. Thus, this is an α-improving step for $\alpha = \frac{x \cdot d(x)}{(x-1) \cdot d(x-1) + d(x)} = \mu(\mathcal{F})$. By symmetry of F, the remaining players can also iteratively improve in the order $\{1, \ldots, 2x - 2\}$ by the same factor. We end up in a state which is similar to s, except that each player is now assigned to the other resource. The theorem follows. $\qquad\square$

3   Symmetric Binary Context

In this section, we consider convergence of α-Nash dynamics for social context congestion games with symmetric binary context.

Theorem 3. *In congestion games under social context, for $|R| = 2$ and $\alpha \geq \sqrt{2n}$, α-Nash dynamics converge to an α-approximate Nash equilibrium.*

The asymptotical tightness follows from the next theorem.

Theorem 4. *There exists a singleton congestion game with symmetric binary social context, where α-Nash dynamics cycle for $\alpha = \frac{1}{3\sqrt{2}} \cdot \sqrt{n}$, even for $|R| = 2$ resources with identical convex latency functions.*

References

[1] Ashlagi, I., Krysta, P., Tennenholtz, M.: Social context games. In: Papadimitriou, C., Zhang, S. (eds.) WINE 2008. LNCS, vol. 5385, pp. 675–683. Springer, Heidelberg (2008)

[2] Caragiannis, I., Fanelli, A., Gravin, N., Skopalik, A.: Efficient computation of approximate pure Nash equilibria in congestion games. In: FOCS, pp. 532–541 (2011)

[3] Caragiannis, I., Fanelli, A., Gravin, N., Skopalik, A.: Approximate pure Nash equilibria in weighted congestion games: existence, efficient computation, and structure. In: EC, pp. 284–301 (2012)

[4] Chen, H.-L., Roughgarden, T.: Network design with weighted players. In: SPAA, pp. 29–38 (2006)

[5] Chien, S., Sinclair, A.: Convergence to approximate Nash equilibria in congestion games. Games and Economic Behavior 71(2), 315–327 (2011)

[6] Christodoulou, G., Koutsoupias, E., Spirakis, P.G.: On the performance of approximate equilibria in congestion games. In: Fiat, A., Sanders, P. (eds.) ESA 2009. LNCS, vol. 5757, pp. 251–262. Springer, Heidelberg (2009)

[7] Fabrikant, A., Papadimitriou, C., Talwar, K.: On the complexity of pure equilibria. In: STOC (2004)

[8] Fotakis, D., Kontogiannis, S.C., Spirakis, P.G.: Selfish unsplittable flows. Theor. Comput. Sci. 348(2-3), 226–239 (2005)

[9] Gairing, M., Klimm, M.: Congestion games with player-specific costs revisited. In: Vöcking, B. (ed.) SAGT 2013. LNCS, vol. 8146, pp. 98–109. Springer, Heidelberg (2013)

[10] Goemans, M.X., Mirrokni, V.S., Vetta, A.: Sink equilibria and convergence. In: FOCS, pp. 142–154 (2005)

[11] Hansknecht, C., Klimm, M., Skopalik, A.: Approximate pure Nash equilibria in weighted congestion games. In: APPROX/RANDOM, pp. 242–257 (2014)

[12] Harks, T., Klimm, M., Möhring, R.H.: Characterizing the existence of potential functions in weighted congestion games. Theory Comput. Syst. 49(1), 46–70 (2011)

[13] Hoefer, M., Skopalik, A.: Social context in potential games. In: Goldberg, P.W. (ed.) WINE 2012. LNCS, vol. 7695, pp. 364–377. Springer, Heidelberg (2012)

[14] Hoefer, M., Skopalik, A.: Altruism in atomic congestion games. ACM Trans. Economics and Comput. 1(4), 21 (2013)

[15] Libman, L., Orda, A.: Atomic Resource Sharing in Noncooperative Networks. Telecommunication Systems 17(4), 385–409 (2001)

[16] Milchtaich, I.: Congestion games with player-specific payoff functions. Games and Economic Behavior 13, 111–124 (1996)

[17] Monderer, D., Shapley, L.: Potential games. Games and Economics Behavior 14, 124–143 (1996)

[18] Rosenthal, R.W.: A class of games possessing pure-strategy Nash equilibria. International Journal of Game Theory 2, 65–67 (1973)

[19] Roughgarden, T.: The price of anarchy is independent of the network topology. J. Comput. Syst. Sci. 67(2), 341–364 (2003)

[20] Skopalik, A., Vöcking, B.: Inapproximability of pure nash equilibria. In: STOC, pp. 355–364 (2008)

Nash Stability in Fractional Hedonic Games*

Vittorio Bilò[1], Angelo Fanelli[2], Michele Flammini[3,4],
Gianpiero Monaco[3], and Luca Moscardelli[5]

[1] Department of Mathematics and Physics - University of Salento, Italy
vittorio.bilo@unisalento.it
[2] CNRS, (UMR-6211), France
angelo.fanelli@unicaen.fr
[3] DISIM - University of L'Aquila, Italy
{michele.flammini,gianpiero.monaco}@univaq.it
[4] Gran Sasso Science Institute, L'Aquila, Italy
[5] Department of Economic Studies - University of Chieti-Pescara, Italy
luca.moscardelli@unich.it

Abstract. Cluster formation games are games in which self-organized groups (or clusters) are created as a result of the strategic interactions of independent and selfish players. We consider fractional hedonic games, that is, cluster formation games in which the happiness of each player in a group is the average value she ascribes to its members. We adopt Nash stable outcomes, where no player can improve her utility by unilaterally changing her own group, as the target solution concept and study their existence, complexity and performance for games played on general and specific graph topologies.

1 Introduction

Hedonic games, introduced in [6], are games in which players have preferences over the set of all possible player partitions (called clusterings). In particular, the utility of each player only depends on the composition or structure of the cluster she belongs to. Cluster formation is of fundamental importance in a variety of social, economic, and political problems. Therefore, a big stream of research considered this topic from a strategic cooperative point of view [5,7,9]. Nevertheless, studying strategic solutions under a non-cooperative scenario becomes important when considering huge environments (like the Internet) lacking a social planner or where the cost of coordination is tremendously high. In this setting, a clustering is Nash stable if no player can improve her utility by unilaterally changing her own cluster. A non-cooperative research on hedonic games can be found in [8].

A notably class of hedonic games is that of *additively separable* ones [2,5], in which the utility of a player is given by the sum of the weights of the edges

---

* This work was partially supported by PRIN 2010–2011 research project ARS Tech-noMedia: "Algorithmics for Social Technological Networks" and by COST Action IC1205 on Computational Social Choice.

T.-Y. Liu et al. (Eds.): WINE 2014, LNCS 8877, pp. 486–491, 2014.
© Springer International Publishing Switzerland 2014

being incident to the other players belonging to the same cluster. Moreover, within this class of games, the *symmetric* case, where the weights are given by an undirected edge-weighted graph in which nodes represent players·and edge weights measure the happiness of the players for belonging to the same cluster, has received significant attention [3,5].

In this paper, we consider the class of (symmetric) *fractional hedonic games* recently introduced in [1]. The main difference with respect to additive separable hedonic games is that, in the fractional model, the utility of each player in a cluster is divided by the number of players belonging to it. In such a way, fractional hedonic games model natural behavioral dynamics in social environments that are not captured by additive separable ones: one usually prefers having a couple of good friends in a cluster composed by few other people rather than being part of a crowded cluster populated by uninteresting guys. We analyze this class of games from a non-cooperative perspective, with the aim of understanding the existence, computability and performance of Nash stable clusterings.

We first show that in presence of negative edge weights, Nash stable clusterings are not guaranteed to exist, while, if edge weights are non-negative, the basic outcome in which all players belong to the same cluster (*basic Nash stable clustering*) is Nash stable. Then, we evaluate their performance by means of the widely used notions of price of anarchy and price of stability. We give an upper bound of $O(n)$ on the price of anarchy for weighted graphs and show that it is asymptotically tight even for unweighted paths. We also prove a lower bound of $\Omega(n)$ on the price of stability holding even for weighted stars. We observe that, being the basic Nash stable clustering the responsible for such a bad performance, one may ask whether Nash stable clusterings of better quality may exist and be efficiently computed. To this aim, we show that Nash stable clusterings may not be reached by independent selfish agents unless some kind of centralized control is enforced in the game (that is, uncoordinated best-response dynamics may not converge to stable outcomes), even for unweighted bipartite graphs. This last result, in particular, rises the question of the existence of efficient algorithms for the determination of good quality Nash stable clusterings. To this aim, however, we prove that computing the best quality Nash stable clustering, as well as an optimal (non necessarily stable) one, is an NP-hard problem. Given the above negative and impossibility results, we focus on fractional hedonic games played on particular graph topologies such as unweighted bipartite graphs and unweighted trees which already pose challenging questions and require non-trivial approaches. For bipartite graphs we show that the price of stability is strictly greater than 1 and provide a polynomial time algorithm computing a Nash stable clustering approximating the social optimum by a factor strictly smaller than 2 (thus proving that 2 is an upper bound to the price of stability in this setting). For trees, we prove that the price of stability is 1 and show how to constructively compute in polynomial time an optimal Nash stable clustering.

Due to space limitations, most of the proofs are omitted. All details can be found in the full version of the paper.

2   Definitions, Notation and Preliminaries

For an integer $n > 0$, denote with $[n]$ the set $\{1, \ldots, n\}$. Let $G = (N, E, w)$, with $w : E \to \mathbb{R}_{>0}$ (we consider positive weights because in Lemma 1 we prove that Nash stable clusterings may not exist with negative weights), be an edge weighted connected undirected graph. We denote with $n = |N|$ and with $w_{u,v}$ the weight of edge $(u, v) \in E$. Furthermore, given any set of edges $X \subseteq E$, let $W(X) = \sum_{(u,v) \in X} w_{u,v}$. We say that G is unweighted when $w_{u,v} = 1$ for each $(u, v) \in E$. Given a subset of nodes $S \subseteq N$, $G_S = (S, E_S)$ is the subgraph of G induced by the set S, i.e., $E_S = \{(u, v) \in E : u, v \in S\}$. $N_u(S)$ denotes the neighbors of u in S, i.e., $N_u(S) = \{v \in S : (u, v) \in E\}$, and $E_u(S)$ the edges in E_S being incident to u, i.e., $E_u(S) = \{(u, v) \in E : (u, v) \in E_S\}$.

The *fractional hedonic game* induced by G, denoted as $\mathcal{G}(G)$, is the non-cooperative strategic game in which each node $u \in N$ is associated with a selfish player (or agent) and each player chooses to join a certain *cluster* (assuming that candidate clusters are numbered from 1 to n). Hence, a state of the game, that we will call in the sequel a *clustering*, is a partition of the agents into n clusters $\mathbf{C} = \{C_1, C_2, \ldots, C_n\}$ such that $C_j \subseteq N$ for each $j \in [n]$, $\bigcup_{j \in [n]} C_j = N$ and $C_i \cap C_j = \emptyset$ for any $i, j \in [n]$ with $i \neq j$. Notice that every cluster does not need to be necessarily non-empty. If $u \in C_i$, we say that u is a member of C_i. We denote by $C(u)$ the cluster in $\mathbf{C}$ of which agent u is a member. In a clustering $\mathbf{C}$, the payoff (or utility) of agent u is defined as $p_u(\mathbf{C}) = \frac{W(E_u(C(u)))}{|C(u)|}$. Each agent chooses the cluster she belongs to with the aim of maximizing her payoff. We denote by $(\mathbf{C}, u, j)$, the new clustering obtained from $\mathbf{C}$ by moving agent u from $C(u)$ to C_j; formally, $(\mathbf{C}, u, j) = \mathbf{C} \setminus \{\mathbf{C}(u), C_j\} \cup \{\mathbf{C}(u) \setminus \{u\}, C_j \cup \{u\}\}$. An agent *deviates* if she changes the cluster she belongs to. Given a clustering $\mathbf{C}$, an *improving move* (or simply a *move*) for player u is a deviation to any cluster C_j that strictly increases her payoff, i.e., $p_u((\mathbf{C}, u, j)) > p_u(\mathbf{C})$. Moreover, player u performs a *best-response* in clustering $\mathbf{C}$ by choosing a cluster providing her the highest possible payoff (notice that a best-response is also a move when there exists a cluster C_j such that $p_u((\mathbf{C}, u, j)) > p_u(\mathbf{C})$). An agent is *stable* if she cannot perform a move; a clustering is *Nash stable* (or is a *Nash equilibrium*) if every agent is stable. An *improving dynamics* is a sequence of moves, while a *best-response dynamics* is a sequence of best-responses. A game has the *finite improvement path property* if it does not admit an improvement dynamics of infinite length. Clearly, a game possessing the finite improvement path property always admits a Nash stable clustering. We denote with $\mathsf{NSC}(\mathcal{G}(G))$ the set of Nash stable clusterings of $\mathcal{G}(G)$. The *social welfare* of a clustering $\mathbf{C}$ is the summation of the players' payoffs, i.e., $\mathsf{SW}(\mathbf{C}) = \sum_{u \in N} p_u(\mathbf{C})$. We overload the social welfare function by applying it also to single clusters to obtain their contribution to the social welfare, i.e., $\mathsf{SW}(C_i) = \sum_{u \in C_i} p_u(\mathbf{C})$ so that $\mathsf{SW}(\mathbf{C}) = \sum_{i \in [n]} \mathsf{SW}(C_i)$.

Given a game $\mathcal{G}(G)$, an *optimal* clustering $\mathbf{C}^*$ is one that maximizes the social welfare of $\mathcal{G}(G)$. We denote $\mathsf{SW}(\mathbf{C}^*)$ as $\mathsf{SW}^*(\mathcal{G}(G))$. A clustering $\mathbf{C}$ is *feasible* if G_{C_i} is connected, for every $i \in [n]$. Notice that an optimal configuration is always feasible. The *price of anarchy* of a fractional hedonic game $\mathcal{G}(G)$ is defined as the worst-case ratio between the social welfare of a Nash stable clustering and the social optimum: $\mathsf{PoA}(\mathcal{G}(G)) = \max_{C \in \mathsf{NSC}(\mathcal{G}(G))} \frac{\mathsf{SW}^*(\mathcal{G}(G))}{\mathsf{SW}(C)}$. Analogously, the *price of stability* of $\mathcal{G}(G)$ is defined as the best-case ratio between the social welfare of a Nash stable clustering and the social optimum: $\mathsf{PoS}(\mathcal{G}(G)) = \min_{C \in \mathsf{NSC}(\mathcal{G}(G))} \frac{\mathsf{SW}^*(\mathcal{G}(G))}{\mathsf{SW}(C)}$.

Next two lemmas characterize the existence of Nash stable clustering in fractional hedonic games.

Lemma 1. *There exists a graph G containing edges with negative weights such that $\mathcal{G}(G)$ admits no Nash stable clusterings.*

Lemma 2. *For any weighted graph G (with positive weights), $\mathsf{NSC}(\mathcal{G}(G)) \neq \emptyset$.*

3   General Graphs

This section is devoted to results concerning general graph topologies.

Theorem 1. *For any weighted graph G, $\mathsf{PoA}(\mathcal{G}(G)) \leq n - 1$.*

Theorem 2. *For any integer $n \geq 2$, there exists an unweighted path G_n such that $\mathsf{PoA}(\mathcal{G}(G_n)) = \Omega(n)$.*

Theorem 3. *For any integer $n \geq 2$, there exists a weighted star G_n such that $\mathsf{PoS}(\mathcal{G}(G_n)) = \Omega(n)$.*

Theorem 4. *There exists an unweighted bipartite graph G such that $\mathcal{G}(G)$ does not possess the finite improvement path property even under best-response dynamics.*

Theorem 5. *Given a fractional hedonic game, the problem of computing a Nash stable clustering of maximum social welfare is NP-hard, as well as the problem of computing an optimal (not necessarily stable) clustering.*

4   Bipartite Graphs

In this section, we focus on games played on unweighted bipartite graphs.

Theorem 6. *There exists an unweighted bipartite graph G such that $\mathsf{PoS}(\mathcal{G}(G)) > 1$.*

We now show how to constructively compute in polynomial time a Nash stable clustering for such graph topology with good social welfare. As an implication, we obtain an upper bound to the price of stability. Given an unweighted bipartite graph G, let VC be a minimum vertex cover of G, and let $\overline{VC} = N \setminus VC$. It is well known that $\overline{VC}$ is a maximum independent set of G. Moreover, due to the König's theorem, we know that, in a bipartite graph, the number of vertices in a minimum vertex cover equals the number of edges in a maximum matching and the minimum vertex cover can be computed in polynomial time. We will construct a Nash stable clustering that is composed by $|VC|$ non-empty clusters where, for each player $u \in VC$, we have a different cluster C_u that is a star graph having node u as its center. We obtain such a clustering by considering a particular dynamics of the game $\mathcal{G}(G)$. Candidate clusters are numbered from 1 to $|VC|$, that is, one cluster for each node in VC. Let C_u be the cluster associated to player $u \in VC$. We fix the strategy of each player $u \in VC$ to C_u and let only players in $\overline{VC}$ move in the dynamics. The strategy set of a player $u \in \overline{VC}$ is $\{C_v | (u, v) \in E\}$. We consider the dynamics starting from a clustering where each cluster contains at least 2 nodes whose existence is guaranteed by König's theorem, i.e., for each edge (u, v) of the maximum matching associated to VC, without loss of generality we assume $u \in VC$ and $v \in \overline{VC}$, therefore we have a cluster C_u and the starting strategy of $v \in \overline{VC}$ is the cluster C_u. In this section, we refer to such a dynamics as $\mathcal{D}$. The following property holds.

Property 1. At each step of the dynamics $\mathcal{D}$, for each $u \in VC$, we have $|C_u| \geq 2$.

Lemma 3. *The dynamics $\mathcal{D}$ converges after a number of moves which is polynomial in the number of players.*

Next lemma claims that, once the dynamics reaches a stable clustering (which is guaranteed by Lemma 3) henceforth called $\mathbf{C}^{\mathcal{D}}$, the players in VC are also stable and therefore $\mathbf{C}^{\mathcal{D}}$ is Nash stable for the game $\mathcal{G}(G)$.

Lemma 4. $\mathbf{C}^{\mathcal{D}}$ *is Nash stable for $\mathcal{G}(G)$.*

We conclude by proving the approximation guarantee yielded by $\mathbf{C}^{\mathcal{D}}$

Theorem 7. *The Nash stable clustering $\mathbf{C}^{\mathcal{D}}$ is such that $\frac{\mathsf{SW}(\mathbf{C}^*)}{\mathsf{SW}(\mathbf{C}^{\mathcal{D}})} < 2$.*

Proof. Let VC be the minimum vertex cover of G used to define the dynamics $\mathcal{D}$. By Property 1, we get that the contribution to the social welfare of any cluster $C^{\mathcal{D}}(u)$, where $u \in VC$, is at least 1, i.e., $\mathsf{SW}(C^{\mathcal{D}}(u)) \geq 1$ for any $u \in VC$. Let C_i^* be a non-empty cluster of an optimal clustering $\mathbf{C}^*$. We partition the nodes of C_i^* in two sets $X_i^{VC} = C_i^* \cap VC$ and $X_i^{\overline{VC}} = C_i^* \cap \overline{VC}$. We distinguish between two cases:

i) $X_i^{VC} = \emptyset$; it follows that $C_i^* \subseteq \overline{VC}$. Therefore, since $\overline{VC}$ is an independent set, it follows that $\mathsf{SW}(C_i^*) = 0$.

ii) $X_i^{VC} \neq \emptyset$; in this case the total number of edges in C_i^* is at most $|X_i^{VC}||X_i^{\overline{VC}}| + \frac{1}{2}|X_i^{VC}|^2$.

Hence, the contribution to the optimal social welfare of cluster C_i^* verifies

$$\mathsf{SW}(C_i^*) \leq 2\frac{|X_i^{VC}||X_i^{\overline{VC}}| + \frac{1}{2}|X_i^{VC}|^2}{|X_i^{VC}| + |X_i^{\overline{VC}}|} = 2|X_i^{VC}|\frac{|X_i^{\overline{VC}}| + \frac{1}{2}|X_i^{VC}|}{|X_i^{VC}| + |X_i^{\overline{VC}}|}. \quad (1)$$

On the other hand, in the Nash stable clustering $\mathbf{C}^{\mathcal{D}}$, for any $u \in X_i^{VC}$, there is a cluster $C^{\mathcal{D}}(u)$ whose contribution to the social welfare is at least one; thus, we get

$$\sum_{u \in X_i^{VC}} \mathsf{SW}(C^{\mathcal{D}}(u)) \geq |X_i^{VC}|. \tag{2}$$

Dividing (1) by (2) we obtain

$$\frac{\mathsf{SW}(C_i^*)}{\sum_{u \in X_i^{VC}} \mathsf{SW}(C^{\mathcal{D}}(u))} \leq 2 \frac{|X_i^{\overline{VC}}| + \frac{1}{2}|X_i^{VC}|}{|X_i^{\overline{VC}}| + |X_i^{VC}|} < 2.$$

By summing over all the non-empty clusters C_i^* of the optimal clustering $\mathbf{C}^*$ the theorem follows. □

5 Trees

In this section, we focus on games played on unweighted trees.

Theorem 8. *For any unweighted tree graph G, $\mathsf{PoS}(\mathcal{G}(G)) = 1$. Moreover, an optimal clustering for $\mathcal{G}(G)$ can be computed in polynomial time.*

6 Conclusions

There are several open problems that still need to be addressed. For instance, some of the provided upper and lower bounds are not tight, so there are some gaps that need to be closed. Among them, the major one is that requiring the determination of significant bounds to the price of stability for general unweighted graphs. Another interesting research direction would be considering directed graphs where the weight of a directed arc (u, v) denotes the value player u has for player v.

References

1. Aziz, H., Brandt, F., Harrenstein, P.: Fractional hedonic games. In: AAMAS, pp. 5–12 (2014)
2. Aziz, H., Brandt, F., Seedig, H.G.: Stable partitions in additively separable hedonic games. In: AAMAS, pp. 183–190 (2011)
3. Ballester, C.: NP-completeness in hedonic games. Games and Economic Behavior 49(1), 1–30 (2004)
4. Bloch, F., Diamantoudi, E.: Noncooperative formation of coalitions in hedonic games. International Journal of Game Theory 40(2), 262–280 (2010)
5. Bogomolnaia, A., Jackson, M.O.: The stability of hedonic coalition structures. Games and Economic Behavior 38, 201–230 (2002)
6. Dréze, J.H., Greenberg, J.: Hedonic coalitions: optimality and stability. Econometrica 48(4), 987–1003 (1980)
7. Elkind, E., Wooldridge, M.: Hedonic coalition nets. In: AAMAS, pp. 417–424 (2009)
8. Feldman, M., Lewin-Eytan, L., Naor, J.(S.): Hedonic clustering games. In: SPAA, pp. 267–276 (2012)
9. Gairing, M., Savani, R.: Computing stable outcomes in hedonic games. In: Kontogiannis, S., Koutsoupias, E., Spirakis, P.G. (eds.) SAGT 2010. LNCS, vol. 6386, pp. 174–185. Springer, Heidelberg (2010)

The Role of Common and Private Signals in Two-Sided Matching with Interviews

Sanmay Das and Zhuoshu Li

Washington University in St. Louis, St. Louis, USA
sanmay@seas.wustl.edu, zhuoshuli@wustl.edu

Abstract. We study two-sided matching markets where the matching is preceded by a costly interviewing stage in which firms acquire information about the qualities of candidates. Our focus is on the impact of the signals of quality available prior to the interviewing stage. Using a mixture of simulation, numerical, and empirical game theoretic analysis, we show that more commonality in the quality signals can be harmful, yielding fewer matches as some firms make the same mistakes in choosing whom to interview. Relatively high and medium quality candidates are most likely to suffer lower match probabilities. The effect can be mitigated when firms use "more rational" interviewing strategies, or through the availability of private signals of candidate quality to the firms.

Keywords: matching, information acquisition, empirical game analysis.

1 Introduction

The matching literature typically assumes that agents know their own preferences before the mechanism is run. Recently, there have been some papers that try to relax this stringent assumption [1,2,7], or to look at cases where the mechanism does not wish to elicit complete preference information [4]. In one-shot settings, agents come into the matching setting with unknown (or partially known) true preferences, but can learn more through a costly information acquisition (*interviewing*) stage before the actual matching happens (for example, academic job markets) [7,13]; in repeated settings, the "match" is not final, but conveys information to participants on quality [5,2].

Lee and Schwartz proposed what may be the first model of matching with an interviewing stage, where employers first simultaneously choose a subset of workers to interview, and then, in a second stage, submit preferences to a (Gale-Shapley) matching algorithm that then forms the matching [7]. The basic question that Lee and Schwartz ask is about the employer's decision of whom to interview, given that interviews are costly and all employers and workers on either side of the market are ex ante identical. The main complexity is then that the marginal benefit of interviewing a worker goes down as her number of other interviews goes up. The major result is that in symmetric equilibria (where each employer and worker has the same number of interviews), the number of agents

T.-Y. Liu et al. (Eds.): WINE 2014, LNCS 8877, pp. 492–497, 2014.
© Springer International Publishing Switzerland 2014

matched goes up in the overlap, a measure characterizing the number of common interview partners among agents.

Our focus is on labor markets with interviewing, and in particular, the role of information in the interviewing and matching process. Consider the matching process that academic departments go through when interviewing and hiring faculty candidates. Typically, departments have a budget, say they can interview three or four candidates for a position. They start off the process by receiving a noisy signal about their preferences over candidates – CVs, letters of recommendation, and word-of-mouth can yield much information about candidates, but not nearly as much as an in-person interview. Once they have received these noisy signals, each department chooses which candidates to interview. Following Lee and Schwartz [7], after all the interviews have taken place, we can model the matching process as Gale-Shapley matching with departments submitting ranked lists of the candidates they interviewed. While this ignores some frictions (like exploding offers [3,8]) that can be important, those are likely to be a second-order effect compared with the choice of candidates to interview. In contrast with Lee and Schwartz, who consider ex ante identical firms and workers, we are interested in situations where firms and workers are of different qualities, and some quality signals are available prior to the interviewing stage.

We look at a stylized model where there is a universally shared, common knowledge ranking of all firms, and there is a "true" universally shared ranking of all candidates, but this true ranking is not known – instead, firms receive different signals of candidates' rankings or qualities. If the true ranking were known to everyone, there would be only one stable matching, the assortative one, and any rational interviewing process would lead to the stable outcome in the matching stage. When signals of quality or ranking are noisy, firms must reason both about the true quality of candidates and about strategic issues in deciding whom to interview. This can lead to inefficiencies, where some candidates and firms do not end up getting matched whereas they would have with better information; these inefficiencies may fall disproportionately on some portion of the population of candidates and firms.

We are particularly interested in the roles of *common* and *private* information on aggregate and distributional outcomes in such matching markets. Common signals are shared across firms – for example, the quality of a CV, number of publications, LinkedIn endorsements, or public contributions to open source projects, can all be thought of as common signals of varying precision. Private signals can be generated through phone screens, preliminary interviews, etc. We assume that common and private signals are conditionally independent given the true ranking or value of the candidate. The central question of this paper is the effect of the relative precision of common signals and private signals on market outcomes. While a perfect common signal would reduce the problem to one with known rankings of both firms and candidates (and lead to the assortative matching and no inefficiencies under any reasonable model), our main finding is that the presence of a strong, but imperfect, common signal in addition to existing private signals can actually have significant negative effects, with fewer matchings occurring than with a private signal alone. The burden of this is typically borne by the candidates who are ranked relatively high (but not in the highest echelon). The mechanism is interesting – when these candidates end up with a common signal that is "too high", they interview at firms that are ranked too high for their actual quality. The firms that are closer to their true range choose not to interview them, but when these candidates' true qualities are revealed, they often don't get offers from the places that did interview them.

These findings are robust to several different choices of how signals of rankings and values are generated, and to different strategic choices by firms of whom to interview. The latter question is independently interesting – we demonstrate the intuition for our main result with a simple, but realistic, interviewing strategy where firms interview candidates "around" their true ranking. We then turn to a form of empirical game theoretic analysis [14] to explore a richer space of interviewing strategies, yielding "more rational" strategic decisions. This can alleviate the problem, with more agents being matched when there is only a common signal, but does not provide much benefit in terms of the number of agents matched when firms have access to both common and private signals.

2   Model and Inference

There are n workers and n firms, represented by the sets $W = \{w_1, ..., w_n\}$ and $F = \{f_1, ..., f_n\}$. The matching market operates in two stages, following the model of Lee and Schwarz [7]. In the first stage, each firm selects k workers (or candidates) to interview; this decision is made on the basis of information present in the signals received by firms (described below). During the interview process, the true ranking of the set of candidates that is interviewed is revealed to each firm. The second stage can then be thought of as a Gale-Shapley matching where each firm submits a ranked list of the candidates it interviewed (others are unacceptable), and each candidate submits a ranked list of firms.

All workers know their preference rankings over employers with certainty. We assume that the workers all have exactly the same preferences over potential employers. Further, there exists a universal "true" ranking of all the workers as well, but this ranking is unobserved. Employers receive a private signal of their preferences as well as a common signal. In this paper we consider two possibilities. In **random-utility models** w_i has a true value v_i (which is drawn from a normal distribution). f_j's private signal $\mathbf{s_j} = (s_1, s_2, ... s_n)$. Each $s_i, 1 \leq i \leq n$ is a noisy realization of the true value of v_i, corrupted by zero-mean Gaussian or uniform noise. The common signal, received by all employers, is a single (noisy) vector $\mathbf{z_C} = (z_1, z_2, ... z_n)$.

In the **Mallows model** [11], signals are directly over the ranking space. Following Lu and Boutilier's [9] description of its form, we say that each employer's private signal is a *ranking* Γ_j sampled from the distribution which assigns $\Pr(\Gamma_j | \Gamma, \phi_p) = \frac{1}{Z} \phi_p{}^{d(\Gamma_j, \Gamma)}$, where Γ is the modal (true) ranking, $\phi_p \in (0, 1]$ is a dispersion parameter such that the smaller ϕ_p is, the more the distribution will be concentrated around the modal ranking, d is a distance function between rankings (we use the Kendall tau distance), and Z is a normalizing factor. The common signal, Γ_C is sampled from a Mallows model with the same modal ranking Γ and a possibly different dispersion parameter ϕ_C. In both cases, we assume common knowledge of all the relevant parameters of the distributions; the only unknowns are the true values or rankings.

In both the random utility and Mallows models, it is computationally difficult to perform full Bayesian reasoning over the whole space of possible posterior rankings, so we assume that firms compute the single most likely posterior ranking from the common and private signals, which we denote as $\widetilde{\Gamma}_j$, and use this single ranking for interviewing decisions. We defer details of the inference procedures to a longer version of this paper, but note that, in the random utility models, the procedures follow from those developed by MacQueen [10], while in the Mallows model, we use an algorithm based on the one devised by Qin *et al* [12] in the coset-permutation distance based stagewise (CPS) model (which is equivalent to the Mallows model using the Kendall tau distance).

3 Results

We first examine outcomes in a market where firms all use the same simple and intuitive interviewing strategy. They each compute their posterior ranking based on the available signals, and then interview the k candidates who are ranked "around" the firms own ranking (e.g. with $k = 5$, the firm ranked 11 interviews candidates 9 through 13), with the firms at the top and bottom of the rankings adjusting their interview sets downwards and upwards as needed. We run 50000 simulations for each of the random utility and Mallows models; each simulation is of a market with 30 firms and 30 workers, each with interview budget 5. In each run, we hold the private signal parameters fixed, which are σ_p, b_p in the random utility models and ϕ_p in the Mallows model, and vary the common signal parameters, which are σ_C, b_C in the random utility models and ϕ_C in the Mallows model.

Based on the observation that the only stable matching if true preferences were known is the assortative matching, and that adding a common signal gives everyone more information about the true ranking, one would assume that adding the common signal always leads to more agents being matched. At the extreme, this is obvious – suppose the common signal had no noise and contained perfect information. Then the rational inference is just to use that signal. In this case, the assortative match would occur for sure.

But it turns out that, as the signal becomes less precise, the number of unmatched agents goes up sharply, and quickly exceeds the expected number of unmatched agents when no common signal is present! Surprisingly, on the candidates' side, the candidates who are less likely to get matched are actually the higher ranked ones (except for the very top ranked ones) (see Figures 1 and 2). What is the mechanism at play? In a more coordinated environment, as created by a common signal, the correlation between employers' estimates of a workers desirability is higher. Thus, it is more likely that several employers *all* make the

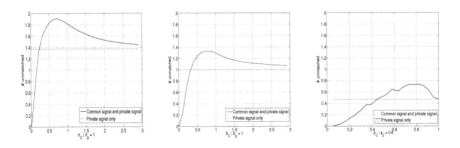

Fig. 1. Average number of agents left unmatched (Y axis) versus (decreasing) "precision" of the common signal (σ_C for Gaussian noise (**left**), b_C for uniform noise (**middle**), and ϕ_C for the Mallows model (**right**)), holding the precision of private signals fixed. The dashed line shows the number that are left unmatched when there is no common signal.

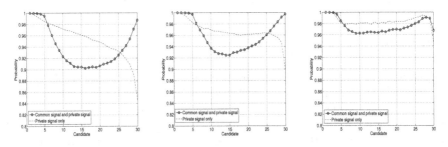

Fig. 2. The probability that the candidate of a particular rank is matched when firms have access to both a common signal and a private signal. Left: Gaussian noise ($\sigma_C = 0.6, \sigma_p = 0.5$), Center: Uniform noise ($b_C = 0.6, b_p = 0.5$), Right: Mallows model ($\phi_C = 0.7, \phi_p = 0.6$).

mistake of thinking a particular worker is too good or too bad for them. For candidates, the truth-revealing nature of the interview phase means that it can be disadvantageous to "place too high" in the first (interview selection) stage.[1] When opinions are more independent, as is the case when the private signal is stronger, it is less likely that someone will fall through the cracks in this manner. Therefore, more homogeneity of opinion, with even a little bit of noise, can create worse outcomes!

Alternative Interviewing Strategies. Our results thus far apply to a simple interviewing strategy. What if employers used more sophisticated strategies? We analyze this using the basic idea of empirical game theoretic analysis [14,6]. The fundamental strategic decision faced by a firm is to choose a set of k candidates

---

[1] For example, suppose a middle-ranked candidate gets early "buzz" on the job market, he may not get interviews from departments actually ranked in his vicinity because they think he is out of reach, but may not get offers once he is interviewed by higher ranked places and they realize he isn't quite at their level.

to interview. Game-theoretically, an (ex-ante) Bayes-Nash equilibrium would be one where each firm would not change the set of candidates it chose to interview, given the strategies of other firms, and the information available to them prior to the interview stage. Unfortunately, this game is very complex to analyze. Therefore, we restrict our attention to a manageable set of strategies: each firm can decide on any set of k contiguously ranked candidates (in its posterior private ranking). We can determine (approximate) equilibrium firm strategies using an iterative empirical method (since firm i's best strategy depends only on the choices of the firms ranked above i, and also has no effect on the utilities of those firms).

Can these "more rational" interviewing strategies resolve some of the inefficiency in terms of the number of participants left unmatched? Our initial experiments (available in a longer version of this paper) indicate that with only common signals, when the penalty for being unmatched is high enough, the better strategies, do, in fact, reduce the number left unmatched. However, with both common and private signals, the more complex strategies do not provide much, if any, societal benefit.

References

1. Chade, H.: Matching with noise and the acceptance curse. Journal of Economic Theory 129(1), 81–113 (2006)
2. Das, S., Kamenica, E.: Two-sided bandits and the dating market. In: Proceedings of IJCAI, pp. 947–952 (2005)
3. Das, S., Tsitsiklis, J.N.: When is it important to know you've been rejected? A search problem with probabilistic appearance of offers. Journal of Economic Behavior and Organization 74, 104–122 (2010)
4. Drummond, J., Boutilier, C.: Elicitation and approximately stable matching with partial preferences. In: Proceedings of IJCAI (2013)
5. Ho, C.-J., Slivkins, A., Vaughan, J.W.: Adaptive contract design for crowdsourcing markets: Bandit algorithms for repeated principal-agent problems. In: Proceedings of ACM EC, pp. 359–376 (2014)
6. Jordan, P.R., Vorobeychik, Y., Wellman, M.P.: Searching for approximate equilibria in empirical games. In: Proceedings of AAMAS, pp. 1063–1070 (2008)
7. Lee, R.S., Schwarz, M.: Interviewing in two-sided matching markets. Technical report, National Bureau of Economic Research (2009)
8. Lippman, S.A., Mamer, J.W.: Exploding offers. Decision Analysis 9(1), 6–21 (2012)
9. Lu, T., Boutilier, C.: Learning Mallows models with pairwise preferences. In: Proceedings of ICML, pp. 145–152 (2011)
10. MacQueen, J.B.: Optimal policies for a class of search and evaluation problems. Management Science 10(4), 746–759 (1964)
11. Mallows, C.L.: Non-null ranking models. I. Biometrika 44(1/2), 114–130 (1957)
12. Qin, T., Geng, X., Liu, T.-Y.: A new probabilistic model for rank aggregation. In: NIPS, pp. 1948–1956 (2010)
13. Rastegari, B., Condon, A., Immorlica, N., Leyton-Brown, K.: Two-sided matching with partial information. In: Proceedings of ACM EC, pp. 733–750 (2013)
14. Wellman, M.P.: Methods for empirical game-theoretic analysis. In: Proceedings of AAAI, vol. 21, pp. 1552–1555 (2006)

Author Index